*For my parents,*
*Isaac, son of Hersch Zvi,*
*and Ida, daughter of Josef Jam,*
*with love and gratitude*

# CONTENTS

# ACKNOWLEDGMENTS

The great part of the work on the present study was carried out with the help of a Fellowship from the John Simon Guggenheim Memorial Foundation. Grateful acknowledgments are also made of summer research grants received over a period of years from the American Council of Learned Societies and the Social Science Research Council, as well as from the Russian and East European Institute of Indiana University. The Russian and East European Center of the University of Illinois at Urbana-Champaign has helped defray some of the expenses in the preparation of the manuscript.

I have benefited immensely from access to the excellent collection of Soviet periodicals at Radio Liberty in New York, and from the help of Dr. Andrew Turchyn, the Slavic librarian at Indiana University, and of Laurence H. Miller and Marianna T. Choldin, Slavic librarians at the University of Illinois at Urbana-Champaign.

I am also indebted to Dr. Howard Goldman and to Mrs. Constance Antony for their painstaking assistance in gathering the data on which this book is based, and to Mrs. Niza Uslan and Mrs. Victoria Lockwood for typing the manuscript.

My greatest debt is to the late Ernest J. Simmons, under whose guidance I wrote a dissertation which was the basis for my *Russian Classics in Soviet Jackets* (Columbia University Press, 1962). The present study is intended as a companion to my earlier one. Together, they deal with the wider problem of non-Soviet literature in Soviet society.

# A DECADE OF
# EUPHORIA

*Western Literature in Post-Stalin Russia, 1954-64*

# INTRODUCTION

There exists a branch of literary scholarship that is concerned with the penetration and critical reception of individual authors and even major works outside the confines of their native lands. Not a few investigations of this kind deal with the fate of various Western writers in Russia, both prerevolutionary and Soviet. Deming Brown's *Soviet Attitudes toward American Writing,* which examines official and officially-inspired Soviet reactions toward an entire national literature of a major "capitalist" country between 1918 and 1960, is the most ambitious and successful such study to date.[1] Yet it appeared to this writer that an even broader investigation should be undertaken, which would encompass *all* of Western literature since, in the final analysis, Soviet literary criticism and publishing—the first reflecting powerful ideological pressures and the latter actually a monopoly of the state—view all of Western writing as an identifiable entity. That this is indeed the case is evident from Soviet textbooks and publishing statistics, which routinely divide all literature into Soviet, prerevolutionary Russian, and foreign, with the last category occasionally subdivided into "classics" and "modern." The common denominator of foreign books is not that they are translations—so are, after all, many books by hundreds of non-Russian authors, both Soviet and those who lived in Imperial Russia—but that they are consistently viewed by Soviet critics and publishers alike as carriers, in varying degrees, of non-Soviet values (or, in Soviet parlance, "bourgeois ideology") and are thus to be treated with particular caution.

The present book deals with the publication and official reception of the entire corpus of Western writing in post-Stalin Russia, particularly during the stormy decade 1954–64. The emphasis here on translations from the English, French, Spanish, German, and Italian (though not to the exclusion of other Western languages, which range from Latin to Norwegian and from Portuguese to Icelandic) reflects the fact that translations from these five constituted the lion's share of Western literature then published in the USSR. At the same time every effort was made to gather all available published evidence, however scattered and fragmentary, on the popularity

1. Deming Brown, *Soviet Attitudes toward American Writing* (Princeton, N.J.: Princeton University Press, 1962).

of and reactions to Western writing on the part of the Soviet reading public, an important subject that, for a variety of reasons, has been largely avoided by Western and Soviet scholars alike. Even incomplete and selective data on the subject, it was felt, would be of significant value in imparting a degree of concreteness and perspective to an analysis of "official" Soviet literary criticism and publishing statistics. The problem this book sets out to examine is admittedly vast and complex. Perhaps, as is true for so many other areas of study concerning the USSR, some guidelines may be suggested by pre-Soviet Russian history.

Three centuries ago, in 1672, Tsar Alexis summoned Dr. Gregori, the Lutheran pastor of Moscow's foreign colony, and commanded him to establish a troupe of amateur players. This event marked the birth of the Russian theater. The repertory of Dr. Gregori's ensemble consisted of German plays translated into Slavonic by scribes from the Russian Foreign Office. Thus, as it were, the Muscovite monarch began three traditions which persist to this day in Soviet Russia—those of government initiative and controls in matters cultural, of literary translation as an important activity subsidized by the authorities, and of close links between the availability of Russian renditions of foreign writing and the policies of the state, domestic as well as foreign. In the eighteenth century, ties between literature and the state were strong. Constructive achievements and military triumphs of Peter I and Catherine II, who both were later found deserving of the epithet "the Great," were extolled by the two foremost poets of the age, Lomonosov and Deržavin; indeed, the empress herself was a gifted woman of letters.

The nineteenth century saw a weakening of the connection between literature and the state. This period was marked by the rapid growth of privately owned publishing and the gradual relaxation of government censorship. The few important writers who combined literary activities with government service, such as Griboedov, Goncharov, Tjutčev, and Leont'ev, kept their two careers distinctly separated.[2] Toward the end of the nineteenth century, the government's influence on the literary market place, including translations, was confined by and large to erratic and mostly ineffectual interference by censorship (Karl Marx's *Das Kapital* was allowed to appear, presumably because it impressed the censors as an obtuse scholarly treatise) and to the selection of foreign books, mostly fiction, which formed part of government-controlled school curricula. Otherwise, translators, publishers, bookstores, and importers of foreign publications were left pretty much to their own devices. The demand for translations of

2. Ivan Goncharov, the author of *Oblomov*, was associated with the censorship office. The playwright Aleksandr Griboedov, the poet Fëdor Tjutčev, and the novelist and critic Konstantin Leont'ev were all in the diplomatic service.

West European and, later, also American literature was exceptionally high in a country where the term "European" (as in "he is a real European") was regarded as flattery. It should also be noted that knowledge of foreign languages, particularly French and German, was widespread in prerevolutionary Russia where it was viewed as an obligatory attribute of reasonably educated people; as a result, prior to 1917 Russia was a major importer of West European books and journals.[3]

Incongruously, in the wake of the Revolution of November 7, 1917, the status of foreign writing in Russia, in translation as well as in the original languages, gradually became strangely reminiscent of what it had been in medieval Muscovy. Within days after the Bolshevik seizure of power, a decree of the Council of People's Commissars reinstituted a far-reaching system of censorship which affected all forms of the printed word, including fiction, poetry, and drama. The decree emphasized the temporary character of the measure, promising it would be rescinded as soon as conditions returned to normal; this has never occurred, and the institution of *Glavlit*, in various forms, persists to this day.[4] Privately owned publishing houses continued to exist until the late 1920s, and a few publishing cooperatives survived for several years before being taken over by the state, which, *de facto*, through a multitude of its agencies, is now the country's *only* publisher.[5] Imported books are accorded special treatment. A Soviet researcher points out that special bookstores in "Moscow, Leningrad, and other cities" sell books from the People's Democracies;[6] it should be noted, however, that even such books are censored for their contents, as are foreign Communist periodicals. As for books from the non-Soviet world, an American scholar states unequivocally that "there is not a single bookstore in the Soviet Union" which sells books published in the West. Moreover, "Russians cannot order books from stores abroad either, partly because it is unlawful to possess foreign currency and impossible to exchange it."[7] (A far weightier reason, it may be added, is the unwillingness of the Soviet authorities to countenance the uncontrolled penetration of uncensored foreign books.) Finally, one may even uncover analogies between seventeenth-century Russia, where scribes in the Foreign Office of Tsar Alexis laboriously trans-

3. Russian memoirs and literary works suggest that, until the late eighteenth century, some Russian aristocrats read almost exclusively Western literature in the original languages. In Pushkin's *Queen of Spades* the old countess inquires, incredulously, whether Russian novels really do exist.

4. The best source of information on the subject is Martin Dewhirst and Robert Farrell (eds.), *The Soviet Censorship* (Metuchen, N.J.: The Scarecrow Press, 1973).

5. For details, see this writer's *Russian Classics in Soviet Jackets* (New York: Columbia University Press, 1962), pp. 20–26.

6. B. G. Reznikov, *Rabota prodavca v knižnom magazine* (Moscow: Iskusstvo, 1960), p. 42.

7. Carl R. Proffer (ed.), *Soviet Criticism of American Literature in the Sixties* (Ann Arbor, Mich.: Ardis, 1972), p. xiii.

lated German drama, and the present-day USSR. A few years before becoming head of the Soviet delegation to the United Nations in the mid-1960s, Nikolaj T. Fedorenko edited and lovingly annotated an impressive anthology of Chinese verse, lavishing particular praise on the poet Mao Tse-tung, a literary accomplishment now, alas, undeservedly forgotten for crass nonliterary reasons.[8]

A wide variety and large quantities of Western writing were published in the early postrevolutionary years. Two theoretical considerations argued for this policy. The Soviet state was committed to making accessible to the masses those treasures of world culture that poverty and illiteracy placed beyond their reach under the old regime. At the same time the doctrine of proletarian internationalism, with its slogans of universal brotherhood of workers and peasants, encouraged the publication of those works of modern foreign literature that portrayed the plight and hopefully also the revolutionary aspirations of the toiling masses in the West. As a result, Soviet readers had access to most of the Western literary classics, and to a more selective but nonetheless large body of modern West European and American writing. Allowing for fluctuations in foreign and domestic policy which affected the assortment and quantities of such books (for instance, the relative priorities assigned individual themes, and authors), these general guidelines were to remain in effect until the end of World War II, and to some degree thereafter. Thus, in the 1920s Soviet publishers favored Western writing about World War I exposing the senseless slaughter that, it was alleged, benefited capitalists alone. In the 1930s, there were many Soviet translations of works depicting America's Great Depression, mass unemployment, and the consequent rise of class consciousness. Anti-Nazi novels and plays were brought out in the late 1930s, but their publication stopped abruptly with the signing of the Nazi-Soviet friendship pact. Anti-German works of every description were disseminated during World War II.

It is important to reiterate that in conditions of monopolistic Soviet publishing and the unavailability of non-Soviet books, the authorities can easily regulate the supply of different types of books, while the Soviet reading public is only very occasionally able to affect this supply by demonstrating demand. Thus Deming Brown's observation, made in 1962 with

8. *Antologija kitajskoj poèzii,* perevod s kitajskogo pod obščej redakciej Go Mo-žo i N. T. Fedorenko, 4 vols. (Moscow: Goslitizdat, 1957–58). Mao's poetry and Fedorenko's commentary appear in Vol. IV on pp. 5–23 and 317–24, respectively. It is worth noting that Fedorenko devotes seven pages of commentary to the eighteen pages of Mao's verse. The other thirty modern Chinese poets represented in the volume occupy, it is true, 290 pages of text, but receive only five pages of Dr. Fedorenko's notes. The commentary to Vol. IV, which deals with the modern period of Chinese poetry, is the only one signed by Dr. Fedorenko. The notes to the other volumes are unsigned.

reference to American writing, is equally applicable to all translated literature in the USSR from the 1920s to the present:

> We can be sure that if a work of American literature has been issued repeat-
> edly in the Soviet Union, the public likes it. But the small printing of a book,
> or failure to print it at all, does not necessarily indicate that Soviet readers
> do not or would not like it. It is reasonably certain, for example, that the
> works of Thomas Wolfe, F. Scott Fitzgerald, James T. Farrell, and Thornton
> Wilder would find many enthusiastic readers in the Soviet Union. Yet they
> have never been published there.[9]

The low ebb in the fortunes of West European and American literature
in the USSR was reached in the later 1940s when the country that had only
recently played a decisive role in the defeat of Nazism embarked on a
virulently nationalistic, xenophobic course. The "anti-cosmopolitan" campaign with its bitter denunciations of "servility to the West" all but destroyed any serious study of Western writing and could not fail to affect the
publication of translated Western literature. For all intents and purposes
publication of the latter was confined to the reprinting of venerable classics;
living foreign writers were restricted, by and large, to those whose pro-
Soviet sympathies, particularly as reflected in their writings, compensated
for their foreign citizenship. Literary merit and readers' interest were given
scant consideration. Seething official hatred of all things Western was so
pervasive that it prompted a Western scholar to ask whether the USSR was,
indeed, intent on withdrawing from Western civilization.[10]

The situation began to change rapidly within weeks after the death of
Joseph Stalin on March 5, 1953. The freeing of a group of Jewish physicians
arrested in January of that year on charges of conspiring to murder leading
Soviet political figures was accompanied by the first denunciation of ethnic
hatred to appear in print in years. Some of the most outlandish claims of
Russia's cultural supremacy (such as ascribing to the Russians innumerable
discoveries in science) began to be questioned. Suggestions of Russia's past
indebtedness to Western culture, though still unfashionable, ceased to be
regarded as near-treason. Slowly and cautiously, Soviet Russia began to
reaffirm her membership in the community of Western culture. Not unex-

---

9. Deming Brown, *Soviet Attitudes toward American Writing*, p. 7. Most of the authors cited,
it so happens, were published in the USSR in the ensuing decade. This does not, however,
invalidate Brown's argument; other names could be substituted easily enough. Fitzgerald's
*The Great Gatsby* appeared in the USSR in 1965, and *Tender is the Night* in 1971; two short
stories of Thomas Wolfe were translated in 1958 and one more in 1962; Wilder's novel *The
Bridge of San Luis Rey* was printed in *Novyj mir* in December 1971. But thirteen years after
the appearance of Deming Brown's study, no evidence could be found of publication of any
work by Farrell.

10. W. W. Kulski, "Can Russia Withdraw from Civilization?" *Foreign Affairs,* Vol. XXVIII,
No. 4 (July 1950), pp. 623–43.

pectedly, among the first beneficiaries of the more hospitable atmosphere for Western literature were the older and hence ideologically safer classics. On December 26, 1953, the journal *Sovetskaja kul'tura* reminded its readers that in recent years *Othello* and *Twelfth Night* were produced on Soviet stages, but not *Hamlet, Macbeth,* or *King Lear*; it also expressed dismay that "for a long time" there had been no performances of Molière, Schiller, Ibsen, and Shaw. As anybody could guess, this was a signal that this intolerable state of affairs would soon be rectified.

For some years after World War II the World Peace Council, a Soviet-dominated organization, would periodically proclaim anniversary years for famous writers of the past, thus providing Soviet propaganda with an opportunity to claim those writers for the Soviet cause by insisting that the USSR alone embodied a given author's noble hopes and aspirations, while the Soviet Union's adversaries personified everything the writer held in contempt. Such primitive exercises continued well beyond Stalin's death. Thus, in 1954 the World Peace Council called for worldwide observances of the 2400th anniversary of the birth of Aristophanes and of the bicentennial of Henry Fielding.[11] People of goodwill throughout the world were asked to take note of Fielding's "impassionate protests against bloody militarist adventures of tyrants and oppressors of nations, his contempt for the selfishness of moneyed classes." Analogous claims were made a decade later on the occasion of the 400th anniversary of the birth of Shakespeare: "To us, this giant of the Renaissance was never merely a classical relic, an object of veneration. He has always been regarded as a contemporary, a participant in the mighty struggle waged by the Soviet people for mankind's glorious future."[12]

Relatively new and significant in its impact on the fate of Western literature in Russia in the decade after 1954 was the increasingly frequent use of that literature as a public relations device in the much emphasized posture of peaceful coexistence with the West. Translated foreign literature was thus to become a not unimportant element in the conduct of Soviet foreign policy, a cultural dimension of the *détente* to which the USSR was to become committed abroad and consequently, if only to a lesser degree, in the eyes of its own citizenry.[13] Typical early examples of this kind of

11. The anniversary of Aristophanes was discussed in *Izvestija,* December 29, 1954, and the bicentennial of Fielding in *Pravda,* October 9, 1954.

12. *Pravda,* April 23, 1964.

13. Cultural activity as an arm of foreign policy is not an entirely new phenomenon. Probably best known are the activities of the Alliance Française and, more recently, the British Council. These bodies, however, strive to promote their countries' national interests through the use of *their own* culture, e.g., by sponsoring language courses, reading rooms, lending libraries, lectures, films, etc. The USSR engages in similar activities abroad. As far as can be ascertained, it is the only major country also to make extensive use of *other* countries' cultures for similar

diplomacy by means of foreign literature included a public commemoration of the bicentennial of Montesquieu's death, which was attended by senior officials from the French embassy;[14] a similar event in honor of the centennial of Walt Whitman's *Leaves of Grass* attended by ranking American diplomats as well as "American athletes visiting Moscow"—who may or may not have heard of Whitman's work before;[15] and assistance to a visiting British delegation in the production of a film of their visit to the USSR: "The head of the delegation could see this [great interest in English literature] for himself. On the library shelves of the Stalin Automobile Factory he saw the works of Shakespeare, Galsworthy, Burns, Thackeray, Byron, Walter Scott, Shaw, and Dickens."[16] At the same time, as a result of warmer relations between the USSR and Western Europe, the Soviet public could see a larger selection of Italian films,[17] and, for the first time, live performances by a major Western European theatre, the Comédie Française.[18]

Most importantly, 1955 saw the inception of the monthly *Inostrannaja literatura* (Foreign Literature), a successor to the defunct *Internacional'naja literatura* (International Literature), also a monthly, which was published prior to World War II. *Inostrannaja literatura* is now the USSR's only periodical devoted almost entirely to foreign literature and the arts, with occasional articles and polemical reviews dealing with sociopolitical subjects; its editor in the early 1970s was the former ambassador to the United Nations, Nikolaj T. Fedorenko. *Inostrannaja literatura* does not

purposes. An example familiar to millions in the West is the practice by Soviet song and dance ensembles of always including in their performances one or two songs and dances of the *host* country. The device is apparently effective: it invariably brings forth applause.

14. *Pravda*, March 16, 1955.

15. *Pravda*, June 14, 1955. Two days earlier, *Izvestija* printed an obviously commissioned article on Whitman by the eminent critic and translator Kornej Čukovskij. The decision to celebrate the centennial of Walt Whitman's masterpiece emanated from the World Peace Council, which proclaimed the date "a great cultural festival of all progressive mankind."

16. *Sovetskaja kul'tura*, October 2, 1954. On November 24, 1954, *Pravda* reported a speech by Professor A. I. Denisov, delivered on the occasion of the 30th anniversary of Britain's Society for Cultural Relations with the USSR. Since the establishment of the Soviet state, according to Professor Denisov, more than 2,000 books by British authors were published in the USSR in 53 languages, a total of over 35 million copies.

17. The festival of Italian films was scheduled to be held in Moscow, Leningrad, Stalingrad (since renamed Volgograd), and the capitals of the fourteen union republics from March 16 to 26, 1954. It was to feature two new Italian films, both noted for their message of social protest, *Rome Eleven O'Clock* and *Two Cents Worth of Hope*. At the same time a number of previously released Italian films were to be shown again (although no information was given on either the past or the envisaged new showings, e.g., where, how long, expected sizes of audiences, etc.). Films in the latter group included *Four Steps in the Clouds, Return to Sorrento, Favorite Arias, The Young Caruso, The Love Potion, The Millionaire of Naples, No Peace Under the Olive Trees, Pagliacci, Under Sicilian Skies,* and *The Bicycle Thief.* See *Izvestija*, March 9, 1954.

18. The visit of the Comédie Française began with a performance of Molière's *Tartuffe.* Also included in the program were Molière's *Le Bourgeois Gentilhomme,* Corneille's *Le Cid,* and a modern play, an adaptation of Jules Renard's *Carrots,* a story of a sensitive boy facing a world of bullies. See *Pravda,* April 9 and 18, 1954.

deal exclusively with Western writing; its coverage includes all countries outside the USSR proper, and occasionally entire issues are devoted not only to Africa or Asia, but even to Slavic literatures of Eastern Europe. Since access to foreign books and periodicals is allowed only to a handful of specialists, the importance of *Inostrannaja literatura* is hard to overestimate.[19] One of the items featured in the first issue, Jean-Paul Sartre's *La Putain respectueuse (The Respectable Prostitute)*, offered a glimpse of some of the qualities that were to characterize much of the journal's contents in years to come. The play was political; its author was known for his leftist views; the work in question was strongly anti-American; the text was slightly edited to suit Soviet tastes (in this case, by the author himself); and, lastly, the play's title was changed to *Lizzie:* Soviet journals do not tolerate "pornography," not even in titles of works by foreign authors.

The year 1955 also marked the beginning of a rapid expansion in the publication of Western writing. As if to compensate for years of neglect, the public was offered large quantities of works by old favorites, supplemented by first issues of books never before printed in the USSR. Such works were often sold out in a matter of hours. It is common knowledge among Soviet citizens that newly published books, and particularly foreign ones, are *deficitnyj tovar,* merchandise in short supply. Even foreigners who buy Soviet publications abroad are aware that few Soviet books are kept in print.

Our discussion will be centered primarily around literary works published in book form. It will deal mainly with translations into Russian, which account for most of the foreign writing printed in the USSR, but translations into the other languages of the Soviet Union will also be considered. Additionally, we will take into account West European and American books published in their original languages in the USSR: fearful of penetration into the country of *any* books from abroad, Soviet authorities regularly resort to this stratagem (it should be noted that most such publications are not texts adapted for school use, except insofar as they are supplied with appropriate Russian introductions).

19. "For example, *The Atlantic Monthly* and *Harper's Magazine* are in a 'special repository' at the Moscow Library of Foreign Literatures, and they can be read only with special permission (a document to the effect that the item is connected with the reader's scholarly work)." Proffer, *Soviet Criticism of American Literature,* p. xiv. A very curious bimonthly *Sovremennaja xudožestvennaja literatura za rubežom (Modern Writing Abroad)* is published by the State Library of Foreign Literature in Moscow. It is printed in only six thousand copies (early issues were mimeographed) and seems to have been launched around 1960 (the July–August 1974 issue bears the number 106). The 150-page journal prints *"obzory, recenzii, annotacii"*—surveys, reviews, and annotations of foreign books not yet published in the USSR, and perhaps never to be published there. Most of its contents are tendentious plot summaries, but even these must be interesting to Soviet readers with no easy access to foreign books. The bulletin appears to have occasional difficulties with the censorship; No. 1, 1972, and No. 4, 1973, were held up for four months, and some of the others for three months.

The decision to focus attention on books, rather than on the contents of journals, was suggested by several considerations. Books are "permanent" acquisitions; they are not, as a rule, discarded after reading. Hence, a book purchased by an individual may be read and re-read by more people than the same work published in a journal, this in spite of the fact that the press runs of some of the Soviet Russian literary journals which publish Western writing (there are about a dozen important ones) reach six hundred thousand copies, much more than that of an average book. (The series *Roman-gazeta,* almost every issue of which is a separate large-format paperback, with a circulation of up to a million copies, will be considered in the category of books.) Also, ordinary libraries do not keep old periodicals, and in those that do store them, bound periodicals cannot be taken out. Finally, only persons with access to bibliographies can track down the contents of old journals, while books are listed in card catalogues.[20]

Nevertheless, we shall not entirely exclude literary journals from discussion. Besides *Inostrannaja literatura,* we have examined the contents of all issues for 1954 to 1964 of the foremost "liberal" monthly of the period, *Novyj mir,* of the "moderate" *Moskva,* "conservative" *Neva* and *Zvezda,* the "neo-Stalinist" *Oktjabr',* and selected issues of others.[21] In addition, careful study was made of *Voprosy literatury,* the Soviet Union's leading scholarly literary journal (which includes discussions of foreign literature), as well as of the general press, particularly *Literaturnaja gazeta* (only partly devoted to literature), and the two central daily newspapers, *Izvestija* and *Pravda.* Most of the literary journals publish some translations of West European and American writing (although journals appearing in Central Asia, even those printed in Russian, often feature translations of Arabic, Turkish, Hindi, and other Asian authors). Many do so apparently to brighten up their tables of contents. This is sometimes accomplished by printing, in five pages or so, samples of verse by a like number of foreign poets.[22] More often, however, the translations are shorter prose works; some are serious literature, others are aimed at less sophisticated tastes, but all share one common feature—high reader appeal—and hence all are lucrative to the journal.[23]

20. With some exceptions, ideologically sensitive books are not, as a rule, found in the general card catalogues of Soviet libraries, but only in "special" catalogues. The books themselves are stored in restricted sections of the larger Soviet libraries, with access by special permission only.

21. These include *Prostor, Ural, Sibirskie ogni, Volga, Junost', Don, Polymja,* and *Neman.*

22. Thus, in *Moskva* (No. 12, 1959, pp. 126–31) there were poems by Robert Frost, Carl Sandburg, Jack Spicer, and Lawrence Ferlinghetti.

23. E.g., the staunchly Stalinist monthly *Don* has published over the years an exceptionally large number of translations from the English. These included works by such very different authors as J. B. Priestley, C. P. Snow, William Faulkner, Isaac Asimov, James Thurber, Agatha Christie, and Ellery Queen. Published in Rostov, the journal is regarded as being under the influence of the conservative novelist Mixail Šoloxov, the author of *Silent Don* (one member of its editorial board bore the politically schizoid name Šoloxov-Sinjavskij). Western

Western literature in translation, while occasionally dubious ideologically, is a great moneymaker. In all of our research we did not come across a single complaint about the unprofitability of Western literature, theater, and cinema. On the contrary, hundreds of speeches and articles inveighed against promoters of Western imports whose thirst for cheap popularity and easy profits, it was claimed, blinded them to the social and political cost involved. The dilemma contained in the earthy old Russian saying, *kapital priobresti i nevinnost' sobljusti,* how to make a fast ruble without losing one's virginity, to reconcile capitalist greed and Communist purity, is not easy to solve. Its implications will be discussed in chapter nine.

Most of the statistical data on the publication of West European and American literature in the USSR were obtained from *Knižnaja letopis' (Book Annals)* a weekly publication purporting to list all books and pamphlets printed in the USSR. As a rule, *Knižnaja letopis'* indicates the number of copies in which each item was published, although there are occasional omissions.[24] Collecting statistics from about six hundred issues of this journal was a laborious undertaking, but there was, unfortunately, no alternative. (The weekly *Novye knigi* merely announces books *scheduled* for publication; some of these never materialize). No overall Soviet bibliography of all foreign books, in translation as well as in the original, exists. Most bibliographies are limited to the output of a single publisher or lack information on sizes of press runs. Occasionally, even bibliographies published

---

detective stories, particularly by Georges Simenon, the French creator of Inspector Maigret, appear occasionally in *Znamja, Zvezda, Neman,* and *Polymja.* Though officially frowned upon, such stories are very popular with Soviet readers and are clearly intended to boost the journals' circulations.

24. Questions have been raised in the West about the reliability of Soviet publishing statistics in general, with suggestions that these are sometimes falsified for a variety of reasons, but evidence is inconclusive. What is certain is that until the late 1960s Soviet statistics lumped together new books and reprints, as well as pamphlets, catalogues, and industrial manuals (many distributed free of charge), and also counted each translation into the scores of languages spoken in the USSR as well as every separate volume in a set; the statistics were thus grossly inflated. This could be ascertained from data cited in Soviet sources in those years. Thus, a Soviet study cited the number of titles published in the USSR in 1958 as 63,000. A few pages later, however, it asserted, "Every year, some 30,000 new book titles [*naimenovanij*] are offered for sale," thus revealing a discrepancy of over fifty percent between "statistical" books and those actually sold in bookstores. See Reznikov, *Rabota prodavca,* pp. 4, 17. Now, however, more meaningful comparisons are possible, and the new data dispels the myth that the USSR is the world's largest book publisher, both in terms of book production per capita as well as in absolute figures. True, Soviet publishing statistics still include reprints as well as individual volumes in multivolume sets, but pamphlets are now listed separately from books, which are defined as publications of at least 49 pages. In 1969, the USSR published 41,317 titles in this category, with a total of 921,191,000 copies; this was 3.8 copies *printed* per capita. The corresponding 1969 figure for the United States was 1,435,000,000 copies actually *sold,* or 7.1 copies per capita (no data is available on the number of titles). It should, of course, be remembered that the American figure does not include publications of the federal, state, and local governments. Thus, the actual per capita consumption of books in the U.S. is really nearly twice that of the Soviet Union. See *Book Publishing in the USSR,* Reports of the Delegations of U.S. Book Publishers Visiting the USSR, October 21–November 4, 1970, August 20– September 17, 1962, 2nd ed., enlarged (Cambridge, Mass.: Harvard University Press, 1971), p. 16.

under the most impressive auspices are carelessly compiled and cannot be entirely relied upon.[25] Much more seriously, such bibliographies betray interference on the part of Soviet censorship. Thus, a bibliography of American literature published by the USSR Academy of Sciences in 1970 retroactively suppresses all data on the publication of works by Howard Fast. Writes Deming Brown, "No American writer has ever enjoyed more Soviet adulation in his own lifetime than Howard Fast. From 1948 to 1957, over 2,500,000 copies of his works were printed, in twelve languages of the USSR."[26] It appears that Fast's break with the Communist movement resulted also in the American novelist's expulsion from a scholarly bibliography published in an era of alleged de-Stalinization and *détente*.

The Western literary works examined in this book were originally written in fifteen languages. Our data, however, were limited to Russian titles of works and crudely phonetic and exasperatingly inconsistent Cyrillic transcriptions of their authors' names, hopelessly confused because of the variety of languages involved.[27] Every effort was made to ascertain the proper spelling of names, but this was sometimes impossible since in a number of cases they could not be found in any non-Cyrillic reference work. Similarly there were cases when English translations of individual titles could not be found, a particularly vexing detail when the original was written, say, in Icelandic, or Italian, or Finnish. Indeed, some of these books may not have been translated into English; citing their titles in the original language (assuming *these* could be

25. For example, a bibliography of Russian translations of American literature which purports to include twentieth-century American writers as well as "translations of works of those writers whose lives and careers fall mainly in the nineteenth-century, but end in the present century" was compiled by V. A. Libman and edited by A. N. Nikoljukin for the Institute of World Literature of the USSR Academy of Sciences. The bibliography "includes translations published up to 1968, inclusive." "Bibliografija. Literatura S.Š.A. v russkix perevodax (XX vek)," in M. O. Mendel'son, A. N. Nikoljukin, R. M. Samarin (eds.), *Problemy literatury S.Š.A. XX veka*, Akademija Nauk SSSR, Institut Mirovoj Literatury im. A. M. Gor'kogo (Moscow: Nauka, 1970), pp. 391–519. The quotations are on p. 391. It includes such very marginally twentieth-century American authors as Bret Harte (1836–1902), Lafcadio Hearn (1850–1904), Frank Norris (1870–1902), and Stephen Crane (1871–1900). In a number of cases, no information is given on dates of birth and death. Inexplicably, compilers missed such recent Soviet publications as Saul Bellow's *The Gonzaga Manuscripts* (*Neva*, No. 7, 1961) and *Oni požnut burju* (apparently, "They Will Inherit the Wind") by Elizabeth Littleton and Herbert Sturtz (precise spelling unknown), both identified as Americans in a preface to the Russian translation of their novel about life in Franco Spain (*Moskva*, Nos. 8 and 9, 1961). Very likely, the number of such omissions was far greater. No attempt at a systematic check was made.

26. Deming Brown, *Soviet Attitudes toward American Writing*, p. 281.

27. In the scholarly bibliography of American literature referred to in note 25, Woodrow Wilson's name is spelled *Vil'son*, but Mitchell Wilson's, *Uilson;* Richard Wright is *Rajt;* Herman Wouk is *Vuk*, but Tennessee Williams is *Uil'jams*. Bret Harte is *Gart*, Robert Herrick is *Gerrik*, and Joseph Hergesheimer is, for some reason, *Geršsgejmer;* William Heywood is *Xejvud*, Ben Hecht is *Xekt*, Joseph Heller is *Xeller*, Lillian Hellman is *Xellman*, and Ernest Hemingway is *Xeminguèj*. And this is within a single book dealing with a single language! See *Problemy literatury SŠA XX veka*.

found) was not an ideal solution. Also, as in all countries, translations in the USSR often appear under titles that do not resemble the originals. Apologies are offered in advance for any errors that may have resulted.

In order to impart greater clarity to the vast subject under consideration, the book begins with two chapters that highlight, so to speak, its two extremes. Chapter one, "The Red Pencil," illustrates the most brazen manifestation of the Soviet state's interference in the dissemination of translated Western literature in the USSR, the censoring of the texts themselves. Unacknowledged as a rule to Soviet readers and unauthorized by Western authors, such censorship illustrates the rigidity of political controls over literature and publishing in the USSR. Indeed, the fact that most of the textual changes thus introduced are relatively minor only serves to illustrate the thoroughness of these controls. At the other pole is chapter two, "Western Writing and Soviet Readers," which examines available data, admittedly selective and incomplete, on "spontaneous" reader reactions to Western writing, on tastes and preferences of various categories of the reading public, however restricted to books that state-controlled publishers choose to make available.

Subsequent chapters examine the publication in the USSR of various types of Western prose, poetry, and drama by grouping them into categories corresponding roughly to the labels affixed to them in popularly written Soviet literary criticism and mass-circulation literary journalism, in textbooks, and in reference works. In the course of our discussion we shall refer frequently to the *Theatrical Encyclopedia* (*Teatral'naja ènciklopedija,* five volumes, 1961–67) and particularly to the *Literary Encyclopedia* (*Kratkaja literaturnaja ènciklopedija,* eight volumes, 1962–75, abbreviated in the notes as KL). Both works were published by the "Sovetskaja Ènciklopedija" Publishing House. Each is the standard reference work on its subject currently in use. Contributors include major critics as well as novices. While admittedly not particularly perceptive aesthetically, this kind of politically-oriented Soviet literary criticism is most reflective of the official thinking that ultimately determines whether a certain foreign author or even a *type* of writing (say, James Joyce or the French *nouveau roman*) is to be published at all, and if so, in how many copies. In this connection, it should be borne in mind that the circulations of Soviet literary journals are determined not by public demand, but by arbitrarily assigned allocations of paper; debates about "excessive" printings of certain Western authors usually revolve around their ideological value, not their artistic merit. In some measure, such crudely political considerations, quite openly expressed, may be viewed as a counterpart of sorts to crass commercialism in Western publishing at its worst.[28] The analogy cannot be pursued too far, however, because, unlike the West, in the Soviet Union there is not a single independent publisher, however small and impoverished, not a single "little magazine" operating on a shoestring (save for the strictly illegal *samizdat*), not one amateur theater with a repertory free of any controls.

Like it or not, an examination of the quasi-official attitudes of Soviet literary critics and the quite official publishing policies in that country must be formulated in the categories employed by the makers of these policies —and these categories, as will be seen, are often crudely political. Hence, at the risk of some incongruity, we shall examine some of Hemingway's works as mere pacifist novels and others as juvenile reading, Boccaccio and Rabelais as enemies of religion, Balzac and Dickens as ordinary accusers of capitalism, and Faulkner as just another author exposing racism and the general squalor of American life. Serious, sensitive, and even original Soviet responses to these and other foreign authors' art do exist, but these are ordinarily quite unrelated to decisions about their publication and press runs. If a culinary simile be permitted, the heavily ideological decision making in Soviet publishing of Western literature is reminiscent of the behavior in a restaurant of some unfortunates, who, before considering the taste or even price of a given dish, must first ascertain the cholesterol content of Peking duck, the carbohydrate value of lasagna, and the number of calories in baked Alaska. Literary gourmets in the West may sneer at such coarseness, but Soviet readers are well aware that their reading fare must first pass such scrutiny.[29]

Chapters three and four examine two types of Western writing that Soviet criticism views as relatively apolitical. The former examines a number of venerable classics, particularly poetry, as well as light reading of recent origin, while the latter deals with the vast assortment of books for younger readers, from pre-schoolers to adolescents. While no serious ideological value is attached to either group, the advisability of making merely enter-

28. Even scholarly publications are not exempt. A publisher's blurb in *Problemy literatury SŠA XX veka* (p. 2) informs: "This book examines the work of a number of modern U.S. writers, Bellow, Updike, Cheever, Mailer, Lowell, Williams, whose best works, notwithstanding the bourgeois limitations of their authors, criticize antihumane and soulless capitalist society." And the modest salesman in a bookstore is also expected to do his share: "He should know the ideological significance and political timeliness of a particular publication . . . in order to suggest it to a customer when necessary." Reznikov, *Rabota prodavca,* p. 19.

29. My first attempts to study Soviet readers' reactions to literature, Russian and foreign, and to Soviet literary criticism were based on several hundred interviews conducted shortly after the war by the Russian Research Center of Harvard University. The results were published in two articles, "Russian Writers and Soviet Readers," *The American Slavic and East European Review,* Vol. XIV, No. 1 (February 1955), pp. 108–21, and "Foreign Authors and Soviet Readers," *The Russian Review,* Vol. XIII, No. 4 (October 1954), pp. 266–75. More recently, I discussed the subject with approximately three hundred new arrivals in Israel from the Soviet Union. These conversations were published as a pamphlet, *Why They Left: A Survey of Soviet Jewish Emigrants* (New York: Academic Committee on Soviet Jewry, 1972).

taining reading available to adults is often questioned. On the other hand, similar reading for children and adolescents is viewed positively as being educational in the broader sense of the word—building character, acquainting with far-away times and places, and contributing to an appreciation of literary values.

Chapters five, six, and seven discuss the publication of literature that pursues openly didactic goals, hopefully reaching all audiences. These books, directly or indirectly, support the image of non-Soviet societies projected by the Soviet media and taught in Soviet schools. Included are works that expose a wide variety of evils allegedly endemic to capitalism, ranging from economic injustice to religious fanaticism, from racist persecution to feelings of alienation and drift, from unemployment to war. Some of these works were written by friends of the Soviet Union and sympathizers of the Communist cause. The authors of others may have regarded their writing as loyal, constructive criticism of the less attractive sides of their societies. Still others may not have consciously pursued any social goals. Yet regardless of their authors' intentions, these books are published in the USSR for reasons that are often openly utilitarian. They are presented as illustrations of the thesis that life under capitalism is morally repugnant, economically perilous, and psychologically alien to the nature of man. Chapter eight, by contrast, concerns Western authors who remain unpublished for obvious political reasons (such as, for instance, vocal opponents of Soviet policies or former Communists) as well as others whose limited publication is allowed in spite of many misgivings about their ideological message and even objectionable artistic form (such as, for instance, rebellion against the traditional canons of realism that are favored in Soviet literature). Chapter nine focuses on some of the political perils and social and moral paradoxes inherent in the dissemination of nonconformist and rebellious Western literature critical of social conventions and institutions in an authoritarian and conservative Soviet society.

The relative abundance and variety of translated literature from the Western world were among the hallmarks of the cultural vitality and excitement that characterized the first post-Stalin years. A Russian critic's memorable essay of nearly a century ago bestowed the proud name of a marvelous decade on the extraordinarily fruitful ten years in the history of Russian literature that followed, ironically, the death of Pushkin, its greatest poet.[30] The years 1954–64 did not produce a Lermontov or a Gogol. The decade may, however, be at least partly deserving of the title "marvelous," particularly when viewed against the depressing background of the Stalinist period.

30. P. A. Annenkov, *Zamečatel'noe desjatiletie (1838–1848)*, published in 1880.

The process of cultural ferment that began in the mid-1950s continued, with less energy, under Khrushchev's successors. Some, although not quite as many, interesting Soviet books appeared, as well as a substantial number of new translations of Western authors. But surprises were relatively few; the general patterns and guidelines had already been established. Gone were the great expectations and the heady atmosphere of the marvelous post-Stalin decade, the decade of shortlived euphoria.

In a simile that became famous in Russian history, Peter the Great's founding of a new capital was likened to the opening of a window to Europe. The simile retains a degree of validity when applied to the tumultuous events in Russia's cultural life in the decade that followed Stalin's death, including the sudden expansion of the variety and quantity of foreign writing available to the public. While the aging dictator was alive, windows to the non-Soviet world had been tightly shut, and the atmosphere within the USSR was stifling, as many prominent cultural figures later admitted. At first the window to the West was opened only a crack, but because of pressures from within the country, where access to Western culture became a barometer of the progress of de-Stalinization, as well as from abroad, where this was viewed as evidence of the sincerity of the politics of "peaceful coexistence," the cracks grew progressively wider. At no time, to be sure, was the window anywhere near fully open, but the impact of the fresh air was ever more widely felt. Within a decade of the old tyrant's demise, complaints grew louder that the window was causing drafts in the decorous and static Soviet society, creating restlessness among its young. The simplest way to deal with the problem might have been to shut the window again, but this was no longer feasible. And so the window to the West remained half-open. It was, however, equipped with wind-deflectors and screens to reduce the inflow of troublesome Western culture and thus to minimize the damage it might cause.

# CHAPTER

# I

# *The Red Pencil*

Until very recently, the structure and operations of Soviet publishing attracted little interest abroad for the understandable reason that they did not in any way affect the fortunes of Western authors and booksellers.[1] In the absence of any copyright agreement, Soviet journals and publishers felt free to print any foreign books without even the courtesy of informing their authors. The situation changed abruptly with the Soviet accession in February 1973 to the Universal Copyright Convention. On January 1, 1974, a Soviet copyright agency, VAAP (an acronym of its formal Russian name, *Vsesojuznoe agentstvo avtorskix prav,* the All-Union Agency for Authors' Rights) was officially established. Less than two years later, its Moscow headquarters employed some four hundred persons, with additional offices in the various Soviet republics and representatives in several foreign countries. Lured by the prospect of royalties, foreign publishers and authors alike have exhibited considerable curiosity about this organization.[2] These legitimate interests, however, need not concern us here. Suffice it to point out that royalties will be paid only on works published abroad since May 27, 1973, and that it will therefore be some years before the impact of the new policy will be felt.[3] Nevertheless, a brief sketch of the organization and

1. Among the few academic investigations of the subject is Boris I. Gorokhoff, *Publishing in the USSR,* Slavic and East European Series, Vol. XIX (Bloomington: Russian and East European Institute, Indiana University, 1959).

2. An interesting, if somewhat politically naive account of conversations with officials in the Soviet agency is Herbert R. Lottman, "Inside VAAP," *Publishers' Weekly,* September 8, 1975, pp. 28–33.

3. Some indications, however, are discernible from the information conveyed to Mr. Lottman by the Soviet officials. Thus, for instance, the organization's deputy chairman Vasilij Sitnikov (previously deputy director of the Soviet Academy of Sciences' Institute for the Study of the USA and Canada) informed Mr. Lottman that VAAP decided against acquiring the rights to Heinrich Böll's *Katharina Blum,* ostensibly because of the author's exorbitant financial demands: "So we'll wait till it's less of a best seller and the author is less demanding" (Ibid., p. 30). A more likely reason for the decision may have been a desire to punish Böll for his defense of Soviet dissident authors and his much-publicized welcome of Solzhenitsyn after the

operation of Soviet publishing may be useful at this point. A succinct and remarkably candid description is given in a Soviet history of the subject:

> Soviet book publishing operates on principles of economic self-sufficiency and socialist [!-MF] profit. It is equally alien to the spirit of subsidies and to crude commercialism. *Still, while economic factors are strictly observed, its primary function in society is that of an ideological enterprise,* the activities of which rest on the unshakable foundation of profound Party spirit, popular appeal, strict scholarly standards and planning. *In its daily activities, it* [Soviet book publishing] *is guided by the policies of the Communist Party.* Its ideological banner is Marxism-Leninism which points to the only correct path to the reshaping of the world. Soviet publishing has no reason to conceal its political creed or its ideological affiliation under a shabby cloak of "nonpartisanship," as bourgeois publishers are fond of doing in order to cover up their class nature.... *Prior to accepting a manuscript and sending it to the printer's, every* [Soviet] *publishing house must arrive at a firm opinion: how useful will this particular manuscript be to the overall cause of the building of Communism, and how helpful will it be in the solving of current tasks.*[4]

Clearly, the description is a projection of hopes and aspirations rather than of present-day realities in the Soviet Union's 236 publishing houses,[5] whose operations are, of course, more pragmatic and flexible.[6]

Like most Soviet institutions, publishing houses are subject to several levels of control. Most are officially attached to a variety of local organizations which range from affiliates of the Writers' Union to a variety of industrial enterprises and from branches of the Communist Party to educational establishments. Thus, their books should advance the goals, or at least fall within the purview of these institutions. At the same time, how-

latter's deportation to Germany two years earlier. That VAAP, in addition to its legitimate functions as protector of the financial interests of both Soviet and foreign artists, will also serve as yet another lever of Soviet censorship controls may be seen from the following observations by Sitnikov to his American visitor: "Of course, an [Soviet] author shouldn't send his manuscripts abroad directly if he wishes us to protect his rights. *And we need an opportunity to have the book examined by serious critics to see if it has any value. Then we have an organization that looks at books to see if they contain state secrets. We do advise authors not to turn over manuscripts directly because they can get into trouble*" (Ibid., Emphasis added). The organization will also, naturally, use its leverage on Western publishers as well: "Certainly, the publisher of dissident [Soviet] writers won't have our sympathy, but we'll continue to deal with him. ... Publishers interested in our literature should publish those who accept the Soviet way of life, not those who reject it" (Ibid., p. 31).

4. A. I. Nazarov, *Kniga v sovetskom obščestve. Očerk istorii knigoizdatel'skogo dela v SSSR* (Moscow: Nauka, 1964), pp. 83–84. Italics added.

5. The figure for 1975 cited in Herbert R. Lottman, *Publishers' Weekly,* September 8, 1975, p. 30.

6. For some of the "inside" details of operations of Soviet publishing the author is indebted to Mr. Ilya Suslov, a graduate of the Moscow Institute of Printing and Publishing. Mr. Suslov served as department chief at the Children's Publishing House (Detizdat) from 1956 to 1960. Between 1960 and 1965 he was managing editor of *Junost',* an important monthly, and from 1967 to 1973 he was humor and satire editor of *Literaturnaja gazeta.* Mr. Suslov now lives in the United States.

ever, local Party organizations are expected to offer these provincial publishers a degree of supervision and guidance. At a higher level, all publishing houses are controlled by the State Committee for Printing and Publishing of the USSR Council of Ministers. The committee exercises control over the primarily technical and commercial aspects of publishing, while problems of a political nature, however indirect, are dealt with by the Ideological Commission of the Central Committee of the Communist Party. Normally, the two organizations collaborate harmoniously, but occasional conflicts are inevitable. When these occur political considerations ultimately prevail.

The possibility of such conflicts always exists because the principal leverage of control exerted by the State Committee on Printing and Publishing involves the technical and commercial aspects of book publishing; it is this body, for instance, that decides on the all-important problem of allocation of paper to individual publishers. The publishers, in turn, must put this paper to good use, and their principal tangible indicator of success is financial profit. Hence they have a natural tendency to favor books that are proven money-makers, such as translated foreign fiction, which always sells well and which, until 1973, involved no payment of royalties. These books, however, are not necessarily the most desirable ones politically, and a "game" is thus set in motion. The publishers try to guess to what extent they can afford to neglect the ideological dimensions of publishing, a particularly ticklish decision considering they must operate within fixed allocations of paper. Meanwhile, the Ideological Commission and its various spokesmen, both official and unofficial, attempt to maximize the ideological value of the book output without, however, destroying altogether the publishers' economic viability. The balance is always precarious.[7] Hence, in Soviet conditions, censorship in the usual meaning of the term is only one of many mechanisms enforcing the state's control over literature and the arts; indeed, the others are actually much more effective, and censorship as such may be said to play only an auxiliary role.[8]

The state's monopoly in publishing assures that no really objectionable work is allowed to appear, while questionable works may be printed in insignificant quantities, which restricts their circulation; similar procedures obtain in theatrical repertories and in the cinema. At the same time, political pressures—not necessarily overt—minimize the degree of ideological latitude tolerated in Soviet literary criticism. Much of this is accomplished without recourse to formal censorship. Experienced Soviet critics, editors, and publishing officials can in most cases be depended upon to observe

7. We shall return to this subject in the Conclusions.
8. The best bibliography of the subject is found in Martin Dewhirst and Robert Farrell (eds.), *The Soviet Censorship* (Metuchen, N. J.: The Scarecrow Press, 1973).

proclaimed policies and also to sense the implications of newspaper editorials and pronouncements by Soviet leaders that may, however remotely, relate to matters within their jurisdiction, thus, again, making formal intervention by the censorship unnecessary. Significantly, no published Soviet source acknowledges the existence of any censorship apparatus within the USSR, but, as shall be demonstrated below, oblique references to it do occasionally appear in print. It may safely be assumed that hardly any Soviet citizen would be shocked by the disclosure that there *are* Soviet censors except, perhaps, by an *official admission* of the fact itself. The presence of the censorship is attested by the data that appears on the reverse side of the title page or on the last page of most books published in the USSR. (Books destined for export are among the exceptions.) This information usually includes the dates on which the book cleared preliminary and final censorship as well as the censor's code number. This applies in equal measure to new books and to reprints, as well as to translations from foreign languages; to reiterate, books printed abroad are for all intents and purposes not available in the USSR. With rare exceptions of some imports from Communist bloc countries, they are not sold in bookstores and may be found only in specialized libraries inaccessible to most readers.

Curiously, in Imperial Russia, where the existence of censorship was freely acknowledged, foreign books were treated on the whole with greater leniency than writings by Russian authors. Thus, the first privately owned printing establishment, founded in St. Petersburg in 1771, was authorized to print *only* foreign books—provided, of course, these were not blasphemous or seditious. The French Revolution and the alarming spread of Freemasonry in Russia frightened the Imperial authorities into establishing in 1796 special censorship committees charged with examination of foreign books at ports of entry; in fact, an edict of 1800 briefly prohibited the import of all foreign books. After the Decembrist revolt of 1825 a revised code banned literary works dangerous to the throne, to the Orthodox Church, and to public morals. A double standard was imposed on foreign books: works over 160 pages in length were exempted from prepublication censorship if printed in the original, but in the case of translations only those over 320 pages were exempted.[9] The double standard was clearly aimed at preventing the dissemination of objectionable reading matter among the less educated strata of the population, a policy that was also to be pursued in the decades to come. The gradual weakening of tsarist censorship (and also its singular inconsistency: some overt socialist propaganda was published quite legally,

9. Leon I. Twarog, "Literary Censorship in Russia and the Soviet Union," *Essays on Russian Intellectual History,* Leon Borden Blair (ed.) (Austin: University of Texas Press, 1971), pp. 100–101.

while obstacles were placed in the way of Leo Tolstoy's moralizing tales) contributed to the fact that in Russia at the turn of the century translations of foreign literature were abundant and very popular with all classes of readers.

Since censorship is usually exercised in the USSR at an early stage, when a foreign book is being considered for possible translation or a play for production in the theater, its interference remains largely invisible. Works are rarely banned after their appearance (although, as will be seen, there are exceptions), but some are simply not chosen for translation or production on stage. In conditions of a state monopoly in publishing, this procedure, however outwardly legitimate and whatever the ostensible reasons, also embodies and conceals censorship controls. Those who dissent from the opinion (if one was indeed given as a reason for an unfavorable decision) that a certain work by a foreign poet, novelist, or playwright is of no interest to the Soviet public cannot publish a small edition of the book at their own expense and risk, or collect private funds to underwrite a performance in an experimental theater or even by an amateur group requiring little or no financial backing.

Foreign books that Soviet censors find essentially unobjectionable are usually published or performed with their texts intact or subjected only to what may be described as minor cosmetic surgery. Still, the latter procedure deserves some attention because it attests to the extreme thoroughness of the Soviet censorship controls. Hardly anything in the slightest way objectionable politically or otherwise, however seemingly insignificant—be it but a chance remark by the author or a literary character, sometimes only a single word—is allowed to slip through. Also, in view of the fact that such minor textual emendations of works by non-Soviet authors are, as a rule, unacknowledged (admittedly abridged works will be considered separately), Soviet readers are being deceived into believing that the Western writers they are allowed to read observe (apparently of their own free will!) taboos and conventions that are enforced on the Soviet Union's own authors. Soviet translations of Western writing never *openly* disagree, if only fleetingly, with any of the basic articles of the Soviet faith and never overtly question the Soviet version of history; they never speak with disrespect of Soviet leaders or of the Communist movement; and they follow the rules of Victorian prudery that are still stringently adhered to by Soviet authors. Most Soviet readers are well aware that writers in their own country are frequently pressured into, to paraphrase Mayakovsky, stepping on the throats of their own songs. Such pressures from above (and subsequent recantations and even expressions of gratitude to the Party for its paternal firmness and guidance) are occasionally widely publicized, *pour encourager les autres.*

It is unlikely that most Soviet readers are similarly aware that prior to 1973 Western books were often published and sometimes censored in the USSR without their authors' knowledge, let alone consent. Yet this was then the common Soviet practice. Thus, Kurt Vonnegut, Jr., in reply to this writer's query declared that he was unaware that his books were being published in the USSR, let alone that their texts were censored, sometimes rather heavily. Similar replies were received from Joseph Heller, Arthur Miller, and Gore Vidal. Only Alan Sillitoe was consulted, but even he was misled into believing that the very minor textual changes in the Russian translation of *Key to the Door* were aimed at toning down a bit his overly blunt descriptions of sex, although, as will be seen later in this chapter, most of the changes were clearly political in nature. It is also worth noting that the failure to inform Heller, Vonnegut, Vidal, or Miller that their works were being translated was a clear violation of Soviet laws then in effect. Prior to Soviet accession to the Universal Copyright Convention (the "Geneva Convention" of September 6, 1952) on February 21, 1973, the legislation on copyright was the Soviet law of 1928, reconfirmed in 1964, which provided that "any published work can be translated into another language *without the consent but with the knowledge of the author,* provided that the integrity and the sense of the work are preserved." The latter *caveat* was obviously meant to allow the editor-censors a degree of latitude in effecting minor changes in the text.[10]

10. "To the best of my knowledge, the books of mine which have been published in the Soviet Union are *Utopia-14 (Player Piano), Cat's Cradle,* and *Slaughterhouse-5.* I was not consulted at all about their translation. I was not even informed that they were being published." Letter from Kurt Vonnegut, Jr., to Maurice Friedberg, September 12, 1974.

"I was not aware that changes *had* been made in the Russian version of *Catch-22.* The answer to your question, therefore, is that they were not made with my consent. Nor was approval sought for the right to publish at all." Letter from Joseph Heller to Maurice Friedberg, July 19, 1974.

"No request was ever made to me from any Soviet source to make changes in my works produced or published there. As you doubtless know, they have not ordinarily asked permission to produce or publish foreign works either, and never did in my case." Letter from Arthur Miller to Maurice Friedberg, June 6, 1975.

"I had no idea that *Washington, D.C.* had been published in the Soviet [Union] until I started getting fan mail from Estonia. Needless to say, I never gave them any right to publish and they have never even sent me a copy, assuming no doubt that I am like Jack London and with the majority." Letter from Gore Vidal to Maurice Friedberg, postmarked Rome, August 11, 1975.

"I forget the date when it [*Key to the Door*] appeared in Russian, but you no doubt know this. I do recollect, however, that some time before this event I received a letter from some person who was to be involved in it (or it may have been done by word of mouth when that person—I don't remember who it was, in any case—came to London), enquiring from me as to whether or not I would mind if they took out an odd paragraph here and there due to the fact that some sections of the novel were too sexually explicit. I was assured that this would involve very few omissions, and on this I gave my consent. I did not, however, give anything more than that—certainly no permission to remove matter which may have been objectionable

Before World War II little was known of the workings of Soviet literary censorship. Western authors affected by it were, for the most part, friendly to the USSR (others were rarely published there) and they preferred to overlook this unpleasant fact together with other warts of Soviet life. After all, a great many stubbornly closed their eyes even to such large-scale horrors as the Great Purges and the establishment of a huge network of prison camps. According to David Caute,

> Artistic censorship [in the USSR] tended to distress the fellow-travellers though the Webbs [Sidney and Beatrice] made no mention of it. [The German poet and playwright Ernst] Toller was upset to discover that a satire written by the German Communist Egon Erwin Kisch had been cut by a humourless Russian censor, and that both Wagner and Pirandello were banned. Stanislavsky told Dreiser that he would have willingly produced his plays in Russian had the censors not intervened, and a writer thus thwarted usually concludes: if they censor *me,* something must be wrong. The American novelist also saw productions of Schiller's *The Robbers* and of *Uncle Tom's Cabin* which had been "edited" and mutilated for propaganda reasons, leaving him with the impression that the Soviet government was enslaving and betraying the arts.[11]

In 1969 Arthur Miller complained to Yekaterina Furtseva, then Soviet Minister of Culture, about the numerous changes made by Soviet translators (or editor-censors?) in the text of one of his plays: "Nothing is left to be developed and discovered, everything is stated at the outset, and rather crudely at that. I could not understand why the play was such a success."[12] Miller's complaints referred to the Soviet version of *A View from the Bridge.* It appears that he was unaware of the much more severe political censorship a decade earlier of another of his plays, *The Crucible,* which will be discussed later in this chapter.[13]

Arthur Miller was not the only Western dramatist to have his plays censored in the USSR. Those whose plays were thoroughly edited included Lillian Hellman and Jean-Paul Sartre: "In Sartre's *La Putain respectueuse,*

---

to the regime." Letter from Alan Sillitoe to Maurice Friedberg, November 16, 1975.

For text of the law, see *Graždanskij kodeks RSFSR* (Moscow, 1972), p. 129. Italics added.

11. David Caute, *The Fellow Travellers: A Postscript to the Enlightenment* (New York: Macmillan, 1973), p. 94.

12. Arthur Miller, "In Russia," *Harper's Magazine,* September 1969, p. 44.

13. Still another, and very ingenious, device was employed in the Soviet translation of Arthur Miller's *Death of a Salesman,* which appeared in the February 1956 issue of *Novyj mir.* The translation was entitled *Čelovek kotoromu tak vezlo,* "The Man Who Had All the Luck," which heightened the play's ironic portrayal of American "success." The Soviet title also introduces some confusion because it coincides with the title of another play by the American dramatist, one that has never been produced. Miller refers to *The Man Who Had All the Luck* as "a failure" and a "desk-drawer play." See the author's introduction to *Arthur Miller's Collected Plays* (New York: Viking Press, 1973), p. 13.

decently renamed Lizzy MacKay, the ideologically reformed heroine ended by joining the ranks of the Peace Movement."[14] The case of Sartre's play was unusual in that the changes were made by the author himself: "When Sartre learned that his play was being considered by a Soviet theater, he revised it and introduced a new ending. . . . In this version, which was written specifically for the Mossoviet Theater, the play is most effective. Sartre's sensitivity to dialogue and to the specific requirements of the stage are apparent in this treatment of the motif of the triumph of human dignity over the bias and hypocrisy of spokesmen for bourgeois morals."[15]

That foreign films shown in the USSR are often "edited" for political reasons has been known for some decades. Unable to prevent this practice, American filmmakers made an attempt to eliminate at least one of its most pernicious features, the addition to foreign films of scenes written and produced in the USSR:

> In 1948 Mr. Eric Johnston, as President of the Motion Picture Association, contracted with the Soviet film-import office for the sale of twenty-five American films. . . . *The agreement authorized Soviet censors to delete scenes from films purchased, but stipulated that editors would refrain from making any additions.* . . . American films exhibited in the USSR have not always been obtained by official transactions, nor has tampering by editors invariably rested on permission of the producers. In the postwar period the Soviet use of two American motion pictures led to high-level diplomatic discussions between the USA and the USSR. On January 17, 1951, American Ambassador Alan G. Kirk delivered a note to the USSR Ministry of Foreign Affairs

14. François de Liencourt, "The Repertoire of the Fifties," *Literature and Revolution in Soviet Russia 1917–62,* Max Hayward and Leopold Labedz (eds.) (London: Oxford University Press, 1963), p. 161. Tampering with a play's text is an extreme measure. In the hands of a skillful director many plays may acquire political overtones without any alteration of the text itself. This stratagem has been developed into a fine art in the USSR, and the results do not always please the authorities. Thus, on June 30, 1967, *Komsomol'skaja pravda* reported "persistent rumors" that A. K. Tolstoj's nineteenth-century play *Death of Ivan the Terrible* was not allowed to be staged because some persons detected in it "allusions and comparisons" (presumably, with Stalin). The newspaper offered no comment on the rumors but strongly condemned a production of Aleksandr Suxovo-Kobylin's *Death of Tarelkin* which, it claimed, was artificially "modernized." As will be seen in chapter 8, Suxovo-Kobylin's grotesque comedy is a biting exposé of a police state.

15. *Izvestija,* February 10, 1956. Similarly, when Miguel Angel Asturias's novel *His Green Holiness* was published in *Inostrannaja literatura* (No. 12, 1960), readers were informed that the text was "condensed with the author's permission." The novel is a caustic account of the enslavement of a small Latin American republic by Yankee imperialists, acting through the medium of a large company (reminiscent of United Fruit) with the connivance of mercenary local traitors. Asturias is well known in the USSR as the author of *A Week-End in Guatemala* and *El Señor Presidente.*

The case of Anatolij Kuznecov is probably unique. While still in the USSR, he successfully sued a French Catholic publisher for allegedly mutilating the text of his novel *Sequel to a Legend (Prodolženie legendy;* KL, Vol. III [1966], p. 876). Subsequently, Kuznecov defected to the West, where he accused the Soviet authorities of censoring *Babi Yar,* another of his novels. An uncensored version of the latter work was brought out indicating by means of italics those sections, sentences, and individual words that were either deleted or inserted by Soviet censors. See A. Anatolij (Kuznecov), *Babij Jar.* Roman-dokument. (Frankfurt/Main: Possev, 1970).

regarding two films then being exhibited publicly in Moscow. . . . Both films involved were produced by the Columbia Pictures Corporation during the thirties.

The first, entitled *Mr. Smith Goes to Washington,* was being shown in the USSR under the title *Senator.* Although at least one Soviet film review actually described the film's so-called "fairy-tale ending" to the readers of *Sovetskoye iskusstvo* (Soviet Art), this ending had apparently been omitted in public exhibition of the film. According to the press officer of the U.S. Department of State, both films were being screened in "mutilated and distorted" versions. The second film, *Mr. Deeds Goes to Town,* was definitely shorn of its "happy ending"—a loss certain to leave an impression upon the audience quite different from that intended by the producers.

According to State Department officials, the Soviet government had claimed possession of both films as trophies of war captured in Germany.[16]

Among the many great expectations awakened by Stalin's death on March 5, 1953, was the faint hope that it might also herald the end of literary censorship—the abolition perhaps not of all political controls (to hope for *that* would have been far too unrealistic), but at least of one of the crudest and most humiliating practices—the petty rewriting of individual words and passages of otherwise acceptable works, both new and old, to assure their complete conformity with the letter as well as the spirit of current Party policies. Relatively rare in the days of Lenin, such practices were largely a phenomenon of the Stalin era; it was therefore not entirely unreasonable to trust that they might be abandoned together with other excesses of Stalinism.[17] Such hopes were expressed, for instance, in an article in *Literaturnaja gazeta,* December 21, 1954, which condemned "all kinds of liberties on the part of translators and editors" even though these might allegedly be aimed at "improving the text." Works that are unacceptable, the argument went, "should not be translated." The article was a summary of a speech delivered at the Second Congress of the Union of Soviet Writers, the first to be held since the founding congress of the organization in 1934.

It soon became apparent that such hopes were to be disappointed. On the contrary, the important reversals in a number of Soviet policies that followed in rapid succession in the wake of Stalin's death argued for the

16. Paul Babitsky and John Rimberg, *The Soviet Film Industry* (New York: Frederick A. Praeger, 1955), pp. 256–57. Italics added. Alexander Solzhenitsyn's *Cancer Ward* (Bantam Books, 1972, p. 264) contains a reference to "a new 'Trophy' film" and a translator's note: "Western films captured by the Red Army in Germany in 1945 and shown throughout Russia for many years after the war."

17. The practice of rewriting older works of Soviet literature is discussed in two articles by this writer, "New Editions of Soviet Belles Letters: A Study in Politics and Palimpsests," *The American Slavic and East European Review,* Vol. XIII, No. 1 (February 1954), pp. 72–88; and "Soviet Literature and Retroactive Truth," *Problems of Communism,* Vol. III, No. 1 (January–February 1954), pp. 31–39.

necessity of *more* censorship, not less. The Party's new truth was to be, as always, the only truth, thus making the gospels of the Stalin era insidious heresies. These were to be destroyed in the same manner as heretical books of preceding eras of Soviet history, through the traditional procedure of library purges. On September 22, 1959 (that is, during the post-Stalin "liberal" era), a resolution of the Central Committee of the Communist Party of the Soviet Union instructed the USSR Ministry of Culture and other appropriate organizations "to take the necessary measures for the removal of obsolete publications [*ustarevšie izdanija*] from library holdings."[18] Thus, the procedure by which Stalin's propaganda materials were to be disposed of was itself traditionally Stalinist, just as the manner in which Stalin's secret police chief Lavrentij Berija was removed in 1953 (to many, at that time, a sign that there would be no more lawlessness or terror) was exactly the same as the fate of his many victims: execution shrouded in mystery, without any public trial, with exact date of death undisclosed.

Paradoxically, a strengthening rather than a slackening of the Soviet censorship's vigilance was also to be expected as a result of the greatly expanded publication of translations of Western books, fiction as well as nonfiction. Translations, a Soviet military newspaper warned in 1958, represent a real danger because of their inevitable procapitalist and often also anti-Soviet bias. The newspaper appealed for greater care in the selection of titles to be translated and emphasized the necessity of supplying every such book with prefaces, introductions, and commentaries in order "to enable the reader to understand it correctly, to demonstrate to him what is valuable in a given work, and what is tendentious and false."[19] A year later, the desiderata of the armed forces' newspaper were to become official policy. On June 4, 1959, a resolution of the Central Committee of the Communist Party decreed that Soviet translations of Western books in the social sciences "be published in limited printings" and that such translations "are to be supplied with lengthy introductions and annotations." Furthermore, an explicit order was issued to censor their texts: *"Passages of no scholarly or practical interest are to be deleted."* That the 1959 resolution is presumably still in force is indicated by its reproduction in a compilation of documents printed in 1972. Had the resolution been officially withdrawn (or simply ceased to be enforced), normal Soviet procedure would preclude its republication.[20]

18. *KPSS o kul'ture, prosveščenii i nauke.* Sbornik dokumentov. (Moscow: Izdatel'stvo Politiceskoj literatury, 1963), p. 278.
19. *Krasnaja zvezda,* June 25, 1958.
20. *O partijnoj i sovetskoj pečati, radioveščanii i televidenii,* Sbornik dokumentov i materialov. (Moscow: Mysl', 1972), p. 462. Italics added.

That passages and entire books which the authorities, to paraphrase the Central Committee's formula, consider to be of no artistic or practical interest, have arbitrarily been denied publication in the post-Stalin era is attested by Alexander Solzhenitsyn's open letter of May 16, 1967 to the Fourth Soviet Writer's Congress. Solzhenitsyn, then already in disgrace but officially still a member of the Union of Soviet Writers, wrote:

' To the Presidium and the delegates to the Congress, to members of the Soviet Writer's Union, and to the editors of literary newspapers and magazines:

Not having access to the platform at this Congress, I ask that the Congress discuss:

1. The no longer tolerable oppression, in the form of censorship, which our literature has endured for decades, and which the Union of Writers can no longer accept.

Under the obfuscating label of GLAVLIT, this censorship—which is not provided for in the Constitution and is therefore illegal, and which is nowhere publicly labelled as such—imposes a yoke on our literature and gives people unversed in literature arbitrary control over writers. A survival of the Middle Ages, the censorship has managed, Methuselah-like, to drag out its existence almost to the twenty-first century. Of fleeting significance, it attempts to appropriate to itself the role of unfleeting time—of separating good books from bad. . . .

Works that might express the mature thinking of the people, that might have a timely and salutary influence on the realm of the spirit or on the development of a social conscience, are proscribed or distorted by censorship on the basis of considerations that are petty, egotistical, and—from the national point of view—shortsighted. Outstanding manuscripts by young authors, as yet entirely unknown, are nowadays rejected by editors solely on the grounds that they "will not pass." Many members of the [Writers'] Union, and even many of the delegates at this Congress, know how they themselves have bowed to the pressures of the censorship and made concessions in the structure and concept of their books—changing chapters, pages, paragraphs, or sentences, giving them innocuous titles—just for the sake of seeing them finally in print, even if it meant distorting them irremediably. It is an understood quality of literature that gifted works suffer [most] disastrously from all these distortions, while untalented works are not affected by them. Indeed, it is the best of our literature that is published in mutilated form. . . .

Literature cannot develop in between the categories of "permitted" and "not permitted," "about this you may write" and "about this you may not." Literature that is not the breath of contemporary society, that dares not transmit the pains and fears of that society, that does not warn in time against threatening moral and social dangers—such literature does not deserve the name of literature; it is only a facade. Such literature loses the confidence of its own people, and its published works are used as wastepaper instead of being read. . . .

*I propose that the Congress adopt a resolution which would demand and ensure the abolition of all censorship, open or hidden, of all fictional writing,*

*and which would release publishing houses from the obligation to obtain autho-
rization for the publication of every printed page.*[21]

The censorship restrictions discussed by Solzhenitsyn continue to the
present and extend also to translations of Western writing.[22] And the Central Committee's admonitions regarding the need to excise from translated
foreign books "passages of no scholarly or practical interest" are also
scrupulously observed by the country's literary periodicals and publishers
of West European and American fiction and drama.

In essence, there are two kinds of censorship interference, overt and
unacknowledged. The first may be described as brutal but, in a way, "honest"; the second is doubly reprehensible, since it clearly aims at deceiving
the reader into believing that he is reading the complete and authentic
version of a work by a "bourgeois" writer. In most cases, abridgements are
to be viewed as "honestly" censored works since the majority of them are
attempts not merely to conserve space or to give the reader the most
interesting parts of a long work, but to avoid the publication of undesirable
portions of the original text affecting in the process sometimes only a
negligible saving of space. One example of perfectly legitimate, if extreme,
abridgement are the thirty-odd pages chosen from Carlos Baker's seven-
hundred-page biography of Hemingway that were printed in a Soviet journal.[23] The selection included condensations of several chapters from the
book, mainly passages generally suggesting that Hemingway admired Communists (however inconsistently) or providing background material to some
of his novels. Clearly, this was one way to avoid translating the pages in
Baker's biography which tell of Hemingway's clashes with Soviet critics and
other Communists, but the important thing to remember is that no Soviet
reader could possibly have believed that the thirty pages were anything but
a very small sample of Baker's book, or that the selection of material was
the American biographer's, rather than the Soviet editor's.

More questionable was the honesty of the condensation of Studs Terkel's
*Division Street, America.*[24] The book is a profile of Chicago which emerges
from scores of interviews with inhabitants of that city from every walk of

21. *Solzhenitsyn: A Documentary Record,* Enlarged Edition with the Nobel Lecture in
Literature, edited and with an introduction by Leopold Labedz (Bloomington: Indiana University Press, 1973), pp. 106–9. Italics in the original. The text of Solzhenitsyn's letter was
originally printed in *The New York Times,* June 5, 1967.
22. It is too early to determine whether Soviet accession to the Universal Copyright Convention on February 21, 1973, will result in discontinuation of earlier practices of affecting textual
changes in translations of Western literary works, a practice forbidden under the Convention's
terms.
23. *Inostrannaja literatura,* Nos. 5, 6, and 7, 1969, selections from Carlos Baker, *Ernest
Hemingway: A Life Story* (New York: Charles Scribner, 1969).
24. *Inostrannaja literatura,* Nos. 8 and 9, 1969. The original was Studs Terkel, *Division
Street, America* (New York: Pantheon Books, 1967).

life. The Russian translation was introduced by S. Višnevskij, a Soviet journalist who spent six years in the United States; Višnevskij vouched for the authenticity of the picture of a typical American city that Terkel's interviews provide. The Soviet journal did acknowledge that the translation was an abridgement of the original book. This could have been accomplished straightforwardly, since Terkel's volume consists of a great many disjointed individual statements by a large number of respondents, some identified and others anonymous, commenting on various aspects of life in Chicago of the 1960s. A slanted selection of these statements would have given Soviet editors more than ample opportunity to indulge their predilection for caustic criticism of various aspects of American life and their aversion to printing more benign appraisals of it. Not content with that, the Soviet editors also censored the contents of many individual interviews, cutting some and actually rewriting others (none of which classifies as abridgement in the ordinary sense of the term). As for Studs Terkel's own introduction, one page or so was left of the five in the English original.

Truman Capote's *In Cold Blood,* a documentary account of a vicious murder of a Kansas farmer and his family, appeared in 1965; within a year an abridged version of the book appeared in a Soviet journal.[25] The Russian translation was entitled *An Ordinary Murder (Obyknovennoe ubijstvo)* with its suggestion that murder in the United States has become commonplace.[26] The abridgement of the novel followed a consistent pattern. Deleted were most of the references to the farmer's prosperity (e.g., the information, on p. 9 of the original, that he lived in a fourteen-room house, a luxury unheard of in the Soviet Union; that Clutter, though a farmer, was a college graduate —on p. 79; that his daughter played the piano as well as the clarinet and went horseback riding—on p. 18; and even that bed linen was changed twice a week—on p. 28). Also gone were many other allusions to normal middle-class habits and possessions (for instance, the almost universal ownership of automobiles). Though such textual revisions may have minimized the image of the American farmer's prosperity (particularly shocking in comparison with his Soviet counterpart), it accomplished this end by destroying much of the central motif of Truman Capote's book, which rests on his detailed account of human actions as well as physical surroundings. The impact of Capote's work is generated by the monstrous incon-

25. *Inostrannaja literatura,* Nos. 2 and 3, 1966. The original was Truman Capote, *In Cold Blood: A True Account of a Multiple Murder and Its Consequences* (New York: Random House, 1965).
26. "Murder becomes commonplace" was both the title and the conclusion of Raisa Orlova's review of Capote's novel in *Novyj mir,* No. 9, 1966.

gruity of a horrid murder in the placid, prosperous surroundings of rich American farmland. In Truman Capote's book the senseless crime had to be committed in cold blood. In the Soviet translation the murder did, indeed, appear more ordinary and almost commonplace.

Soviet censorship is not confined to politics, however broadly defined. It also acts (as did its tsarist predecessor) as a guardian of public morals, and materials considered offensive are not allowed to appear. Dissemination of pornography is a legal offense in the USSR, and few overtly erotic works, except for such old classics as Boccaccio, Maupassant, and Rabelais, are published. It should be noted, incidentally, that to some extent we are witnessing here genuine cultural differences between the USSR and the West, differences that have widened in the last half century. Until the 1920s, Russian literature was about as explicit in its treatment of sex as was Western writing at the time. Stalinist prudery was somewhat relaxed in the post-Stalin period, but by then Western treatment of the subject had become so unrestrained that a degree of censorship could not be avoided, especially in the case of most recent Western prose and drama. Curiously, very little of the unofficial Soviet writing disseminated through *samizdat* channels— that is, of the writing of the Soviet dissidents—is strongly erotic, let alone pornographic, by any Western standards of the 1970s.

Offensive passages, or even individual words in otherwise acceptable Western works, are either omitted or softened in translation into Russian. The procedure is not unlike that employed by American television in "editing" recent "adult" films in order to make them acceptable as family entertainment, a technique described in a recent newspaper headline as "How the Gosh-darn Networks Edit the Heck Out of Movies."[27]

The methods employed by Soviet translators and editors intent on stamping out the "obscenity" and "intolerable" sexual suggestiveness of modern Western writing vary and span the entire range from the ingenious to downright silliness. Thus, Kurt Vonnegut's *Slaughterhouse-Five* contains some language that was until quite recently considered unprintable even in the United States:

27. *The New York Times,* January 26, 1975, Arts and Leisure section, p. 1. Curiously, a mirror-image procedure was followed in an English translation of Solzhenitsyn's *One Day in the Life of Ivan Denisovich* (New York: Praeger Publishers, 1972). Max Hayward and Ronald Hingley decided not to duplicate the disguises of common Russian obscenities: "The translators of this version have thought it best to ignore the prudish conventions of Soviet publishing and spell out the English equivalents in full" (p. xvii). Significantly, Alexander Tvardovsky, the editor of *Novyj mir,* the journal in which the original Russian text was printed, feared that even in their bashfully concealed form "certain words and expressions typical of the [prison camp] setting in which the hero lived and worked may offend a particularly fastidious taste" (p. xxiv).

Roland Weary and the scouts were safe in a ditch, and Weary growled at Billy, "Get out of the road, you dumb motherfucker." The last word was still a novelty in the speech of white people in 1944. It was fresh and astonishing to Billy, who had never fucked anybody—and it did its job.[28]

The Russian translation omitted the reference to the double standard of speech among America's blacks and whites, but succeeded admirably in reproducing the obscenity without actually resorting to the term itself:

Roland Weary and the scouts were already safe in the ditch, and Weary growled at Billy, "Get out of the road, blankety-blank [*tram-tararam*] your mother," At that time, in 1944, that verb was rarely uttered aloud. Billy was very surprised, as he had never blankety-blanked [*tram-tararam*] anybody. The words sounded fresh and did their job.[29]

Less imaginative was the rendition of "No matter how, a man alone ain't got no bloody fucking chance," a sentence found in Hemingway's *To Have and Have Not.* The Russian rendition was "Still, a man alone can't do a damn thing" [*ne možet ni čerta*]. Both the original and the published Russian translation were cited in a generally serious Soviet study of Hemingway, but the accompanying comment, curiously, treated the translation as *the norm,* and the original as a *departure* from it: "In the original, Harry's last sentence is lexically sharply strengthened."[30] Hemingway's "Moorish tart," a major character in *The Fifth Column,* was obviously offensive on two counts, as an obscenity as well as a racial slur; in the Russian version she appears as a "Moroccan woman."[31] The "bare-assed plain" from Hemingway's *Across the River and into the Trees* became, in the USSR, "bare like a bald spot."[32] In *For Whom the Bell Tolls* the

28. Kurt Vonnegut, *Slaughterhouse-Five, or The Children's Crusade* (New York: Delacorte Press, 1969), p. 29.

29. *Novyj mir,* No. 3, 1970, p. 92. Elsewhere in the original version a bawdy song concludes with "Oh, I'll never fuck a Polack anymore" (Vonnegut, *Slaughterhouse-Five,* p. 134). Apparently, the translators took exception both to the predicate and to the direct object. Both were omitted (*Novyj mir,* No. 4, 1970, p. 155). An amusing mistranslation is found in the Russian version of Vonnegut's other work translated in the USSR. In the original, the morals of a group of American engineers are described as "resolutely monogamous." In the Russian translation this became "strictly monotonous" [*strogo monotonnoe*]. See Kurt Vonnegut, Jr., *Player Piano* (New York: Charles Scribner's Sons, 1952), p. 30; Kurt Vonnegut, *Utopija 14* (Moscow: Izdatel'stvo C.K.V.L.K.S.M. "Molodaja gvardija," 1967), p. 64.

30. Ju. Ja. Lidskij, *Tvorčestvo È. Xeminguèja* (Kiev: Naukova dumka, 1973), p. 290. The source of the original is cited as Ernest Hemingway, *To Have and Have Not* (New York, 1937), p. 225. The translation is found in Èrnest Xeminguèj, *Sobranie sočinenij v četyrex tomax.* Pod obščej redakciej E. Kalašnikovoj, K. Simonova, A. Starceva (Moscow: Goslitizdat, 1968), Vol. II, pp. 631–32.

31. Ibid., Vol. III; Hemingway, *The Fifth Column* (London: Jonathan Cape, 1939; reissued 1968).

32. Xeminguèj, *Sobranie sočinenij,* Vol. IV, p. 27; Hemingway, *Across the River and into the Trees* (New York: Charles Scribner's Sons, 1950), p. 31.

Fascists scream at the Republican soldiers, "Red swine. Mother rapers. Eaters of the milk of thy father." Notwithstanding the fact that the foul language is used by the novel's villains, it was excised from the Russian translation.[33] And an endearingly old-fashioned device was employed elsewhere in the same novel. Two Spanish sentences, *"Me cago en su puta madre"* (I shit on your whore mother) and *"Hijo de la gran puta"* (Son of a great whore) were left untranslated, with a footnote explaining that these are "Spanish oaths."[34] It is unlikely that this was unnoticed by Russian readers, since ordinarily Soviet editions of Western novels carefully translate even such sentences as "yes, sir," "merçi, madame," and "guten Morgen."

In Samuel Beckett's *Waiting for Godot*, "the mother had the clap"; in the Russian version her affliction is more in keeping with the dignity of her age —"the mother had a wart" *(borodavka)*.[35] In John Steinbeck's *The Winter of Our Discontent* a divorcee worries that her alimony payments may stop coming "if the son of a bitch should die"; in the Russian version the woman's capitalist greed is left intact, but her language is more ladylike— "but what if the first husband should die!"[36] In Gore Vidal's *Washington, D.C.* a woman is "douching herself"; the Russian version discreetly refers to a "procedure," which could just as well be the setting of curlers or the application of facial cream.[37] More drastic steps were taken to protect Soviet readers from the "smut" found elsewhere in the same novel. Three pages were cut which related the story of an American college boy who had thought that he would be tormented in hell for the deadly sin of masturbation, an activity later discontinued by an enterprising girl from Richmond, Virginia, who robbed him of his virginity.[38] In Graham Greene's *The Comedians,*

> There was a great yellow moon and a girl was making love in the pool. She had her breasts pressed against the side and I couldn't see the man behind her.[39]

33. Hemingway, *For Whom the Bell Tolls* (New York: Charles Scribner's Sons, 1944), p. 314. Xeminguèj, *Sobranie sočinenij*, Vol. III, p. 441.
34. Hemingway, *For Whom the Bell Tolls*, p. 421. Xeminguèj, *Sobranie sočinenij*, Vol. III, p. 554.
35. Samuel Beckett, *Waiting for Godot* (New York: Grove Press, 1954), p. 15, right side; *Inostrannaja literatura*, No. 10, 1966, p. 170.
36. John Steinbeck, *The Winter of Our Discontent* (New York: Viking, 1961), p. 197; *Inostrannaja literatura*, No. 3, 1962, p. 19.
37. Gore Vidal, *Washington, D. C.* (London: Heinemann, 1967), p. 99; *Inostrannaja literatura*, No. 11, 1968, p. 149.
38. Vidal, *Washington, D. C.*, pp. 63–66. Omitted from the Russian version.
39. Graham Greene, *The Comedians* (New York: Viking, 1966), p. 49.

The Russian version was more modest but also less educational:

> There was a great yellow moon over the trees, and a girl was embracing some man. I could not see him.[40]

Few readers and critics in the West consider Sir Charles Snow's *Corridors of Power* particularly sexually suggestive. Apparently, some Soviet editors do, for the following passage was omitted in the novel's Russian translation:

> There was one glint of original sin, as Arthur saw Margaret and me getting ready to go. He might have been talking with extreme purity; but he was not above using his charm on Margaret, persuading her to invite Penelope to stay in our flat and, as it were coincidentally, him too. I suppose he was trying to get her out of the atmosphere of the Cambridge house. But I was feeling corrupt that night, and it occurred to me that, like most of the very rich people I had known, he was trying to save money.[41]

A translation of Arthur Miller's *Incident at Vichy* was published in the July 1965 issue of *Inostrannaja literatura*. The translation appeared after some delays which, it was rumored, were caused by the play's subject matter: in the mid-1960s, when the issue of anti-Jewish discrimination in the USSR was widely debated in the West, Soviet literary journals preferred to avoid the theme of anti-Semitism, including even persecution of the Jews by the Nazis in works by Western authors. Incredibly, among the few textual revisions in the Russian version all but one were aimed at Arthur Miller's "obscene" language. Thus one scene in the original text was deleted, presumably because Soviet editors objected to the detailed explanation (by a Nazi professor!) that circumcised penises are not to be construed as definite proof of Jewishness, and that an "accidental" glance at a German officer's maleness revealed circumcision.[42] "Looking at penises" on p. 45 of the original was changed to "taking the pants off," and "we look at your cocks" (p. 55) was transformed into "we look between your legs." The Soviet Union is surely one of the very few places on earth where a work by Arthur Miller would be censored for alleged obscenity—*Arthur* Miller, we repeat, not *Henry* Miller.

The ultimate decision to translate Arthur Miller's *Incident at Vichy* was in all likelihood facilitated by the fact that the play is not so much an attempt to record an episode from the story of Jewish martyrdom during the Nazi Holocaust (as are, say, some of the books of Elie Wiesel, a Franco-

40. *Inostrannaja literatura*, No. 9, 1966, p. 38.
41. C. P. Snow, *Corridors of Power* (London: Macmillan, 1964), p. 120. Omitted in *Inostrannaja literatura*, No. 11, 1966, p. 126.
42. Arthur Miller, *Incident at Vichy* (New York: The Viking Press, 1966), p. 41.

American novelist not published in the USSR) as it is an indictment of man's irrational inhumanity to man. This was, of course, duly emphasized in the Soviet introduction to the Russian translation of the play. Indeed, readers' attention was called to the fact that in Miller's play "even those most persecuted," that is the Jews, look down at a gypsy, a traditional pariah in Western society, while the freeing by the Nazis of one of the arrested Jewish businessmen was cited as evidence supporting the familiar Soviet claim that Nazi anti-Semitism was aimed only at working class Jews, not at the Jewish bourgeoisie: "This class unity of a collaborationist and a Fascist, which disregards even racial barriers, is striking illustration of the class nature of Fascism."[43]

Significantly, while Arthur Miller's pronouncements on the Jewish problem (his own as well as those of his fictional personages—Soviet critics very often refuse to distinguish between the two) were found unobjectionable, one *general* observation on the subject of national character was obviously thought intolerable. According to one of the play's dramatis personae, "Whenever a people starts to work hard, watch out, they're going to kill somebody."[44] In the context of *Incident at Vichy* the remark was obviously directed at the industrious Germans. Yet Soviet editors must have felt that it also fit all too well the Soviet work ethic. The Russian sentence reads: "When *a man* starts to work *without rest,* watch out, he's going to kill somebody."

While Soviet accounts of the Nazi era consistently minimize Hitler's annihilation of the Jews, they suppress altogether the Nazis' persecution of another minority, one that was neither ethnic nor political—homosexuals. Homosexuality is a legal offense in the USSR, and Soviet editors and censors were understandably loath to admit that the Nazis viewed homosexuals as much the same criminals as the Communists (it is bad enough that they were bracketed together with the Jews).[45] Kurt Vonnegut's *Slaughterhouse-Five* informs that in Nazi camps "the candles and the soap were made from the fat of rendered Jews and Gypsies and fairies and Communists, and other enemies of the State."[46] In the Soviet version the word "fairies" was replaced with "vagrants" and "the State" was replaced with the more specific "Fas-

43. T. Kudrjavceva's introduction, *Inostrannaja literatura,* No. 7, 1965, pp. 152–53.
44. Arthur Miller, *Incident at Vichy,* p. 10.
45. For additional discussion of the subject of homosexuality, see the section about André Gide in chapter 8 and the reference to Oscar Wilde in chapter 6. In this connection, one should also recall Khrushchev's angry outburst in 1962 at an exhibition of paintings. Addressing Željtovskij, whose abstract canvases displeased him, the then Prime Minister of the USSR exclaimed, "Are you a pederast or a normal man?" and then, speaking to all of the abstract painters, "Judging by these [artistic] experiments, I am entitled to think that you are pederasts, and for that you can get 10 years. . . . Gentlemen, we are declaring war on you." Priscilla Johnson and Leopold Labedz (eds.), *Khrushchev and the Arts,* pp. 102–3, 105.
46. Kurt Vonnegut, *Slaughterhouse-Five,* p. 83.

cist state."[47] An entire chapter (No. 9, "Two Kinds of Alienation") was omitted from what purported to be an unabridged Russian translation of Sir Charles Snow's *Corridors of Power,* presumably because of its portrayal of young people cynically indifferent to any and all ideologies and of a crazed alcoholic of rightist views who hates "the Jews, the Reds, the Pansies."[48] In Gore Vidal's *Washington, D.C.* a witness dreams of testifying before the Un-American Activities Committee during the McCarthy era. The witness is obviously hostile to the committee, and his imaginary speech is filled with transparent irony:

> Now, let us ponder the struggle for men's minds outside the land of the free. The Communists offer a Utopian vision which is particularly attractive to two types: the ignorant and the degenerate. In fact, since for statistical purposes all ignorant dupes and sexual degenerates are *ipso facto* Communists we may then assume that *any* sexual degenerate is by definition not only an ignorant dupe, but a Communist or at the very least a fellow-traveller. Since the Senator has established that all State Department personnel are homosexual, it can hardly surprise us that they are simultaneously ignorant dupes as well as Communists in need of rooting out.[49]

Obviously, Soviet censors found such linking of Communists and homosexuals (even though occurring only in fantasy, and intended as an attack on anti-Communist American politicians!) sacrilegious. The speech was deleted from what, again, purported to be a complete translation of a foreign novel.[50] This was, by the way, only one of a number of excisions in the Russian version of *Washington, D.C.,* a novel that is, essentially, directed against mindless anti-Communist hysteria in American government circles both before and after World War II. Others included references to the fact that the Stalin-Hitler pact of 1939 resulted in many defections from the American Communist Party, particularly among writers and journalists— but that such men and women remained socialists. Of the two, it is likely that the latter assertion was thought more insidious: those who desert the Party must be regarded as Fascists, revisionists, Zionists—but never socialists.[51] Also deleted was a sentence informing matter-of-factly that

47. *Novyj mir,* No. 3, 1970, p. 116. Another minor political slip of Kurt Vonnegut's was corrected in a Soviet translation of *Player Piano.* In the original, a character in the novel declares that a Ghost Shirt is "childish—like Hitler's Brown Shirts, like Mussolini's Black Shirts. Childish like any uniform." In the translation the first sentence was omitted. See Kurt Vonnegut, *Player Piano* (New York: Charles Scribner's Sons, 1952), p. 251; Kurt Vonnegut, *Utopija 14* (Moscow: Izdatel'stvo C.K.V.L.K.S.M. "Molodaja gvardija," 1967), p. 341.
48. *Inostrannaja literatura,* No. 11, 1966, p. 105 contains no indication that the text of Snow's *Corridors of Power* was abridged or otherwise edited.
49. Gore Vidal, *Washington, D.C.,* p. 270.
50. *Inostrannaja literatura,* No. 12, 1968, p. 134.
51. Gore Vidal, *Washington, D.C.,* p. 156; omitted in *Inostrannaja literatura,* No. 12, 1968, p. 70.

"Communist units have already crossed the thirty-eighth parallel" in
Korea; according to the Soviet version of history, it was South Korea
that attacked the Communist North.[52] A casual remark by one of the
characters about an archvillain of Soviet history ("I hadn't realized
that Trotsky was such a . . . well, such a force still") disappeared in
translation.[53] So did some irreverent banter about the changes in Communist slogans during World War II, when pragmatism displaced some
of the old dogmas.[54]

Most important, however, were those changes that distorted a basic
impression created by the original text of Gore Vidal's novel, which was
that while anti-Soviet and anti-Communist paranoia in the United States
was an irrational obsession that was ultimately damaging to the country's
best interests, the paranoia was an outgrowth of a genuine dislike and
suspicion of Communism and the USSR on the part of a large segment of
the American people. Systematic removal from the Soviet text of references
to this important fact deprived *Washington, D.C.* of much of its literary
logic, to say nothing of its documentary value. Examples range from incidental remarks by the novel's various characters to observations that appear
to reflect the author's own views. Thus, a seemingly innocent aside ("Now
she's nothing but a Communist married to a cripple. Oh, it's sad! It *is*
sad, what life does.") was omitted, perhaps because the naive expression of sympathy for the woman's double misfortune bespoke a *sincere*
opinion of Communism as a misfortune to be pitied; that the remark was
presented in an ironical context mattered little to Soviet editors.[55] An
American politician's concern that his daughter's involvement with a
man of leftist views may damage his own political future falls in much
the same category:

> The Senator smiled his beyond-tragedy smile. "We shall discover that when
> I am up for re-election and my opponent announces that my son-in-law is a
> Soviet agent."

—as does his interlocutor's answer: "I don't think even the Russians
would want him." The fact that in the United States Communist sympathies were linked in the public mind with Soviet *espionage* (a taboo
subject, by and large, except for wartime intelligence work against the

52. Gore Vidal, *Washington, D.C.,* p. 275; omitted in *Inostrannaja literatura,* No. 12, 1968,
p. 137.
53. Gore Vidal, *Washington, D.C.,* p. 195; omitted in *Inostrannaja literatura,* No. 12, 1968,
p. 91.
54. Gore Vidal, *Washington, D.C.,* p. 216; omitted in *Inostrannaja literatura,* No. 12, 1968,
p. 102.
55. Gore Vidal, *Washington, D.C.,* p. 145; omitted in *Inostrannaja literatura,* No. 12, 1968,
p. 64.

Nazis) made the excision of the passage almost inevitable.[56] Finally, and in some ways most revealingly, there was the suppression of some general reflections appearing at the end of Gore Vidal's *Washington, D.C.* on the paradox of "disillusioned absolutists of the Left," i.e., Communists, who then seek political and spiritual solace in the authoritarian brand of Roman Catholicism, and of the observation by an American liberal that Senator Joseph McCarthy may have demonstrated, at most, "how small and poorly organized the Communist conspiracy was."[57]

An editorial note to a Russian translation of John Le Carré's *A Small Town in Germany* praised the novel for such virtues as its exposure of the revival of Nazi influence in West Germany, but also warned that Le Carré often views the world through "a smudged glass of anti-Communist propaganda."[58] It was therefore not surprising that the thriller's spectacles were to be cleaned up a bit before, to use the title of another of Le Carré's books, the spy could be allowed to come in from the cold into Soviet libraries and apartments. The changes were insignificant, but again they serve to emphasize the extreme political sensitivity of Soviet censors. Thus, in the supposedly unabridged translation, Soviet readers would not find the original's reference to a possible secret deal between Bonn and Moscow.[59] A casual aside was crossed out which suggested that the tailoring of West German officials' attire was reminiscent of Russian tunics and therefore aroused suspicion.[60] Elsewhere, a West German intelligence chief speculates:

> "The Yanks would fight in Saigon," he declared, "but they wouldn't fight in Berlin. Seems a bit of a pity they didn't build the Berlin Wall in Saigon."

The reference to the Berlin Wall, which was built by Communist East Germany to prevent escapes to the West, was deleted.[61] Also amended was the following classic sample of spy thriller prose:

> Christ: had he really slept with [Jennie] Pargiter? There are certain sacrifices, General Shlobodovitch, which not even Leo Harting will make in the service of Mother Russia.[62]

---

56. Gore Vidal, *Washington, D.C.*, p. 98; omitted in *Inostrannaja literatura*, No. 11, 1968, p. 49.

57. Gore Vidal, *Washington, D.C.*, pp. 314–15; omitted in *Inostrannaja literatura*, No. 12, 1968, p. 162.

58. Ibid., No. 3, 1970, p. 143.

59. John Le Carré, *A Small Town in Germany* (New York: Coward-McCann, 1968), pp. 34–35.

60. Ibid., p. 188; omitted in *Inostrannaja literatura*, No. 2, 1970, p. 164.

61. Le Carré, *A Small Town in Germany*, p. 211; omitted in *Inostrannaja literatura*, No. 2, 1970, p. 177.

62. Le Carré, *A Small Town in Germany*, p. 196.

Clearly, no such disrespectful remarks could be tolerated either about Mother Russia or about generals of the Soviet military intelligence. The Soviet version reads: "Good Lord! Had he really slept with Jennie Pargiter? One must make sacrifices . . ."[63] So one must indeed, to get a Western novel of international intrigue past the Soviet censors.

As a rule, passages that portray the Soviet Union or the Communist movement in an unfavorable light are censored; this applies equally to authorial speech and to pronouncements by fictional characters. Thus, we read in the original text of Kurt Vonnegut's *Slaughterhouse-Five:* "I remembered two Russian soldiers who had looted a clock factory. They had a horse-drawn wagon full of clocks." Vonnegut's recollections deal with a German city just occupied by the Soviet army; looting in such conditions is not a particularly shocking occurrence. Nevertheless, the words "who had looted a clock factory" were deleted from the Russian translation.[64]

An impressive Soviet study of Hemingway notes that in the play *The Fifth Column* "Hemingway shows that there are things in the [Spanish] Republican camp which are less than attractive, but that it is not these that should determine an honest man's attitude toward the cause."[65] More importantly, Hemingway himself foresaw that such objections would be raised, and he wrote in the introduction to the play: "Some fanatical defenders of the Spanish Republic, and fanatics do not make good friends for a cause, will criticize the play because it admits that Fifth Column members [i.e., Spanish Fascists—MF] were shot."[66] Clearly, Soviet editors and censors are among the fanatics performing a disservice to the "cause," to Hemingway and to his Russian readers. In the Soviet translation the truncated sentence reads: "Some people will criticize the play because it admits that Fifth Column members were shot." Having conceded that much, Soviet editors and censors proceeded to minimize the grounds for any such objections by cutting most of the first scene of the second act of *The Fifth Column* in which Antonio tells Philip of the executions carried out by the Spanish Republicans, including the Socialists among them, and how their victims—Fascists, enemy soldiers, Catholic priests, and even some people arrested by mistake—died with dignity and courage.[67]

Occasionally, textual emendations introduced by Soviet literary guardians can only be described as ludicrous, even though they are obviously not

63. *Inostrannaja literatura,* No. 2, 1970, p. 170.

64. Kurt Vonnegut, *Slaughterhouse-Five,* p. 12; omitted in *Novyj mir,* No. 3, 1970, p. 84. It should, perhaps, be noted that in 1944–45 the Soviet troops' seemingly unbridled passion for "liberating" watches and clocks of every description was the subject of innumerable anecdotes throughout Eastern Europe.

65. Ju. Ja. Lidskij, *Tvorčestvo È. Xeminguèja,* p. 302.

66. Ernest Hemingway, *The Fifth Column,* p. 8.

67. Ibid., pp. 50–52; omitted in Èrnest Xeminguèj, *Sobranie sočinenij,* Vol. III, p. 59.

viewed as such by the Soviet bureaucrats. Thus, in Kingsley Amis's *Lucky Jim* Dixon, one of the novel's characters, "might as well be thinking of Monte Carlo or Chinese Turkestan."[68] In the Russian text the latter is replaced with Tierra del Fuego (in Russian, *Ognennaja zemlja*), which is located off the coast of Chile and Argentina.[69] Normally, such substitution would be considered quite proper, since Tierra del Fuego is, to a Russian reader, very exotic (as Chinese Turkestan is to an Englishman), while Turkestan is not. Still, suspicion lingers that artistic effect was not the only reason: it so happens that Turkestan has, for some time now, been disputed territory between China and Russia, and it may have been thought that using the term "Chinese Turkestan" would therefore be inadvisable. Lest this line of reasoning appear extreme, the same novel offers another example. Dixon plans on sending an acquaintance "a box of twenty-five Balkan Sobranie (Imperial Russian blend)."[70] In the Soviet version this becomes simply "cigars," as if the editors wished to suppress the information that Imperial Russia is remembered in the West, if only as a brand name of tobacco.[71] Things have certainly changed for the worse since the 1920s, when Vladimir Mayakovsky, a great Soviet poet who on occasion also wrote advertising copy, confidently predicted that while the Revolution might sweep aside everything linked to the *ancien régime,* an exception would be made for one brand of cigarettes *(Nami ostavljajutsja ot starogo mira tol'ko —papirosy "Ira").*[72]

John Steinbeck's *Travels With Charley in Search of America,* an account of the novelist's journey by car across the country with a faithful dog as his only companion, was published in 1962; prior to its appearance in book form some chapters were printed in *Holiday* magazine. In the March 1963 issue of *Inostrannaja literatura* Soviet readers were given an opportunity to read some of the travelogue's other chapters, those which, as Soviet editors broadly hinted, were suppressed by *American* censors on the staff of *Holiday:* "We publish those chapters from Steinbeck's novel which *Holiday* magazine, *for obvious reasons,* did not include in its selection."[73] The chapters chosen by Soviet editors dealt with Steinbeck's visit to New Orleans, where he witnessed an angry white mob trying, in defiance of court orders, to prevent two little black girls from entering what had once been an all-white school; Steinbeck is called a "nigger-lover." The claim that American censors may have tried to prevent the publication of these chapters must

68. Kingsley Amis, *Lucky Jim* (London: Victor Gollancz, 1957), p. 65.
69. *Inostrannaja literatura,* No. 10, 1958, p. 49.
70. Kingsley Amis, *Lucky Jim,* p. 153.
71. *Inostrannaja literatura,* No. 11, 1958, p. 202.
72. Vladimir Majakovskij, *Polnoe sobranie sočinenij v trinadcati tomax* (Moscow: Goslitizdat, 1957), Vol. V, p. 285.
73. *Inostrannaja literatura,* No. 3, 1963, p. 187. Emphasis added.

have appeared convincing enough to Soviet readers.

Two years later the full text of Steinbeck's *Travels With Charley* appeared in Russian in book form. *Almost* full, that is. Early in the narrative Steinbeck tells of a chance conversation at a roadside stop:

> Khrushchev was at the United Nations, one of the few reasons I would have liked to be in New York. I asked, "Have you listened to the radio today?"
> "Five-o'clock report."
> "What happened at the U.N.? I forgot to listen."
> "You wouldn't believe it," he said, "Mr. K. took off his shoe and pounded the table."
> "What for?"
> "Didn't like what was being said."
> "Seems a strange way to protest."
> "Well, it got attention. That's about all the news talked about."
> "They should have given him a gavel so he could keep his shoes on."
> "That's a good idea. Maybe it could be in the shape of a shoe so he wouldn't be embarrassed."[74]

In the Russian version the scene was reduced to the following:

> I asked, "Have you listened to the radio today?"
> "Five-o'clock report."
> "What happened at the U.N.? I forgot to listen."[75]

The answer was silence. By the time the translation had cleared the office of the first Soviet censor (December 14, 1964) Khrushchev had already been deposed. By the time permission was given to roll the book off the presses (February 16, 1965) he was already well on his way to becoming a historical unperson, just another Soviet retiree. No purpose would have been served by allowing his embarrassing antics to remain part of historical record, even if only as the subject of lighthearted banter in an American novelist's book.

We have been considering so far two of the most common *types* of textual changes in Soviet translations of Western writing, those aimed at shielding the Soviet reader's ideological purity from defilement by Western political heresies, and those intended to eliminate the kind of eroticism or simply earthiness that is nowadays commonly accepted in the West even in books for adolescents. The latter type of censorship is particularly senseless in view of the fact that in everyday speech most Russians are no more decorous and prudish than are ordinary people elsewhere, and the great and mighty Russian tongue is more than adequate for a faithful rendition of any kind

74. John Steinbeck, *Travels With Charley in Search of America* (New York: Bantam Books, 1966), p. 30.
75. Džon Stejnbek, *Putešestvie s Čarli v poiskax Ameriki* (Moscow: Progress, 1965), p. 40.

of slang, oath, or expletive. In the final analysis both of these types of censorship, but especially when viewed together with the major and the most drastic kind, that which completely prevents the appearance of entire categories of Western writing, recall the frightening prophecy made over half a century ago by Yevgeni Zamiatin, the author of *We,* a Russian predecessor of Orwell's *1984.* Four years after the Revolution of 1917 Zamiatin wrote:

> I am afraid that we won't have real literature as long as Russia's citizenry is looked upon as a child whose innocence must be protected. I am afraid that we won't have real literature until we cure ourselves of a certain new Catholicism which fears every word of heresy in no lesser degree than the old.[76]

Zamiatin's warnings were directed at the future of Russian literature, and it is in Soviet Russian literature that his jeremiads have proven all too accurate. Yet, to some extent, they are also applicable to the fate of translated West European and American literature in Soviet Russia.

Having discussed censorship interference, so to speak, generically, let us now turn to a few case studies of individual books that were heavily censored, translations that bring to mind a quip well known in literary circles of the Soviet bloc: a telegraph pole is a thoroughly edited tree. As will be seen, there is a catch to the Soviet translation of Joseph Heller's *Catch-22* and James Jones's progress is less than smooth on the Soviet stretch of the road *From Here to Eternity;* the chimes ring a bit differently in *For Whom the Bell Tolls* and someone has been tampering with Alan Sillitoe's *Key to the Door.* Finally, mysterious Soviet witch-hunters applied evil magic to the account of the Salem trial of 1692 in Arthur Miller's *The Crucible.*

Translations of two of these works, Heller's *Catch-22* and Jones's *From Here to Eternity,* could not be obtained, perhaps because their mutilation by "translators" was denounced in the Soviet press as counterproductive; the possibility should not be excluded that the two translations were subsequently quietly withdrawn from circulation, particularly abroad. We shall therefore have to rely on secondary sources. The accounts are quite instructive.

According to Carl R. Proffer, *Catch-22* appeared in 1967 with the notation on the title page that this was an abridged version of the novel.[77] An article by two Soviet scholars in the September 1972 issue of *Novyj mir* provides some details. Heller's novel was published in 50,000 copies by the

76. E. Zamjatin, *Lica* (New York: Izdatel'stvo imeni Čexova, 1955), pp. 189–90.
77. Carl R. Proffer (ed.), *Soviet Criticism of American Literature in the Sixties,* pp. xxiv–xxv, xxx.

Publishing House of the USSR Ministry of Defense.[78] (This, incidentally, may explain the translators'—or censors'—excessive zeal: the book was intended primarily for Soviet soldiers.) The translation had already been criticized by M. Lorie in 1970 in *Masterstvo perevoda,* an anthology dealing with problems of translation, which raises the question why it was decided to revive the issue again in 1972, five years after its appearance. According to the two Soviet critics, "many passages in the book were simply incorrectly translated and others were omitted for no apparent reason."[79] Thus, for instance, the translators are said to have omitted the opening lines of Chapter II, presumably the following:

> In a way, the C.J.D. man was pretty lucky, because outside the hospital the war was still going on. Men went mad and were rewarded with medals. All over the world, boys on every side of the bomb line were laying down their lives for what they had been told was their country, and no one seemed to mind, least of all the boys who were laying down their lives. There was no end in sight.[80]

In the Soviet version, "They [the translators] simply dropped the paragraph just cited, lest the reader, God forbid, suspect the author of rotten pacifism, of failing to comprehend the true goals of the people's struggle against Fascism."[81] Also "mercilessly" excised were the novel's "erotic" scenes.[82] To cite Carl R. Proffer:

> But where these cuts are and how substantial they are the Soviet reader cannot generally determine. For example, about fifty pages is cut from *Catch-22,* including most of the plot line involving Nately's whore, her sister and Yossarian—so the ending of the novel is quite puzzling to Russian readers ("who is this female, where does she come from, why is she trying to kill Yossarian?").[83]

78. N. Anastas'ev and A. Zverev, "Zametki na poljax perevodnoj prozy," *Novyj mir,* No. 9, 1972, pp. 244–53.
79. Ibid., p. 244.
80. Robert M. Scotto (ed.), *Joseph Heller's Catch-22: A Critical Edition* (New York: Dell, 1973), p. 16.
81. N. Anastas'ev and A. Zverev, in *Novyj mir,* No. 9, 1972, p. 246.
82. Ibid., p. 245.
83. Carl R. Proffer, *Soviet Criticism of American Literature in the Sixties,* p. xxv. As an example of "erotica" censored out of Heller, Proffer cites the following: "He [Yossarian] rolled a piece of lint out of his navel."
Arbitrary and unacknowledged cutting of translated Western literary works is bad enough. Things are far worse in Soviet literary criticism of Western literature where, in addition to cutting, Proffer reports some instances of Soviet editors

> *adding things on their own.* If the reader discovers seemingly irrelevant sentences of abuse in the text of an essay, he may suspect that this is an editorial interpolation. The beginnings and endings of the articles are especially susceptible to editorial revision. ... Along with the abridgment of translations by editors, this practice of critics is the

The two Soviet critics' disapproval of the censoring of Joseph Heller's *Catch-22* was not prompted by an abhorrence of censorship as such. Their objections were grounded in more pragmatic considerations, specifically in the belief that the crude censoring of Heller's text actually *detracted* from its value as anti-American propaganda. Thus, the omission of the novel's erotic scenes resulted, in their view, in a "distortion of the ideological essence of the work."[84] *Catch-22,* although ostensibly a novel about the U.S. Air Force during the closing months of World War II, is "least of all military literature," nor is its cognitive value of historical interest only: the book "exposes a slice of *present-day* conditions in American society."[85] It therefore stands to reason that the cutting of scenes in *Catch-22* that depict the *demoralization* of American troops was propagandistically counterproductive; it was this that triggered the Soviet critics' indignation.

A similar line of reasoning was followed in their disapproval of an equally clumsy job of censoring James Jones's *From Here to Eternity,* which was published in 200,000 copies by the same Soviet military publishers:

> The translators [or censors?—MF], apparently, consider the author [James Jones] merely as one who did the preliminary chores for their own activities. The creators of the Russian version, with enviable courage, correct the author wherever, in their opinion, he falls into error; they change around those artistic solutions which they find unconvincing, and throw out from the novel pages which they find superfluous. With all that, they did not even deem it necessary to indicate on the title page that the Russian edition is an abridged translation of the novel. Only the reader who will take the trouble to read A. Ševčenko's introduction will find there, at the very end and in a subordinate clause of a sentence, a carelessly dropped *mention of the fact that the novel "is being printed in Russian with some excisions." "Some" indeed! After all, what we are talking about here is the excision of over one third of the text.*

The Soviet text of the novel, according to the two critics, is patched up without any rhyme or reason. Occasionally, entire chapters are missing; at other times, sentences are chopped off in the middle. The Russian version of *From Here to Eternity* ". . . systematically crosses out all scenes, sentences, and remarks that do not correspond to the notion of the book's translators and publishers of what a novel exposing the American army

---

least praiseworthy feature of Soviet treatment of American and other foreign literatures. (Ibid., p. xxvi; emphasis added.)

This writer finds Proffer's gentle rebuke overly charitable. In our view, the Soviet editorial practice of arbitrary cutting of literary texts (as distinct from the common misdemeanor of quoting out of context), and particularly of *adding* of editorial comments as alleged parts of the literary text, is despicable and barbarous.

84. N. Anastas'ev and A. Zverev, in *Novyj mir,* No. 9, 1972, p. 245. Emphasis in the original.
85. Ibid., p. 244. Emphasis in the original.

ought to be like."[86] Again, the concern of the two Soviet critics was not the integrity of a literary text, but the belief that the censored translation served to weaken the impact of James Jones's novel (which, like Joseph Heller's, is set during World War II) as an exposé of the American military, a task made particularly timely by the American presence in Vietnam.[87] The two critics implied that emphasizing, not playing down, of the novel's portrayal of American troops' hatred of the war, cynicism, alcoholism, and obsession with sex would have accomplished that end more effectively. The complete (or perhaps only lightly censored) text of James Jones's *From Here to Eternity* would have advanced that end more effectively.

Ernest Hemingway's *For Whom the Bell Tolls* was first translated into Russian more than a quarter of a century after its appearance in the original and thirteen years after the resumption of publication of Hemingway's works in the USSR in 1955. It was printed in a four-volume set of the novelist's works which had a press run of 200,000 copies per volume. The novel was vulnerable to intervention by the Soviet censorship because both its author and its central protagonist Robert Jordan display occasional irreverence—not antipathy, but irreverence—when commenting on Communism and the Communists, and also because it contains information that is at variance with the official Soviet version of the history of the Spanish Civil War.[88] Let us examine several examples.

To this day, Soviet sources perpetuate the fiction that there was no direct Soviet involvement in the Spanish Civil War, that the few Russians who

86. Ibid., p. 247–48. Emphasis added. The term "publishers" may well be an oblique reference to formal censorship. The translators of James Jones's *From Here to Eternity* were also criticized for their inept way of dealing with the obscene material in the novel. This should be done, the critics intoned, "without losing anything essential, but also with a feeling for propriety and artistic sense of proportion." The translators were told to study the successful manner in which a colleague handled the "outspoken pages" in Robert Penn Warren's *All the King's Men,* the story of Huey Long, the once legendary boss of Louisiana.

87. Ibid., p. 246. James Jones's novel was credited with "conveying with an epic sweep and great power of realism the truth about the American army, how it cripples the soul and destroys man's noblest aspirations. Jones's artistic intuition discerned long before others did the mounting threat of Fascism in American life, the menace of the growing 'military-industrial complex.' "

88. The post-Stalin version, incidentally, is considerably closer to the historical record than the one obligatory prior to the dictator's death. Thus, for example, Hemingway's Karkov is modeled after Mixail Kol'cov, a Soviet journalist and prose writer and a participant in the Spanish Civil War. Kol'cov was arrested during the Great Purges and either was executed or died in prison. He was posthumously exonerated of all charges against him only after Stalin's death. Had *For Whom the Bell Tolls* been published earlier, it would have entailed the additional embarrassment of portraying a historical "un-person." The usual procedure in such cases (as practiced in reissues of Soviet novels) was either to drop the character altogether or at least omit mention of his name. Neither would have been easy in view of Karkov's role in Hemingway's novel. See this writer's two articles cited in footnote 10. That Kol'cov served as a prototype for Karkov is attested by Ju. Ja. Lidskij, *Tvorčestvo É. Xeminguèja* (1973), p. 368.

An illegal *samizdat* translation of *For Whom the Bell Tolls* (presumably, faithful to the original) circulated in the USSR some years prior to the appearance of the censored printed version in 1968. Solzhenitsyn reports reading the *samizdat* version in Moscow in 1961. See A. Solženicyn, *Bodalsja telënok s dubom. Očerki literaturnoj žizni* (Paris: YMCA Press, 1975), p. 23.

were actually there were merely volunteers, acting presumably as individuals, much as the Western Communists from the International Brigade, and that the Soviet role in the war was minimal. This myth is contradicted by a number of passages and incidents in *For Whom the Bell Tolls*—in the original version of the novel. Not so in the Soviet translation. Early in the novel Golz says to Robert Jordan: "You never think only about girls. I never think at all. Why should I? *I am Général Soviétique. I never think. Do not try to trap me into thinking.* "[89] The underlined sentences are missing from the Russian version.[90]

In the original version of the novel Karkov, the *Pravda* correspondent, was said to be "in direct communication with Stalin, [and] was at this moment one of the three most important men in Spain." The deletion in the Soviet version of two little words—"the three"—effectively minimized Karkov's, and the Soviet Union's, role in the embattled country.[91] The original version informs that Spaniards who fled to the USSR after 1934 were sent to the military academy "and to the Lenin Institute of the Comintern." The Soviet translation refers only to the military academy. The same page in English and Russian contains another telling discrepancy. The English reads:

> *The Comintern had educated them* [the Spaniards—MF] *there* [in the USSR —MF]. In a revolution you could not admit to outsiders who helped you nor that anyone knew more than he was supposed to know. He [Jordan] had learned that. If a thing was right fundamentally the lying was not supposed to matter. *There was a lot of lying though. He did not care for the lying at first. He hated it. Then later he had come to like it. It was part of being an insider, but was a very corrupting business.*

Again, the underlined sentences were omitted in the Russian translation of Hemingway's novel.[92]

The most explicit example is probably the following. In the English text,

> He [Jordan] could not see Miaja on a bicycle, but Karkov said it was true. *But then he had written it for Russian papers so he probably wanted to believe it was true after writing it.*

89. Ernest Hemingway, *For Whom the Bell Tolls*, p. 8.
90. Xeminguèj, *Sobranie sočinenij*, Vol. III, p. 117. Curiously, the missing sentences were cited in Ju. Ja. Lidskij, *Tvorčestvo É. Xeminguèja* (1973), p. 360. The Soviet critic needed them in order to make a point, and therefore cited them, doing the translating himself from an English edition of the novel, although elsewhere the references were to the four-volume Soviet set of Hemingway. Naturally, Lidskij made no mention of the fact that the sentences he quoted are not to be found in the Soviet version of *For Whom the Bell Tolls*.
91. Ernest Hemingway, *For Whom the Bell Tolls*, p. 424. Omitted in Xeminguèj, *Sobranie sočinenij*, Vol. III, p. 556.
92. Ernest Hemingway, *For Whom the Bell Tolls*, p. 229. Omitted in Xeminguèj, *Sobranie sočinenij*, Vol. III, p. 354.

But there was another story that Karkov had not written. He had three wounded Russians in the Palace Hotel for whom he was responsible. They were two tank drivers and a flyer too bad to be moved, and *since, at that time, it was of the greatest importance that there should be no evidence to justify an open intervention by the fascists,* it was Karkov's responsibility that these wounded should not fall into the hands of the fascists in case the city should be abandoned.

Apparently, some people in authority in the USSR continue to believe that such evidence must still be suppressed. The underlined parts were omitted from the Russian text, as was also the indication immediately following that all evidence of Russian presence would be destroyed if the city were to be evacuated.[93]

There were also more conventional deletions, i.e., of material portraying Communists in an unfavorable light. Thus, a reference to the fact that Karkov had a promiscuous mistress as well as perhaps two wives was cut, as were the sentences about another Russian: "Kashkin has only been tolerated there. There was something wrong with Kashkin evidently and he was working it out in Spain."[94] Of the Communist units within the Spanish Republican forces we read the following in the English text of *For Whom the Bell Tolls:*

> In few armies since the Tartar's first invasion of the West were men executed summarily for as little reason as they were under his [Lister's] command.

The comment is missing from the Soviet edition.[95] Robert Jordan muses in the original version of the novel about men who retain

> . . . the first chastity of mind about their work that young doctors, young priests, and young soldiers usually started with. The priests certainly kept it, or they got out. *I suppose the Nazis keep it, he [Jordan] thought, and the Communists who have a severe enough self-discipline.*

Clearly, mentioning the Nazis and the Communists in the same breath could not be tolerated; the last sentence was cut.[96] So was a transparent reference to the Soviet purges of "enemies of the people" in the late 1930s; a Soviet journalist threatens the French Communist André Marty with

93. Ernest Hemingway, *For Whom the Bell Tolls,* pp. 237–38. Omitted in Xeminguèj, *Sobranie sočinenij.* Vol. III, p. 362.

94. Ernest Hemingway, *For Whom the Bell Tolls,* pp. 231–32. Omitted in Xeminguèj, *Sobranie sočinenij.* Vol. III, p. 357.

95. Ernest Hemingway, *For Whom the Bell Tolls,* p. 234. Omitted in Xeminguèj, *Sobranie sočinenij,* Vol. III, p. 359.

96. Ernest Hemingway, *For Whom the Bell Tolls,* p. 239. Omitted in Xeminguèj, *Sobranie sočinenij,* Vol. III, p. 364.

having his status reviewed in the USSR.[97]

Alan Sillitoe's *Key to the Door* was one postwar British novel that was certain to appeal to official Soviet tastes. It described in grim realistic detail the squalor and brutality of Nottingham's working class life, and then related its hero's army experiences in the Far East, where he learns that the Malayan Communists he is called upon to fight are decent and patriotic people worthy of admiration. True, by Soviet standards Sillitoe's novel had too much sex, and it was most unfortunate that the heroine through whom the novel's central protagonist learns of the virtues of Communism was a prostitute by trade, but one cannot, after all, expect perfection from Western writing. *Key to the Door,* which appeared in English in 1961, was serialized in a Soviet journal two years later and was subsequently printed in what appears to be the highest figure for any single printing of a Western novel, one million copies.[98] In itself, the million-copy edition is conclusive evidence of the Soviet authorities' admiration for Sillitoe's novel. Yet the admiration was not entirely uncritical. Although there is no inkling of this fact in the Russian translation that appeared in the literary monthly, some "improvements" were made in the British novelist's text. Most were cuts affecting either material that was objectionable or, more frequently, passages and entire pages *that contributed nothing* to the novel's ideological impact. In addition, there were a few minor changes in the wording of the text. Let us examine how this affects the overall impression of the novel.

There was no compelling reason, political or otherwise, for the omission of the novel's second and third chapters.[99] What the reader learns from them are simply details of the rough courtship and brutal working class marriage from which issued Brian Seaton, the novel's central hero. But then there was no special reason to retain them, so they were cut. By contrast, the omission of a three-page episode rid the Russian translation of the following somewhat embarrassing passage:

> He [Abb Fowler, one of the workers] carried a ragged copy of the [Communist] *Daily Worker* and talked about the war in Abyssinia not long finished and the war in Spain not long begun. Every Thursday for months he'd thought of volunteering to fight in Spain, but never did. "I'm a Communist, 'Arold," he would say, "and I don't mind gettin' shot at, if you want to know, but not in Spain. It's the bleeders in this country *I* want to stand up against a wall.[100]

97. "I would like to know if it could not be possible to change the name of the tractor factory"—i.e., dropping André Marty's name, a regular practice whereby the public in the USSR would first learn of a famous Bolshevik's downfall. See Ernest Hemingway, *For Whom the Bell Tolls,* p. 426; omitted in Xeminguèj, *Sobranie sočinenij,* Vol. III, p. 559.
98. *Inostrannaja literatura,* Nos. 5, 6, and 7, 1963.
99. Alan Sillitoe, *Key to the Door* (London: W. H. Allen, 1961), pp. 22–56.
100. Ibid., p. 129. The excision affected pp. 128–31.

Most of another twelve-page excision affected material that Soviet editor-censors probably viewed simply as superfluous.[101] But the cutting also removed an interesting conversation between a little boy and his devout grandmother—the kind of conversation that is reportedly not uncommon in the USSR, where children of working parents are often left in the care of a *babushka:*

"Why do we have to worship God?" he asked in the same tone.
"So that He'll love you."
"What does it matter if God loves us?"
"Because if He does," she catechised, "you'll grow up strong and won't ever come to harm."
"I don't want God to love me," he said.
"Ay," she ended it slowly, "you don't now, but you might some day."[102]

Somewhat later in the novel six pages disappeared from the Russian translation for no apparent reason, and another two presumably because of their references to pornographic books that may have offended the sensitivities of blue-stocking editors in Moscow.[103] Some fifty pages later, however, simple cutting would also have deprived the novel of some politically valuable material, and it was therefore decided to resort instead to "cosmetic surgery" which would eliminate obscenity but leave the politics intact. In the English text the imaginary file compiled on Brian Seaton by the British military authorities reads as follows:

POLITICS: socialist, used to read *Soviet Weekly.*
SEX LIFE: plenty until he fell foul of the authorities and received his two years. Five-fingered widow now.[104]

101. Ibid., pp. 137–51.
102. Ibid., p. 141. In Kornej Čukovskij's magnificent study of children's language between the ages of two and five, we find the following observation:

Occasionally, two mutually contradictory notions very peacefully coexist in his [a child's] mind. This may be seen, for instance, in this astounding declaration by a four-year old girl in Moscow:
—God exists, but I, of course, don't believe in him.
Her grandmother has preached to her the dogmas of the Orthodox faith, while her father, on the contrary, instilled in her godlessness. In an attempt to make both of them happy, she expressed simultaneously in one tiny sentence both the belief and the disbelief in God, demonstrating great resourcefulness and (in this case!) very little concern for the truth:
—God exists, but I, of course, don't believe in him.
Expressing two mutually exclusive propositions, the child failed to notice that the result was absurd.
—Does God know, that we don't believe him?

Kornej Čukovskij, *Sobranie sočinenij v šesti tomax* (Moscow: Goslitizdat, 1965), Vol. I, pp. 447–48.
103. Alan Sillitoe, *Key to the Door,* pp. 158–64, 166–67.
104. Ibid., p. 211.

In the Soviet version, the reference to masturbation was dropped and, while they were at it, a small political improvement was introduced by the editors: the reading of the *Soviet Weekly* was given in the present instead of the past tense:

> POLITICS: socialist, reads *Soviet Weekly.*
> PERSONAL LIFE: disorganized; as a result stopped respecting authorities and received his two years.[105]

Another thirty "superfluous" pages were arbitrarily omitted a little later,[106] and then the same procedure was followed in another politically valuable passage marred by regrettable "obscenity." In the original version a character muses:

> England.
> This syphilitic island.
> This seat of majesty.
> This lump of excrement.[107]

It is the Russian text that is the more Victorian:

> England.
> This lousy island
> This seat of majesty.
> This stinking dump.[108]

Thus improved upon, Alan Sillitoe's novel was widely publicized and disseminated in the USSR. Soviet readers were not informed that, before being issued a Soviet visa, Sillitoe's unruly hero was significantly "civilized," in the sense that Mark Twain's Aunt Polly used to "civilize" Tom Sawyer for church on Sunday. Sillitoe's Brian Seaton was told to wash his mouth with soap, mind his manners, curb his tongue a bit when speaking of things he knew little about (such as politics)—and also not to waste time when telling his story to busy Soviet folks.

Arthur Miller's play *The Crucible* was among the first harbingers of the wave of new translations that literally flooded the USSR after the years of Stalinist drought. A translator's note in the theatrical journal where it appeared vaguely described the Russian version as "somewhat abridged": "remarks not directly related to the action were partly abridged," as were

105. *Inostrannaja literatura,* No. 6, 1963, p. 51.
106. Alan Sillitoe, *Key to the Door,* pp. 296–327.
107. Ibid., p. 427.
108. *Inostrannaja literatura,* No. 7, 1963, p. 186.

some details of beliefs and rituals that would not be understood by modern readers; it was mentioned that the new ending of Act II, added by Miller after the play had been staged, was omitted.[109] The Soviet translator's (or editor's) note was not merely an understatement. It was a deliberate attempt to deceive. Not only was the play's dialogue freely mutilated. The systematic blotting out of authorial comment, which forms an integral part of *The Crucible*'s text, makes this translation one of the most heavily censored to appear in the USSR in the first post-Stalin decade. Indeed, it may be argued that the suppression of Arthur Miller's comments distorted the play's meaning almost beyond recognition, particularly for an audience of readers and spectators unfamiliar with American history. Ignorant of the play's historical setting, this audience needed some information on America's Puritans and on the Witches' Trial in Salem, Massachusetts, in the year 1692 far more than did the audiences in Miller's native America. Yet it was this background commentary, interwoven with the texture of the dialogue that was—for obvious reasons—suppressed by the Soviet censors. Without these comments Arthur Miller's play, a generalized parable on the evils of suspicion, fanaticism, and vicious terror as weeds that spring up from what might once have been a pure faith, was reduced to little more than costume drama.

At the outset of Act I of *The Crucible* Arthur Miller explains to his audiences the origins of Colonial America's Puritans:

Their fathers had, of course, been persecuted in England. So now they and their church found it necessary to deny any other sect its freedom, lest their New Jerusalem be defiled and corrupted by wrong ways and deceitful ideas. . . . Massachusetts tried to kill off the Puritans, but they combined; they set up a communal society which, in the beginning, was little more than an armed camp with an autocratic and very devoted leadership. It was, however, an autocracy by consent, for they were united from top to bottom by a commonly held ideology whose perpetuation was the reason and justification for all their sufferings. So their self-denial, their purposefulness, their suspicion of all vain pursuits, their hard-handed justice, were altogether perfect instruments for the conquest of this space so antagonistic to man. . . . The Salem tragedy, which is about to begin in these pages, developed from a paradox. It is a paradox in whose grip we still live, and there is no prospect yet that we will discover its resolution. Simply, it was this: for good purposes, even high purposes, the people of Salem developed a theocracy, a combine of state and religious power whose function was to keep the community together, and to prevent any kind of disunity that might open it to destruction by material or ideological enemies. It was forged for a necessary purpose and accomplished that purpose. But all organization is and must be grounded on the idea of exclusion and prohibition, just as two objects cannot occupy the same space.

109. *Teatr,* No. 6, 1955, p. 3. In Miller's new ending Proctor tries in vain to induce Abigail to refute the false charges made against her by Elizabeth.

Evidently the time came in New England when the repressions of order were
heavier than seemed warranted by the dangers against which the order was
organized. The witch-hunt was a perverse manifestation of panic which set
in among all classes when the balance began to turn toward greater individual
freedom.[110]

The applicability of Arthur Miller's remarks to the Soviet Union's own
history, specifically to the degeneration of Lenin's authoritarianism of the
early revolutionary years into the reign of terror of the Stalin era, was far
too transparent. The profoundly subversive passage was not allowed to
stand in the Soviet version of the play. Neither were Miller's explicit comments on the applicability of the experience of the Salem witch-hunts of the
eighteenth century to the fate of nonconformists in our days, *both* in Western countries and in Communist ones:

> In the countries of the Communist ideology, all resistance of any import is
> linked to the totally malign capitalist succubi, and in America any man who
> is not reactionary in his views is open to the charge of alliance with the Red
> hell. Political opposition, thereby, is given an inhumane overlay which then
> justifies the abrogation of all normally applied customs of civilized inter-
> course. A political policy is equated with moral right, and opposition to it
> with diabolical malevolence. Once such equation is effectively made, society
> becomes a congerie of plots and counterplots, and the main role of govern-
> ments changes from that of the arbiter to that of the scourge of God. The
> results of this procedure are no different now from what they were, except
> in the degree of cruelty inflicted, and not always even in that depart-
> ment. . . . Sex, sin and the Devil were early linked, and so they continue to
> be in Salem, and are today. From all accounts, there are no more puritanical
> mores in the world than those enforced by the Communists in Russia, where
> women's fashions, for instance, are as prudent and all-covering as any Ameri-
> can Baptist would desire.[111]

Stripped of Arthur Miller's authorial comment, *The Crucible*, in all
likelihood, made little sense to a Soviet audience. It was pretty much ruined
as drama, and not very effective as a document on barbarity in early America. To many, no doubt, Arthur Miller's *The Trial of Salem (Salemskij
process)*, which was the Russian title of the perfectly realistic play on a
historical subject, probably appeared less comprehensible than the few plays
of the theater of the absurd that were to appear in the USSR in the years
that followed.

Another extreme case of censorship involves an old Hungarian-Viennese
operetta by Paul Abrahams. Though Abrahams was still alive in the United

110. Arthur Miller, *Arthur Miller's Collected Plays,* with an introduction [by the author]
(New York: The Viking Press, 1957), pp. 227–228.
111. Ibid., pp. 249–50.

States (he died in 1960), some Soviet theatrical authorities, dissatisfied with the operetta's libretto, simply *commissioned a new one*. E. Šatunovskij's new libretto was certainly an ideological improvement over the old "bourgeois" text:

> The new libretto . . . naturally leaves out the more indecent situations of the original operetta. An attempt was even made to expose the shenanigans of the bourgeois press . . . and a representative of the lower classes was introduced into the play—Daisy's uncle Celestin, an active member of the waiters' union. An attempt was also made to depict "class antagonisms."

As it turned out, even the new Soviet libretto was unsatisfactory. According to *Pravda,* April 12, 1957, it extolled "the 'charms' of 'chic' bourgeois life, with its hypocrisy and immorality" and that, in turn, could not "fail to evoke fears regarding the theater's fidelity to the ideological and artistic achievements of the Soviet operetta." But then, it might be argued, the theatrical authorities should have known that it would be as difficult to produce a nonbourgeois, nondecadent, "progressive" Hungarian-Viennese operetta in the USSR as it would have been to stage a proletarian factory drama in the old Hapsburg Empire.

A further method of intervention used by the censorship is the total withdrawal from sale, circulation, or public performance of books, plays, and films that had once been given its blessings but had later become an embarrassment, or were even officially anathemized by the Party's guardians of faith.

Two early instances of this procedure—the temporary withdrawal of anti-Nazi films based on Lion Feuchtwanger's novels and the retroactive eradication of previous publication of books by the "turncoat" Howard Fast —are discussed elsewhere.[112] A more recent instance, involving a production of Shakespeare's *Richard III* in 1965–66, was reported by Natalia Belinkova, a Soviet editor now living in the United States. It appears that Shakespeare's play aroused the apprehensions of Yekaterina Furtseva, the late Soviet Minister of Culture. Commented Belinkova:

> They [the Soviet theaters—MF] chose works that they felt would be above suspicion and began to prepare productions of Shakespeare. But Furtseva heard about this, called together the chief producers of various theaters and said: "Do you think we don't realize why you have chosen plays by Shakespeare? We know it's because they are all about rulers and the struggle for power!" And that was the end of several productions of Shakespeare's plays.[113]

112. For the Feuchtwanger episode, see chapter 7; for the story of Fast, see chapter 8.
113. Martin Dewhirst and Robert Farrell (eds.), *The Soviet Censorship,* p. 90.

The years 1965–66 were, indeed, marked by a struggle for power among Khrushchev's successors, and this, in turn, must have evoked memories of a similar struggle a decade earlier among Stalin's heirs. That Furtseva's fears were not altogether groundless is attested by the following summary of *Richard III* in a Soviet reference work:

> [Richard III] is an intelligent, impassioned and courageous man, yet at the same time he is a physical and moral monster. Power-hungry, cunning, and cruel, Richard turns into a criminal and cynical usurper of power who marches toward the throne over corpses of old men and infants, cursed by bereaved mothers and orphaned sons and daughters. The disastrous anarchy brought about by the activities of Richard III is tearing England apart, growing ever more ominous. Neither the nobility nor the people support the hated murderer and despot during the uprising launched by Richmond. Shakespeare depicts Richard's death and Richmond's victory as the triumph of forces of order over anarchy and the feudal internecine wars that tore England apart in the fifteenth century.[114]

The incident thus serves, as it were, to illustrate the aptness of the title of Jan Kott's Polish book, *Shakespeare, Our Contemporary.*

Book burning, often masquerading under such euphemisms as "clearing library shelves of obsolete materials," has a long and inglorious history in the USSR.[115] A Soviet manual for bookstore salesmen offers some matter-of-fact advice on procedures to be followed upon the receipt of "orders from superior organizations" that specific items are no longer to be sold to the public. First of all, bookstore employees are reminded to "carefully search the storage room" to make sure none of the "withdrawn" books (or pamphlets or issues of journals) are inadvertently forgotten. Following that,

> Publications listed in the circular [*akt*] are to be stricken from the book inventory and are to be delivered as scrap to organizations dealing with pulping. Prior to their delivery for pulping, book jackets, covers, and title pages are to be torn off them, and illustrations [*izoprodukcija*] are to be torn up.[116]

114. *Osnovnye proizvedenija inostrannoj xudožestvennoj literatury.* Literaturno-bibliografičeskij spravočnik. 2nd rev. ed. (Moscow: Kniga, 1965), pp. 41–42. For a more detailed treatmentofthepoliticalpotentialoftheplay,seeV.P.Komarova," 'RičardIII'Šekspira kak političeskaja tragedija," *Filologičeskie nauki*, No. 5, 1971, pp. 40–53. A few years later M. Minkovič, Soviet Belorussia's Minister of Culture, expressed some misgivings about "modern" allusions in a recent production of Hamlet. See *Izvestija*, January 9, 1969.

115. As early as 1920 the Commissariat of Education had issued an order "to purge the public libraries of obsolescent literature." See Bertram D. Wolfe, "Krupskaya Purges the People's Libraries," *Survey* (London), No. 72 (Summer 1969), p. 141. For additional discussion of the subject, see chapter 8.

116. B. G. Reznikov, *Rabota prodavca v knižnom magazine*, 1960, pp. 75–76.

The extreme thoroughness of the procedure betrays the fact that this is no mere routine commercial disposal of waste.

A number of books by Somerset Maugham that were published in the late 1950s were apparently regarded as harmless enough reading, and their appearance was consonant with the relatively relaxed atmosphere of those years.[117] Among these was a translation of *The Summing Up*, which contains Maugham's opinions on literary and sundry matters, many of them quite unconventional, as befitted a British novelist then already in his seventies examining with a jaundiced eye the follies of the young; some pages in the book recall La Rochefoucauld's wistful observation, *si jeunesse savait, si vieillesse pouvait*. Normally such books, when published in the USSR, cause a mild flurry of excitement among the intelligentsia, delighted to see in print some opinions they would never dare express in public—not that this would be tolerated. There are reasons to assume that the appearance of such books (the best *Soviet* example is, of course, the controversial memoirs of Ilya Ehrenburg) is partly intended to serve as a safety valve for similar sentiments, an opportunity for a vicarious expression of unorthodox grievances and aspirations for a small circle of *literati*. Unexpectedly, Somerset Maugham's *The Summing Up* produced an angry outburst—not merely from some Stalinist critics, but from the Central Committee of the Communist Party of the Soviet Union. In a resolution adopted on June 4, 1959, Maugham's *The Summing Up* was indignantly denounced as a book "which may only bring harm to the cause of the ideological-political education of the working masses."[118] (At that time Maugham was still alive; he died in 1965.) Leonid Finkelstein, a Soviet journalist now living in the West, recalls what was obviously a response to a circular inspired by that resolution:

> On another occasion, Somerset Maugham's *The Summing Up* had just reached the bookshops when it was suddenly banned. Telex messages were sent out at once, but the bookshops had been open for half an hour and nobody could prove how many copies had already been sold. The bookshop managers are no fools: they returned one or two copies and kept the remaining 150 or so, selling them for three times the price to trusted customers.[119]

The Central Committee's denunciation of a single book by Somerset Maugham is overshadowed by the far more important resolution by the

117. See chapter 3.
118. *O partijnoj i sovetskoj pečati, radioveščanii i televidenii,* 1972, p. 461.
119. Martin Dewhirst and Robert Farrell (eds.), *The Soviet Censorship,* p. 71. It is possible that the Central Committee's formal resolution on Maugham's *The Summing Up* was not made public at the time. Finkelstein makes no reference to it, mentioning only the instructions to the bookstores.

same body adopted a year earlier, on April 5, 1958, condemning as a major ideological blunder the publication by *Goslitizdat,* the country's largest publisher of fiction, of four volumes by Upton Sinclair. The appearance of these books, especially without appropriate introductions, was declared a very serious mistake in view of "Sinclair's ideological positions in recent years and of certain features of the works themselves [which] require fundamental criticism."[120] As in the case of Maugham, the author in question was still alive; Sinclair died in 1968. Because the Central Committee's resolution affected books that, together with their author, had been famous in Russia for half a century, some historical background may be useful here.

Upton Sinclair's renown in Russia antedates the Revolution. *The Jungle,* which described the horrors of Chicago's slaughterhouses at the turn of the century, was translated into Russian very soon after its appearance in 1906. Tolstoy praised the novel, although he disapproved of its socialist bias. On the other hand, Lenin expressed serious misgivings about Upton Sinclair's "intuitive" non-Marxist brand of socialism:

> Sinclair is an emotional socialist without theoretical grounding. He attacks the question "simply"; he is indignant over the approaching war and seeks refuge from it in socialism . . . he is naive because he ignores the half-century-old development of mass socialism, the struggle of currents within it; because he does not see that an objectively revolutionary situation as well as a revolutionary organization are prerequisites for the growth of an active revolutionary movement. This cannot be replaced by "sentiment."[121]

Lenin's reservations notwithstanding, Upton Sinclair rapidly became one of the favorite Western authors in the young Soviet Republic. To cite Deming Brown:

> Upton Sinclair seems to have been made to order for Russian readers in the early years of the Soviet regime. . . . Ever sympathetic toward the underprivileged, and perpetually shocked by social injustice, he made his writing a fervent protest against America's inadequacies. His works often graphically supported the generalizations about American life which appeared in the Soviet press, for his opinions coincided closely with those that were being fostered in the Russian public.[122]

The Soviet authorities' esteem for the radical American novelist resulted in the production, in 1931, of a Soviet film based on one of his books, making

120. *O partijnoj i sovestkoj pečati, radioveščanii i televidenii,* p. 449.
121. V. I. Lenin, "English Pacifism and Dislike of Theory," *The Imperialist War, Collected Works* (New York: 1930), Vol. XVIII, pp. 165–66. Cited in Deming Brown, *Soviet Attitudes Toward American Writing,* pp. 205–6.
122. Ibid., p. 202.

Sinclair one of a very few living foreign writers to be accorded this kind of recognition: "The hero of the film *Jimmie Higgins,* adapted from the novel by Upton Sinclair, a young man strangling in the conditions of capitalism, searches for a way out and finally finds it in the political slogans of Communism."[123]

The publication of Upton Sinclair's writings fluctuated with changing political conditions within the USSR, and also with changes in Sinclair's own political activities. Widely published between 1921 and 1931, he was boycotted during the Great Depression for "selling out" to the Establishment.[124] Restored to grace in the late 1930s as a valiant anti-Fascist, he was anathematized once more in 1949:

> Discovering that he had come out in support of the Atlantic Pact, the Russians revealed that he had "long been well known as a careerist and businessman of literature, who at one time flirted with 'socialist' ideas." . . . When in 1951 Sinclair suggested that working conditions in the United States were now improved over those he had portrayed in *The Jungle* in 1906, he was met with a howl of derision. The Russians knew better![125]

Deming Brown concludes:

> We have seen that Soviet enthusiasm for Sinclair was in direct proportion to his agreement with current official ideology. In his works the critics have sought documentation in support of their own preconceptions about America . . . The story of Sinclair in the Soviet Union, then, serves to emphasize the simple, naked obligation that underlines all Soviet criticism: to respect, first and foremost, the political line of the Communist Party.[126]

The entry for Upton Sinclair which appears in the sixth volume of the *Literary Encyclopedia* published in 1971, and which takes due note of the novelist's death in 1968, lists in its bibliography only one book for the period from 1954 to 1964, a reprint of the novel *Sylvia.*[127] Significantly, the reprint's date is given as 1957, i.e., prior to the Central Committee's resolution. The encyclopedia's bibliography, it is true, does not aspire to completeness. Yet the USSR Academy of Science's allegedly all-inclusive bibliography of twentieth-century American authors published in the USSR up to 1968 lists, for 1954–64, only the novel *Sylvia,* a 1965 political pamphlet, and an article written by Upton Sinclair on the occasion of the fiftieth anniversary of

123. Paul Babitsky and John Rimberg, *The Soviet Film Industry,* p. 167. See also Appendix A.

124. Deming Brown, *Soviet Attitudes Toward American Writing,* p. 208.

125. Ibid., pp. 209–11.

126. Ibid., pp. 215, 218. Apparently, Deming Brown was unaware of the Central Committee's 1958 resolution assailing the republication of Upton Sinclair's works.

127. KL, Vol. VI (1971), pp. 855–59.

Tolstoy's death in 1960.[128] Our own research, based on the weekly listings in *Knižnaja letopis' (Book Annals),* which are, as a rule, recorded immediately upon each book's appearance, demonstrates that at least six other books by Upton Sinclair had been published (the Central Committee's resolution, it will be recalled, referred only to four). The six were: *Jimmie Higgins* (300,000 copies); *The Metropolis; 100%: The Story of a Patriot; The Flivver King* (250,000 each); *The Jungle* (165,000); and *King Coal* (150,000). Retroactive suppression of data on their publication strongly suggests an analogy with the fate of Somerset Maugham's *The Summing Up.* All of these books by Upton Sinclair (or only four of them? If so, which ones?) were probably withdrawn from sale and circulation and presumably destroyed.[129]

Literary censorship and other restrictions on freedom of circulation of books almost inevitably result in the appearance of a black market where such books may be purchased at exorbitant prices. In the 1920s and 1930s, for instance, erotic and pornographic books, many of them printed by Olympia Press in Paris, were being smuggled from France to "puritanical" England and the "repressive" United States. With the relaxation of anti-obscenity laws in Great Britain and America in the 1960s—and with their stiffening in de Gaulle's France—the direction of the traffic was reversed, reportedly to the great humiliation of many Frenchmen. In tsarist Russia, there was always a brisk trade in "forbidden" books, many of them printed in Russian abroad. The tradition continues to this day. Scores of titles printed in Russian in the West, and ranging from the Bible and philosophical tracts to the novels of Solzhenitsyn and Nabokov's *Lolita,* find their way to the USSR; the same is true of other kinds of books printed outside the USSR. Together, these may be classified as "illegal" reading matter. Somewhere between this category of books and those currently sold in Soviet bookstores are the old and second-hand books, some printed in prerevolutionary Russia, others in the early years of the regime; these are sold by the *bukinisty,* state-owned stores specializing in old books. Such books form a "gray" area—not forbidden, but often containing materials of which the authorities disapprove. Finally, there are the very legal books which were published in such inadequate amounts that they are almost immediately

---

128. *Problemy literatury S.Š.A. XX veka,* 1970, p. 464.

129. That Upton Sinclair may once again return to official favor is suggested by a highly equivocal entry in the *Literary Encyclopedia* in 1971 which lists the strong as well as the weak sides of his work (it praises *Jimmie Higgins,* hesitates about *The Jungle,* and denounces the Lanny Budd series) and also his praiseworthy and shameful political pronouncements. Significantly, the article ends on a hopeful note, recording Upton Sinclair's "positive" actions in the 1960s, i.e., *after* his condemnation by the Central Committee, such as his opposition to the nuclear arms race and to the anti-Communist Smith-McCarran Act, and citing Sinclair's letter viewing "hopefully" developments in the USSR. KL, Vol. VI (1971), pp. 857–58. A children's story by Upton Sinclair was published in 1971 in 100,000 copies.

available only on the black market. Two examples of the latter, books by Kafka and Saint-Exupéry, are discussed elsewhere.[130]

The semi-legal status of second-hand books was made apparent in an article printed in *Izvestija* on November 14, 1953, which described a black marketeer enriching himself on "rare editions." The list included authors very infrequently reprinted in the USSR, such as Plato and Nietzsche. As far as the clearly illegal books are concerned, Soviet law enforcement agencies do their duty. On May 14, 1964, *Večernjaja Moskva* reported the smashing in Moscow of a ring of black marketeers specializing in "erotica and viciously anti-Soviet stuff . . . from Madrid, Munich, and New York publishers." The "anti-Soviet stuff" was identified as poetry by Marina Cvetaeva and Nikolaj Gumilev (the first has since been republished in the USSR). As for the erotica, Soviet readers were titillated with a portrait of an Orthodox priest "slobberingly gorging himself on salacious obscenity, such as, for instance, the novel, *Lady Chatterley's Lover.*" (One almost feels nostalgic: there is still a country where D. H. Lawrence's work is considered salaciously obscene.) The Soviet police may have won a battle, but not the war. On February 26, 1975, *Literaturnaja gazeta* published a sensational exposé of an international conspiracy of Westerners and Russian émigrés aimed at smuggling into the USSR "subversive" books in Russian and other languages. The tone of the article was that of injured innocence, which was perhaps quite appropriate. The Soviet Union requires no such conspiracies. Soviet books, pamphlets and periodicals can be freely purchased or ordered by mail almost anywhere in the Western world. A black market in books will exist in the USSR for exactly as long as the state's monopoly in publishing and the Soviet literary censorship—and not a day longer.

130. See chapter 8.

# CHAPTER

# 2

# *Western Writing and*
# *Soviet Readers*

Before embarking on a detailed description of the publication in the USSR of West European and American writing we should perhaps examine, however briefly, the available evidence on the Soviet readers of that literature.

Attempts at a study of Russia's reading public, of its tastes and preferences, as well as of the impact of these on book publishing, go back to the latter part of the nineteenth century. Among these, perhaps the most noteworthy are the writings of Nikolaj Aleksandrovič Rubakin (1862–1946), bibliophile, publisher, and founder of "bibliological psychology."[1] Today, many of Rubakin's theories, methods, and findings appear naive as well as obsolete;[2] nevertheless, for some forty years these were among the very few investigations of the subject. Just as sociology began to emerge as an independent discipline in the USSR only after Stalin's death, so did the more specialized field of research in reading habits and predilections languish until the late 1960s, quite possibly because of apprehensions that the verified data might be at variance with those optimistically projected by politicized Soviet theory.[3] Be that as it may, in 1968 the USSR Academy of Sciences

1. Rubakin's *Etjudy o russkoj čitajuščej publike: Fakty, cifry, nabljudenija* appeared in St. Petersburg in 1895 and was reprinted in three volumes in 1911–15. The two-volume N. Roubakine, *Introduction à la psychologie bibliologique,* was published in Paris in 1922. A Russian edition, *Čto takoe bibliologičeskaja psixologija,* was printed in Leningrad in 1924, and *Psixologija čitatelja i knigi* followed in 1929. See KL, Vol. VI (1971), pp. 409–10. There is also a book-length popular biography, A. N. Rubakin, *Rubakin. Locman knižnogo morja* (Moscow, 1967).
2. A recent Soviet study deprecates somewhat Rubakin's pioneering efforts. See B. S. Mejlax (ed.), *Xudožestvennoe vosprijatie.* Sbornik I. Akademija Nauk SSSR. Naučnyj sovet po istorii mirovoj kul'tury. Komissija kompleksnogo izučenija xudožestvennogo tvorčestva (Leningrad: Nauka, 1971), p. 14.
3. "A period of autonomous development [of sociology in the USSR and most of Eastern Europe—MF] in the 19th and early 20th century was followed (from 1945 to about 1960) by

convened a symposium "at which, for the first time, problems of the reception of literature and the arts were formulated from different perspectives, including points of convergence of individual scholarly disciplines." One of the results of the symposium was the emergence of a Commission for Interdisciplinary Study of Literature and the Arts of the USSR Academy of Sciences.[4] The legitimization of this dormant field of inquiry was long overdue. According to M. B. Xrapčenko, a Soviet critic of some eminence and the author of studies of Gogol, Tolstoy, and literary theory, "So far, no really serious attempts have been made, alas, to probe literature's active role, its socio-aesthetic role; this is a special task of literary scholarship." Xrapčenko defined the task as a historical-functional approach" [*istoriko-funkcional'nyj podxod*]: "the historical-functional approach is the study of literary phenomena that exert a significant impact on the reading public and also, of course, if one may use the expression, of literary works with the highest degree of vitality [*najbolee žiznesposobnyx*]."[5]

Thus, after decades of a virtual ban on field work by literary and general sociologists (Soviet as well as Western), some statistical data based on interviews and questionnaires relating to reading habits are being published in the USSR.[6] The findings are often understandably fragmentary and the conclusions tentative, but many are nevertheless quite revealing.

Because the Soviet Union is a multiethnic and multilingual country (according to the 1970 census, Russians now comprise less than 55 percent of the population, and may soon account for less than half of the total because of the higher birth rate among the Turkic peoples), translations of Western writing are published in languages other than Russian. As will be demonstrated in the chapters that follow, ability to read some of these languages (such as Latvian and Estonian) is occasionally a distinct boon,

one of converging processes with a hostile attitude to sociology. This hostility tended to recede gradually after the mid-1950s." *Marxism, Communism and Western Society: A Comparative Encyclopedia,* C. D. Kernig (ed.) (New York: Herder and Herder, 1973), Vol. VIII, pp. 40–41.

4. The body's Russian name is *Komissija kompleksnogo izučenija xudožestvennogo tvorčestva AN SSSR*. See B. S. Mejlax, *Xudožestvennoe vosprijatie,* p. 147.

5. Ibid., pp. 40–41.

6. The new atmosphere also encouraged historical studies of the subject, e.g., B. V. Bank, *Ob izučenii čitatelja v Rossii (XIX v.)* (Moscow: Kniga, 1969). The present writer, though not a sociologist himself, made use of the data on reading habits and literary tastes that were found in the several hundred interviews and questionnaires conducted and prepared by the Russian Research Center of Harvard University. The respondents were displaced persons from the USSR, and the questions and findings pertained to 1940, their last peacetime year in the Soviet Union. My findings appeared in two articles: "Foreign Authors and Soviet Readers," *The Russian Review,* Vol XIII, No. IV (October 1954), pp. 266–75, and "Russian Writers and Soviet Readers," *The American Slavic and East European Review,* Vol. XIV, No. 1 (February 1955), pp. 108–21. Allowing for the great disparity in sampling and methodology, to say nothing of the internal changes within the USSR in the quarter of a century separating the two sets of interviews, the findings that emerge from the data collected by the Harvard interview project are remarkably consistent with those reported by Soviet investigators in the late 1960s and early 1970s, which will be considered in this chapter as well as in chapter 9.

because a significant number of translations (particularly from the Scandinavian languages) appear in these languages alone. Conversely, a command of the Turkic languages offers little advantage, and speakers of these languages who do not read Russian are restricted to a selection of Western writing that bears much resemblance to what was available in Russian during the Stalin era. Still, Soviet statistics do not allow us to determine with any significant degree of precision the number of non-Russians who can also read the Russian translations. One recent study of the Soviet reading public, published in 1968, estimates that approximately three-quarters of the Soviet population know Russian well enough to read books in that language, but emphasizes that the distribution of such bilingual readers is uneven.[7] It stands to reason, for instance, that Ukrainians and Belorussians can acquire a reading knowledge of Russian with reasonable ease. The 1968 study also points out that in non-Russian areas Russian books are read most commonly in large cities, a reflection, no doubt, of the fact that urban dwellers tend to be much better educated, but also certainly of another factor, the presence of many Russians and other Slavs. Thus, a 1964 survey in Riga revealed that 53 percent of indigenous Latvians, speakers of a non-Slavic language, read Russian without difficulty; the corresponding figure for a small Armenian town was only 10 percent. In Baku, the capital of Soviet Azerbaidzhan, most library patrons borrowed books in both Russian and Azerbaidzhani, a Turkic language (presumably, this referred to Azerbaidzhani readers alone, as relatively few Russians take the trouble to learn the local language); yet in a village library in the same republic a collection of ten thousand Russian books remained practically untouched. (That the existence of the collection is evidence of a wasteful and clumsy policy of Russification of minority ethnic groups is, of course, another matter.)

A survey of leisure activities conducted in the early 1970s in several large cities in the European part of the USSR confirmed the hypothesis that less educated persons read fewer books and vice versa. Thus, among manual workers of both sexes, slightly over one-half reported reading at least one book a month, while ten percent read three or more books.[8] Formulated in another way, this may mean that nearly one-half read no books at all. More unexpected is the finding of the 1968 study that rural dwellers (who have less access to other types of entertainment, such as the cinema) consistently

7. *Sovetskij čitatel'.* Opyt konkretno-sociologičeskogo issledovanija. Sbornik statej (Moscow: Kniga, 1968). This is probably the most important study of the subject to date. It is based on 6,682 questionnaires, 1,030 individual library cards *(kartoteki čtenija)* with records of books checked out, 400 "readers' autobiographies," 83 readers' conferences, and 54 library reports. Ibid., p. 10.

8. L. A. Gordon, E. V. Klopov, *Čelovek posle raboty: social'nye problemy byta i vnerabočego vremeni* (Moscow: Nauka, 1972), p. 170.

read less than their urban counterparts with approximately equal education. It is difficult to estimate the extent to which this is related to the availability of books in the villages, although there can be no doubt of the importance of this factor. To turn to the primary interest of our study:

> The data of the questionnaire demonstrates that foreign literature is little read in the villages. Only thirteen names of nineteenth and twentieth-century authors were cited, but not a single name of a foreign author still active was mentioned. All of the writers cited were mentioned but once, except for Theodore Dreiser and Jack London who received five votes apiece, and Émile Zola who was mentioned three times.

The findings were confirmed by records in the library of one Russian village, which revealed that within the span of approximately one year, 150 library patrons read all in all merely ten foreign authors, but of these only three were living writers. The three were Heinrich Böll, the Australian leftist Dymphna Cusack, and the East German Dieter Noll.[9] (It should be mentioned, however, that things were very different in a village in Latvia, an independent state prior to World War II, where of a sample of 40 readers, 31 read a total of 46 foreign books. The nine who read none were all persons with no high school education.[10]) As with other population groups, it was the young who showed most interest in foreign literature, although, as we shall see, here too the difference between urban and rural readers was quite pronounced. When first questioned, students in the upper grades of the village school reported having read only Ethel Voynich's *Gadfly,* Victor Hugo's *Les Misérables,* George Sand's *Consuelo,* and an unspecified book by Jules Verne. When asked again some time later, they also volunteered the names of Alexandre Dumas and Jack London, both old favorites of Russian children, as well as such "adult" authors as Theodore Dreiser, the French Communist novelist Elsa Triolet, Erich Maria Remarque, and two modern science fiction writers, the American Ray Bradbury and the Pole Stanislaw Lem.[11] It may well be that repeated questioning elicited at least some name-dropping, and it is the first rather than the augmented second list that is the more reliable.

9. *Sovetskij čitatel',* p. 138. Altogether, the collective farmers mentioned 126 different authors. Of this number, 99 were Soviet (the Russians most frequently cited among them were Sholokhov, Simonov, Ostrovskij, and Fadeev, in that order; the most prominent non-Russians were the Latvian V. Lācis, the Ukrainian O. Hončar, and the Kirgiz Č. Ajtmatov). Of the fourteen prerevolutionary Russian authors, the six most frequently cited were (again, in that order) Tolstoy, Pushkin, Chekhov, Lermontov, Nekrasov, and Turgenev. The study emphasized that all of the writers mentioned, Russian, Soviet, and foreign, were little read. Ibid., pp. 137–38.

10. Ibid., p. 138.

11. Ibid., p. 139. In this and other books on the subject, translations from other Soviet-bloc countries were very rarely mentioned. Thus, references to foreign literature are nearly synonymous with Western writing.

A study of reading habits and preferences in several towns with populations below 50,000 contains little specific data on the reading of foreign literature, but it does offer some valuable insights on more general questions that are also applicable to that specific problem. Thus, for instance, 95 percent of respondents identified themselves as readers of fiction, drama, and verse; only 5 percent declared that they had "no use for literature." Of the 95 percent of readers, 58 percent considered themselves "regular readers"; by contrast, in Western Europe, according to the Soviet study, the percentage of "regular" readers is estimated between three and five.[12] Perhaps here, too, a degree of caution is called for. The reading of fiction, drama, and verse is an important status symbol in Soviet society, a hallmark of *kul'turnost'* (which it is not necessarily in the West), and few respondents might have been expected to so brazenly defy all conventions as to actually deny having "any use" for literature. It should be recalled that well over a century ago, Xlestakov, the central character in Gogol's great comedy *Inspector General,* flabbergasted Russian provincials (fictional ancestors of the subjects in the Soviet sociological survey!) by pretending to be a man of letters and a friend of Pushkin's; the awe was even greater than that evoked by his impersonating an important government official. While allowance should be made for this possible upward bias in claiming the status of readers and regular readers of *belles lettres,* the book also contains much data probably quite unaffected by it. Thus, 60 percent of respondents in the towns surveyed reported reading such popular illustrated periodicals as *Ogonëk, Smena, Rabotnica,* and *Sovetskaja ženščina;* 55 percent subscribed to one or more of them. Our skepticism regarding the high percentages of alleged "regular readers" of literature was not dispelled by the number of subscriptions to literary and semi-literary monthlies in one town of less than 50,000, Ostrogožsk. There were seventeen subscriptions to *Molodaja gvardija,* a youth journal (the figure, as the others, includes libraries); ten to *Oktjabr',* then the leading Stalinist literary periodical; eight to the middle-of-the-road *Znamja;* seven to the then liberal *Novyj mir;* and five to *Inostrannaja literatura.* Incidentally, in the entire town of nearly 50,000 inhabitants only one library subscribed to the country's single journal devoted to translated foreign literature.[13] A table illustrates preferences for various types of literature; percentages refer to the numbers of respondents (presumably of all ages and backgrounds) in the town of Ostrogožsk and in several other towns of similar size who named a given category of books as their favorite reading.[14]

12. *Kniga i čtenie v žizni nebol'šix gorodov.* Po materialam issledovanija čtenija i čitatel'skix interesov. (Moscow: Kniga, 1973), p. 74.
13. Ibid.
14. Ibid., p. 78.

| CATEGORY OF LITERATURE | PERCENTAGE IN OSTROGOŽSK | PERCENTAGE IN OTHER TOWNS |
|---|---|---|
| Prerevolutionary Russian | 10 | 10 |
| Soviet Russian | 65 | 62 |
| Other Soviet | 9 | 9 |
| Pre-World War II foreign | 11 | 13 |
| Postwar foreign | 5 | 6 |

Taken together, the two categories of foreign books (which, as suggested earlier, are overwhelmingly *Western* since only a small fraction of the *postwar* foreign books are books from Soviet-bloc countries) the figures are 16 percent for Ostrogožsk and 19 percent for other towns of comparable size, suggesting that the popularity of Western literature is greater among urban than among rural readers which, to reiterate, may be partly a reflection of its greater availability. The popularity of Western literature (in fact, of the older Western writing alone) is second only to that of Soviet Russian literature. Western books are more widely read than are the Russian classics or translations of non-Russian Soviet authors. Viewed in another way, the table indicates that books by non-Soviet authors (the Russian classics plus foreign books) were the favorite reading of slightly over one-quarter of all respondents in several "typical" Soviet towns with populations below 50,000.

Unfortunately, no comparable overall information could be found for large cities, but there are, as will be seen, good reasons to believe that the trend toward greater interest in Western literature would be even more pronounced among the highly urbanized and better educated readers. This assumption is supported, for instance, by the findings of another poll, in which two groups of respondents, ordinary workers and engineers and technicians, were asked to name their favorite literary periodical. While the percentages preferring other periodicals were quite close for both groups, there was one very significant exception. Nearly three times as many engineers and technicians named *Inostrannaja literatura,* although the journal ranked low for both groups.[15] The figures were as follows:

15. *Sovetskij čitatel',* p. 104. Since the totals exceed 100, we must assume that some of the respondents named more than one periodical. The table reveals also a number of other facts. Thus, for instance, two of the listed periodicals, *Junost'* and *Molodaja gvardija,* are published specifically for young readers. Of the two, *Junost'* was, in the mid-1960s, by far the more literate and artistically interesting, as well as politically more liberal. Both groups preferred it to *Molodaja gvardija,* but by very different margins. Engineers and technicians preferred *Junost'* by a ratio of 4 to 1, while the figure for workers was only 2.5 to 1; also, *Molodaja gvardija,* an official journal of the Young Communist League, was the only publication listed preferred by more workers than engineers and technicians. It is also worth noting that both groups preferred the neo-Stalinist literary monthly *Neva* to the liberal *Novyj mir,* although by different margins (21 and 2 percent, respectively, for workers, and 24 and 14 engineers and technicians).

| PERIODICAL | PREFERRED BY WORKERS, PERCENT | PREFERRED BY ENGINEERS AND TECHNICIANS, PERCENT |
|---|---|---|
| Junost' | 22 | 28 |
| Neva | 21 | 24 |
| Znamja | 16 | 18 |
| Moskva | 11 | 13 |
| Oktjabr' | 11 | 15 |
| Molodaja gvardija | 9 | 7 |
| Novyj mir | 9 | 14 |
| Zvezda | 8 | 8 |
| Inostrannaja literatura | 4 | 11 |

That foreign literature is generally preferred by the younger and better educated Soviet readers is also apparent from another poll, although it must be emphasized that the categories of books were arranged in a manner that heavily favored Soviet literature: in the mid-1960s, respondents were asked to choose between all of Soviet literature—that is, all literature written in the USSR within a half century—and "modern" foreign literature written since World War II, that is, within a period about half that long. Furthermore, it must be remembered that at the time of the interviews, modern foreign literature was just being introduced into the school curriculum,[16] and that postwar Western literature began to be published on an appreciable scale only in the late 1950s. In view of these factors, the percentage of readers in all categories indicating their preference for contemporary foreign writing is impressive.[17]

| GROUP OF READERS | PREFER SOVIET LITERATURE, PERCENT | PREFER POSTWAR FOREIGN LITERATURE, PERCENT |
|---|---|---|
| Workers | 77 | 39 |
| Engineers and technicians | 72 | 47 |
| Language and literature teachers | 86 | 27 |
| Science teachers | 64 | 18 |
| College and university students | 56 | 59 |
| Secondary and trade school students | 88 | 30 |

The most striking finding, of course, is that one crucial group of respon-

16. B. S. Mejlax (ed.), *Xudožestvennoe vosprijatie,* p. 155.
17. *Sovetskij čitatel',* p. 282. Again, in a number of cases percentage figures add up to more or less than 100, indicating that some respondents chose both categories, while a number of respondents among the science teachers chose neither. The information on the size of the sample and the location of interviews was quite vague.

dents—college and university students—that is, the upcoming generation of the country's élite, actually preferred modern foreign writing to Soviet literature, and considering the biased nature of the poll referred to earlier, probably preferred it by a much wider margin than indicated in the table. We shall return to the problem below.

Various sources yield additonal, though occasionally only fragmentary, information on occupational groups of readers. Thus, for workers as well as engineers and technicians we have a list of favorite authors divided into four categories: prerevolutionary Russian, Soviet (Russian and non-Russian both), prewar foreign literature (identified as "classics of foreign literature") and, separately, "contemporary foreign writers." The latter two groups are somewhat confusing, because certain twentieth-century Western authors (e.g., Romain Rolland and Theodore Dreiser) are listed as "classics," while their contemporaries (such as Erich Maria Remarque and Ernest Hemingway) are listed with the "moderns."[18]

*Classics of Foreign Literature Rated "Most Popular"*

| AUTHOR | AMONG WORKERS, PERCENT | AMONG ENGINEERS AND TECHNICIANS, PERCENT |
|---|---|---|
| Theodore Dreiser | 18 | 20 |
| Jack London | 16 | 21 |
| Émile Zola | 16 | 14 |
| Honoré de Balzac | 11 | 14 |
| Guy de Maupassant | 11 | 10 |
| Victor Hugo | 9 | 12 |
| William Shakespeare | 6 | 6 |
| Romain Rolland | 3 | 6 |

It may be safely assumed that Dreiser's place on the list (first for workers, second for engineers and technicians) attests to readers' curiosity about life in the United States which attracted them to the socioeconomic documentary emphasis of his novels, and that the figures for Shakespeare as favorite *reading* (not theater) may have been inflated somewhat because of the status attached to appreciating the bard's works. The other names on the list confirm the old popularity of Jack London's tales of adventure (their American settings may be an additional attraction), a partiality for the

18. One rationale for this apparent incongruity may have been the fact that Dreiser and Rolland, then both deceased, were published during the Stalin era, while the then living authors Remarque and Hemingway reappeared in the USSR after an interruption of many years. In any case, only more confusion would be created if we attempted to "correct" the classification created by Soviet interviewers. Once again attention is called to the fact that the list of contemporary foreign authors includes only one author from a Soviet-bloc country, the East German Dieter Noll, who furthermore appears at the very bottom of the list, which supports our thesis that, in practice, the term "foreign author" nearly coincides with "Western author." Regarding the totals of percentages, see footnote 17.

rather massive traditional French social novels (Balzac, Zola, Hugo, Rolland—but not, for instance, Flaubert) and, as entertainment, for Maupassant's novellas, which were among the most *risqué* books available in the USSR in the 1950s and 1960s. The list of most popular contemporary foreign authors was as follows:

| AUTHOR | AMONG WORKERS, PERCENT | AMONG ENGINEERS AND TECHNICIANS, PERCENT |
|---|---|---|
| Erich Maria Remarque | 11 | 18 |
| Ernest Hemingway | 4 | 10 |
| Ellen Dymphna Cusack | 3 | 3 |
| James Aldridge | 2 | 4 |
| Mitchell Wilson | 1 | 4 |
| Heinrich Böll | 1 | 3 |
| Archibald Cronin | 1 | 4 |
| Dieter Noll | 1 | 2 |

The list of "favorite" modern foreign authors demonstrates, first of all, that relatively few workers were sufficiently acquainted with recent foreign writing even to name a particular author. While the percentage of workers expressing preferences for a foreign classic was ninety (although some of these were probably duplications—i.e., naming more than one author—this was most likely offset by those who may have cast scattered votes for authors other than the eight appearing on the list), the corresponding figure for modern foreign authors was only twenty-four, or about one-quarter. This included four authors each of whom was preferred by only one percent of responding workers, which permits us to assume that the large majority had no favorite modern foreign authors at all. To a lesser extent, this was also true of responding engineers and technicians. The total of their responses in the list of older Western authors was 103 (which presupposes, of course, duplications), while the figure for modern foreign writers was 48, less than half of the former. Other than that, the list reflects, above all, the realities of Soviet book publishing of the first post-Stalin decade, although even within their confines some genuine preferences are discernible. The pacifist novels of Remarque and Hemingway's prose with its often captivating plots and exotic settings, were the favorites of both groups of readers. It is also worth noting that the American Mitchell Wilson, who often writes about the problems of science and technology, was cited by four percent of the engineers and technicians, but only one percent of the workers. That Ellen Dymphna Cusack, a pro-Communist Australian author relatively little known in the West, and James Aldridge, a similarly political British novelist (whose name does not appear in standard Western literary reference works) are listed immediately after Remarque and Hemingway, is simply evidence that in Soviet conditions the availability of books induces demand and can also to an extent create "preferences," although, as we shall see, this is not always the case.[19]

Secondary school teachers of science and mathematics have educational backgrounds not very different from those of engineers and technicians, but appear to be less interested in foreign writing. Only 21 percent reported reading foreign prose (85 percent read Soviet literature). The two Western authors mentioned most frequently were a "classic," Theodore Dreiser, and a recent newcomer, Heinrich Böll, whose novels describing the horrors of war and the aimless prosperity of postwar West Germany were then being published in the USSR. Teachers of science and mathematics also expressed interest in Harper Lee's *To Kill a Mockingbird,* an American novel about racism in the South that was recently printed in a million copies. Only rarely did they mention such old favorites as London and Balzac.[20]

Secondary school teachers of language and literature for the most part also read books by Soviet authors. A Soviet scholar comments: "This is quite logical. Pupils must first be acquainted with Soviet literature; it is the ideas of Soviet literature that influence the shaping of ideological and moral values of man in our society. Still, it is disquieting that works by foreign authors occupy an insignificant place in the reading of this group."[21] Of the sample of language and literature teachers, 27 percent reported reading modern (i.e., postwar) foreign prose, and 3 percent modern foreign verse; but only 6 percent referred to specific authors when questioned about books read during the previous year. Twenty percent said they read *Inostrannaja literatura,* while 5 percent actually subscribed to the journal,[22] a figure incongruously high considering that only 6 percent of all respondents cited one or more specific foreign authors read in the last year. A number of respondents

19. The two tables appear in *Sovetskij čitatel',* p. 97. See also Appendix B. A sociological study conducted in the large industrial city of Chelyabinsk and the smaller industrial towns Zlatoust and Troitsk indicates that the bookstores there were short of many kinds of books. The three Western authors whose books were unavailable were Jack London, Theodore Dreiser, and Walter Scott, all of them widely published at the time. When asked about their preference, a group of young workers (exact ages and numbers of respondents unspecified) "named more than 120 titles of literary works they read during that month. Unfortunately, these included not only genuinely artistic works, but also a number of inferior ones, predominantly of the detective genre." The latter were, presumably, predominantly translations. M. T. Iovčuk and L. N. Kogan, *Duxovnyj mir sovetskogo raboč̌ego. Opyt konkretno-sociologičeskogo issledovanija* (Moscow: Mysl', 1972), p. 339.

20. *Sovetskij čitatel',* pp. 174–75.

21. Ibid., pp. 195–96.

22. Ibid. The same figures are cited by V. D. Stel'max, "Iz opyta izučenija čitatel'skix interesov," in B. S. Mejlax (ed.), *Xudožestvennoe vosprijatie,* p. 155. Stel'max emphasizes that until recently (i.e., before 1971) modern foreign literature was not taught in Soviet schools.

declared themselves fans of a particular modern Western author, saying that they "follow" his works. Of those who did so, the study cited only several: Heinrich Böll, 29 respondents (22 percent of the sample); J. D. Salinger, 16 (12 percent); James Aldridge, 13 (10 percent); Erich Maria Remarque, 8 (6 percent); Mitchell Wilson, 3 (2 percent); and William Faulkner, one (less than one percent). That the reading of foreign literature is more prevalent in urban centers, particularly in the two largest cities, may be seen from the following table in which all of the respondents were secondary school teachers of language and literature:[23]

|  | MOSCOW AND LENINGRAD | OTHER CITIES OF THE RUSSIAN FEDERATION | VILLAGES |
|---|---|---|---|
| "Keep up" with modern foreign prose | 45% | 19% | 13% |
| "Keep up" with modern foreign poetry | 4% | 4% | 1% |
| Mentioned specific foreign authors read during last year | 11% | 7% | 5% |

The present and recent pupils of these language and literature teachers are the country's most voracious readers of translated foreign writing, notwithstanding the fact that presumably little effort was made to awaken their interest in them—or, possibly, partly for that very reason.[24] Among secondary school pupils in cities with populations below 50,000, only nine percent expressed preference for the Russian classics—perhaps a reaction to the massive doses of them in the school curriculum and, more importantly, to the boring, doctrinaire way in which they are taught; another factor is the relative paucity among the classics of reading matter suitable for juveniles.[25] Most popular with junior high school students is Soviet literature, rated favorite by 75 percent. In contrast to prerevolutionary

23. *Sovetskij čitatel'*, p. 197. The fact that the total adds up to only slightly over 52 percent, and that the authors of the report did cite the three votes for Mitchell Wilson and even the single vote received by Faulkner, suggests that some of the other respondents may have cited authors whom the Soviet scholar preferred not to cite by name. Thus, it may have been thought "undignified" to have teachers of literature declare themselves fans of authors of detective novels or even "naive" science fiction.

24. In a survey of subscribers to *Literaturnaja gazeta*, *Inostrannaja literatura* emerged as the fourth most popular journal (it was preceded by *Junost'*, *Novyj mir*, and the illustrated mass circulation magazines *Ogonëk* and *Smena*). Its largest group of readers were "cultural workers," which presumably includes teachers, librarians, artists, etc. They accounted for 28.9 percent of *Inostrannaja literatura*'s readers. Another 27 percent were scientists, scholars, writers, and journalists. *Inostrannaja literatura* was least popular with professional Communist Party personnel; they constituted only 4.9 percent of the journal's subscribers. See *Literaturnaja gazeta*, No. 40, 1968, and No. 19, 1969, and Appendix C.

25. See chapter 4.

Russian writing, the corpus of Soviet literature contains hundreds of books written expressly for this audience. Indeed, it may be argued that some of the most important features of Soviet books written ostensibly for adults and often cited by Western observers as evidence of artistic weakness of the bulk of Soviet writing—such as its unabashed didacticism, primitive psychological motivation, clearcut division of protagonists into heroes and villains, artificial happy endings, and even the predilection for pseudo-documentary forms—make *adult* Soviet books attractive as reading for adolescents. Finally, foreign literature was the favorite of 16 percent of the sample of secondary school boys and girls.[26] This does not mean that only one out of six junior high school students read it. Among twelve- and thirteen-year-olds, as many as 70 percent said that they liked foreign literature.[27] The three authors most frequently mentioned were Mayne Reid, Alexandre Dumas, and Jules Verne—the same threesome that captivated their grandparents in the *gimnazii* of tsarist Russia.

The common denominator of Western juvenile fiction and Soviet literature of high ideological seriousness becomes apparent in the following finding of Soviet sociologists:

> Our data for 1948–50 and for a later period, 1965–66, demonstrates that the following books have acquired the stature of a singular spiritual influence on our [adolescent—MF] readers: N. Ostrovskij's *How the Steel Was Tempered,* E. L. Voynich's *The Gadfly,* and A. Dumas's *The Count of Monte Cristo.*[28]

The two nineteenth-century novels and Nikolaj Ostrovskij's Soviet classic share one important feature: a young central character whose devotion to the cause of justice inspires him to nearly superhuman heroism, imbues him with undying hatred of oppressors, and causes him to place common goals above personal considerations. All three have interesting if simplistic plots and all eschew literary refinements that might complicate the clear-cut division of causes and protagonists into forces of good and evil. These traits unite the three novels with very different settings, making Alexandre Dumas's French sailor, Ethel Voynich's nineteenth-century Italian revolutionary, and Nikolaj Ostrovskij's youthful Russian Communist equally attractive literary heroes for Soviet teenagers.

26. Of that number, 12 percent expressed a preference for "older" foreign writing, and 4 percent for "modern" foreign literature. See *Kniga i čtenie v žizni nebol'šix gorodov,* 1973, p. 133.

27. Ibid., p. 199.

28. O. I. Nikiforova, *Psixologija vosprijatija xudožestvennoj literatury* (Moscow: Kniga, 1972), p. 137. For a *samizdat* lampoon on Ethel Voynich's novel as a "spiritual influence," see Appendix F.

Understandably, the literary tastes of somewhat older readers are more sophisticated. This is attested by a study of 1,601 senior secondary school students ranging in age from fifteen to seventeen that was conducted in a number of Soviet cities.[29] Soviet literature was still their favorite reading, but the gap separating it from the other categories of books was much narrower: 88 percent were regular readers of Soviet writing, 63 of the Russian classics, and 76 of translated foreign literature.[30] Alexandre Dumas, beloved by their younger schoolmates, retained only some of his appeal; quite a few of these older high school students found him superficial.[31] It is not clear whether respondents were specifically asked to name their favorite author or authors, merely encouraged to do so, or whether such names were volunteered spontaneously. A total of 1,880 specific responses was cited, more than one for each person interviewed. Actually, the number must have been significantly larger, since individual writers identified by name appear to have been subjectively chosen by the authors of the report. No author receiving fewer than two percent of the total vote was listed; Alexandre Dumas, whose constituency, however shrunken, must still have been considerable, was not listed; and there were no specific authors of detective stories, even though the study indicated that many of the fifteen-to seventeen-year-old readers were devotees of the genre.[32] Of the tabulated votes, 1,222 (or 76 percent of the 1,601 persons interviewed) were cast for Soviet authors, and 658 (42 percent) for foreign authors, all of them Western. The list of Soviet authors resembled the one emerging from the study of reading preferences of engineers and technicians referred to earlier in this chapter.[33] The one major (and somewhat paradoxical) difference was that the youngsters showed considerable interest in science fiction as well as in Soviet novels about scientists, engineers, and technicians. Apparently Soviet engineers and technicians were not interested in reading novels about themselves; they might conceivably have found them boring if "truthful" and irritating if "untruthful" in their portrayal of technological realia and, more importantly, of psychological motivations of protagonists they knew from first-hand experience. They exhibited curiosity, however, about their American counterparts who populate the novels of Mitchell Wilson.[34] The list of foreign authors read by the fifteen- to seventeen-year-olds was not very different from that of favorite writers of the two adult groups (of

29. *Sovetskij čitatel'*, pp. 220–21. Of that number, 146 attended trade schools; the others were from academic senior high schools.
30. Ibid., p. 228.
31. Ibid., p. 230.
32. Ibid.
33. See footnote 19.
34. See Appendix D.

workers and of engineers and technicians), except that it included two of the perennial favorites of Russian adolescents, Ethel Voynich and Mayne Reid:[35]

| AUTHOR | NUMBER OF RESPONDENTS | PERCENT OF TOTAL |
|---|---|---|
| Jack London | 183 | 12 |
| Ethel Voynich | 80 | 5 |
| Theodore Dreiser | 70 | 5 |
| William Shakespeare | 63 | 4 |
| Émile Zola | 62 | 4 |
| Mayne Reid | 51 | 3 |
| Erich Maria Remarque | 46 | 3 |
| Honoré de Balzac | 38 | 2 |
| Victor Hugo | 36 | 2 |
| Stefan Zweig | 29 | 2 |

College and university students are the one group that prefers postwar foreign literature to Soviet writing. Actually, among this group of readers the popularity of Soviet literature also trails that of the Russian classics and of prewar West European and American writing.[36] Interviews with 767 students conducted in 25 Soviet institutions of higher learning in various parts of the country disclose that 78 percent of the respondents read the Russian classics; 73 percent, older works of foreign literature; 59 percent, modern foreign literature; and only 56 percent, Soviet literature.[37] *In other words, Soviet college students showed a clear preference for all categories of non-Soviet writing over Soviet literature.* This may explain the persistent official concern in the USSR about the "excessive" popularity of Western culture, which will be discussed in chapter nine, "A Problematic Coexistence: Western Culture in Soviet Society." Suffice it to point out here that, however selectively published and tendentiously interpreted, non-Soviet writing is in the final analysis a carrier of non-Soviet ideas.

The college students' tastes in Soviet literature were not, on the whole, very different from those of other readers.[38] The most significant change was observed in attitudes toward the Russian classics: in secondary school they had found them boring.[39] While a part of the blame surely rests with the

35. *Sovetskij čitatel'*, p. 235. For additional discussion of the subject see chapter 4.
36. Since prior to World War II there were no Communist countries other than the USSR proper, the Soviet term "classical foreign literature" is in practice nearly synonymous with Western writing. Judging by all evidence, translations of older works of non-Western literatures, such as Asian and African, account only for an insignificant proportion of translated foreign literature of the prewar period published in the USSR.
37. *Sovetskij čitatel'*, pp. 248–50.
38. See Appendix E.
39. *Sovetskij čitatel'*, p. 257.

doctrinaire and unimaginative manner in which the Russian classics are taught in Soviet schools,[40] there is no denying the fact that many of the masterpieces of nineteenth-century Russian literature are much too subtle for children and young adolescents. Unable to appreciate the intricacies of the art of the great Russian poets or the sophisticated thought of some of the masterpieces of the Russian novel, many juvenile readers probably read them for their plots alone. When judged by such criteria, *Eugene Onegin* or *Anna Karenina* may in fact appear inferior to *The Three Musketeers* or even a primitive Soviet novel set during the Civil War or describing the exploits of the Soviet intelligence service. Upon "rediscovery" of the Russian classics at the university—where they are no longer required reading that must simply be endured and often even memorized—the students chose some of the best Russian prose but, curiously, ignored the poets.[41]

"A greedy interest in classical foreign literature is characteristic of student readers," a Soviet scholar reports.[42] The hunger for foreign writing extends also, of course, to modern Western writing of every description and includes translated poetry, which contrasts with the apparent lack of interest in Russian verse.[43] By far the most popular type of reading was translations of foreign thrillers, preferred by 34 percent of the 767 college students.[44] The "classics of foreign literature" ranked in order of their popularity among the Soviet college students were as follows:[45]

40. For a detailed treatment of the subject see N. N. Shneidman, *Literature and Ideology in Soviet Education* (Toronto: D. C. Heath/Lexington Books, 1973).

41. The incomplete list, with some of the 767 respondents obviously citing more than one author, was headed by Leo Tolstoy (50 percent of the entire sample), followed by Chekhov (36 percent), Kuprin (21 percent), and Turgenev and Dostoyevsky (18 percent each). *Sovetskij čitatel'*, p. 257. The figure for Dostoyevsky, an author systematically neglected in the school curriculum for ideological reasons, is particularly noteworthy. Although only eighth on a workers' list of favorite classical Russian authors and sharing seventh place with Gogol on a similar list for engineers and technicians, Dostoyevsky was fourth in popularity (together with Turgenév) among the college students. Dostoyevsky occupied only the ninth place among the prerevolutionary authors published in 1956–62. (See footnote 19.) It should also be kept in mind that in the preceding period Dostoyevsky fared even worse. He occupied only the fifteenth place among the Russian classics printed in 1918–57. See this writer's *Russian Classics in Soviet Jackets*, p. 190.

The absence from the list of students' favorites of the nineteenth-century Russian poets paradoxically parallels the dislike of poetry by readers with less than seven grades of schooling (a reaction to the enforced memorization of poetry in school?). In sharp contrast to the students, however, these less educated readers also often dislike foreign literature in general. As one such reader explained, "I am having trouble remembering the [foreign literary protagonists'] names and I don't understand their life." V. D. Stel'max, "Iz opyta izučenija čitatel'skix interesov," in B. S. Mejlax (ed.), *Xudožestvennoe vosprijatie,* pp. 157–58.

42. *Sovetskij čitatel'*, p. 259.

43. It should be emphasized that the Soviet source's failure to include any Russian poets, classical as well as modern, in the list of authors favored by the Russian students, is contradicted by testimonies of scores of witnesses who are nearly unanimous in reporting that Soviet college students are voracious readers of poetry, particularly of modern verse. This was also the opinion of many Soviet authors expressed in conversations with this writer.

44. *Sovetskij čitatel'*, p. 260.

45. Ibid., pp. 259–60. Again, respondents must have named more than one author.

| AUTHOR | PERCENT OF TOTAL SAMPLE |
|---|---|
| Honoré de Balzac | 24 |
| Jack London | 22 |
| Émile Zola | 21 |
| Theodore Dreiser | 20 |
| William Shakespeare | 15 |
| Victor Hugo | 14 |
| Guy de Maupassant | 14 |
| Jules Verne | 12 |
| Romain Rolland | 10 |
| Stendhal | 9 |
| Charles Dickens | 8 |
| George Byron | 7 |
| Mayne Reid | 6 |
| Alexandre Dumas | 6 |
| Johann Wolfgang Goethe | 4 |
| Robert Burns | 2 |

Modern foreign authors were listed in the following order:

| AUTHOR | PERCENT OF TOTAL SAMPLE |
|---|---|
| Erich Maria Remarque | 19 |
| Ernest Hemingway | 18 |
| Ray Bradbury | 9 |
| Heinrich Böll | 8 |
| J. D. Salinger | 5 |
| H. G. Wells | 4 |

Finally, 24 percent—or every fourth college student—was a reader of *Inostrannaja literatura,* another eloquent testimony to the truly extraordinary interest in foreign writing among Soviet college students.[46]

A comparison with similar lists emerging from interviews with workers as well as with technicians and engineers (the latter, of course, themselves college graduates) reveals a number of interesting discrepancies. First of all, the students reveal a far greater degree of literary sophistication than the engineers and technicians, to say nothing of the workers. Among the students, the favorite on the list of older foreign authors was Balzac; among the others, Balzac ran a distant third to Dreiser and Jack London. Stendhal, Dickens, and Byron did not appear on the nonstudents' list. The students read far more of Hemingway and also read Salinger (who did not appear on the other lists), and conversely, displayed little or no interest in the

46. Ibid. Only two periodicals were more popular with this group of readers, the youth-oriented *Junost'* (54 percent) and, strangely, the neo-Stalinist *Neva* (26 percent). The popularity of the latter may be due to the rather frequent appearance in it of novels glorifying the exploits of the Soviet military and police, subject matter of considerable appeal to younger readers.

primitive propagandistic novels of James Aldridge and Ellen Dymphna
Cusack. At the same time the students refused to part with their childhood
companions, such as Mayne Reid and Dumas, and retained a strong interest
in science fiction, old and new (Bradbury, Jules Verne, H. G. Wells).[47]
Finally, discounting the 34 percent of respondents favoring detective fiction
(most of which is Western), a list of twelve authors most popular with Soviet
students includes only *one* Soviet writer, Sholokhov:

| AUTHOR | PERCENT OF TOTAL SAMPLE |
| --- | --- |
| Leo Tolstoy | 50 |
| Chekhov | 36 |
| Sholokhov | 25 |
| Balzac | 24 |
| London | 22 |
| Zola | 21 |
| Kuprin | 21 |
| Dreiser | 20 |
| Remarque | 19 |
| Hemingway | 18 |
| Turgenev | 18 |
| Dostoyevsky | 18 |

The almost demonstrative boycott of the bulk of Soviet writing by the
young men and women who will in the near future constitute the Soviet
intelligentsia must be viewed with concern by the Soviet authorities; some
vocal expressions of this concern will be discussed in chapter nine. This
rejection of Communist-inspired literature in favor of what Soviet college
students probably regard as apolitical Western books brings to mind the
behavior of Soviet authors who in the oppressive years of Stalinism sought
ways to evade producing the ideological potboilers then being manufactured
by most of their colleagues. It recalls the career of Mixail Prišvin, whose
books describe forests and animals while avoiding much comment about
Soviet humanity. It reminds one of the novels of Aleksandr Grin, most of
them set in the never-never land called Grinland. It brings to mind the
many Soviet authors who sought a degree of safety in writing fairy tales and
nursery rhymes, occasionally (as in the case of the playwright Evgenij
Švarc) destined only ostensibly for children. One also discerns some links
with Soviet writers whose original works ceased to be published and who
found shelter in writing stage and screen adaptations of safe old classics (as
did Mikhail Bulgakov and Isaac Babel) or in literary translation. Boris

47. Another juvenile favorite, Jack London, retains his appeal with other adult readers as
well. In general, college students said they prefer foreign writing with "sharply delineated
plots" *(ostrosjužetnye),* preferably accounts of adventure *(priključenčeskie).* V. D. Stel'max,
"Iz opyta izučenija čitatel'skix interesov," B. S. Mejlax (ed.), *Xudožestvennoe vosprijatie,* pp.
157–58.

Pasternak is said to have observed that whereas Mayakovsky shot himself, he, Pasternak, translated. One recognizes, too, a distant echo of an observation made on the eve of World War I by Georgi Plekhanov, Russia's most eminent pre-Soviet Marxist literary critic. Writing at a time when many of his country's leading authors rebelled against the demand that literature be a carrier of political ideas, Plekhanov commented:

> The belief in art for art's sake arises and takes root wherever people engaged in art are hopelessly out of harmony with their social environment. This disharmony reflects favourably on artistic production to the extent that it helps the artists to rise above their environment.[48]

One wonders whether Plekhanov's rather dogmatic observations about creators of art do not also contain a measure of applicability to similar phenomena among consumers of art. That rejection of much of Soviet literature by Soviet college students "reflects favorably on artistic consumption" is obvious from the list of their twelve favorite authors. Not more than two or three are artistically inferior to *any* writers of Soviet prose. Can it be that the consistent preference for non-Soviet writing indicates also a degree of disharmony with the values of their highly politicized social environment?

Reference was made earlier to the fact that in conditions of monopolistic Soviet publishing the selection of titles to be translated and the sizes of printings are often quite unrelated to public demand; more specifically, that small printings of certain translations of Western literature (or the failure to publish others altogether) are not to be taken as indicators of a lack of interest in them.[49] That the Soviet authorities are perfectly aware of the kinds of books for which there exists a large demand that is chronically ignored by the publishing authorities is illustrated by a fascinating episode that took place late in 1974.

The Soviet Union has long been plagued by paper shortages. Collecting scrap paper for recycling by usual means did not prove very effective: few people bothered to turn it in since the price paid for scrap was only two kopeks (slightly over two cents) per kilogram (2.2 pounds). Then, in September 1974, government agencies announced that nine book titles would

48. G. Plekhanov, *Unaddressed Letters. Art and Social Life* (Moscow: Foreign Languages Publishing House, 1957), p. 184. Plekhanov warned, however, that ultimately this stance of ideological aloofness is self-defeating, because it also blinds its adherents to the struggle that is being waged by others against the values and conditions they all oppose. Ibid., p. 185.

49. The reverse is, of course, also true but only within limits. Thus, certain works of Soviet literature (to say nothing of overtly propagandistic nonfiction) are not only given much publicity and are strikingly inexpensive, but bookstores are pressured and libraries are often in effect forced to order large quantities of such books. Nevertheless, there are limits beyond which this procedure inevitably produces economically intolerable oversupplies of such books.

be printed in half a million copies each, but would not be sold through regular commercial channels. To obtain a copy of any of these, one would have to deliver to a storehouse twenty kilograms of scrap paper (forty-four pounds). The economic rationale for the operation was as follows:

> Thus the state will receive some 70,000 tons of waste paper, having used only about 1,500 tons of paper (the average weight of a 350-page book is 0.4 kg.). Allowing for the loss of some 25 percent during the pulping process, approximately 50,000 tons of new paper will be obtained; this figure is over 13 percent above the annual production of paper for printing. This measure will undoubtedly assist fulfillment of the Five-Year Plan for paper production.
>
> Furthermore, millions of unsold and unwanted books, which will come back in the form of pulp, will be partly bought up by the purchasers of the new series of books. This is a form of exchanging unpopular books for works that are in great demand. In this way, two birds are killed with one stone: supplies of unpurchased literature are partially disposed of, and approximately 70,000 tons of pulp paper are obtained free of charge.[50]

Additional information was provided by N. V. Ksintaris, a senior official of the Council of Ministers, in an interview printed in *Pravda* on October 25, 1974. Stores exchanging forty-four pounds of scrap paper for one copy of any of the nine books were to be set up in ten major cities.[51] The list of books that were to lure Soviet citizens into collecting and hauling the heavy bundles of old newspapers, magazines, and unwanted volumes was as follows:[52]

Il'f and Petrov, *The Twelve Chairs*
Aleksej N. Tolstoy, *Aelita* and *Engineer Garin's Hyperboloid*
Hans Christian Andersen, *Fairy Tales* (in two volumes)
Ethel Voynich, *The Gadfly*
Arthur Conan Doyle, *The Hound of the Baskervilles*
Wilkie Collins, *The Woman in White*
Georges Simenon, *The Maigret Stories*
Alexandre Dumas, *Queen Margot*

Of the nine titles, only three were by Soviet authors. The two novels by Aleksej N. Tolstoy are both science fiction with elements of social anti-utopia, a combination very rare in Soviet writing, and *The Twelve Chairs* is one of the few Soviet comic novels. The other six were all translations of Western literature, half of them thrillers.

50. Radio Liberty Dispatch, RL 318/74, New York, October 2, 1974. The Soviet sources are *Socialističeskaja industrija,* September 14, 1974, and *Literaturnaja gazeta,* No. 34, 1974, p. 10.
51. The cities were Moscow, Leningrad, Kiev, Alma Ata, Sverdlovsk, Gorky, Novosibirsk, Kemerovo, Krasnoyarsk, and Donetsk.
52. Radio Liberty Dispatch, and *Literaturnaja gazeta,* No. 4 (December 4, 1974), p. 12.

The overwhelming success of the scheme surpassed all expectations. One newspaper correspondent reported long lines of people of all ages and backgrounds waiting in front of stores exchanging scrap paper for books, with young women pushing baby carriages loaded with old books and papers; there were also many automobiles with out-of-town license plates, showing that numerous customers traveled long distances to obtain a copy of one of the coveted books. Alexandre Dumas's *Queen Margot,* the first title to be printed, was soon being sold on the black market for twenty-five rubles (close to thirty dollars).[53] Another newspaper revealed that in order to get a copy of *Queen Margot* or *The Hound of the Baskervilles* some people were bringing as part of the required forty-four pounds of scrap paper volumes of Gogol, Chekhov, Tolstoy, and Dostoyevsky, to say nothing of Soviet authors.[54] This does not, of course, indicate that the Russian classics are unread, but only that they are more readily available and hence can be replaced. It does, on the other hand, loudly attest to the great hunger for light, entertaining Western reading matter that is not being satisfied by Soviet publishing houses. One may reasonably expect that *Anna Karenina* and *Dead Souls* will be republished soon enough. But it is wiser not to take any chances with French historical romances or the adventures of London and Paris detectives; one never knows when these might become available again to Soviet readers.

Apologies were made in the Introduction for the somewhat crude lumping together of literary works of shockingly unequal merit in some of the chapters that followed, with the political slant of their contents as the decisive criterion. That objections would be raised to classifying Faulkner as a chronicler of racism in the American South (thus placing him side by side with a number of admittedly second-rate authors) and listing Boccaccio with some crude antireligious doggerel was not difficult to foresee. The justification offered was that Soviet criticism (or rather literary journalism) aimed at mass audiences often treats foreign authors in this manner, and it is therefore reasonable to assume that the less sophisticated readers are conditioned to view them in a similar manner. Our hypothesis is borne out by the 1973 study of Soviet readers in small towns (with fewer than 50,000 inhabitants) already referred to in this chapter. More than half of all respondents (58 percent) appeared quite indifferent to the artistic merit of literary works. Their likes and dislikes were determined by a book's setting, plot, and protagonists—in short, by nonaesthetic factors.[55] A typical case reported was that of a young woman of twenty-one with a secondary

53. *Literaturnaja gazeta,* No. 52, 1974, p. 12.
54. Boris Goduncov, "Talon na 'Korolevu Margo'," *Sovetskaja kul'tura,* December 27, 1974.
55. *Kniga i čtenie v žizni nebol'šix gorodov,* pp. 90–91.

education, who was equally pleased with *Anna Karenina,* with Dreiser's *Sister Carrie,* and with two Soviet potboilers, Natal'ja Davydova's *Ljubov' inženera Izotova* (The Love of Engineer Izotov, 1960) and Pavel Luknickij's *Nisso* (1946). To her, these were all novels "about love."[56]

While no detailed sociological studies are available of the popular reception and probable impact of Western literature in Soviet society (the subject is, understandably, politically sensitive), significant indirect evidence may be deduced from a survey of readers' motivations and of their criteria in evaluating all types of literary works. The survey was based on interviews with 1,200 persons of different ages, occupations, and educational backgrounds.[57] Among the most important findings were the following.

The strongest single impetus for the reading of fiction, poetry, and drama was what the Soviet researcher called a "Columbus complex." Respondents read literary works "in order to obtain information about various phenomena of life, about [different historical] periods, [foreign] countries, the lives and work of outstanding people, etc. This [motivation] was found among readers of all ages and backgrounds." Fully 54 percent of all respondents—more than half—gave it as one reason for the reading of literature.[58] Next in order of importance was a literary work's "truthfulness" and authenticity, a logical enough extension of the "Columbus complex"; these factors were emphasized by a nearly identical proportion of the sample, 49 percent.[59] This was followed by a desire to find the purpose and meaning of life (45 percent), which may also be interpreted as a sublimated quasi-religious quest familiar to readers of Tolstoy and Dostoyevsky.[60] Another consideration was a desire to learn more about human nature (30 percent); this group of readers was attracted to what the researcher called "psychologism," a quality they found in the writings of Dostoyevsky and Chekhov.[61] Other important reasons were a search for moral ideals (25 percent; this, too, may be an expression of spiritual hunger) and the desire to "become educated," to acquire status (22 percent). And 22 percent declared that they like books in which conclusions are *implied* rather than openly stated.[62]

56. Ibid., p. 95. The respondent's classification was not unlike that of the Soviet *Literary Encyclopedia,* where the entry for Davydova informs that her works "deal chiefly with the subjects of love, friendship, and family relations," but makes no comment at all on their aesthetic merit or even artistic manner (KL, Vol. II [1964], p. 489).

57. L. I. Beljaeva, "Motivy čtenija i kriterii ocenok proizvedenij xudožestvennoj literatury u različnyx kategorij čitatelej," in B. S. Mejlax (ed.), *Xudožestvennoe vosprijatie,* pp. 162–76.

58. Ibid., p. 168.

59. Ibid., p. 175.

60. Ibid., pp. 168–69.

61. Ibid., p. 169.

62. Ibid., p. 173. Additional findings included:

21 percent enjoy the experience of reading in itself; such respondents read almost anything indiscriminately. 20 percent read literature in order to improve their own personalities. 19 percent seek concrete information about life in our time; this group favors Soviet writing *and also most recent foreign literature* (Ibid., p. 169). 16 percent

The last preference, clearly, is an oblique criticism of the great bulk of Soviet literature which is notoriously preachy. The "Columbus complex," which was the most frequently cited reason for the reading of literature, also implies a preference for non-Soviet writing. As for the insistence that literature be "truthful," suffice it to recall that the opening salvo aimed at the Soviet writing of the Stalin era and published within months of the dictator's death accused it of contrivance and falsehood and demanded that literature be "sincere."[63] That is not to say that all of the preferences tend to favor non-Soviet writing, both Western and prerevolutionary Russian. Some are in fact more readily satisfied by Soviet books. Status seekers, for instance, presumably read the latest Soviet best sellers, as do those who wish to find in literature projections of their own problems and aspirations. Nevertheless, the general tendency favors works that are serious without being didactic, preferably offering a degree of authentic information on a variety of subjects, and probing some moral problems. Surprisingly few respondents prized literature for its entertainment value alone.[64]

While the absence of hard data excludes the possibility of gauging the actual impact of Western literature on Soviet audiences, evidence presented earlier as well as that which will be cited in the concluding chapter offers sufficient grounds for a number of hypotheses. In the first place, it is quite obvious that for significant numbers of readers Western literature serves as a means of escape from the persistent, annoying didacticism of the overwhelming part of Soviet writing, theater, and the cinema, to say nothing of the shrill propagandistic tone of the Soviet press, radio, and television. Such "escapism" may be viewed as innocent enough in most parts of the world, but it is regarded with considerable suspicion by the Soviet state which expects from its citizenry not merely passive allegiance, but also vocal enthusiasm for its policies (often advanced, by the way, in "timely" productions of Soviet literature) and, above all, undivided attention. Thus, infatuation with foreign settings (except on the part of the young, for whom it may

---

read for relaxation and entertainment; this category of readers favored, for instance, "thrillers." 10 percent read literature to gain better insight into their own psyches. 10 percent seek confirmation of their own ideas about life. 7 percent believe literature enriches one's spiritual life. 7 percent seek in literature affirmation of their own values.

63. Vladimir Pomerancev, "Ob iskrennosti v literature," *Novyj mir,* No. 12, 1953.

64. This does not necessarily contradict the sensational demand for such light reading as the romances of Alexandre Dumas and the exploits of Sherlock Holmes. Such books may be appreciated for their honesty, nondoctrinaire tone, and, last but not least, for the "authenticity" of their foreign settings. The latter consideration need not be dismissed as improbable. This writer has encountered scores of American undergraduates who believed that Dostoyevsky's Raskolnikov was probably a "typical" Russian student.

As for the preference for "factual" information in literature, it may well be a result of the manner in which literature is taught in Soviet schools and interpreted in most of Soviet criticism. This predilection is reflected in the work of the great majority of Soviet authors, including the nonconformists among them. Thus, Solzhenitsyn's *Cancer Ward* offers a wealth of clinical details on the diagnosis and treatment of the disease.

be regarded as a useful supplement to formal geography courses) implies, however faintly, a disinterest in Soviet subject matter, and may thus be viewed with a concern similar to that evoked by refusal to read Soviet newspapers and excuses to evade attending propaganda meetings that are a regular feature of Soviet life.

Second, the virtual boycott of conventional Soviet writing on the part of college students, especially when examined in conjunction with the 22 percent of readers from all walks of life who dislike "preachy" literature, indicates that a significant segment of the reading public resents crudely didactic writing, preferring literature that poses problems—moral, social, and psychological—without imposing on the reader ready-made solutions. That part of the reading public may be said to regard literature as a stimulus for *independent* thought, an activity not encouraged by Soviet schools and Soviet society in general. Such readers' attraction to non-Soviet literature must be a cause for some disquiet in the Soviet Establishment, since the formulation of these problems in Western writing is not always conducive to arriving at "desirable" conclusions. Uneducated readers, on the other hand seem less resentful of such authorial encroachment on their right to personal evaluations of problems and conflicts discussed in literature; they may in fact welcome such assistance. It is, however, this group of readers —particularly those in the countryside—who also show the least interest in foreign literature. Schoolchildren do read selected works of Western literature and are probably quite receptive to the "message" contained in them. That message is often broadly educational rather than narrowly political. It may promote such general virtues as hard work, courage, resourcefulness, and loyalty. More overt ideological appeals are less frequent; besides, these are supplied by Soviet literature which appears to be this group's favorite reading matter.

Carefully selected works of West European and American literature provide Soviet readers with a very unflattering image of the non-Soviet world, and as pointed out, the majority of them sift literary works for factual information about life in societies other than their own. It may well be that some readers are skeptical about such consistently gloomy and hostile descriptions of life outside the USSR.[65] The majority, however, probably accept them as true, disregarding the factor of selectivity and, more importantly, ignoring that writers in the West normally regard their

65. Thus, we read in Solzhenitsyn's *The First Circle:* "There was also a book on the stool, *American Tales* by a progressive author. Khorobrov was in no position to verify them against real life, but the selection was strange. Every tale contained some obligatory slur about America. Assembled with venom, they presented such a nightmarish picture that one could only wonder why the Americans had not all fled their country or hanged themselves." Aleksandr Solženicyn, *V kruge pervom* (S. Fischer Verlag, Switzerland, 1968), p. 150.

proper roles as those of critics of their societies, rather than extollers of their virtues. (Can one readily imagine an American novel hailing the wisdom of President Ford, or a British play glorifying that country's system of socialized medicine, or a West German poet singing the praises of the high productivity of labor at the Volkswagen plant?) It is likely that many Soviet readers note that Western writing criticizes such evils as social inequality, intolerance of dissent, society's disregard for the rights of the individual to his private little happiness, and the hypocrisy of official pieties—and decide that life in the West is indeed intolerable (there may be some confusion here, because the Soviet press also repeatedly informs them that the standard of living in the West, particularly in the United States, is still higher than in the USSR). At the same time, however, many of these readers probably note that most of these problems (except, say, unemployment) are also to be found in Soviet society, although they are rarely raised in Soviet literature and their very existence is denied. Similarly, as we shall see, not all Soviet readers are convinced that anti-militarist sentiments are appropriate only when directed against the *foreign* military and "imperialist" wars. Paradoxically, such reactions are most likely to be evoked by Western left-wing and Communist authors. One possible response, then, may well be an attitude of cynicism and resignation with regard to the social ills of both Soviet and non-Soviet societies. A Soviet quip comes to mind: "Is there life on Mars? No—there is no life on Mars, either."[66]

66. The Russian original goes, *"Est' li žizn' na Marse? Tože net."*

# CHAPTER

# 3

# Extremes That Meet:
# Venerable Classics and
# Modern Entertainment

The theory of "continuity and change" ranks among the more enduring and intellectually respectable approaches to the study of the Soviet Union.[1] It argues, in effect, that serious study of Russia's prerevolutionary old institutions and modes of behavior sheds much light on those features of Soviet life that might otherwise appear incomprehensible or bizarre. Whatever the theory's merits in other problems, its application to a survey of Soviet tastes and predilections in Western literature does, indeed, offer many valuable insights. Preferences that can be traced directly to Communist politics aside, translations of the older works of foreign writing that are made available in the USSR bear a strong resemblance to what a private library of a liberal or radical member of the intelligentsia might have contained at the turn of the century. Insulated since 1917 from normal cultural contacts with the West, Soviet readers remain faithful to hundreds of Western authors and thousands of books that changing fashions have long consigned to oblivion in their own countries.[2]

The Russian literary landscape abounds in such living fossils, and the phenomenon was illuminated with striking clarity in the early post-Stalin

1. See, e.g., the major collection of essays, Ernest J. Simmons (ed.), *Continuity and Change in Russian and Soviet Thought* (Cambridge, Mass.: Harvard University Press, 1955).
2. A pioneering study, and one of the few serious attempts at a serious investigation of the subject, is Levin L. Schücking, *The Sociology of Literary Taste* (London: Routledge and Kegan Paul, 1966). This is a thoroughly revised version of an essay first published in 1923. A Russian translation appeared in 1928 under the imprint of "Academia" publishers in Moscow. Unfortunately, Schücking's 100-page book has very little to say about Russia.

era when some of the "new" Western books were those that, abroad, are best described by Mark Twain's definition from *The Disappearance of Literature:* "A classic is something that everybody wants to have read and nobody wants to read." The strikingly antiquated artistic outlook of most Soviet writing—not the few exceptions that are translated abroad because *they* may appeal to the Western public—is, in a way, a mirror image of this state of affairs. How many American youngsters still read Jack London, how many British boys still devour Mayne Reid? Or, for that matter, how many adults? Yet millions of Russians do.[3] Not that our *new* books are artistically or intellectually necessarily superior to those now collecting dust in libraries and attics; most, in fact, are not. We merely wish to call attention to the relatively static assortment of titles that is characteristic of both Soviet book production and of reading preferences.

When after years of neglect foreign literature began to be printed again on a large scale shortly after Stalin's death, a curious Rip Van Winkle process set in: the primary beneficiaries of the "thaw" were authors and books that were being read in Russia at the time the "freeze" began, i.e., those that were fashionable decades earlier. This lag, it should be noted, is further reinforced by the country's uniform school curriculum which, aside from politically motivated revisions in the selection of "progressive" modern authors represented, is otherwise remarkably stable, emphasizing traditional nineteenth-century European realists (particularly those critical of their societies) and shunning foreign writers, of whatever ideological stripe, who employ "modernistic" techniques. While the issues in this particular case are not exclusively related to artistic predilections, it is worth noting that the first Soviet edition of Franz Kafka appeared in 1965, i.e., at a time when, after decades of great popularity and critical acclaim, Kafka's works had begun to vanish from reading lists in freshman literature courses abroad. On the other hand, a writer like Hans Fallada, "little known nowadays" according to *The Penguin Companion to Literature,* is still going strong in the USSR: well over half a million copies published during the first post-Stalin decade.[4] So are countless other traditionalist writers, great and

3. A recent study of reading habits in Soviet small towns (with fewer than 50,000 inhabitants) cites the case of a fifth-grader, the most bookish boy in his class, whose favorite books, as reported on three different occasions, were *all* foreign—and were all old favorites, books that were read by schoolboys in Russia at the turn of the century. The authors and titles cited were Mayne Reid's *The Headless Horseman* (cited on all three occasions), Alexandre Dumas's *The Count of Monte Cristo* and *The Three Musketeers,* and Giovagnoli's *Spartacus. (Kniga i čtenie v žizni nebol'šix gorodov,* 1973, p. 241). For a detailed discussion of the subject see chapter 4.

4. *The Penguin Companion to Literature* (Baltimore, Md., 1969), Vol. II, p. 262. Throughout this study, *The Penguin Companion* and similar standard reference books will be referred to both for the purely factual information they contain and for what may be regarded as the closest approximation of generally accepted views (or "conventional wisdom") in Western literary scholarship, less controversial and opinionated than longer works by individual critics.

not so great, poets, playwrights, and authors of children's books, adventure stories and *Bildungsromanen,* particularly those with a "humanist" bent, counterparts as it were of pre-Soviet Russia's own "philanthropic" literature, those that denounce cruelty and oppression and champion the cause of society's underdog. These works tend to be artistically simple (in the non-derogatory sense of the term), rational, and didactic; mostly realistic, they also include some of the great Romantic classics.

Paradoxically, these are the same books that were favored by Communism's founding fathers themselves. Karl Marx and Friedrich Engels may have been revolutionaries in their politics, but in literature their tastes were nearly impeccably traditional; they cherished the great classics of antiquity and, among more recent writers, the same authors that most cultivated Germans of their times esteemed. Only rarely did they express any great enthusiasm for the revolutionary authors of the day.[5] Similarly, Lenin's artistic preferences were no different from those of most "bourgeois" intellectuals of the time; he loved the great Russian and foreign classics and had little patience for the various "experimental" types of writing (Futurist, Symbolist) then in vogue, however sympathetic he may have found some of them politically.

As pointed out, because of the monopolistic nature of Soviet publishing and the general unavailability of books printed abroad, one cannot equate supply with freely expressed demand. Yet, however involuntary or induced or artifically created, the demand for old-fashioned Western writing continues to be strong, a testimony of sorts to Russia's continued membership in the European culture that produced it. It is also evidence of the essentially superficial impact on the contemporary average Russian's artistic tastes of some of the great post-realist prose writers, highly innovative poets, and unconventional playwrights of the first decades of this century, of such towering figures as Aleksandr Blok, Fëdor Sologub, Vladimir Mayakovsky, Boris Pasternak, and Isaac Babel.

Readers who favor modern West European and American writing, particularly of the stylistically more unconventional variety are, indeed, under-

---

Such Western reference sources will be cited not as irrefutable authoritative pronouncements, but merely to bring into sharper focus the overtly politicized opinions of Soviet evaluations of Western writing. *The Penguin Companion to Literature* is a four-volume reference work: Vol. I, *British and Commonwealth Literature,* ed. David Daiches (Baltimore, Md.: Penguin Books, 1971); Vol. II, *European Literature,* ed. Anthony Thorlby (Baltimore, Md.: Penguin Books, 1969); Vol. III, *United States and Latin American Literature,* ed. M. Bradbury, E. Mottram, and J. Franco (Baltimore, Md.: Penguin Books, 1971); Vol. IV, *Classical and Byzantine, Oriental and African Literature,* ed. D. R. Dudley and D. M. Lang (Baltimore, Md.: Penguin Books, 1969).

5. The best treatment of the subject is Peter Demetz, *Marx, Engels and the Poets: Origins of Marxist Literary Criticism,* revised and enlarged by the author and translated by Jeffrey L. Sammons (Chicago: University of Chicago Press, 1967).

privileged in the USSR. Only on very rare occasions can they indulge their tastes—even when the authors in question are, politically, friends. On the other hand, devotees of older literature are singularly fortunate if they know Russian. (The benefits apply, of course, also to such persons outside the USSR, where Soviet books are, as a rule, freely available, and some are, indeed, easier to obtain than in the USSR proper.) Older West European and American literature is regularly issued in huge editions (although, as we shall see, even those are not sufficient to meet the seemingly insatiable demand). Very large printings of prose, verse, and drama are published in single volumes as well as multivolume sets, as modest if not shabby paper-backs and in resplendent de luxe editions, as straight reprints of the texts themselves and in volumes supplied with an elaborate scholarly apparatus.

Often foreign books are brought out in new translations—a reflection of Russia's traditional excellence in that activity, one that goes back, in fact, to the beginning of the nineteenth century. That tradition was not inter-rupted by the Revolution. On the contrary, among the ambitious (and subsequently abandoned) projects of the early postrevolutionary years was a plan to publish, under the patronage of Maxim Gorky, new translations of nearly all of the greatest monuments of the art of writing. The high esteem for the literary translator's work continued in the years that fol-lowed; Kornej Čukovskij, an eminent scholar, children's poet, and transla-tor himself, called it *vysokoe iskusstvo*—"the lofty art." Literary transla-tions are well paid in the USSR, and what is equally important, are recognized as artistic achievements in their own right, much as in a major musical recording in the West the laurels are shared by the composer and the performer. On the other hand, in a more negative vein, literary transla-tions have unwittingly benefited from the political restrictions imposed in the USSR on the publication of original literary works. As a result, Soviet authors who could not at varying times hope to have their own work appear in print, have sought refuge in translations. One famous name stands out, that of Boris Pasternak, who during his years of public disfavor created a new Russian *Hamlet*.

Primarily, we shall be considering in this chapter books (most of them quite old or, paradoxically, very new) for which relatively few extravagant political claims are made in Soviet literary criticism; an exception will be made for a small number of authors and titles brought out, it seems, because of the fondness for them of Karl Marx and other founding fathers. It should be emphasized that other books may be, objectively, just as apolitical. They will, however, be discussed elsewhere because Soviet critics do consider them political and make periodic attempts to harness their real or alleged political potential for the Soviet cause. The thrust of the present study argues for the logic of following, for purposes of discussion, whatever ground rules are established by the Soviet critics and publishers. Thus, in chapter four, "For the Young and Adventurous," we shall accept, for the time being, the views of those Soviet publishers that induced them to print Melville's *Moby Dick* because it is, ostensibly, a nice wholesome book about whaling—which, on reflection, it *also* is.

Most of the works discussed in this chapter are not from the Soviet publishers' vantage point, ideologically worthwhile. Indeed, quite a number are published in spite of expressed reservations about their ideological implications. In the case of the older classics, this indulgence may be accepted as the authorities' gesture to *kul'tura,* and the only indirect benefit accruing may well be the desire to demonstrate that the USSR is a patron and protector of high culture of all times, whatever its ideology, a line of reasoning occasionally also pursued in the publication of the prerevolutionary Russian classics.[6] Writers in this category are relatively unaffected by minor vicissitudes of Soviet politics, although more books of this type get published during relatively permissive periods in Soviet cultural policies. At the other end of the spectrum—in the chronological sense and sometimes also in artistic stature—are the contemporary works of light, entertaining reading that are made available at times when the authorities are apparently satisfied that no major harm would be done by indulging somewhat the Soviet reading public's taste for some foreign literary cotton candy.

A large proportion of the older part of this politically quite inert reading matter consists of translations of poetry. All evidence suggests that Soviet citizens read more verse, including translations, than most Europeans and Americans. Again, the art of translation of poetry is a firmly established tradition in Russia, and many of the country's foremost poets tried their hand at rendering foreign verse into Russian, either from the originals or from interlinear prose translations *(podstročniki);* among twentieth century Russian poets active as translators, in addition to Pasternak one must also mention Ivan Bunin, Anna Axmatova, Valerij Brjusov, Vladislav Xodasevič, and Samuil Maršak. To a degree, verse as a genre is less susceptible to politics than prose, both because of the brevity of most of its forms, and also because excessive ideological baggage runs the risk of reducing it to doggerel. And poetry, in Pushkin's quip, "must be a little on the stupid side" *("A poezija, prosti Gospodi, dolžna byt' glupovata").*[7] As for plays, in the hands of a skillful director and actors, they may, *on stage,* acquire a wide range of political resonance—frequently, indeed, quite different from that

6. See this writer's *Russian Classics in Soviet Jackets* (New York: Columbia University Press, 1962).
7. Letter to P. A. Vjazemskij, May 1826, in A. S. Puškin, *Polnoe sobranie sočinenij v desjati tomax* (Moscow: Akademija Nauk SSSR, 1949), Vol. X, p. 207.

intended by their creators. Their printed texts, however (again, partly because of their relative brevity, the absence of an omniscient narrator, etc.), are less versatile carriers of ideas than longer works of prose. For this reason many foreign plays that are rarely performed are frequently published in large printings.

Adherents of the theory of continuity and change interested in the problem of the evolution of reading tastes and preferences in Russia may wish perhaps to begin with one of the most famous early statements on the subject, a stanza in *Eugene Onegin* where the poet informs that, as a youth, he was infatuated with Apuleius but had no use for Cicero *("Čital oxotno Apuleja, a Cicerona ne čital")*. With some correctives introduced by readers more mature in years, Pushkin's preferences are still by and large those of Russians today. All of the extant works of Apuleius were republished in 1959, in over 150,000 copies. We found no evidence of the publication of Cicero during the first post-Stalin decade, although a three-volume set of his writing had appeared (significantly?) at the height of Stalinism, in 1949–51.[8] Only a few Greek and Roman classics were published, on a relatively modest scale, perhaps partly a result of the fact that Latin and ancient Greek are seldom taught in the country's colleges, and then only to a handful of specialists. The literature of classical antiquity was represented by Aeschylus' *Prometheus Bound* (a very large total printing, over 400,000 copies), about 100,000 copies each of *The Iliad* and *The Odyssey,* and over half a million copies of collections of ancient Greek myths. Other books were printed in relatively small quantities.

A number of West European writers have, in a manner of speaking, acquired Russian citizenship by virtue of the prolonged close association of their names with Russian literature proper. A good example is Alain-René Lesage, the eighteenth-century French author of plays that are reminiscent of Molière's, and of picaresque novels of which *Gil Blas* is one of the finest of all time. The nearly half a million copies of Lesage's works were doubtless published because of their intrinsic merits—they are lively, clever, and funny,[9] yet it does not appear farfetched to assume that Lesage's long-standing popularity with Russian readers was reinforced by the existence of an 1814 Russian imitation, Vasilij Narežnyj's *Rossijskij Zilblaz.* Jean-Jacques Rousseau, whose name is insepara-

8. Cicero's reputation is quite solid: "Outstanding orator, jurist, author, and political figure in ancient Rome; the last major ideologist of the Roman republic." *Bol'šaja sovetskaja enciklopedija,* 2nd ed., Vol. 46 (1957), pp. 663–64. A collection of articles about Cicero was published in 1959 to mark the 2000th anniversary of his death.

9. These included 150,000 copies of *Moon Flocks,* 120,000 of *The Lame Devil* (of which 40,000 in Lithuanian; the novel is also known in English under the title *Asmodeus*), over 120,000 of *Gil Blas* itself (including 30,000 in Latvian), and 7,000 of *Crispin, Rival of His Master.*

ble from the history of Russian Sentimentalism, appeared in a three-volume set, at 100,000 per volume.

Prosper Mérimée, a friend of Turgenev, a translator of Pushkin into French, and one of the first major foreign authors to be influenced by the Russians, was published on a generous scale: a six-volume set was launched at 350,000 copies per volume, and a two-volume set at 300,000 was completed. In addition, there were smaller printings of Mérimée's individual works, in Russian, in other languages of the USSR, as well as in the original French.

Another name inextricably linked with the annals of Russian literature and literary criticism is George Sand whose espousal of feminism and mild socialism contributed to the enormous popularity of her works in Russia where they were translated immediately after their appearance in France. Turgenev called George Sand "one of our saints," insisting that she was the single most influential person in *Russian* literature and social thought. Dostoyevsky, who rarely agreed with Turgenev, confirmed that she was, indeed, the most influential single author (though he apparently had reservations about Sand's role as a social theorist). The largest single printing for any of Sand's novels was of *Consuelo* (over 800,000), a novel depicting Bohemia's oppressed peasants; this was followed by half a million copies of *Indiana,* "an impassioned appeal in defense of women's rights. The novel's rather strange plot is combined with a truthful theme, that of a woman who was first her father's slave and then her husband's."[10] Other works of George Sand published included *The Sin of Monsieur Antoine, Horace,* and *The Miller of Angibault* (150,000 each). George Sand's compatriot (and onetime lover) Alfred de Musset was similarly published on an impressive scale: a quarter of a million copies of *La Confession d'un enfant du siècle* (which describes the liaison with Sand), half a million of "Mimi Pinson" (a romantic novella about students and midinettes familiar to millions as the libretto of Puccini's *La Bohème*), and a two-volume set of selected writings, at 150,000 per volume.[11]

Of West European literatures, the most widely read in Russia has traditionally been that of France, and in the nineteenth century French was also the most widely known foreign language. A number of the established French classics are reissued periodically, in varying numbers of copies. Thus, Marie-Madeleine La Fayette's seventeenth-century study of a woman in love, *The Princess of Clèves,* appeared in 75,000 copies. Abbé Prévost's eighteenth-century *Manon Lescaut* was reprinted in five times that

10. KL, Vol. VI (1971), p. 641.
11. The faint praise accorded Musset's politics is typical of Soviet evaluations of writers dealt with in this chapter: "Musset was not at all close to the democratic forces of his time, but he was incapable of adhering to this position with consistency." KL, Vol. V (1968), p. 50.

amount,[12] while the total reached by the works of brothers Goncourt was twice again as large.[13]

The two most illustrious Frenchmen in this group are Flaubert and Stendhal. Gustave Flaubert was a great artist and an admirer of Russian literature, particularly of Tolstoy; he was also a close friend of Turgenev. Ideologically, however, Flaubert's work had some serious limitations: "Profoundly disappointed in bourgeois culture and politics, Flaubert hated the narrow-mindedness of the French middle class and the impoverished bourgeoisie, the vulgar existence of which is so brilliantly described in his novels. Yet Flaubert was deeply pessimistic in his outlook on life because he did not believe in the possibility of fundamental social change."[14] And yet, in spite of such deficiencies in his *Weltanschauung,* the works of Flaubert were made available in exceptionally large quantities. There was a five-volume set at 250,000 copies per volume, over 800,000 copies of *Salammbô,* a novel set in ancient Carthage, over half a million copies of *Madame Bovary,* as well as smaller printings of other titles.[15]

As in the case of Flaubert, the Soviet appraisal of Stendhal is uneven; while commended for his enmity toward the Catholic Church, contempt for the aristocracy, and love of freedom, Stendhal is rarely portrayed as particularly "progressive," and the ideological contradictions in his works are not entirely glossed over.[16] Still, the first post-Stalin decade saw the publication of an ambitious edition of Stendhal's works, a fifteen-volume set, at 340,000 copies per volume. Nor were the individual works neglected: 800,000 copies in six languages of *The Charterhouse of Parma,* 300,000 in five languages of *The Red and the Black* (also 15,000 in the original), the same amount of *L'Abbesse de Castro,* over half a million of *Vanina Vanini* (then required reading in secondary schools), a quarter of a million of *Lucien Leuwen,* and over half a million of a volume of novellas (also 16,000 in a French edition).

Among the most interesting examples of the characteristically Soviet art of resorting to what is ostensibly a discussion of pre-Soviet and even non-Russian literature for the purpose of advocacy of contemporary causes—and not necessarily literary at that—was a 1958 essay by Ilya Ehrenburg

12. And also 10,000 copies in the original French. Again, no exaggerated claims were made for the ideological importance of the work: "It [*Manon Lescaut*] depicts the tragedy of love in a society based on social inequality. Society refuses to sanction the love of Chevalier des Grieux, a young nobleman, for a 'fallen woman,' because that love runs counter to prejudices canonized by the law." Ibid., p. 954.

13. The brothers Goncourt were not only apolitical but in fact anti-Marxist (fortunately, *avant la lettre*): "The brothers Goncourt seek the clues to man's destiny not in the laws that govern society, but in biology and physiology." KL, Vol. II (1964), p. 256.

14. *Osnovnye proizvedenija,* 1965, p. 464.

15. Including nearly 150,000 copies of *Sentimental Education,* the story of gradual disillusionment of an idealistic young man (there was also an edition in the original French). *Madame Bovary* appeared in Russian, Lithuanian, Latvian, Ukrainian, as well as in French.

16. See, e.g., the entry for Stendhal in KL, Vol. VII (1972), pp. 163–65.

entitled "Lessons of Stendhal." A Soviet novelist and public figure with a highly controversial past that included early opposition to the regime followed by many years of faithful service as Stalin's unofficial ambassador to the Western cultural establishment, Ehrenburg saw, and tacitly accepted, some of the worst outrages of the Stalin era. Yet, after the dictator's death and until his own, Ehrenburg was one of the most eloquent champions of the liberal Soviet intelligentsia.[17] His "Lessons of Stendhal" was transparently an *apologia pro vita sua.*[18] Thus, for instance, Ehrenburg emphasized that "Stendhal demonstrates that neither tendentiousness nor politics detract from a novel's stature, provided the author is able to feel, see, and think with a profundity that is appropriate to art"—an apparent answer to Ehrenburg's Western critics who had accused him of precisely that over many years. At the same time—while ostensibly commenting on *The Red and the Black*—Ehrenburg answered his Stalinist critics who had more than once charged him of taking some liberties in his novels with basic articles of the Communist faith: "However precise the analysis of social evolution, however subservient the individual to general processes, the universe of the novel differs from philosophical generalization, government blueprints and statistical data."

Older English novelists with relatively apolitical Soviet reputations were published on a more modest scale than the French authors, a reflection in part of their lesser popularity in prerevolutionary Russia. Thus, Henry Fielding was represented by unspecified printings of his two plays, *Love in Several Masks* and *The Old Debauchees or the Jesuit Caught* and less than 200,000 copies of *Tom Jones,* a brilliant satire in the opinion of a Soviet critic, but unfortunately marred by Fielding's naive belief in the existence of ideal gentlemen-farmers like the novel's Mr. Wilson.[19] Another English novel that suffers from its author's "erroneous" views was Oliver Goldsmith's *The Vicar of Wakefield.* Its tale of the harassment of a poor village pastor by a landowner was praiseworthy, but its sentimental idealization of the patriarchal life in England's countryside was not;[20] the novel was nevertheless printed in a quarter of a million copies. George Eliot's *Silas Marner* and *The Mill on the Floss* were found sufficiently worthy to warrant republication in 150,000 and 50,000 copies respectively; still, readers were warned, the English novelist's artistic merits (particularly her sophistication as a psychologist) must not be allowed to obscure her insufficiently critical view

17. Ehrenburg died in 1967. For a discussion of his career see this writer's "Ilya Grigorevich Ehrenburg," *Soviet Leaders,* George W. Simmonds (ed.) (New York: Thomas Y. Crowell, 1967), pp. 272–81.
18. Il'ja Ėrenburg, "Uroki Stendalja," *Sobranie sočinenij v devjati tomax,* Vol. VI, (Moscow: Goslitizdat, 1965), pp. 445, 453.
19. KL, Vol. VII (1972), p. 958.
20. KL, Vol. II (1964), p. 225.

of reality, a defect aggravated by Eliot's moralizing tone.[21]

A number of classic German, Spanish, and Finnish novels were published in editions of varying size. Works of the nineteenth-century Swiss writer Gottfried Keller, author of *Bildungsromanen* critical of bourgeois society, were published in three quarters of a million copies, including a half million copies of *Forger of His Happiness* and two anthologies in the original German. Novels by two German chroniclers of peasant life, Wilhelm Polenz and Theodor Storm, were published in small editions in Armenian and Lithuanian, respectively.[22] One possible objection to Storm may have been his portrayal of peasants as a conservative social class.[23] An evaluation of *The Life Story of Buscón,* a seventeenth-century picaresque novel by Francisco Quevedo y Villegas republished in 200,000 copies, follows the pattern referred to earlier: good observation marred by "faulty" analysis and prognosis. We read: "[*The Life Story of Buscón*] comprises an autobiography of a rogue who travels in different social circles; everywhere, he finds moral decay and power wielded by gold. The novel reveals its author's pessimistic philosophy, his lack of faith in man's ability to embark on the path of virtue. This imparts to the novel's realism a cruel and somber quality."[24] *La Celestina,* a great fifteenth-century picaresque novel by Fernando de Rojas was brought out in a mere 75,000 copies, somewhat surprising in view of the novel's warm portrayal of old Spain's lower classes. Finally, there were two small editions of Alexis Kivi, described by a Western source as "the best loved and most intensively studied of all Finnish authors."[25] The novel *Seven Brothers* appeared in 30,000 copies in Latvia, where much of the literature of Finland is regularly translated; the play *The Shoemakers Nummi* was printed in Russian, but in a miniscule edition of 2,500 copies. Perhaps the blame rests with Soviet critics' unhappiness with Kivi's tendency in his works to seek solutions to social problems not in politics, but in education and—a horrid thought!—religion.[26]

Poetry, Russian as well as translated, forms an important part of Soviet school curricula, and the name of George Gordon Byron may well be more familiar to present-day Russian schoolchildren (references to the English poet are unavoidable in any discussion of Pushkin and Lermontov) than to their English-speaking contemporaries. At one time, as mentioned earlier, Byron was not only the single most important literary influence in Russia, but even something of a folk hero, though understandably less so than in

21. *Osnovnye proizvedenija,* p. 79.
22. Polenz's *The Peasant Büttner* was printed only in 30,000 copies in Armenian, and Storm's *The White Horseman* in a mere 15,000, in Lithuanian.
23. *Osnovnye proizvedenija,* pp. 271–72.
24. KL, Vol. III (1966), p. 475.
25. *The Penguin Companion,* Vol. II, p. 432.
26. *Teatral'naja enciklopedija,* Vol. III (1964), p. 11.

Greece. Even now, a century and a half after his death, Byron is held in higher esteem in Slavic countries than in his native land; his works are still studied in school (many stubbornly consider him the greatest English poet) and are regularly reprinted. The figures for 1954–64 are close to 300,000 in nine languages (exclusive of textbooks).

Friedrich Schiller's appeal, though less intense perhaps, was broader because it extended to drama; his plays are still being performed in the USSR. His Romantic verse and plays are also very popular with the country's non-Russian readers. Recent multivolume editions of Schiller included two in Russian (a seven-volume set and a two-volume one, each at 75,000 copies per volume) and also a three-volume set in Georgian at 7,000; Georgia's own poetic tradition is strongly Romantic, which may explain the affinity to the German poet. A wide variety of anthologies and individual titles account for an additional 350,000 copies of Schiller's writings in nine languages.

While the popularity of American poetry is, obviously, a more recent phenomenon, two American poets are firmly established among the foreign poets that are not only quite widely read but also held in high esteem by the Russian critics. Henry Wadsworth Longfellow is approvingly described in a Soviet literary encyclopedia as a Romantic who "extolled patriarchal customs, idealized America's past and the life of her indigenous population, the Indians";[27] Longfellow's success with Russian readers, however, was more likely enhanced by the availability of good translations. In particular, Ivan Bunin's magnificent rendition of *The Song of Hiawatha* (with retention of the original meter), belongs to the select few poetic translations that are memorized by Russian schoolchildren.[28] Walt Whitman's fame reached Russia early; the first Russian article about the American poet appeared in 1861, and the 1907 anthology of Kornej Čukovskij's translations has been frequently reissued.[29] Russia's liberal and secular intelligentsia found Whitman's paeans to labor, science, and democracy congenial. He is still read, and a larger than usual number of translations appeared in 1955 in observance of the centennial of *Leaves of Grass*.[30] A more recent American poet, Robert Frost, began to gain in popularity in the late 1950s and became quite well known after his visit to the USSR in 1962 at the age of eighty-eight, only a year before his

27. KL, Vol. IV (1967), p. 416.

28. *The Song of Hiawatha* was published in 130,000 copies in Russian, 10,000 each in Armenian and Estonian, and 8,000 in Ukrainian. A Russian anthology of Longfellow's verse was printed in 25,000 copies.

29. KL, Vol. VII (1972), pp. 749–53.

30. There was a separate edition of *Leaves of Grass* (45,000 copies) and also an anthology of Whitman's verse (25,000). Also, as is customary on such occasions, selections of Whitman's poetry were printed in literary journals, e.g., in *Novyj mir*, No. 7, 1955.

death.[31] No attempt was made—an exception to what is all too often the practice—to claim the poet as a sympathizer of the Soviet cause. Considered an official cultural ambassador of the United States, he was, on the whole, described quite fairly as an honest and great poet, a man of rugged integrity, and a believer in peaceful coexistence.[32]

Other translations of verse that were apparently brought out for largely unideological reasons included a volume of fourteenth-century Spanish fables by Infante don Juan Manuel (their suitability for children probably accounts for the large printing of 100,000 copies), a small edition of 7,000 copies of the modernist Mexican poet Manuel Gutiérrez Nájera, 25,000 copies of Sweden's greatest poet Esaias Tegnér, and 35,000 of the Chilean Gabriela Mistral. The *Literary Encyclopedia* praises Mistral for her efforts on behalf of the "struggle for peace";[33] in her case, however, unlike so many others, it appears to have been the intrinsic merits of her verse and genuine reader interest that prompted the publication of the volume. Her politics were clearly of secondary importance.

Scholars, actors, and ordinary theatergoers are equally aware of an old problem plaguing Russia's theater, namely the chasm between the country's rich staging traditions and the large number of theaters (distinguished professional groups as well as collectives of enthusiastic amateurs) and the relatively small repertory of Russian plays. A Russian theatrical director has at his disposal only two good neo-classical Russian comedies, both of them by Denis Fonvizin, and no tragedies that are worthy of staging. In the nineteenth century, too, the achievements of Russian drama were modest indeed in comparison to the magnificent harvest of poetry and prose written in the same period. A number of great plays stand out—Griboedov's *Woe from Wit,* Gogol's *Inspector General,* Turgenev's *A Month in the Country,* Tolstoy's *The Power of Darkness*—but until the advent of Chekhov Russia produced only two really important playwrights, Aleksandr Ostrovskij and Aleksandr Suxovo-Kobylin. Thus, it was not only receptivity to foreign art that explains the Russian theater's traditional hospitality to Western drama;

31. Six pages of Robert Frost's verse appeared in *Novyj mir,* No. 6, 1960; another five were printed in No. 8, 1962. An anthology (143 pages) entitled *From Nine Books* was published in 1963; no information on the press run is available. Robert Frost, *Iz devjati knig. Pod redakciej i s predisloviem M. A. Zenkeviča* (Moscow, Izdatel'stvo Inostrannoj literatury, 1963).

32. "[Frost] was one of those masters whose voice is emphatically subdued, whose verse does not glitter with innovations. The power of his work lies in its sincerity, intimacy, ability to see the essence of seemingly the most ordinary phenomena. . . . The most attractive features of Frost's poetry are his unusual kindness toward people, his humanity, and his accessibility —which have nothing in common with a quest for cheap popularity. . . . He loves his country, he welcomes progress (e.g., in "Science Fiction"), he affirms the right of every nation to choose its own destiny, he glorifies peace on earth. Frost's pure, strong, and poetic faith in man stands in contrast to all kinds of modernistic 'dehumanizing' concepts in the art of the West." *Osnovnye proizvedenija,* 1965, pp. 402–3.

33. KL, Vol. IV (1967), p. 869.

an important factor was the compelling practical need of finding suitable plays for the repertories. In essence, a similar situation prevails in Soviet theaters at present.[34]

A number of the foreign playwrights performed on the Russian stage have become popular with the reading public. Shakespeare, for example, has been widely read as well as performed ever since the early nineteenth century when Russia's Romantics discovered him as a progenitor of their own views of art and society; a strong Shakespearean influence pervades, for example, Pushkin's *Boris Godunov.* Two Shakespearean anniversaries may have contributed significantly to the lavish scale of republication of his writings, the 400th of his birth in 1964 and the 350th of his death in 1966.[35] There appeared an eight-volume set of Shakespeare's complete works in Russian at 225,000 copies per volume, a seven-volume set in Estonian at 10,000, and a six-volume one in Latvian at 15,000. Of individual works, the largest figures were reached by *Hamlet*—650,000 copies in six languages. Other works, including anthologies, account for the remaining half a million copies. The works of Shakespeare's two less famous contemporaries, Christopher Marlowe and Thomas Heywood, were republished as well. There appeared an anthology of Marlowe's writings (50,000 copies), as well as separate issues of *Edward II* (10,000) and *Dr. Faustus* (4,000) and of Heywood's comedies *The Fair Maid of the*

34. Foreign plays in the repertory of Soviet theaters during 1954–64 will also be discussed in subsequent chapters, particularly the last.

35. Generally, anniversary observances of important writers coincide in the USSR with much intensified publication of their works. Thus, the Academy of Sciences' edition of Pushkin was scheduled to coincide with the centennial of the poet's death in 1937, and other important editions were brought out in time for the sesquicentennial of his birth in 1949. The single most impressive Soviet edition of any writer's works to date is the jubilee edition *(jubilejnoe izdanie)* of Tolstoy's works launched to coincide with the centennial of the novelist's birth in 1928. The ninety-volume set comprising three series (fiction and nonfiction, diaries, and correspondence) was completed in 1959. See this writer's *Russian Classics in Soviet Jackets,* pp. 42–80.

That anniversaries are a serious consideration is attested by the publication, in 1965, of a 54-page pamphlet listing all important anniversaries of births and deaths by foreign writers for the coming year (*Kalendar' pamjatnyx dat po zarubežnoj xudožestvennoj literature na 1966 god* [Moscow: Kniga, 1966]). Among the entries were such obvious ones as the 350th anniversary of the death of Cervantes, as well as Shakespeare, and, less expectedly, of Shakespeare's contemporary Francis Beaumont. Also noted were the centennial of the death of the American radical writer Lincoln Steffens, the sesquicentennial of the birth of Charlotte Brontë, the bicentennial of Madame de Staël, and the 400th anniversary of Louise Labé, known for her French sonnets. Others included the approaching sesquicentennial of Sheridan, the centennial of H. G. Wells, the 75th anniversary of Herman Melville, and the 50th of both Jack London and Emile Verhaeren. Anniversaries were listed by month and day. In the case of writers particularly favored in the USSR, note was also taken of birthdays of living authors, not necessarily "round" ones (e.g., 60th, 65th, 70th, etc.).

Observing anniversaries formally is one thing, but doing something about them is quite another. Thus the calendar noted the 25th anniversary of James Joyce's death, but Joyce remains unpublished in book form. Also recorded was the 50th anniversary of the death of Henry James, praised for his polished style and sophisticated psychology, but no work of James was published in 1966 (or 1967 or 1968). In fact, Henry James had not been published in the USSR before that, either. He was last printed in Russia in 1908, and reappeared in print only in 1973. For a Soviet lampoon of literary jubilee observances, see this writer's *Russian Classics in Soviet Jackets,* pp. 203–6.

*West* (10,000) and *The Wise Woman of Hogsdon* (2,000).

Molière was first translated into Russian early in the eighteenth century and was frequently performed on the Russian stage. His popularity continued after the Revolution. Molière's plays were, in fact, among the first to be produced in the new Soviet Republic. While the Civil War was still in progress and the future of the Bolshevik regime was in doubt, amateur theaters of the Red Guards staged *The Doctor in Spite of Himself* and *Les Fourberies de Scapin.* These plays, as well as *Tartuffe, Le Malade imaginaire,* and *Le Bourgeois Gentilhomme,* are still frequently performed in Soviet theaters.[36] Molière's comedies have been viewed with favor by the Soviet authorities because, in their estimate, they "exposed the social pathology of the aristocratic-bourgeois society from progressive, popular, humanist positions."[37] The fortunate coincident of official and popular favor is reflected in the publication of their texts. A two-volume set of his works appeared in 150,000 copies per volume and *Les Précieuses ridicules* and *The Doctor in Spite of Himself* in 75,000 each. There were also small printings of four plays in Estonian (in 5,000 copies each) and the same number of copies of a Ukrainian anthology. Of Molière's compatriot and contemporary Jean François Regnard, there were 9,000 copies of collected comedies, 5,000 of *The Gambler,* and 75,000 of *The Unexpected Return.*[38]

Lope de Vega may well be the most prolific playwright of all time. While some Western estimates are much lower, the *Literary Encyclopedia* credits him with writing two thousand plays and publishing five hundred, with two hundred additional texts yet to be discovered.[39] Still, according to a Soviet source, in the second half of the nineteenth century Russia was one of the few countries outside the playwright's native Spain where Lope de Vega's plays were performed.[40] They are still being staged in the USSR, and they also appear in print. A six-volume set of Lope de Vega's drama and prose was published in Russian, at 50,000 copies per volume, and also two anthologies of undisclosed printings. His novellas were published in 150,000 copies, with additional reprints of both plays and prose in several other languages.

Some rather overly enthusiastic claims have been made for the politically

36. See *Teatral'naja ènciklopedija,* Vol. III (1964), p. 898.
37. Ibid., p. 892.
38. Soviet critics have reservations about Regnard's comedies, in particular about their insufficient didacticism: "They are, for the most part, merely entertaining, even though their comic inventiveness appears inexhaustible" (KL, Vol. VI [1971], p. 261). Other critics are more charitable. While conceding that *The Gambler* may be just a portrait of the idle rich squandering money, *The Only Heir,* for instance, is said to convey "the all-powerful and destructive power of money in feudal-bourgeois society." *Teatral'naja ènciklopedija,* Vol. IV (1965), p. 596.
39. KL, Vol. I (1962), p. 879.
40. *Teatral'naja ènciklopedija,* Vol. I (1961), pp. 879–80.

"progressive" nature of Carlo Goldoni's eighteenth-century plays.[41] It seems, however, that such claims may be a *consequence* rather than a *cause* of Goldoni's great popularity in the USSR, not only on the Russian stage and with Russian readers, but apparently even more in the Ukraine, the Caucasus, and Central Asia. Goldoni was first performed in Russia in 1759 and his colorful and—for Russia—very exotic settings and situations have remained popular ever since. The *Theatrical Encyclopedia* proudly notes, "More performances of Goldoni are given in the USSR than anywhere in the world, including the playwright's homeland, Italy."[42] Between 1954 and 1964 his plays were published at least four times, in close to 100,000 copies. By contrast, the plays of Goldoni's German contemporary, Gotthold Ephraim Lessing, were printed in only 18,000 copies. True, some Soviet critics are, ideologically, less extravagant in their praise of Lessing, one of the towering figures of the German Enlightenment.[43] Their reservations, however, are of much the same kind as those voiced with regard to such Russian writers as Tolstoy. The lesser popularity of Lessing may, again, be genuine; he is didactic and serious, while Goldoni is colorful and amusing. Soviet readers and theatergoers may simply find in Goldoni's plays a welcome contrast to the moods and preoccupations of their native theatrical repertory, particularly that of the Soviet period. No such relief is forthcoming from Lessing. Finally, 10,000 copies were issued of Ludwig Holberg's eighteenth-century comedies. Held in high esteem by Marx and Engels, they were also often staged in eighteenth-century Russia.[44]

Also republished were three West European playwrights, all famous in Russia at the turn of the century. Indeed, the impact of Henrik Ibsen transcended the theater: "Early in the twentieth century he became one of the foremost influences on the Russian intelligentsia."[45] Widely performed in Russia both before and after the Revolution,[46] Ibsen's plays, with their criticism of bourgeois hypocrisy and conventions, attract readers as well, particularly since, when viewed against the background of most Russian and Soviet drama, they emerge as quite "modern." A four-volume set appeared in 150,000 copies per volume and there were another 100,000

41. One example: "The works of the mature Goldoni contain the kind of cutting democratic critique of the beastly philistine kingdom of bourgeois tyrants that is not often to be found even among the most progressive ideologists of the third estate" (KL, Vol. II [1964], p. 237). Another: "Goldoni was an impassioned foe of serfdom and of all of its survivals, a defender of enlightenment, self-rule, and freedom, a friend of the people" (*Teatral'naja ènciklopedija*, Vol. II [1963], p. 50).
42. Ibid., p. 52.
43. "Lessing's enlightened realism is somewhat circumscribed. He attempted to solve political problems on a moral plane alone. In Lessing's view, the moral perfection of society would lead to the uprooting of social evil." Ibid., Vol. III (1964), p. 516.
44. Ibid., Vol. V (1967), p. 634.
45. KL, Vol. III (1966), p. 33.
46. *Teatral'naja ènciklopedija*, Vol. II (1963), p. 824.

copies of other editions. Maurice Maeterlinck's fame in Russia coincided with Ibsen's; he was particularly popular with audiences that favored Russia's own Symbolist theater, which he strongly influenced.[47] Artistically, Maeterlinck was close to the "Decadents" of whom Soviet critics disapprove; politically, however, things looked brighter. There was, for instance, Gorky's weighty testimony that Maeterlinck moved toward socialism.[48] In any case, there were no insurmountable obstacles to Maeterlinck's publication on a modest scale. The *Mayor of Stilmonde* and *Salt of Life* came out together in 75,000 copies, with 25,000 additional copies of an anthology. Lastly, there were about 100,000 copies of both prose and plays of Bjørnstjerne Bjørnson, a Norwegian writer popular in Russia at the turn of the century: a twelve-volume set of his works appeared in Russian in 1893–97, and a seven-volume one in 1910–14. He was also frequently performed on the Russian stage.[49] Bjørnson, Soviet critics caution, has serious ideological limitations. In his works, for instance, one finds repeatedly the suggestion that harmony may be established between social classes—and that class warfare, which Marxism views as an inevitability, may be averted.[50] Again, it was apparently thought that no major harm would be done by very limited republication of Bjørnson's old-fashioned writing, particularly if half of the total amount was to appear in Latvian and Estonian, where classics of Scandinavian literature are held in reverence.

The Soviet practice of harnessing the ideological potential of literary denunciations of social injustice in the past to enhance the credibility of justifications for present Soviet policies will be discussed in a separate chapter. We should mention here a small group of writers whose value in this respect is rather marginal, but whose works are published as an act of filial piety, so to speak, usually in recognition of their past services to the revolutionary cause or in deference to the high opinion in which the authors were held by Marx or Engels.[51] Considerations of this kind may have brought about the publication of a small edition of 25,000 copies of the German poet Georg Herwegh. An associate of Karl Marx, Herwegh was an opponent of Prussian militarism and a sympathizer of the French revolu-

47. Ibid., Vol. III (1964), p. 811.
48. KL, Vol. IV (1967), p. 800. Curiously, in 1920 Maeterlinck was viewed as clear and present danger to the Soviet cause, and his works were to be removed from library shelves. See photograph of the circular in Bertram D. Wolfe, "Krupskaya Purges the People's Libraries," *Survey* (London), No. 72 (Summer 1969).
49. *Teatral'naja ènciklopedija,* Vol. I (1961), p. 782.
50. KL, Vol. I (1962), p. 805.
51. Occasionally, an endorsement by Communism's Founding Fathers is used as justification for the publication of writers with otherwise dubious political credentials. Thus, La Rochefoucauld's cynical but ideologically quite conservative *Maximes* (1665) were described as "pessimistic" (in the Soviet lexicon of criticism a distinctly derogatory term), but were republished nevertheless in an edition of 75,000 copies. In La Rochefoucauld's favor was that Marx quoted him in a letter to Engels. KL, Vol. IV (1967), pp. 35–36.

tion. He translated Garibaldi's anthem and wrote the party song for Ferdinand Lassalle's Socialist Union of German Workers. He may also have been the first advocate of *partijnost'* in poetry, which is now a basic concept of the Soviet doctrine of Socialist Realism and which should perhaps be translated as "Communist inspirational content."[52]

A contemporary of Herwegh, Hermann Ferdinand Freiligrath, a poet of "left-wing liberal views," was the author of *Neue politische und soziale Gedichte* which "contains some of the best German revolutionary poetry."[53] At one time there was, in fact, "an extremely close collaboration" between Freiligrath, Marx, and Engels.[54] It was at that period, presumably, that he had "created in his poems striking, realistic portraits of proletarians, the gravediggers of the bourgeoisie, the heroes of future revolutions." True, subsequently Freiligrath's ardor for the revolutionary cause cooled, prompting a Soviet commentator to note that "he had outlived his talent."[55] Still, in generous recognition of his past, his verse was republished in 35,000 copies. A third German poet in that group was Georg Weerth. His political biography is apparently without blemish. A founding member of the Union of Communists, a close associate of both Marx and Engels, described by Engels as "the first and most important poet of the German working class," George Weerth is now considered "an early forerunner of the literature of Socialist Realism."[56] His verse was republished in three languages, about 100,000 copies in all.

Beyond doubt, the French songwriter Eugène Pottier is the single best known revolutionary poet of all time: it was Pottier who in 1871 wrote the lyrics to the *Internationale.* To quote the *Literary Encyclopedia:* "Pottier was a poet-propagandist [*agitator*]. Capable of discerning the innermost socioeconomic and political essence of events and of their artistic reflection, Pottier was, in Lenin's words, 'one of the greatest propagandists through the medium of song.' He was one of the forerunners of Socialist Realism in the poetry of France."[57] Still, the didactic value of Eugène Pottier's satirical songs at this time is surely rather slight, and the quarter million copies of these were more likely printed for reasons of revolutionary nostalgia.

Memories of the glorious revolutionary past may also have played a leading role in the decision to reprint, in 200,000 copies, the novel *Poverty (La Misère)* of which Louise Michel was coauthor. Nicknamed "the Red

---

52. Ibid., Vol. II (1964), p. 132.
53. *The Penguin Companion,* Vol. II, p. 282.
54. Peter Demetz, *Marx, Engels and the Poets,* p. 95.
55. *Osnovnye proizvedenija,* pp. 269–70.
56. KL, Vol. I (1962), pp. 883–84.
57. Ibid., Vol. V (1968), p. 922.

Maid of Montmartre," Michel fought on the barricades of the Paris Commune as an anarchist follower of Bakunin. She was equally militant in her
writings: "Denouncing religion and capitalism, she defended the humanist
principles of French literature."[58] The search for revolutionary ancestors
was also a probable impetus in the republication (in 100,000 Russian copies,
with an additional 10,000 in the original English) of another old classic,
William Godwin's *Caleb Williams. Caleb Williams* was translated into
Russian in 1838 and was praised by one of the leading Russian radical critics
of the nineteenth century: "Highly regarded by N. G. Černyševskij, the
novel describes the fate of a poor man slandered by an aristocrat. The
author's intention is absolutely clear: [he wishes to demonstrate that] the
law sanctions oppression by the rich and cements the helplessness of the
poor." It is also reasonable to assume that the publication of *Caleb Williams*
was made easier by the fact that quite another work by the same author,
*An Enquiry Concerning Political Justice,* contains views that, in the authoritative estimate of Friedrich Engels himself, "border on Communism."[59]

Evidence presented thus far and documentation found in the chapters to
follow demonstrate quite unmistakably that Soviet book publishers and
literary critics are obsessed with political considerations, real and sometimes rather far-fetched, to a degree quite unknown in the West. As a result,
in our attempt to follow the stated or implied line of reasoning of Soviet
critics and publishers, time and again authors of patently nonpolitical books
are subjected in this study to careful scrutiny for their works' ideological
potential, very broadly understood, in an effort to explain their fortunes in
the USSR. (Indeed, as we shall see in the concluding chapter, excessively
generous publication of translations with *no* apparent ideological overtones
at all was *itself* passionately debated as a serious ideological issue.) It is
therefore with some relief (and misgiving: what if these, too, are somehow
"political"?) that we shall consider another category of works that are by
and large ideologically neuter. These are books for adults that correspond
most closely to the type of reading about which Mark Twain wrote face-
tiously in a prefatory note to *The Adventures of Huckleberry Finn:* "Persons
attempting to find a motive in this narrative will be prosecuted; persons
attempting to find a moral in it will be banished; persons attempting to find
a plot in it will be shot."

Works considered earlier in the chapter, while essentially nonideological,
may be said to have been published in part as a dutiful gesture of homage
to the very great classics of world literature or, occasionally, to works that
were treasured by the prophets of the Communist faith. The books to be

58. Ibid., Vol. IV (1967), p. 898.
59. Ibid., Vol. II (1964), p. 220.

discussed now are less venerable. Although some are respected, as for instance the writings of O. Henry, they do not evoke the obligatory awe elicited in a status-conscious USSR by mere mention of the names of Shakespeare or Goethe (only Mayakovsky dared, more than a half century ago, in his reckless Futurist youth, to suggest the shooting of Pushkin). These books come closest to what may be defined as "merely" enjoyable reading for adult audiences with average, unrefined tastes, books that are not particularly useful ideologically or intellectually, or especially elevating aesthetically and spiritually, books that require little prompting from teachers and critics urging that they be read. In short, books that make, above all, enjoyable reading, books that are fun.

Since the 1920s books of this kind have not been very plentiful in the USSR. Not many were written by Soviet authors who were constantly exhorted to create works reflecting, in one way or another, the majesty and effort of building and defending Soviet Russia, didactic books that would chastize and inspire, lead and teach. Stalin's apocryphal but much cited definition of writers as "engineers of human souls" implied the writing of "useful" books. It was not conducive to the creation of literature that was above all a commentary on the human condition, to say nothing of works that were primarily entertainment. Nineteenth-century Russian writing contains much of the Western world's literature of high seriousness. Alas, all too many Russian authors of that period whose artistic gifts were not equal to the task were not content to create "merely" entertaining reading matter, with the result that their works were often boring instead of serious, and annoyingly didactic instead of intellectually challenging. A famous incident in the history of Russian literature concerns a letter from the aging novelist D. V. Grigorovič to Anton Chekhov, urging the young writer to stop squandering his talent on superficially entertaining short stories (and pornography!) and concentrate instead on "truly artistic works."[60] The truth of the matter is that even without such advice, Chekhov would, in all likelihood, have developed into a great writer, although perhaps of a different mold; he might, perhaps, have become a great humorist and author of comedies in the more traditional sense. Grigorovič, on the other hand, and hundreds of "serious" writers like him are remembered chiefly for their noble aspirations. While disdaining the modest role of literary entertainers, they failed to become Tolstoys and Dostoyevskys, forgetting also, apparently, the latter's admonition: "The very best book—no matter what its subject and what kind of book it is—is the interesting book."[61] Thus, in

60. The text of the letter is reproduced in Ernest J. Simmons, *Chekhov: A Biography* (Boston: Little, Brown, 1962), pp. 95–97.

61. Quoted in M. N. Kufaev, *Istorija russkoj knigi v XIX veke* (Leningrad: Kul'turno-Prosvetitel'noe Izdatel'stvo "Načatki znanij," 1927), p. 207.

essence, pre-Soviet Russian literature consists, one might say, of some immortal masterpieces and a large number of quite unreadable books; it has no appreciable body of average writing without pretensions to greatness but satisfying enough as light reading. Or, in the words of a nursery rhyme, "when she was good, she was very, very good; and when she was bad, she was horrid."

Traditionally, therefore, Russian readers had to rely on translations of West European and American literature for much of their light reading; similarly, Russian theaters could hardly do without translated melodramas and bedroom farces. There were times, most notably in the last years of Stalin's life, when very few books and plays of this type were printed or produced. This did not mean that there was no demand for them, but simply that the authorities pretended a demand did not exist. That this was indeed the case was demonstrated by the spectacular comeback staged by this "useless" reading after 1954 when restrictions were relaxed. Prudently, many Soviet publishers brought out much of this type of reading—particularly novels of adventure and historical romances—as books ostensibly destined for adolescents.[62] It was more difficult to maintain this pretense in the case of another genre, the thriller. Yet an increasing amount of escapist reading began to be made available in the more permissive mid-1950s, a development coinciding with the reappearance on Soviet stages of such "empty" entertainment as the old comedies and melodramas of Eugène Scribe and Victorien Sardou.

As pointed out, O. Henry's poignant, succinct stories of turn-of-the-century America were viewed respectfully enough by Russian critics (indeed, some Formalists used them to illustrate theories of the structure of the short story), but O. Henry was not regarded as a "great" and therefore somewhat forbidding classic. Russian readers still obviously enjoy these sad and funny tales about ordinary Americans. Their partiality for O. Henry may well be enhanced by interest in his American settings (one of the most successful of all Soviet books is Il'f and Petrov's *Little Golden America*, no literary masterpiece but a rare travel account of the United States). O. Henry's short stories were published in close to 2,500,000 copies, most of them anthologies (in eight languages, including English), and also as a two-volume set at 150,000 copies per volume.

Humor is one quality in which Soviet literature, for some of the reasons suggested earlier, is particularly deficient; the finest Soviet writer of humor and satire, Mikhail Zoshchenko, was silenced in 1946 on charges of slandering Soviet life. Hence the thirst for translated comic writing is greater in

62. See chapter 4.

the USSR than for most other types of literature. The stories of British life
of Jerome K. Jerome, which span the range from subdued chuckles to
hilarious laughter, were published in the years 1954–64 in nearly 1,500,000
copies, in six languages (including a printing of 40,000 in the original). Half
of this amount consisted of translations of *Three Men in a Boat;* the other
half was a two-volume set. Even so, witnesses report, obtaining a copy of
Jerome was most difficult; the books were sold out within days.

A number of old favorites were made available again. George du Maurier's *Trilby,* a novel about the hypnotist Svengali set against the background of the bohemia of Paris, was reprinted in 150,000 copies; 200,000
copies were printed of *The Marriage of Laucha,* a picaresque novel by the
Argentine author and socialist journalist Roberto Jorge Payró (1867–1928);
50,000 of Jens Peter Jacobsen's *Marie Grubbe,* a Danish novel set in the
seventeenth century and describing a variety of social strata from royalty
to peasants; a more recent work with a similarly exotic historical setting—
fourteenth-century Norway—was *Christine, Lawrence's Daughter,* by the
anti-Nazi Sigrid Undset (1882–1949). The novel was published in half a
million copies. Edward Bulwer-Lytton's *Pelham,* a satire on nineteenth-
century British fashionable society, came out in 150,000 copies; the same
author's *The Last Days of Pompeii,* a novel reminiscent of Sienkiewicz's
*Quo Vadis,* was printed in Armenian in 50,000 copies,[63] and his not overly
profound but entertaining plays in 25,000. Also revived were the gay farces
of Eugène-Marie Labiche, very popular in nineteenth-century Russia (22,-
000 in Russian, 2,000 in Armenian), and Henri Alain-Fournier's *The Lost
Domain,* a wistful evocation of a lost love set in the French provinces a
century ago, reprinted in 170,000 copies.

As suggested earlier, reissuing books previously published, particularly
by authors no longer alive, is politically far less risky than bringing out new
books, especially works by living foreign writers.[64] Publication in the USSR
of nonpolitical works of scores of living foreign authors not necessarily
known for their pro-Soviet sympathies, many of them for the first time, was
significant evidence of political liberalization during the post-Stalin "thaw."
Even though the writers concerned did not always receive notification that
their books had appeared in the USSR, to say nothing of royalty payments,
publication of these works was equally telling testimony to the improvement
of relations between the USSR and the non-Communist world, and it

63. This, in spite of the fact that the novel "also has the Christian message that the eruption
[of the volcano] was well deserved." *The Penguin Companion,* Vol. I, p. 326.
64. Political considerations will now be supplemented by financial ones. As a result of Soviet
accession in 1973 to the Universal Copyright Convention, Soviet publishers will henceforth
have to contend with the problem of royalties, which, as a rule, were not paid until that time,
except as tokens of particular favor.

received considerable publicity abroad. Some of the authors were first introduced to Soviet readers in journals through a short story or an excerpt from longer works, which later appeared in their entirety. Not all of the works were new, but they were greeted as such by Soviet readers. Let us cite a few examples.

Hjalmar Bergman's *God's Orchid,* a comic novel about a small town in Sweden, was forty years old when it was finally published in Russian in 75,000 copies. Irving Stone's *Lust for Life,* a 1934 biography of Van Gogh, was translated into Russian in 1961, when it was issued in 200,000 copies.[65] A 1922 novel by Enrique Larreta, *The Glory of Don Ramiro,* which describes Spain's Moorish communities in the sixteenth century (i.e., after the Inquisition) and is based on thorough historical research, was first published in Russian in 100,000 copies in 1961, the year of the author's death.[66] Even though many of W. Somerset Maugham's works suffer, in Soviet critics' view, from undue pessimism about humanity's prospects,[67] several of them were published, including *Of Human Bondage, The Moon and Sixpence,* and *The Land of Promise.*[68]

The texts of five plays newly translated from the English and performed in Soviet theaters were also published in book form, though in small editions. These included Noel Coward's *The Nude With a Violin,* A. A. Milne's *Mr. Pim Passes By,* Raymond E. Lawler's *The Summer of the Seventeenth Doll,* Jerome Quilty's *Dear Liar,* and William Gibson's *Two for the Seesaw.* All were comedies recently successfully performed on Western stages; all were quite apolitical.[69] Yet two of them, Gibson's and Quilty's, were soon to be at the center of an ideological controversy.[70] A number of new Western books of no special political interest also were translated into Russian. Most important among these were three tales from Jack Kerouac's *On the Road,* which were printed in a special youth issue of *Inostrannaja literatura* (No. 10, 1960). The world they described must have charmed Soviet readers with its exoticism—a world of jazz, of carefree travel, of odd jobs, of dignified Mexicans and

65. Short excerpts from Irving Stone's *The Agony and the Ecstasy* appeared in several periodicals, while the text of the first book of the novel was printed in *Neva,* No. 3, 1964.
66. Enrique Larreta, an Argentine diplomat as well as a writer, was identified as "politically, a conservative," but this failing was apparently compensated by the novel itself, which "criticizes the Catholic Church which, in his [the author's] view, has abandoned the true faith." KL, Vol. IV (1967), p. 37.
67. KL, Vol. IV (1967), p. 999.
68. Insufficient information available on press runs. For the story of Maugham's *The Summing Up,* see chapter 1. A number of Maugham's shorter works appeared in the literary monthlies, e.g., "The Kite" was printed in *Moskva,* No. 7, 1962.
69. Lawler's play dealt with an unexpected emotional crisis produced by a *seventeenth* annual summertime love affair; Quilty's was about G. B. Shaw's romance with Mrs. Patrick Campbell.
70. See chapter 9.

silly gringos. It was truly literature from the New World.

Of the various types of "useless" entertaining reading, thrillers are far and away the most popular, although, as will be seen, they are frequently the subject of ideological controversy. Most are translations, but the genre also has a Russian tradition. In 1779 a book appeared in Russia bearing the intriguing title *A Detailed and True Description of Deeds Good and Evil of the Russian Scoundrel, Thief, Robber, and Former Moscow Detective Van'ka Kain, of His Entire Life and Strange Adventures.*[71] Little is known about the author, Matvej Komarov, but there is considerable information about the hero of the narrative:

> Ivan Osipov, a peasant known under the nickname Kain [Cain], was one of the most famous and popular brigands in the eighteenth century. After many daring robberies in Moscow and on the Volga River, he appeared one day of his own free will in the Investigative Chambers pretending to offer his services to the police. He was not, however, in the least intent on ceasing his activities. On the contrary, having bribed the entire Investigative Chamber, in 1748 he unleashed terror among Moscow's rich, burning and robbing their houses at will. Some of them fled to Petersburg, others spent nights in open fields.
>
> Ordinary folk viewed Kain as an avenger punishing their real oppressors, and unquestionably regarded him with sympathy. When he was, at last, arrested, workers from a textile factory attempted to free him. Komarov succeeded in seeing Van'ka Kain while the latter was under arrest in the Investigative Chambers. On the basis of Van'ka Kain's tales of his adventures and his "autobiography," which at first circulated in manuscript but was later published as well, Komarov composed his *Description*, to which he subsequently added a collection of Kain's and his comrades' favorite songs, which opens with the famous "Rustle Not, oh Mother Oak Grove Green."[72]

Komarov's *Van'ka Kain* was an immediate success. In fact, it may have been the first native best seller: fifteen editions were issued in the last third of the eighteenth century.[73] It may also be partly responsible for the subsequent Russian addiction to detective stories, a continuing addiction that requires, in conditions of the near absence of satisfactory domestic products, a steady supply of this imported opiate for the masses craving thrillers.

71. The Russian title is *Obstojatel'noe i vernoe opisanie dobryx i zlyx del rossijskogo mošennika, vora, razbojnika i byvšego moskovskogo syščika Van'ki Kaina, vsej ego žizni i strannyx poxoždenij.*

72. D. D. Blagoj, *Istorija russkoj literatury XVIII veka,* 2nd ed. rev. (Moscow: Učpedgiz, 1951), pp. 478–79. The brigand song "Ne šumi, mati zelënaja dubravuška" is cited in full in Pushkin's *Captain's Daughter,* a novel set against the background of the eighteenth-century peasant revolt of Emeljan Pugačev. See A. S. Puškin, *Sobranie sočinenij v desjati tomax,* Vol. V (Moscow: Goslitizdat, 1960), pp. 348–49.

73. D. S. Mirsky, *A History of Russian Literature,* Francis J. Whitfield (ed.) (New York: Alfred A. Knopf, 1949), p. 38. Equally successful was Komarov's *Tale of an Adventure of the English Mylord George and of the Brandenburg Countess Frederica-Louise, the Above Supplemented by the Story of Marcimiris, a Former Turkish Vizier, and of Theresia, the Queen of Sardinia* (1782).

The existence of a void created by the unavailability of Soviet books about spies, criminals, and upright heroes intent on foiling their insidious designs was recognized within months after Stalin's death. An article in *Komsomol'-skaja pravda,* a youth newspaper, of December 16, 1953, called on Soviet writers to create such books because "they instill in the young a love for the heroic calling of a Soviet intelligence officer." The ensuing discussion continued for years and is by no means over. In 1964 opinions were still very much divided. Some critics maintained that detective stories serve the useful function of heightening the reader's, particularly the young reader's, awareness of danger and evil in the world and the need for all people of goodwill (not just Soviet people) to stand up and fight that evil. Soviet books of this genre, it was noted (in an apparent allusion to the enormous popularity abroad of the tales of James Bond, a *Western* agent), would have the additional advantage of serving as "powerful means of advertising the advantages of the Soviet way of life."[74] Other writers objected, insisting that the detective story is essentially harmful and that if more interesting works could be produced in established genres such as travel and biography there would be no need for detective stories.[75] Still others attempted to strike a conciliatory note by saying, in effect, that there are bad and harmful detective stories (Western ones), but that the genre itself is not beyond redemption, calling on Soviet writers to produce detective tales and thrillers that are uplifting and patriotic.[76]

While the polemics continued, some Soviet novelists proceeded to create novels of crime and international intrigue. Lev Šejnin, an old practitioner of the genre, brought out new plays and prose about Soviet detectives tracking down violators of Soviet laws; Vadim Koževnikov wrote a massive novel *The Shield and the Sword (Ščit i meč)* which extolled the wartime heroism of Soviet intelligence agents.[77] At the same time, Western thrillers and detective stories were gradually becoming available as a result of two factors that favored the process—a slackening of political vigilance during the post-Stalin thaw and the consequent readiness of Soviet publishers to make an easy profit on books for which there was not simply demand but real hunger.

74. I. Višnevskaja in *Komsomol'skaja pravda,* March 31, 1964. In any case, the critic implied, attempts to uproot detective novels are doomed to fail since these "have been and are being read by professors and laborers, farmers and great statesmen, schoolboys and retirees."
75. Rimma Žukova, an eminent sportswoman, ibid., May 22, 1964.
76. Arkadij Adamov, ibid., June 10, 1964.
77. Somewhat later, novels of this kind began to acquire rather ominous overtones by suggesting the existence of links between American and Israeli intelligence and liberal Soviet intellectuals and Jews. Such were, for instance, two novels by Ivan Ševcov, both published in 1970, *In the Name of the Father and the Son (Vo imja otca i syna)* and *Love and Hate (Ljubov' i nenavist').* The latter appeared in 200,000 copies under the imprint of the publishing house of the Ministry of Defense (Voenizdat).

While some of the thrillers and detective stories were printed on a relatively modest scale (e.g., 18,000 copies of Daphne du Maurier's *Rebecca* in
the original English; or 250,000 copies of the entertaining detective yarns
of Gilbert K. Chesterton), two British masters of the genre, Wilkie Collins
and Arthur Conan Doyle, were brought out in printings that would place
them within the reach of a large reading public, although still insufficient
to satisfy demand.[78]

Wilkie Collins was a friend of Charles Dickens with whom, in fact, he
collaborated on a few books. Like Dickens, Collins sympathized with society's underdogs. The preceding facts are duly pointed out in the *Literary
Encyclopedia.*[79] Collins was not, however, primarily interested in social
problems. His sentimental melodramas and, above all, his detective stories
earned him his popularity in prerevolutionary Russia. They continue to be
widely read in the USSR a century after their original publication. Thus,
*Moonstone,* a story about the mysterious disappearance of a precious stone,
appeared in close to a million copies; *Hide and Seek* in 350,000; *The Woman
in White* in 200,000; and a collection of short stories in 75,000 copies.

Arthur Conan Doyle's name is synonymous with the detective story. Less
known is the fact that Doyle was also a pioneer writer of science fiction,
and it was these works that were most published in the USSR: one and a
half million copies of *The Lost World,* with its memorable portrait of
Professor Challenger, an eccentric explorer and scientist, and another half
million of *The Marracot Deep,* of an anthology of science fiction, and of tales
about the sea. These are the books favored by the authorities as educational
reading for the young.[80] Not so the Soviet reading public. There is massive
evidence that Arthur Conan Doyle, not unexpectedly, is popular first and
foremost as the author of detective stories about the immortal sleuth Sherlock Holmes, his close companion Dr. John Watson, and their archenemy
Professor Moriarty. The approximately one and a quarter million copies of
these tales actually printed did not begin to satisfy public demand. Still,
issuing the Sherlock Holmes tales on such a large scale required some
justification on the part of the publishing establishment. In essence, the
argument chosen was that the adventures of the English detective are, in
a way, educational, and that in any case they are vastly preferable to the
horrid newer specimens of the genre: "Sherlock Holmes, who unravels
complex crimes with his uncommon logic, powers of observation, and
attention to details that escape others, stands in sharp contrast to many
heroes of twentieth-century bourgeois literature with their amoral traits and

78. See chapter 2.
79. KL, Vol. III (1966), pp. 659–60.
80. The problem of science fiction is discussed in chapter 4.

readiness to resort to any means in order to achieve desired ends. Therein lies the cause of his [Sherlock Holmes's] popularity in many countries of the world."[81]

Apparently it was felt that the adventures of Sherlock Holmes were not, alone, sufficient to satisfy the public's craving for foreign detective stories and had to be supplemented with other books. The trickle of Soviet novels of the same genre was not an adequate supplement. The danger posed by the Western detective story was, in essence, that it provided the Soviet reader with *escapist* reading, with entertainment that did not contain the required dosage of educational content. (Works with openly anti-Soviet overtones, such as those of Ian Fleming, the creator of Agent 007, were, obviously, not translated.) In the years that followed, limited quantities of carefully selected Western thrillers by various authors were printed in book form or appeared in literary monthlies intent on boosting their circulations.[82] Gradually, an approved hero of the Western detective story emerged in the person of Inspector Maigret, the creation of Georges Simenon, a living French author. Simenon's "sociopsychological" novels, in a Soviet critic's estimate, "relate the tragic destinies of men in contemporary bourgeois society, their loneliness, painful searches for a way out from the dead end, and the disintegration of the bourgeois family." Simenon was also praised for condemning Fascism, racism, colonialism, and *American* gangsters.[83] While only scattered information is available on press runs, Simenon's works appear to be widely published. *Le Président* was published in Russian in 1960; "One Does Not Kill a Poor Man" appeared in August 1964 in *Inostrannaja literatura.* Numerous translations of Simenon's novels and short stories subsequently made their way into print.[84] Thus, in the USSR, the mantle of Sherlock Holmes was inherited by Inspector Maigret, a mildly "progressive" French policeman.

81. KL, Vol. II (1964), pp. 729–30. The device of neutralizing possible objections to a non-Soviet author's work by contrasting them favorably with the writings of other authors that are far more objectionable, is also systematically employed in Soviet commentaries on prerevolutionary Russian writers. See this writer's *Russian Classics in Soviet Jackets,* pp. 113–15.
82. For instance, in 1968 the orthodox journal *Don* serialized a novel by Agatha Christie.
83. KL, Vol. VI (1971), pp. 840–41.
84. Simenon's *Brothers Rico* was translated in 1965; *Maigret's First Case* was first serialized in *Don* in 1967 and was published in book form the following year; *La Prison* appeared in 1968. Other works by Simenon were published in *Neva* (Nos. 6 and 7, 1968), in *Inostrannaja literatura* (No. 8, 1967; No. 8, 1968), and in other journals.

# CHAPTER

# 4

# *For the Young and Adventurous*

Except for a brief period during the 1920s when, in a flush of revolutionary fervor, fairy tales were rejected by some Soviet educators as bourgeois fantasies harmful to proletarian children, books printed for juvenile readers in the USSR have always included many juvenile classics, both Russian and foreign. While newer children's books, Soviet or translated, were exposed to thorough scrutiny for their ideological contents (and also, to some degree, for acceptability of their authors' personae), few such precautions were seemingly observed in the republication of older children's favorites. One major factor that may have brought about this inconsistency was that, like most parents and educators, the men and women responsible for Soviet publishing policies apparently believed and continue to believe that books good enough for them as children should be equally beneficial and interesting to the younger Soviet generation.

Another, weightier reason for the continued publication of non-Soviet juvenile writing probably was that, political rhetoric notwithstanding, many of the basic values that the Soviet educational establishment attempted to instill in children and adolescents paralleled those associated with the traditional nineteenth-century Western ethos. In the succeeding decades Soviet society grew more conservative. Today, many Westerners would find Soviet families and schools downright Victorian. Thus, in the 1970s Soviet youngsters continue to be taught the virtues of hard work, obedience to authority, patriotism, and self-denial. Since these values are championed in the didactic older works of West European and American children's literature, these books further reinforce the efforts of Soviet schoolteachers. Given sufficient care and skill in selection and interpretation, old-fashioned "bourgeois" children's books need not impede efforts at a specifically Soviet socialization of the young.[1]

Assuming these beliefs, it was inevitable that even in earlier years, when shrill Communist rhetoric advocated rejection of the 'bourgeois' values contained in works written for 'bourgeois' children, Soviet books printed for teen-age readers should have included a very large number of translations from the West European languages. Besides, there was simply not enough in the Russian literary heritage to fill the void that would have been created by failure to reprint translated juvenile classics. Recent Soviet writing would not have sufficed to compensate for a number of traditional deficiencies in Russian literature, such as the near absence of novels of adventure, particularly with exotic settings, tales of sea voyages, science fiction, and stories of suspense. As some Russian critics were to note in the 1920s, Russian literature has all too often neglected the plot, a shortcoming particularly harmful to writing for juvenile audiences, to say nothing of such genres as the detective story. Thus, translated literature for children continued to be reissued on a large scale even in periods of extreme xenophobia, such as Stalin's declining years, when Western books destined for adult readers were, for all intents and purposes, restricted to translations of venerable classics and of living writers with impeccably pro-Soviet credentials.

In the wake of Stalin's death, translations of West European and American books for children and adolescents benefited from the liberal policies of the "thaw," multiplying in numbers and press runs. Paradoxically, because they have always been treated more generously than similar books for adults, they were also the principal beneficiaries of the liberalized publishing policies. Not surprisingly, those in authority in book publishing felt it was safer to bring out more *copies* of books already on bookshelves, or to publish for the first time titles reassuringly similar in content, than to be the first to break long-standing taboos on specific authors or subject matter.[2]

In spite of all efforts, this writer could not identify some foreign authors published by Detizdat and other Soviet publishers specializing in juvenile books.[3] Their number, however, was not large enough to appreciably affect the overall picture. A more serious *caveat* pertains to interpretation of the

1. Significantly, Soviet educators and editors prefer the authoritarian work ethic of West European and American children's literature of earlier years to many recent books that they find overly permissive, contributing to the breakdown of discipline, sanctioning selfishness, etc. This may well account for the lack of enthusiasm in the USSR for some of America's children's television series.

2. The problem will be discussed in some detail elsewhere; see, in particular, chapter 4.

3. The difficulty of identifying little known foreign authors published in the USSR is compounded by the highly erratic Soviet system of quasi-phonetic transliteration of names from Latin into Cyrillic script.

data on quantities printed. Until the late 1960s, Soviet publishing statistics classified quite indiscriminately as "books" not only new titles as well as reprints, but also each volume from a multivolume set, every translation (an important factor in a multilingual state such as the USSR), and, most confusing of all, pamphlets of only several pages. The latter accounted for a very considerable portion of all children's books. Often these were picture books not unlike those published in the United States for pre-school children; most frequently the pamphlets consisted of a single fable or fairy tale, although sometimes they were separate issues of individual chapters from longer novels, occasionally in edited form.[4] Thus, if judged by Western statistical standards, the picture would appear far less impressive; the problem of inflated statistics was common to all Soviet publishing figures, but was particularly serious in dealing with data on children's books. It is to be hoped that the situation will improve in the future, but a spot check of statistics for the early 1970s still reveals much inconsistency and confusion.

Russian folklore is one of the world's richest, and fairy tales are among its favorite genres. Some of these were turned into famous poems by Alexander Pushkin, who heard them from his peasant nurse Arina Rodionovna. As for West European "literary" tales, it is more than likely that these were introduced in Russia primarily through the efforts of the thousands of French, German, and English tutors and governesses whose portraits survive in scores of nineteenth-century novels and memoirs. Gradually these stories acquired, as it were, Russian citizenship and even Russian names: thus, Cinderella became Zoluška. Translated fairy tales became indispensable companions of Russian childhood.

The four great names associated with fairy tales are, of course, Jakob and Wilhelm Grimm, Charles Perrault, and Hans Christian Andersen, all of them old favorites in Russia. A four-volume set of Grimm was published

4. An example is Balzac's *Gobseck,* which is a 50-page fragment from the second volume of *La Comédie humaine.* Gobseck is a usurer who lives in squalor but gloats in the knowledge that his huge fortune makes him more powerful than any of the proud aristocrats; the story was clearly intended to provide young Soviet readers with an abhorrent picture of a capitalist exploiter obsessed with the power of money. It is one of only a few works of foreign literature that are required reading in Soviet public schools. A complete list of works of foreign literature studied by Soviet schoolchildren was recently compiled by N. N. Shneidman of the University of Toronto (*Literature and Ideology in Soviet Education,* [Toronto: Lexington Books, D. C. Heath and Co., 1973], pp. 77–90). It includes the following:

GRADE 4: Andersen, "The Snow Queen" (required); Perrault, "Cinderella" (recommended).
GRADE 5: Longfellow, excerpt from "Hiawatha" (recommended).
GRADE 8: Molière, *Le Bourgeois Gentilhomme;* Byron, excerpts from *Childe Harold's Pilgrimage,* and several of Byron's poems.
GRADE 9: Shakespeare, *Hamlet;* Goethe, *Faust;* Balzac, *Gobseck;* Stendhal, *Vanina Vanini.*

The last item, a novella of some twenty-five pages, is frequently published as a separate book. It is about an Italian patriot who breaks with the woman he loves when she, in order to save his life, betrays his comrades to the enemy.

in 1908–12, and the first Russian translation of Perrault appeared as long ago as 1768. The year 1955 marked the sesquicentennial of Hans Christian Andersen's death, and this, no doubt, contributed to the zeal of Soviet publishers.[5] Andersen's tales, it was noted, "are filled with the love and work of ordinary folk. . . . They are full of delicate humor and of biting satire aimed at the conceited rich who stand ready to sacrifice feelings and common sense to wealth and social position."[6] Andersen's fairy tales, long popular in Russia (a four-volume set was published in 1894–95), were printed during the first post-Stalin decade in twenty languages (a record apparently not approached by any foreign author at the time except the Grimm brothers). Over 4,000,000 copies of the Dane's fairy tales were published in Russian and 500,000 more in nineteen other languages. As for individual tales, *Princess on a Pea* held the lead with 2,500,000 copies, followed by 2,000,000 of *The Steadfast Tin Soldier,* and somewhat fewer of *The Ugly Duckling.*[7] Of course, the 11,000,000 copies of all titles by Hans Christian Andersen made him by far the most widely published Scandinavian author in the USSR, although the vast majority of his "books" did not really deserve the appellation: all too often they were pamphlets containing only a single tale. Much the same was true of the runner-up in the category of fairy tales, the Grimm brothers, with 10,000,000 copies, also in twenty languages of Soviet ethnic groups. Charles Perrault's tales were published in a similar manner in approximately 6,000,000 copies. The largest single item was *Cinderella* (3,000,000), followed by *Little Red Riding Hood* (1,500,000), and *The Sleeping Beauty* (slightly over 1,000,000). Others were far behind: thus, there were only 350,000 copies of *Puss in Boots.*

The fairy tales of Wilhelm Hauff, an author remembered chiefly for historical romances written in the manner of Walter Scott, were republished in about 650,000 copies. Per Christian Asbjörnsen's collection of Norwegian legends and folk tales was brought out in a modest edition of 125,000 copies. No data was available on the two printings of French fairy tales by Christian Pineau, a common statistical omission when living authors are

5. As already indicated, Soviet publishers are very sensitive to literary anniversaries, but are occasionally quite inconsistent in paying homage to great writers of the past. Thus, international observances of Hans Christian Andersen's sesquicentennial were widely publicized, while the 250th anniversary of Charles Perrault's death in 1958 seems to have received little notice.

6. *Novyj mir,* No. 4, 1955, p. 159. The *Literary Encyclopedia* notes with approval, "In a number of cases Andersen eschews the tradition of happy endings in fairy tales. His heroes become victims of social injustice." KL, Vol. I (1962), p. 223.

7. The other fairy tales were printed in relatively small quantities—300,000 of *The Snow Queen,* 230,000 of *The Wild Swans,* and 200,000 of *The Emperor's Nightingale.* Of course, many of these may have appeared in general anthologies of fairy tales or in other collections. Thus, *The Snow Queen,* which was at the time required reading for all fourth-grade pupils, must have been printed in general textbooks.

involved.[8] Somewhat apart stands L. Frank Baum's *The Wonderful Wizard of Oz,* a "serious" fantastic tale first published in 1900 and thus lacking the longer tradition of Hauff and others. It was printed in 125,000 copies.[9]

Besides their value as wholesome entertainment, many books for the very young serve the explicit or incidental purpose of familiarizing little boys and girls with exotic flora and fauna.[10] A number of famous Soviet writers, among them Kornej Čukovskij and Samuil Maršak, have written works of this kind; their creations and works of this genre by prerevolutionary Russian writers as well as from Russian folkore have been systematically supplemented by translations of Western writers. Falling in this category are the works of two Britons, Edward Lear and Beatrix Potter, the first writing in verse and the second in prose (100,000 and 325,000 copies respectively). Maurice Carême, a contemporary Belgian poet, endeared himself to a Soviet critic with his "healthy, optimistic vision of the world" and by being "an enemy of formalist experiments," i.e., by writing in a traditional manner.[11] Carême's poem for young children, "My Snake," was printed in half a million copies. Similar pedagogical goals probably argued for the publication of works by two modern Canadian authors, Sir Charles Roberts and Ernest Thompson Seton. Stories by the former were printed in approximately a quarter of a million copies, while those by Seton, the famous conservationist and founder of the Boy Scout movement, reached a figure of two million. But then, Ernest Thompson Seton has been well known in Russia since early in this century. Several of his books, such as *Wild Animals I Have Known, Two Little Savages,* and *Rolf in the Woods,* were repeatedly reissued. Seton's works, most of them filled with factual material and also with Indian and Eskimo lore, were published in Russia in 1910 in a ten-volume set.[12]

Another foreign author of works treating exotic flora and fauna who was well known in prerevolutionary Russia was Rudyard Kipling; a four-volume set of Kipling's works came out in 1908 and a twenty-volume collection appeared in 1916. Yet, for political reasons, the publication even

8. Born in 1904, Pineau was active in the Resistance and also in the French Socialist Party. His fairy tales, published in France in 1952 and in Russian in 1959, are described by the *Literary Encyclopedia* as "lyrical, satirical, and parable-like, filled with criticism of the bourgeoisie and alluding to many social problems of our times." KL, Vol. V, (1968), p. 748.

9. This is somewhat surprising in view of the story's didactic—and even political—potential. One non-Soviet source, for instance, points to the fact that the characters and situations of *The Wonderful Wizard of Oz* "satirize chauvinism in this [American] 'melting pot' of races" (*The Penguin Companion,* Vol. III, p. 27). Normally, Soviet educators (and literary critics as well as publishing policy makers) miss no opportunity to criticize America's racial problems.

10. Rudiments of botany and zoology are taught in Soviet primary schools.

11. KL, Vol. III (1966), p. 405.

12. The Soviet Union has no Boy Scout or Girl Scout movements as such; scouting existed in tsarist Russia but was abolished after 1917 as "bourgeois." The highly politicized Soviet organizations of Young Octobrists (for the very young) and Pioneers (for older children) incorporate in their activities many features of scouting.

of his animal stories in the USSR seems somewhat surprising: a standard non-Soviet reference work identifies him as a "poet, short story writer, journalist, and imperialist."[13] Kipling's characterization in the Soviet *Literary Encyclopedia* is quite uncomplimentary. He was, indeed, an imperialist and worse; "Kipling glorified the 'civilizing' mission of the Anglo-Saxon race among the 'backward' nations of the East," he "extolled the actions of Britain's armed forces," and so forth.[14] Kipling's collected writings fill some thirty-five volumes, but the only works of his that are reprinted in the USSR are the tales of Mowgli, an "uncivilized" boy who appears in *The Jungle Book* and *The Second Jungle Book,* and some short stories about wild beasts. Most of these are printed in thin pamphlets often consisting of a single tale. Nearly 1,750,000 copies of Kipling's tales have been issued in nine languages.

Compilers of collections of readings for the very young can avail themselves of the huge treasure of Russian folk tales. The situation grows more difficult when one attempts to set up a library of books appropriate for older children. Folklore is less helpful here, and relatively little is found in the writings of Russian authors of the last century. Although there are many Soviet books aimed at this age group (indeed, some well known Soviet authors, such as Arkadij Gajdar, Venjamin Kaverin, and Lev Kassil' address themselves primarily to this audience), things would be difficult indeed without recourse to translated juvenile fiction. Some of the works published, such as Carlo Collodi's *Adventures of Pinocchio* (115,000 copies) have long ago achieved the status of children's classics; others, such as Giovanni Pirelli's *Giovannino and Pulcerosa* (160,000) are less well known. Some of the authors represented, for instance Edmondo de Amicis (*The Heart of a Boy* and a few travel books, 300,000) are known as children's writers; others, such as Katherine Mansfield wrote primarily for adults and only incidentally for younger readers (her Chekhovian tales for children were printed in 90,000 copies in Russian and 35,000 in the original English). Many of the books published for older children, such as Lewis Carroll's *Alice's Adventures in Wonderland* (250,000 copies) or the less famous children's novels of Mary Mapes Dodge (over 600,000 copies of *Hans Brinker* and other titles) have long been known to Russian readers; others, such as Antoine de Saint-Exupéry's poetic tale *The Little Prince* (nearly 250,000) are very popular newcomers.[15]

13. *The Penguin Companion,* Vol. I, p. 294.
14. KL, Vol III (1966), p. 521. Curiously, the Soviet encyclopedia fails to notice in Kipling what would, in the USSR, normally accrue to a foreign writer's credit, namely his "extreme anti-Americanism" (*The Penguin Companion,* Vol. I, p. 295).
15. *The Little Prince* was hailed by a Soviet critic because its story demonstrates the importance of kindness and goodwill. (Vera Smirnova in *Moskva,* No. 8, 1959, pp. 121–23). Other works of Saint Exupéry will be discussed below.

The common denominator of most of the foreign literature published for older children appears to be, first, the building of character (e.g., teaching fairness, honesty, understanding) and, second, a healthy dose of useful information on a variety of subjects formally taught in Soviet schools. A prime example of the latter was Selma Lagerlöf's *The Wonderful Adventures of Nils,* of which more than a quarter of a million copies were brought out in Russian and three other languages. The novel was, in fact, originally commissioned by the Swedish government as an aid for teaching Swedish geography in the public schools; its author conceived—before the advent of aviation—the original idea of having a little boy fly over the country on "gooseback."[16] Character-building rather than the imparting of factual information was probably the decisive factor in bringing out two other Swedish novels—*Adventures of Detective Kalle Blomkvist,* which describes homeless waifs (125,000 copies) and the semi-fantastic *Little Boy Karlsson Who Lives on the Roof* (100,000)—both by Astrid Lindgren, and three French novels—Jules Renard's *Carrots,* a portrait of a child's encounter with the cruel realities of the adult world (150,000), and two novels by Hector Malot: *Without a Family* (*Sans famille,* 125,000 of the complete text and 250,000 adapted for children) and *Romain Kalbris* (30,000). Both of Malot's novels have been available in Russian since the 1880s.

As pointed out earlier, Soviet publishers often bring out under separate cover individual chapters from longer works, particularly those that make good reading for children (in earlier years such pamphlets were also aimed at semi-literate workers and peasants; with the improvement of adult literacy, the practice was gradually phased out).[17] Not many nonspecialists would instantly recognize two titles attributed to Victor Hugo, *Kozet* and *Gavroš* (nearly 200,000 copies of the first, in five languages; 150,000 of the second, in two languages). Both are excerpts from *Les Misérables.* Cosette is a prostitute's daughter protected by Jean Valjean, the central character in the novel, from mistreatment by a sadistic tavern keeper; Gavroche is a street urchin who dies while helping the insurgents manning the barricades.[18]

There are many writers, great and less than great, who are almost unknown outside their own countries, and not necessarily because of the language barrier. Conversely, some writers are better known abroad than among their own countrymen, again for a variety of reasons. Two of the

16. Also printed were 200,000 copies of the same author's *The Story of Gösta Berling,* a good novel about brigands with many folk legends woven into the narrative.

17. For a discussion of such editions see this writer's *Russian Classics in Soviet Jackets,* pp. 61–67.

18. In addition, a condensed version of the entire novel was printed in a quarter of a million copies.

most striking examples, Jack London and Mitchell Wilson, will be discussed later in this chapter. Another, less known, example is the British writer James Greenwood (1833–1929), author of *The True History of a Little Ragamuffin* (1866). The novella's fortunes in Russia were strikingly better than in its author's homeland:

> While in England it was republished but once, in 1884, it became enormously popular in Russia. Translated into Russian by the [Ukrainian and Russian] writer Marko Vovčok, it was reprinted approximately forty times. Greenwood's little boy Jim is a realistic personification of the impoverished children of London. In his *In the World* [Maxim] Gorky recalls how captivated he was with *The Little Ragamuffin:* ". . . its very first page brought out in my soul a smile of delight."[19]

Greenwood's novella remains popular in the USSR. During the first post-Stalin decade it was republished at least seven times in Russian (over 500,000 copies of the full text and 50,000 of an adaptation) and was also printed in Ukrainian (45,000), Turkmen (10,000), Tatar (8,000), and Tadzhik (5,000).

A distinctive feature of Soviet publishing of translated literature is the systematic promotion of specific authors and individual works for transparently political reasons; similar considerations also result in the blacklisting of other writers and titles. Both problems are discussed in some detail elsewhere in this book. One particular case, however, deals specifically with children's literature and will be considered here.

Gianni Rodari emerged from our research as far and away the best-selling Italian author in the USSR. No other Italian writer has been printed on a scale at all comparable. The titles of Rodari's books, their publishers, and, especially, their huge printings all suggested that these were children's books. Thus, *Adventures of Cipollino* was issued in Russian in 1,500,000 copies, with 300,000 additional copies in fifteen languages; similar figures were reached by *What Are Different Trades Like*. In addition, *The Journey of the Blue Arrow* was printed in some 750,000 copies, *Gelsomino in the Land of Lies* in 400,000, plus 500,000 copies of other tales. But who was Gianni Rodari? His name was not to be found in standard reference works, including *Dizionario Letterario Bompiani,* which lists six thousand Italian authors. Ultimately, a Soviet newspaper confirmed our suspicions and subsequently additional documentation was found in a newly published volume of the Soviet literary encyclopedia. Gianni Rodari, born in 1920, a Communist, writes children's stories and nur-

19. KL, Vol. II (1964), p. 391. The quotation is from M. Gor'kij, *Sobranie sočinenij,* Vol. XIII (Moscow, 1957), p. 342.

sery rhymes for *L'Unità,* the Italian Communist daily.[20]

Of all foreign novels featuring resourceful boys with whom young Soviet readers can identify, the most popular are—and have been practically since their appearance in Russian—*The Adventures of Tom Sawyer* and *The Adventures of Huckleberry Finn.*[21] A recent Soviet bibliographic reference work hails *Tom Sawyer* as "one of the most beloved books among all of the world's young readers," and *Huckleberry Finn* as "a no less beloved and wise book, reflecting Twain's talents." The latter work, moreover, is credited with greater ideological value: "A description of the vices of American life, the writer's realistic art and democratic sympathies impart a special significance and charm to this book, so very popular with young readers."[22] Not unexpectedly, the same source also had kind words for *The Prince and the Pauper:* "Saturated with great love for the oppressed and ruined people, the book invariably makes a profound impression on young readers."[23] Whatever the reasons, Mark Twain continues to enjoy a wide following in the USSR. A twelve-volume set of his works was published at 300,000 per volume, while *Huckleberry Finn, Tom Sawyer,* and *The Prince and the Pauper* were reissued in a total of nearly 2,000,000 copies, supplemented by a similar printing of anthologies.[24]

While over the years Twain's Tom and Huck have been holding the same fascination for young European readers as for their American contemporaries, to many, Twain's most interesting and puzzling figure was the run-away

20. KL, Vol. VI (1971), pp. 322–23.

21. A lonely voice of dissent, cowardly hiding behind a pseudonym, was heard forty-odd years ago. See L. G., "S Tomom Soerom pioneru ne po puti" (Tom Sawyer Is Not Befitting Company for a [Soviet] Young Pioneer) in *Kniga i proletarskaja revoljucija,* No. 2–3, 1932, pp. 194–96.

22. *Osnovnye proizvedenija,* 1965, pp. 388–89.

23. Ibid., p. 389.

24. It is more than likely that Mark Twain's popularity in the USSR induced Soviet publishers to bring out a novel *about* him: Miriam Mason's *A Boy from the Great Mississippi,* in 120,000 copies. A characteristic, if somewhat extreme, attempt to make political capital of Mark Twain, was the publication in 1961 of the American writer's *King Leopold's Soliloquy.* The decision to bring out the translation was quite candidly dictated by political circumstances. In 1961, the former Belgian Congo was embroiled in a civil war. The Soviet Union supported the regime of Patrice Lumumba (Moscow's special university for Afro-Asian students now bears his name). Belgium, and to a degree the United States, showed sympathy for the secessionist regime of the Katanga province headed by Moise Tchombe. Mark Twain's caustic lampoon of the Belgian monarch was written over half a century earlier. It attacked, in the words of the Soviet editors, the man who had the audacity to proclaim himself "personal ruler of [the Congo] a huge country with a population of 25 million." To make certain that Soviet readers' righteous indignation not be squandered on Belgium alone, the editors emphasized that the "United States was the first to support Leopold's bloody regime in the Congo." Explicit comment followed: "Today, when Belgian imperialists, supported by world imperialism, have unleashed a new tragedy in the Congo, Mark Twain's tract acquires an exceptionally timely quality. It is for that reason that some people in the writer's homeland saw to it [?— MF] that the tract be forgotten. Unfortunately, until recently it was also unknown to Russian readers. This is the first Russian publication of the complete text." (*Zvezda,* No. 5, 1961, p. 149). Projecting Soviet practices to the United States, a Soviet reader would thus assume that *King Leopold's Soliloquy* is banned in America, and cannot, at the very least, be found in bookstores and libraries. There was even a hint that American censorship had long succeeded in concealing Mark Twain's work from *Russian* readers!

slave Jim. The mystery of his social position was compounded by the exoticism of his race: millions of East Europeans had never seen a black man.[25] In recent decades most juvenile books with Negro protagonists published in the USSR have been translations of works by modern African writers, many of them little known beyond their own countries; as pointed out earlier, these are outside the scope of this study. Two old favorites by white American authors, however, continue to be reprinted. Harriet Beecher Stowe's *Uncle Tom's Cabin,* the famous abolitionist novel, was first published in Russia in 1858 (by curious coincidence, it appeared the same year as Ivan Turgenev's *Sportsman's Sketches,* a book that played a similar role in the movement to abolish serfdom in Russia). A Soviet encyclopedia assures that "This novel remains a very popular children's book in our days as well,"[26] and the claim is borne out by statistics; nearly 1,500,000 copies of *Uncle Tom's Cabin* were printed in eight languages. The fact that Mrs. Stowe's novel, once widely regarded as political dynamite, has now come to be considered harmless reading for children is, of course, a manifestation of a socioliterary metamorphosis common to many books whose political scent has evaporated with the passage of time. The ideological controversy once engendered by such children's classics as *Robinson Crusoe* and *Gulliver's Travels* (both referred to later in this chapter) is now remembered only by scholars. By contrast, Joel Chandler Harris's *Uncle Remus, His Songs and His Sayings* was always, it seems, viewed simply as good reading (or listening) for children, although here, too, it can be safely assumed that for many young Russians the contents of the book also served as an introduction to the life of the American Negro. The book appeared in over a million copies.

Popular though such works may have been, their appeal to Russia's children does not compare with the truly hypnotic fascination of generations of that country's young with books that sang the glories of a romanticized American Indian and of the courage and adventure in that mythical land, the American Wild West. Such reading matter was truly, to paraphrase Karl Marx's famous dictum about religion, a narcotic for the masses of Russian children—not so much for those fortunate few who grew up in the manors of gentlefolk lovingly immortalized by Tolstoy, as for the many more who populated the drab secondary schools ruled over, if not quite by the demented Peredonovs from Fëdor Sologub's *Petty Demon,* then cer-

25. I speak also from personal experience. A Polish translation of *Huckleberry Finn* was the first book I ever read, and I recall vividly how, at the age of six, I could not understand the novel's references to racial segregation, although I had no trouble comprehending the fact that Jim was oppressed on "ethnic" grounds. A Jewish child in a virulently anti-Semitic country could understand that easily enough.

26. KL, Vol. I (1962), p. 631.

tainly by thousands of real-life replicas of Chekhov's Belikov, the misan-
thropic and disciplinarian teacher of Greek in "A Man in a Case." Statistics
may well be superfluous here; abundant testimony is found in memoirs and
in Russia's own literature. Perhaps the closest parallel is that of the epidemic proportions of the reading of courtly romances in Western Europe
of the fifteenth or sixteenth century. Monumental testimony to the phenomenon is found in *Don Quixote* which, whatever its other attributes, is also
a towering portrait of a poor hidalgo gone mad from excessive reading of
medieval escapist novels. Two youthful Russian victims of a similar affliction appear in "The Boys," a sad and comic short story written by Chekhov
in 1887. Overwhelmed by the allure of America's Wild West and its Indian
warriors as depicted in the novels of Mayne Reid, two Russian schoolboys
conspire to seek fame and fortune in that far-away country.[27] And, like
Cervantes' pathetic hero, they are ultimately apprehended and returned to
the humdrum realities of their home surroundings.

The biography of Thomas Mayne Reid (1818–83), a writer now far more
famous in Slavic countries than in the English-speaking world, is filled with
nearly as many improbable adventures as are his novels. Born in Ireland,
the son of a Protestant minister, he went to America in the late 1830s, where
he wrote his many romances about the American frontier. He took part in
the Mexican war of 1846–48 and returned to Europe in time to fight in the
Hungarian Revolution of 1848. During his lifetime his novels enjoyed huge
success both abroad (in Russia many were translated soon after their appearance in the original) and in England. At his death on October 22, 1883,
the London *Times* printed a moving obituary which began, "Every schoolboy, and everyone who has ever been a schoolboy, will learn with sorrow
of the death of Captain Mayne Reid."[28]

Soviet critics, of course, find rationalizations for the continued publication in their country of Mayne Reid's writings. They assure their readers
that his "novels of adventure are thematically linked to the suffering and
struggle of America's oppressed peoples"; that *The Rifle Rangers* depicts

27. One of the boys in Chekhov's story, who pointedly inquires whether his friend's sister
had ever read Mayne Reid, introduces himself as "Montigomo, the Hawk's Claw" and refers
to his friend Volodja as "my paleface brother." Volodja's two prosaic sisters, Katja and Sonja,
who had never read the master's creations, eavesdrop on the boys' conversation:

> The things they found out! The boys were getting ready to run away somewhere in
> America to dig for gold. They had everything ready for the journey: a pistol, two knives,
> biscuits, a magnifying glass to make fire with, a compass and four rubles in cash. They
> learned that the boys would have to walk on foot a few thousand miles, fighting off
> tigers and savages on the way, then dig for gold and hunt for ivory, kill enemies, join
> the pirates, drink gin, and finally marry beautiful maidens and cultivate plantations.

A. P. Čexov, *Sobranie sočinenij v dvenadcati tomax,* (Moscow: Goslitizdat, 1955), Vol. V,
p. 449.
28. Quoted in Brian Doyle (ed.), *The Who's Who of Children's Literature* (London: Hugh
Evelyn, 1968), p. 234.

"resistance to an American invasion"; that *The Quadroon* lays bare "the horrors of the slave trade, characteristic of America's South"; that in *The White Chief* and in *Osceola the Seminole* "Reid portrayed sympathetically the Indian's struggle against white colonizers."[29] It is unlikely, however, that these are the real reasons for Reid's continued popularity with Soviet readers. A six-volume set of Reid's creations, published in the late 1950s at 300,000 per volume, was, by many accounts, soon selling briskly on the black market. *The Headless Horseman* was published separately in about 700,000 copies, and the combined printings of Reid's other books reached a million. This excessive enthusiasm for Mayne Reid caused some concern to the Soviet authorities who had good reasons to believe that Reid was being read by adolescents (and also by adults) at the expense of more "useful" books.

James Willard Schultz (1859–1947) is regularly published, though not quite on the scale of Reid. His *Lone Bull's Mistake, With the Indians in the Rockies, A Son of the Navajo Tribe,* and other writings appeared in about three quarters of a million copies. Schultz's books have documentary value. One of the first white men to explore what is now the Glacier National Park, Schultz lived in Montana with the Blackfeet Indians; his wife was a Pikuni. Schultz described a way of life he knew well.[30]

Together with most Europeans, the Russians have long been admirers of James Fenimore Cooper who has been steadily published in their country since the 1820s. During the first post-Stalin decade over 6,000,000 copies of his works were printed in six languages, including 2,000,000 of a six-volume Russian set, 1,500,000 of *The Prairie,* over 500,000 of *The Deerslayer,* 300,000 each of *The Spy* and *The Pioneers,* and lesser quantities of other works and of anthologies. Cooper's tales of Indians, of virgin forests, and of sturdy American pioneers have doubtlessly, over the years, served much the same purposes as the writings of Mayne Reid, James Schultz, and many of the authors who will be discussed below. They were, and continue to be, good escapist literature providing juvenile, and not only juvenile, readers with vicarious adventures in distant lands. But they may also have found particularly responsive readers among the Russians, whose feeling of kinship with Cooper's heroes and locales may be traced partly to the fact that, alone among the Europeans, they live in a country that still has a wild frontier—Siberia—and vast unexplored spaces, and indigenous tribes of hunters and fishermen, thus making the romance of

29. Unfortunately for the critic, the best that could be claimed for *The Headless Horseman,* Reid's most popular single work in Russia, is that it contains "realistic scenes of life and customs in Texas." KL, Vol. VI (1971), pp. 283–84.
30. Martha E. Ward and Dorothy A. Marquardt, *Authors of Books for Young People* (Metuchen, N. J.: The Scarecrow Press, 1971), p. 456.

Cooper's America simultaneously distant and relevant.

A shelf labeled "travel" is a permanent fixture of nearly every modest public library in the United States. Yet, even if they were to try hard, Russian librarians would not find it easy to stock a similar section of their collection without recourse to a substantial number of translations from Western languages. The truth of the matter is that Russia was never a major maritime nation, it had no overseas colonies, and it was still relatively isolated and inaccessible in 1917; Peter the Great's famous "window to Europe" was opened only in the eighteenth century. Russian novels offer memorable scenes of horses and sleighs and carriages braving the successively dusty, muddy, and snow-covered highways and byways that crisscross the vast expanse of land. But literature of the sea and of adventure at sea? *Two* names—Goncharov and Stanjukovič—come readily to mind in all of prerevolutionary Russian fiction, and less than a score in the Soviet period. Indeed, a surprising number of major Russian writers of the pre-Soviet period and, until very recently, an overwhelming majority of Soviet writers had never set foot outside their native land.

It may well be that the thirst for literature of travel is greater among Soviet citizens of all ages, and most particularly the young, than, say, in America or in Western Europe precisely because car ownership is still a rarity in the USSR and because government restrictions make a journey abroad an impossible dream to all but a privileged handful. Film travelogues and books about distant lands are the only consolation available to people whose curiosity has been whetted by the formal study of geography (unlike in this country, an integral and important part of the school curriculum). It may also be argued, however, that books about travel, far from satisfying the urge to visit distant places, actually reinforce it. Some support for this conjecture may be found in the fact that until Stalin's death most translated travel fiction consisted of venerable classics set in the previous century or earlier, thus dampening, perhaps, the reader's desire to go and see for himself the exotic places depicted; the historical distance detracted, as it were, from the setting's reality and accessibility. The modest relaxation of obstacles on travel abroad in the post-Stalin period was accompanied by a freer flow of travel literature set in the present, although the change was slow in coming. Thus, on March 23, 1956, *Komsomol'skaja pravda,* a newspaper for younger readers, expressed regret that the "wonderful travel book" *Kon-Tiki* appeared in Russian only after a delay of several years.[31]

Jonathan Swift's *Gulliver's Travels* and Daniel Defoe's *Robinson Crusoe* have been available in Russian translations for more than two centuries.

31. Thor Heyerdahl's *Across the Pacific by Raft,* a factual account by a Norwegian explorer, was published in America in 1950.

*Gulliver's Travels* appeared during the first post-Stalin decade in nine languages, a total of nearly one and a half million copies.[32] The total printing of *Robinson Crusoe* was just slightly larger, and the number of languages identical.[33] A third old favorite is Rudolf-Erich Raspe's tales of Baron Münchhausen (half a million copies in ten languages). The legendary eighteenth-century liar's exploits have considerable local appeal in the USSR because of their settings: the book's full title is *Baron Münchhausen's Narrative of His Marvelous Travels and Campaigns in Russia.*

Also in the category of old staples of travel literature in Russia are the French novels of Louis Boussenard, an astoundingly prolific writer: a Russian edition of his works published in 1911, a year after his death, filled *forty* volumes. Politically, there was little to recommend Boussenard to Soviet publishers; his entry in the *Literary Encyclopedia* is strongly reminiscent of the article on Kipling who, as pointed out earlier, is selectively published notwithstanding his "imperialist" aberrations:

> He [Boussenard] traveled a great deal on business, and having thus collected his data, he began in 1877 to publish novels with swiftly moving plots and filled with factual material describing flora and fauna as well as history and geography. Ordinarily, his heroes are young Frenchmen who perform miracles of courage and resourcefulness in little explored countries. . . . In spite of the fact that some of Boussenard's writings contain elements of colonialist ideology, his work as a whole is permeated with humane sentiments and makes fascinating reading for the young. Toward the end of his life he wrote novels of adventure filled with compassion for oppressed peoples, such as *Le Capitaine Casse-Cou* (1901, Russian translation 1956) which deals with the Anglo-Boer war.[34]

The latter novel was printed in a million copies, with another half a million of *Diamond Thieves.*

The last of the classic writers of travel literature whose fame in Russia reaches back to the nineteenth century is Robert Louis Stevenson. Nearly all of his novels were translated into Russian immediately after their appearance in England. A twenty-volume set of Stevenson's complete works was published in Russia on the eve of World War I. Although the usual perfunctory claims crediting Stevenson with anticolonialism, antiracism, and other

32. There was also a Soviet edition of 4,500 copies in English. Swift's *A Tale of A Tub* was printed in 115,000 copies.

33. Soviet moviegoers could hear excerpts from *Robinson Crusoe* in the soundtrack of Grigori Čuxraj's 1956 film *Sorok pervyj* (based on a story by Boris Lavrenev) in which passages from the English novel are used to set the stage, as it were, for the film's own tale of shipwreck and sojourn on an uninhabited island during the Civil War.

34. KL, Vol. I (1962), p. 788. The encyclopedia's reference is apparently to the date of the most recent Russian translation. The novel, translated under the title *Kapitan Sorvi-golova*, has been available in Russian for over a half a century.

virtues may be found in Soviet sources, their hollow, ritualistic ring is readily apparent.[35] Some ideological justification appears to have been needed for the repeated republication of *Treasure Island, The Black Arrow,* and *The Wrecker,* a total of two million volumes. A five-volume set of Robert Louis Stevenson was published in 1967.

More political capital could be made from the Dutch writer Multatuli (real name Eduard Douwes Dekker, 1820–87), quite well known in prerevolutionary Russia, particularly for his *Max Havelaer, or the Coffee Auctions of the Dutch Trading Company.* Multatuli, whose pseudonym means "I have suffered much" (reminiscent of the pseudonym of a famous Russian writer, Gor'kij, which means "bitter") exposes the cruel exploitation of Java's indigenous population by colonialist masters. The novel and Multatuli's children's tales appeared in some 700,000 copies.

Travel, adventure, and ideological significance were the qualities that once endeared the writings of Bret Harte to Soviet publishers; an edition of Harte's complete works came out in 1928. Harte's world of rugged Wild West prospectors, miners, and social outcasts, victims of "rapacious American capitalism," provided the Soviet reader, it was felt, with material that was both enjoyable and instructive. While the earlier ardor for Harte may have cooled somewhat, recent reprints of his writing still reach the respectable total of three quarters of a million copies, not bad for a writer who emerges in Soviet criticism as a kind of minor-league Jack London.

Together with Twain, Cooper, and Dreiser, Jack London has long shared the distinction of being among the American authors most widely printed in Russia. Indeed, far more famous there than in the United States, he has been for many decades the object of a minor cult. In many ways London's career paralleled that of his Russian contemporary Maxim Gorky: both were restless young men continually changing occupations, constantly on the move (both were, in fact, former hoboes), horrified of and yet fascinated by violence, filled with pity for the weak yet in awe of the strong, intellectually attached to Marxist socialism yet sometimes under the spell of classical Marxism's antichrist, Nietzsche. (Lenin was fond of both writers, but was later to quarrel with his onetime friend Gorky.[36]) Such inconsistencies and

35. An original ideological note is injected in the praise accorded *The Black Arrow* and a few of Stevenson's other novels for their "nonacceptance of modern bourgeois civilization, projected into the past" (KL, Vol. VII [1972], p. 178). (The sentence is reminiscent of the Soviet historian Pokrovskij's characterization of history as politics projected into the past.) By this reasoning, feudal lords and slaveowners may, with some ideological ingenuity, be found worthy of praise for *their* opposition to bourgeois values. The device was also used in recent years by Soviet propaganda to extol a number of anti-Western but otherwise rigidly royalist, religious, authoritarian regimes in Asia and Africa, particularly Arab ones.

36. According to Lenin's widow, Nadežda Krupskaja, Lenin liked London's *Love of Life* (1906, published in Russian the following year under the title *Iskra žizni*). KL, Vol. IV (1967), p. 419. For some of the ideological reasons underlying the conflict between Lenin and Gorky, see Maxim Gorky, *Untimely Thoughts: Essays on Revolution, Culture and the Bolsheviks*

contradictions are, as a rule, glossed over in Soviet Gorky criticism, particularly in works written on a popular level and aimed at general audiences, including students, and little wonder: Gorky remains enshrined as the founding father of Soviet literature and creator of the concept of Socialist Realism, that literature's official creed. To tarnish the icon of Gorky would be clearly counterproductive.[37]

Similarly, there is a tendency to overlook aspects of Jack London's work that might complicate the simplistic Soviet view of the American writer as a socialist enemy of bourgeois America and a friend of the oppressed whose views find reflection in his enormously popular adventure novels.[38] We do not mean to suggest that there is *no* truth in such characterizations of London; not a few aspects of Soviet evaluations of the American novelist are shared by Western criticism, which is, of course, free of the obligatory bias of published Soviet works. We merely wish to call attention to the Soviet tendency to deny in London's works the complexity that sets them above lesser specimens of the genre.[39] To Soviet critics writing for their country's *only* current literary encyclopedia (there was only one published earlier, in the 1920s; it was abandoned, unfinished, in the early 1930s), *The Iron Heel,* for instance, is a straightforward political tract: "This is a book about the people's struggle against the tyranny of monopolistic capital, against the financial oligarchy. . . . The novel affirms scientific socialism's teachings about revolution."[40] In view of Jack London's large and devoted following in Russia prior to the revolution, the aim of Soviet London criticism should be viewed as an attempt to harness for the Soviet cause the ideological potential of his politically-oriented works—works that are known to be widely read and enjoyed. This approach is also evident in Soviet evaluations of other foreign writers that are equally popular; it is similarly characteristic of Soviet appraisals of classics of prerevolutionary Russian literature.[41] It appears appropriate for Jack London whose published works, during the first post-Stalin decade in Russia, included a

*1917–18,* translated from the Russian, with an introduction and notes by Herman Ermolaev (N. Y.: Paul S. Eriksson, 1968). Note the parallel with Jack London whom KL (IV [1967], p. 421) describes as "one of the first proletarian writers of the West, . . . the founder of revolutionary literature in the U.S.A."

37. The collection cited in note 36 consists of materials that were, and continue to be, wilfully suppressed in the USSR. They do not appear in Soviet editions of Gorky's *complete* works. In addition to Gorky's differences with Lenin, these include essays on harassment (and worse) of political dissenters, denunciations of anti-Semitism, etc.

38. For an excellent discussion of the subject see Deming Brown, *Soviet Attitudes Toward American Writing,* pp. 219–38.

39. Thus, for instance, a popular British reference work points to the fact that Jack London's *Martin Eden* "dramatizes his own rise into the moneyed class as a betrayal of idealism," thus crediting the novel, as it were, with the "complicating" factor of a successful radical writer's personal dilemma. See *The Penguin Companion,* Vol. III, p. 157.

40. KL, Vol. IV (1967), p. 420.

41. The problem is discussed at length in my *Russian Classics in Soviet Jackets.*

fourteen-volume set (a total of 3,500,000 copies), a seven-volume set (2,750,000), a two-volume set (600,000), well over 1,000,000 copies in six languages of *Martin Eden,* and a film version of *The Fighter,* the story of a young Mexican who becomes a prize-fighter in the United States in order to earn money for the revolutionary cause.[42]

Jack London was probably most responsible for awakening among the Russians an awareness of the romantic appeal of the North, of its snow-covered wastelands and the chilly waters of its seas. Adventure books with Arctic settings included also Theodor Mügge's German tales (in a modest 65,000 copies) and a collection of stories by the Danish Arctic explorer Peter Freuchen entitled *The Whale Hunters from Melville Bay* (100,000 copies).

Herman Melville himself presents a fascinating case of a very belated literary discovery. As indicated in this and other chapters, American literature has on the whole, fared extremely well in Russia ever since the 1820s. Melville's example points to curious exceptions. *Typee,* written in 1846, was first translated into Russian more than a century later, in 1958, as was that novel's sequel *Omoo* (165,000 copies). The neglect of Melville prior to 1917 does not concern us here, but failure of Soviet publishers to bring it out earlier was surely a serious political oversight if, as Soviet critics claim, *Omoo* does, indeed, "indict white colonizers and missionaries"![43] As for *Moby Dick,* it was first translated into Russian in 1961, 110 years after its appearance in English; the exact number of copies issued could not be ascertained. The two printings of the novel appeared with a thoughtful introduction by A. I. Starcev, a distinguished and sensitive critic.[44] That is all the more reason to note that the decision to publish Melville's great novel at long last was probably influenced by the apparent conviction of some Soviet editors that no harm would be done by bringing out a nice book about whale-hunting to provide Soviet teen-agers with wholesome and instructive reading. *Moby Dick* appeared in the series "Novels of Adventure" printed by the Geography Publishing House and catering to juvenile tastes.

There is some irony in the fact that among translations of English novels describing adventures at sea which, as suggested earlier, owe much of their

42. Three decades earlier *Martin Eden* was made into a film by the great Soviet poet Vladimir Mayakovsky, who also played a part in it. KL, Vol. IV (1967), p. 421. For a list of Soviet films based on Western literary works, see Appendix A.

43. Ibid., p. 746.

44. A number of the more serious (and therefore not always very representative) essays by Soviet critics of American writing are reproduced in English in Carl R. Proffer (ed.), *Soviet Criticism of American Literature in the Sixties* (Ann Arbor, Mich.: Ardis, 1972). Abel' Starcev is represented by his article on Fitzgerald. A 1965 pamphlet listing upcoming anniversaries of foreign writers identified Herman Melville (the 75th anniversary of whose death fell in 1966) as "an American Romantic writer who rejected bourgeois civilization; author of the monumental allegorical novel *Moby Dick,*" *Kalendar' pamjatnyx dat po zarubežnoj xudožestvennoj literature na 1966 god* (Moscow: Kniga, 1965), p. 35.

popularity to the near absence of similar reading matter in the corpus of Russian writing, are the works of the Russian-born Pole Joseph Conrad.[45] Conrad has been read in Russia since early in this century. In 1954–64 a two-volume set of his works was published in half a million copies. There was also a large printing of *'Twixt Land and Sea* (250,000), a smaller one of a volume including "The Duel" and other stories (100,000), and a very small one of *Lord Jim.*[46]

Some of the juvenile favorites with exotic settings were discussed earlier. Henry Rider Haggard's *King Solomon's Mines* and other tales of African safaris have been known in Russian for decades; an anthology of these was reprinted in half a million copies. Relatively new to Russia are books with Latin American locales, as, for that matter, are all books by Latin American writers. Translations of South American writers are now rapidly increasing. Among those with special appeal for younger readers were three authors of works depicting man pitted against treacherous jungles. Horacio Quiroga, a Uruguayan, is the author of tales reminiscent of E. A. Poe; nearly a half million copies of these and of his fairy tales were published. José Eustasio Rivera, a Colombian, is more civic-minded. His novel *Vortex* contains pictures of the frightening exploitation of rubber plantation workers in the Amazon river basin; it was printed in 75,000 copies, with 30,000 more of an anthology. Rómulo Gallegos, president of Venezuela from 1941 to 1948, was represented by two novels, *Canaima* (75,000) and *Doña Barbara* (30,000). There were also translations of two Argentine authors. Ricardo Güiraldes's *Don Segundo Sombra,* a romanticized novel about the gauchos published in 1926, was translated into Russian in 1960 and printed in 180,000 copies. *The Birds of Prey of "Florida,"* a 1916 novel by Benito Lynch, was translated into Russian in 1963 and printed in 100,000 copies. Lynch, even according to Soviet sources, was a nonpolitical writer. In the novel in question, "as always in Lynch's novels, the civilized European brings conflict and unhappiness into the otherwise simple rustic world."[47]

At first glance it may appear somewhat shocking to see a novelist of Ernest Hemingway's sophistication discussed together with so many unpretentious books for children and adolescents. The decision to do so may be justified on several grounds. To begin with, whatever Hemingway's other attributes, he is *also* a writer of novels of adventure, much as Dostoyevsky is *also* a writer of thrillers (to some of his detractors, such as Vladimir Nabokov, he is indeed little more than an author of Gothic novels). Second,

---

45. Conrad was born Korzeniowski in the little town of Berdičev in the Ukraine. Once the "capital" of Ukraine's Jewry, Berdičev (which is far removed from any sea) has one other foreign literary connection: it was there that Balzac married a Polish noblewoman.
46. 20,000 in Lithuanian and 17,000 in the original English; none in Russian.
47. *The Penguin Companion,* Vol. III, p. 345.

he is frequently treated as such in Soviet publishing and criticism, a parallel with the case of *Moby Dick* referred to earlier; thus, one recent collection of Hemingway's short works was brought out under the title *Stories About Sports.* Moreover, most of Hemingway's works published in the USSR belong in this category: they extol courage, adventure, daring. His more introspective and political works, notably *For Whom the Bell Tolls,* are rarely printed; these are discussed elsewhere.[48] The largest printing for any of his books was achieved by Hemingway's then recent work, *The Old Man and the Sea,* a half million copies in eleven languages. Nearly 300,000 copies of *The Green Hills of Africa* and a two-volume set of Hemingway at 300,000 per volume were issued. Hemingway was a major Soviet literary "rediscovery" of the late 1950s and early 1960s; his works, boycotted during the previous decade, were also then being frequently published in Soviet literary periodicals. Thus, *Across the River and into the Trees* was serialized in 1960 in *Moskva.* Selections from *The Fifth Column and the First 49 Stories* were printed in 1961 by *Novyj mir.* Chapters from *The Dangerous Summer* recounting Hemingway's encounters with the celebrated matador Manolete were published in *Inostrannaja literatura* in 1961.

Antoine de Saint-Exupéry was represented primarily by *Le Petit Prince.* Some Soviet editors apparently thought that the tale might also interest adult readers; in 1959 it was featured in the sober, unillustrated monthly *Moskva.* Saint-Exupéry, whose writings are so unlike the traditional realism of Soviet prose, was very much in vogue at the time, and his books sold briskly on the black market.[49] The legend of the man may have been as attractive as his writings. A military as well as a commercial pilot, Saint-Exupéry died while on a mission during World War II. His works, mostly describing the danger, adventure, and loneliness of flying, many with patriotic and anti-Nazi overtones, found many Soviet readers. They were printed on a rather modest scale in book form but appeared frequently in literary periodicals. *Southern Mail* was printed in 1963 in *Neva,* a monthly with a press run of 200,000, while *Airman's Odyssey* appeared in 1962 in *Moskva,* press run 100,000.

It may be said that the best novels of adventure and travel are great

48. *For Whom the Bell Tolls* appeared in Russian only in 1968 in a four-volume set of Hemingway's works. A reviewer in *Literaturnaja gazeta* (May 7, 1969) noted, "One cannot, of course, forget that Robert Jordan [the novel's central hero] is not a Communist." Actually, an effort was made by Soviet censors to make forgetting this fact easier. The text of the novel was subjected to cuts resulting in the removal of "anti-Communist" passages. The subject was discussed in some detail in chapter 1. Another of Hemingway's novels, *A Farewell to Arms,* will be dealt with in the chapter examining the possible impact of foreign literature on Soviet society.

49. This was confirmed in a Soviet journal. See G. Somov, "Princ i niščie" (The Prince and the Paupers), *Molodoj kommunist,* No. 1, 1966, pp. 74–79. Admissions of this kind are very rare.

literature; this in itself is reason to encourage their reading among the young. Yet works of this genre that have little claim to literary distinction also have their pedagogical uses. Many provide the young reader with vivid and detailed descriptions of faraway lands, their climates, vegetation, and the livelihoods of their inhabitants, and thus serve as a valuable supplement to what is learned in Soviet geography classes. A somewhat similar appraisal may be made of another category of books which take their readers to distant times rather than remote locales. Again, some of the authors and titles in this group are celebrated masterpieces of the art of writing; others are aesthetically undistinguished. All, however, presumably provide entertaining reading and in the process acquaint the reader—who is most likely, though not necessarily, young—if not with solid historical information, then at least with the flavors and colors and smells of life as it was lived in ages gone by. The greatest name in this category is doubtless Cervantes; the most widely read authors are Sir Walter Scott and Alexandre Dumas-*père*.

*Don Quixote,* first published in Russian in 1791, that is, prior to the appearance of any significant body of original *Russian* writing, has traditionally been popular with Russian readers and influential among the country's writers.[50] Approximately a million copies of *Don Quixote* were printed in Russian and a fourth of that number in six other languages. In addition, there was a five-volume set of Cervantes' writings at 350,000 copies per volume. Clearly, the multivolume set was not aimed at juvenile readers, nor were its buyers presumably limited to scholars, libraries, and bibliophiles. Rather it suggests that, as in the case of so many other foreign authors, a significant number of Soviet readers retain a sufficient fondness for a writer first read in their youth to purchase a set that includes his less important works. This, it should be noted, involves not only parting with one's money (Soviet books, particularly multivolume sets, are quite expensive relative to Soviet earnings) but also, no less importantly, allocating a part of precious space on one's bookshelves, a serious consideration in conditions of overcrowded Soviet housing.

Sir Walter Scott, a writer of lesser stature than Cervantes, has traditionally been at least equally influential with Russian authors and vastly more popular with the reading public: "In Russia Scott was already well known in the 1820s. . . . As a novelist, Scott influenced the historical prose of Russian writers, particularly N. V. Gogol' *(Taras Bul'ba)* and others."[51] An eighteen-volume set of Scott was published in Russia in 1896–99, and a

---

50. Thus, Ivan Turgenev's essay *Hamlet and Don Quixote* (1860) is one of the most important theoretical contributions by any Russian novelist. For a detailed study of the fortunes of the Spanish novelist in Russia, see Ludmilla Turkevich, *Cervantes in Russia,* (Princeton, N. J.: Princeton University Press, 1950).

51. KL, Vol. VI (1971), p. 900.

twelve-volume set in 1904–5. The two important Soviet editions of Sir Walter Scott were the fourteen-volume set of 1928–29 and the twenty-volume set brought out between 1960 and 1965, the latter in 300,000 copies per volume. Separate issues of Scott's individual works brought out at about the same time totaled approximately 2,500,000 copies. The larger printings, averaging 400,000, were of *Ivanhoe, The Edinburgh Dungeon, Quentin Durward,* and *Rob Roy;* there were also more modest quantities of *The Puritans, Richard the Lion Hearted,* and *The Fair Maid of Perth.*

The *Literary Encyclopedia* emphasizes that "Soviet scholars advance the thesis of a profoundly contemporary quality of Scott's legacy," and examples of retroactive projection of the Soviet view of history to the work of a British novelist of nearly two centuries ago may indeed be found in the very same article. Thus, readers are informed that Sir Walter Scott "saw the negative sides both of feudalism and of the newly formed bourgeois state. He sympathized with the masses and ascribed to the [common] people a significant role in the shaping of history. Scott's novels are centered around events that are, in one way or another, linked to major sociohistorical conflicts."[52] More specifically, *Rob Roy,* a novel about Scotland's Robin Hood, was said to expose "class contradictions" and "social injustice." Conversely, *Ivanhoe,* in the Soviet critic's opinion, should not be approached as a social document, since the novel's strength lies in its use of folklore rather than realism.[53] It is unlikely, of course, that many Soviet readers study *Rob Roy* in order to learn about class contradictions in feudal England. The Soviet state sees to it that they find ample opportunities for that elsewhere, in and out of school. Still, the quasi-official Soviet view of Scott is worth noting because it provides some notion of the kind of ideological justification that is deemed necessary presumably to offer some guidance to Soviet publishers and also a degree of reassurance to perplexed librarians and schoolteachers wondering whether reading about the adventures of English feudal lords, noble brigands, and damsels in distress is compatible with Communist upbringing of the young.

To the relatively apolitical eye of a Western observer, the fortunes of the Count of Monte Cristo and the exploits of the three musketeers might appear quite unlikely to provoke a major political controversy in the USSR. The fact is that the printing of approximately five million copies of novels by Alexandre Dumas-*père* stirred violent passions, this in spite of the French novelist's impressive references: "Among those who highly valued Dumas were K. Marx, L. Tolstoj, M. Gor'kij, [the chemist] D. Mendeleev, [the Soviet Commissar of Education] A. V. Lunačarskij, and other out-

52. Ibid., p. 897.
53. Ibid., p. 899.

standing figures."[54] The storm generated by the publication of vast quantities of books by Alexandre Dumas-*père* will be discussed in the concluding chapter.

Other historical romances published during the period included 140,000 copies of *The Chronicles of Captain Blood* by Rafael Sabatini, a twentieth-century Anglo-Italian author reminiscent of Dumas; 50,000 copies of *Ettore Fieramosca,* a sentimental novel about nineteenth-century Italian wars of independence by Massimo d'Azeglio; and 180,000 copies of *Captain Fracasse,* Théophile Gautier's novel about the theater of *commedia dell'arte,* which was read in Russia long before the Revolution both in translation and in the French original. Matteo Bandello's sixteenth-century Italian novellas, considered the best after Boccaccio, appeared in 315,000 copies, and a volume of Charles Nodier, the author of *Jean Sbogar,* the story of a romantic outlaw of whom Pushkin's Tatjana was fond, was published in 100,000 copies. Finally, there were 2,000,000 Russian copies (with additional small quantities in six other languages) of Raffaello Giovagnoli's *Spartacus,* a nineteenth-century Italian romance about an uprising of slaves and gladiators in ancient Rome. The popularity of the novel is closely related to that of its subject, who is sometimes described as the leader of the first class-war in history and hence a fitting subject for veneration in a Marxist state. (The name Spartacus [*Spartak*] was chosen by Moscow's leading soccer team, and the nationwide Soviet Olympics were called *Spartakiady.*) Chronologically, the most distant setting occurred in the translations from the French of four novels by the brothers Rosny, Joseph (1856–1940) and Seraphin (1859–1948). Highly prolific writers, the Rosnys produced about a hundred books on a wide variety of subjects and of uniformly scant artistic merit. The titles published in the USSR (in well over a million copies) all dealt with prehistoric man. Thoroughly grounded in scientific data, they were printed most likely because of their educational value.[55]

Translations of foreign science fiction have long been a staple of juvenile reading in Russia, and the novels of Jules Verne have been consistently the most popular examples of this genre. The reading of Verne's works continues to be encouraged, as they are believed to awaken in the young an interest in science, and thus serve an important utilitarian function. The article on Verne in the *Literary Encyclopedia* credits his works with influencing some of Russia's and the West's greatest scientists: "Verne's works, which were inspired by the great scientific discoveries of the nineteenth century, influenced in turn many noted scientists, inventors, and explorers (D. I.

54. KL, Vol. II (1964), p. 840.
55. The four volumes were entitled *Vamireh, the Man from the Stone Age; The Struggle for Fire; The Cave Lion;* and *Toward New Lands.*

Mendeleev, N. E. Žukovskij, K. E. Ciolkovskij, V. A. Obručev, F. Nansen, and others). Not only did they regard Verne's works highly, but they also, to some degree, owed to him their choices of life's callings and a number of specific and, on occasion, very significant scientific ideas. . . . In the USSR Verne is one of the most widely read and beloved foreign writers."[56] Publishing statistics bear out the encyclopedia's assertions. In addition to a twelve-volume set of Jules Verne's writings (at 390,000 copies per volume—a total of 4,700,000 copies!), there were 700,000 copies each of *Children of Captain Grant* and *The Fifteen-Year Old Captain,* 500,000 copies of *The Mysterious Island,* and 2,500,000 copies of other titles.

H. G. Wells, whom a British reference work identifies as a "novelist, reformer, and controversialist"[57]—a characterization similar to the one given G. B. Shaw—would appear, at first, to have all the positive attributes of Jules Verne and also to hold some additional attractions. Verne died in 1905, Wells in 1946. Since most of Wells's important books were written some thirty years after Verne's, Wells's science is more up-to-date. In addition, H. G. Wells was a devoted friend of the Soviet Union. His *Russia In the Shadows* (1920) recounts his once celebrated conversations with Lenin. Yet publication figures for Wells, though impressive, totaling approximately four million copies, trail behind those for Jules Verne.[58] One reason for this incongruity, paradoxically, may be traced to H. G. Wells's preoccupation with the *political* implications of scientific progress. Several of Wells's books warn of *unspecified* dictators who might harness science for their evil purposes or of invasions from other planets which might expose the follies of the social fabric designed by *Man* on Earth. Such ambiguities may well cause slight discomfort among Soviet editors; they open the way to far too many parallels in interpretation. Jules Verne is much safer after all.

Soviet literary critics, editors, and educators prize science fiction as useful supplementary reading to secondary school courses in science and mathematics. At the same time, they eye suspiciously writings suggesting that advances in science might also bring about changes in human and social, and hence also political, relationships. Soviet ideology does not presume to predict in detail the evolution of scientific thought (although on a number of important occasions the Soviet state did interfere in various areas of

56. KL, Vol. I (1962), p. 933.
57. *The Penguin Companion,* Vol. I, p. 548.
58. Individual works of H. G. Wells published in 1954–64 included *The Invisible Man* (about 650,000 copies), *The War of the Worlds* (half a million), *The First Men in the Moon* (100,000) and *The Autocracy of Mr. Parham* (100,000). In addition there was a three-volume set of his science fiction (750,000), two one-volume anthologies of the same (over 300,000) and one and a half million copies of anthologies with unspecified contents, though presumably including much the same selections.

science, ranging from genetics to physics, on the grounds that specific theories, such as heredity and relativity, were incompatible with its interpretation of Marxism). On the other hand, the Soviet Union does claim to be the guardian of what it regards as the only true blueprint of social evolution, which envisages an orderly transition from capitalism to socialism and from socialism to communism (at which point, presumably, social evolution would come to a grinding halt). To suggest that mere technological progress might invalidate this blueprint is insidious doctrinal heresy. For that reason some of the Western books most *feared* by the ideologically very sensitive Soviet literary and publishing Establishment are about social utopias often mixed with elements of science fiction, such as George Orwell's *1984* and *Animal Farm* or Aldous Huxley's *Brave New World.*

Similarly, some of the most famous books by Soviet Russian authors still suppressed in the USSR two decades after Stalin's death also belong to the genre of social utopia set against the background of science fiction. Best known among these is Yevgeni Zamiatin's *We,* a novel in many respects similar to Orwell's *1984,* which it antedates. Mikhail Bulgakov, who died prior to World War II, was partly restored to grace in the 1960s; a number of his works were printed for the first time, though at least one of them, *The Master and Margarita,* appeared only in censored form. (An unexpurgated edition was subsequently published in 1973.) There was, however, one work of Bulgakov that was not allowed to appear at all. *The Heart of a Dog,* an irreverent tale of unhappy attempts to graft onto a dog some of the traits of Soviet humanity of the 1920s, was printed only abroad. Indeed, during Stalin's lifetime two plays by an author whom Stalin himself had proclaimed the greatest Soviet poet were banished from the Soviet stage. Vladimir Mayakovsky's *The Bathhouse* and *The Bedbug,* both combining science fiction with disrespectful commentary on present and future Soviet society, returned to the Soviet repertory only in the mid-1950s.

The sensitive position of science fiction in the USSR, still evident in the 1970s, may be traceable to the difficulty of effecting a total separation between the genres of science fiction and social utopia. The Soviet novelist is thus faced with the risky task of portraying future society, however hazy its outlines, in a manner unobjectionable to Communist ideologues. This may well be one reason why so much Western science fiction is translated in the USSR. Western authors are not likely to refer to human values and social ties in a future society on earth (or on Mars, as the case may be) in terms that would be ideologically entirely acceptable. Unlike Soviet writers, however, *they are not expected to;* as non-Soviet authors, they may *not* know what the future holds. Never having had the benefit of a Soviet upbringing, foreign writers *may* err. But their errors can be patiently explained to Soviet readers who will treat them with indulgence. And a non-Soviet writer can certainly be forgiven for taking still another way out of the dilemma—one not permitted, alas, to a Soviet author of science fiction—namely, the avoidance of all references to socially meaningful human activity in a fantastic future world where Man has conquered nature and displaced God as King of the Universe.

Significant amounts of modern science fiction continue to be translated. Some works appear in anthologies (thus, a volume of American science fiction was published in 1960; there were two more in 1965); many are printed in periodicals;[59] still others appear as separate volumes (e.g., Isaac Asimov's *I, a Robot* in 1964; Asimov also appears frequently in Soviet periodicals). Of contemporary writers of science fiction, Americans seem to be most frequently translated, and the list is headed by Ray Bradbury. His most popular works in the USSR in the 1960s were *The Silver Locust,* which is set on Mars in the twenty-first century and has social overtones (blacks at long last agree to accept whites as equals), and *Fahrenheit 451.* The latter is usually presented to Soviet readers as science fiction, pure and simple. The novel's real subject, book burning ($451°$ F is the temperature at which paper catches fire), is understandably somewhat delicate in the USSR, although some Soviet critics did emphasize self-righteously that book burning, a vicious practice, is endemic to capitalism and fascism.

Social aspects of science are the central subject of the works of Mitchell Wilson, an American writer very widely read in the USSR, far more so than in his own country. Several of Wilson's novels were serialized in Soviet journals prior to their appearance in book form.[60] At least one, *Davy Mallory,* a sequel to *My Brother, My Enemy,* was received by a Soviet journal from the author in manuscript form.[61] *Live with Lightning* was first published in the USSR in 1951, two years after the novel's appearance in English, at a time when translation of modern Western authors, except for works by foreign Communists and ardent apologists for Stalin's policies, was very rare. Yet Mitchell Wilson, though not unfriendly to the USSR, did not fit this description. In fact, the staunchly Stalinist Soviet critic Roman Samarin was quite right in emphasizing in 1961 that "Wilson is in no way an adherent of socialism. He makes this quite clear through the character of Horvath [in *Meeting at a Far Meridian*] who confidently proclaims the stability of America's capitalist system."[62]

59. Typically, in *Inostrannaja literatura.* Thus, Robert Sheckley's "Therapy" (a short story from a 1956 collection of the American author's works) set in the year 2103 with a conflict built around the psychological differences between Martians and Man, was printed in No. 1, 1967.

60. Thus, *Meeting at a Far Meridian* was first printed in four consecutive issues (Nos. 1, 2, 3, and 4, 1961) of *Inostrannaja literatura.*

61. Published in *Inostrannaja literatura,* Nos. 6 and 7, 1959.

62. *Izvestija,* June 21, 1961. The comment is also to be viewed as more authoritative by virtue

What, then, induced Soviet publishers to bring out Mitchell Wilson's works in the darkest days of Stalinism and to continue publishing them thereafter? The figures are more than impressive in book form alone: in 1954–64, over 750,000 copies of *My Brother, My Enemy,* half that amount of *Live with Lightning,* and large printings of *Meeting at a Far Meridian.* Some clue may be found in a Soviet encyclopedia's comments on the latter work. In that novel, readers are told, "Shaken by an atomic explosion, a [American] physicist is disenchanted with his calling, with society, and with himself. His spiritual recovery begins during his trip to the USSR (Wilson himself has been to the USSR several times, and his works are better known here than in his country). Concentrating on problems of science and ethics, Wilson's novels are simultaneously valuable for their scientifically cognitive aspects."[63] Mitchell Wilson's novels are widely disseminated in the USSR because books dealing with science are thought to be useful, because they are genuinely popular, and also because the Soviet authorities apparently believe that readers in the USSR can be convinced that the ethical conflicts and crises of conscience described in Wilson's novels exist only in American and other capitalist societies. It is, of course, true that conflicts between science and *private business* in the USA do not have *exact* Soviet analogies. Still, analogies that make allowances for different social structures can and probably are made by some Soviet readers. As Deming Brown perceptively notes, there *are* conflicts between pure science and the interests of specific Soviet industrial enterprises; one such conflict was described in a famous post-Stalin novel, Vladimir Dudincev's *Not By Bread Alone,* in which a scientific discovery is suppressed because it would interfere with the commercial operations of a Soviet plant.[64] And a very famous Soviet scientist, Academician Andrei Sakharov, often called the father of the Soviet hydrogen bomb, did, obviously, experience some serious spiritual torment. In the early 1970s Sakharov was the unofficial head of the Soviet movement for

---

of its appearance in the official daily newspaper of the Soviet government rather than in an ordinary literary journal.

The Soviet critic's opinion of Mitchell Wilson's politics was confirmed by the American novelist's assertion that *My Brother, My Enemy* was *not* intended as a novel about conflicts between American scientists and their capitalist employers. Rather, wrote Mitchell Wilson, it is a study of two contrasting groups of scientists in the United States: the idealists and those merely interested in money. See *Inostrannaja literatura,* No. 7, 1956.

63. KL, Vol. VII (1972), p. 745. At one time plans were discussed for a joint Soviet-American film based on the novel, but the project was apparently abandoned.

64. "Despite their spectacular achievements, Soviet science and technology face impediments that are remarkably similar to those on which the tension of Wilson's novels is based. . . . This is in part the reason why Wilson's novels are so popular in Russia. For the Soviet reader does not view with pitying detachment the troubles of the American scientist, fighting to capture his own individual vision of the truth. The reader's own experience has taught him to recognize these troubles, and to feel a close sense of identification with them." Deming Brown, *Soviet Attitudes Toward American Writing,* pp. 188–89. Curiously, Mitchell Wilson is more popular with Soviet students than with engineers and technicians. See chapter 2.

democratic rights, a movement that also protested Soviet contributions to the world arms race; these activities earned him the Nobel Peace Prize in 1975.

Official benevolence toward Western writing about science was successfully exploited by unscrupulous Soviet publishers bent on making a quick profit. A translation of André Maspain's French novel *The Radioactive Cobalt Affair* was printed in 580,000 copies before the authorities caught on. It appears that the little-known author's book (Maspain is not listed in several standard Western reference works) is not about science at all. It is really about the dissolute life among the science jet set in France. Its scientific background was provided, it seems, to impart to it "redeeming social value," much as this was done, in less permissive days, with pornographic novels and films in the United States. There is no evidence of any indignant protests by the Soviet public, or that André Maspain's novel had to be pulped for lack of sales.[65]

A somewhat special case is that of Edgar Allan Poe who has, for many decades, enjoyed in Russia a degree of popularity nearly as great as in his native America (a twelve-volume set of his works was published in St. Petersburg in 1914). Moreover, Poe has been held in high esteem by Russian critics as a sophisticated craftsman. Edgar Allan Poe's poetry and his tales of horror and suspense, of which there are a number of successful Russian renditions, have their devotees. One can, however, also claim for Poe some educational significance; thus, *The Purloined Letter* was recently praised by a Western critic for its "analytical seriousness, an intellectual and semi-scientific bent."[66] *Hans Phaall* is prized by many as an outstanding example of science-fiction writing. These considerations may well have induced Soviet publishers to bring out, in 400,000 copies, a volume consisting of these two works and of *The Murders in the Rue Morgue*. There were also three anthologies of Poe's works, a total of over 300,000 copies.[67]

Throughout this chapter we have tacitly assumed that Soviet publishers were correct in believing that "juvenile" books, in a looser sense of the term,

65. The swindle was exposed in *Izvestija* on June 8, 1963. André Maspain's *Atomic Story*, originally published in French in 1961, was renamed by Soviet publishers *The Radioactive Cobalt Affair* and brought out in Russian in 1963. An introduction stated the novel's purpose as familiarizing "schoolchildren in the upper grades" with Western practices in such serious endeavors as "the application of nuclear energy in industry and in research" and peaceful uses of the atom in general. Such noble intentions, *Izvestija* argued, are not borne out by the contents of Maspain's novel, much of which is taken up with detailed accounts of life among France's hedonistic youth and loving descriptions of luxurious living conditions among segments of French society. There really was no need, *Izvestija* complained, to allow Soviet youngsters to read such paeans to the bourgeois way of life simply in order to learn what the peaceful atom is all about.

66. *The Penguin Companion*, Vol. III, p. 206.

67. For a detailed discussion, see Joan Delaney Grossman, *Edgar Allan Poe in Russia: A Study in Legend and Literary Influence* (Würzburg: Jal-Verlag, 1973).

including travel, adventure, science fiction, etc., were being read by an overwhelmingly juvenile audience. That such was the intent of Soviet cultural planners may be deduced from the fact that huge quantities of such books appeared either under the imprint of publishing houses that catered to this market (such as Detizdat, the Children's Publishing House, or the Young Communist League's Molodaja gvardija) or in series whose titles revealed that they were aimed at young readers (such as "Novels of Adventure" printed by the Geography Publishing House). As suggested in this chapter, many translations of ideologically dubious Western books were printed in the USSR apparently because they were expected to broaden young readers' cultural horizons, acquaint them with far-away times and distant lands, teach them resourcefulness, awaken scientific curiosity, encourage persistence and daring. The expectation was that such books would be read by a predominantly student audience, by young people who also, while attending school, read a great deal of ideologically solid Soviet literature under the watchful guidance of Soviet pedagogues.

There is, however, significant evidence that these objectives were not always attained and that books intended for Soviet adolescents were read by large numbers of adults. (Ironically, this state of affairs is a mirror image of the situation that obtains in the United States, where merchandise on sale in so-called "adult bookstores," i.e., pornography, often attracts juvenile customers.) It appears that large quantities of "juvenile" books were bought and read by people who were too old to profit from their positive educational features. Reports from bookstores and lending libraries suggested that translated West European and American adventure and travel books were being read, in part, at the expense of Soviet books published for adults. The reports were confirmed by attendance figures for cinemas showing similar Western imports as contrasted with theaters exhibiting Soviet films. Clearly, at the very least, juvenile Western books and films were to many Soviet adults an escape from Soviet literature and the cinema, perhaps even from Soviet values. At the same time, the impact of such Western books on adults would differ from their impact on children. An attempt was made earlier to suggest some possible reactions on the part of *adult* Soviet readers to the books of H. G. Wells and Mitchell Wilson. All of this raised a number of important questions and suggested serious implications, some of which were discussed in the pages of Soviet journals in 1957–58, in 1963–64, and in the years that followed. A few even impelled formal pronouncements by leading figures in the Soviet government, including N. S. Khrushchev himself. The subject will be examined in the closing chapter of this study.

# CHAPTER

# 5

# *Three Scourges of Mankind:*
# *Religion, Racism, War*

We shall now turn to one category of books favored by Soviet publishers for overtly political reasons, namely works that indirectly illustrate the claim that *Soviet* society, whatever its temporary imperfections, is already free of such ancient plagues as religious prejudice, racial injustice, and wars waged in the interests of exploiting social classes. After all, as every schoolchild is taught, in the USSR religious hatred and racial discrimination are both outlawed, while exploiting social classes disappeared after the October Revolution of 1917.

"Religion is the opium of the people"; this sentence from Karl Marx's *Introduction to a Critique of the Hegelian Philosophy of Right* has been invoked regularly in the USSR ever since the Revolution of 1917 in the unending campaign to stamp out religion. Less frequently cited is the sentence that immediately precedes it and that provides a clue to the reasons for the failure of the Soviet regime to accomplish that goal. The sentence reads: "Religion is the sign of the oppressed creature, the feelings of a heartless world, just as it is the spirit of unspiritual conditions."

Soviet antireligious propaganda is, as a rule, very crude. In that respect, there is little difference between the contents of the atheistic journal of the 1920s and 1930s, *Bezbožnik* (The Godless) and the present *Nauka i religija* (Science and Religion), except that the former was occasionally bawdy while the latter is always earnest. Other changeless features of Soviet antireligious polemics are failure to distinguish between religious faith and the churches as institutions and refusal to concede that religion in our time is not the same as it was centuries ago. Whenever this must be admitted, such changes are explained by the *weakness* of religious institutions and thus their *inability* to enforce what are supposedly their unchanging aims, although exceptions are occasionally made for individual friendly clerics.[1] On the whole, however, religion and the churches (the concepts are used interchangeably) continue to be identified, actually or potentially, with political reaction, intolerance, corruption, and anti-intellectualism.

The lack of distinction between opposition to religion and criticism of the clergy, between attacks on obscurantism and superstition and enmity toward faith in God, makes it possible to enlist in the antireligious campaigns scores of works of Western literature that are in some way critical of religious institutions and observances. In fact, prior to World War II the All-Union Society of Militant Atheists, the publisher of the magazine *Bezbož-nik,* operated a publishing house that printed much translated West European literature.[2] At least one translated novel, Harald Alfred Bergstedt's *St. Jurgen's Day,* was made into an antireligious Soviet film.[3]

That translations of Western literature continue to be used as antireligious propaganda in the post-Stalin period is attested by the July 7, 1954, resolution of the Central Committee of the Communist Party of the Soviet Union entitled "On Serious Shortcomings in Scientific-Atheistic Propaganda and Measures for Its Improvement." Among steps to be taken were the following:

> 5. To propose [*predložit'*] to the USSR Academy of Sciences Publishing House to bring out works and excerpts from works by thinkers of antiquity and of the French Enlightenment, and to supply them with popularly presented introductions.

1. Thus, for example, Hewlett Johnson (1874–1968), the Dean of Canterbury, was also one of the most active apologists for Stalin's policies in the West: "So great was the mutual admiration of the Dean and the Soviet authorities that, to his slight embarrassment, he was accorded more lines in the *Soviet Encyclopedia* than Jesus Christ." David Caute, *The Fellow-Travellers: A Postscript to the Enlightenment* (New York: Macmillan, 1973), p. 248.

2. There was also a separate Anti-Religious Library of Fiction, sponsored by the publishing house of the Young Communist League, and the Anti-Religious Library of the Military Publishing House (Voenizdat). See this writer's *Russian Classics in Soviet Jackets,* p. 79.

3. Bergstedt's Danish novel, first published in 1919, "is a satire on the hypocrisy of the church and of the clergy (this work was filmed in the USSR)." KL, Vol. I (1962), p. 556. During World War II Bergstedt collaborated with the Nazis, and was subsequently sentenced to a prison term, a fact duly noted in the Soviet encyclopedia. Nevertheless, *St. Jurgen's Day* was apparently considered so valuable as antireligious ammunition that it was republished in the USSR in 150,000 copies, a decision made easier by Bergstedt's death in 1955. There is at least one other case of literary amnesty of a convicted Nazi collaborator: a multivolume set of the Norwegian novelist Knut Hamsun was launched in 1970 under the editorship of the late Boris Sučkov.

7. To direct [*objazat'*] the Foreign Languages Publishing House to bring out the best works by foreign scholars and writers on the subject of religion and atheism.

8. To direct the State Publishing House of Literature [Goslitizdat] to arrange for mass publication of inexpensive editions of classics of Russian and foreign literature dealing with atheist subject matter as well as for the publication of fairy tales, folk songs, proverbs, and sayings directed against religion.[4]

The overwhelming majority of translated literary works with anticlerical and antireligious motifs originated in Roman Catholic countries: France, Italy, Spain, and, more recently, Latin America. On the one hand, this argues for greater receptivity to such works in Russia, a country with a strong anti-Catholic tradition perpetuated in her own literary heritage. At the same time this consideration may limit the didactic effectiveness of literary works that mock or criticize customs and institutions quite different from those of Russian Orthodoxy, such as, for instance, priestly celibacy (Russian priests do marry). More importantly, translated antireligious literature is largely ineffective in the USSR because, given the distance in time and the remoteness of the specific objects of criticism, it is unlikely to shake the faith of true believers, while the number of inert churchgoers who cling to religious observance because of habit and social pressures is very low in a country committed to atheism. Furthermore, such people are to be found, for the most part, among the older and less educated citizens, i.e., those who do not read many books. Indeed, it is more than likely that the Soviet publishing authorities' attempts to exploit the antireligious potential of West European and American writing ultimately benefit Soviet readers, because they result in the publication and dissemination of many literary works, ranging from classics to recent Western best sellers, that otherwise might not have been made available.

There is no work of Russian literature remotely comparable to Giovanni Boccaccio's *Decameron,* which appeared in 1954–64 in well over half a million copies in four languages. A Soviet critic was quite correct in his evaluation of the fourteenth-century collection of tales as "a book, one of whose central themes is criticism of the Catholic church, mockery of the Catholic clergy, of priests and monks, and of the Papal court."[5] More likely of central interest to Soviet readers is *Decameron's* vivid eroticism; the fact that the seducers are the ostensibly celibate monks and priests is, in all

4. *KPSS o kul'ture, prosveščenii i nauke.* Sbornik dokumentov (Moscow: Izdatel'stvo politi-českoj literatury, 1963), p. 235.
5. KL, Vol. I (1962), p. 671.

probability, of little import. Boccaccio's less famous countryman and contemporary, Franco Sacchetti, wrote novellas quite similar in subject matter
and tendency. These were printed in 320,000 copies; the *Literary Encyclopedia* notes with approval that Sacchetti's works have been on the Catholic
Index of forbidden books since the eighteenth century.[6] Benvenuto Cellini's
sixteenth-century Italian autobiography, filled with accounts of adventure
and amorous escapades and containing numerous gibes at the Catholic
church, appeared in 150,000 copies.

The sensuous and often anticlerical verse of François Villon has many
admirers among the Soviet intelligentsia. Still, fifteenth-century French
poetry is not likely to have mass appeal in translation; a volume of Villon
was printed in 25,000 copies. Prose is quite another matter. M. N. Ljubimov's 1961 translation into Russian of *Gargantua and Pantagruel* is likely
to make François Rabelais even more popular in years to come—assuming
the book remains in print. The 850,000 copies of the novel attest that the
earthy and irreverent humor of Rabelais is appreciated by the Russian
public, while the fact that the book attacks the church may prompt Soviet
publishers to assure its availability.[7]

Varying degrees of criticism of religion and the church were a factor
in the republication of three famous French authors of the eighteenth
century. Indeed, their appearance was a direct response to the July 7,
1954, resolution of the Central Committee of the Communist Party referred to earlier. Charles Louis de Montesquieu's *Persian Letters* (first
published in Russian in 1789) were issued in 150,000 copies; religion and
the church rank high among the foibles and vices of French society
noted in the book by two visitors from distant Persia. More pointed
criticism of religious institutions could be found in the writings of Denis
Diderot whose ties to Russia were strong. Among his admirers was
Catherine II, and it was upon her invitation that Diderot lived in
Russia in 1773–74, a stay that inspired a number of his essays. Recent
Soviet editions of Diderot include nearly 250,000 copies of *Rameau's
Nephew*, a portrait of an upper class parasite and his milieu; 100,000
copies of *Jacques le fataliste*, a mock-picaresque novel; and 175,000 of
*The Nun*, the latter an account of a girl's forcible incarceration in a
convent. While a Western critic may argue that *The Nun* "is less an an-
ticlerical satire" than "a fictional examination of moral and psychologi-

6. Ibid., Vol. VI (1971), p. 608.
7. "*Pantagruelisme* rejects suppression of sensual needs, and any kind of asceticism, be it
religious, moral, economic, or political. It also rejects any limits on spiritual freedom and any
kind of dogmatism." KL, Vol. VI (1971), p. 130. An important study of Rabelais was written
by M. M. Baxtin, best known as the author of a major monograph on Dostoyevsky.

cal aberrations,"[8] to Soviet critics as well as readers, the novel's message is more self-evident. Apparently it was felt that Diderot's writings would be particularly effective in combating religion; this is suggested by the publication, in 1956, of a volume of Diderot entitled *Selected Atheistic Works.*[9] Still, it comes as no surprise that Diderot's stature as a foe of religion is overshadowed by Voltaire's. Of Voltaire's works, most widely printed was *The Simpleton* (over half a million copies); the work, Soviet readers were informed, "attacks religious intolerance and obscurantism," an accurate enough description.[10] There was also an edition of *Philosophical Tales* (75,000 copies) and small printings of *The Maid of Orleans* ("a biting anticlerical satire"[11]) and of *The Babylonian Princess,* which denounces religious fanaticism.

Four nineteenth-century West European poets—three Frenchmen and one Italian—may have been published, in part, because of the strongly anticlerical tendency of their verse. There were anthologies (25,000 copies each) of Giosué Carducci, "a steadfast opponent of Christianity, which he views as an obstacle to historical progress,"[12] and of Charles Leconte de Lisle who "rejects religion, particularly Catholicism—'the beast in purple' —as a moral justification of bourgeois society."[13] That the publishing fortunes of foreign authors in the USSR are affected by many considerations can be seen from the vast disparity in the press runs of Pierre-Jean de Béranger and Arthur Rimbaud. The poetry of both is rich in criticism of the Church. While in Béranger's verse that criticism most often assumes the form of carefree bawdiness, the tone of Rimbaud's verse is, by contrast, serious: even a non-Soviet source describes it as "violently anticlerical and anti-Christian."[14] Politically, both were equally "progressive" for their time. "[Rimbaud] sympathized with the [Paris] Commune and strove to participate personally in the struggle. Rimbaud dedicated to the Commune verses that are the supreme achievement of French revolutionary poetry."[15] Béranger's credentials are no less impressive, and his satirical barbs at the clergy, the royalists, and the bourgeoisie received what must be to Soviet critics supreme recognition: "Karl Marx called Béranger 'immortal.'"[16] And yet Rimbaud is very rarely published in the USSR (even though his verse has

8. *The Penguin Companion,* Vol. II, p. 227.
9. D. Didro, *Izbrannye ateističeskie proizvedenija* (Moscow, 1956). No information available on the press run. Similar use was made of four stories by Guy de Maupassant which were published as a single volume entitled *Ateističeskie rasskazy.*
10. KL, Vol. I (1962), p. 1030.
11. Ibid., p. 1033.
12. Ibid., Vol. III (1966), p. 402.
13. Ibid., Vol. IV (1967), pp. 102–03.
14. *The Penguin Companion,* Vol. II, p. 655.
15. KL, Vol. VI (1971), p. 250.
16. Ibid., Vol. I (1962), p. 551.

been often translated by some of Russia's most eminent modern poets), and then only on a modest scale: the post-Stalin anthology was printed in 25,000 copies. By contrast, Béranger is published frequently and—for translations of poetry—in editions destined for wide dissemination: over 500,000 copies in 1954–64, in Russian, Estonian, Belorussian, and Ukrainian, as well as 8,000 in the original French. A likely reason for this enormous disparity in the availability in the USSR of Rimbaud's and Béranger's works is to be sought in the aesthetics of the two poets. Rimbaud's poetry is complex and his view of reality is reminiscent of the Russian Symbolists whose acceptance by Soviet literary criticism is only halfhearted. Béranger, on the other hand, is simple and clear, and the "message" of his songs is quite unambiguous; he is, in short, closer to the Socialist Realist ideal of poetry. No doubt, the simplicity of Béranger's work makes him attractive also to a larger number of readers than the artistically sophisticated poetry of Rimbaud. Yet in the final analysis no true comparison is really possible. There is every reason to believe that the 25,000 copies of Rimbaud that were made available did not begin to satisfy the readers' demand. Indeed, this may also be true even of the much larger printings of Béranger.

Juan Valera has personal ties to Russia, where he served for a time as the ambassador of Spain. His novel *Pepita Jiménez* makes for enjoyable reading: it is a tale of a lusty young widow who seduces a seminarian and forces him to marry her, stealing him, as it were, from the Church. The novel appeared in 150,000 copies.[17] More pointedly antireligious is *Doña Perfecta,* a novel by Benito Pérez Galdós first published in Russia in 1882: it is a partly autobiographical account of the misery of a young liberal in a fanatically religious Spanish town. A new Russian translation was made in 1956 and published in 90,000 copies; an additional 7,000 copies were printed in Lithuanian, the language of the only sizable Roman Catholic group in the USSR. Other works by Pérez Galdós include 150,000 copies of *Torquemada,* a cycle of four novels that show the social climbing of a usurer obsessed with the idea that his dead son was a god, and two novels about the Spanish-Napoleonic wars, *Trafalgar* (100,000) and *Cadiz* (15,000). Leopoldo Àlas y Ureña's *Farewell Cordera,* a humorous, good-natured tale mildly critical of aristocrats and the clergy and appealing for religious tolerance, was printed in 250,000 copies.

Conrad Ferdinand Meyer, a nineteenth-century Swiss author writing in German, is remembered chiefly for the novel *Jürg Jenatsch* and the novella *Plautus in a Convent. Jürg Jenatsch* is about a seventeenth-century Luth-

---

17. The *Literary Encyclopedia* summarizes the novel in more dignified language: "In the novels *Pepita Jiménez* and *Doña Luz,* he [Valera] expressed his opposition to religious asceticism, defended man's physical joys and the life of the senses." Ibid., p. 835.

eran pastor who is a patriot and a hero in Switzerland's struggle for independence; the *Literary Encyclopedia* criticizes the novel because it "ignores the role of the people in historical events."[18] Curiously, this *positive* portrait of a Lutheran pastor was published in 30,000 copies in Latvian, the language of one of the two Lutheran ethnic groups in the USSR, an oversight, no doubt, on the part of the ideological watchdogs in the Baltic republic. Meyer's *Plautus in a Convent,* of which more than 500,000 copies were printed in Russian and another 115,000 in Ukrainian, is a mildly anticlerical tale of intrigue, although the verdict of the *Literary Encyclopedia* is more emphatic: "The novella *Plautus in a Convent* unmasks the corrupt morals of the Catholic Church and portrays the triumph of humanistic principles."[19]

Roger Martin du Gard's *Jean Barois,* a novel depicting "an intellectual torn . . . between religious faith and scientific skepticism,"[20] was published in 250,000 copies. The Colombian poet Luis Carlos Lopez is known chiefly for his ironic verse about provincial life in his country. The colors were darker when viewed through the lens of the *Literary Encyclopedia:* Lopez is said to have satirized the authorities and "oppression by the clergy."[21] An anthology of his verse appeared in 10,000 copies. The eminent Spanish writer and philosopher Miguel de Unamuno was represented by 100,000 copies of an anthology of his novellas; aside from their intrinsic merits, the decision to bring them out may have been influenced by the fact that "many of Unamuno's works are banned by the Catholic Church."[22] The March 1959 issue of *Novyj mir* featured the first Russian translations of two short stories by the recently deceased Italian writer Corrado Alvaro (1895–1956). One of the stories, "Our Neighborhood," is reminiscent of Dostoyevsky's "Legend of the Grand Inquisitor." A young Italian priest, despondent over the accounts of sins he hears at confession, asks for a transfer, but a cardinal turns down his request on the grounds that sin is eternal.

Finally, we should mention four authors then living, all writing in French, whose works were published during the period 1954–64. Jacques Prévert is a poet in the tradition of François Villon; he also writes children's verse. A volume of his poetry appeared, but no information is available on the press run.[23] Daniel Gillès de Pelichy, a Belgian, is the author of *State of Grace,* "an anticlerical novel," and of *Coupon No. 44,* in which "Gillès exposes with considerable power the collapse of the mercenary Belgian

18. Ibid., Vol. IV (1967), p. 733.
19. Ibid.
20. *The Penguin Companion,* Vol. II, p. 515.
21. KL, Vol. IV (1967), p. 422.
22. Ibid., Vol. VII (1972), p. 808.
23. His verse is described antibourgeois, anticolonialist, and anticlerical. KL, Vol. V (1968), pp. 953–54.

bourgeoisie, which had betrayed [to the Nazis] the country's resistance movement." Again, no statistics are available on press runs.[24] Beti Mongo (pseudonym of Alexandre Biyidi) is an African writer from the Cameroons who now lives in France. His *Poor Christ from Bomba,* which satirizes missionary activity in Africa, was printed in an unspecified number of copies.[25] And Roger Peyrefitte's *The Keys of St. Peter,* "a tract directed against the Catholic Church and the Pope,"[26] was printed in 20,000 copies, but only in Lithuanian. The purpose of the publication was thus made obvious: the book, it was hoped, would help discredit Roman Catholicism in the Soviet Union's only republic with a predominantly Catholic population.

Whether Peyrefitte's sensationalist book, which attacks present-day Catholicism, had the intended impact on its Catholic readers in Soviet Lithuania is difficult to say. As suggested earlier, the overall effectiveness of anticlerical Western literature as an aid in combatting religion in the USSR is very much open to question, particularly since most of its likely readers are in any case indifferent to religion. More probably, the majority of Soviet readers are attracted to anticlerical West European and American writing because of a number of its characteristic features, which set it apart from modern Soviet literature. Much of this translated writing consists of comic and satirical prose and verse, of which there is little in Soviet Russia's own literature. Much of it is irreverent and iconoclastic, both literally and figuratively—again, in contrast to Soviet writing which is, for the most part, respectful of official dogmas and authorities. Nor should one overlook another attraction that Western anticlerical writing may hold for Soviet readers. Unbelievable as this may seem in the 1970s, Boccaccio's *Decameron,* Rabelais's *Gargantua and Pantagruel,* and even Diderot's *The Nun* contain some of the most explicit descriptions of sex available in Soviet bookstores and libraries, thus tempting readers with a degree of eroticism that would never be tolerated in Soviet novels.[27]

The subject of racial injustice ranks high on the Soviet list of evils of the capitalist world, and foreign novels, poetry, and plays that deal with the subject are viewed favorably by Soviet critics and publishers. Many of these were written by authors prominently identified with pro-Soviet causes; these will be discussed in a separate chapter.[28] Since most West European and

24. KL, Vol. II (1964), p. 939.

25. Another book by the same author, *Mission Accomplished,* was printed in Russian in 85,000 copies, and in 30,000 in Estonian.

26. KL, Vol. V (1968), p. 639.

27. Curiously, the only *religious* work found in a post-Stalin Soviet periodical were some excerpts from the biblical Song of Songs, a love poem. It appeared in the Ukrainian literary journal *Dnipro,* No. 12, 1970.

28. See chapter 7. Non-Soviet authors in that category are treated somewhat differently from others. For that reason works dealing with the subject of racism are discussed in two different

American books that raise the problem of racial discrimination address themselves specifically to the plight of the black, it is easy enough for Soviet critics, as well as readers, to identify racism with the non-Soviet world: there are no blacks in the USSR. On the other hand, there seems to have been a conscious effort to avoid the publication of books that might suggest some undesirable parallels with Soviet policies. Thus, in spite of the abundance in Western writing of literary treatment of anti-Semitism, very few books were published that fit that description. In fact, avoidance of the subject extended even to militantly anti-Nazi works describing the martyrdom and heroism of Jews during the Hitler era. A mere 15,000 copies of *The Diary of Anne Frank,* a document of a Jewish girl in Nazi-occupied Europe, was among the few exceptions.[29]

A number of works that deal with the oppression of blacks, including *Uncle Tom's Cabin,* were discussed in chapter four. Other works with historical settings include *Cecilia Valdés,* a Cuban abolitionist novel by Cirilo Villaverde (50,000 copies); a volume of verse describing the horrors of slavery by the nineteenth-century Brazilian poet Antônio de Castro Alves (10,000); *Juyungo,* a picaresque novel from Ecuador by Adalberto Ortiz (25,000); and a very small printing (2,500 copies) of Dubose Heyward's *Porgy.* The last was probably printed in connection with a very successful tour of the USSR by an American company that featured George Gershwin's opera *Porgy and Bess,* based on Heyward's story about Negro life in old Charleston, South Carolina. The tour, which began in December 1955, was the first ever in the USSR by American artists.

Most of the antiracist books published were set either in South Africa or in the United States. Of the former, there was a surprisingly small press run of a collection of Alan Paton's writings (15,000 in Ukrainian),[30] and of *I and My Son,* a Swedish novel by Sara Lidman.[31] Much larger were the figures for *Let the Day Perish,* a novel by the South African novelist Gerald Gordon. The *Literary Encyclopedia* notes with disappointment that Gordon fails to demonstrate who are the *real* opponents of racism (i.e., the Communists), but finds the novel, nevertheless, a good documentary ac-

---

chapters, an unsatisfactory but probably unavoidable solution.

29. It was published with an introduction by Ilya Ehrenburg. For general information on the subject see Lionel Kochan (ed.), *The Jews in Soviet Russia Since 1917,* 2nd ed. rev. (London: Oxford University Press, 1972).

30. A Soviet reference work finds Alan Paton's fiction and journalism rather moderate (KL, Vol. V [1968], p. 639). This stands in contrast to his appraisal in a Western source, which describes *Cry, the Beloved Country:* "It is a passionately propagandist novel about a black man's country and the white man's laws. . . . Paton is not afraid to shout, or to preach." *The Penguin Companion,* Vol. I, p. 415. There was also a collection of South African short stories entitled *Debbi, uxodi domoj,* (Debbie, Go Home), after Paton's story in the volume.

31. Printed in 20,000 copies. Another novel by the same author, *The Land of Mosquitos,* was printed in Latvian in 15,000 copies. The latter work "emphasizes the position of women in capitalist society." KL, Vol. IV (1967), p. 192.

count of the plight of people of mixed blood in South Africa. *Let the Day Perish* was printed in four languages in 250,000 copies, as well as in 20,000 in the original English.[32] No information is available on the press run of Jack Cope's *The Fair House,* which described the unequal struggle between South Africa's white soldiers and Zulu tribesmen driven off their land, or on a collection of his short stories.[33]

The most important single new work dealing with the problem of racism in the United States in a contemporary setting was Harper Lee's sensitive novel, *To Kill a Mockingbird.* The plot of the novel conforms to a stereotype: a black man is accused in Alabama of raping a white woman. The novel's effectiveness stems in large part from the choice of vantage point. The "naive" narrator is a child, a daughter of the white lawyer who defends the black in court. *To Kill a Mockingbird* was first printed in the journal *Inostrannaja literatura,* and was then published as a paperback in the *Roman-gazeta* series in one million copies.[34] The estimated propaganda value of Harper Lee's novel, and thus the justification for the exceptionally large press run, is apparent from a plot summary published for the benefit of Soviet librarians and schoolteachers: "The author shows how Jean-Louise and Jim [characters in the novel] begin to understand . . . that in America, killing a mockingbird is considered a sin, but taking a man's life only because his skin happens to be black is a civic duty."[35]

A number of other important works on the subject of race in the United States also appeared in *Inostrannaja literatura;* these included James Baldwin's *Blues for Mr. Charlie,*[36] Lorraine Hansberry's play *A Raisin in the Sun,*[37] and Tennessee Williams's play *Orpheus Descending.*[38] An interesting story by William Eastlake, "In A While, Crocodile," combined the problems of *two* American minorities: a black musician sells his instrument to help poor Indians, but then dies of starvation himself.[39]

Both institutionalized religion and racism are treated by Soviet sources as attributes of non-Soviet societies, as age-old scourges of mankind that have no place in a Soviet state where, it is claimed, they linger on only as

32. Ibid., Vol. II (1964), p. 277.
33. Shorter anti-racist works are occasionally printed in journals, e.g., Ronald Segal's *The Tokolosh* in *Inostrannaja literatura,* No. 5, 1961.
34. *Inostrannaja literatura,* No. 3, 1963.
35. *Xudožestvennaja literatura, literaturovedenie, iskusstvo. Rekomedatel'nyj ukazatel' novinok* (April–June 1963) (Moscow: Ministerstvo Kul'tury RSFSR, 1963), p. 70.
36. *Inostrannaja literatura,* No. 11, 1964.
37. Ibid., No. 11, 1959.
38. Ibid., No. 7, 1960. While the main protagonists of Tennessee Williams's *Orpheus Descending* are not black, racial tensions are very much in evidence: a white who helps blacks is harassed, a "nigger-loving" white woman is refused service in stores, etc.
39. *Novyj mir,* No. 5, 1963. It seems that the story was published in Russian five months prior to its appearance in the original. Gerald Haslam, *William Eastlake* (Austin, Texas: Steck-Vaugh Co., 1970), p. 43, lists the story's publication in English in *Cavalcade,* XVI (October 1963).

vestigial superstitions and prejudices among backward elements of the population. Clearly, no such simplistic claims are possible with reference to the
third and most terrible affliction of mankind—war. The contradictions
inherent in the Soviet treatment of the subject will be discussed at some
length in the concluding chapter of this study, devoted to an analysis of the
desired and possible effects of the publication and reading of translated
foreign literature in the USSR. For the time being we shall merely note the
Soviet view that "Marxism-Leninism distinguishes between two kinds of
war, the just and the unjust, the progressive and the reactionary. . . . Unjust
wars are extensions of a policy of social and national oppression, while just
wars are extensions of a policy of struggle for liberation from class and
national oppression and of defense of a people from the threat of enslavement."[40] Dissemination of translated antimilitaristic literature is thus a
problem of considerable complexity and involves serious risks. While instill-
ing hatred and contempt for "unjust" wars and for armies defending "unjust" causes is, needless to say, much to be desired, Soviet publishers, critics,
and ideologues must make every effort to prevent possible extension of such
sentiments to *all* armies and *all* wars.

Like most Western literary traditions, prerevolutionary Russian writing
includes works that extol the heroism and travail of war as well as books
that emphasize the senselessness of human slaughter and the boredom of
military routine. The latter tendency became stronger at the beginning of
the twentieth century and is best exemplified by Alexander Kuprin's *The
Duel.* Kuprin's novel appeared in 1905, shortly after the stunning defeat of
the Russian navy by tne Japanese, and became very popular in part because
of its outspoken antimilitarism. By contrast, antimilitarism in Soviet literature, particularly since the 1930s, is found only in portrayals of "unjust"
wars waged in the name of "unjust" causes, with foreign or historically
distant settings. In works that describe wars against the Soviet state, enemy
forces are, as a rule, depicted in crudely unflattering terms; only very rarely
can a sensitive Soviet writer allow that the adversaries might have been
misguided men fighting for a lost cause. Mikhail Bulgakov's *The White
Guard* is one such exception, though it must be noted that the novel
had originally appeared abroad in the more tolerant atmosphere of the
1920s. Mikhail Sholokhov's *Silent Don* (1928–40) is also a partial exception to this rule. By and large, however, Soviet prose, drama, and verse
dealing with military subject matter, even works that describe Soviet de-
feats in the early stages of World War II, emphasize the heroism and
patriotism of the Soviet soldier. In all of Soviet literature, there is not

40. *Sovetskaja istoričeskaja ènciklopedija,* Vol. III (Moscow: Gosudarstvennoe Naučnoe
Izdatel'stvo "Sovetskaja ènciklopedija," 1963), pp. 625–26.

a single work that actually satirizes the Soviet military.[41]

Not unexpectedly, most of the antimilitaristic literature published in the Soviet Union deals with World War II, much of it written by German authors. In the USSR, where in the 1950s and 1960s memories of the horror of that war were still vivid among all but the very young, such books must have been of singular interest: they showed the war through the eyes of former enemies, thus complementing in a way the vast body of Soviet writing on the same subject. The majority of authors were East Germans, and their books are thus outside the scope of this study.[42] West German writers were fewer. Most important among them was Heinrich Böll. Two of Böll's novels with wartime settings were published: *Adam, Where Art Thou?* and *Billiards at Half Past Nine.* The first describes the horrors and futility of war. The Soviet evaluation of the novel is more pointed. *Adam, Where Art Thou?,* which portrays worn-out German soldiers toward the end of the war, is said to emphasize "the personal responsibility of his [Böll's] compatriots for crimes they committed during the war unleashed by Hitler."[43] Of the second, a Western critic writes: "It is Böll's matter-of-fact presentation of the brutalities of racial persecution, the lethal vacuity of *Wehrmacht* life, and the grim aspects of daily existence under the Nazis, which allows the full horror of recent German history to emerge on the pages of these tales."[44]

Another West German, Hans Werner Richter, a founder of Gruppe-47, a loose association of left-wing writers, was represented by the novel *Thou Shalt Not Kill.* The *Literary Encyclopedia* describes this work as "permeated with antiwar pathos; it relates the story of a German family that was almost entirely wiped out by the war."[45] Still another was the young novelist Manfred Gregor (b. 1929), author of *The Bridge,* a pathetic account

41. One of the better known Soviet plays of the prewar period, with a Civil War setting (and describing a Soviet defeat), bore a characteristic title, *The Optimistic Tragedy* (by Vsevolod Višnevskij). In 1949 Jurij German's novel *Podpolkovnik medicinskoj služby (Lieutenant Colonel of the Medical Corps)* was discontinued after the appearance of the first installment in the journal *Zvezda* because its hero was overly introspective and insufficiently heroic. During the post-Stalin "thaw" a number of works were criticized for similar shortcomings, notably Konstantin Simonov's *Živye i mertvye* (*The Living And the Dead,* 1959). Significantly, the first Soviet novel to treat the Soviet army without due reverence circulated in the USSR in the 1970s in *samizdat* and was ultimately published in the West: Vladimir Vojnovič, *Žizn' i neobyknovennye priključenija soldata Ivana Čonkina.* Roman-anekdot v pjati častjax. (Paris: YMCA Press, 1975).
42. Similarly, we shall not consider what is probably the most important single antimilitarist novel available in the USSR, Jaroslav Hašek's *Good Soldier Schweik,* a biting Czech satire of the old Austro-Hungarian army. The effectiveness of this novel may be gauged from its numerous editions, as well as adaptations for the stage and film, and also from reports that at different times military authorities in various countries sought to prevent the novel's dissemination among soldiers.
43. *Xudožestvennaja literatura,* (October–December 1963) (Moscow, 1964), p. 52.
44. *Encyclopedia of World Literature in the 20th Century,* Vol. I, p. 149. No information is available on the press run of either title.
45. KL, Vol. VI (1971), p. 310.

of a group of German boys, almost children, who are drafted into the army
and ordered to defend the Third Reich in the closing days of the war.[46]

The most important Western novel with a wartime setting was *Le Commandant Watrin* by Armand Lanoux. Within a year after its publication
abroad it was issued in Russian in half a million copies, with an additional
13,000 in Ukrainian and 8,000 in the original French. The preferential
treatment accorded *Le Commandant Watrin* is explained by two of its
features: criticism of pacifist ideas (i.e., objections to participation even in
"just" wars) and the singling out of a Communist as a symbol of resistance
to the Nazis. According to the *Literary Encyclopedia* the novel, which is
set in a German camp for French prisoners early in the war, has two central
characters: "One of them is a lieutenant, formerly a schoolteacher, struggling with his pacifist scruples. The other, a career officer, in May 1940 had
carried out orders to execute a Communist soldier. Now he realizes that
blind obedience had made him a tool of traitors to his country. The heroes
of the novel begin to understand the necessity of fighting for the liberation
of France."[47]

A similar work by another French author, Robert Merle's *La Mort est
mon métier (Death is My Profession)*, a novel about Rudolf Lang, the
notorious SS commandant of Auschwitz, was given an interpretation
closely resembling that of Lanoux's *Le Commandant Watrin.* In the opinion of a Soviet critic, the novel about the henchman of Auschwitz belongs
with those works of Robert Merle which examine "the problem of violence,
of attitudes toward war, of man's personal responsibility for everything
taking place in society at large. . . . Merle progresses from pacifism and an
abstract humanism toward an understanding of revolutionary violence. *La
Mort est mon métier* is an anti-Fascist book aimed against the Prussian cult
of militarism and blind obedience to 'superhuman' leaders."[48]

Finally, there were some works that dealt with two favorite themes of
Soviet propaganda in the years preceding West Germany's rapprochement
with the USSR, namely the claim that, unlike socialist East Germany, in
capitalist and "revanchist" West Germany the old Nazis continued to
prosper and there was an ominous revival of German militarism. Günther
Weisenborn's novel *Der Velforger (The Avenger)* described attempts to
uncover Nazi criminals that were never brought to trial.[49] Marcello Ven-

46. The novel (which was also made into a successful film in Western Europe) was published
in *Inostrannaja literatura,* Nos. 10 and 11, 1960.
47. KL, Vol. IV (1967), p. 27. The dating of the execution of the French Communist soldier
is somewhat unusual. In May 1940, i.e., at the height of the Nazi-Soviet honeymoon, French
Communists generally abstained from anti-Nazi activity. They became active in the Resistance
following Hitler's attack on Russia on June 22, 1941.
48. KL, Vol. IV (1967), p. 784. The novel was published in Ukrainian in 65,000 copies. There
was also an undisclosed number of copies of a Russian play based on the novel.
49. *Inostrannaja literatura,* No. 1, 1963.

turi's novella *Vacanza tedesca (A German Vacation)* told of a former SS-man who could not tolerate the thought that a comrade of his was buried in Italy and made plans to bring his remains for reburial in Germany. The old SS-man's young German wife cannot understand his Nazi fanaticism and sympathizes with the Italian villagers, who meet them with open hostility.[50] Wolfdietrich Schnurre's *Eine Rechnung die nicht aufgeht* (roughly, *The Figures Won't Balance*) was a spoof on the new German *Reichswehr*: a herd of sheep ruins army maneuvers, and a general is nearly killed by a wounded ram.[51]

The most important Western book dealing with Soviet Russia's involvement in a war other than World War II published in 1954–64 was Väinö Linna's Finnish trilogy *Pohjantähden alla*, translated into Russian under the title *Zdes', pod Poljarnoj zvezdoju (Here, Under the Polar Star)*. A Western critic writes:

> His [Linna's] particular field of interest has been the Finnish Civil War of 1918 and the complicated tangle of causes behind it. He shows in detail how the seeds of the war lay in a system of land tenure bristling with inequalities and the unrealistic idealism of an intelligentsia devoid of any genuine understanding. He brings out the lack of political foresight with which the socialists behaved and which helped make the tragedy inevitable. His political comments in, and in subsequent defense of, *Pohjantähden alla*, a trilogy (1959–62), have given rise to much controversy: he accuses the historians of countenancing a "white lie" by perpetuating the myth of a "war of liberation" [from Russia—MF] and of a white army actuated by purely idealistic motives.[52]

The implication of Linna's views was that Finland might have been better served by remaining a part of the Russian state, then already a Soviet Republic. His attack on the "myth" of the nobility of the Finnish cause was further emphasized by descriptions of White atrocities of which the Reds were the victims. Linna's case was the more persuasive because he was not a Communist, but considered himself a spokesman for Finland's smallholding peasants. One can almost sense a feeling of hidden satisfaction in the *Literary Encyclopedia*'s complaint that Linna "was not inclined to recognize the enormous role played by Finland's Communists in the struggle against reaction in the period between the 1920s and the 1940s."[53] It was apparently felt that Linna's non-Communist credentials enhanced the effectiveness of his pro-Soviet, "revisionist" view of Finnish history.

In a way, the case of Väinö Linna embodies the essence of one major

50. *Ibid.*, No. 10, 1962.
51. *Novyj mir*, No. 6, 1960.
52. *The Penguin Companion*, Vol. II, p. 480.
53. KL, Vol. IV (1967), p. 203. No information was given on the press run of Linna's novel.

feature of Western literature that accounts for its attractiveness to Soviet publishers and educators. Given appropriate selectivity in the choice of authors and works, and also consistently biased Soviet commentaries on them, Western writing offers an opportunity to provide Soviet readers with a picture of life in the capitalist West that is unattractive enough to make even Soviet conditions look tolerable by comparison. Frightening accounts of life under capitalism are, of course, a regular feature of Soviet journalism; there are also many Soviet literary works that perform a similar function. Not unreasonably, however, such accounts must be suspected of bias by a Soviet public that has, over the decades, grown accustomed to the all-pervasiveness of state propaganda with its frequently proven exaggerations and downright falsehoods. By contrast, similarly grim pictures of life in the "bourgeois" world are more likely to be believed when drawn by non-Soviet writers, and their trustworthiness is certainly considered greater if their authors are themselves "bourgeois."

In all likelihood, Soviet readers of books exposing the horrors of a war that was unleashed within their memory by the Nazis identify quite spontaneously and strongly with the victims and foes of Nazism. They also probably agree with the implied message of many such works, namely that armed resistance was the only way to liberate mankind from the Nazi plague. On the other hand, their response to literary works condemning wars further removed from personal experience—indeed, often quite distant in terms of both history and geography—is more problematic. Not only are the lines separating the Leninist categories of "just" and "unjust" wars often hazy; more importantly, the Soviet reader's emotional involvement with either of the clashing armies and causes may be rather ambivalent. And it is precisely that kind of neutral stance that is conducive to an "indiscriminately" pacifist reader response, a possibility further strengthened by the nonnationalistic, detached vantage point characteristic of much of this type of writing.

Somewhere along in the school curriculum every Soviet child is taught that in the American Civil War the abolitionist North led by President Lincoln stood for justice, while the South wanted slavery to endure. And yet Stephen Crane's *The Red Badge of Courage,* even in the estimate of a Soviet critic, is essentially not a partisan book, but the tale of one man, and how "the government had dragged him into a war and then mercilessly shipped him off to slaughter."[54] The most important group of pacifist works dealt with the already distant events of World War I and its aftermath. The

54. KL, Vol. III (1966), p. 813. The volume containing *The Red Badge of Courage* and a few of Stephen Crane's tales about the squalor of New York's Bowery was printed in 85,000 copies.

distinction between the forces of darkness and light in that war was by no means obvious in a famous novel by another American author, then still alive and enjoying a revival in the USSR. Ernest Hemingway's *A Farewell to Arms*, published in nearly a quarter of a million copies in Russian and four other languages, clearly posed the kind of danger that Western pacifist novels present to the cause of Soviet patriotism. In the words of a Soviet critic, "The novel is filled with hatred of and revulsion for war, *any kind of war.*"[55]

Probably the most famous antiwar novel of all time was *All Quiet on the Western Front* by Hemingway's contemporary, the expatriate anti-Nazi German, Erich Maria Remarque. Like Hemingway, Remarque was still active in the 1950s and his works were being republished in the USSR after an interruption of many years. Originally published in 1929, *All Quiet on the Western Front* was translated into twenty-five languages, selling what was at that time a sensational total of two and a half million copies within eighteen months. While its artistic merits are average at best, Remarque's novel is a shattering human document, and its account of the numbing violence and despair of a world war now overshadowed by the one that followed retains much power. The ambivalence of the political message of *All Quiet on the Western Front* was apparent from its original reception by the press in the Weimar Republic. The political Right charged Remarque with slander of heroic German soldiers, while the Left faulted him for failing to expose the social and economic factors that were at the root of the war.[56] It was symptomatic of the relative permissiveness of the post-Stalin "thaw" that a work of such dubious political value (and of its political *potential* there could be little doubt in a country then still recovering from the ravages of war) was allowed to appear in nearly a million copies, including 21,000 in the original German.[57] The largest press run, however —about two million copies, over three-quarters of it in Russian and the rest in four other languages, including the original German—was reached by Remarque's 1937 novel *Three Comrades*. Although set in Germany of the 1920s, *Three Comrades* must have struck a responsive note in the hearts of

55. *Osnovnye proizvedenija*, 1965, p. 407. Emphasis added.
56. Jürgen Rühle, *Literature and Revolution: A Critical Study of the Writer and Communism in the Twentieth Century*, translated and edited by Jean Steinberg (New York: Frederick A. Praeger, 1969), p. 155.
57. More understandable was the appearance, also in a million copies but in five languages, of Remarque's 1954 novel *A Time to Live and a Time to Die* in which a German soldier on home leave has a clearer premonition of Nazism's defeat than his comrades can in the chaos of battle. Boris Sučkov, a noted Soviet specialist on German literature, observed that in contrast to Remarque's other novels, which are marred by the general passivity of their characters, *A Time to Live and a Time to Die* is ideologically a marked improvement: "Love for man should be active, sometimes even violence may lead to the good—such are the conclusions approached by the author after much reflection." B. Sučkov, "Kniga, kotoraja sudit," *Inostrannaja literatura*, No. 4, 1955, p. 207.

many Soviet veterans of World War II: the novel portrays the chaos and drift of a society just emerging from the travail of a war, where only personal ties of love or comradeship in the army provide a measure of security and solace.[58]

The writings of the British novelist Richard Aldington (1892–1962) closely parallel Remarque's both in themes and in attitudes. Aldington's *All Men Are Enemies,* first published in 1933 and translated into Russian four years later, is in many ways reminiscent of *Three Comrades.* It describes in angry tones a generation of Englishmen trying to find happiness in a callous country only recently emerged from the upheavals of World War I. *All Men Are Enemies* was printed in 600,000 Russian copies, and also in 25,000 in Lithuanian. The extreme pain and anger of his 1929 novel *Death of a Hero* are not merely a product of artistic imagination. They may be readily traced to Aldington's personal memories of a war during which he was buried in an explosion, with the trauma of shellshock lingering long after. According to a Soviet critic, *Death of a Hero* "showed the insanity and criminality of war," and was "the best English antiwar novel of the time."[59] It was printed in 100,000 copies in Russian as well as 20,000 copies in the original.

Other works that may be classified broadly as falling within the antiwar category include William Faulkner's "About Face," about an ordinary young officer with the American forces in Europe during World War I whose only real interest appears to be whiskey, but who is, posthumously, declared a hero because this serves the purposes of big brass.[60] A recent American novel, Mac Hyman's *No Time for Sergeants,* a comic account of the misadventures of a hillbilly recruit in the U.S. Army, was published in 115,000 copies. Finally, there were 375,000 copies of *Si tous les gars du monde,* an antiwar novel by Gilbert Remy, author of books about de Gaulle and the wartime French Resistance.[61]

Most of the American films shown in the USSR in the post-Stalin years were either outwardly innocent entertainment or critical commentary on various aspects of American life; even these, however, were often regarded with much suspicion by Soviet officialdom. Curiously, the two antiwar motion pictures among them appear to have been shown only to limited audiences. *The Bridge on the River Kwai* was shown in 1958 to a select group

58. A fourth novel by Remarque, *The Black Obelisk* (1956), set in a small German town in the 1920s, with a hero reminiscent of a central character in *All Quiet on the Western Front,* was first translated in *Inostrannaja literatura,* No. 8, 1957; the editors described it as an antiwar novel. *The Black Obelisk* then appeared in an apparently large Russian edition under separate cover, with an additional 115,000 copies in Ukrainian.

59. KL, Vol. V (1968), p. 415. Aldington was also lauded for exposing the fraudulence of the heroic myth of Lawrence of Arabia.

60. The story was printed in *Moskva,* No. 2, 1960.

61. Gilbert Remy's novel was also made into a successful French film.

of Soviet officials and celebrities from the world of film; those present also included the ambassador of the United States.[62] The film, magnificently acted by a distinguished group of performers from several countries (including Alec Guiness) and filmed in dazzling color, depicts a group of allied soldiers in a Japanese prisoner-of-war camp. The prisoners are building a bridge, and the camera focuses the spectator's attention on the conflict between man's urge to build and his natural pride in his work (a trait that was, incidentally, to lie at the center of Alexander Solzhenitsyn's *One Day in the Life of Ivan Denisovich,* his only novel to appear legally in the USSR) and the awareness that this productive work would benefit the enemy's war machine. The film thus illuminated an incongruity that only a war could produce. Perhaps it was felt that the opposing sides in the film—the British and the Japanese—and the war they fought in the jungles of Asia, were so far removed from the Soviet spectator's memories and associations that the most likely response to the film might be that *all* wars are stupid, cruel, and destructive. The undesirability of such conclusions may have argued against wide distribution of the film.

Stanley Kramer's film *On the Beach,* based on Nevil Shute's novel, was a frightening story of a counted few survivors of a nuclear holocaust that destroys most of our planet. A Soviet reviewer took mild exception to the film's fatalism but generally had high praise for it, expressing the hope that the future would bring more antiwar *American* films like this one. At the same time the reviewer expressed confidence that *Soviet* films would, for their part, "show us a glimpse of the future of mankind."[63] The seemingly slight difference in expectations—future American films should continue to condemn all wars, while Soviet films should address themselves to other subjects—was actually rooted in the more serious problem of the double standard by which Soviet critics view all art and life in the West and in their own country. Religion is to be roundly condemned, unless it is the secular faith of Communism, its dogmas, rituals, and high priests; relics are to be ridiculed except for the one that reposes in the mausoleum on Moscow's Red Square.[64] Racism must be excoriated when its victims are blacks, of whom there are none in the USSR; it had better not be dealt with at length when affecting the yellow races, lest it raise some embarrassing questions

62. *Izvestija,* February 20, 1958.
63. *Izvestija,* December 18, 1959.
64. This taboo was violated by an anonymous work that was circulated illegally in the USSR in the early 1970s. *Smuta novejšego vremeni, ili Udivitel'nye poxoždenija Vani Čmotanova* (A Modern Time of Troubles, or The Amazing Adventures of Vanja Čmotanov) relates the story of a petty thief who steals Lenin's head from his embalmed body on the assumption that since it is so closely guarded, it must be worth a lot, perhaps to foreign governments. The Soviet authorities thereupon enlist living actors to impersonate Lenin's corpse. To top off the outrage, the manuscript was ascribed to Vsevolod Kočetov, a symbol of Communist orthodoxy among Soviet novelists.

about the Sino-Soviet propaganda war that often acquires racial overtones, or about the tensions between the Slavic settlers and the indigenous population in Soviet Central Asia; and it had best be avoided altogether when the racism in question is anti-Semitism.[65] Finally, wars—past, present and future—must be denounced when "unjust," as wars waged by imperialism and the bourgeoisie always have been, are, and will be. More circumspection, however, is advisable when dealing with "just" wars. And it goes without saying that, as in the past, any future war that the Soviet Union may have to wage, would also be purely defensive, patriotic, and "just." This double standard is consistently reflected in the policies of Soviet publishing houses. The works of the "bourgeois" authors which they print normally criticize "bourgeois" society, while books by Soviet writers usually extol the virtues of their own "socialist" society.

65. For this reason, the subject of anti-Semitism is one of the important concerns of *samizdat* literature circulated illegally in the USSR, such as the writings of Andrej Sinjavskij ("Abram Tertz"), a non-Jewish writer and critic now living in the West, and Julij Daniel' ("Nikolai Arzhak"), a Jew, who still lives in the USSR. Raising the problem of anti-Semitism in their works figured as a major offense in their trial in 1966, at which they were both sentenced to long prison terms. Some of their writings are available in English: Abram Tertz, *The Trial Begins* and *On Socialist Realism* (New York: Vintage Books, 1960), and Yuli Daniel (Nikolai Arzhak), *This Is Moscow Speaking and Other Stories* (New York: Collier Books, 1968). For a transcript of their trial, see *On Trial: The Soviet State versus "Abram Tertz" and "Nikolai Arzhak,"* translated, edited, and with an introduction by Max Hayward (New York: Harper & Row, 1966). There exists a large anthology of Russian poetry dealing with Jewish subject matter, Aleksandr Donat, *Neopalimaja kupina: evrejskie sjužety v russkoj poezii, antologija* (New York University Press, 1973).

# CHAPTER

# 6

# *The Evils of Capitalism*

Religious fanaticism, racial persecution, and "unjust" wars do not exhaust the list of misfortunes which, according to official Communist dogma, are endemic to non-Soviet societies. There are many others, ranging from economic injustice to a nagging sense of void and drift. These will be examined in the present chapter.

It is said of Hillel, the ancient Hebrew sage, that when asked to summarize in an instant the essence of his faith, he replied, "Love your neighbor as yourself; the rest is commentary; now go and study." Similarly, and with parallel caveats regarding the complexity of commentaries and the need for further consideration of the subject, one might start with the obvious observation that most Western literature is concerned with the human condition and how that condition is affected, by, among other things, man's social institutions. In much of Western writing since the nineteenth century, of which the Russian is of course an integral part, the social setting against which man is portrayed is subjected to critical scrutiny. That skeptical stance is one of the hallmarks of the literature of modernity and sets it apart from the writing of earlier periods which, as often as not, espoused a fatalistic conception of human destiny, viewing it as an inevitable consequence of what it regarded as immutable attributes of life itself, such as human frailty, an unchanging social structure, and divine will.

A posture of social agnosticism has been characteristic of literature born in societies undergoing rapid change—secularization, urbanization, abolition of caste privilege, and recognition, at least in theory, of claims to dignity of persons hitherto implicitly and sometimes explicitly denied human status, most often because of faith or condition of servitude. Of course, ideals were not always observed in actual practice; but then the former were never universally shared, while the latter varied, reflecting local conditions at a given time. The disparity between reality and aspirations was thus obvious. Hence the preoccupation of modern literature with injustice, pretense, hypocrisy. With time, indeed, many writers have come to believe that it is their *duty*—not mere privilege—to expose such evils and incongruities, and gradually, if at times grudgingly, most Western societies have acquiesced in the writer's role as critic, ideally loyal or at least not overly subversive of their most sacred values. Some of these societies have been reasonably tolerant and benign; others blatantly oppressive. Politically, since the early nineteenth century, the states of Western Europe and the Americas ranged from absolute monarchies to parliamentary democracies. In the Soviet view, however, they were and are essentially alike: post-feudal bourgeois (or bourgeois-aristocratic) capitalist states with the allegedly endemic traits of capitalism, such as economic exploitation and social injustice. Degrees may vary but not enough, it is claimed, to affect the principle itself.

Since the literature of the modern West is, whatever the personal allegiances of the writers themselves, overwhelmingly critical of some features of its social fabric (unlike in the eighteenth century, not many authors would have agreed with Voltaire's Candide that theirs was the best of all possible worlds), a claim made by Soviet criticism with a truly monotonous persistence is that the literature of the West (and of nineteenth-century Russia) exposes the evils of capitalism. In the words of Aleksandr Anikst, one of the Soviet Union's foremost authorities on Western writing: "All of nineteenth-century European realism is usually called [in Soviet sources— MF] *critical,* and that is justified because it portrays the inappropriateness of the bourgeois system to human norms."[1] It is symptomatic that in the highly politicized Soviet aesthetics, only two qualifying adjectives are used with the term "realism"—"critical" and "socialist"—the latter denoting the sole literary creed recognized in the USSR, in spite of the fact that it is applied perforce to works of dubious realism.[2] In contrast to "critical" realism, which essentially questions the premises and practices of human and social relations in modern Western society, Socialist Realism consistently glorifies Soviet norms and institutions in a candid effort to advance the Soviet cause. As I wrote nearly two decades ago, Soviet literature has

1. KL, Vol. VI (1971), p. 215.
2. Attempts to extend recognition to a "Socialist Romanticism" in the post-Stalin era were unsuccessful apparently because of apprehension that this might erode the political dimension of Socialist Realism: departures from its current interpretations might then be justified on ostensibly aesthetic grounds, thus introducing dangerous political diversity.

much less in common with nineteenth-century realism than with the neo-classicism of the preceding century. As neoclassicism, Soviet literature favors a division of protagonists into idealized heroes and repugnant villains, advocates the supremacy of reason over feelings, extols the wisdom of the reigning monarch, and demands subjugation of private interests to those of the State.[3] These attributes of Stalinist literature remain largely in force to this time.

The essential disparity between Soviet literature and prerevolutionary Russian and Western writing since the demise of neoclassicism imparts an air of legitimacy to the Soviet claim that such traditional concerns of "critical realism" as the defense of the downtrodden, championship of the nonconformist, and other portrayals of injustice or hypocrisy shown against the background of "bourgeois" settings can and should be interpreted as attacks on "capitalism" and the "bourgeois" way of life as a whole.[4] The claim acquires particular importance when considered together with a basic premise of Soviet ideology which holds that the essential nature of both is immutable. With due allowances for technological advances and "concessions" allegedly thrust upon them by the growing forces of progress, human and social relations in "bourgeois" societies and under whatever brand of capitalism are said to have remained essentially unchanged. To claim otherwise is to be guilty of any of a number of pernicious heresies, from those of the nineteenth- and twentieth-century "reformist" Social Democrats down to such recent ideological "diversions" as the theory projecting an eventual convergence of Soviet and Western-type systems, or at least a permanent blunting of their contrasts, or the belief that the doctrine of peaceful coexistence between states should somehow extend to ideologies as well.[5] The implication of such beliefs is crucial to an understanding of Soviet publishing policies with regard to translated Western writing and of evaluations of Western literature in ideologically-centered Soviet criticism. In the Soviet view, criticism of human relations and social realities contained in the Western literature of "critical realism," however oblique, however distant in time and regardless of whether its specific targets have undergone basic changes (or, indeed, are still in existence), constitutes a valid indict-

3. *Russian Classics in Soviet Jackets*, p. 164. My book was published in 1962, but the copyrighted dissertation on which it is based was defended at Columbia University in 1958. Significantly, two years later much the same point was made quite independently by the then anonymous Soviet critic using the pseudonym Abram Tertz: "In its content and spirit, as in its central figure, socialist realism is much closer to the eighteenth century than to the nineteenth. . . . Like ourselves, the eighteenth century had the idea of political purposefulness, the feeling of its own superiority, and a clear consciousness that 'God is with us.' " See Abram Tertz, *The Trial Begins* and *On Socialist Realism* (New York: Vintage Books, 1960), p. 195.

4. Such subject matter did reappear briefly in Soviet literature during the post-Stalin "thaw" (e.g., in the works of Ilya Ehrenburg, Jurij Kazakov, Solzhenitsyn) but was not allowed to strike roots as a recognized major theme, appropriate for a significant body of Soviet writing.

5. Attacks on the latter error will be discussed in chapter 9.

ment of "bourgeois" society and the "capitalist" system as they exist today. In other words, the writings of Western "critical realists," even if over a century old, can properly be used as ammunition in Communism's incessant ideological struggle against present-day non-Soviet societies. That the same can and must be done with similar writing of more recent origin goes without saying.

## Marx, Engels, and the Great Victorians; Galsworthy and Wilde

While the belief in the broad applicability of literary indictments of "bourgeois" conditions is a Soviet concept, the idea that imaginative literature is valid and accurate sociopolitical evidence has a longer history. Thus, a hundred years ago Karl Marx and Friedrich Engels praised "the brilliant constellation of contemporary English novelists who in their striking and eloquent books discovered for the world more political and social truths than all the professional politicians, journalists, and moralizers taken together; they created descriptions of every segment of the bourgeoisie."[6] Foremost among the English novelists lauded by Communism's founding fathers were Charles Dickens and William Thackeray. Dickens, with a total of well over twenty million copies printed between 1954 and 1964, was definitely the most widely published English-language writer in the USSR. A thirty-volume set of Dickens was brought out in 1957–63 in 550,000 copies per volume, which alone accounts for seventeen million copies. There were also many anthologies in Russian, in English, and in various languages of the peoples of the USSR. Among individual titles, there were over a million copies of *David Copperfield* and over half a million each of *The Posthumous Papers of the Pickwick Club, Oliver Twist,* and *Cricket on the Hearth.* The publication of the thirty-volume set with a press run more common for individual paperbacks is convincing testimony of the high esteem in the USSR for the novelist now "rather unjustly neglected" in his native land.[7]

That the reasons for the Soviet partiality to Dickens are not entirely aesthetic is suggested by a Soviet critic: "The great English realist Dickens introduced into literature descriptions of lower social strata, of the 'bottom' of capitalist society. He strikingly depicted social antagonisms and the emergence of the proletariat on the stage of history."[8] Another critic pro-

6. K. Marks, F. Engel's, *Ob iskusstve,* Vol. I (1967), p. 487. Cited in KL, Vol. VI (1971), p. 214.
7. *The Penguin Companion,* Vol. I, p. 146.
8. KL, Vol. VI (1971), p. 214.

vides capsule characterizations of Dickens's individual works. The *Sketches by Boz* are cited as the first example of "Dickens's realistic satire, with its strikingly antibourgeois tone, joyous humor, and sentimental pathos rooted in social compassion. Most of his descriptions of manners and morals are characterized first and foremost by a sentimental compassion for the poor. Dickens demonstrates how human individuality is depersonalized in a vast capitalist city and makes an attempt at interceding on behalf of the dispossessed."[9] Much the same appraisal is given *The Pickwick Papers:* "For all their imperfections, Dickens's comic heroes become carriers of the writer's optimistic faith in man's nobler attributes; at the same time, they become evidence for an indirect criticism of the bourgeois world."[10] *Oliver Twist,* which a Western critic described as an artistic study of "crime as a violent disorder of a loveless society,"[11] gained approval from the Soviet critic for its indignation over the mistreatment of the poor, but also received a mild rebuke for its ending, which he believed was marred by the depiction of a "good" capitalist who assumes responsibility for the poor waif.[12] *Martin Chuzzlewit,* a satire critical of the United States, and *Nicholas Nickleby,* which portrays corrupt politicians and the horrors of Yorkshire schools, were praised, as was *Dombey and Son,* a novel described as centered around "a portrait of a cruel proprietor, whose desire to have his firm prosper dislodges from his soul all human feelings. The enormous power of the satirical portrait imparts to it the stature of a symbol for everything that is obscurantist, evil, and inimical to man, and which was begotten by the forces of capitalism."[13] *David Copperfield* with its partly autobiographical accounts of hardships was dealt with in a relatively restrained manner. More passions were stirred by *Hard Times,* which was described as a novel depicting workers and vicious capitalists in a mythical coal mining town. The more pity, in the Soviet critic's view, that in this as well as in other works, "Dickens fails to demonstrate any understanding of the necessity of the revolutionary struggle of the working class. Instead, he chose for his positive heroes workers who preach humility and Christian forgiveness."[14] *Little Dorrit,* with its description of the somber debtors' prison where the author's father was jailed, was summarized approvingly: "The Dorrit family . . . serves as a symbolically generalized description of those mysterious, sinister laws of capitalism which transform a human individual into a plaything of unknown, hostile forces."[15] By contrast, rather strong reserva-

9. Ibid., Vol. II (1964), p. 685.
10. Ibid., p. 686.
11. *The Penguin Companion,* Vol. I, p. 146.
12. KL, Vol. II (1964), p. 686.
13. Ibid., pp. 687–88.
14. Ibid., p. 689.
15. Ibid.

tions were expressed about *A Tale of Two Cities* because of an ambivalence
that allegedly detracts from the novel: while the author's sympathies "with
the people" are unquestionable, there is also said to be in the novel an
underlying fear of actions by that same people.[16] The article concluded:

> Dickens was from the very beginning a vocal opponent of capitalism and its
> filthy money-grabbing practices. . . . Nevertheless, the writer's liberal-demo-
> cratic views prevented him from becoming a conscious partisan of Chartism,
> the revolutionary English labor movement. Dickens was never successful in
> his repeated attempts to suggest positive solutions to the problem of the
> revolution. At the same time, the inner logic of realistic portrayals of life
> suggested to the writer conclusions about the futility of all attempts to peace-
> fully restructure bourgeois society, *thus creating preconditions for a deeper
> understanding of laws of contemporary life.*[17]

The closing circumlocution is vaguely reminiscent of traditional Christian views of the Old Testament as worthy of reverence not so much for its
own sake as for its role as a preamble of sorts to the real Holy Writ, the
Gospels. So it is also with Soviet evaluations of the cognitive significance
of Western writing critical of certain features of life under capitalism. While
not in itself sufficient for a formation by the reader of a personal view of
the nature of the bourgeois system (indeed, if read alone it may suggest
profoundly erroneous conclusions), it enhances his receptivity to "laws of
contemporary life" which, as every Soviet schoolchild knows, are embodied
in the teachings of Marxism-Leninism.

It would be wrong, however, to attribute the popularity of Charles Dickens in the USSR to his value in anticapitalist polemics. Dickens has been
very popular in Russia since the early 1840s, with *The Pickwick Papers,
Dombey and Son, David Copperfield,* and *Our Mutual Friend* among his
most widely read works. Dostoyevsky, a writer quite at variance with many
Soviet values, observed: "I am certain that we understand Dickens in Russian almost as well as the English themselves do, perhaps even with all of
the nuances."[18] This was not, of course, meant as a compliment to the
quality of translation. Rather, it was a claim, undoubtedly valid, that Dickens's descriptions of injustice and cruelty and his appeals for compassion
and understanding struck a responsive chord in Russian readers. Dickens's
writing was, after all, remarkably similar in its interests and sympathies to
much *Russian* literature of the time, which the Russian public and critics

16. Ibid., pp. 689–90. No evidence was found of publication of *A Tale of Two Cities,* except
in multivolume sets.
17. Ibid., p. 690. Emphasis added.
18. F. M. Dostoevskij, *Polnoe sobranie xudožestvennyx proizvedenij,* Vol. XI (1929), p. 271.
Quoted in KL, Vol. II (1964), p. 691.

perceived as directly reflective of their own concerns. Russian writing of that time championed the cause of downtrodden peasants, humiliated clerks, the unemployed, social pariahs, and dreamy seekers after truth and justice. It is little wonder that the author of *Poor Folk* and *The Insulted and the Injured,* the creator of the Marmeladovs and of a gallery of martyred children, thought that he and his compatriots could readily understand Dickens. That similar concerns come to the fore in Soviet literature whenever ideological controls are relaxed—as in the second post-Stalin "thaw" of the early 1960s—and that such works invariably stir up discussion about the humane traditions of Russian writing, suggests that these concerns are still very much alive in the USSR. Most of the time, however, they are not voiced by the Spartan, heroic, neoclassical writers of Socialist Realism. It is partly for that reason that pre-Soviet Russian literature retains much of its appeal in the Soviet Union—as do the old-fashioned sentimental novels of Charles Dickens.

William Thackeray was also popular in prerevolutionary Russia. A twelve-volume set of Thackeray's works was published in 1894–95. Friedrich Engels emphasized the documentary quality of Thackeray's novels, and they were also praised by Karl Marx.[19] The *Literary Encyclopedia* points out that "in contrast to bourgeois literary scholarship, Soviet scholars emphasize the democratic character of Thackeray's work, his satirical exposés, and his masterful creation of social types." *Vanity Fair,* first translated into Russian in 1850, was reprinted in 1954–64 in about one and a half million copies; a stage adaptation is performed in Soviet theaters. The *Literary Encyclopedia* has high praise for the great satirical novel: "All are equally depraved in a bourgeois world where everyone is constantly trying to get rich, in which everything is filled with snobbery, vanity, and selfishness. . . . Thackeray brushes aside the official elegant exterior of history and sees behind its façade the ordeal of the masses, the panic of the bourgeoisie, the orgy of predatory instincts." *The Virginians,* printed in a quarter of a million copies, was attractive to Soviet publishers apparently because it could be interpreted as simultaneously anti-British, anticolonialist, and anti-American: "In his descriptions of the American war of independence Thackeray satirizes the ignorant landed gentry of New England and condemns Britain's colonialist policies." *The Luck of Barry Lyndon* (100,000 copies) "depicts the corrupting power of money which is the cause of murders, robberies, and frame-ups. He [Thackeray] exposes wars waged for the sake of spoils and feudal despotism." Much the same was said of *The History of Henry Esmond, Esq.* (150,000), *Pendennis*

19. Ibid., Vol. VII (1972), p. 443.

(30,000 in English), and *The Book of Snobs* (15,000).

All of this recalls Jonathan Swift's definition of satire in the preface to *The Battle of the Books:* "Satire is a sort of glass wherein beholders do generally discover everybody's face but their own." One wonders whether Soviet readers are completely reassured by Soviet commentaries on the works of Thackeray, Rabelais, Voltaire, and Swift himself, which claim that the caustic observations of these writers apply, in effect, to all societies, past and present, with the sole exception of their own homeland.

Other nineteenth-century English classics included works by the Brontë sisters. The summary given in the *Literary Encyclopedia* of Charlotte Brontë's *Jane Eyre*, read in Russia for well over a century (it was translated in 1849, two years after its original appearance), reveals the combination of sentimentality and social protest that the Russian liberal intelligentsia once favored in a novel: "Partly autobiographical, the novel relates the fortunes of a poor governess who defends her independence and human dignity. The novel is permeated with protest against social injustice, against the idle rich lording it over honest working people."[20] *Jane Eyre* was published in over a million copies in Russian alone, with additional printings in Estonian, Lithuanian, and Armenian, as well as 10,000 copies in the original English, an indication perhaps of a fortunate convergence of official favor and remarkably traditional popular tastes. *Shirley*, the novel that probably induced Marx to rate Charlotte Brontë alongside Dickens and Thackeray, was brought out in 100,000 copies (with 20,000 additional in the original): "Brontë portrays the life of her heroes against the background of the struggle of the Luddites, the destroyers of machines. While sympathizing with the workers, the author rejects revolutionary tactics." Emily Brontë's *Wuthering Heights*, published in over half a million copies, also fused motifs of personal and social misfortune: "[Emily] Brontë's novel is a history of the tragic love of a hired hand, an orphan foundling, and the daughter of his employer. . . . The novel's significance lies in its truthful portrayal of the cruel world of provincial English estates."[21] A third English woman novelist published was Margaret Harkness:

Harkness is the author of the novella *A City Girl* (1887; Russian translations 1888, 1940) which tells the story of a seamstress who is seduced by a gentleman masquerading as a "friend of the workers." In his letter to Harkness written in early April of 1888, F. Engels expressed his high regard for the truthfulness of the novel, but criticized the limitations of Harkness, her inability to see "the revolutionary rebuke of the working class to the oppressors."[22]

20. Ibid., Vol. I (1962), p. 746.
21. Ibid., p. 747.
22. Ibid., Vol. II (1964), p. 68.

A work of scant literary merit, *A City Girl* was nevertheless reprinted in 300,000 copies, probably as an act of revolutionary piety.

Fortunately, ideological considerations occasionally encourage Soviet publishers to bring out works of great artistic stature as well as reader appeal. Among recent beneficiaries are the writings of Thomas Hardy. Thus, *The Mayor of Casterbridge* was printed in 500,000 copies and *Tess of the d'Urbervilles* in 400,000; both depict human tragedy resulting from a clash between the old-fashioned rural existence and the new forces of industrialization, aggravated by society's adherence to rigid codes of behavior. A Soviet critic's summary of *Tess of the d'Urbervilles* makes it out to be far more political: "The tragic fate of Tess, a wonderful country girl who dies a victim of cruel and inhuman bourgeois morality, is shown against the background of the general ruin and degeneracy of once mighty aristocratic families and the impoverishment of villages."[23] There was also an anthology of Hardy's writings, published in 250,000 copies. *Jude the Obscure* was printed in only 34,000 copies: 15,000 in Latvian and 19,000 in the original English.

John Galsworthy is another author whose writings combine subject matter favored by Soviet publishers—a critical view of England's bourgeoisie —and literary attributes favored by the country's reading public. Galsworthy's most famous work, *The Forsyte Saga* is a shrewd study of Britain's sturdy and prosperous middle classes, of their extreme conservatism and greed, as well as their industriousness and fierce family loyalties. A novel of formidable size—a double trilogy—it is also a family chronicle, a format popular in Russian literature. Finally, it is worth remembering that Russian readers probably find Galsworthy's mode of narration congenial. Young Galsworthy was strongly influenced by Turgenev, and residues of that influence may also be discerned in Galsworthy's later works. Notwithstanding Galsworthy's ideological limitations and personal sympathies, *The Forsyte Saga* earned high praise from a Soviet critic:

> Under Galsworthy's pen the story of a single bourgeois family rises to the stature of a broad canvas of the destinies of an entire social class. And even though Galsworthy's views are circumscribed by his belief in the stability of the bourgeois system which in his opinion reflected, so to speak, man's individualist nature, his faithfulness to realism made his panorama of bourgeois England an accurate reflection of the gradual decline of its former might.[24]

23. *Osnovnye proizvedenija,* p. 87.
24. KL, Vol. II (1964), p. 234.

Various parts of *The Forsyte Saga* were published in over two million copies in Russian, 100,000 copies each in Lithuanian and Estonian, and 50,000 in the original English. A sixteen-volume set of Galsworthy's collected writings appeared in 375,000 copies per volume. There were also approximately two million additional copies of anthologies and individual titles of Galsworthy's prose and drama, making him one of the most widely printed Western authors in the USSR. An aristocrat by background and rather conservative in politics, Galsworthy was preferred by Soviet publishers to many radical debunkers of capitalism because he could conceivably be viewed as a latter-day, minor-league Balzac whose works, whatever their author's intention, acquainted readers with many unseemly features of capitalism. As for the Soviet public, in all probability they were drawn to Galsworthy by the same features that in the 1970s kept millions of viewers in Great Britain and elsewhere glued to their television screens for a period of weeks when the British Broadcasting Corporation's adaptation of *The Forsyte Saga* was serialized. No literary masterpiece, Galsworthy's trilogy tells a long succession of good stories about parents and children, tyrants and lovers, money and conventions, secrets and gossip. Not many novels offer that much, and few offer more.

Oscar Wilde retains his popularity in the USSR. A two-volume set of his writings was printed in a total of 400,000 copies, with another 60,000 of anthologies. There was also a 25,000-copy edition of plays in English and (also in English) 66,000 copies of *The Picture of Dorian Gray,* described in a Western reference work as "a novel about a beautiful hedonist who miraculously retains his youth while his portrait shows the ravages of time and unnamed dissipations."[25] The *Literary Encyclopedia*'s entry, written by Aleksandr Anikst, a reputable Soviet scholar, is a rather labored attempt at demonstrating that for all of his ostentatious amoralism Oscar Wilde really appealed for adherence to *true* morality. Nothing was said, of course, of the fact that what England's bourgeoisie found particularly shocking was Wilde's homosexuality—which is just as shocking to the bourgeoisie of the USSR, where homosexuality is a legal offense.[26] One of the few important works of earlier American literature published was Nathaniel Hawthorne's *The Scarlet Letter* (165,000 copies plus 11,000 in English). It was duly described as a study in hypocrisy and selfishness in bourgeois society.[27]

25. *The Penguin Companion,* Vol. I, p. 554.
26. KL, Vol. VII (1972), pp. 715–18. *Teatral'naja ènciklopedija* (Vol. V [1967], pp. 306–7) notes that Oscar Wilde was tried for "immorality," but bashfully refrains from specifying the charge of homosexuality. One of Wilde's plays, *Lady Windermere's Fan,* was staged in 1959 by the Malyj Theater, one of Moscow's best.
27. *Osnovnye proizvedenija,* pp. 383–84.

## The Lessons of Balzac, the Limitations of Zola, and Other Testimony on French Capitalism

Of the great nineteenth-century French novelists, Stendhal and Flaubert are treated in Soviet criticism with relative restraint; since comparatively few extravagant claims are made about their ideological significance, and they were discussed in chapter three, which deals with nonideological literature. The evaluations of Hugo, Zola, and, above all, Balzac are much more politicized.

The decade 1954–64 saw the launching of a fifteen-volume edition of Victor Hugo, at 150,000 copies per volume. There were further about a quarter of a million copies of *The Year 1893*, half a million of *Les Travailleurs de la mer*, and 750,000 of *Notre Dame de Paris*. The first of these was praised for its admiration of the Jacobins, but criticized for "failing to understand" the significance of revolutionary violence and for preaching "charity"; the second, notwithstanding its message of Christian sacrifice, was lauded as a paean to labor; the third was described as an expression "of anticlericalism that is new for Hugo."[28] In *Notre Dame de Paris*, "The somber outlines of the cathedral are shown in the novel as a frightening symbol of Catholicism which has been oppressing man for centuries."[29] The largest press run for any single work by Hugo was the one and a half million copies of *Les Misérables:* "In relating the tale of his hero's fortunes—one of them unemployed, sent to prison for stealing a roll to feed his hungry children, the other a young seamstress who sells her body in order to save her child—Hugo has demonstrated that crime and poverty are inevitable consequences of capitalism."[30]

Emile Zola was influential among the prerevolutionary Russian intelligentsia both as a novelist and as a public figure, particularly in connection with his role in the Dreyfus affair which was followed in Russia with avid interest. As for his fame as a novelist, suffice it to recall that, incredible as this may seem, "Since 1872, Zola's works had been occasionally printed in Russia prior to their appearance in France."[31] He is still published on a vast scale. Two multivolume editions of Zola's writing were launched during the first post-Stalin decade, an eighteen-volume set at 273,000 copies per volume, and a twenty-six volume set at 300,000. There were also over two million copies of individual titles in several languages. Yet, curiously, in spite of these very impressive figures, Soviet critics are restrained in their

28. KL, Vol. II (1964), pp. 472–76.
29. Ibid., pp. 472–73.
30. Ibid., p. 474. Excerpts from *Les Misérables* were also printed under separate cover. See chapter 4.
31. KL, Vol. II (1964), p. 1041.

praise of Zola. It is pointed out, for example, that Engels preferred Balzac to Zola because of Zola's naturalism.[32] On the one hand it is admitted that Zola's writings "showed the unseemly countenance of [the post-Napoleonic French] bourgeois republican demogoguery and hypocritical lies about harmony between social classes. [In the work of Zola—MF] the worker was and remains a prisoner of poverty, a slave of accident. Society is, as expected, ruled by the power of gold."[33] It is also admitted that "E. Zola has greatly broadened realism's scope by having shown an exceptionally rich variety of social types, the growing antagonism between labor and capital, the struggle of workers against exploiters (e.g., in *Germinal*). He has devised an original structure of the novel, in the center of which lie major 'economic organisms,' such as the market, the coal mine, etc."[34] Nevertheless: "On the other hand, even the most attractive personages in Zola's works bear the stamp of mediocrity and spiritual poverty. In his canvas of the world, man is to some extent crowded out by objects and action by descriptions. These weak sides of Zola's artistic method are closely linked to the theory of *naturalism* which he set forth and which was formed under the direct influence of positivist philosophy."[35]

Politically, Balzac was considerably to the right of Zola. While Zola was closely identified with libertarian and republican causes, Balzac was a royalist. Chekhov was an admirer of Zola and it was over the Dreyfus case (in which he took the side of Zola, whose famous essay "J'accuse" rallied the defenders of the Jewish captain in the French army) that Chekhov broke with Suvorin, his longtime publisher and friend. As for Chekhov's attitude toward the politically rightist Balzac, it may not be entirely accidental that the "news" item chosen in his *Three Sisters* to illustrate the inanity of the press (it is cited by Čebutykin, the incompetent old doctor) states that Balzac was married in Berdyčev, then a small Jewish town in the Russian Pale of Settlement. Yet Balzac's books, as pointed out, were more to the liking of Friedrich Engels who wrote:

> In my view, one of the greatest victories of realism and one of the greatest features of old Balzac is that Balzac . . . was forced to resist his own class sympathies and political bias, *saw* the inevitability of a downfall of his beloved aristocrats, and described them as men unworthy of a better fate; also, he *saw* the real men of the future there where alone at that time they could be found.[36]

32. Ibid., p. 1039. This, incidentally, makes for some confusion because in the lexicon of Soviet criticism, "naturalism" is a common euphemism for overly frank portrayal of sex.
33. Ibid., p. 1038.
34. Ibid., Vol. VI (1971), pp. 217–18.
35. Ibid.
36. K. Marks, F. Engel's, *Ob iskusstve,* Vol. I (1967), p. 8. Cited in KL, Vol. VI (1971), p. 209.

Of *La Comédie humaine,* a broad canvas of French society between 1816 and 1848, Engels said:

> I learned more [from it—MF], even about economic details (such as, for example, the redistribution after the revolution of personal property and of real estate) than from the books of all the specialists on that period—historians, economists, statisticians—taken together.[37]

Apparently taking his cue from Engels, a Soviet critic emphasized that "Balzac condemned the power of money, which had become the sole criterion determining human relations, he condemned selfishness, anarchy, and arbitrariness in the economic evolution of society, the impoverishment of the people, etc."[38] All these ideological considerations, combined with Balzac's stature and undoubted popularity with the reading public, result in Balzac's fairly steady distinction of being the most widely published French author in the USSR. A twenty-four volume set of his works was printed at 350,000 per volume; the most widely reprinted single item appears to be *The Droll Stories,* of which nearly a million copies were printed. Two titles were published in the original French, in 10,000 copies each: *Le Père Goriot* and *Le Peau de chagrin.* The total number of copies of all of Balzac's works printed exceeds thirteen million.

One official justification for the favor in which Guy de Maupassant is held in the USSR is his usefulness in unmasking the sham of capitalism: "His work is firmly grounded in a profoundly critical attitude toward capitalist conditions, a sober lack of illusions with regard to the human relations characteristic of those conditions, to the hypocrisy of bourgeois democracy and the filthy political deals of the Third [French] Republic, to the slime of militarism and colonialist adventures."[39] More specifically, the novel *Bel Ami,* printed in a half a million copies, was said to depict "the mercenary character of all social milieux and the moral degeneration of the individual bourgeois"; *Pierre et Jean,* with roughly the same press run, was described as a study in "proprietary instincts which destroy family ties."[40] In contrast, Maupassant's attitude toward the lower classes was sympathetic and respectful. Thus, "In novellas about the Franco-Prussian war it is precisely simple folk, sometimes the pariahs and rejects of bourgeois society who—unlike the cowardly and selfish bourgeois—are capable of heroism and patriotic sentiments."[41] A collection of four tales ("My Uncle Sostin,"

37. Ibid., Vol. I (1962), p. 431.
38. Ibid.
39. Ibid., Vol. IV (1967), p. 958.
40. Ibid., p. 961.
41. Ibid., p. 960.

"Moiron," "The Christening," and "The Normandian") was published under an eloquent title: *Atheist Tales.*[42] Then there are, of course, the many tales of Maupassant where he "speaks with irony and bitterness about the desecration of love which was transformed into a subject of purchase and sale or filthy games, into a means of deception, profit, enslavement, about adultery and prostitution—those invariable companions of bourgeois conjugal deals—and about the tragedy of abandoned children."[43] It is more than likely that the last feature of Maupassant's writings is what most attracted Soviet buyers and readers of the nearly seven million copies of Maupassant's books, including a twelve-volume set at 310,000 copies per volume and eight books in French.[44] To put it bluntly, they wanted to read good racy stories about "filthy games," about prostitution and adultery, the more so because no such stories are to be found in stodgy and puritanical Soviet literature. It is unlikely that the personal observations of Soviet readers bear out the notion that prostitution and adultery are engendered only by bourgeois family structure. In any case few readers probably gave it much thought. At least one Russian reader's reaction suggests this, Isaac Babel's magnificent short story "Guy de Maupassant."

Alphonse Daudet was not nearly as popular a storyteller in Russia as Maupassant. The usual claims are made in the *Literary Encyclopedia* about Daudet's "progressive" features. Of his *Tartarin de Tarascon* it is said, "The trilogy mocks the obsession with making money in the colonies"— a dual indictment, as it were, of colonialism and capitalism.[45] *L'Immortel* is a "biting satire on the French Academy and on the sterility of official learning that is far removed from the people." There is even genuflection to a patristic source, properly footnoted: Lenin makes two references to Daudet's braggart Tarascon in the seventeenth volume of his writings (on pages 359 and 489).[46] Most of the nearly one and a half million copies of Daudet's works consists of *Fromont jeune et Risler aîné,* which describes a wallpaper factory in Paris and a scheming wife who ruins a business partnership (300,000 copies plus 21,000 in French); *Jack* (400,000, mostly adaptations for children); and the tall tales of Tartarin, the French Münchhausen.

Less known nineteenth-century French authors published at the time

42. For a discussion of this subject see chapter 5.
43. KL, Vol. IV (1967), p. 960.
44. *Bel Ami*, 10,000 copies; *Oriol*, 10,000; *As Strong as Death*, 10,000; four anthologies, 38,000.
45. KL, Vol. II (1964), p. 728.
46. Ibid.

include Camille Lemonnier,[47] Claude Tillier,[48] and Henri Becque.[49] Finally, mention should be made of Jules Vallès, a participant in the French Commune and member of the First International. His autobiographical trilogy, *Jacques Vingtras,* is described by a Western source as filled with "savage indignation at injustice and inequality and his profound pity for the disinherited."[50] It appeared in some 200,000 copies, mostly one excerpt from the long work; the autobiographical *Le Bachelier* was printed in half a million copies; there were also 5,000 copies of Vallès's articles and pamphlets in the original French.

## Other Nineteenth-Century Europeans; the Latin Americans

Most of the better known German writers "exposing the bourgeoisie" wrote early in the twentieth century and will be considered elsewhere.[51] Suffice it to mention here Hermann Sudermann, a dramatist who wrote about social injustice (his *Voyage to Tilsit* appeared in 15,000 copies in Lithuanian), and the Austrian author of novellas Adalbert Stifter ("The Old Stamp" was printed in 150,000 copies).[52]

Italian literature was represented by two authors. Giovanni Verga's novellas describing the hard life of Sicilian peasants were printed in 250,000 copies. There were about 200,000 copies of short stories and an undisclosed press run of one play, *The Pleasure of Honesty,* by Luigi Pirandello, described as a complex writer who deals with the theme of hardships endured in the modern world by "the little man." Minna Canth's Finnish novella *Poor Folk,* which sounds a strong note of social protest, was published in 15,000 copies in Estonian, a language in which much of Scandinavian writing appears in the USSR.[53] There was a similar small edition of another Finnish author, Väinö Kataja, who describes impoverished landless peasants, and a 75,000-copy printing of an anthology of Alexander Kielland:

47. 80,000 copies. Lemonnier's *La Fin de bourgeois* is, of course, "about the degeneration of the bourgeoisie," KL, Vol. IV (1967), p. 113.
48. A French edition of *Mon oncle Benjamin* (15,000 copies). "The edge of Tillier's satire is directed not only against class prejudices but also against the deadening impact of bourgeois morality and its selfishness." KL, Vol. II (1972), p. 500.
49. A very small edition of his play *The Vultures* was described in an old Soviet metaphor: "In his portrayal of bourgeois society he observes in it only greedy business sharks—the predators and their victims." KL, Vol. I (1962), p. 499.
50. *The Penguin Companion,* Vol. II, p. 790.
51. See chapter 7.
52. *Teatral'naja ènciklopedija,* Vol. II (1963), pp. 813–14.
53. A Soviet source writes that Minna Canth "depicts the destitution and oppression of Finland's working folk, and the growing protest against corruption." KL, Vol. III (1966), p. 371.

Kielland, whom Norwegian literary scholarship includes in the "four great," is one of the few Norwegian writers who correctly understood the nature of class contradictions. . . . Kielland unmasks the economic and political adventurism of the bourgeoisie, depicts the hard living conditions of the workers, the shakiness and impermanence of ideological and ethical principles of certain segments of Norway's intelligentsia, and the corrupting influence of capitalism on the hearts and minds of the young.[54]

The workings of Spain's capitalist society were reflected in the short stories of Joaquin Dicenta, one of which "depicted a worker struggling for his rights against the employer";[55] a collection of Dicenta's stories appeared in 50,000 copies. And the two worlds, the Old and the New, were bridged, as it were, by Ramón del Valle-Inclán, the Spanish author of *Tirano Banderas;* this satire on the Mexican dictator of the 1920s, Primo de Rivera, was published in 75,000 copies.

Literatures of Latin America, younger than those of Western Europe, began to penetrate Russia relatively late, and then frequently in translations from third languages, usually French, rather than from the original Spanish or Portuguese. Large scale publication of Latin American writing is a recent development in the USSR and coincides with the rapid expansion of Soviet diplomatic and other contacts with the countries of South America during the post-Stalin era. It was intensified in the 1960s in the wake of the establishment of a Communist regime in Cuba and the growth of left-wing activity in Chile and other countries. Most of the Latin American authors published in the USSR (and their number is very large indeed) are Marxists or at least opponents of "Yankee imperialism"; the majority of them are still active writers.[56] The publication of authors of the older generation is both a natural extension of interest in contemporary writing and an attempt to provide Soviet readers with historical perspective on the political and social evolution of Latin America. The picture that emerges from these works is of a continent plagued by the evils of capitalism made even more pernicious by economic backwardness and a colonial relationship with Europe and the United States.

Two Brazilian novels were published. *Don Casmurro* by Joaquim Maria Machado de Assis describes, according to a Soviet source, the cruelty of the newly enriched capitalist during the modernization of the vast semicolonial country.[57] Aluisio Azevedo's *O cortiço (The Slum),* published in 1890, was

54. *Osnovnye proizvedenija,* p. 316.
55. KL, Vol. II (1964), p. 700.
56. Their works will be discussed in chapter 7.
57. KL, Vol. IV (1967), pp. 706–7. No data are available on the press run.

translated into Russian in 1960 and brought out in 100,000 copies. A Soviet critic approved of the novel's descriptions but expressed reservations about its implied evaluations: "Azevedo raises critical problems, both social and ethical, exposes racial prejudice, portrays the decline of morals in a bourgeois-artistocratic society. Still, even in *The Slum,* which offers a striking picture of the life of the urban poor and a picturesque portrait of a *nouveau riche* who cruelly oppresses the people, one senses a tendency to explain away social vices with biological laws."[58]

Two Chilean authors were published, each in 50,000 copies. Alberto Blest Gana's *Martín Rivas* was said to depict the destructive powers of money, how it kills love and family loyalties—a familiar theme from the West European literature of "critical realism."[59] Baldomero Lillo's tale "Outpost No. 12" is probably among those of his works which, "simple and concise, are filled with a profound sympathy for working people and hatred for the exploiters."[60] Mariano Azuela's Mexican novel *Los de abajo (The Underdogs)* appeared in 100,000 copies, and *La maldición (The Curse)* in 13,000 in Ukrainian; Azuela focused on the social injustices that persisted in Mexico in spite of the revolution. Manuel de Jesús Galvan is a Dominican author. His *Enriquello* (published in 1879, it was translated into Russian only in 1963), an account of an Indian rebellion against Spanish oppressors, was printed in 50,000 copies. And José Marmol's Argentine novel *Amalia,* which describes the horrors of life under his country's nineteenth-century dictator Juan Manuel Rosas, was issued in 100,000 copies. Two poets whose works were published were the Cuban patriot José Martí (140,000 copies, of which 50,000 were of *North American Scenes,* which includes much caustic comment about the United States) and Rubén Darío, a modernist Nicaraguan poet (credited, in fact, with coining the term "modernism"). Darió's nonaesthetic virtues included dislike of "soulless North American [i.e., United States] civilization."[61] An anthology of Darío's verse was printed in 10,000 copies.

58. KL, Vol. I (1962), p. 94. The novel appeared in English under the title *The Brazilian Tenement.* See L. A. Šur, *Xudožestvennaja literatura Latinskoj Ameriki v russkoj pečati* (Annotirovannaja bibliografija russkix perevodov i kritičeskoj literatury na russkom jazyke, 1960–1964) (Moscow: Kniga, 1966), p. 49. The book also has a Spanish title page: L. A. Shur, *Literatura Latinoamericana en la Imprenta Rusa* (Bibliografia de las obras traducidas al ruso y ensayos criticos, 1960–1964) (Moscú: Editorial "Kniga," 1966).
59. KL, Vol. I (1962), p. 641.
60. Ibid., Vol. IV (1967), p. 198.
61. Ibid., Vol. II (1964), p. 527. An annotated Soviet bibliography noted with approval that in the 1880s José Martí had "unmasked such revolting features of North American life as exploitation of man by man, the power of money, the cult of brute force and spiritual decline." At the same time, the Latin American poet and patriot "J. Martí admires the courage and optimism of the American people and unmasks politicians and capitalists who cruelly oppress the American workers." *Xudožestvennaja literatura,* 1963, (April–June 1963), p. 77.

## *The Twentieth Century*

Not unexpectedly, Soviet publishing and criticism of Western writing with
recent and contemporary settings is heavily politicized. In a society where
readers are conditioned to accept literature of non-Soviet origin as a faithful
mirror of life, this kind of prose, drama, and verse is intimately linked to
the highly sensitive problem of shaping a public image of the non-Soviet
world in general and of specific countries in particular. The formation of
that image is the more critical because, in the case of all but a handful of
Soviet citizens, it cannot be "verified" by such traditional means as travel
abroad or even the reading of foreign newspapers and magazines. At the
same time it is hoped that the image presented by the translated literature
will reinforce (and certainly, in no case contradict) that projected by the
Soviet media. Portrayals of Western societies in the Soviet press are not
entirely uniform and tend to fluctuate with changing Soviet foreign policies
(e.g., France has emerged recently as a relatively benign capitalist country,
while the United States, the *détente* notwithstanding, appears as the prototype of the evils of capitalism). Normally, of course, Communist authors
in the West can be relied upon to live up to such requirements; their writings
will be considered elsewhere.[62] In the final analysis, naturally, what matters
more are the contents of books, not the political sympathies of their authors,
which may at times be rather at variance with them—the royalist Balzac,
as pointed out, was credited by Engels with not allowing his political
sympathies to obstruct his artistic vision, and much the same was said of
Tolstoy by Lenin. Still, there are certain minimal requirements; thus, if he
is to be published in the USSR, a living Western author cannot be overtly
identified with anti-Soviet views and causes, however desirable his writings.
Most likely, this consideration will be weighed even more carefully now that
the USSR, as a result of its accession in 1973 to the Universal Copyright
Convention, is no longer free to censor the texts of published translations
and will have to pay royalties.

Nevertheless, publication of Western authors not necessarily sympathetic
to the Soviet Union does offer some very important advantages in addition
to the obvious one of providing a wider selection of good writing to Soviet
readers and, it might be added, substantial profits to Soviet publishers.
Works that are at all critical of any features of life in Western society are
particularly effective as supporting evidence of Soviet denunciations of the
non-Soviet way of life because of their non-Soviet and non-Communist
origin. Furthermore, by projecting to the West some of the attributes of

62. See chapter 7, which also includes a discussion of the criteria followed in assigning
Western authors to that category.

Soviet writing, it is not unlikely that many Soviet readers believe that authors in Western societies create under somewhat similar conditions, and that their criticism of life in their own countries is, if anything, understated (or else it would not have been printed there!) and written only as a result of extreme provocation. One would not, naturally, expect Soviet readers to know that the writer in the West often views himself (and is largely viewed by others) as a well-meaning critic of what were once called the mob, the philistines, the bourgeoisie; that, in sharp contrast to Soviet literature, "embellishing" reality is very uncommon in Western writing; and that even those very rare authors in the West who by and large agree with the values and practices of their societies are likely to warn, at least, against the threat of complacency. As a result, a reasonably *representative* selection of modern writing of Western Europe and the Americas lends itself quite readily to the Soviet interpretation of it as "exposé." From then on, it becomes only a question of emphasis of the alleged validity of this writing as an indictment of the non-Soviet way of life as a whole.

In earlier times, contemporary Western literary works emphasized economic deprivation as a feature of life in the non-Soviet world. Such works are still being printed and reprinted, with new titles originating mainly in poorer regions such as Latin America, Spain, or the Italian South. One does, however, discern a visible shift in emphasis, particularly in the selection of works with present-day settings in one of the industrial nations of Western Europe or in the United States. The reasons are not too hard to guess. Soviet readers may be impressed by the lack of economic security in the West, i.e., the threat of unemployment, but not by poverty as such. What is poverty in some of the West's industrial nations may appear as reasonable affluence to a Soviet reader whose normal living conditions still include a monotonous diet and extremely overcrowded housing, and to whom the possession of any kind of automobile is great luxury. In recent years, the assortment of translations of newer Western writing made available to Soviet citizenry emphasizes instead such features of non-Soviet life as social injustice amid conditions of relative prosperity and, above all, various kinds of psychological malaise. It is not so much poverty that emerges from these works as characteristic of Western life (Marxist predictions notwithstanding, the rich have not all grown richer, and the paupers have not become poorer but have, on the contrary, often become members of the middle class) but rather feelings of nagging alienation, aimlessness, and boredom.[63]

63. That these are sometimes described in recent Western fiction as finding their expression in sexual promiscuity (not merely suggested, but portrayed in lengthy and frequent detail) is a source of perpetual embarrassment to Soviet critics and publishers, particularly when the offenders are otherwise "progressive" West European and American authors. Occasionally it appears that certain works are not published because of such reservations. In borderline cases,

## Some Contemporary Latin Americans and
## West Europeans

As mentioned, books, both old and new, emphasizing such traditional features of "bourgeois" society as destitution are often translations from the Spanish and Portuguese, of European as well as Latin American origin. Of Spanish authors, the most frequently published is the émigré novelist Juan Goytisolo, an implacable opponent of the Franco regime. Goytisolo's *The Devil in Paradise,* set during the Spanish Civil War, was printed in 100,000 copies; in the rather florid phrase of the normally bland *Literary Encyclopedia,* the 1955 novel "resounded like an impassionate curse to a war unleashed by the Fascists."[64] *The Surf,* which describes the bourgeoisie in Barcelona, was printed in 27,000 copies; Goytisolo's shorter works portraying Spain's desperately poor peasants and exploited workers appeared in literary journals.[65] An earlier anti-Franco émigré, the noted poet Antonio Machado y Ruiz, much of whose verse describes land-hungry peasants, was represented by a volume with a press run of 10,000. No information was available on the sizes of the editions of four other Iberian authors. Juan Antonio de Zunzunegui's *Running in the Dark* focuses on some of the absurdities of Spanish life, including the situation of the working classes. Dolores Medio's *A Civil Servant* "depicts realistically the condition of the people in Franco Spain. Her chief protagonists are the working folk of Madrid, clerks, laborers."[66] Jose Maria Ferreira de Castro, a Portuguese writer as well as a public figure with leftist leanings, was represented by the novel *A lã e a neve (Wool and Snow),* which shows the struggle of the country's workers for their rights.[67] Aquilino Ribeiro, also an active opponent of the Salazar regime, had his *Quando os lobos uivam (When the Wolves Are Howling),* an attack on social injustice in Portugal, translated into Russian in 1963.[68]

Much the same picture of oppression and want emerges from Latin American writing. Alfonso Hernández Cata, a Cuban who lived in Spain, represents a bridge between the Old and the New World. Many of the short stories in Cata's 100,000-copy anthology attack dictators. *El Señor Presi-*

---

when a good work can be salvaged with only minor "editing," certain cuts may be made in the text, and euphemisms and circumlocutions used. For a more detailed discussion, see chapter 1.

64. KL, Vol. II (1964), p. 222.

65. The novel *La resaca,* which depicts the wretched existence of Spanish workers, appeared in *Inostrannaja literatura,* No. 6, 1961. Two short stories with rural settings were printed in *Novyj mir,* No. 7, 1962, and No. 4, 1963. The first was *Campos de Nijar* (1960) and the second *La Chanca* (1962).

66. KL, Vol. IV (1967), p. 725.

67. Ibid., Vol. VII (1972), p. 940.

68. Ibid., Vol. VI (1971), pp. 278–79.

*dente* "exposes the cruelty of a tyrannical regime," that of Guatemala's dictator Estrada Cabrera. Its author, Miguel Angel Asturias, left the country after a coup ousted Guatemala's leftist Arbenz regime; "his books were burned by the authorities."[69] *El Señor Presidente* was printed in 150,000 copies. Many more—probably half a million—were printed of the Nobel Prize winning author's collection of short stories with strong anti-American overtones, *A Weekend in Guatemala*. Writers from four other Latin American countries portrayed the hard struggle for existence of people in their lands. Miguel Otero Silva's novel *Casas muertas (Dead Houses)* "paints a dismal canvas of the misfortunes of inhabitants of a small provincial town in Venezuela."[70] *Corral Abierto,* a novel by the Uruguayan author Enrique Amorim, "described the life of the inhabitants of a 'rat city,' one of the settlements that serves as a haven for the down-and-outs among the poor."[71] Ernesto L. Castro is an Argentine writer: "Castro's central theme, the hard life of peasants and fishermen, a life full of deprivations and the concerns and disappointments of 'little men,' is particularly striking in the novel *Los isleros* [The Islanders]. . . . *Campo arado* [*The Ploughed Field*] is a history of Argentina's *pampas* during the lifespans of three generations of settlers."[72] *Los Isleros* was published in 200,000 copies; the press run of *Campo arado* is unknown. There was no information on the press run of Eduardo Caballero Calderón's Colombian novel *Siervo sin tierra (Siervo the Landless)* and on a volume of tales by the Chilean Francisco A. Coloane. One of the tales, describing a rebellion of farmhands in the 1920s, was printed in *Novyj mir,* No. 6, 1956. A much performed play (it was also published) was *The Plague Is Coming from Milos* by the Argentine Osvaldo Dragún. Although set in ancient Greece, the play was said to deal actually with contemporary issues: "The play is aimed against war and the predatory policies of imperialist states."[73]

Among contemporary Italian authors not openly identified with Communist causes, the most widely published was Alberto Moravia. This is not to say that Moravia's political views are regarded as unfriendly; on the contrary, he is described as invariably coming out "in defense of peace, freedom, and democracy."[74] By Soviet standards for Italians, however, this is mild praise. *La Ciociara* was published on a large, but unspecified scale in Russian and also in other languages: 80,000 in Georgian, 15,000 each in Armenian and Lithuanian. *Roman Tales* were, similarly, printed in Russian

69. Ibid., Vol. I (1962), p. 348.
70. Ibid., Vol. V (1968), p. 507. No information available on the press run.
71. Ibid., Vol. I (1962), p. 187. There were 150,000 copies of the novel. Another work by Amorim, *The Lumberjacks,* was printed in 15,000.
72. KL, Vol. III (1966), pp. 434–35.
73. *Teatral'naja ènciklopedija,* Vol. II (1963), pp. 500–501.
74. KL, Vol. IV (1967), p. 965.

in probably close to half a million copies, with additional amounts in six other languages of the USSR.[75] The *Roman Tales* were described quite accurately in the *Literary Encyclopedia* as a canvas of the squalor of the city's slums with their homeless and unemployed dwellers. More far-reaching claims were made for *La Ciociara:* "His [Moravia's] heroine, after many trials to which fate subjected her, acquires both national and class consciousness, and *the author has her deliver his condemnation of war as a crime against mankind.*"[76] Alberto Moravia has his limitations. He is, for instance, a prime example of a "progressive" writer embarrassingly—by Soviet standards—obsessed with sex. Still, he is frequently published in Soviet literary periodicals.[77]

The list of modern Italian authors describing the economic hardships suffered by their compatriots, particularly in the countryside, is a long one. Most widely published were Carlo Montella (*Fire in the Land Administration,* 100,000; anthologies, 150,000 in Russian as well as 19,000 in Ukrainian and 16,000 in Estonian) and Silvia-Maggi Bonfanti (*A Sunny Valley,* 350,-000, and *Speranza* [*Hope*], in Latvian, 15,000).[78] Eduardo de Filippo was published many times, but almost no data are available on press runs of his sentimental works which "tell about the hard life of Italy's ordinary people."[79] Eduardo de Filippo's theater visited Moscow, and his comedies, which are said to reveal "the implacable hostility of bourgeois society to human happiness," were for a time the most widely performed modern Western plays in the repertory of Soviet theaters.[80] Other Italian authors in

75. 80,000 copies in Georgian, 20,000 in Estonian, 15,000 each in Lithuanian, Latvian and Azerbaidzhani, and 4,000 in Moldavian.

76. KL, Vol. IV (1967), p. 965. Emphasis added. The identification of a literary protagonist's views with those of the author, considered quite inadmissible in Western literary scholarship, is common in the USSR. It was used as legal evidence at the 1966 trial of Abram Tertz (pseudonym of Andrej Sinjavskij) and Nikolaj Arzhak (pseudonym of Julij Daniel').

77. *La Ciociara,* a well-known novel showing the misery and violence in Nazi-occupied Italy, appeared originally in *Inostrannaja literatura,* Nos. 1 and 2, 1958. The same periodical had earlier printed selections from his *Épidemia (Epidemic),* which was later incorporated in the *Roman Tales. Epidemia* has some mildly anti-American passages. An example: "True, mass-circulation illustrated periodicals from time to time featured photographs and articles which maintained that while happiness may not be littering the streets in the United States, it is nevertheless within one's reach." (*Inostrannaja literatura,* No. 6, 1957, p. 45.) Also in the same journal (Nos. 9 and 10, 1963) appeared Moravia's novel *Il disprezzo (Contempt),* about a writer's wife who realizes that her husband actually wants her to become the mistress of an influential movie producer. The first Russian translations of Moravia, a few of the *Roman Tales,* appeared in *Novyj mir,* No. 10, 1955. Another story by Moravia, which described the wretched existence in Rome of a worker from the south who is mocked for not even being able to speak Italian properly, was printed in *Moskva,* No. 1, 1959.

78. The latter was also serialized in Russian in *Inostrannaja literatura,* Nos. 3 and 4, 1955, and subsequently was apparently published separately in that language.

79. KL, Vol. II (1964), p. 622. *Questi fantasmi* appeared in Russian in 1956, *Napoli milionaria* in 1959, and *Filumena Marturano* was printed in Russian at least twice.

80. Thus, *Filumena Marturano* was staged in Moscow in 1956 by the Vakhtangov Theater, and subsequently in many other cities. *Lies Have Long Legs* was performed by the Moscow Theater of Satire, the Leningrad Theater of Comedy, and others. *My Family* was staged in Moscow, Leningrad, Riga, Murmansk, and Arkhangelsk; *Questi fantasmi* by the Theater of Drama and Comedy, and *De Pretore Vincenzo* by such important theaters as Sovremennik

this group included Raffaele Viviani,[81] Gian Paolo Callegari,[82] Elio Vittorini,[83] and Corrado Alvaro.[84] Works by Franco Solinas, Antonio Mallardi, and Leonardo Sciascia were published in literary journals.[85]

A significant amount of modern Greek writing, particularly poetry, was published. Most of it, however, was blatantly political even by Soviet standards. An exception was Nikos Kazantzakis's *Christ Recrucified,* described as an "expression of protest against injustice"; it was printed in 180,000 copies.[86] Scandinavian representation was modest: 10,000 copies of an Estonian translation of the Finnish author Toivo Pekkanen, who "realistically describes the hard life of urban workers,"[87] and a large printing (150,000 copies) of *Katrina,* a novel set in the Åland Islands and describing "the poorest of peasants and their struggle against capitalist landowners";[88] its author, Sally Salminen, is a Swedo-Finnish novelist. An anthology of Danish short stories by Hans Christian Branner, a writer said to criticize the greed and hypocrisy of the bourgeoisie, had an undisclosed press run.[89] Finally, there were 30,000 copies of a Ukrainian translation of the Flemish author of parodies and satires of manners and morals, Willem Elsschot.

---

(The Contemporary, then considered the most daringly innovative in the country) and the Stanislavskij Theater of Drama. (*Teatral'naja ènciklopedija,* Vol. II [1963], pp. 394–95.) Eduardo de Filippo's plays also appeared in literary periodicals (e.g., *Neva,* No. 12, 1962).

81. Raffaele Viviani (1888–1950), whose early work earned the approval of Gorky, wrote much about the waterfront of Naples. There were three editions of his plays; no information is available on press runs of two of them. The third was 13,000 copies.

82. *La ragazze bruciate verdi,* a novel about cynical tough adolescents; press run undisclosed.

83. A 20,000-copy anthology in Georgian. *Erica,* a novella about a teen-age girl forced by extreme poverty into prostitution, appeared in *Inostrannaja literatura,* No. 9, 1960.

84. "Alvaro is one of the few Italian writers who realistically depicted peasant life during the Fascist period." KL, Vol. II (1964), p. 171. An Estonian anthology was published in 15,000 copies. No information is available on the press run of the Russian.

85. Solinas's *Squarciò the Fisherman* appeared in *Inostrannaja literatura,* No. 11, 1958; Leonardo Sciascia's *Il giorno della civetta,* a novel about Sicily's poor whose attempts to establish a cooperative are thwarted by the rich and the Mafia, both protected by the authorities, was printed in the same journal, No. 4, 1962. Antonio Mallardi's *Levantazzo,* which portrays penniless fishermen, was translated in *Novyj mir,* No. 7, 1963. From time to time Soviet journals print "mini-anthologies" of foreign writing. Two such collections of Italian writing appeared in *Inostrannaja literatura.* The one assembled in No. 1, 1960, included short stories by Carlo Bernari, the first translation of his work into Russian (from the 1951 collection *Siamo tutti bambini*), Alberto Moravia, Vasco Pratolini, Italo Calvino, and Renata Vigano. The last two contributions were sent by the authors in manuscript, i.e., they were probably commissioned by the Soviet editors. Italo Calvino's warned against the menace of a resurgence of Nazism and the danger of war; Renata Vigano's related an episode from the anti-Nazi resistance. The second such collection also included one commissioned item, a story by Carlo Levi, as well as translations of stories by Calvino, Dino Buzzati, Tommaso Landolfi, and Carlo Emilio Gadda (ibid., No. 9, 1962). A similar "mini-anthology" of Scandinavian short stories was featured in *Neva,* No. 8, 1960.

86. KL, Vol. III (1966), p. 294. Not that the Soviet authorities found Kazantzakis's novel politically worthless: it was awarded the 1956 prize of the World Peace Council, a Soviet-dominated body.

87. KL, Vol. V (1968), p. 640.

88. Ibid., Vol. VI (1971), p. 617.

89. Ibid., Vol. I (1962), p. 724. Another Danish collection of short stories, *Det Blodige Sand (The Bloody Sand)* by Jurgen Petersen, denounced French rule in Algeria (*Moskva,* No. 6, 1961).

German literature appearing in the USSR between 1954 and 1964, i.e., prior to the improvement in West German-Soviet relations, consisted by and large of translations of East German authors (which are outside the scope of this study), venerable classics and juvenile books, books dealing with events of World War II, or works by anti-Nazi German émigrés, all of them considered elsewhere.[90] Other kinds of postwar German writing began to be published on an appreciable scale in the mid-1960s. The first West German author to achieve renown in the USSR was Heinrich Böll. Böll's novels with war settings are dealt with elsewhere. His works set in postwar Germany include *Acquainted With the Night,*[91] *The Unguarded House,* the long story "The Bread of Our Early Years," and *Dr. Murkes gesammeltes Schweigen,* all of them describing the moral squalor hidden behind the economic prosperity in postwar Germany. All were published.[92] A preface to the first Russian translations of Böll to appear in the USSR introduced him to Soviet readers as an author who had his limitations (e.g., "humanism" marred by frequently religious overtones, but it was acknowledged that "the passion with which Böll denounces the evils of capitalist society, his hatred of injustice, and, last but not least, the strongly antimilitaristic tendency of his books endear Böll's work to all progressive people in Germany."[93]

Paul Schallük's novel *Engelbert Reineke* combined flashbacks of the war with realistic descriptions of life in postwar Germany.[94] By contrast, Ursula Rütt's *In Sachen Mensch* was shrill in tone; according to Soviet editors, the exposé of West Germany as a corrupt neo-Nazi state was banned in that country as libelous:

> Ursula Rütt, who knows well the life and customs of the high and the mighty, succeeded in exposing in a sharply satirical, distinct manner the hypocrisy and falsehood of the so-called bourgeois-democratic self-government, which serves as a cover for the resurrected system of Fascist barracks. Using as an example the lives of ordinary people and petty officials in a small town, the author demonstrated that the entire Bonn state serves the interests of a small group of "interested persons," that its entire apparatus is filled with a milita-

90. See especially chapters 5 and 7. Among the rare exceptions was a 12,000 copy German-language anthology of Erich Mühsam, a poet, satirist, and playwright of leftist views who died in a Nazi camp in 1934.
91. It was published in the original German (about 20,000 copies), in Lithuanian (15,000), Estonian (20,000), Moldavian (5,000) and Russian (press run undisclosed).
92. *The Unguarded House* appeared in Russian (150,000 copies), Ukrainian (18,000), and Lithuanian (12,000). "The Bread of Our Early Years" appeared in book form in an undisclosed press run. Selections from *Dr. Murkes gesammeltes Schweigen* were published in *Inostrannaja literatura,* No. 6, 1959.
93. *Novyj mir,* No. 4, 1956, p. 175.
94. *Inostrannaja literatura,* Nos. 11 and 12, 1963.

ristic spirit, that old Nazi officials and Nazi regulations remain intact, that from top to bottom there is corruption, careerism, greed, and bureaucracy, which destroy anyone attempting to assert his Humanity.[95]

Finally, in the late 1950s Soviet readers and theatergoers were introduced to the Swiss German playwright Friedrich Dürrenmatt. The first translation of Dürrenmatt into Russian, it seems, was the play *The Visit* (*Inostrannaja literatura,* No. 3, 1958), in which an old lady, because of her wealth, becomes a virtual dictator in a small town and even settles scores with a former lover. While it is true that Dürrenmatt is often very critical of "bourgeois reality," his likely long-range impact will probably be felt in the Russian theater itself. Because of their "anticapitalist" tendency, Dürrenmatt's plays imparted a degree of respectability—or at least provided a measure of safety—to attempts on the part of a number of Soviet playwrights and directors to inject some "modernist" techniques in a drama and theater that, since the early 1930s, not only have tolerated no innovation in form both in their repertory and staging, but have actually repudiated their own avant-garde directors and dramatists of the 1920s, including Vsevolod Meyerhold and—incongruously—the country's Communist poet-laureate Vladimir Mayakovsky.[96]

Most contemporary French authors are discussed elsewhere.[97] Two writers of the older generation still alive in the post-Stalin decade—François Mauriac and André Maurois—reappeared in print after a long absence; neither was considered particularly "progressive" in his politics. Indeed, Mauriac was a profoundly religious writer. In the estimate of a Western critic, Mauriac "vividly evokes a dark world in which human love seems impure and unsatisfactory and where sinful creatures struggle toward the light that only God's grace can grant."[98] A Soviet evaluation of Mauriac is

95. Spelled with a capital H. Ibid., No. 7, 1957, p. 83.
96. Vsevolod Meyerhold (1874–1940), the greatest innovator in the Soviet theater, was arrested in 1939 and died in prison. His theater was closed in 1938. He has since been half-heartedly "rehabilitated," and the closing of the theater as "politically hostile to Soviet reality" is blamed on the Stalin "cult of personality." (See *Teatral'naja ènciklopedija,* Vol. III [1964], pp. 775–76.) Still, Meyerhold's "formalism" continues to be frowned upon. Mayakovsky's two famous plays, *The Bathhouse* and *The Bedbug,* were not performed in the USSR at a time when the poet's propagandistic verse was memorized by every Soviet schoolchild, that is during those years when, in the words of Pasternak, a cult of Mayakovsky was being implanted by force, "as were potatoes under Catherine the Great." *The Bathhouse* and *The Bedbug* reappeared on the Soviet stage after Stalin's death (together, incidentally with the plays of Bertolt Brecht, another author whose political acceptability was long apparently insufficient to outweigh Socialist Realism's objections to the artistic form of his drama). In recent years, incidentally, Brecht's name is occasionally invoked as evidence that Socialist Realism is compatible with artistic innovation. This must be viewed as a polemical device. By all evidence, the influence of Brecht on Soviet drama and theater is tolerated more in theory than in practice. Thus, for example, Aleksej Arbuzov's 1959 play *Irkutskaja istorija,* one of the best in the post-Stalin repertory and one of the more "innovationist," daringly resembles a number of features of Thornton Wilder's *Our Town* (1938), a reasonably conventional play.
97. See, especially, chapter 7.
98. *The Penguin Companion,* Vol. II, p. 521.

very different: Mauriac's novels "depict the life of the provincial French bourgeoisie, the nobility, clergy, and students, and the spiritual and religious quests of the young; they discuss problems of marriage and the family. A steadfast Catholic, Mauriac demonstrates that in its daily conduct the bourgeoisie flouts the principles of Christian morality. Mauriac's unmasking of the pathology of human relations under capitalism continues traditions of nineteenth-century critical realism."[99] Mauriac's two most widely published novels were *The Unknown Sea* and *Viper's Nest,* the latter published in a quarter of a million copies in Russian. "Le Drôle," a good story about a spoiled rich boy who is finally tamed by a clever governess, appeared in *Inostrannaja literatura.*[100]

A similarly effective exposé of mercenary bourgeois family relations emerges from a selection of Maurois's short stories published in *Inostrannaja literatura,* No. 4, 1963. The stories were chosen from the 1960 collection *Pour piano seul.* "Our Husband" relates how two successive wives of a famous writer jointly exploit their memories of the man after his death by making a deal with a Hollywood producer. Another of the stories is about an eccentric old couple who never leave their hotel room together; it turns out that they are guarding a suitcase filled with money.

While no exact statistics are available, it appears that Maurice Druon was one of the most important younger French writers favored by Soviet publishers in the 1954–64 period because of his portrayals of the injustices of capitalism. His novel *Les Grandes Familles,* which describes the disintegration of France's upper classes that contributed to the country's capitulation, was naturally favorably received in the USSR.[101] *The Accursed Kings* is a historical novel set in the fourteenth century: "The protagonists of *The Accursed Kings* bear the names and titles of men who ruled medieval France, but their actions and ethics are similar to the moral code of contemporary capitalism."[102]

There were 115,000 copies of a novel by Georges Conchon: *"In the Final*

99. KL, Vol. IV (1967), p. 974.

100. There was also a 2,000-copy edition in Estonian. *Viper's Nest,* which was previously published in 1932 and 1934, "exposes" a basic bourgeois social institution: "All members of a family (grandfather, father, children, grandchildren) poison each other with a venom of hatred and lies" (ibid.). *The Unknown Sea* appeared in Latvian (30,000 copies) and also apparently in a large Russian edition (press run unspecified). "Le Drôle" appeared in *Inostrannaja literatura* No. 10, 1962.

101. *Les Grandes Familles* was first serialized in *Inostrannaja literatura* (Nos. 4, 5, and 6, 1960) and was subsequently published in book form.

102. KL, Vol. II (1964), p. 809. The Soviet characterization of Druon's novel bears remarkable resemblance to Heinrich Mann's own evaluation of his *Henry IV, King of France;* see chapter 7. No information is available on the press runs of this series of Druon's novels (which includes *Le Roi de fer,* translated into Russian in 1957, and *La Reine etranglée,* translated in 1960). In the 1960s, one could occasionally see in Soviet periodicals Druon's cartoons suggested by biblical stories, which depicted God as a kindly but silly old man. Druon is a member of the pro-Communist National Committee of French Writers.

*Analysis* (*Tous comptes faits,* 1957, Russian translation 1961) depicts the world of banking manipulators in present-day France. Business sharpies, fond of liberal phrases, turn out to be the same kind of predators as their associates who had collaborated with the Nazis during the occupation."[103] The writings of Maurice Pons were of such immediate political value that one of them was made into a Soviet film, a distinction achieved only by a handful of foreign authors: "In the novel *Le Cordonnier Aristote* (1958, Russian translation 1961) one finds realistic portrayals of young [French] intellectuals facing a colonial war. The short novel *Le Passager de la nuit* (1960, Russian translations 1961, 1962) describes the upheaval in the heart of an apolitical newspaperman brought about by witnessing the heroic struggle of the Algerian [Arab] underground and of the Frenchmen who help it. *Le Passager de la nuit* was made into a film in the USSR."[104]

## Recent Writing from the British Commonwealth

Because of certain features of their works, a number of the more important debunkers of British "bourgeois" values and institutions are discussed else-where.[105] One modern British author published in the USSR on an exceptionally large scale was A. J. Cronin, whose dual traits of social awareness and sentimentality endeared him simultaneously to Soviet publishers and critics, as well as to the reading public. Most widely printed of all Cronin's novels was *The Stars Look Down* (nearly 2,000,000 copies in Russian, 50,000 in Lithuanian, and 40,000 in Latvian), the story of an ambitious coal miner who wants to be elected to Parliament:

> In the mid-1930s, at the height of the general democratic anti-Fascist struggle, Cronin wrote one of his most important novels, *The Stars Look Down* (1935, Russian translation 1937) which highlights the striking contradictions of modern bourgeois society. The writer's sympathies are entirely on the side of the masses. In the center of the novel stands a wonderful portrait of David Fanwick, a folk hero. A man of integrity, he attracts readers by his rich spirituality, notwithstanding the fact that neither he nor his heroes know how to fight for the people's interests. Following in the footsteps of critical realism, Cronin unmasks the capitalist Richard Barras, the manipulator Joe Gowlen, and the opportunistic leaders of the Labor Party.[106]

103. KL, Vol. III (1966), p. 719.
104. Ibid., Vol. V (1968), p. 880. The novel was also printed in 150,000 copies; there are no statistics on the Russian edition of *Le Cordonnier Aristote* (the Estonian version appeared in 20,000 copies and the Ukrainian in 15,000). Neither Maurice Pons nor Georges Conchon was listed in the standard Western literary reference works, but both appear in *Qui est qui en France 1973–74.*
105. Thus, for H. G. Wells, see chapter 4, and for G. B. Shaw, chapter 7.
106. KL, Vol. III (1966), p. 835.

Similarly welcome were Cronin's other works. *The Hatter's Castle,* first translated in 1938, "tells the tragic story of the Browdie family, which suffers under the despotic rule of its head, James Browdie, a typical bourgeois property owner."[107] *The Hatter's Castle* was reprinted in some 400,000 copies in Russian, 25,000 in Lithuanian, and a like number in the original English with a Russian introduction. *The Citadel,* which advocates medical insurance for workers and, according to a Soviet critic, "unfolds the tragic conflict between the scientist and bourgeois society, between science and the capitalist thirst for profits,"[108] was reprinted in close to a quarter of a million copies, including 50,000 in Latvian and 20,000 in English. *The Northern Light,* a recent work (1957) was first translated in a literary journal,[109] and then came out in book form in over half a million copies (including 15,000 in Lithuanian). The novel exposes the crass commercialism of British journalism thus intimating that the proud concept of a free press is really hollow mockery. No information is available on press runs of other works by A. J. Cronin then published; these included *Crusader's Tomb, Shannon's Way,* and *The Green Years.*

For a time, during the Cold War, J. B. Priestley was out of favor in the USSR and Soviet journalists referred to him as "the former writer Priestley." Now Priestley was restored to grace. His older works were reprinted, such as *The Angel Pavement* which, dealing with the world of London business, "quite expressively depicts the contradictions inside capitalist England."[110] *Wonder Hero* was reissued in 300,000 copies, and several of his plays were reprinted as well (e.g., *Laburnum Grove*). At the same time Priestley's recent works were translated, such as *Mr. Kettle and Mrs. Moon* (1955) and the short story *June 31.*[111] Symptomatic of Priestley's return to official favor was the appearance in 1958 of the play *Now Let Him Go,* which was received from the author in manuscript (i.e., it was presumably commissioned by the Soviet editors).[112]

A major new arrival in the post-Stalin period was Graham Greene. *Our Man in Havana* was printed in a Soviet periodical before Castro's revolution in Cuba and was subsequently reprinted in book form at least twice.[113] There were at least three printings of *The Quiet American,* about 150,000 copies

107. Ibid.
108. Ibid.
109. *Inostrannaja literatura,* Nos. 1 and 2, 1959.
110. KL, Vol. VI (1971), p. 18. It was reprinted in 150,000 copies.
111. In the story a fairy-tale princess from medieval England exposes the pretenses of modern British society, its cowardice, hypocrisy, greed, etc. The title is "magic": June has only thirty days. The story was printed in *Inostrannaja literatura,* No. 9, 1962.
112. Ibid., No. 2, 1958. The play is about an old artist who is so disgusted with the vulgarity and commercialism of London that he runs away with his paintings. He dies during his journey.
113. Ibid., Nos. 3 and 4, 1959. No press runs available on the two Russian reprints of the book. It was also printed in Estonian (18,000 copies), Latvian (15,000), and Moldavian (3,500).

of short stories and, intriguingly, 75,000 copies of a Ukrainian translation of *The Third Man*.[114] Graham Greene's writing also appeared in Soviet literary journals.[115] Greene's attraction was strong because he combined lively storytelling with contemporary settings and a strongly political flavor, usually very critical of Western institutions and policies: "Notwithstanding the fact that in 1926 Greene, in his quest for positive ideals, converted to Catholicism, his novels expose the inhuman essence of religion. Social criticism, characteristic of nearly all of his work, grows noticeably stronger starting with his novel *The Quiet American*, in which Greene condemns not only the 'dirty war' in Vietnam, but all of imperialism's policies of enslavement of nations. . . . In the novel *Our Man in Havana* Greene opposes militarism. The novel is an impassioned political tract."[116] Opposition to Western policies induced the Military Publishing House to bring out a translation of *Darkness Visible*, a satirical novel by Norman Lewis, a British writer of the older generation. The novel was good reading for Soviet soldiers: "[it] offers frightening pictures of the 'dirty war' in Algeria, exposés of French colonialists, and of the monopolists who inspire their 'activities'."[117]

It stands to reason that in their search for literary works that would provide evidence for Soviet propaganda's claims about the repugnant nature of life under capitalist conditions, Soviet editors and publishers would show particular interest in works with contemporary settings, writings that would not require any propping up with claims that conditions have not *really* changed that much since the writing of the book in question. Not surprisingly, during the first post-Stalin decade they were attracted to a group of British authors that came to the fore after World War II, in particular the so-called "angry young men." They were not proletarian, let alone Communist writers in the proper sense of the term. They exhibited, from the Soviet point of view, many of the ideological limitations characteristic of "critical realism," most importantly an inability to understand that the "correct" solution to the social ills described in their works with so much genuine indignation is the Communist one. A Soviet critic pointed out this shortcoming in a discussion of John B. Wain and Kingsley Amis published in 1956, i.e., before the appearance of most of such works in the USSR: "The books provide no answers to the most specific, ordinary problems that

114. *The Third Man*, a thriller set in occupied Vienna at the height of the Cold War, has some anti-Soviet overtones. It is possible that the text was censored by Soviet editors.
115. Thus, e.g., three stories appeared in *Zvezda* (No. 8, 1963). To Soviet readers, all were interesting because of their subject matter alone. One was set in exotic Africa, another dealt with the problem of Nazis in France, and the third titillated with its protagonist, a madam of a London brothel.
116. *KL*, Vol. II (1964), pp. 388–89.
117. Ibid., Vol. IV (1967), p. 471. It was published in 15,000 copies. Normally the Military Publishing House offers no data on press runs, which are, presumably, considered state secrets.

agitate ordinary people throughout the world. What is one to do in our time, when so much depends on the path that millions of these ordinary people will choose. . . . These writers underestimate their heroes, they doom them to remain 'little people' forever and ever."[118]

Nevertheless, such works were translated. *Lucky Jim,* with its portrayal of a young man driven to exasperation by the stupidity and hypocrisy of British universities, was published in spite of its "naive" belief that happy endings are possible, and that "good" rich men really do exist. These failings were, in a Soviet critic's estimate, redeemed by the novel's depiction of the vulgarity, greed, and aimlessness of bourgeois existence.[119] John B. Wain's *Hurry on Down* (a novel showing an upper-class young man contemptuous of his milieu who cannot, ironically, escape assuming a privileged position in that society) was serialized in another journal a year later and was also published in book form.[120] Typical of Soviet appraisals of books by the "angry young men" was this evaluation of John Braine's *Room at the Top:* "The novel's hero forsakes the woman who sincerely loves him because of the allure of marrying a rich man's daughter. And even though Braine fails to point to any way out of bourgeois conditions, the strength of his novel is contained in his condemnation of the protagonist and of bourgeois society that is hospitable to egotists and opportunists."[121] Absence of "positive" ideology was also said to mar John Osborne's play *Look Back in Anger:* "It depicts England's postwar youth, who reject traditional bourgeois values with bitterness and sarcasm, but see no goals worth fighting for."[122] Even so, the play was published, though probably in relatively modest editions.[123]

It is possible that the relative restraint displayed both in the publication and in the evaluation of most of the works by Britain's "angry young men" may be traced in part to what is sometimes referred to in Soviet political writings as "anarchistic individualism." There is an ambivalence in Soviet attitudes toward proponents of such tendencies. On the one hand, their bitter enmity toward the capitalist system is generally applauded. On the

118. V. Rubin, "Malen'kie ljudi," *Inostrannaja literatura,* No. 10, 1956, p. 189.

119. P. Palievskij, "Ščastlivčik Džim Kingsli Ejmisa," *Inostrannaja literatura,* No. 12, 1958, pp. 228–29. *Lucky Jim* was printed in Nos. 10, 11, and 12, 1958, of the same journal.

120. *Novyj mir,* Nos. 8, 9, and 10, 1959. No data available on the press run of the book.

121. KL, Vol. I (1962), p. 731. *Room at the Top* was printed in Estonian (20,000 copies), Lithuanian (15,000), in the original English (25,000), as well as in Russian (statistics unavailable). An early collection of Angus Wilson's short stories, *The Wrong Set* (1949) "exposed the hypocrisy and cruelty of the outwardly respectable 'middle class.' " (Ibid., Vol. VII [1972], p. 746.) It had a small run, only 20,000 copies.

122. Ibid., Vol. V (1968), p. 474.

123. There was an Estonian translation (20,000 copies), while the size of the Russian edition was unspecified. Most plays, however, tend to be printed in small editions. A formal attraction of Osborne's plays to Soviet editors (and theatrical directors) may have been the fact that they are artistically quite conventional.

other hand, it is feared that their positive features may in the final analysis be outweighed by the danger they pose: themselves mostly of bourgeois and intelligentsia backgrounds, they distract the working class from meaningful class warfare under the aegis of the Communist Party. Recent examples of this ambivalence are the equivocal Soviet, and generally Communist, attitudes toward the European and American New Left in the late 1960s. It may well be that the "angry young men" were suspected of being that movement's literary spokesmen.

It is perhaps for that reason that simultaneously with guarded praise and limited dissemination of works by young British authors that portray bitter and disillusioned members of the middle classes—or, to call a spade a spade, the bourgeoisie—there was an effort to promote the works of one "angry young man" whose moods may have been similar to the others but whose protagonists were workers. As the *Literary Encyclopedia* points out: "One of the central subjects of Sillitoe's writings is the English worker's moral and social dissatisfaction with bourgeois conditions."[124] The workers may be hedonistic and brutal, but workers they are, and *their* wrath, it may have been assumed, would evoke in a Soviet reader positive *associations* with such proletarian novels as Maxim Gorky's *Mother.* Sillitoe's novel *Key to the Door* depicts a worker whose life is reduced to fistfights, whiskey, army, and sex. (The latter, incidentally, was deplored as a "naturalistic tendency.") *Key to the Door* was first serialized in a journal[125] and a few months later was published in the paperbound series *Roman-gazeta* in a million copies, the largest single print run used by Soviet publishers for foreign literature and an indicator of rare favor.[126]

Another author from an English-speaking country published at the time was the Irish actor and prose writer Walter Macken. His two collections, *The Green Hills and Other Stories* and *Boat Races,* "depict the hard life and work of Irish fishermen, their lonely struggle with nature."[127] Also published (90,000 copies in Russian and 15,000 in Lithuanian) was the novel *Rain on the Wind,* the hero of which, an old fisherman, "sees the poverty and injustice around him, and a feeling of protest begins to awaken in him."[128] While Macken's and other serious authors' writings were somber in tone, those of the Canadian Stephen Leacock (175,000 copies in Russian,

124. KL, Vol. VI (1971), p. 823.

125. *Inostrannaja literatura,* Nos. 5, 6, and 7, 1963.

126. For a detailed discussion of Sillitoe's *Key to the Door* and the censoring of its text, see chapter 1. At the same time shorter works by Sillitoe were published in journals. Thus, a story from the 1963 collection *The Ragman's Daughter* appeared in ibid., No. 4, 1964. The story described the grief and loneliness of a working class couple who had recently lost their son.

127. *Boat Races* was printed in 150,000 copies; no information is available about the press run of the other volume.

128. KL, Vol. V (1968) p. 41. A few items from *God Made Sunday and Other Stories* appeared in *Novyj mir,* No. 9, 1963.

plus 20,000 in English) were ostensibly gay. Yet, in the view of a Soviet critic, their final effect was similar. All, in the final analysis, helped expose bourgeois society for what it is: "Leacock laughs at the moral conventions, dubious entertainment, smugness and superstitions of the bourgeoisie. . . . In his tales about the American electoral system, British parliamentary procedure, and anti-Soviet propaganda, Leacock rises to the stature of a political satirist. . . . During World War II Leacock proved to be a friend of the USSR."[129]

## *American Writing As an Indictment of the American Way of Life*

To Soviet leaders and ordinary citizens alike, the archetypal capitalist country is, of course, the United States of America. The United States, in the nearly unanimous view of Soviet writers, embodies the essence of everything evil in a "bourgeois democracy." At the same time America is also a symbol of efficiency and technological progress, hence the Soviet theory about the "internal contradictions" of American capitalism, which are manifested in such phenomena as wealth and poverty coexisting side by side, millions of automobiles and fear of unemployment, alleged mass dissatisfaction with the country's political system—and failure to abolish that system by whatever means necessary. These contradictions, however, also result in a schizoid Soviet view of the United States, a curious blend of hostility and envy that has occasional overtones of admiration; the Soviet slogan of the early 1930s, "catch up with and overtake America," and Soviet industrial goals of the Khrushchev years sometimes stated in similar terms, are eloquent examples of this ambivalence.

The tension between the two conflicting views of the United States was further aggravated in the post-Stalin years. America was cast in a dual role —as a state with which the USSR was eager to develop good diplomatic and commercial relations and simultaneously as the mightiest citadel of capitalism and bourgeois values, which the Soviet Union was ideologically committed to oppose. These "internal contradictions" in Soviet attitudes toward the United States were clearly reflected in the publication and interpretation of American literature during the first post-Stalin decade. There was a dramatic expansion in the publication of American writing, particularly striking when contrasted with the years that preceded it. Cold War taboos, although applying to all Western literature, were then most

129. KL, Vol. IV (1967), p. 194.

stringently observed with regard to American literature; for a time, American books brought out in the USSR were, for all intents and purposes, limited to old classics (preferably accessible to juvenile readers) and to works by Communist and pro-Soviet authors. The expansion benefited these categories of books, but the relaxation of tensions within the USSR and the policy of detente and peaceful coexistence also argued for the publication of modern American authors who were not overtly political, including some of this country's most distinguished prose writers, poets, and dramatists. At the same time Soviet criticism of American writing began to concern itself once again with literary values. All of this, however, was kept within bounds. Periodic exhortations of critics and editors to remain on guard against the danger of penetration into the USSR of "alien bourgeois ideology," and reiteration by the country's leaders (including Khrushchev himself) of the insistence that no peaceful coexistence is possible with the non-Soviet world in the ideological sphere, served to prop up the temporarily shaken foundations of the traditional Soviet politicized criticism of American literature.

Both types of criticism survive in the 1970s but the political variety is incomparably more influential and continues to enjoy overwhelming predominance in such crucial areas as reference works, textbooks, and the general press. Soviet critics and editors soon discovered that American literature of the 1960s, taken as a whole, reflected much of the painful reexamination of American values, institutions, and policies that was characteristic of the latter period of racial conflict and unrest, as well as the national trauma of Vietnam. All of these could be, and were, pointed to as evidence of instability and demoralization within a country that was universally regarded as the Soviet Union's capitalist antipode, her chief rival as a great power and the world center of bourgeois ideology. That the American authors of such works were by and large loyal critics of their society was ignored in the USSR, a country where the concept of loyal opposition is not widely recognized. That most chose not to dwell on what were to them, and to their readers, self-evident positive aspects of life in America went unmentioned. To have pointed this out would have been politically counterproductive, and it probably would not have been widely believed in a society whose literature dutifully emphasizes the positive. That most of the writers in question were not particularly enamored of the USSR was passed over in discreet silence.[130] Carefully selected and tendentiously interpreted, American writing of the 1950s and 1960s published in the USSR

130. Works by radical critics of American society, many with pro-Soviet sympathies, also strongly contribute to the negative picture of the United States that emerges from translations of American writing accessible to Soviet readers. See chapter 7.

helped foster in the Soviet reader's mind an image of America as a land of racial oppression, economic injustice, and spiritual void. Thus, it blended harmoniously with the image of the United States that was projected by older works of American literature that had been published during the Stalin era and continued to be reprinted on a large scale after the dictator's death. Indeed, such older books continued to be recommended to Soviet readers as documents of American life that had somehow escaped obsolescence and retained their original validity. As Deming Brown writes:

> The Soviet choice of [older] translations contributed abundantly to a distorted impression of America. The high percentage of politically biased works of left-wing, and often Communist, orientation, simply misinformed the Russian public about the political climate and tendencies of the United States. . . . Moreover, this image was badly outdated. In the 1950s, for example, the works of Dreiser became for Soviet readers the highest American authority on the details of life in the United States—the workings of its social system, the operation of its economy, the psychology of its classes—whereas in actuality the country had changed profoundly in many respects since Dreiser's time. Sinclair's *The Jungle,* describing a situation that had existed half a century ago, continued to be published as a valid and timely document. In passing off such works as true descriptions of contemporary America, the publishers performed a twofold service to Soviet propaganda. First, they helped perpetuate the image of a mythical America that was totally vulnerable to the classic nineteenth-century Marxist critique of capitalism, and, second, they showed the America of the days of the horseless carriage, thus obscuring the improvements in her standard of living and the increasingly equalitarian distribution of her wealth.[131]

The time limits of our discussion overlap only slightly with Deming Brown's: it must be remembered, however, that his comment is a summary of the entire period between 1917 and 1960. During the first post-Stalin decade, and particularly in its latter part, there were some shifts of emphasis. Works that portrayed America's high standard of living (even among workers and blacks) were published, provided that economic "embarrassment" was "redeemed" by portrayal of other negative features of American life, for instance race discrimination or even a nagging feeling of boredom and futility of life in "bourgeois" society. The squalor, in other words, need no longer be material; it could also be psychological. Inferences that the United States was indeed vulnerable to a Marxist critique of capitalism that might be drawn from individual works of American literature were significantly expanded. They now included such themes as inequality in the midst of plenty, as well as the relatively new concept (new, that is, in the USSR)

131. Deming Brown, *Soviet Attitudes toward American Writing,* pp. 317–18.

of the alienation of man from his social environment, even if the literary protagonists illustrating this thesis were not always themselves members of the oppressed classes. To be sure, Theodore Dreiser's earnest novels continued to be printed but their position was now a more modest one.[132]

Frank Norris's novel *Octopus* and his collection of short stories *A Deal in Wheat* depict the ruin of California farmers by the moguls of the Southern Pacific Railroad. Both books are now three quarters of a century old. Their literary merit alone would hardly warrant republication in a quarter of a million copies (and 13,000 in the original English). A likely reason may have been a desire to suggest to Soviet readers that the dog-eat-dog "free enterprise" described by Norris and such other features of turn of the century America as police corruption are still pretty much the same in America of the 1960s.

The *Literary Encyclopedia*'s entry for Sinclair Lewis rebuked American critics for their downgrading of Lewis, with the insinuation that their views reflected a conscious political bias: "Characteristically, bourgeois American criticism considers Lewis a mediocre artist, an 'uninspired' journalist who created 'caricatures' of America. In the USSR and other socialist countries Lewis's works are being constantly reissued."[133] That is not to say that the Soviet critics themselves attributed to Lewis great artistic merit. Rather, they considered the problem secondary in view of Sinclair Lewis's importance as a chronicler of the workings of American society whose accounts retain much of their validity half a century later. Thus, *Babbitt* was printed in a quarter of a million copies in Russian (as well as 15,000 in Latvian and 20,000 in English): "In the novel *Babbitt* (1922; Russian translations 1926, 1959) Lewis created a classic type of an American manipulator and philistine."[134] *Arrowsmith* was reissued in twice that amount (also 30,000 copies in Estonian); the novel was described as a portrait of a positive counterpart of Babbitt, a medical researcher who stands up to greedy and unscrupulous scientific enterpreneurs. *Kingsblood Royal* (165,000 copies) was called a denunciation of racism. Elmer Gantry was described as "a 'salesman of God's word,' an American Tartuffe, an ignorant and lecherous pastor." (*Elmer Gantry* was printed in English, with a Russian introduction, in 10,000 copies.) As for Lewis's *Main Street,* a novel frequently published in earlier years, it continued to be highly praised: "The writer's power is demonstrated in his satirical mockery of the spiritual poverty of 'one-storied America' [the title of Il'f and Petrov's popular Soviet account of travels in the U.S.A.—MF], of religious charlatans, political demagogues, and merce-

132. See chapter 7.
133. KL, Vol. IV (1967), pp. 472–73. A nine-volume set of Sinclair Lewis's writings appeared in 1965.
134. Ibid., p. 471.

nary spirit, which fills all the pores of American society." But it was reprinted in a mere 30,000 copies.[135] The story "Willow Walk" was printed in over 300,000 copies in Russian, 40,000 in Georgian, and 16,000 in Estonian, even though its political value is scant.

Erskine Caldwell is known in the USSR chiefly for his *Tobacco Road,* which was translated in 1938 and, by reputation, as a friendly foreign correspondent, author of two books of wartime reportage and a novel about the Soviet guerrilla movement.[136] His autobiographical *Georgia Boy,* which portrays the poor of the rural South, appeared in 350,000 copies (including 15,000 copies in Latvian, 12,000 in Lithuanian, and 7,000 in Turkmen); there were also approximately a half million copies in Russian (and 15,000 in Armenian) of Caldwell's short stories, many of which describe such perennial American ills as racism and unemployment—two problems that have no exact Soviet parallels and are therefore effective criticism of "bourgeois American way of life."[137] There were several anthologies (about 200,000 copies in all, including 15,000 each in Armenian and Estonian) of Sherwood Anderson. In his stories, Soviet readers were promised, they would find "realistic portrayals of the American backwoods, of their spiritual poverty, of crippled human destinies. Anderson creates grotesque portraits of eccentrics who live in a world where objects crush men."[138] Objects crush men in many of the poems of Ogden Nash also. Soviet readers were told in an editorial note to the seven pages of his verse in *Novyj mir* (No. 1, 1963) that for all of his mocking humor, Nash is really a sad observer of his surroundings. This assertion was supported by those of Nash's poems that were printed; they dealt with such subjects as the lack of moral scruples and the power of the almighty dollar.

Eccentrics and failures abound in the writings of William Saroyan. In the words of a Western critic, "His bitter sentimentalities are not cynical or political in the twenties or thirties manner, but his derelicts and humble men and women struggle in the same Depression with a warmth which is heroic, on a small scale."[139] Viewed through the politicized prism of Soviet criticism, Saroyan's works "depict people alien to bourgeois greed and the crash of illusions about America as a country of universal well-being. Saroyan's

135. Ibid., pp. 471–72.
136. The novel *All Night Long* appeared in 1942, as did the two other volumes, *Moscow Under Fire* and *All-out on the Road to Smolensk.* KL, Vol. III (1966), p. 652.
137. Two of Caldwell's recent novels appeared in *Inostrannaja literatura: Jenny by Nature,* about a bigoted and hypocritical small-town clergyman intent on ruining a decent elderly woman and her boarder, driven to prostitution by an unhappy love affair (the disaster is averted by an honest old lawyer; No. 12, 1962); and *Close to Home,* which describes some horrors of life in the American South, particularly those rooted in race problems (Nos. 10 and 11, 1963).
138. KL, Vol. I (1962), p. 227.
139. *The Penguin Companion,* Vol. III, pp. 228–29.

heroes are the 'little people' of America's small towns, many of them destitute. Yet even when they become rich, they do not become happy."[140] The last sentence, a reflection of the broadened concept of America as an oppressive society that was referred to earlier was also echoed in the preface to three of Saroyan's stories newly translated in a Soviet journal: "Saroyan's heroes are nearly always simple people, forced to wage an embittered struggle for existence, and the writer strives to portray the rich, complex, poetic inner world of these people in its clash with the soulless prose of the 'civilization' created by American capitalism."[141] Saroyan's works were printed in a total probably approaching 750,000 copies. The play *My Heart Is in the Highlands* was published in Armenian (3,000 copies) as was *The Human Comedy,* a novel (10,000): himself of Armenian origin, Saroyan frequently uses Armenian motifs in his work. The Russian edition of *The Human Comedy* was issued in 150,000 copies (also 12,000 in Lithuanian); there were also two Russian printings of *The Adventures of Wesley Jackson* of unspecified size, but presumably large. Anthologies of Saroyan's short stories were published in some 300,000 copies in Russian and three other languages (Estonian, 20,000; Lithuanian, 12,000; and Turkmen, 5,500).

John Steinbeck's *Grapes of Wrath* was first published in the USSR in 1940; he continued to be printed until the middle of the war (the last work of his, *The Moon Is Down,* a novel about the Norwegian anti-Nazi resistance was published, incongruously, in 1943 in Magadan, the capital of the Soviet concentration camp empire, the *Gulag Archipelago* later made famous by Solzhenitsyn. After that, no work of Steinbeck's was printed until the post-Stalin "thaw," when *The Pearl,* a parable about a Mexican Indian made unhappy by the discovery of a gem, was translated. The nonpolitical *The Pearl* was printed in Russian and three other languages (Estonian, 20,000; Armenian, 20,000; Georgian, 10,000), in a total of about 350,000 copies.[142] There was also a 100,000-copy edition of excerpts from that work and from a sentimentalized novel about poor Americans, *Tortilla Flat.*[143] *The Winter of Our Discontent,* a new work at the time (published in English in 1961, it was brought out in Russian within a year), was understood by a Soviet critic to illustrate the "crash of the American dream"[144] and (in spite of its references to the Gospels) was given one of the widest disseminations

140. KL, Vol. VI (1971), pp. 661–62. Saroyan's sentimentality and avoidance of unpleasant subjects were deplored.
141. *Zvezda,* No. 4 (1956), p. 84. Earlier, four stories by Saroyan had appeared in *Novyj mir,* No. 11, 1955.
142. One Russian printing was 150,000 copies, the press run of the other was not disclosed.
143. Again, the Soviet appraisal was more politicized. According to a Soviet critic, *Tortilla Flat* is a book reminiscent of at least two of Maxim Gorky's works. It is said to portray "men rejected by society, inhabitants of its 'lower depths,' strikers driven to despair." KL, Vol. VII (1972), p. 156.
144. Ibid., p. 157.

of any single work by a foreign author. It was first serialized in a journal,[145] then printed in half a million copies in the paperback series *Roman-gazeta,* and reprinted at least once more in an unspecified number of copies. The critic Raisa Orlova was particularly impressed by Steinbeck's kindly shopkeeper's transformation into an unscrupulous and dishonest man: "Money vs. humanity—this is the crux of the new novel [*The Winter of Our Discontent*]. This is an old head-on collision in American life and American culture—old, but not obsolete. This is also the *leitmotif* of John Steinbeck's work—old, perhaps, but not at all obsolete."[146]

*Grapes of Wrath* was reprinted in a quarter of a million copies in Russian and 30,000 in Latvian, rather modest amounts for an old classic called "a tragic epic of the American people; his [Steinbeck's] ruined farmers are the heroes of a saga."[147] There were also some 120,000 copies of anthologies of Steinbeck's short stories. At the same time some of his older writings were appearing in literary periodicals; thus a dramatization of *Of Mice and Men,* a novel written in 1937, was published in Russian in 1963: "In it [*Of Mice and Men*] the writer describes the destinies of ordinary workers, farm hands, whose life he knew well, as he also knew the locale where the story is set, the area around Salinas, in California, where he was born and in his youth had worked for a time on a ranch, just as his protagonists do. Steinbeck's novella is filled with great love for downtrodden Americans, it is filled with sympathy for their tragic destinies."[148]

Finally, an abridged version of *Travels With Charley* was serialized in a Soviet journal immediately after the novel's appearance in the United States in 1962; a separate edition of the entire novel was printed in 1965.[149] Probably anticipating Western criticism of the tendentious selection of parts of Steinbeck's novel in the Soviet journal, Soviet publishers decided that the best defense is offense: they accused *American* editors of doing just that in the selections from *Travels With Charley* that were printed in an American magazine.[150] Steinbeck's popularity with the Soviet establishment was not to last much longer. On July 7, 1966, the Soviet poet Yevgeni Yevtushenko, whose role as the Soviet Union's envoy to the Western intelligentsia bears much resemblance to the activities of Ilya Ehrenburg during the Stalin era, published a letter in *Literaturnaja gazeta* calling on Steinbeck to denounce

145. *Inostrannaja literatura,* Nos. 1, 2, and 3, 1962.
146. Ibid., No. 3, 1962, p. 198.
147. KL, Vol. VII (1972), p. 157. The neglect of the book is particularly striking in view of the fact that the 300,000 copies of *The Grapes of Wrath* brought out in 1941 were "by far the largest single printing an American work had ever enjoyed in Russia." Deming Brown, *Soviet Attitudes toward American Writing,* p. 74.
148. *Moskva,* No. 8 (1963), p. 61. Three short stories by Steinbeck appeared in the same year in *Novyj mir* (No. 12, 1963).
149. *Zvezda,* No. 4, 1962, and Nos. 5 and 6, 1963.
150. The full text of *Travels With Charley* was slightly censored. See chapter 1.

the American presence in Vietnam. Instead, Steinbeck printed an answer in *Newsday* defending American policies in Southeast Asia. On February 5, 1967, Steinbeck was excommunicated in *Pravda:* "Service to an antihuman cause has nullified Steinbeck's reputation both as a citizen and as a writer."[151]

That older and recent American works were viewed by Soviet publishers as complementing each other and advancing the same pedagogical goals is illustrated by two American films that were released in the USSR in the late 1950s. Reference was made earlier to West European and American films shown in the USSR to special invited audiences.[152] More care is exercised in the selection of films shown to general audiences: "Foreign films shown publicly in the USSR are selected not only on the basis of their artistic merits, their value as entertainment or education, and their box-office earnings, but also with an eye to their possible usefulness as reinforcement of domestic propaganda concerning the non-Soviet world."[153] Two films released in the late 1950s illustrated the traditional and the new features in the image of the United States that were to be supported by evidence contained in American films. The old claim that the United States is a country of impoverished and exploited workers was illustrated by a film produced in America by the International Union of Mine, Mill, and Smelter Workers that was dubbed into Russian, presumably for wide distribution. *Salt of the Earth* was praised in *Pravda:* "This film accurately describes the struggle of American workers for an improvement of living and working conditions."[154] Friendlier relations with the United States encouraged a Soviet critic to praise the humane message of *Marty,* a moving film about a lonely middle-aged American bachelor then being shown in Moscow. At the same time *Marty* was commended for demonstrating the shallowness of Americans whose spiritual nourishment consisted of primitive detective novels and girlie magazines, that is for confirming the newer emphasis of Soviet characterizations of the United States as a

151. The following appeared in the *Literary Encyclopedia* in 1972: "In 1966 Steinbeck declared himself a defender of American aggression in Vietnam at a time when the American intelligentsia spoke up in opposition to the government's militaristic policies." KL, Vol. III (1972), p. 157. Steinbeck died in 1968; it is likely that with time his transgression will be forgotten, or written off as a vagary of old age, and that his works will be republished. Such procedures are common enough, even with regard to the writings of such bitterly anti-Soviet émigrés as Ivan Bunin, now widely published in the USSR.

152. See the Introduction and chapter 5.

153. Paul Babitsky and John Rimberg, *The Soviet Film Industry* (New York: Frederick A. Praeger, 1955), pp. 247–48.

154. *Pravda,* April 24, 1957. Three years earlier, a Soviet journal had reported the film's American première. *The Salt of the Earth* was hailed as "the first truthful film about the life of the working class in the history of the American cinema; it was produced by progressive artists expelled from Hollywood. The story of the film itself is as dramatic as is the event it describes, the fifteen-month strike of American miners of Mexican origin." *Novyj mir,* No. 7, 1954, p. 140.

land of little culture, boredom, and purposeless existence.[155]

Of all the belated Soviet discoveries of American writers in the late 1950s and 1960s, none is more startling than that of William Faulkner, then already a patriarch of American literature. In previous decades Faulkner either was dismissed as a decadent antirealist obsessed with pathology (and a racist at that) or, what was more common, was totally ignored. The admission of Faulkner to the ranks of publishable American authors during the post-Stalin thaw raises a question: Why publish Faulkner at all? Why not simply continue ignoring him, though dispensing perhaps, in the more civilized atmosphere of the post-Stalin "thaw," with the abuse that had regularly been heaped on him in preceding decades? Why not dismiss him as an author who, like Joyce and Proust, is of no interest to Soviet readers and therefore not worth printing?

Perhaps some clues to the problem may be found in Soviet publication statistics for the two giants of prerevolutionary Russian prose, Tolstoy and Dostoyevsky. Ideological reasons, implied and candidly stated, favored the publication of Tolstoy and resulted in consistent discrimination against Dostoyevsky; the former's books and shorter works were studied by every schoolchild in the country, while the latter was treated at best as a minor and flawed novelist. A list of fifteen prerevolutionary Russian authors ranked in order of the total number of copies printed by Soviet publishers between 1918 and the beginning of World War II is headed by Tolstoy. Dostoyevsky's name is last on that list; he is outranked by such second-rate Russian authors as Uspenskij, Korolenko, and Mamin-Sibirjak.[156] Between 1918 and 1957, government-owned Soviet publishing firms brought out 1,652 titles by Tolstoy in 80 languages, with a total press run of 76,272,000. The corresponding figures for Dostoyevsky were 138 titles, 13 languages and 6,911,000 copies; Tolstoy's name was second on this list (he was outranked by Pushkin), and Dostoyevsky's was again fifteenth.[157] It was not until after Stalin's death that the blatant inequality in the treatment of the two novelists began to be moderated. Tolstoy continued to be favored heavily, but the gap was getting narrower. In 1956–62 Tolstoy was still first, with 313 titles in 53 languages and 36,374,000 copies, but Dostoyevsky moved up to eighth place, with 68 titles in 14 languages and 7,494,000 copies.[158]

A somewhat similar imbalance obtained in the mid–1950s in the Soviet

155. *Izvestija,* November 11, 1959. Paddy Chayefsky, the author of the film's script, was soon to lose favor with the Soviet authorities, in part at least because of his activities on behalf of Soviet Jews, and his play about Stalin, *The Passion of Joseph D.*
156. *Maurice Friedberg, Russian Classics in Soviet Jackets,* p. 189.
157. Ibid., p. 190.
158. Maurice Friedberg, "Literary Output: 1956–1962," *Soviet Literature in the Sixties: An International Symposium,* Max Hayward and Edward L. Crowley, eds. (New York and London: Frederick A. Praeger, 1964), pp. 174, 176.

treatment of the two greatest living American writers, Hemingway and Faulkner (incidentally, one a very "Tolstoyan" and the other a strikingly "Dostoyevskian" novelist). Both politically and artistically, Hemingway was the more congenial of the two, and many Soviet readers remembered his writings that were published in the USSR in the 1930s. With the translation in 1955 of *The Old Man and the Sea* Hemingway's books reappeared in Soviet bookstores and libraries. In an atmosphere of "peaceful coexistence" it was simply untenable to continue a total boycott of America's other leading novelist. The first story of Faulkner, from the collection *Knight's Gambit,* appeared in a literary journal in 1957, a year after its publication in English.[159] This was followed by several novellas printed, curiously, in the more conservative journals.[160] *The Mansion* was serialized in *Inostrannaja literatura,* but a few years later *Soldier's Pay* was printed by a rather Stalinist literary monthly.[161] Simultaneously, Faulkner's writings began to be published in book form. There was an anthology of his short stories in 1958, and another one the following year (one was printed in 150,000 copies; the press run of the other is unavailable). *The Hamlet* came out in 1964 in 100,000 copies, the same number as *The Town* a year later.[162]

Again, there was a parallel with the guarded readmission of Dostoyevsky into the official pantheon of Russian literature. Side by side with a small body of serious criticism intent on studying the "rehabilitated" author's art, there were more numerous attempts to justify this amnesty on political grounds, to provide the reader with antidotes to the ideologically harmful contents and objectionable artistic form of Faulkner, and even to find in his writings isolated incidents and themes of "progressive" character. Thus, Raisa Orlova and Lev Kopelev in an article published in 1958 pointed to the "positive" fact that Faulkner describes in his works the destruction of the patriarchal old South by a new breed of rapacious, ruthless businessmen— a traditional concern of good critical realism—even though his moral analysis of the process, in contrast to a sociopolitical analysis, is, of course, wrong.[163] An annotated bibliography of foreign literature intended for li-

159. *Inostrannaja literatura,* No. 12, 1957.
160. Thus, for example, "By the People" appeared in *Znamja,* No. 10, 1960; "About Turn," in *Moskva,* No. 2, 1960; "Bear Hunt," in *Znamja* No. 12, 1961; and "Artist at Home" was printed in *Neva,* No. 5, 1963, shortly after Faulkner's death in 1962.
161. *The Mansion* was printed in *Inostrannaja literatura,* Nos. 9, 10, 11, and 12, 1961. *Soldier's Pay* appeared in *Don,* Nos. 4, 5, and 6, 1966.
162. *The Mansion* appeared under separate cover in 1965, and *Intruder in the Dust* was translated in *Inostrannaja literatura,* Nos. 1 and 2, 1968.
163. R. Orlova, L. Kopelev, "Mify i pravda amerikanskogo juga; zametki o tvorčestve Folknera," *Inostrannaja literatura,* No. 3, 1958, pp. 206–20. Raisa Orlova is a specialist in American literature. Her essay on Hemingway's *For Whom the Bell Tolls* is reproduced in English translation in Carl R. Proffer, *Soviet Criticism of American Literature* pp. 117–48. Lev Kopelev, Orlova's husband, writes primarily about German literature. Kopelev is widely

brarians, teachers, and the reading public noted that Faulkner's realism is marred by impressionism, a feverish quality of narration, and a tendency to get readers "forcibly sucked into the whirlwind of events"—blemishes that are frequently, by the way, also attributed to Dostoyevsky. Still, readers were reassured about a number of Faulkner's "positive" attributes: he describes the rampant racism of the South and reflects its atmosphere of helplessness and fear; in his trilogy the Snopeses are the symbol of the "parasitic plutocracy, the growth of the forces of fascism in the USA." It was significant to the compilers of the bibliography that Linda, who helps to kill Faulkner's villain Flem Snopes, is a Communist. In conclusion, readers were told that while Faulkner's short stories reflect racism in America, *The Town, The Mansion,* and *The Hamlet* demonstrate that "American society lacks moral values with which it could oppose fascism."[164] Foreign writers—even living ones—are quite defenseless in such cases. Hardly ever does a Soviet journal allow a Western author to publish a rejoinder to a particularly preposterous claim by a Soviet critic.

As already suggested, Soviet publishers and critics prefer dead Western writers to living ones. The dead do not stir, whatever position they are given in the procrustean bed of Soviet criticism. The living may, and often do stir, risking excommunication, although their sins may be forgiven, most often posthumously. A number of such anathemized Western authors will be considered elsewhere.[165]

While the writings of the recently deceased conservative Mississippian were rapidly gaining acceptance in the USSR (although, to be sure, with more than the usual degree of biased interpretation), a living American playwright of equal eminence, known for his liberal views and leftist associations, was gradually losing favor in the Soviet Union for reasons that were clearly political. The first play of Arthur Miller, *All My Sons,* was translated in 1948, at the height of Stalinist xenophobia.[166] *The Crucible,* with its transparent allusions to the atmosphere of suspicion and fear of the McCarthy period, appeared in 1955.[167] Then came *Death of a Salesman:* "The play depicts the tragedy of an average American family whose faith

believed to have served as the prototype for Rubin, the brilliant but dogmatic Communist, one of the central characters in Alexander Solzhenitsyn's *The First Circle.* Thus, Dimitrij Panin, who now lives in the West, and who himself served as a prototype of another major character in the novel (Sologdin, Rubin's ideological opponent), writes, "Our disputes were to be described later by Solzhenitsyn in *The First Circle,* where Lev Kopelev was the prototype for Rubin." D. Panin, *Zapiski Sologdina* (Frankfurt/Main: Possev, 1973), p. 418. A book of Kopelev's memoirs was recently published in the United States: *Xranit' večno* (Ann Arbor, Mich.: Ardis, 1975).

164. *Osnovnye proizvedenija,* 1965, pp. 404–5.
165. See chapter 8.
166. *Zvezda,* No. 2, 1948.
167. *Teatr,* No. 6, 1955. The play's Russian title was *Salemskij process (The Trial of Salem).* The Soviet text was heavily censored. See chapter 1.

in the saving powers of 'private enterprise' is crumbling."[168] *Death of a Salesman* was followed in 1957 by *A View from the Bridge* which portrays a renegade and informer, and later by *A Memory of Two Mondays.*[169] Next appeared an anthology of plays published earlier (no press run available) and, in 1965, *Incident at Vichy.*[170] The latter play was published after some delay; by then, the Soviet authorities had become weary of publishing *any* works by foreign writers that dealt with the problem of anti-Semitism, even persecution of the Jews by the Nazis, the subject of Miller's drama. Earlier, Miller's plays had been widely performed, and Miller himself was praised in a 1964 volume of the *Theatrical Encyclopedia* as a progressive playwright, conscious of social problems, and heir to the best traditions of American drama.[171] By 1967, the *Literary Encyclopedia's* praise became more restrained; Miller was only a "liberal democrat."[172] Another play, *The Price,* was translated in 1968.[173] In 1969, however, Miller's book *In Russia,* with photographs by his wife Inge Morath, provoked severe criticism in the USSR; there was also resentment of Miller's activities on behalf of dissident Soviet writers and intellectuals as well as of Soviet Jews. Works by the living liberal Arthur Miller had become distinctly less welcome in the USSR than those of the deceased bard of the traditional American South William Faulkner.[174]

168. *Novyj mir,* No. 2, 1956, p. 157. The *Literary Encyclopedia* said much the same thing eleven years later: "In the tragedy *Death of a Salesman* (1949, Russian translation 1956) Miller departs from conventional norms of the theater in order to unearth the sources of illusions of American 'success' and the crash of these illusions." KL, Vol. IV (1967), p. 833. Curiously, the *Novyj mir* translation of *Death of a Salesman* was entitled *The Man Who Had All the Luck (Čelovek kotoromu tak vezlo),* probably to heighten the impact of its irony directed at American "success." The change of title is confusing, because it is also the title of *another* play by Arthur Miller, which the playwright called "a preparation, and possibly a necessary one, for those that followed, especially *All My Sons* and *Death of a Salesman,* and this for many reasons" (Arthur Miller, "Introduction," *Arthur Miller's Collected Plays* [New York: The Viking Press, 1957], p. 14). The book version of the play bore the correct title, *Smert' kommivojažera (Death of a Salesman)* (Moscow: Iskusstvo, 1956). It was printed in 10,000 copies.
169. The first appeared in *Inostrannaja literatura,* No. 4, 1957, and also as a separate book; the second in the anthology *Sovremennaja dramaturgija,* No. 4, 1958.
170. *Inostrannaja literatura,* No. 7, 1965. Also see chapter 1.
171. *Teatral'naja ènciklopedija,* Vol. III (1964), pp. 828–29. *All My Sons* was staged by the Moscow Theater of Drama in 1958; *Death of a Salesman* by the Leningrad Pushkin Theater of Drama in 1958 and by the world-famous Moscow Art Theater in 1960. The Moscow Theater of Drama presented *A View from the Bridge* in 1959, and *The Crucible* was staged in 1962 by the Moscow Stanislavsky Theater.
172. KL, Vol. IV (1967), p. 834.
173. *Inostrannaja literatura,* No. 6, 1968.
174. An older playwright, Lillian Hellman, had her works published in two anthologies (no publication figures given); her plays were given high marks for their "striking portraits of capitalist predators and their victims," "the responsibility of democratic bourgeois governments and the progressive intelligentsia for the outbreak of World War II" and for showing "the spiritual universe of man in modern capitalist society." *Teatral'naja ènciklopedija,* Vol. V (1967), p. 599. For a time it appeared that the young American playwright Edward Albee might earn a secure place in the Soviet repertory. *The Death of Bessie Smith* was published in *Inostrannaja literatura,* No. 4, 1965, and his Americanized version of the British playwright Giles Cooper's *Everything in the Garden* in ibid., No. 1, 1969. He was praised in 1965 for "unmasking race hatred and fanaticism," and for his "angry mockery of the cruelty, smugness

Arthur Miller first received favorable attention in the USSR in the late 1940s, and much of his erstwhile popularity can be traced to his defiance of Congressional committees then investigating left-wing activities. The credentials of Dorothy Parker were much older: "In the 1920s and 1930s [Parker] participated in the progressive movement of the American intelligentsia. She was persecuted for her beliefs in the early 1950s. . . . Many of Parker's novellas, written in an informal, ironic vein, are permeated with contempt for the bourgeois way of life, with hatred of the hypocrisy, cruelty, humiliation of human dignity, selfishness, and greed of her milieu."[175] J. P. Marquand's *H. M. Pulham, Esq.,* brought out in 50,000 copies, was described as "A broad canvas of the life of the ruling classes . . . in which a man who lives in accordance with the values of bourgeois circles sacrifices his love for the sake of success in his career."[176] More overtly political were the works by Jay Deiss. His novel *The Blue Chips,* which was serialized in a journal, had the attraction of an industrial setting with much technological detail used as background for a politically "valuable" conflict. As the story unfolds, it becomes apparent that the real concern of a pharmaceuticals manufacturer is not scientific progress or providing people with effective drugs, but simply making money for the stockholders, the owners of the blue chips.[177] Another novel by the same author, *A Washington Story,* was translated at least in part in order to demonstrate that "average Americans live in fear of being accused of Communist or democratic activity."[178] It was printed in 150,000 copies.

John Cheever was introduced to Soviet readers in 1961. His stories about the demise of a simpler America coupled with satirical barbs at the synthetic, commercialized civilization replacing it, were printed in periodicals and also published in separate collections. Among the first to appear was

and emptiness of an average American family's life" (*Teatral'naja ènciklopedija,* Vol. IV [1965], p. 150). Still, his close ties to the theater of the absurd, the excessive sexuality of many of his plays, and perhaps also political factors (his *Box-Mao-Box,* a 1968 play, while critical of American life, employs *Quotations from Chairman Mao!*) appear to have made such prospects unlikely. In October 1973, at an international conference on cultural exchanges with the Soviet Union in Salzburg, Austria, Albee attacked literary contacts with the USSR as a sham.

175. KL, Vol. V (1968), p. 599. There were two anthologies of Dorothy Parker's stories, one printed in 75,000 copies, the press run of the other unknown; 10,000 copies were printed in the original English.

176. Ibid., Vol. IV (1967), p. 622. A curious double standard obtains here, as sacrificing love for the sake of one's career is a motif not entirely unknown in Soviet literature. The best example is the Communist hero Davydov in Sholokhov's *Virgin Soil Upturned,* who is prevailed upon to break with a Cossack woman because the liaison endangers the success of a campaign to organize a collective farm. In Soviet conditions, however, such resolutions of conflicts are treated as laudatory triumphs of reason over superficial physical attraction for an unworthy person who would interfere with the call of duty, a line of reasoning even more Spartan than that characteristic of neoclassic tragedies.

177. *Inostrannaja literatura,* Nos. 1, 2, and 3, 1960.

178. KL, Vol. II (1964), p. 502. See chapter 1.

"The Superintendent," a story from Cheever's 1953 collection *The Enormous Radio and Other Stories,* which describes genteel poor tenants who are forced to move to make room for the vulgar newly rich. It was printed in *Novyj mir,* No. 4, 1961. The title story of the collection appeared in *Znamja* (No. 5, 1961), as did "The Season of Divorce" (No. 1, 1961). The entire volume was published in 1962 (no information is available on the press run). Cheever's works continued to be published in later years.[179]

Of all American writers of the younger generation first published in the USSR in the 1960s, J. D. Salinger may well be the most important and influential. *The Catcher in the Rye* was the first to appear, though Rita Rajt-Kovaleva's translation took some liberties with Salinger's text to avoid scandalizing Soviet prudes.[180] This was followed by several of Salinger's shorter works published in the then "liberal" monthly *Novyj mir.*[181] A volume of short stories came out in 1963 in 113,000 copies (there was also one in Armenian in 15,000, and a Georgian translation of *The Catcher in the Rye* in 20,000), and two printings of an anthology comprising *The Catcher in the Rye;* "Raise High the Roof Beam, Carpenters"; "A Perfect Day for Bananafish"; "The Laughing Man"; "De Daumier-Smith's Blue Period"; and "Uncle Wiggily in Connecticut." Each printing appeared in 100,000 copies.[182]

In many ways, Soviet interpretations of Salinger embody the approach to recent Western writing that is not overtly political at all, that does not reflect any of the traditional horrors of capitalism (such as grinding poverty, unemployment, or discrimination), but which, in the belief of Soviet critics and publishers, can nevertheless be used as an aid in the indoctrination of Soviet readers about the evils of the bourgeois way of life. As the noted Soviet novelist Vera Panova observed in her introduction to the first Soviet publication of *The Catcher in the Rye,* Salinger's Holden Caulfield comes from a reasonably wealthy and well educated family; it is not poverty and ignorance that oppress him. He is, however, a victim of a society in which

179. There are, however, other important American authors who are quite ignored for any number of reasons. Thus, we have come across only one Russian translation of Saul Bellow, "Gonzaga's Manuscripts," a story about an American's visit to Spain in search of manuscripts of a Spanish poet. The visitor feels the hostility of Spaniards for Americans, and his room is searched by the police—which must have struck some Soviet readers as incongruous *(Franco's* police mistreats *Americans?).* Bellow's story appeared in *Neva,* No. 7, 1961.
180. "While the adolescent bluntness of Holden Caulfield's language is often bowdlerized in the translation, enough of the original remained for the diction and frankness to come as a pleasant shock to the Soviet reader." Carl R. Proffer, *Soviet Criticism of American Literature in the Sixties,* p. 3. The translation first appeared in *Inostrannaja literatura,* No. 11, 1960.
181. "For Esmé, With Love and Squalor," a sensitive story of an encounter between an American soldier and a British teen-age girl during the war, was printed in *Novyj mir,* No. 3, 1961; "The Laughing Man" and "Down at the Dinghy," in No. 4, 1962; "De Daumier-Smith's Blue Period," a good tale about a would-be young painter's brief career at a fictitious art school, in No. 11, 1963.
182. The 1965 edition is listed in the Soviet bibliography of American writing, but the 1967 is not, again a telling commentary on its reliability.

everything is "phoney" (a favorite expression of Salinger's juvenile hero) and where even the innocent and the pure at heart must don the protective mask of cynicism in order to conform.[183] Rita Rajt-Kovaleva's rather shrill introduction to the 1967 anthology of Salinger provides a telling illustration of the approach and deserves to be extensively quoted:

> The name of the author of this book is well known in our country, and our readers have long understood that J. D. Salinger is far from being the least important among America's progressive writers. All those who read him attentively and thoughtfully understand at once which side he is on—with those who sink humanity into ever more mass slaughters, those who wearing the hoods of the Ku Klux Klan murder people at night for the black color of their skin, or with those millions who in all the countries of the world (and hence, also in the USA, Salinger's homeland) raise their angry voices against war, against racial discrimination, against violence, famine, and poverty.
>
> And while it is true that Salinger never shows us his compatriots in direct struggle with that which corrodes America today, he can, better than anyone else, lead our reader into a world so distant from us, a world we often know only from hearsay, that is ruled by the "American way of life."
>
> In that world Salinger has been repeatedly denounced for unmasking that way of life with too much candor and passion, for allegedly distorting it by viewing it through the eyes of an adolescent or a young man incapable of adjusting to his environment.
>
> The fact is, however, that this is precisely what Salinger is writing about —that his young protagonists had no wholesome, normal childhoods, that they hardly knew of ordinary, wholesome relations among people.
>
> He writes about a world where the most important thing is money, where everything is for sale, even a girl "with the skinniest shoulders."
>
> He writes about a world engulfed in dishonesty and lies, what the hero of the novel The Catcher in the Rye calls phoniness and make-believe.
>
> He tells us how man is tied by advertising that gushes from all sides, how sharp businessmen undertake to teach, in absentia, absolutely anything to everybody: the Spanish language, the writing of film scripts, the management of a stockholding business, the art of playing the guitar, painting pictures, being attractive to girls, writing verse, and manufacturing elegant porch furniture.
>
> He writes about a world where, for money, they offer to tidy up not only one's external life, but one's inner life as well.
>
> If your spiritual world is not in good shape, if you cannot find yourself, if you cannot "adjust" to a boring and sometimes even dishonest job, if you are dissatisfied with something, or have doubts about one thing or another—don't you worry! There is a vast army of people, some of them even with medical training who (for a substantial consideration!) will clean and tidy up your soul, just as one cleans a garden or a garage. They will train you to be tolerant of what revolts you, they will teach you to adjust to life—in short, they will

183. *Inostrannaja literatura,* No. 11, 1960, pp. 138–41.

turn you into a member of society in good standing, one who knows how to tolerate not only bribery in the office, but also racist violence, and even an unloved wife.

In this book you will read how Salinger hates in every way the vulgarization of the arts and sciences that is so common in America.

And while the desecration of art is treated only ironically in the story "De Daumier-Smith's Blue Period," of "healers of souls" he says directly that "those headshrinks" have pushed one of his heroes to suicide, and he mockingly relates the tale of a society matron who runs to "her" analyst as one goes to a beauty parlor.

Perhaps Salinger will be reproached for failing to notice complex events of world significance, for his escape into a primitive, childish perception of the world, into what many call "the myth of childhood," where everything is allegedly viewed with the unobstructed, sharp eye of child, free of any residues of "adult" attitudes toward one's environment that are imposed by life.

Apparently, however, the sound of the voice of an adolescent, the voice of a youth—say, a poet or a young artist, whom you will meet in this book— is to readers like the voice of that truth that is "spoken through the mouths of babes." The reason Salinger has now become so close to young readers of many countries is apparently to be sought in the fact that all history testifies to the advent of mankind's liberation from the yoke of exploiters and warmongers, that it awakens in young people an identical hatred of war and of oppression of man by man.[184]

Assuming no drastic changes in the nature of popular Soviet literary criticism, or more precisely the kind of literary-political journalism that often passes for serious criticism, it seems reasonable to assume that, allowing for shifts in emphasis, it will continue to hold up much of nineteenth- and twentieth-century Western writing as evidence of the "inappropriateness of the bourgeois system to human norms."[185] Capitalism will continue to be blamed for a seemingly endless variety of social ills as these are portrayed by Western authors—including destitution, crime, discrimination—and of ills that can be viewed as extensions of more abstract phenomena, such as the alienation of the individual from social organisms and processes. As suggested by a number of the examples cited in this chapter, even such ostensibly timeless human vices and foibles as greed, vanity, dishonesty, and disloyalty will, in all likelihood, continue to be interpreted as evidence, however indirect, of the corrupting influence of capitalism on human nature. This is not to say, however, that such claims are necessarily accepted by Soviet readers or that they will be in the future.

184. R. Rajt-Kovaleva, "Predislovie," Dž. D, Selindžer, *Nad propast'ju vo rži—Vyše stropila, plotniki—Xorošo lovitsja rybka-bananka—Čelovek, kotoryj smejalsja—Goluboj period de Dom'e-Smita—Lapa-rastjapa.* Perevod s anglijskogo i predislovie R. Rajt-Kovalevoj (Moscow: Izdatel'stvo C.K.V.L.K.S.M. "Molodaja gvardija," 1967), pp. 3–5.
185. KL, Vol. VI (1971), p. 215.

# CHAPTER

# 7

# Comrades, Friends,
# and Kindred Spirits

As suggested in the preceding chapters, descriptions of the evils of capitalism are often to be found in the works of authors otherwise viewed by Soviet
critics as themselves quite "bourgeois." Not surprisingly, similar descriptions of the seamy sides of life in non-Soviet societies abound in the writings
of Western authors who are *treated* by Soviet critics as true Communists,
trusted allies, and faithful "fellow travelers." These will be discussed in the
present chapter.

The term "fellow traveler" has a curious history. Although introduced
in the United States much earlier, it acquired notoriety in the postwar years,
particularly in connection with the late Senator Joseph McCarthy's investigations of a few real and a great many imaginary Reds. Essentially, the
expression "fellow traveler" was used to describe loosely those who, while
not Communists themselves, were *too* sympathetic to Communism for the
Senator's taste. The irony, unnoticed by most, was that the political term
"fellow traveler" was itself a Communist coinage; though endowed with a
similar flavor of condescension and disapproval, it was originally meant to
identify persons who were *insufficiently* Communist in their allegiances.
The term *poputčik* was used by Trotsky half a century ago to describe
Russian writers who sought accommodation with the Soviet regime without
actually becoming converted to the Soviet cause.[1] Originally, however, the
term was—and still is—used without any political connotations at all. The
standard Russian dictionary of Vladimir Dal' defines *poputčik* as one who
happens to be going in the same general direction, adding that at the

1. See Leon Trotsky, *Literature and Revolution* (New York: Russell & Russell, 1925).

crossroads the paths of the *poputčiki* may part.[2]

A cliché of the Romantic tradition juxtaposed the proud and solitary artist with the fickle and vulgar mob. With the passage of time the concept of the mob became synonymous with those of the "philistine" and the "bourgeois," while specifically excluding the similarly nebulous "people." The former categories became all but obligatory objects of the artist's scorn; to celebrate their virtues was unthinkable—unless, of course, it was a writer's conscious intention to shock. On the other hand, the "people" was to be worshipped. In the nineteenth century the cause, indeed the concept, of the "people" was somewhat abstract. By contrast, in the early decades of the twentieth century, two major political movements, equally "antibourgeois" and claiming equally to represent the true interests of the "people," came to power in major European states. Both of these movements attracted artists emotionally ready to join forces with other opponents of the despised middle class values: "Writers like d'Annunzio, Marinetti, Benn, Jünger, Hamsun, Pound, Motherland, and Giono were drawn to Fascism, and others like Dos Passos, Brecht, Becher and Seghers made common cause with the Communists."[3] The lines were not always clearly drawn. Thus, for example, Ludwig Renn, a member of the German Communist Party since 1928 (it seems that he was attracted to Communism chiefly by Lenin's denunciations of imperialist wars), was also courted by the Nazis who appreciated his *positive* view of the experience of battle.[4] After spending the war in Mexico, Renn became a respected member of Communist East Germany's literary establishment and his works are lauded in the *Literary Encyclopedia* for their "hatred of fascism and imperialist wars."[5] Harald Alfred Bergstedt's *St. Jurgen's Day,* an antireligious novel published in 1919, was held in high esteem in the USSR and was even, as already mentioned, made into a Soviet film. During World War II Bergstedt collaborated with the Nazis and was then sentenced to a prison term by a Danish court. Subsequently, his novel was republished in the USSR, the author's tarnished reputation notwithstanding.[6]

The number of West European and American authors attracted to Communism in the 1920s and 1930s far surpassed that of Fascist sympathizers;

2. *Tolkovyj slovar' živago velikorusskago jazyka Vladimira Dalja,* 2nd ed., Vol. III (Moscow and St. Petersburg: M. O. Vol'f, 1882), p. 308.

3. Jürgen Rühle, *Literature and Revolution: A Critical Study of the Writer and Communism in the Twentieth Century,* translated and edited by Jean Steinberg (New York: Frederick A. Praeger, 1969), p. 201.

4. Ibid., pp. 155–56.

5. KL, Vol. VI (1971), p. 258. According to Rühle, Renn grew disenchanted and "began to devote himself to historical and remote subjects, to juvenile literature, and to studies on art and ethnology. Several of his books, including his memoirs, were allowed to appear only after substantial revisions." Rühle, *Literature and Revolution,* p. 157.

6. KL, Vol. I (1962), p. 556. See chapter 5.

this was true even in Germany and Italy. Some writers had little choice. Several were Jews (among German writers alone, Jakob Wassermann, Lion Feuchtwanger, Arnold and Stefan Zweig). Others may have found specific features of the Communist idea particularly appealing. There can also be no doubt that a great many considered the anti-intellectualism of the Fascists particularly repugnant: bonfires of books in Nazi Germany were well known, while few were aware of similar measures in the USSR. In contrast to the Fascists, the Communists held literature in high esteem and this was a matter of public record. Many writers in the West, all too keenly aware of their own insecure position in society, could not fail to be impressed by the attention that was lavished on literature in the USSR, the huge press runs of books, and the public recognition and honors bestowed on many authors by the Soviet state. Some Western writers may have suspected or even been aware that many Soviet authors paid a price for this privileged status, such as submission to a degree of control by the Party and the state, even a measure of censorship (that some paid with their lives was not well known, or at least not believed, until much later). Still, what mattered most was that, in contrast to "bourgeois" states, the Soviet state *cared* about the arts, and the arts were assigned an important place in its blueprint for the future.

Many Western authors may also have been impressed with the recognition accorded their own writings in the USSR. Thus, in 1936, just prior to his arrival in the USSR, nine of Lion Feuchtwanger's books were brought out by Soviet publishers. Romain Rolland and Upton Sinclair must have been gratified by the circulations of their works, nearly two million copies of the former and three million of the latter by mid-1930s. Some Western authors, not entirely liberated from capitalist instincts, may also have been pleased by the incomes thus derived. Until 1928, i.e., prior to his recognition as a major pro-Soviet novelist, Theodore Dreiser's books were simply pirated in the USSR; thereafter he began collecting ten per cent in royalties. David Caute is correct in emphasizing: "Such men could not, of course, be 'bought.' What these figures represent is not so much money as recognition; and the writer's life, after all, is a constant striving after recognition not only for himself, but also for what he takes his work to represent."[7] Not that personal gain should be entirely overlooked; authors, after all, must earn their livelihoods from writing. (Pushkin once observed that he wrote for himself, but published for the sake of money.) Idealistic and practical reasons were equally important to Heinrich Mann who wrote in 1943: "I love the Soviet Union. It is close to me—and I to it. I am widely read there,

---

7. David Caute, *The Fellow-Travellers: A Postscript to the Enlightenment* (New York: Macmillan, 1973), p. 13.

it affords me a living, and I look upon it as though it were already posterity that knows me."[8] The most important single reason, however, was clearly ideological, a vague admiration for the egalitarian goals of Communism and a growing concern over the menace of Fascism. Thus, Jürgen Rühle writes about German authors:

> The reason that some of them, men like Thomas and Heinrich Mann, Keller-mann, Feuchtwanger, Arnold Zweig, and Leonhard Frank, were attracted to Communism is not hard to understand. For one, they yearned for an ideal society, which they presumed existed in far-off Russia. Then, too, there was the fellowship of the anti-Fascist groups. Finally, there was the recognition accorded them by the Communists as fellow fighters against Fascism and as fellow realists, recognition that took the form of public acclaim, literary awards, and the enthusiastic reception and wide dissemination of their writings in the Communist orbit.[9]

In many ways, these German authors fit quite accurately Trotsky's definition of the term "fellow traveler." But there was an important difference: they all lived outside the USSR and were thus in a position to determine freely the extent to which their public acts and published writings were to coincide with the desires of the Communist Party, an advantage not enjoyed by the "fellow travelers" in the USSR and, later, in other countries of the Soviet bloc:

> Yet none of these writers actually became a Communist. Thomas Mann, Feuchtwanger, and Leonhard Frank indulged in their flirtation with Communism from a safe distance—from Switzerland, the United States, and West Germany, respectively. Kellermann and Arnold Zweig settled in East Germany. There Kellermann, who died in 1951, lived out his days in obscurity, while the aged Zweig retreated into a kind of make-believe Communism he was careful not to test against reality. Heinrich Mann, after much hesitation, finally decided to move to East Germany, but he died in 1950 in the United States, just before making his planned move.[10]

Thus, these German writers, together with other West Europeans and Americans, also fall within the traditional meaning of the Russian expression *poputčiki.* They "traveled" with the Communists because for much of the first half of the twentieth century they were brought together by the danger of Nazism. Like many traveling companions (at least as remembered

---

8. Rühle, *Literature and Revolution,* p. 152. Rühle observes: "At the heights of his delusions, Heinrich Mann even saw the Moscow trials as proof of the intellectual essence of the Revolution, and the embarrassing interrogation of Stalin's enemy Radek by Vyshinsky—'a psychological battle for the possession of buried truth'—appeared to him of Dostoevskian dimensions."
9. Ibid., p. 151.
10. Ibid., p. 152.

from old novels describing the more leisurely modes of transportation by ship, rail, and carriage), these voyagers developed friendships, seeking each other's support and companionship during the long and arduous journey. Yet one must not be deceived by the apparent intimacy of such camaraderie; it could vanish as suddenly as it began, when the time came for one of the passengers to get off. Most of the Western writers of the interwar period known for their sympathy for Communism and friendship for the USSR (and even, occasionally, as admirers of Stalin) were quite sincere antitotalitarian liberals and democrats. It was simply that their deep hostility to the Fascism of Adolf Hitler blinded them or induced them to consciously disregard some of the Fascist features of Stalinism at a time when many felt that clearcut choices had to be made.

The superficiality of many Western authors' self-proclaimed loyalty to the Soviet cause is often tacitly recognized by Soviet critics who prefer to avoid identifying these writers too closely with Communist goals, partly because this would entail bestowing an official *imprimatur* on their often erratic, and occasionally downright heretical, views. This reticence extends even to those few who had actually been members of the Communist Party, such as Theodore Dreiser who, like so many confirmed sinners in the Middle Ages, took the vows shortly before his death. Considering such authors as mere "progressives" and "friends," rather than full-fledged comrades, makes it possible to excuse and explain their ideological errors—and also, paradoxically, enhances the effectiveness of their "useful" books with Soviet readers on the grounds of their authors' implied political neutrality.[11] At the same time, the great prestige of these writers, who include a number of famous names in modern literature, is assiduously exploited, both to maximize the significance of their praise of the USSR and of the Communist dream, and to add weight to their denunciations of the injustices and incongruities of the bourgeois way of life.

While there is, understandably, no "official" classification of foreign authors, a number of patterns may be discerned in their publication and evaluations. These are often quite subjective and may appear arbitrary, sometimes even unjustified, to a foreign observer. No useful purpose would be served by trying to challenge the logic of Soviet critics and publishers;

11. Occasionally, this stratagem is employed in the USSR proper. Thus, on March 8, 1963, Khrushchev excoriated some Soviet artists and writers for believing in the possibility of peaceful coexistence with the West in the ideological sphere, as opposed to the mere diplomatic and military spheres, i.e., for renouncing the idea of converting all of mankind to the Communist faith: "This bait has unfortunately been taken by some Communists—writers and artists —and even by some of the leading workers in the creative organizations. It should be noted at the same time that such nonparty men as Comrade Leonid Sobolev, for instance, have been staunchly defending the party line in literature and art." *Khrushchev And the Arts: The Politics of Soviet Culture, 1962–1964.* Text by Priscilla Johnson. Documents selected and edited by Priscilla Johnson and Leopold Labedz (Cambridge, Mass.: MIT Press, 1965), pp. 168–69.

their approaches, however, should be noted because they affect the availability and reception of many Western authors. In this chapter we will consider books by West European and American writers whose pro-Soviet views are emphasized (other authors who hold similar views but are not so identified are considered elsewhere, as are authors of works that fall under specific categories, e.g., children's books). Some of these authors are labeled "progressive," in Soviet usage normally a synonym for pro-Soviet and pro-Communist; occasionally the term is a gross understatement for an author very active in Communist Party affairs, much as the term "Christian" would be considered inadequate for a member of the Church hierarchy. Others are described as Communists, which normally denotes recognition of the authenticity of their views and affiliations, which is by no means automatic; as pointed out, often there is a stubborn reticence to recognize such claims in sources aimed at Soviet readers. In other cases different code words are employed—e.g., "active in the struggle for peace"—which denote a similar degree of guarded praise: the author is a kindred spirit, but not a comrade. A limited number of Western authors, usually Party members, are accorded the highest accolade by being identified as Socialist Realists, that is, in effect, as creators of *Soviet* literature who happen to be residing abroad. Thus, a political-literary doctrine that was born in the USSR in 1934 and has since enjoyed the status of the only artistic and ideological creed to which all Soviet artists must subscribe (adherents of others were silenced and worse) is now being endowed with an international status. Furthermore, its adherents are now said to be found not only in the countries of Eastern Europe (where Socialist Realism has been gradually imposed as part of their transformation into People's Democracies), but also among writers in the West, where Socialist Realism boasts of a number of voluntary converts, some of them of impressive stature. Thus, the honorific "Socialist Realist" is bestowed by Soviet critics on particularly distinguished Western authors judged politically deserving (for instance, Theodore Dreiser, Pablo Neruda, Jorge Amado, Louis Aragon).[12] Indeed, an effort is made to impart to the procedure a degree of respectability by concocting a prehistory of sorts of Socialist Realism in *Western literature.*[13] One such progenitor is the British radical Robert Tressall (ca. 1870–1911):

12. A collection of essays on the origins of Socialist Realism in literatures of the West was published by the USSR Academy of Sciences: T. V. Balašova, F. S. Narkir'er, R. M. Samarin, S. V. Turaev (eds.), *Genezis socialističeskogo realizma v literaturax stran Zapada* (Moscow: Nauka, 1965).

13. The historical validity of the effort is somewhat dubious. The doctrine of Socialist Realism was formally proclaimed at the First Congress of the Union of Soviet Writers in 1934, while "the term 'Socialist Realism' was itself used for the first time in the Soviet press in 1932 (*Literaturnaja gazeta,* May 23)." Attempts to find beginnings of Socialist Realism "at the turn of the twentieth century" are unconvincing. See the entry "Socialističeskij realizm," KL, Vol. VII (1972), pp. 92–101.

Between 1905 and 1910 Tressall wrote *The Ragged Trousered Philanthropists,* a novel about the life and struggle of workers (condensed edition, 1914; full text, 1955; Russian translation, 1924) which became a historical landmark in the evolution of England's Socialist Realist literature. The novel's hero is a socialist worker. He serves as a mouthpiece for Tressall's condemnation of reformism, for the painting of a panorama of future socialist society, and for the glorification of free labor.[14]

Tressall's book is now of purely historical interest. It was published in 10,000 copies in the original English only, as was another relic of a heroic past, *Communism Was My Waking Time,* by Rupert John Cornford, a leader of Britain's Young Communist League who died in the Spanish Civil War.[15]

The implications of the Socialist Realist label when applied to Western authors are reasonably obvious. The honorific assumes that in the opinion of authoritative Soviet critics, a given Western writer is sufficiently selective in his choice of subject matter and protagonists and in the resolution of conflicts, all of which are suitably politicized; that his frankly partisan Communist inspirational bias *(partijnost')* is consistently in evidence; and that his mode of presentation is generally accessible to the average reader. Books by Western authors *identified* in Soviet sources as Socialist Realists, Communist Party members, "progressives," or activists in various pro-Soviet organizations ("peace groups" and others) are considered separately in this chapter. Conferral of such recognition implies varying degrees of quasi-official endorsement of those of the authors' writings that are published in the USSR, and particularly of their sociopolitical contents. That this recognition is by no means automatic may be seen from the fact that many Western writers whose political sympathies and even official affiliations would seem to place them in this category are not so designated in Soviet sources because the contents (and sometimes the form) of their works are not deemed worthy of such endorsement, or because of recent questionable behavior (for instance, public disagreement with certain Soviet policies). Conceivably, identifying such books as written by Communist or even "progressive" authors may suggest to many readers that various heresies—political and artistic—are compatible with allegiance to Communism, a conclusion Soviet authorities understandably wish to avoid.

The range of artistic merit of authors in this category is wider than in any other. Some of the writers represented occupy distinguished places in the literatures of their countries (e.g., Louis Aragon, Pablo Neruda) and their Communist politics are thus to be viewed merely as an additional factor

14. KL, Vol. VII (1972), p. 612.
15. KL, Vol. III (1966), pp. 751–52.

favoring the dissemination of their books in the USSR; occasionally, such political considerations may override artistic objections to their work, such as "modernistic" techniques, or overly frank descriptions of sex. (At other times, they are considered insufficient. Thus, for example, the political pronouncements of Pablo Picasso and Diego Rivera have for years been praised in the USSR, but not their painting, which is considered too "abstract." Many Soviet citizens who know Picasso as a "progressive" public figure have never seen a reproduction of any of his works, except the "Peace Dove.") Others are obscure authors, unlisted in the most detailed literary reference works in their own countries, unknown even to specialists; these authors obviously owe their publication in the USSR to political considerations: the Italian children's writer Gianni Rodari, a staff member of *Unità,* the Communist Party daily, is an example.[16] There are many, in fact, who are really journalists, if not simply party functionaries, and whose literary and semiliterary creations are printed in effect as tokens of special favor. Unrecognized in their own lands, these men and women are praised in the USSR as important writers and are also, of course, rewarded with royalties, literary prizes, and trips to the Soviet Union—all this in contrast to ordinary Western "bourgeois" writers whose works, until 1973, were as a rule printed in the USSR without their knowledge and consent, not to mention payment.[17]

Communist and "progressive" foreign authors form, not unexpectedly, the largest group of writers whose works appear in Soviet periodicals with the notation "received in manuscript form," which indicates that the work was probably commissioned by the Soviet editors. Royalties for such commissioned writings may often account for a significant part of a foreign author's earnings (especially when combined with income from Soviet translations of works initially published outside the USSR and from performances in the theater). A reading of approximately thirty prose works and plays identified as having been "received in manuscript" and a comparison of these with works by the same authors that were not commissioned reveals, not unexpectedly, that the former were written with Soviet audiences (and editors) in mind. The commissioned items often bore a strong resemblance to *Soviet* literature. They were written simply, avoided morally offensive material, and, as a rule, had a transparently political message. Some of these commissioned works, though not all, may have subsequently appeared in the original abroad. It is curious that hundreds of such works sent to the USSR by Western leftist authors were openly printed and

16. See chapter 4.

17. In 1973 the USSR joined the Universal Copyright Convention, which should presumably end this type of piracy. So far, evidence is too scanty to predict how strictly the Convention's provisions will be enforced.

proudly publicized at a time when two Soviet authors, Andrej Sinjavskij ("Abram Tertz") and Julij Daniel' ("Nikolaj Arzhak"), were publicly vilified, and (simultaneously!) tried and sentenced to prison terms by Soviet courts for doing exactly the same thing—sending for publication abroad writings which they could not publish in their own country.[18]

The advantages of publication in the USSR of books by Western Communists and Soviet sympathizers—or, more precisely, writers so identified by Soviet sources—are not limited to their propaganda value. It should be noted that the impact of these books is probably enhanced by a systematic effort at publicizing their authors in the USSR as important writers in the West—claims that Soviet readers cannot, of course, verify. Such books further serve the purpose of indirectly building up *abroad* the prestige of their writers and, by extension, of the political movements with which they are associated. There are indications that this stratagem is particularly effective in the case of Afro-Asian and, to a lesser extent, some Latin American authors, i.e., writers in countries where international recognition is taken the more seriously because it is relatively rarely received.

The transparently politicized criteria by which the stature of foreign authors is measured in the USSR are illustrated by the list of "great living foreign authors" that appeared in *Literaturnaja gazeta* on September 20, 1955. The list was compiled by Aleksandr Fadeev, then just demoted from the position of Secretary General of the Union of Soviet Writers (following Khrushchev's denunciation of Stalin, Fadeev committed suicide in May 1956). While the authors on Fadeev's list are of very unequal literary merit, they were nearly all then considered comrades, or at least friends and kindred spirits, in the USSR. The list read as follows:

> *French:* Aragon, Éluard, Stil, Roger Vailland, Sartre, Vercors, Robert Merle, and Pierre Gascard
> *German:* Becher, Brecht, Seghers, Arnold Zweig, Remarque, Feuchtwanger
> *American:* Fast, Caldwell, Lillian Hellman, Hemingway
> *British:* Aldridge, O'Casey, Coppard, Lindsay
> *Italian:* Prattolini, Moravia
> *Australian:* Prichard, Frank Hardy
> *Latin American:* Neruda, Amado, Guillen
> *Indian:* Krishan Chandar
> *Icelandic:* Laxness

18. An account of the trial and a postscript of the court proceedings of February 10 to 14, 1966, is found in *On Trial: The Soviet State versus "Abram Tertz" and "Nikolai Arzhak,"* translated, edited, and with an introduction by Max Hayward (New York: Harper & Row, 1966).

Of course, any such list reflects the subjective predilections of its compiler, some of which may be extreme. Still, a list that includes among the "great" Erskine Caldwell but not William Faulkner, Jack Lindsay but not T. S. Eliot, can only be described as absurd.

Yet with all this, books by Western Communist and pro-Soviet authors must be approached with caution by the Soviet literary establishment. Unlike the conservative and disciplined Soviet Communists, Western Communists are often rebels disrespectful of all authority, skeptics and iconoclasts. Their works—again, in sharp distinction to those of their Soviet comrades—normally defend society's victims, the poor, the despised, the failures. Such concerns are not encouraged among Soviet authors, while disrespect of established authority is not tolerated. Thus, unless it can be made clear that the critical attitude of these Western Communists is specifically directed at *bourgeois* institutions and *capitalist* injustices, Soviet critics prefer to minimize their Communist ties.

A number of major realists of the interwar period, nearly all of them now dead, are usually treated somewhat apart from other authors portraying the decline and evils of capitalism. As a rule, they are identified as great realists, great democrats, great anti-Fascists, and great friends of the Soviet Union (*bol'šoj drug SSSR*).

## Early French Admirers: France, Rolland, Barbusse

In contrast to a number of authors whose rapprochement with Communism was considerably influenced by the rise of Fascism, Anatole France (who died in 1924), seems to have perceived Communism and the USSR as natural, if more radical, extensions of the socialist cause he had long championed. Like Theodore Dreiser, Anatole France joined the Communist Party practically on his deathbed, at the age of eighty.[19] A frequent contributor to *L'Humanité*, France was one of the Communist Party's foremost literary spokesmen (the others were Romain Rolland and Henri Barbusse). A skeptic and an iconoclast, Anatole France satirized various institutions of modern society and human foibles in general, but he was particularly indignant about the hypocrisy of bourgeois values and was virulently anticlerical. In the USSR, the largest circulation for any single work of France (over half a million copies) was attained in 1954–64 by "Crainquebille," a tale about a street vendor who annually insults a police-

19. As in the case of Dreiser, a Soviet source prefers to overlook this act of formal conversion: "The example of the October Revolution smashed his [Anatole France's] bitter skepticism and, toward the end of his life, led him to a *rapprochement with* the French Communist Party." *Osnovnye proizvedenija,* p. 482. Emphasis added.

man in order to spend the winter in a warm jail. *The Revolt of the Angels,* described by a Western critic as "an ambitious satire of Christianity,"[20] was published, somewhat surprisingly, on a relatively modest scale: 150,000 copies in Russian, 30,000 in Latvian, and 16,000 in Ukrainian. Perhaps it was felt that some aspects of the work, though declared blasphemous by the Catholic Church, might suggest undesirable parallels to Soviet readers: "Indignant over God's despotism, angels descend on earth in order to learn from humans how revolutions are made. They assume human guise, and are on the verge of revolt. But their leader Satan sees in a dream how, having defeated God's armies and replaced God on the throne, he gradually acquires himself all the repugnant features of the coarse tyrant. He then calls off the revolt."[21] The writings of Anatole France were widely published, mostly as anthologies of short stories in Russian, in other languages of the USSR, and also in the original; about a million copies of these were printed all told. There was also an eight-volume set printed in 240,000 per volume, making for a grand total of some three and a half million volumes of Anatole France.

Romain Rolland was another French writer considered a "great friend of the USSR." Although disapproving of the Soviet use of terror to silence dissent, he was drawn to Communist ideals and was a great admirer of Stalin. Rühle relates that

> while visiting the Soviet Union in 1935, the seventy-year-old pacifist Rolland was overwhelmed by the "triumphant demonstrations of a people filled with joy and pride," particularly the mass demonstrations in Red Square. . . . In leaving Russia, Rolland wrote to "dear Comrade Stalin": "I depart with the firm conviction, which I sensed even before I came, that world progress is inextricably bound up with the fate of the USSR, and that the USSR is the fiery crucible of the proletarian international in which all mankind must and shall generate itself."[22]

With over a million copies in Russian alone, *The Soul Enchanted* was by far the most widely published of Rolland's works. Notes the *Literary Encyclopedia:* "Completed on the eve of the Nazi putsch in Germany, the novel warns humanity against the danger of Fascism. . . . The novel's heroes frequently refer in their thoughts and discussions to the Soviet experience. Rolland glorifies 'the life-giving energy of the USSR, the energy of those who act.' "[23] Among individual titles, *Colas Breugnon,* a historical novel set in seventeenth-century Burgundy, was printed in half a million copies, and

20. *The Penguin Companion,* Vol. II, p. 279. For a discussion of this subject see chapter 5.
21. *Osnovnye proizvedenija,* p. 484.
22. Rühle, *Literature and Revolution,* p. 325.
23. KL, Vol. VI (1971), p. 346.

nearly the same amount was published in several languages of *Jean-Christophe,* a huge novel with a contemporary setting.[24] There was a fourteen-volume Russian set of Romain Rolland's collected works at 240,000 copies per volume.[25]

Roger Martin du Gard was not politically active, although he did sign a number of anti-Fascist manifestos circulated in the 1930s among the French intelligentsia.[26] He is best known for the seven-volume opus *The World of the Thibaults,* a family chronicle about a sternly bourgeois father and his two sons, one of whom abandons Catholicism and becomes a socialist, while the other ends up questioning all of Western civilization. As suggested elsewhere, such massive novels (Galsworthy's *The Forsyte Saga* is another example) are still widely popular in the USSR, a country quite untouched by the newer fashions in literature and the arts. Soviet publishers, on the other hand, prized *The World of the Thibaults* sufficiently to bring out its various parts in over a million copies: "On the pages of Martin du Gard's novel, the story of the disintegration of one bourgeois family turns into the history of the decline of an entire social class. . . . Martin du Gard's Jacques Thibault is a heroic man who rebelled against bourgeois society, against the rule of forces that unleash wars."[27]

Most militant among this group of French novelists was Henri Barbusse, a member of the French Communist Party since 1923. According to Rühle, "Barbusse sincerely respected Stalin. Stalin had recognized Barbusse's importance and had protected him against the suspicions and harassment to which he was subjected by the French [Communist] Party."[28] Another admirer of Barbusse was Lenin. According to Lenin, in Barbusse's two most important novels, *Under Fire* and *Light,* "The transformation of a completely ignorant bourgeois altogether crushed by conventions and prejudices into a revolutionary—a transformation brought about by none other than the war itself—is portrayed with exceptional force, talent and truthfulness."[29] *Under Fire,* which demonstrates that soldiers in a bourgeois army have nothing to gain from a war, was printed in 175,000 copies in Russian, while *Light,* which embodies an appeal to the workers of the world to unite

24. *Jean-Christophe* (1903–10) was said to reflect its author's opposition to chauvinism and to portray the crisis of capitalist society and confusion among the intelligentsia. Ibid., p. 344. It was printed in Latvian (135,000), Ukrainian (75,000), Estonian (60,000), and French (40,-000).

25. A twenty-volume set had been published in 1930–36, a recognition then rarely accorded a living foreign author.

26. KL, Vol. IV (1967), p. 658.

27. Ibid. By coincidence, Thibault was the real name of Anatole France. There were also a quarter of a million copies of *Jean Barois,* a novel about "an intellectual torn, like many of his generation, between religious faith and scientific scepticism: it is notable for its presentation of the Dreyfus case and its unusual dialogue form." *The Penguin Companion,* Vol. II, p. 515.

28. Rühle, *Literature and Revolution,* p. 328.

29. V. I. Lenin, *Sočinenija,* Vol. XXIX, p. 470. Quoted in KL, Vol. I (1962), p. 452.

against the capitalist bosses, appeared in 100,000 copies.[30] His propaganda value diminished with passage of time, Barbusse, a writer of modest gifts, is now in declining favor.

## The German Anti-Nazis

Heinrich Mann, referred to earlier, was a candid believer in the political uses of literature. Of his *Henri IV, King of France* he wrote:

> A league of big landowners and provincial monopolists broke up and destroyed the monarchy—naturally, without openly admitting to their goal. To listen to them, these gentlemen defended a belief, a *Weltanschauung.* Under like circumstances, they now proclaim their anti-Communism. Henri Quatre, the liberator, acted as a revolutionary: now one would call him a Communist. In his time he was called a heretic, and the true events remained shrouded in mystery.[31]

As interpreted by the author, *Henri IV* bears a strong resemblance to such artistic Soviet apologias for Stalin as Aleksej Tolstoj's novel *Peter the Great* and Sergej Eisenstein's film *Ivan the Terrible,* both of which glorify despotic rulers of the past as a way of justifying the cruel reign of a Soviet despot. This consideration may have favored Heinrich Mann's publication in earlier years as much as the author's pro-Soviet politics and his caustic comments about the bourgeois way of life in those of his writings that have more recent settings.[32] He continues to be published on a generous scale. An eight-volume set was printed in a total of 1,250,000 copies.

Heinrich Mann's brother Thomas Mann was well known in Russia before the revolution; a multivolume set of his works was launched in 1910. According to the *Literary Encyclopedia,* "In recent decades, [Thomas] Mann has been one of the most highly valued twentieth-century Western authors in the USSR."[33] While less political than Heinrich Mann, Thomas Mann is the greater writer, and his firm anti-Nazi stand during the war, as well as his postwar pronouncements, gave no grounds for Soviet objections.[34] Thomas Mann's traditional, realistic style, frequently resembling the Russian masters, makes his writing accessible to Soviet readers, while the

30. Barbusse is also the author of biographies of Lenin (1934) and Stalin (1935). The worshipful tone of the latter caused the *Literary Encyclopedia* to cite Barbusse as one of the very few foreign (or, for that matter, Soviet) authors who were deceived by Stalin's "cult of personality." KL, Vol. I (1962), pp. 452–53.

31. Cited in Rühle, *Literature and Revolution,* p. 196.

32. KL, Vol. IV (1967), p. 582.

33. Ibid., p. 588.

34. "Together with other cultural figures of the West he [Thomas Mann] comes out in defense of peace, demands a ban on nuclear tests, and fights reaction, as he always did." Ibid.

contents of his books coincide with the preferences of Soviet publishers. A ten-volume set was published at 140,000 copies per volume. Among individual works, the largest printings were attained by *The Beloved Returns (Lotte in Weimar)*, with its portrait of an old, wise Goethe exposing the evils and folly of chauvinism (330,000 copies; also 10,000 in German), and by *Confessions of Felix Krull, Confidence Man:* "While resembling sixteenth- and seventeenth-century picaresque tales, the novel depicts the complete disintegration of social contacts during the period of imperialism; man's loss of all social stability, indeed of his own identity, transform him into a kind of evil spirit."[35]

An excerpt from Jakob Wassermann's *The World's Illusion* was published under the title *The Gold of Kachamarka* (100,000 Russian copies, 65,000 in Ukrainian): "He [Wassermann] vividly depicted the disintegration of bourgeois family and the inhuman character of bourgeois relations."[36] Much of his impact, however, is vitiated by a blend of eroticism and mysticism that is quite dated, and also unacceptable in the USSR, which may account for the rather modest printings.

The ideological value of the writings of Stefan Zweig is minimal. True, he did support the USSR in the 1930s and he was, in fact, an opponent of Fascism—but that is not saying very much for a German author of Jewish origin during the Hitler era. An annotated Soviet bibliography warns that Stefan Zweig "did not always understand the laws of historical and social evolution" while an 850-page Soviet college textbook of twentieth-century foreign literature does not mention him at all.[37] Thus, the publication of Stefan Zweig's writings on a generous scale should be viewed primarily as a response to reader interest in his fictionalized biographies of writers, artists, explorers, and historical figures, as well as in his novellas. The largest press runs were those of the biography of Magellan (close to a million copies) and of the posthumously published *Stefan Zweig and Friederike Zweig: Their Correspondence 1912–42* (over 500,000 in Russian, and 15,000 each in Lithuanian and Uzbek). There were many anthologies in Russian (over 1,500,000 copies) and in other languages (Estonian, Latvian, Georgian, as well as German), and a seven-volume set at 385,000 copies per

35. Ibid. There was also an undisclosed press run of a separate edition of *Doctor Faustus* (1943): "This is a novel about the spiritual sources of backwardness and reaction that led to the formation of an 'evil Germany,' and generally about the acute crisis of the entire capitalist world and its culture, as well as about the growth and collapse of Fascism." Ibid., p. 587. In addition, there were 15,000 copies of a Latvian translation of *Mephisto*, a satirical novel about Nazi Germany's "decent" citizens who "did not themselves kill, but who were not repelled by the idea of shaking hands with murderers." *Mephisto*'s author, Klaus Mann, was the son of Thomas Mann. Ibid., p. 584.

36. KL, Vol. I (1962), pp. 870–71.

37. *Osnovnye proizvedenija*, p. 34. The textbook is *Istorija zarubežnoj literatury XX veka*, pod redakciej doc. Z. T. Graždanskoj (Moscow: Gosudarstvennoe Učebno-Pedagogičeskoe Izdatel'stvo Ministerstva Prosveščenija RSFSR, 1963).

volume. The grand total was well over six million copies.

Of all the non-Communist German writers of the period, Lion Feuchtwanger was the most political, and his writings were simultaneously the most outspokenly anti-Nazi and pro-Soviet. He spent the year 1936–37 in the USSR and described his experiences in *Moscow 1937,* a book that succeeds in largely overlooking the bloody Stalinist purge then in full swing. In 1936–39, together with Bertolt Brecht and the orthodox Communist Willi Bredel, Feuchtwanger edited the Moscow German journal *Das Wort.* In 1930 Feuchtwanger wrote *Success,* a novel that forty years later was still praised by the *Literary Encyclopedia* for its "profundity of social analysis," which makes it "an important realistic work unmasking Nazism's early manifestations."[38] Even higher accolades were earned by another prewar novel: "A sharply anti-Fascist note is sounded in the novel *The Pretender* (*Der falsche Nero,* 1936, Russian translation, 1937). Feuchtwanger makes use of the historical realia of ancient Rome in order to relate in a parodistic and satirical manner the Nazi clique's accession to power, its bloody terror, and the inevitability of its inglorious collapse."[39] Feuchtwanger was to return to the subject again: "In the novel *Die Brüder Lautensack* (1943) authentic historical personages and events in Germany on the eve of the Nazi *coup d'état* impart to the sociopolitical analysis of events a higher degree of concreteness and depth."[40] Feuchtwanger was not merely a foe of Nazism. His 1952 *'Tis Folly to Be Wise,* a novel about the life and the legacy of Jean-Jacques Rousseau, lent itself to the following interpretation in a Soviet college text:

> In this novel Feuchtwanger makes an effort to give due credit to the French Revolution and to the summit of its revolutionary development, the Jacobin dictatorship. Feuchtwanger sees Jean-Jacques [Rousseau's] greatness in the fact that his teachings "are linked by a line (not always a straight one, to be sure), through the American and the French revolutions to Hegel, Marx, and Engels, to the Paris Commune, and to the [Soviet] October Revolution."[41]

Although Feuchtwanger was once popular as a writer in Western Europe and in America, his stature as an artist is modest: he may be fairly described as a "middle-brow" novelist. Nevertheless, he is being published and republished in the USSR. A twelve-volume set of his writings at 300,000 copies per volume was launched in 1963 and completed in 1968. There were also

38. KL. Vol. VII (1972), p. 923. The novel is an account of the Bavarian Communist revolution of 1919.

39. KL, Vol. VII (1972), p. 924.

40. Ibid. After a delay of fourteen years, the novel was serialized in *Inostrannaja literatura* (Nos. 1, 2, and 3, 1957).

41. *Istorija zarubežnoj literatury XX veka,* 1963, p. 285.

many individual books. Although the total press run cannot be established, it may be guessed at about three million copies. Certain titles were published in large editions. Thus, *Die Brüder Lautensack* appeared in over half a million copies, as did *The Pretender*. Others have no information on the sizes of printings—e.g., in the case of *The Spanish Ballad*, or were published in small editions (e.g., *The Oppermanns*, 75,000 copies), or not at all (e.g., *Power*, German title *Jud Süss*).

Some suggestion as to why certain of Feuchtwanger's novels were neglected is found in the college text just cited. Thus, in discussing *Power*, the Soviet professor comments:

> The novel portrays the cruelty and hypocrisy of Catholicism and Protestantism. However, while subjecting to justified criticism Christian clergy and feudal aristocracy who have, for their selfish interests, propagated religious intolerance, Feuchtwanger idealizes Judaism and the role of the eighteenth-century Jewish community with its leaders, the rabbis and the rich."[42]

*Josephus (Der jüdische Krieg)*, which describes ancient Judea's war with Rome, is no better: "This novel, too, has an ideological shortcoming; it overemphasizes the Jewish national problem and idealizes ancient Hebrew traditions and religion."[43] *The Oppermanns (Die Geschwister Oppenheim)*, which is set in Nazi Germany, suffers from the same problem: "Attention is centered on Fascist anti-Semitism. It is true that anti-Semitism occupied a prominent place in Fascist repression, but this does not nearly exhaust the negative nature of Fascism."[44] Some improvement is found in *Paris Gazette (Exile)*: "The writer abandoned the supraclass notion of 'Jewry.' The businessman Grüngold is used to portray the class nature of the bourgeoisie. Grüngold is an ally of Nazism; even though he is a Jew, he helps the Fascists to liquidate Friedrich Benjamini, a progressive journalist."[45] Yet Feuchtwanger was to backslide again in one of his last novels, *The Spanish Ballad*, published only three years before his death in 1958:

> *The Spanish Ballad* . . . contains some serious ideological shortcomings. Feuchtwanger repeated his earlier nationalist errors. He overestimated the role of national and religious problems in Spanish history. Much is false in his portrait of Raquel. Though a progressive woman, Raquel is forced by the author's will to defend the idea of the 'chosenness' of the Jewish people and

42. Ibid., p. 291.
43. Ibid.
44. Ibid., p. 293.
45. Ibid. This praise of Feuchtwanger for portraying a Jewish accomplice of the Nazis is similar to Khrushchev's speech of March 8, 1963, which advanced the unsubstantiated claim that a Jew served as an interpreter for the Nazi general at Stalingrad, and that not all Jews were anti-Nazis. See Priscilla Johnson and Leopold Labedz, *Khrushchev and the Arts*, pp. 184–85.

the superiority of its faith. The book also idealizes the workings of the Jewish community.[46]

Still, as pointed out, Feuchtwanger continues to be published in the USSR on a rather large scale. The printing of his less controversial works reflected the general 1954–64 policy of providing the Soviet public with entertaining reading matter. Books that portrayed Nazism as a cruel, bloodthirsty phenomenon (such as *The Pretender* or *Die Brüder Lautensack*) were particularly favored, as were all such works by foreign authors, because their value is not merely historical. Tens of millions of Soviet citizens remember and hate Nazism from firsthand experience, and what is more important, *the Nazi system is the only non-Soviet regime about which they have personal knowledge*. Thus, Soviet ideologues may expect that reinforcing such hate may immunize them further against any danger of attraction to a non-Soviet way of life. It may be for that reason that the label "Nazi" is pinned so indiscriminately by Soviet propaganda on any and all current foreign enemies of the USSR—be it Tito's Yugoslavia in 1949–53, or the United States, or, more recently, Israel and Communist China.

As for the criticism of Feuchtwanger's Jewish "nationalism," it parallels very closely the tone of the veritable avalanche of Soviet propaganda maligning Judaism and the Jews that was then being published in the USSR.[47]

It is worth noting that Lion Feuchtwanger's Jewish anti-Nazism had first caused some embarrassment to the Soviet leadership nearly four decades ago. In the 1920s and 1930s Feuchtwanger's "Jewish" novels were widely published in the USSR, and one of them was even made into a Soviet film. The script for *The Oppenheim Family* (1938–39), which portrays a German-Jewish intellectual family during the early years of Nazi rule, was written by Feuchtwanger himself. Upon the signing of the Nazi-Soviet pact in 1939, the film was removed from Soviet screens. Simultaneously, the publication of a multivolume set of Feuchtwanger's works, launched in 1938, came to an abrupt halt after the appearance of only two volumes.[48] In 1939 the

46. *Istorija zarubežnoj literatury XX veka,* 1963, p. 297.

47. The two best treatments of the subject are Lionel Kochan (ed.), *The Jews in Soviet Russia since 1917,* 2nd ed. (London: Oxford University Press, 1972) and William Korey, *The Soviet Cage: Anti-Semitism in Russia* (New York: Viking Press, 1973). Not surprisingly, some Soviet Jews were attracted by Feuchtwanger's "Zionism." See chapter 9.

48. Only volumes I and VIII were published; the edition was never resumed. KL, Vol. VII (1972), p. 925. An amusing but revealing incident is found in Andrej Sinjavskij's (Abram Tertz's) novel *The Makepeace Experiment (Ljubimov).* The heroine wishes to include in the school curriculum two novels by Feuchtwanger, *The Ugly Duchess* and *Power* (in Russian, *Evrej Zjuss—The Jew Süss*) as well as Hemingway's *The Sun Also Rises:* "These books had been removed from the public library at the proper time, but were accidentally left under a bookcase." The novel's fantastic hero, now the dictator of an imaginary Soviet town, tries to reason with his wife that this is out of the question: "We cannot introduce in the curriculum either Feuchtwanger with Hemingway or Hemingway with Feuchtwanger. This would amount to a peaceful coexistence of two different ideologies. What will Mao Tse-tung say, what will Togliatti [the Italian Communist leader] think when they find out that in a Ljubimov high

pro-Soviet German-Jewish novelist Feuchtwanger created some awkward-ness in the USSR because he was too anti-Nazi; in post-Stalin Russia the anti-Nazi writer became an embarrassment because he was too Jewish.

The only major modern Spanish writer in the group was Vicente Blasco Ibañez whose works "speak with sympathy about the people and expose social injustice."[49] Blasco Ibañez was well known in Russia before the revolution; a sixteen-volume set of his writings appeared in 1910–12. The *Literary Encyclopedia* notes with regret that during World War I Blasco Ibañez was temporarily led astray by chauvinist slogans, "which accounts for the artistic [!] failure of his novels *The Four Horsemen of the Apocalypse* and *Mare nostrum.*"[50] Later, however, Blasco Ibañez was to redeem him-self, by making "many pronouncements in favor of the young Soviet state."[51] His writings, which combine a strong note of social protest, anti-clericalism, and, to Russian readers, exotic locales (thus, for instance, *Blood and Sand,* published in Russian in 100,000 copies, with 30,000 more in Georgian and 20,000 in Lithuanian, is the story of a bullfighter) continue to be published on a wide scale. There was a three-volume set of his writings and also several anthologies, making for a total of nearly one and a half million copies.

## *The Older Anglo-American "Progressives": Shaw, Dreiser, and Others*

George Bernard Shaw delighted in shocking the public; a British reference work identifies him as a "dramatist, controversialist, critic and wit," thus implying comparable degrees of importance to his vocations and attrib-utes.[52] One suspects that it was a desire to scandalize his countrymen and admirers that prompted Shaw to declare in 1948, at the age of ninety-two, that

> Stalin is the great defender of peace. It is to him the Soviet Union owes its strength and unity, and it is this strength that guarantees world peace. I have often said that Communism is the basis of all civilization and the

---

school Feuchtwanger coexists with Hemingway, and they don't fight each other, and do not squeeze each other out?" Abram Terc, *Fantastičeskij mir Abrama Terca* (New York: Inter-Language Literary Associates, 1967), pp. 376–77. The novel is available in English: Abram Tertz, *The Makepeace Experiment,* translated from the Russian and with an introduction by Manya Harari (New York, 1965).

49. KL, Vol. I (1962), p. 637.
50. Ibid., p. 638. Soviet literary criticism routinely ascribes artistic failure to unacceptable ideological positions of the author.
51. Ibid., p. 637.
52. *The Penguin Companion,* Vol. I, p. 471.

guarantor of peace. It is a matter of life and death. Therefore, I repeat: I am for Stalin.[53]

True, on another occasion Shaw warned that "Marxism is not only useless but disastrous as a guide to the practice of government" and equated it with "Mormonism, fascism, imperialism, and indeed all the would-be Catholicisms."[54] Worse: an admirer of Stalin, "He had heaped similar praise on Mussolini, and even on Hitler. As late as 1944, he wrote: 'Mein Kampf contains a good many sound ideas.' "[55] It is thus not very surprising that Shaw's self-professed Communism was not taken very seriously by the London *Daily Worker,* which wrote in Shaw's obituary in 1950: "Bernard Shaw lived and died a socialist. Throughout his many years he labored to bring the ideas of socialism to the British people and to all the peoples of the world. *He called himself a Communist.* From the beginning, he enthusiastically supported the Russian Revolution. He remained a friend of the Soviet state to the end."[56] An appraisal of Shaw's career in the *Theatrical Encyclopedia* emphasizes his political activities:

> A socialist in his political views, Shaw has, from the very beginning of his literary career, denounced capitalist vices and declared that the bourgeois system must be replaced with a Communist one. In early stages of his literary career Shaw espoused reformist views. Later, however, particularly under the influence of the October Revolution, he recognized the validity of revolutionary violence. In his many public appearances Shaw supported the policies of the Soviet government, and rebutted the anti-Soviet slander of the yellow press.[57]

These activities were closely linked to Shaw's plays: "Shaw's sociopolitical views were expressed in his drama. . . . Unlike other philosopher-playwrights, Shaw's ideas are clad in a jocular garb. Laughter is to Shaw a means for the affirmation of ideas hostile to the bourgeois way of life. . . . The central place in his work is occupied by contradictions. These arise because the way of life created by capitalism is inimical to human nature and to natural notions of justice."[58]

As pointed out elsewhere, translations of foreign drama are usually published on a relatively modest scale, and Shaw is no exception. There were 150,000 copies of a two-volume set, and several anthologies and individual

53. Quoted in Rühle, *Literature and Revolution,* p. 315.
54. Quoted in ibid., p. 318.
55. Ibid., p. 316.
56. Cited in *Novyj mir,* No. 7, 1956, p. 146. Italics added. The preceding was quoted in an introduction to a translation of *O'Flaherty, V.C.:* "Shaw's play, with its vivid satirical tendentiousness, is directed against militarism and ethnic oppression." Ibid.
57. *Teatral'naja ènciklopedija,* Vol. V (1967), p. 913.
58. Ibid., p. 914.

plays in Russian, Ukrainian, Lithuanian, and Georgian, as well as in English. To compensate, Shaw's plays were widely performed in Soviet theaters.[59]

Other considerations being equal, Soviet publishers and theater directors strongly favor traditional realistic drama over "modernist." A telling illustration is provided by a comparison of publication and production data for George Bernard Shaw and Sean O'Casey. The artistic stature of the two dramatists is equally recognized. Furthermore, while Shaw's politics were quite erratic, the *Literary Encyclopedia* notes that "O'Casey remained a staunch Communist until the end of his life."[60] O'Casey's plays "depict the life of Dublin's slum dwellers," attack British imperialism, bourgeois liberalism, and other 'evils.' " In at least one of them, *Red Roses for Me,* "O'Casey turns to the subject of the revolution, creates a heroic figure of a fighter for socialism, and draws a canvas of a bright future in a romantic, lofty style."[61] Yet with all of these positive attributes, O'Casey's complex plays, filled with symbols and allusions, are rarely printed in the USSR, and then only in small editions, a striking contrast with the treatment of the formally conventional comedies of Shaw.

Of the twentieth-century American authors popular in the USSR before the war, most were to fall into official disfavor.[62] Only a few escaped that fate. Carl Sandburg, the great urban poet, has been published occasionally in the USSR since 1927, mostly in literary periodicals. None of his verse was printed during the Cold War, but he began to be translated again in 1956. A slim volume of Sandburg's poetry (86 pages) appeared in 1959, and the large volume *Lincoln* came out in 1961. Sandburg is described as a democrat and an anti-Fascist: "A social theme has always resounded in Sandburg's verse. He wrote about the majesty of labor, about life and its tribulations, about the dignity of America's ordinary people, thus earning the reputation of America's people's poet."[63]

Generations of Soviet readers were taught to view Theodore Dreiser's novels as documentary evidence of life in the United States; they are still

59. Soviet productions included *Pygmalion* (Leningrad Lensoviet Theater, 1962); *Mrs. Warren's Profession* (Central Theater of the Soviet Army, Leningrad Theater of Comedy, and Moscow Theater of Satire, all in 1956); *The Devil's Disciple* (BDT Theater, Leningrad, 1956; Moscow Art Theater and Stanislavsky Drama Theater, both in 1957); *Caesar and Cleopatra* (Mossoviet Theater and Moscow Theater of Satire, both in 1964); *Heartbreak House* (Moscow Theater of Satire, 1962); *The Millionaires* (Vakhtangov Theater, 1964; Leningrad Komissarzhevskaya Theater, 1965).

60. KL, Vol. V (1968), p. 409. The *Theatrical Encyclopedia* is more restrained. It notes only O'Casey's "rapprochement with the Irish Workers' Party." *Teatral'naja ènciklopedija,* Vol. IV (1965), p. 147.

61. Ibid., p. 148.

62. Erskine Caldwell, William Saroyan, Sinclair Lewis, John Steinbeck, and William Faulkner are discussed in chapter 6, Ernest Hemingway in chapter 5, and Upton Sinclair in Chapter 1.

63. KL, Vol. VII (1972), pp. 302–3.

praised as reliable guides to America. No matter that the America they describe is half a century old. As any reader of Soviet newspapers knows, it is still a land of greedy capitalists, oppressed workers, and class struggle.[64] Almost alone among the left-wing American authors of the 1920s and 1930s, Dreiser has been published without interruption since 1925.[65] A twelve-volume set of Dreiser's writings was launched in 1951, at the time of the fiercest anti-Americanism in Stalin's Russia, and completed in 1955: Dreiser's death in 1945 may have facilitated retention of his status as a "progressive" author.[66] The entire set was reprinted once more in 1955 at 200,000 copies per volume, and several of his novels were reissued in the first post-Stalin decade.[67] Dreiser is among the very few Western writers of the older generation identified as Socialist Realists.[68] His novel *An American Tragedy* is called "the banner of realist American literature of the 1920s." "Ernita," a novella from the cycle *A Gallery of Women,* contains the "first image of a positive Communist hero in American literature," while the central character of *The Financier* and *The Titan* is praised as "the most striking portrait of a capitalist in American literature."[69] Other novels by Theodore Dreiser were lauded for illuminating the destructive power of money in capitalist society. In *Sister Carrie* it ruins two lovers; in *Jennie Gerhardt* it forces a young woman to yield to mammon whose hold over a man's heart is stronger than her own; in *An American Tragedy* it leads to murder; in *The "Genius"* "a talented artist joins an advertising agency. His talent is destroyed by capitalism which prefers financial geniuses to artistic ones."[70] Together with the individual editions of separate books and the twelve-volume set, the total press run of all of Dreiser's works was nearly ten million copies.[71] Among American authors, comparable publication figures were achieved only by Mark Twain and Jack London.

   Twain, London, and Dreiser have long been the most widely published American writers in the USSR; their works are found in abundance in the

64. For a discussion of the subject, see chapter 9.
   65. The fortunes of some of the others are discussed, *inter alia,* in chapters 1 and 8.
   66. As pointed out, at the time of his death Dreiser was a member of the Communist Party. A similar set of Dreiser's collected works was printed in the early 1970s at 375,000 copies per volume, the largest figure for any American author at the time.
   67. Strangely, many are not registered in *Problemy literatury S.Š.A. XX veka,* 1970, p. 435, although their appearance was noted in *Knižnaja letopis'.*
   68. Several others will be discussed later in this chapter.
   69. KL, Vol. II (1964), pp. 775–76.
   70. Ibid.
   71. The larger items included *Jennie Gerhardt,* one and a half million (also in Lithuanian); *The Titan,* one and two-thirds million (also in Lithuanian, Azerbaidzhani and English); *The Stoic,* nearly a million (also in Latvian, Lithuanian and English); *An American Tragedy,* three-quarters of a million (also in Latvian, Moldavian and Kazakh); *The Financier,* two-thirds of a million (also in Latvian and Lithuanian); *Newspaper Days,* over half a million; *The "Genius,"* nearly half a million (also in Armenian, Latvian, Azerbaidzhani, and Lithuanian); and *Sister Carrie,* a third of a million (also in Lithuanian, Estonian, Azerbaidzhani, and English).

libraries and are studied in Soviet schools. As a result, a Soviet citizen intent on visiting the United States vicariously sees that country much of the time through the eyes of little boys from Missouri, adventurers and gold prospectors in Alaska, and greedy capitalist bosses and embittered strikers in the sprawling cities of the Midwest. He sees a country of nearly total racial segregation, grinding poverty, without any job security, and few spiritual values and aspirations. Readers sophisticated enough to realize that this image is dated can avail themselves of those recent works of American literature which, as indicated elsewhere, criticize such modern ills of American society as the breakdown of old moral codes, and a vague feeling of emptiness and drift. Furthermore, they may even ascertain that such books *are* more or less representative of modern American writing. It would be asking too much even of the more informed Soviet readers to make allowances for the fact that the more severe critics of American society also concede the existence in the United States of positive customs and institutions and attractive features of ordinary life, but find it inappropriate or unnecessary to dwell on these in their works, because, in sharp contrast to Soviet writing, modern American authors and Western authors in general rarely celebrate the self-evident virtues of life among them.

## Later French Communist Authors

As pointed out, in a number of cases it was extremely difficult, and sometimes impossible, to establish the identity of modern foreign authors translated in the USSR. One French author was actually described as being "as yet unknown in his homeland, France"; Marc-Louis Gallot (Galleaux? Gallos?) sent in to the Soviet journal a story about French student demonstrations.[72] Jean Freville is known primarily as a French Communist journalist and historian; nevertheless, two of his novellas were printed in 150,000 copies. Jean Kanapa, editor of the French Communist monthly *La Nouvelle Critique,* was described by a British scholar as "the most dogmatic of French Stalinists."[73] Although Kanapa is not known as a writer of fiction, a few stories from his 1962 collection, which describe the horrors of destruction as seen through the eyes of a Communist observer in wartime Italy, were published in a literary monthly.[74]

72. *Novyj mir,* No. 8, 1957, p. 133.
73. David Caute, *Communism and the French Intellectuals 1914–1960* (New York: Macmillan, 1964), p. 169.
74. *Inostrannaja literatura,* No. 8, 1963. The stories had been selected from Jean Kanapa's *Du vin mêlé de myrrhe.*

French Communist journalists fare well in the USSR as published writers of fiction. In fact, one sometimes gets the impression that publication of one's books in the Soviet Union may be a normal fringe benefit enjoyed by members of the editorial staff of *L'Humanité,* the French Communist daily. Paul Vaillant-Couturier, the newspaper's editor-in-chief before World War II and one of the founders of the French Communist Party, is also credited with being a pioneer of Socialist Realism in France.[75] His writings, however, were republished only in very small editions: 8,000 copies of a Lithuanian translation of his autobiographical *Childhood,* 30,000 copies of a Russian anthology, and 5,000 copies of a collection of his writings in the original French.[76] Simone Téry, another of *L'Humanité*'s staff members, was recognized by the publication of 90,000 copies of a Russian translation (and 12,000 copies of a Lithuanian one) of a novel about a young French Communist who died in the Nazi camp at Auschwitz: "The short novel *Du soleil plein le coeur* (1949; Russian translation, 1958) describes the life of Danielle Casanova, the heroine of the French people."[77] Georges Soria covered the Spanish Civil War for *L'Humanité* and during World War II was the newspaper's correspondent in Moscow; he is well known as a translator of Soviet literature and is director of an organization that disseminates Soviet art and books in France. Soria is a dramatist. His Soviet debut was a translation into Russian in 1955 of *La Peur (Fear),* a play about Julius and Ethel Rosenberg, the Americans executed on charges of stealing atomic secrets for the USSR. *L'Orgueil et la nuée (The Pride and the Cloud)* deals with "the problem of destinies and tasks of science in capitalist society, with the moral countenance of a scientist who comes to realize the fatal consequences of his work in nuclear physics."[78] *L'Étrangère dans l'île (The Foreign Lady)* was a "polemical play" even by the rigorous standards of a Soviet encyclopedia, which described it as "dedicated to the struggle for liberation of the people of Cyprus."[79] Finally, *La Dernière Chance (The Last Chance)* dealt with the war in Algeria, with the playwright's sympathies entirely on the Arab side; the play was "received by the editors in manuscript," i.e., it presumably was commissioned.[80] The French Communist journalists from *L'Humanité* have even produced metaliterature of sorts, a novel *about* French Communist journalists from *L'Humanité*. Hélène Parmelin's *Noir sur blanc (Black on White)* "describes the life and work of

75. KL, Vol. I (1962), pp. 831–32.
76. Perhaps this consisted of Vaillant-Couturier's journalism, which may have been published as an aid for students of French. This would combine good pedagogy with impeccable ideology.
77. KL, Vol. VII (1972), p. 477.
78. *Teatral'naja ènciklopedija,* Vol. IV (1965), p. 1042.
79. Ibid.
80. *Inostrannaja literatura,* No. 8, 1958. *L'Orgueil et la nuée* was printed in 5,000 copies, an average for translated drama. No information available on the press runs of the other plays.

*L'Humanité*'s editors during the Korean war."[81]

Hélène Parmelin's colleague Pierre Courtade, a member of the Central Committee of the French Communist Party, wrote editorials on foreign affairs for *L'Humanité* from 1946 to 1958.[82] Considering the time span involved, Courtade's adaptability to changing political circumstances must have been highly respected by the Party's leadership. During this period, he had to justify to French readers the Soviet excesses of the Cold War— and then "peaceful coexistence"; Soviet praise, excommunication, and then renewed praise of Tito's Yugoslavia; the Soviet invasion of Hungary, and many similar turnabouts in Soviet foreign policy. Following Khrushchev's famous "secret" speech at the Twentieth Congress of the Communist Party of the Soviet Union in which Stalin's crimes were denounced, Courtade retreated slowly and cautiously from his own earlier glorification of the Soviet dictator:

> Pierre Courtade . . . argued that Stalin's policy had been "fundamentally just, even if certain of its aspects ought to be revised in the light of new facts," and he attempted to pass off most of the odium on to Beria. Temporarily the general in the camp of the Stalinist intellectuals, he conducted a spirited campaign in which elements of retreat were barely perceptible. . . . As late as 1961, he persisted in the view that Stalin, despite his faults, had been a father to millions, and that his radio speech in July 1941 would never be forgotten. With more cunning than conviction, he attempted to explain away the French Party's commitment to Stalinism by arguing that when comrades had cried *Vive Staline!* they had meant long live the Red Army, communism, and even France.[83]

The last observations are from Pierre Courtade's 1961 novel *La Place rouge (Red Square)*. They coincided perfectly with the official view of Stalin and Stalinism in the USSR, to wit that all "mistakes" notwithstanding (the word "crimes" was studiously avoided), and in spite of all "violations of socialist legality" that took place in the period of the "cult of personality," the Stalin era must be viewed in a positive light, particularly because it included the proudest pages in the nation's and the party's history, the victorious war against Hitler. Within a year Courtade's novel was serialized in a journal, and soon thereafter it was published in book form in two large edi-

---

81. KL, Vol. V (1968), p. 599. The novel appeared in 15,000 copies in Ukrainian. Like so many other French Communist authors published in the USSR, Hélène Parmelin is known in her country as a newspaperwoman rather than a novelist. Her name appears in *Qui est qui en France* but not in the three-volume *Dictionnaire des littératures,* publié sous la direction de Philippe van Tieghem, avec la collaboration de Pierre Josserand (Paris: Presses Universitaires de France, 1968).

82. This information was contained in Pierre Courtade's autobiographical note prefacing a Russian translation of four of his short stories in the conservative literary monthly *Zvezda,* No. 6, 1958, p. 94.

83. David Caute, *Communism and the French Intellectuals,* pp. 224–25.

tions.[84] *La Place rouge* spans nearly a quarter of a century; the narrative begins in 1935 and concludes in 1957, i.e., after Khrushchev's denunciation of Stalin. Its manner is often reminiscent of television documentaries in which generalized commentary on social and political conditions in France is occasionally livened up with fragments of old newsreels: thus the reader gets to see closeups of de Gaulle, André Gide (anti-Soviet *and* homosexual!), and others. Courtade's novel was intended to provide support for the Soviet version of recent history as of 1962. The *Literary Encyclopedia* comments:

> After the unmasking of Stalin's cult of personality, Courtade created the psychologically complex portrait of a Communist in *La Place rouge* (1961), a novel directed against dogmatism [i.e., rigid Stalinism—MF] and supporting dialectics and historicism in thought [i.e., the official Soviet views at the time of writing—MF]. This is a political novel, and also an autobiographical one (since 1960, Courtade has been the Moscow correspondent of *L'Humanité*). Courtade links the life story of the Communist intellectual Simon Borde with the contradictory movement of history over the span of a quarter of a century, and links the events in France with events in the land of the Soviets.[85]

Pierre Courtade's political novel, however orthodox Communist from a Western point of view, probably impressed many Soviet readers as remarkably candid; it was also made more attractive by its French locale. Soviet publishers may have decided that a somewhat greater degree of outspokenness on a number of political subjects could be tolerated in *La Place rouge:* after all, Courtade was a *foreign* writer. What really mattered, in the final analysis, was the probable overall impact; and that impact was apparently judged positive.[86]

Pierre Courtade was outranked on the staff of *L'Humanité* by André Stil, who was the newspaper's editor-in-chief from 1950 to 1959, a period that included both the height of the Stalinist terror and the anti-Stalinist "thaw"; subsequently Stil was demoted to head of *L'Humanité*'s literary department. In 1951 Stil became the first Frenchman to win the Stalin Prize.[87] The prize was awarded for Stil's *Le Premier Choc,* a novel in three volumes, which, according to David Caute,

84. *Inostrannaja literatura,* Nos. 6, 7, and 8, 1962. The exact press runs of the book could not be ascertained.

85. KL, Vol. III (1964), pp. 923–24. There were also two Estonian translations of Courtade's writings, a book entitled *Cigarettes* (16,000 copies), and an anthology of short stories (20,000). Courtade died in 1963.

86. There may have been one or two similar books. Thus, for instance, *Knižnaja letopis'* listed a volume by the French Communist journalist Yves Farge, but no other information was given.

87. David Caute, *Communism and the French Intellectuals,* p. 194.

took as its theme the struggle of [French] dockers in an Atlantic seaport against the American "occupation." The immediate relevance to the Party line is everywhere clear. The Americans rape, dispossess peasants and small owners of their fields and houses, produce unemployment, incorporate ex-Nazis into their forces and stock France with arms in preparation for a war against the USSR, all with the support and connivance of the French upper classes and their hired agents, the police.[88]

In the words of the *Literary Encyclopedia,* "Stil depicts the struggle of [French] longshoremen against the turning of France into an American military base, and the rallying of all of the nation's patriotic forces in defense of the national interests. Stil draws impressive portraits of Communists, those organizers of the masses, who assume responsibility for the future."[89] The novel, as its summary suggests, obviously lost some of its political timeliness with the advent of *détente* in Soviet-American relations. Widely published in 1952–53, it was apparently no longer being reprinted in Russian, but it was still being published in the languages of Soviet Central Asia and the Transcaucasus: 50,000 copies in Azerbaidzhani Turkic (a very large printing), 15,000 in Uzbek, 5,000 in Tadzhik, and an undisclosed press run in Turkmen.[90] Instead, there were two new books by André Stil that translated into the medium of the novel one of the chief concerns of his *L'Humanité* editorials. *Nous nous aimerons demain* (We Shall Love Each Other Tomorrow, 1957; Russian translation 1961) and *Le Foudroyage* (The Avalanche, 1960; Russian translation 1961) "unmask the criminal character of the war in Algeria."[91] Since at that time domestic Soviet propaganda devoted considerable effort to making the same point, i.e., lending moral support to the Arab rebels and denouncing the French *colons,* André Stil's novels, whatever their literary merits or reader appeal, were worth bringing out for that reason alone. *Le Foudroyage* was first serialized in a journal and then brought out under separate cover.[92] A Russian translation of *Nous nous aimerons demain*

88. Ibid., p. 333.

89. KL, Vol. VII (1972), p. 197.

90. Translations of Western writing into some of the minority languages are often made from the originals; this is the case with the three Baltic languages (Latvian, Lithuanian, Estonian) and Ukrainian. By contrast, translations into the Turkic languages (Azerbaidzhani, Kazakh, Kirgiz, Uzbek), Tadzhik (related to Persian), Tatar, and others are most often made from Russian translations. This results in a time lag: books that are no longer printed in Russian continue to appear for some time in these languages. Occasionally, reluctance to sacrifice a large investment in money and effort results in the publication of books that are no longer *allowed* to appear in Russian. Thus, the *last* books by Howard Fast to be published in the USSR after his break with the Communist movement in 1957 were all translations into the languages of the ethnic minorities. Some came out in 1957. See chapter 8, "Traitors, Kafka, and Other Undesirables." Conversely, readers of these languages must, of course, wait for many books that are available in Russian to appear in their languages—if they ever do.

91. KL, Vol. VII (1972), p. 197.

92. *Inostrannaja literatura,* Nos. 4 and 5, 1961. The press run of the Russian edition could

was brought out in approximately a million copies, one of the largest press runs for a Communist political novel.[93] Within a year, however, the war in Algeria was over; by 1962 Algeria had become an independent state, and this made André Stil's novels politically obsolete. There is no evidence of their republication or, with one exception, translation into the other languages of the USSR.[94]

However political, André Stil is a bona fide novelist; his entry in *Qui est qui en France, 1973–74*, which describes him as *"homme de lettres, journaliste,"* is equally applicable to many writers in France where, in contrast to the United States, the two vocations are often pursued together. Pierre Gamarra is called a Socialist Realist—politically, the highest praise—but not much of his work is published in the USSR.[95] Martine Monod's novels are also a hybrid of literature and political journalism. According to the *Literary Encyclopedia,* "The novel *Le Whisky de la reine* (separate edition, 1954; Russian translation, 1958) is permeated with a Marxist understanding of history. The novel *Le Nuage* (1955, Russian translation 1958) is directed against American nuclear tests. In 1960 Monod wrote the novel *Normandie-Niémen* (Russian translation, 1962) dedicated to Soviet-French collaboration during World War II."[96] All were published in book form.[97] A Russian translation of Roger Vailland's *Beau masque* (1954) was first published in a journal in 1955, and soon thereafter in book form as well.[98] *Beau masque* is a political novel; Vailland "creates a striking portrait of a Communist

not be determined, but indications were that it was large. There were also 25,000 copies of a Ukrainian translation of the same novel.

93. There were two printings of the Russian version; of these, one was half a million copies, while the press run of the second was not indicated. It is usual that when two printings are brought out in close succession, the editions are of roughly the same size. There were also 7,000 copies of the novel in the original French. These were printed in the USSR: the principle of not importing books for general audiences was observed even with respect to a novel by the editor-in-chief of the official daily newspaper of the French Communist Party.

94. A book entitled *Children of the French Waterfront* was published in 15,000 each in Ukrainian and Uzbek, and 7,000 in Tadzhik. In all probability, this is an excerpt from André Stil's *Le Premier Choc*, perhaps of the following incident: "In a carefully constructed scene, he [Stil] even condoned as healthy the nationalist hostility shown by French schoolboys toward their American fellow-pupils. Children, he wrote, are in politics up to their necks." David Caute, *Communism and the French Intellectuals*, pp. 194–95. In addition, there were two anthologies of André Stil's writings in Russian (40,000 copies of one, the press run of the other unknown), 12,000 in Moldavian, and 5,000 each in Lithuanian and Azerbaidzhani.

95. KL, Vol. II (1964), p. 51. Two collections of children's stories and verse appeared in Russian in 90,000 copies, while the press run of the third is not known. There were also translations into Latvian (30,000), Ukrainian (20,000), Estonian (15,000), Tatar (8,000), and Tadzhik (5,000). Gamarra also appears in periodicals, e.g., *Zvezda*, No. 3, 1960.

96. KL, Vol. IV (1967), p. 946.

97. There were two printings of *Normandie-Niémen*, a novel about French pilots in the USSR; no press runs available. *Le Whisky de la reine* was printed in 120,000 copies, and *Le Nuage* in approximately 100,000.

98. *Inostrannaja literatura*, Nos. 2 and 4, 1955, under the title *P'eretta Amabl'*. No information is available on the press run of the Russian edition of the book. The Ukrainian translation was printed in 22,500 copies and the Latvian in 15,000. There were also 12,500 copies of the original French text of *Beau masque*, printed in the USSR.

woman, the real heroine of the [postwar] period."[99] Vailland's *325,000 francs,* a novel about a worker who succumbs to gold fever, was printed in a journal.[100] Emmanuel d'Astier de la Vigerie, a Lenin Prize winner, was represented by a book of memoirs and a novel. *Sept fois sept jours* (1947; Russian translation, 1961) is described as "a truthful chronicle of the French people's struggle in the Resistance written as a quasi-diary."[101] *L'Été n'en finit pas,* although a novel, contains much documentary material on French political and social movements between 1947 and 1954 and also features portraits of "bourgeois" politicians such as General de Gaulle and Vincent Auriol, President of France: "They are contrasted with portraits of Communists, courageous fighters for the future of France."[102]

Much of the writing by French Communist writers was strongly political, and the two dominant themes were the anti-Nazi Resistance and its extension, as it were, after the collapse of Nazism—opposition to the "Americanization" of France. By portraying French Communists as leaders and most active participants in both, these writers had hoped to portray the Communists as the most *patriotic* of Frenchmen—even if this necessitated glossing over the embarrassing period between 1939 (the signing of the Nazi-Soviet pact) and 1941 (Germany's attack on the USSR) when most of France's Communists refrained from anti-Nazi activity. Typical in that respect was Jean Laffitte's trilogy of which one volume, *We Will Return for Jonquils,* was published in the USSR in 1949 at the height of Stalinism, while the concluding part, *Les Hirondelles du printemps (Swallows of Spring),* was translated in 1958. According to the *Literary Encyclopedia,* the former "truthfully describes the heroic role of the Communists in the anti-Nazi resistance. In *Les Hirondelles du printemps . . .* Laffitte turns for the first time to postwar subject matter, describing the activities of the French Communists in 1953, their struggle against the European Defense Community, and their participation in the Peace Movement."[103]

Vercors (pseudonym of Jean Bruller), though not a Communist, was chairman of the National Committee of French Writers and "a member of other progressive organizations." He is best known as the author of a short work about the anti-Nazi underground, *Le Silence de la mer* (1942); his later

99. KL, Vol. I (1962), p. 831. Vailland joined the Communist Party but "after 1956 the writer felt a renewed attraction for anarchist-individualistic moods." Ibid.

100. *Zvezda,* No. 7, 1956.

101. KL, Vol. I (1962), p. 349.

102. Ibid. Chapters from the novel appeared in *Inostrannaja literatura,* No. 8, 1958. No information is available on the press runs of either of the novels.

103. KL, Vol. IV (1967), p. 69. The European Defense Communisty was a NATO-like organization, while the "Peace Movement" was sponsored by the USSR. *Les Hirondelles du printemps* was printed in Russian (press run not disclosed) and in Ukrainian in 15,000 copies. The earlier volume was also printed in Ukrainian in the same amount, but there is no record of a new Russian edition. Presumably, it had been printed in sufficient quantities prior to 1954.

writings include, *Plus ou moins homme* (1949) and *Les Animaux dénaturés* (1952; Russian translation, 1957), a novel which "champions the cause of human dignity in the struggle against reactionary forces."[104] The first, published in Russian prior to 1954, now appeared in Armenian translation in 10,000 copies, as did an anthology of Vercors's short stories; there was an undisclosed printing of the second in Russian, and also of a volume of tales; 20,000 copies of a collection were printed in Estonian.[105] If Vercors was the most famous prose writer of the Resistance, Paul Éluard (pseudonym of Eugène Grindel) was its greatest poet. Formerly an apolitical Surrealist, he joined the Communist Party in 1942 and apparently remained a sincere Communist until his death.[106] His most famous works about the Resistance were *Poésie et vérité* (1942) and *Au rendez-vous allemand* (1944); subsequently, duty and conviction led him to produce some obsequious Communist doggerel.[107] On the whole, Éluard's modernist verse makes him unacceptable as a model of Socialist Realist poetry; on the other hand, his impeccable political credentials make it difficult to reject him completely. In post-Stalin Russia the legacy of Éluard has become something of a weapon in a tug of war between the conservatives and the liberals within the literary establishment. He is being published, although on a relatively modest scale, partly as a result of pressures from those who would rather limit the influence of his verse, particularly of the earlier, experimental period.[108] On the other hand, he is usually highly praised by the "liberals" who would like to see a broadening of the artistic limits considered permissible by current interpretations of the doctrine of Socialist Realism (thus, Ilya Ehrenburg was among Éluard's admirers) and, while prudently emphasizing Éluard's Communist orthodoxy in politics, point to the sophistication and daring of his verse.[109]

104. KL, Vol. I (1962), p. 928.
105. Several short stories by Vercors were printed in *Inostrannaja literatura*, No. 4, 1956.
106. *The Penguin Companion*, Vol. II, p. 251.
107. Consider, e.g., the following poem originally printed in *L'Humanité* of April 26, 1949:

Frères l'U.R.S.S. est le seul chemin libre
Par où nous passerons pour atteindre la paix
Une paix favorable au doux désir de vivre
La nuit se fait toute petite
Et la terre reflète un avenir sans tache.
(Cited in David Caute, *Communism and the French Intellectuals*, p. 167.)

Éluard's death in 1952 spared him the embarrassment of seeing the following reprinted after 1956:

And for us Stalin will be present tomorrow
And Stalin today dissipates sorrow
The confidence is the fruit of his loving heart . . .
(Translation cited in Jürgen Rühle, *Literature and Revolution*, pp. 360–61).

108. One anthology was printed in 10,000 copies, while the press run of the second could not be determined. There were also 4,000 copies of Éluard's verse in the original French, with a Russian introduction.
109. See, for example, the almost ecstatic evaluation of his verse in *Osnovnye proizvedenija*,

Curiously, three among the pro-Communist French authors were themselves born in Russia, and at least one, Vladimir Pozner, began his career as a Russian writer. Pozner's works are, even in the opinion of a Soviet critic, "saturated with politics."[110] A collection of Pozner's stories about the alleged criminality of France's war in Algeria was first published in a Russian literary monthly, and then in 20,000 copies in an Estonian translation.[111] Georges Govy, also Russian-born, is a member of the left-wing National Committee of French writers.[112] Govy's writings deal with life in People's Poland and Franco Spain; a volume of his stories was published in an undisclosed number of copies. The Communist novelist Elsa Triolet had personal ties not only to Russia, but to Russian literature as well. She was a sister of Lily Brik, the great love of the poet Vladimir Mayakovsky, and herself inspired an important book, *Zoo, or Letters Not About Love* by Viktor Šklovskij, who was later to achieve fame as a Russian literary theoretician.[113] She also published in Russian. The *Literary Encyclopedia* credits her with much success in popularizing Russian literature, prerevolutionary and Soviet alike, in France. Her various works were published in approximately one million copies in Russian and the three languages of the Baltic republics. Some were reprints and some dealt with the subject of World War II (e.g., *Les Amants d'Avignon, Qui est cet étranger qui n'est pas d'içi?, L'Inspecteur des ruines*); others were for the most part sections from the trilogy *L'Age du nylon,* then in progress. Triolet's works are, on the whole, politically restrained, although there are, of course, exceptions. Thus, *Roses à credit,* which appeared in *Inostrannaja literatura* (No. 12, 1959) prior to its publication in book form in Russian, Lithuanian, Latvian, and Estonian, is about a young Frenchman who leaves his French wife for a rich girl—an American. In *Le Rendez-vous d'étrangers* (1956; Russian translation, 1958), "the themes of fatherland and internationalism are contrasted with racism and cosmopolitanism."[114]

The most important French Communist writer is Louis Aragon, Elsa

---

1965, pp. 491–92. Also, the brief introduction to a selection of Éluard's poems in *Inostrannaja literatura,* No. 11, 1969.

110. KL, Vol. V (1968), pp. 832–33.

111. *Novyj mir,* Nos. 11 and 12, 1960. The greatest novels about the tragic conflict between the French and the Arabs of Algeria, those of Albert Camus, were not translated in the USSR until much later. Although Camus died in 1960, Soviet critics and publishers were slow in forgiving his staunch opposition to Communism. An equivocal article about Camus in a volume of the *Literary Encyclopedia* published in 1966 (KL, Vol. III, pp. 351–52) and written by Ol'ga Il'inskaja, a friend of Boris Pasternak and herself a victim of Soviet intolerance, makes no mention of any Soviet translations of Camus. A Russian translation of *L'Étranger* was published in the West.

112. KL, Vol. II (1964), p. 206.

113. The book is now available in English: Viktor Shklovsky, *Zoo, or Letters Not About Love,* translated by Richard R. Sheldon (Ithaca, N. Y.: Cornell University Press, 1971).

114. KL, Vol. VII (1972), pp. 618–19. Note the equating of "cosmopolitanism" (in Stalin's time, often a euphemism for "Jewishness") with racism.

Triolet's widower. An eleven-volume set of his writings, with varying numbers of copies per volume, accounted for a total of 816,000 copies. The total printings of all of Aragon's books are difficult to ascertain as much of the data is unpublished—a problem that is, for some reason, encountered frequently in the case of living left-wing authors (it may, one suspects, have something to do with problems of prestige and also, perhaps, with royalties, which even before 1973 were being paid most regularly to writers in this category). *The Communists,* a novel written in 1949, is described by a Western critic as "an orthodox party tract" and a "fictionalized patchwork history of the French Communist Party."[115] The *Literary Encyclopedia* is, of course, more complimentary; in the six-volume novel set in 1939–40 "France's bourgeoisie is contrasted with her working class and its vanguard, the Communist Party. The novel's chief merit is its artistic portrayal of the psychology of Communists who sacrifice their effort for their country's sake, and often their lives as well."[116] *The Passion Week* (*La Semaine Sainte,* 1958; Russian translation, 1960) is characterized in the *Literary Encyclopedia* as describing "seven days in March 1815, Napoleon Bonaparte's advance from the Elbe to Paris, the panicky flight of Louis XVIII abroad. . . . [Aragon] describes the masses who suffered equally under both Louis XVIII and Napoleon, the sacrifices of ordinary human beings, their unshakable patriotism. . . . Breaking with traditions of the historical novel, Aragon builds 'bridges' to our own days." In addition, there were 150,000 copies of *L'Aurélien* "which is set in 1922 (with an epilogue in 1940) [and] offers a portrait of a young man of bourgeois background, a *rentier* ruined by the war,"[117] an unspecified number of copies of the long autobiographical poem *The Incomplete Novel* (*Le Roman inachevé,* 1956), an anthology in Armenian (5,000), and 4,000 copies of Aragon's poetry in the original French.

In 1947, Roger Garaudy, then a member of the Politbureau of the French Communist Party and editor of the party's theoretical journal, wrote: "Every class has the literature it deserves. The big bourgeoisie in decay delights in the erotic obsessions of a Henry Miller or the intellectual fornications of a Jean-Paul Sartre."[118] Some twenty years later Henry Miller remains on the Soviet index; but the positions of Garaudy and Sartre are reversed. Garaudy is now in disgrace, while Jean-Paul Sartre is much honored in the USSR. Writes the *Theatrical Encyclopedia:* "In contemporary political struggles Sartre's positions are progressive. He comes out against colonialism and

115. Rühle, *Literature and Revolution,* p. 364.
116. KL, Vol. I (1962), p. 273. No information was given on the press run of the Russian reprint. There were also 20,000 copies of a Latvian translation, and 7,000 of an Estonian one.
117. KL, Vol. I (1962), pp. 272–74. No data on the press run.
118. Quoted in David Caute, *The Fellow-Travellers,* p. 346.

racism and participates in the movement of the partisans of peace (Sartre is a member of the Executive Committee of the World Peace Council). . . . In his play *Nekrassov* (1956) Sartre had himself attacked anti-Soviet propaganda and sarcastically ridiculed its slanderous zeal."[119] The play was printed in 14,000 copies and presumably was also performed. An earlier play, *The Respectable Prostitute* (1946), had been published, as indicated in the Introduction, in the inaugural issue of *Inostrannaja literatura* in 1955, under the chaste title *Lizzie*.

## Other European Leftists: Italians, Spaniards, Greeks, and Scandinavians

While the wartime Resistance and postwar political struggles are the chief subjects of left-wing French writing, the main theme of similar Italian literature is poverty, both in the rural south (Sicily in particular) and in the slums of the industrial north. Another interesting feature of the publication of such Italian literature in the USSR is the more relaxed way of treating the formal political affiliations of authors. Several writers who have quarreled with certain Soviet policies or actually resigned from the party altogether continue to be published. Thus, for example, Italo Calvino is known to have had differences with the Communist Party, but his works continue to appear; one of the two anthologies of his writing was printed in 150,000 copies. Calvino is particularly prized by the *Literary Encyclopedia* as a "progressive satirist" whose political commitment is evident even in his fairy tales.[120] Similarly, Elio Vittorini, once an editor of *Politecnico*, a Communist periodical, continued to be published (a Russian volume and a Georgian anthology in 20,000 copies) in spite of his criticism of Soviet policies. Most widely published is Vasco Pratolini. According to Rühle, "More than any other writer of the Italian Left, Pratolini is politically engaged. *The Tale of Poor Lovers,* which deals with the early years of Fascism, glorifies the fight of the Communists. That this fight, however, is not a matter of ideology but of the heart is made clear in the most moving passage of the book."[121] *The Tale of Poor Lovers* was printed in two large Russian editions (and also 30,000 copies in Latvian and 20,000 each in Estonian and Lithuanian). *Il Quartiere* (100,000 copies) and *Via de' Megaz-*

119. *Teatral'naja ènciklopedija,* Vol. IV (1965), pp. 857–58.

120. KL, Vol. III (1966), p. 331. Calvino also "created a number of works about Italian youth, dedicated to the struggle against domination by American ideology." *Zvezda,* No. 5, 1957, p. 95.

121. Rühle, *Literature and Revolution,* pp. 373–75, 378. Pratolini, a Communist Party member, condemned the Soviet invasion of Hungary in 1956. This did not significantly affect the publication of his works in the USSR.

*zini* (150,000) demonstrate, in a Western critic's view, that "the mere keeping alive against all odds on the one hand, and organized class struggle and political opposition on the other, are two different levels of the same protest of the working classes against the oppressiveness and injustice of society."[122]

Carlo Levi is characterized in the *Literary Encyclopedia* as "an active participant in Italy's progressive social movement"; he was elected to the Senate in 1963 as an independent candidate running on the Communist Party ticket. Two books by Levi were published: *Labyrinth* and *Words Are Stones,* the latter about backwardness and poverty in Sicily.[123] Indignation about the squalor of the southern Italian countryside pervades Maria Giacobbe's *The Diary of a Young Schoolteacher* (90,000 copies), while Domenico Rea's stories described the slums of Naples.[124] Cesare Pavese's *The Comrade* (over 100,000 copies) "depicts a young man of petty bourgeois background named Pablo who becomes a Communist and a fighter in the underground."[125] And Nino Palumbo, a "progressive realistic writer," described in *The Tax Collector* "the tragic fate of a 'little man' in capitalist society."[126] Finally, Elio Pietri, a Communist Italian script writer, provided Soviet cinema-goers with some background information on *Rome, Eleven O'clock,* then being shown in the USSR, which portrays such horrors as two hundred Italian girls applying for a single typist's job and the ensuing caving in of a staircase, with ambulances carrying off the dead and the wounded. Italian reactionaries, Soviet people were told, tried to have this film banned —for obvious reasons.[127]

The great Spanish poet Federico Garcia Lorca is claimed for the Soviet cause by virtue of his membership in the Association of Friends of the USSR and, of course, his death at the hands of Franco's troops.[128] His poetry and drama, very unconventional by traditional Soviet standards, appeared in Russian in 18,000 copies. In many ways, the "problem" of Garcia Lorca parallels that of Paul Éluard. He is genuinely admired by the liberal artistic intelligentsia and tolerated by the conservative establishment.[129] Blas de Otero, a much lesser poet, has better political credentials: "Otero's verse

122. *The Penguin Companion,* Vol. II, p. 624. There were also 11,000 copies of *Metello* which "depicts the period preceding the founding of the Italian Communist Party." KL, Vol. V (1968), p. 952.
123. KL, Vol. IV (1967), p. 83. Sections from *Words Are Stones* were first printed in *Zvezda,* No. 9, 1956. No data available on the press run of either book.
124. A volume of Rea's stories was printed in Estonian in 20,000 copies; no press run figures are available for the Russian edition. A story by Maria Giacobbe was included in a "mini-anthology" of Italian writing, which also included a story by Aldo de Iaco, identified only as an architect and "a great friend of the USSR," apparently an important literary qualification. *Zvezda,* No. 1, 1961, p. 100.
125. KL, Vol. V (1968), p. 523.
126. Ibid., p. 557.
127. *Moskva,* No. 5, 1957 pp. 74–75.
128. KL, Vol. II (1964), pp. 73–75.
129. See, e.g., *Osnovnye proizvedenija,* 1965, pp. 169–70.

deals with the poet's thoughts about the destinies of his country [Spain], about art and folk poetry, about the heroes of the anti-Fascist struggle, and about the Soviet Union. . . . Most of anthologies of Otero's verse were banned by the censorship and were published outside of Spain."[130] There was also an undisclosed number of copies of *Noche de guerra el Museo del Prado,* which is based on a historical incident during the Spanish Civil War. The author, Rafael Alberti, is a Spanish Communist who now lives in Argentina.[131] Another anti-Franco Spanish émigré in Argentina, the playwright Alexandro Casona, "continues anti-Fascist activity and participates in the struggle for peace."[132] His comedy *Trees Die Standing Up* was printed in 7,000 copies and was also performed in Soviet theaters, as were several of his other plays.[133] Armando Lopez Salinas lives in Spain. His novel *The Coal Mine (La mina)* "portrays the hard life of miners, only recently peasants, in contemporary Spain. It depicts the formation of their class consciousness under the influence of a Communist, a veteran of the national-revolutionary war of 1936–39."[134]

The most widely published modern Greek author in the USSR, Alexis Parnis, has the dubious distinction of not being listed even in the eight-volume Soviet *Literary Encyclopedia.* An anthology of his verse was printed in 20,000 copies, but he was widely published in journals. His contributions include a long narrative poem about the Communist-led Civil War in postwar Greece, which includes many anti-American asides;[135] a long anti-British poem about the Cypriote struggle for independence;[136] *The Island of Aphrodite,* a play on the same subject;[137] and some verses about the city of Leningrad.[138] The Lenin-Prize-winning Greek author Kostas Varnalis "made the subject of the people's struggle against exploitation and injustice the central subject of his work."[139] An anthology was printed in 30,000 copies, and his writings were also published in journals, as were the militantly political poems by Petros Anteos, denouncing Fascism and glorifying the USSR.[140] There was also a volume of similar verse by Yiannis Ritsos: "Ritsos's work was strongly influenced by socialist ideas (e.g., his poems

130. KL, Vol. V (1968), p. 506. No data are available on the press run.
131. KL, Vol. I (1962), p. 170.
132. *Teatral'naja ènciklopedija,* Vol. II (1963), p. 1167.
133. *Trees Die Standing Up* was performed in the Leningrad Theater of Comedy and other theaters, *The Third Word* in the Latvian Republic's Theater of Drama, and *Seven Shouts in the Ocean* in the Moscow Drama Theater. *Ibid.*
134. KL, Vol. IV (1967), p. 424. No information available on the press run of the translation.
135. *Novyj mir,* No. 6, 1954, carried a forty-page installment of *The Lay of Nikos Beloiannis;* a second part of the poem was printed in the same journal two years later (No. 6, 1956).
136. *Zvezda,* No. 4, 1959.
137. *Novyj mir,* No. 9, 1960.
138. *Zvezda,* No. 11, 1960.
139. *Novyj mir,* No. 4, 1959, p. 97.
140. *Moskva,* No. 12, 1961. There was also an anthology of Petros Anteos's verse; no information was given on the press run.

dedicated to Karl Marx, to the USSR, and to the struggling proletariat of other countries)."[141] *Mother Maruso,* a play by Georgos Sevastikoglu, was published in 75,000 copies. Sevastikoglu lived in the USSR for sixteen years, from 1949 to 1965; he was director of a theater for Greek political émigrés in the Central Asian city of Tashkent. Nikiforos Vrettakos is a noted Greek poet. The *Literary Encyclopedia* deplored the "neo-Christian" and "pessimistic" quality of his verse, but this was apparently redeemed in part by his opposition to colonialism, and also by Vrettakos's admiration for the "achievements of the Soviet people and their love of peace."[142] The appraisal of his significance thus resembles that of Éluard and Lorca; a volume of Vrettakos's lyric poetry appeared in an unknown number of copies.

Scandinavian literature was well represented. Five Swedish authors portrayed the hardships of working class life in their country. Jan Fridegård's *I, Lars Hård,* an angry novel about a man brutalized and made cynical by unemployment and other social ills, was printed in a quarter of a million copies. Folke Fridell's *The Girl in Grey,* a similarly embittered novel, appeared in 17,000 in Estonian, a not inconsiderable amount for that language; as already pointed out, traditional ties between Latvia and Estonia and Scandinavia are manifested in the fact that a greater variety of Scandinavian literature is available in those languages than in Russian. Ivar Lo-Johansson is identified in a Soviet bibliography as "a proletarian Swedish writer" whose "novels and articles about Sweden's sharecroppers brought about a number of steps on the part of the government aimed at improving the lot of these toilers of the earth."[143] Lo-Johansson's *Grain Is Ripening in Dakota* appeared in 20,000 copies in Estonian; there was also a Russian anthology, press run unknown. Artur Lundkvist's *Vindingevals* (20,000 copies in Estonian) is relatively apolitical, but its author was active in politics: a recipient of the Lenin Prize, Lundkvist was vice-president of the World Peace Council. Moa Martinson's autobiographical novels about Sweden's rural poor, *Mother Gets Married* and *A Church Wedding,* appeared in over 100,000 copies, including 12,000 in Lithuanian.

Of Norwegian leftists, the most widely published is Øivind Bolstad. A Communist Party member, he is known for his tales about Unicorn, the Norwegian national hero, which were published in Estonian in 20,000 copies, under the title *The Joker from the Island of Tosca.* In *The Patriots,* a play written in 1939, Bolstad predicted the Nazi occupation of Norway.[144]

141. KL, Vol. VI (1971), p. 310. No press run figures are available.
142. KL, Vol. I (1962), p. 1057.
143. *Kalendar' pamjatnyx dat po zarubežnoj xudožestvennoj literature na 1966 god* (Moscow: Kniga, 1965), p. 9.
144. KL, Vol. I (1962), p. 684.

The play was twice reprinted in Russian (press runs not indicated); there were also close to 300,000 copies of his short stories.[145] Björn Rongen's *Big Ma* tells the story of a woman who helps her husband, a trade union organizer, "master the theory of socialism, and struggle for worker's rights"; most of the novel describes a strike.[146] Finally, there was a 90,000-copy edition of short stories and a token 1500 copies of *Defeat,* a play about the Paris Commune by Nordahl Grieg, a Norwegian who lived for two years in the USSR and died in action in World War II.

Martti Larni is a militantly pro-Soviet Finnish journalist. Occasionally, he even represents Soviet newspapers abroad (thus, in the absence of diplomatic ties with Israel, Larni visited Israel on behalf of the Soviet press). Martti Larni is also the Finnish writer most famous in the USSR—or at least, the most publicized and widely printed. One of his novels became a Soviet best seller. Although the exact number of copies is unknown, it was reprinted in Russian at least four times within as many years; there was also a Latvian edition (30,000 copies) and a Georgian one (20,000). The following description adequately explains what endeared Larni's novel to Soviet publishers: "The novelistic tract [*roman-pamflet*] *The Fourth Vertebra, or a Crook In Spite of Himself* (*Neljäs nikama eli Veijari vastoin tahtoaan,* 1957; Russian translation, 1959), which brought the author world renown (it was translated into fifteen languages), is a biting satire on the American way of life."[147] There were compelling nonliterary reasons for the publication of Larni's other novel as well: "In the satirical novel *The Beautiful Swineheard, or Memoirs of the Economic Councillor Minna Karlsson-Kanasen* (*Kaunis sikopaimen eli Talousneuvos Minna Karlsson-Kanasen muistelmia,* 1959; Russian translation, 1961) Larni describes bourgeois conditions, exposes the shady deals of bourgeois business sharks, the hypocrisy of 'philanthropists' and blind kowtowing to everything 'Western'."[148] The last expression, incidentally, sadly remembered from the Stalinist "anticosmopolitan" purges of the late 1940s, is now hardly ever used in Soviet criticism or, for that matter, in the Soviet press. Its resurrection in the context of a novel about modern Finland recalls that Soviet intimidation of that little country has given birth to a political label, "Finlandization," which, translated into concrete terms, implies kowtowing to nothing West-

---

145. Two of Øivind Bolstad's more ideological short stories appeared in *Inostrannaja literatura,* No. 6, 1961. One of them suggests that Norwegian capitalists did not really approve of the anti-Nazi resistance; the other one is about a working class girl corrupted by a rich man.

146. *Xudožestvennaja literatura,* (April–June 1963), pp. 72–73.

147. KL, Vol. IV (1967), p. 35. A dramatization of the novel was staged in Soviet theaters. Ibid.

148. Ibid. The novel had appeared first in *Inostrannaja literatura,* Nos. 8 and 9, 1960. This writer attests that even in comparison with Stalinist potboilers, Larni's novel is extremely crude and propagandistic.

ern and tilting toward most everything Soviet.[149]

Elvi Sinervo is the author of political fiction and children's books. "In 1941–44 she was jailed by the reactionary government [of Finland] for participation in organizing a Society for Peace and Friendship with the USSR," the *Literary Encyclopedia* points out.[150] That is understandable since in 1940 the USSR had attacked Finland and seized some of her territory. "Sinervo opposes Fascism, war, and reaction. The central subject of *Comrade, Don't Betray Us!* (*Toveri, älä petä!*, 1947) is the awakening of political consciousness."[151] Sinervo also wrote a book about Gorky's childhood. Her writings appeared in a total of 200,000 copies, including 15,000 in Latvian and 5,000 in Estonian. Iris Uurto, a writer of love stories whose heroes are workers and artists, is also prominently associated with left-wing causes (her husband is the Communist writer Rantala-Ripatti). Her novel *Love and Fear (Rakkaus ja pelko)* was published in 20,000 copies in Estonian. The noted Finnish poetess Katri Vala is known for her experimental verse. Her left-wing politics thus place her in a category similar to that of Éluard and Garcia Lorca.[152] A volume of Estonian renditions of Vala's verse appeared in 15,000 copies. A fourth Finnish woman writer, Hella Wuolijoki, an Estonian by birth, was sentenced to death in 1943 for "activities on behalf of peace," but this was commuted to life imprisonment. After the war she was elected an honorary member of the Finnish-Soviet Friendship Society. Her plays, which portray the old nests of Finland's gentlefolk at the turn of the century, such as *Justine* and *The Bread of Niskavuoren (Niskavuoren leipä)*, are published in the USSR and have entered the repertory of Soviet theaters.[153] Pentti Haanpää's 1928 collection of short stories about the routine of the Finnish army provoked a scandal; Haanpää was charged with "communism, materialism and atheism."[154] His often sardonic tales were printed in Russian (probably 100,000 copies) and Estonian (15,000). Finally, there were the works of Maiju Lassila, considered one of the founders of proletarian literature in Finland, a participant in the planning of the October Revolution in Petrograd, who died a martyr's death in 1918, executed

149. Thus, e.g., in 1974 there were persistent reports that as a result of Soviet pressures, Solzhenitsyn's *Gulag Archipelago* was nearly unobtainable in Finland.

150. KL, Vol. VI (1971), p. 855.

151. Ibid.

152. "In the 1930s she [Katri Vala] drew close to the democratic and labor movement, published articles in defense of the workers, exposed Fascism and militarism. Her poetry also deals with social problems and the unmasking of reaction." KL, Vol. I (1962), p. 833.

153. A collection of Wuolijoki's plays was published in Russian as were two other plays; no press runs were indicated; another play was printed in 3,000 copies in Latvian. *Stone Nest (Niskavuoren naiset)* was first performed in 1957 by the important Maly Theater; *Justine* was staged in 1958 by the Central Theater of the Soviet Army. *Teatral'naja ènciklopedija*, Vol. I (1961), pp. 1042–43. See also KL, Vol. I (1962), p. 1065. Curiously, even though Hella Wuolijoki wrote some of her early works in Estonian, and some of her later writings have Estonian settings, none appear to have been published in Estonian in 1954–64.

154. *The Penguin Companion*, Vol. II, p. 346.

by anti-Communist soldiers.[155] Lassila was a humorist, and his comic novel *To Borrow Some Matches,* considered by many a classic picture of the Finnish people, was translated into Russian by the greatest Soviet humorist, Mikhail Zoshchenko. Lassila's works were printed in nearly a quarter of a million copies: *To Borrow Some Matches* was issued in Russian in 150,000 copies plus 15,000 in Ukrainian, and a Russian anthology in 75,000. Some tenuous claims are made for the ideological message of his work, but the political value in this case is certainly much more in the legend of Lassila himself.

Among the left-wing Danish writers, too, there were those who owed their publication in the USSR primarily to their political activities, and those whose politics were merely another, albeit very strong, point in their favor. Clearly, Hilmar Wulff belongs in the former group. Onetime editor of the journal *Nyt fra Soviet Unionen* (News from the Soviet Union), and politically active, Wulff had two of his novels published; *Bad Weather* was printed in 100,000 copies, as was probably *Sol-vagabonden* (The Solar Tramps). The first was praised for its analysis of social relations in Denmark and the second for its portrayal of the working class.[156] Otto Gelsted, a poet and a member of Denmark's Communist Party, "exposed instigators of a new war."[157] His verse appeared in two anthologies; the press run of one was 10,000 copies, that of the other unknown. The novels of Hans Kirk, an editor of *Land og Folk,* the Communist newspaper, are strongly political; they describe, among other things, "the role of Denmark's Communist Party in the struggle against Fascism and instigators of a new war."[158] Several were published, in Russian, Estonian, Ukrainian, and Tadzhik, a total of some 150,000 copies, probably owing to their educational value.

Hans Scherfig is described in a Western reference book as "a Danish novelist of Marxist views and author of satires of bourgeois society; the latter are often thrillers written in the Anglo-American traditions."[159] Considering the great hunger of the Soviet public for Western detective stories, it is likely that Scherfig's novels enjoy genuine popularity. Probably, too, Soviet publishers prefer to satisfy this demand with books such as Scherfig's, which combine the pleasant with the useful; these appeared in some 200,000 copies. Another consideration may have been Scherfig's past record of pro-Soviet writing. Thus, in 1951 (i.e., during the worst years of Stalinism) Scherfig wrote an admiring account of a visit to the USSR that also con-

155. *Dictionnaire des littératures,* Vol. II, p. 2278. See also KL, Vol. IV (1967), p. 42.
156. KL, Vol. I (1962), p. 1064.
157. KL, Vol. II (1964), pp. 124–25.
158. KL, Vol. III (1966), p. 539.
159. *Dictionnaire des littératures,* Vol. III, p. 3525.

tained attacks on Denmark's "bourgeois" press for spreading "slander" about that happy land. Karin Michaëlis was considered "a friend of the USSR and active in the struggle for peace."[160] This may well be true, but the publication of her novel *Mother (Mor)* in a quarter of a million copies was probably due primarily to its intrinsic interest, which brought her writings about women and girls world fame.

Finally, there are the writings of Martin Andersen-Nexø, the grand old man of Denmark's proletarian literature, a founder of the Danish Communist Party, member of the jury of the Lenin Peace Prize, and *twice* a political émigré: Nexø spent the war years in the USSR and then, after the war, he emigrated again, this time to East Germany, to escape "persecution" by Denmark's "reactionaries." He died in 1954. Nexø is best known as the author of the cycle of four novels *Pelle the Conqueror* and three novels about "Ditte." Taken together, the two large works are, according to a Western reference book, "a working class epos about the Bornholm boy Pelle, a proletarian who becomes a trade unionist and a strike leader, and the girl Ditte, who is defeated and succumbs to the hardships of life."[161] Another of Nexø's works is the semiautobiographical *Morten the Red:* "Morten's trip to the Soviet Union and his study of the teachings of V. I. Lenin strengthen his faith in mankind's socialist future."[162] Nexø's various novels were published in about a million copies, two thirds of these in Russian, and the rest in Ukrainian, Moldavian, and the three Baltic languages.

The Nobel Prize–winning Icelandic novelist Halldór Kiljan Laxness, though often identified with pro-Soviet causes (a member of the World Peace Council, he was also recipient of its prize in 1953), is quite independent-minded.[163] A Western critic notes, "Fierce social criticism runs through all of Laxness's novels and has often alienated his readers. Yet he is not a defender of so-called Socialist Realism but of freedom for the artist as a mouthpiece of the oppressed and the deprived. Laxness's rich lyrical vein, his vigorous symbolism, his psychological insights, his naturalism, his often cynical impartiality, enable him to fuse the characters and Iceland's harsh

160. KL, Vol. IV (1967), pp. 823–24.
161. *The Penguin Companion,* Vol. II, p. 566.
162. KL, Vol. I (1962), p. 225.
163. Thus, Laxness condemned the Soviet invasion of Hungary in 1956. See Rühle, *Literature and Revolution,* p. 400. A Soviet critic noted in 1958 that although Laxness was a good Communist, he was then somewhat confused, hopefully only temporarily. G. Šatkov, "Gumanizm Laksnessa," *Inostrannaja literatura,* No. 6, 1958, pp. 170–81. Just before that, the journal had published Laxness's new novel, *Brekkukots annáll (The Fish Can Sing),* about Reykjavik's humble beginnings at the turn of the century as a large fishing village. Ibid., Nos. 4 and 5, 1958. The Soviet critic's hopeful prognosis did not materialize. Ultimately, Laxness broke with the Communist Party altogether. In the mid-1960s Laxness "for the first time directs an all-out attack against Marxism, Communism, Stalinism, and the Soviet regime." Lewis Nichols, "In and Out of Books," *The New York Times Book Review,* July 19, 1964, p. 8.

landscape into one vast panorama of intensified reality."[164] His various novels, with modern as well as historical settings, were printed in Russian, Ukrainian, and the three Baltic languages in close to half a million copies. All were highly praised, although misgivings were expressed about Laxness's "skepticism" and hence insufficient optimism, an attribute expected of authors whose Communist faith should inspire confidence in mankind's brighter future.[165] Even so, Laxness's works could be used as supporting evidence for *domestic* Soviet politics. Thus, an editorial note to *Gerpla (The Happy Warriors)* praised the author for departing from the traditions of the Viking saga and portraying King Olaf not as a hero, but as a sadistic henchman. In an obvious allusion to the only recently denounced Stalin, the Soviet critic noted approvingly: "The book pushes off the pedestal [*razvenčivaet*] and ridicules the cult of a hero. It demonstrates that ordinary people play the most important role in history."[166]

## The Latin American Marxists

Some of Latin America's most important writers and poets are Communists and leftists. These were published, but so were scores of authors whose artistic distinction is scant but whose devotion to the cause was to be given literary recognition. Carlos Augusto León, longtime Communist deputy in Venezuela's parliament and author among other things, of, *Yo canto a Lenin (Of Lenin I Sing)*, was honored by translation of a volume of his verse,[167] as was the Paraguayan Elvio Romero whose poetry glorifies the heroism of the Soviet Army.[168] Carlos Luis Fallas is the author of *Marcos Ramirez* ("adventures of a little Costa Rican") and of *Mamita Junai,* an autobiographical novel which describes "the struggle against the mighty United Fruit Company"; he is also a leader in Costa Rica's Communist Party. It is difficult to say how influential the latter fact was in the publication of both books.[169] The same applies to *The Island of Love,* a play by the

164. Gertrude C. Schwebell in *Encyclopedia of World Literature in the 20th Century,* Vol. II, p. 259.

165. "Laxness's humanism, shaped under a strong influence of socialism, and his sharp criticism of the bourgeois political system, are sometimes beset with doubts, with thoughts about human limitations." KL, Vol. III (1966), p. 976.

166. *Inostrannaja literatura,* No. 1, 1957, p. 145. Laxness himself could hardly have intended the parallel; *The Happy Warriors* was first published in 1952, a year before Stalin's death. Russian readers may have detected yet another parallel, with the official stinging rebuke received in 1937 (i.e., during the Great Purges) by the orthodox Soviet poet Dem'jan Bednyj for the opera libretto *Bogatyri,* which mocked the legendary heroes of *byliny,* the Russian sagas, in a manner reminiscent of Laxness. To repeat again with the Marxist historian Pokrovskij, history is politics projected into the past.

167. KL, Vol. IV (1967), p. 131. No press run figures available.

168. KL, Vol. VI (1971), pp. 390–91. No press run figures given.

169. *Mamita Junai* was issued in Estonian in 10,000 copies; *Marcos Ramirez* was published

Uruguayan Communist Alfredo Dante Gravina, and to his two novels, *Del miedo al orgullo (From Fear to Pride)* and *Fronteras al viento (Frontiers for Winds),* the subject of the latter being "life on cattle-raising estates and the struggle of hired hands for their rights."[170] Gravina is active in politics, and his books include admiring accounts of travel in the USSR and Eastern Europe. José Mancisidor is considered "the acknowledged leader of Mexico's young proletarian literature." Besides fiction, Mancisidor also wrote studies of Marx, Lenin, Barbusse, and Gorky. His novel *El alba en las simas (Dawn Over the Abyss)* "describes the struggle for the nationalization of Mexico's oil" and *Border Extends Into the Sea (Frontera junto al mar)* is set against the background of "the heroic resistance of the people of Vera Cruz to the American intervention in 1914."[171] No particular political claims were made for the Bolivian writer Jesús Lara other than the fact that his novel *Jawarninchij* (which in the language of the Quechua Indians means "our blood"), an account of growing protest among the exploited landless Quechua, offers some glimpses of Bolivian Communists.[172]

The two Brazilian authors published included a "progressive" who is also an author and a major novelist who happens to be a member of the Communist Party. An anthology of Milton Pedrosa's short stories was described as follows: "These are tales about the struggle of Brazil's Communists for a better future of the country, a class struggle in which all the working people take part, even the old and children."[173] The writings of Jorge Amado, one of South America's most important authors, were brought out in a quarter of a million copies, three fourths of it in Russian, and the rest in Ukrainian, Latvian, Estonian, and Turkmen. The largest items were *São Jorge dos Ilhens* (over 100,000) and *Seara vermelha* (close to 90,000). Of the first, the *Literary Encyclopedia* writes: "The fate of Brazil under the yoke of imperialism is portrayed most dramatically. . . . An important role in the novel is played by a Communist leader."[174] The second novel "bears witness to Amado's maturing as a Socialist Realist. The tragic history of the family of the impoverished peasant Geronimo, one of whose sons had become a Communist, stands as a symbol of the growing revolutionary moods of the Brazilian peasantry."[175] While there may be some exaggeration in these appraisals, the two novels are among Amado's most political, as

in Russian (30,000 copies) and in Lithuanian (10,000).

170. KL, Vol. II (1964), p. 320. No press run figures available for any of the three titles.

171. KL, Vol. IV (1967), p. 592. *Frontera junto al mar* was printed in 15,000 copies; there is no information about the other novel.

172. Ibid., pp. 32–33. No data are available on the press run of this or of Lara's other novel about the Indians of Bolivia, *Janacuna.*

173. *Xudožestvennaja literatura,* (April–June 1963), p. 64.

174. KL, Vol. I (1962), p. 180.

175. Ibid., p. 181.

distinct from his more accomplished, novels. By contrast, *Gabriela (Clove and Cinnamon)* appears to have been printed only in Estonian, in 30,000 copies.

Similarly, the two Chileans whose works appeared included a relatively unknown novelist and a very famous poet. Luis Enrique Délano's novel *La base* (translated under the very Russian title *Olga*) was a portrait of a heroic young woman Communist in Chile.[176] Pablo Neruda, a much honored poet very active in Communist causes, was published twice. One collection was printed in 40,000 copies (a large figure for translations of modern poetry), while the press run of the second is unknown. A complex, ornate, often "baroque" modern poet, Neruda is yet another member of the group of twentieth-century Western poets who appear to be published in the USSR because their political virtues atone for the formal sins of their verse. Thus, of Pablo Neruda's *Canto general,* a narrative poem in fifteen chapters, the *Literary Encyclopedia* writes: "The last part of the book is the confession of a poet who found his path to the people and impassionately expounds the ideals of Communism."[177]

Of writers from Argentina, Raul Larra was the most published; Larra's credentials include a jail sentence for "progressive activities." His books "describe the hard life of working people. Larra was among the first Argentine writers to introduce Communist protagonists in his works."[178] Inexplicably, all of Larra's books appeared in Ukrainian: *Gran Chaco* (23,000), *Le decían Rulo* (15,000), and *Sin tregua* (7,000), A collection of verse by Raul González Tuñon was issued in 10,000 copies: "During World War II González Tuñon wrote verses about the courage of the Soviet people. . . . His postwar verse inspires the people of Argentina in the struggle for peace (e.g., "An Autumn Sonata in Moscow," 1954; "A Clear Voice," 1956, and others)."[179] *Inspired By Hope,* a novel about Argentina's poor who move from the provinces to the big cities in the vain hope of improving their lot, was published in a "conservative" Soviet monthly. Like the poet González Tuñon, Juan Floriani is an admirer of the USSR. He wrote: "In addition to the cultural traditions of the past, our [Argentine writers'—MF] work also draws inspiration from the successes of the principles of Socialist Realism, and particularly from the outstanding achievements of Soviet literature."[180]

The Argentine playwright Agustin Cuzzani is the author of *A Pound of Flesh* ("a biting satire on bourgeois democracy"; published in 3,000 copies),

176. *Inostrannaja literatura*, No. 12, 1960. Also published in book form, press run unknown.
177. KL, Vol. V (1968), p. 244.
178. KL, Vol. IV (1967), p. 37.
179. KL, Vol. II (1964), p. 259.
180. *Neva*, No. 9, 1960, p. 94.

*The Center of Offense Will Die at Dawn* ("unmasks corruption in capitalist society"), and other dramas that "mock the American way of life," "attack the arms race and appeal for peaceful use of nuclear energy." In view of all these virtues it was to be expected that Cuzzani's plays should attract Soviet theater directors. *The Center of Offense* was performed at the Moscow Theater of the Young Communist League, the Kaliningrad (Königsberg) Theater, and elsewhere.[181]

The largest national contingent among the Latin Americans is, understandably, the Cuban. Prior to the Castro revolution of 1959, leftist Cuban authors were translated in the USSR much in the same manner as similar writers from the other countries of the area. After 1959, as Cuba gradually began to acquire the status of a People's Democracy, an ever increasing number of Cuban authors, some of them little known outside their country, began to appear in Russian translation. At present, Cuban literature is the most widely published of all Latin American writing in the USSR.[182] Of course, it should be kept in mind that divisions along strictly national lines are to be treated in this case simply as an identification device; to differentiate between the various Spanish writers of Latin America is as artificial as drawing sharp dividing lines at this time between West German, Austrian, and Swiss authors writing in German. Such divisions are legitimate only when political conditions differ to a degree that clearly and consistently affects the quality of *published* writing—as between German authors of East and West Germany.

Nicolas Guillén was the most widely published Cuban in the USSR both prior to the Castro takeover and in the years that followed. An Afro-Cuban poet whose two central themes are racial and social justice, he is described by a Western critic as "a modern troubadour of the tavern, chanting his tropically glowing ballads and wryly humorous songs of freedom to a rumba rhythm."[183] Active in Communist causes, he lived for a time abroad. The *Literary Encyclopedia* notes: "In 1959, after the victory of the People's Revolution, he returned to Cuba and became extremely active in literary and public affairs. In poems and articles published in the Cuban press he glorifies the people's victory and the building of a new society."[184] A volume of Russian translations of Guillén's verse was printed in 35,000 copies. A winner of the Lenin Prize, he is, moreover, very widely published in Soviet periodicals, probably more so than any other Latin

181. *Teatral'naja ènciklopedija,* Vol III (1964), pp. 344–45.
182. See L. A. Šur, *Xudožestvennaja literatura Latinskoj Ameriki v russkoj pečati, 1960–1964.* Annotirovannaja bibliografija russkix perevodov i kritičeskoj literatury na russkom jazyke (Moscow: Kniga, 1966).
183. Janheinz Jahn in *Encyclopedia of World Literature in the 20th Century,* Vol. II, p. 71.
184. KL, Vol. II (1964), p. 178.

American author. A Soviet bibliography of Nicolas Guillén published in 1964 runs to 99 pages.[185]

Another well-known Cuban was Alejo Carpentier, a musicologist and novelist (incidentally, of French and Russian parentage). Two of his books were published: *The Lost Steps*, about a search for primitive musical instruments in Venezuela, and *The Kingdom of this World*, a novella "based on historical events, which portrays the struggle for independence of Haiti's Negroes and mulattos in the early nineteenth century."[186]

## Other "Progressive" English-Language Writing

Taken as a whole, United States representation was rather modest. The most important American Communist author, Theodore Dreiser, was discussed earlier in this chapter. John Reed, the author of *Ten Days that Shook the World*, an eyewitness report of the Russian Revolution suppressed during the Stalin era, reappeared in print with 150,000 copies of *Insurgent Mexico*, an account of his four months with the guerrillas of Pancho Villa; once again, Reed became "a well-known American Communist writer."[187] Unlike such West European countries as France and Italy (and to some degree, Latin America), in the aftermath of World War II the Communist movement in the United States not only ceased to attract many new adherents, but also suffered a number of defections; some of these authors will be considered elsewhere.[188] The thinned ranks of American leftists (of the Old Left, to be precise; the New Left was to come into its own some years later, and its reception in the USSR was cool) included some familiar names. Rockwell Kent, the chairman of the American-Soviet Friendship Society, had two old books translated into Russian in time for his eightieth birthday in 1962. *N by E* and *Salamina* describe the Arctic world of Greenland: "Filled with humor and optimism, these books offer a vivid picture of the toil and the spiritual world of the Eskimos."[189] A play entitled *Parlor Magic*, by John Howard Lawson, a leftist Hollywood writer jailed during the McCarthy years, was received in manuscript form and published in a

185. L. A. Šur, *Nikolas Gil'en.* Biobibliografičeskij ukazatel'. Vstupitel'naja stat'ja Z. Plavskina (Moscow: Kniga, 1964).
186. KL, Vol III (1966), p. 419. No data available on the press run of either work. Other Cuban authors published in Russian in book form for the first time included Dora Alonso, Raúl Gonzalez de Cascorro, Margarita Crespo López, Ramón Meza, Hilda Perera Soto, and Onelio Jorge Cardoso.
187. *Moskva*, No. 4, 1958, p. 99. The issue contained translations of three stories from the 1927 posthumous collection *The Daughter of the Revolution and Other Stories*. Excerpts from *Ten Days That Shook the World* were printed in *Novyj mir*, No. 11, 1956.
188. See chapter 8.
189. KL, Vol. III (1966), p. 492. *Salamina* was printed in 50,000 copies; no information is available about *N by E*.

journal.[190] Another leftist American playwright revived at the time was
Elmer Rice. His *Street Scene* (1929) was staged in Leningrad and also
published in book form. *The Force of Truth,* by Albert Kahn, a leftist
journalist and frequent contributor to the Soviet press, was issued in 150,000
copies. Martha Dodd, the daughter of the prewar United States ambassador
in Berlin, "became sympathetic to the USSR"; subsequently, "Dodd and
her husband were persecuted for their progressive views and in 1953 they
were forced to leave the country [USA]." Her novel *Sowing the Wind*
"unmasks the chieftains of Nazi Germany and the industrial circles that
supported them"; *The Searching Light* describes the clash between an
honest American scientist accused of spreading Communist propaganda
and " 'a man from Wall Street' and other reactionaries."[191] Albert Maltz,
who became the most important American Marxist author in the USSR
after the defection of Howard Fast, was printed in well over half a million
copies. There were two Russian printings of *The Cross and the Arrow,* a
novel about Germany's anti-Nazi resistance; press run unknown. Also
printed were 115,000 copies of a Russian anthology, 200,000 copies of a story
translated into simplified Russian for non-Russian children, and 10,000 of
a Georgian translation of *The Underground Stream,* a novel that depicts
"the struggle of automobile factory workers under the leadership of a young
Communist." Finally, there was a Russian translation of *A Long Day in a
Short Life,* which "reconstructs a single day in the life of inmates of a large
Washington jail and the awakening of protest and solidarity of blacks and
whites."[192]

Mention was made earlier in this chapter of the several members of
*L'Humanité*'s editorial staff whose books were translated in the USSR.
There was an American parallel: novels by three editors of the Communist
journal *Mainstream* were translated. Philip Bonosky's *Burning Valley,* a
story of the maturing of an adolescent, was issued in 100,000 copies. No

190. *Inostrannaja literatura,* No. 11, 1962. During the war years and their immediate aftermath Lawson was one of the Hollywood screen writers "relied on" by the American Communist Party "to carry on the revolutionary literary tradition." Daniel Aaron, *Writers on the Left*
(New York: Avon Books, 1965), pp. 397–98.
191. KL, Vol. II (1964), p. 727. No data were issued on the press run of either, except that
*The Searching Light* was also issued in 15,000 copies in Latvian.
192. KL, Vol. IV (1967), p. 555. There is an intriguing possibility that Maltz's *A Long Day
in a Short Life* may have influenced Solzhenitsyn's *One Day in the Life of Ivan Denisovich.*
The titles are remarkably similar *(Dlinnyj den' v korotkoj žizni* and *Odin den' Ivana Denisovi-
ča)* and, more strikingly, both works describe a single day in the existence of a motley group
of prison inmates. Solzhenitsyn's novel was published in 1962; the Russian translation of Albert
Maltz's work came out in 1958. Solzhenitsyn may have wished to portray a "socialist" counterpart of Maltz's "capitalist" jail. A curious incident adds credence to this hypothesis. As
reported by *The New York Times,* shortly before Solzhenitsyn's expulsion from the USSR in
February 1974, upon hearing of the Russian author's financial difficulties, Maltz offered Solzhenitsyn some of his Soviet royalties. It is likely that now that Solzhenitsyn is in the West, the
two politically very different authors would prefer to forget the incident. The tale by Albert
Maltz that was adapted for non-Russian children was *Circus Come to Town.*

information was given about the Russian translation of *The Magic Fern* ("about the life of the working class of the USA") and *Brother Bill McKie,* a fictionalized biography of a labor leader.[193] Shirley Graham, a children's writer, is the author of *Your Most Humble Servant,* a novel about Benjamin Banneker, a Negro writer and scientist of the period of America's War of Independence.[194] There was also an undisclosed number of copies of Lloyd Brown's *Iron City,* "which deals with the struggle for Negro rights and the role [of Negroes] in the labor movement."[195] Of the three, Bonosky is white and the others black.

Books by America's new generation of black radicals, many of them implacably hostile to all whites, began to be translated on an appreciable scale in the late 1960s. Previously, black writing translated in the USSR was more conventionally antiracist—such as Lorraine Hansberry's—or, if militant, then from politically, rather than racially, radical positions. William E. B. DuBois, then still alive (he joined the Communist Party at the age of ninety-three and later emigrated to Ghana), had one of his works of fiction translated. *Mansard Builds a School,* one part of a three-part fictionalized history of blacks in America since the Civil War, "unmasks the true nature of American democracy."[196] Langston Hughes, also alive at the time, has been published steadily in the USSR since 1930. As a Soviet periodical informed its readers, "Hughes is not only an outstanding poet. He is an impassioned fighter for peace and for the freedom of the Negro people, and a tested friend of the Soviet Union. His poems and stories are well known among our readers."[197] A volume of his verse appeared in Russian translation (press run unknown). Langston Hughes's satirical stories of Simple, the Harlem philosopher, are often printed in Soviet periodicals.[198] The American basso Paul Robeson, a Lenin Prize winner and member of the World Peace Council, sent a manuscript to a Soviet journal; *Here I Stand,* a book about blacks in the United States, was printed in abridged form.[199] Paul Robeson also wrote the introduction to John Oliver Killen's *Youngblood,* a

193. KL, Vol. I (1962), p. 691.
194. KL, Vol. II (1964), p. 425.
195. KL, Vol. I (1962), p. 724.
196. *Xudožestvennaja literatura,* (April–June 1963), p. 69.
197. *Novyj mir,* No. 12, 1959, p. 148. The issue featured translations of American verse. The poets represented included, in addition to Langston Hughes, Vachel Lindsay, Carl Sandburg, and Robert Frost.
198. A number of satirical stories from the 1957 collection *Simple Stakes a Claim,* some of them containing strong digs at the "free world" where racial injustice is rampant, were printed in *Inostrannaja literatura,* No. 12, 1958. To heighten their effect, the stories were supplied with tendentious, anti-American annotations.
199. *Novyj mir,* No. 4, 1958. The full text of *Here I Stand* was published in the United States the same year (New York, Othello Associates). Soviet journals and book publishers often print abridged versions of foreign works, selecting only the more "useful" parts. Sometimes the fact that the book is printed in abridged from is unacknowledged; the practice must therefore be viewed as censorship. See chapter 1.

novel about two generations of working-class blacks in the United States.[200]

Since most South African authors whose writing is concerned with that country's painful racial problem are not usually described in Soviet sources as pro-Communist, they are considered elsewhere in this study.[201] One South African writer who apparently is regarded as having Communist sympathies is Peter Abrahams. According to the *Literary Encyclopedia,* all the works of this "colored" author who lives in England "deal with the problem of racial discrimination and the struggle for national liberation." They have appeared in virtually every important language spoken in the USSR.[202] The total for all of Abrahams's books was close to 200,000 copies; except for 28,000 copies of *A Wreath for Udomo* and a similar edition of an anthology, all were translations of *The Path of Thunder.* The latter novel also inspired a Soviet ballet.[203]

There was substantial Australian representation. Some of the subject matter of the Australian books was traditional for left-wing writing outside the Soviet bloc. Thus, Vance Edward Packard was described by the *Literary Encyclopedia* as an author who portrays the class struggle and labor leaders who sell out to the bosses;[204] *The Silver Oak* was printed in an impressive edition of 300,000 copies, while *The Rainbow Bird,* a less political work, came out in 20,000 in Estonian. In the more militant writings of John Morrison, a Communist Party member since 1937, one finds such themes as "capitalism's hostility to the interests of the workers, proletarian solidarity, and internationalism, powerfully expressed."[205] A Russian anthology of John Morrison was printed in 150,000 copies, and an Estonian volume in 17,000. *Shares in Murder,* by Judah L. Waten, a Russian-born Australian Communist, though perhaps equally tendentious, presumably made for more interesting reading: "A sociopsychological detective novel, [it] describes the links between big business, the politicians, and the underworld."[206] Henry Lawson (1867–1922), a short-story writer of an earlier period, was praised for his earlier work in which he "denounced capitalism and foretold a proletarian revolution." Subsequently he was said to have

---

200. KL, Vol. III (1966), p. 512. Within a few years, Killens and other literary exponents of Black nationalism were to be violently attacked. For a detailed discussion of the fate of American literature in the USSR in 1970–75 see this writer's "The U.S. in the U.S.S.R.: American Literature through the Filter of Recent Soviet Publishing and Criticism," *Critical Inquiry,* Vol. III, No. 3 (Spring 1976), pp. 519–83.

201. See chapter 5.

202. KL, Vol. I (1962), p. 40. In 1954–64 the novels of Peter Abrahams were published in Russian, Ukrainian, Belorussian, Kirgiz, Moldavian, Estonian, Uzbek, Lithuanian, Georgian, Azerbaidzhani, Chuvash—as well as in the original English with a Russian introduction (36,000 copies).

203. Peter Abrahams is also published in Soviet periodicals. Thus, "It Happened in the Malayan Quarter" appeared in *Neva,* No. 4, 1963.

204. KL, Vol. V (1968), pp. 555–56.

205. KL, Vol. IV (1967), p. 984.

206. KL, Vol. VII (1972), p. 820. No information available on the number of copies.

experienced a decline "both ideologically and artistically"—a familiar claim in Soviet criticism, which considers the two inseparable; this was a reflection of the "moods of social compromise" of the period. Still, it was considered that, all in all, Lawson's "realistic and democratic traditions serve to promote present-day progressive Australian writing."[207] Lawson's prose and verse, which idealize the working man, were published in close to a quarter of a million copies, including translations into Georgian and Azerbaidzhani (6,000 and 10,000 copies respectively). There is nothing political about the two books by Alan Marshall that were printed in the USSR. *I Can Jump the Puddles* contains verses about a boy trying to overcome the handicaps of polio (it appeared in some 70,000 copies in Ukrainian, Lithuanian, and Latvian); and *People of the Dream Time,* which came out in Russian in 15,000 copies, is a collection of legends of Australian aborigines. Their author, however, is vice-president of the Soviet-Australian Friendship Society, which may have favorably impressed Soviet publishers.[208]

Katharine Susannah Prichard (1884–1969), a founder of Australia's Communist Party, was active in political journalism.[209] Prichard is the author of, among others, *The Real Russia* (1935) and a number of orthodox Stalinist pamphlets.[210] The political bias of her fiction, too, occasionally borders on the ludicrous. Thus, in "Communists Are Always Young," an aged Australian woman proudly watches all of her children join the Australian Communist Party. In what reads at times like a bad parody on Gorky's *Mother* (itself not overly subtle), the matriarch and her husband also join the Party.[211] Since little statistical data is available, one can only estimate on the basis of the figures given for the two Russian anthologies of Prichard's works (a quarter of a million) and of the printing of *Coonardoo* (150,000; also 15,000 in Lithuanian) that her books were probably issued in well over a million copies. *Coonardoo,* a novel about an aboriginal girl and a white farmer by whom she has a child, less overtly political, is Prichard's most successful work. The three volumes of Prichard's goldfields trilogy were published: *The Roaring Nineties, Golden Miles,* and *Winged Seeds;* all sound a strong, and sometimes shrill, note of social protest. No press run figures were released, except for the Estonian translation of the last (20,000).

With the demise of the grand old lady of Australia's proletarian literature, her mantle was inherited by Ellen Dymphna Cusack. Cusack's writing

207. KL, Vol. IV (1967), pp. 432–33.
208. Ibid., p. 676.
209. *Moskva,* No. 6, 1959, p. 142. The issue featured a translation of "Josephine Anne Marie," a tale describing the miserable existence of Australia's aborigines.
210. *The Penguin Companion,* Vol. I, p. 429.
211. The story was published in *Neva,* No. 1, 1963. "Christmas Tree" is milder. It relates how Australian banks conspire to ruin the farmers (*Novyj mir,* No. 4, 1955).

career began in the 1930s; she has published novels, plays, and travel impressions of the USSR and the People's Republic of China.[212] Two of her plays were published: *Comets Soon Pass,* which deals with "the social contradictions of capitalist society, with the new fighting Man," and *Pacific Paradise,* which "relates how the inhabitants of a tiny island prevented American soldiery [*voenščina*] from turning their homeland into a nuclear firing range." While no figures were issued for the two plays, the figure for the novel *Say No to Death* was considerable: over 300,000 copies, plus an edition in the original English. The novel was described as "an indictment of a society in which the have-nots are doomed to die." The most spectacular figure was achieved by the 1961 novel *Heatwave in Berlin,* which "unmasks the West German revanchists."[213] It was first printed in the series *Roman-gazeta* in 700,000 copies, and then reprinted. The total press run was thus probably well over a million copies, one of the largest for any new novel in the early 1960s. Ellen Dymphna Cusack may not be a great writer, but apparently Soviet publishers and editors consider her important. To state that her novels and plays were not published and performed for their cultural or even entertainment value alone is to repeat the obvious. During the first post-Stalin decade the writings of Cusack provided supporting literary evidence for some of the central themes of Soviet propaganda.

Not all of the politically "useful" Western authors of the 1950s and 1960s were Communists or even leftists. Some were moderate and even conservative, but certain features of their writing (or of their public activities) were found appealing by Soviet publishers.

In the 1950s and 1960s, in the estimate of a Soviet critic, Gwynn Thomas was to experience an ideological as well as an artistic decline (in the USSR the two, to repeat, are thought to be indivisible); his politics became moderate and his writing experimental. Gwynn Thomas had known better days as a radical Welsh nationalist writer. The *Literary Encyclopedia* notes: "The novels of the late 1940s testify to the author's certainty regarding the final victory of the revolutionary labor movement. . . . A student of the history of his [Welsh] people, Thomas portrays realistically the life of Welsh miners, their class solidarity (*The Dark Philosophers,* 1947; Russian translation, 1958), and recreates heroic events of the Chartist past (*All Things Betray Thee,* 1949; Russian translation, 1959)."[214] These novels were published in the USSR. Sir Compton Mackenzie's politics are not radical. The aging Scottish nationalist would probably have resented seeing himself introduced

212. The latter, *Chinese Women Speak* (Sydney, 1958), is concealed in the *Literary Encyclopedia*'s generalized mention of trips to the "USSR and other countries."
213. KL, Vol. III (1966), pp. 940–41, and *Teatral'naja ènciklopedija,* Vol. III (1964), pp. 356–57.
214. KL, Vol. VII (1972), p. 570. There is no information on the press run of either novel.

in the Soviet journal that published his *Rockets Galore* as "one of the oldest *English* writers and an active participant in the Peace Movement."[215] The novel, which "deals with the movement in defense of peace" (it describes honest Britons who oppose the armaments race that threatens their existence but are ignored by a government obsessed with hatred of Communism), was also printed in Estonian in 10,000 copies.[216] A. E. Coppard, a master of the English short story, was no firebrand either, although some of his tales do "indict the injustices of bourgeois society"—as, one might add, do the writings of most "bourgeois" authors. Coppard's stories were published in 20,000 copies in the original English, a decision favored by the fact that their author was one of the organizers of the Peace Movement. (We should emphasize, perhaps, that the designation, as used by Soviet sources, refers primarily to the Soviet-sponsored Peace Movement launched in the late 1940s rather than to later grassroots movements such as the one that sprang up in opposition to the American presence in Vietnam.)

Doris Lessing, by contrast, is a genuine radical, and was for many years active in a variety of Communist causes.[217] Her preoccupation with racial injustice (a result, no doubt, of her Rhodesian childhood) and with the destructive effects of age on women have made her a fashionable writer in America in the mid-1970s.[218] A Soviet literary journal notes, "Soviet readers know Doris Lessing not only as a gifted writer but also as a progressive public figure."[219] The *Literary Encyclopedia* points out that she is active in the Peace Movement and her novels, such as *Martha Quest,* "expose colonialism."[220] The total press run of Doris Lessing's works was probably close to half a million copies, mostly in Russian, but also in Latvian and Estonian, as well as in the original English.

Jack Lindsay received the highest ideological accolade as a writer who has "contributed to the literature of Britain's Socialist Realism." The overtly propagandistic nature of much of his writing appears to irk even a *Soviet* critic: "The writer is more interested in social contradictions than in the psychology of individual heroes."[221] An editor of the Communist *Marxist Quarterly,* Jack Lindsay is also a frequent contributor to the Soviet press. Clearly, then, it is doctrinal fervor rather than artistic merit that accorded

---

215. The novel was translated within a year of its publication. *Inostrannaja literatura,* Nos. 6 and 7, 1958.
216. KL, Vol. IV (1967), p. 520.
217. *The Penguin Companion,* Vol. I, p. 313.
218. Lionel Trilling noted with dismay that the Modern Language Association now sponsors panel discussions devoted to Doris Lessing's work at its annual conventions (*Commentary,* December 1974).
219. *Neva,* No. 12, 1959, p. 23. The issue features a story by Lessing, "The Second Hut," about the crying injustice of apartheid.
220. KL, Vol. IV (1967), p. 167.
221. Ibid., pp. 200–201.

Lindsay a separate chapter in a Soviet college textbook of modern foreign literature, a distinction shared by only one other living Briton, James Aldridge.[222] A prolific writer, Lindsay is the author of a number of novels with historical as well as modern settings. The total press run may be estimated at half a million copies.

The name (Harold Edward) James Aldridge does not appear in standard Western literary reference books.[223] Yet in the USSR James Aldridge is one of the most widely printed living authors, with a total of some two million copies issued in 1954–64. Born in 1918, he is described as "an anti-Fascist and a friend of the USSR" and an anti-imperialist proponent of peaceful coexistence; he is a recipient of the gold metal of the World Peace Council.[224] A wartime correspondent, he wrote a number of books with foreign settings (such as Greece and Iran); the earlier ones (e.g., *The Sea Eagle*) are anti-Fascist, while those written later are strongly pro-Soviet and anti-American (e.g., *The Diplomat* and the play *The Forty-Ninth State*, a reference to Great Britain); most were republished. The two important new novels of 1954–64 were *I Wish He Would Not Die* and its sequel *The Last Exile*.

*I Wish He Would Not Die* was received by a Soviet journal in manuscript form, which probably means that it was commissioned; it was published in 1957.[225] Set in wartime Egypt, it contrasted odious British colonialists with noble Egyptian fighters for independence; one of them, a particularly attractive young officer, bore the name Gamal. Guessing the real-life model of Gamal was not overly strenuous. As indicated by an epigraph, the novel's title was borrowed from a book by Gamal Abdel Nasser, then Egypt's dictator and a friend of the USSR. After its appearance in a journal, *I Wish He Would Not Die*, a work of fiction glorifying a living head of a friendly foreign state, was issued in book form in a Russian printing of half a million copies. A sequel, *The Last Exile*, appeared a few years later in a large edition (exact figures were not available). *The Last Exile* was an admiring account of Nasser's Egypt and an indictment of the 1956 attack on Egypt by Britain, France, and Israel in the wake of the nationalization of the Suez Canal. Finally, there was a rare item, a short story by a *British* émigré *in* the USSR. William Campbell, a Scot, came to the USSR in 1933 and became a musician in a band and an actor in Soviet films. Currently, Campbell is the *Daily Worker*'s Soviet correspondent and senior announcer for Moscow Radio. Campbell's tale, "A Canary's Happiness," was a labored satire of British bureaucracy, with a nasty

222. *Istorija zarubežnoj literatury XX veka*, 1963, pp. 524–29 and 530–39, respectively.
223. James Aldridge is listed in the 1971–72 edition of the *International Who's Who*.
224. KL, Vol. V (1968), pp. 416–17.
225. *Inostrannaja literatura*, No. 11, 1957.

dig at the United States thrown in for good measure.[226]

Two Canadian Communists were published. An intriguing entry for Joe Wallace is found in the *Literary Encyclopedia:* "In 1941–43 [Wallace] was in prison and in a concentration camp for being a Communist. Since that time Canadian publishers have been boycotting Wallace and his name is not mentioned in studies of Canadian literature."[227] To compensate for this disgraceful treatment of Wallace by a conspiracy of Canada's capitalist publishers and biased or intimidated scholars, Wallace's "civic lyrics" about "workers and fighters for justice" were issued in a volume of Russian translations and in 10,000 copies in the original English (for export to Canada?). Translations were also printed in *Junost'* (No. 8, 1962), a literary monthly for younger readers, which at the time had a circulation of over half a million. No claims of persecution were made for the other Canadian, Dyson Carter. *Fatherless Sons,* which is set in a nickel smelting mill ("the collective becomes the novel's hero") was published in Russian (press run unknown), Ukrainian (14,000), as well as in two English printings, one of which was 10,000 copies. Carter's other novel, *Tomorrow Is With Us,* has a model plot: "His [Carter's] hero Byrd, an engineer, is a victim of a Fascist provocation. Under the guidance of Kirbie, a Communist and the novel's other hero, Byrd's political consciousness is forged at a time when he is trying to demonstrate the truth [i.e., his innocence—MF]."[228]

A major concern of this study has been the ways and means whereby Soviet critics and publishing authorities regulate the availability of Western writing in the USSR with a view to maximizing its "positive" impact on Soviet readers. The term "positive" is used here in a very broad sense. It includes not only reinforcement of the teachings of Soviet schools and the mass media—that is, illustrations confirming the justice and wisdom both of basic Soviet values and of changing propaganda campaigns, but also such considerations as providing the public with books of unquestionable cultural value or, at least, with reading matter that is wholesome entertainment. As suggested in the Introduction and elsewhere, in the case of books by *deceased* writers, the author's personal politics are treated as a matter of secondary importance, as evidenced by the publication, after their deaths, even of intransigently anti-Soviet émigrés and Nazi collaborators, to say nothing of ordinary "reactionaries." It is only their books that live, and these books are judged largely on their own merits; thus no *author* can be described as entirely incapable of eventual reclamation. Camus has been published and so has Kafka, and it is not inconceivable that one day Soviet

226. *Moskva,* No. 10, 1963.
227. KL, Vol. VII (1972), p. 816.
228. KL, Vol. III (1966), p. 424. An Estonian translation was issued in 8,000 copies.

readers may find in their bookstores a careful selection of the writings of Céline and Koestler, Nabokov and Isaac Bashevis Singer.[229]

Things are different with books by living authors. No book of prose, poetry, or drama, however instrinsically progressive, is likely to be translated in the USSR if its author is a consistent and vocal opponent of Soviet policies. In this chapter we have been considering, by and large, "good" books by ideologically congenial authors, and also quite a few politically indifferent books (and even several questionable ones) written by authors whose continued goodwill was in the interests of the Soviet Union. There were even the two novels by James Aldridge that were unabashed flattery of a foreign head of state, Gamal Abdel Nasser.

Examples of Soviet gestures of appreciation and goodwill can be multiplied. Foreign public figures honored in recent years by Soviet editors and publishers included a philosopher, a doctor, and—strange as it may seem in a Communist country—an absolute monarch. "Satan in the Suburbs," a short story by Bertrand Russell, was printed in a Soviet journal clearly as a token of esteem for Russell's numerous activities on behalf of Soviet-sponsored "peace" efforts in postwar years.[230] In announcing the publication of Dr. Benjamin Spock's famous book on baby care, V. J. Maevskij, director of the Medical Publishing House, emphasized that the book was written by an outstanding pediatrician who is also a "progressive American political figure," an allusion to Dr. Spock's strenuous efforts on behalf of antiwar causes culminating in candidacy for the presidency of the United States.[231] And the pseudonymous author of a translated love poem, M. B. B. Shah, was identified by the editors of a Soviet monthly as His Royal Majesty Mahendra Bir Bikram Shah, then King of Nepal.[232] In 1949, it may be recalled, the USSR had blocked that country's entry to the United Nations. By the mid-sixties, however, Nepal's strategic location between India and China (then already the Soviet Union's rival rather than its ally) brought Nepal some Soviet economic assistance—and also Soviet recognition of the literary gifts of its crowned head.

The commitment of modern Western literature to a critical scrutiny of social ills makes its exploitation in the USSR attractive and, superficially at least, relatively easy—provided, of course, that the injustices do not have overly close parallels within Soviet society. Many, indeed, do not. There are no moneyed *classes* in the USSR, even though there is both privilege and deprivation. There is no unemployment, although completely free choice of work does not exist, either (in 1976, forty-odd million Soviet peasants still

229. See chapter 8.
230. *Zvezda,* No. 10, 1963.
231. *Literaturnaja gazeta,* April 24, 1968.
232. *Inostrannaja literatura,* No. 8, 1966.

did not have internal passports, which are indispensable if one wishes to change one's place of residence). Overt racial discrimination is unknown— but covert practices, for instance against the Jews, are a matter of public knowledge. Thus, on the surface it is possible to blame a host of social injustices in a variety of Western societies on their common denominator —their "capitalist" system of government. Even anger and cynicism with regard to official pieties are designated as by-products of a non-Soviet way of life. Hence the official Soviet stance: indictments of social ills in Western societies are to be viewed as an indictment of the "bourgeois system" that begot them.

Only a fraction, though by no means an insignificant one, of Western writers subscribe to this view. Many, however, are impressed with the fact that whereas in their own countries theirs are truly the voices in the wilderness—formally free, perhaps, but all too often ignored—their art and thought are taken seriously in the USSR. Furthermore, with *all* of the Soviet Union's publishing houses, theaters, and literary journals under state control, this interest can be and is expressed in tangible ways. Earlier in this chapter reference was made to Heinrich Mann's observation that in the USSR he is widely read, able to earn a livelihood, and thus, most importantly, influential both as an artist and as a social critic. That Heinrich Mann's observation retains much validity to this day (and also serves to explain much of the attraction the USSR holds for many authors abroad) is illustrated by a brief introduction by an Argentine writer to a selection of his country's short stories appearing in a Soviet journal. Aristobulo Echegería noted with sadness that not a single author in his homeland can support himself entirely with his writing and contrasted this with "the wonderful privileges enjoyed by poets and prose writers of the socialist camp," expressing the hope that one day, perhaps, such privileges might also be enjoyed by his countrymen.[233]

233. *Zvezda,* No. 3, 1959, p. 140. The four Argentine authors represented were Humberto Constantini, whose tale "Say Something, Doctor" described life among the poor; Alvaro Yunque, in whose story "Bulbul Finds a Protector" the boy's protector is a Communist; Gerardo Pisarello and Gregorio Tavoznansky. Curiously, two years later a Soviet journal published a dissenting view by a Swedish writer: "In my conversations with Soviet authors and readers it seemed to me that they do not always clearly understand the situation of writers in other countries. . . . It is true that our economic conditions are often difficult. It is also true that forces hostile to culture are very influential in our countries. It is true that at meetings of our writers' organizations we talk mostly about contracts, advances, and royalties for translations, and little about literature, culture, and humanism. But this is only one side of the coin. On the marketplace where they deal in thoughts, dreams, and ideas, we sell words. But selling words does not imply that we are selling ourselves. . . . We are proud to earn our livelihoods by our literary labors, we are fighting for it, and our pride is similar to that of a farmer or a metal worker who earns his livelihood with his manual labor, and our struggle is similar to his struggle for that right." *Inostrannaja literatura,* No. 7, 1961, p. 250. The writer, Jan Myrdal, believes that "to write means to fight war and destruction, poverty and oppression."

# CHAPTER

# 8

# *Traitors, Kafka,*
# *and Other Undesirables*

The preceding chapter dealt with authors and works whose personae and subject matter make them particularly attractive to Soviet editors, publishers, and critics. The chapter that follows considers, as it were, the opposite end of the spectrum, writers and books that are viewed as objectionable—politically or otherwise—and are therefore rarely if ever published in the USSR.

The concept of the Orwellian "memory hole," a central feature in the nightmare of the totalitarian state of *1984* is now considered by many in the West crude or outdated—at best, yet another relic of the evil days of the Cold War that had better be forgotten. (And *Animal Farm*, it is claimed, was not so much a parody of the Soviet state, as of Britain ruled by a ruthless government of the Labor Party.) That such political-literary revisionism is at best premature and grounded more in wishful thinking than in hard facts is illustrated by the entry for George Orwell in the *Literary Encyclopedia*. The *existence* of the entry, to be sure, demonstrates a degree of progress; in Stalinist days any factual mention of Orwell would have been unthinkable in a Soviet reference work. Yet the contents of the article, and above all the rigid ban on George Orwell's writings suggest that the literary politics of the Cold War, though less strictly enforced, are still very much alive in the USSR:

In the 1930s Orwell demonstratively [!] recognized socialist and anti-Fascist thought and took part in the national-revolutionary war of the Spanish people on the Republican side. In 1937 he published *The Road to Wigan Pier* (an excerpt was translated into Russian in 1937 [in the USSR—MF]), which realistically described living and working conditions of miners in the Lancashire mining town of Wigan. After 1937, however, Orwell broke with the democratic movement and acquired renown as the author of the anti-utopias *Animal Farm* (1945) and *Nineteen-Eighty-Four* (1949) in which he portrays in a grotesque manner life *in a totalitarian state, which he identifies with Socialism.* Bourgeois criticism sees Orwell's merit in the anti-Communist and modernist tendency of his work.[1]

Thus, Soviet critics (unlike some Western scholars) do admit that Orwell's novels are aimed at *their* social system, rather than Great Britain's; presumably, they are in a better position to judge. The somewhat puzzling reference to Orwell's alleged "modernism" was probably inserted to reinforce the impression that stylistic modernism is synonymous with anti-Communism.

The present status of George Orwell is typical of the semi-Orwellian situation that currently prevails in the USSR with reference to political "renegades" among foreign authors. Their names may be mentioned, though only if accompanied by some unflattering observations. There is no serious discussion of their works, and the works themselves are not obtainable in the libraries and are not, of course, published. We shall consider here a number of such authors, once treated as comrades or at least kindred spirits, who have since betrayed the cause. We shall not, however, include other writers who were never known as close friends of the USSR and were never printed there, or whose current bad fortunes in the USSR are not directly related to their lapsed politics.

The change of status from "friend" to "enemy" of the USSR may be sudden, and the retribution swift. An illuminating account of procedures followed in 1957, i.e., at the height of the post-Stalin "liberal" period, was given by the American novelist Howard Fast:

> An airmail letter to the United States from the Soviet Union takes between two and three days to arrive. The interview in which I publicly announced my separation from the Communist Party appeared on the morning of February 1, 1957. On February 4, 1957, I received my last mail from the Soviet Union ... The Soviet post office had quietly and efficiently halted and seized every piece of mail addressed to me; for no one apart from the Party bureaucracy knew that anything was different about Howard Fast ... On February 1, I simply ceased to exist on one-sixth of the earth's surface.[2]

According to Deming Brown, "No American writer has ever enjoyed more Soviet adulation in his own lifetime than Howard Fast," prior to his fall from grace. "From 1948 to 1957 over 2,500,000 copies of his works were

1. KL, Vol. V (1968), p. 467. Italics added.
2. Howard Fast, *The Naked God: The Writer and the Communist Party* (New York: Frederick A. Praeger, 1957), pp. 31–32.

printed, in twelve languages of the USSR. . . . His was clearly a mass popularity, and for a decade he ranked next to Mark Twain, Dreiser, and London as a favorite."[3] As Howard Fast himself recalls,

> Before that time [the break with the Communist Party in 1957—MF] I had been honored by the Soviet Union as were few living writers, Russian or otherwise. Millions of copies of my books had been printed and sold there. One book alone, *The Passion of Sacco and Vanzetti,* had an initial printing of half a million copies. Two of my own plays had been produced there, two other plays had been dramatized from my books, and another book of mine had become the basis for a Soviet opera. Dozens of critical articles had been written about my work, as well as two book-length critical studies that I know of. The Russian critics and the Russian readers were warm, receptive, over-generous and extravagant in their praise. Both praise and affection went far beyond the reality of my work—which is not to say that I was not pleased by it. I know of no writer so objective that extravagant praise beyond the worth of his work is not greeted with pleasure.[4]

Howard Fast's defection was met at first with silence. Then, on August 24, 1957, an article entitled "Desertion Under Fire" appeared in *Literaturnaja gazeta.* On January 30, 1958, the same newspaper published an article by Nikolaj Gribačëv, a Stalinist writer and critic, in which Fast was called a "sexton of revisionism." Finally, in the February 1958 issue of *Inostrannaja literatura,* Boris Izakov, a journalist, informed his readers that a clue to Fast's treachery might be found in *The Gospel of St. John,* an *unpublished* novel of his, which shows Fast's fascination with the idea of betrayal. This, Izakov concluded, went a long way toward explaining Howard Fast's *The Naked God* where, in addition to other outrages, Fast also had the impudence to accuse the USSR of anti-Semitism.[5]

Actually, the last point of Izakov's article contains a clue to the image of Howard Fast in a Soviet reference work that was to emerge fourteen years later. Some Soviet bibliographies do mention Fast; others, as pointed out, suppress such information altogether.[6] As for the *Literary Encyclopedia,*

3. Deming Brown, *Soviet Attitudes Toward American Writing,* pp. 281–82.
4. Howard Fast, *The Naked God,* pp. 30–31.
5. Boris Izakov, "Dve ispovedi Govarda Fasta," *Inostrannaja literatura,* No. 2, 1958, pp. 214–20.
6. Thus, a bibliography published in 1964 (*Problemy istorii literatury S.Š.A.* [Moscow: Nauka, 1964], pp. 373–475) does list Soviet criticism of Fast. The bibliography was also published in Engish in the United States: *Russian Studies of American Literature: A Bibliography,* compiled by Valentina Libman (Gorky Institute), translated by Robert V. Allen (Library of Congress), edited by Clarence Gohdes (Duke University) (Chapel Hill: University of North Carolina Press, 1969). The original text contains a note: "As is well known, in 1957 H. Fast repudiated his socialist convictions and left the progressive forces of the U.S." (p. 79 of the English version). On the other hand, a Soviet bibliography published six years later under the same auspices, the USSR Academy of Sciences, and, incidentally, compiled by the same bibliographer (*Problemy literatury S.Š.A. XX veka,* [Moscow: Nauka, 1970]), which purports to list *all* Soviet publication of twentieth-century American

it hurls at Fast an accusation that is regularly used by Soviet propaganda as an "answer" to those who criticize the USSR for its mistreatment of Jews. It now turns out that Howard Fast is, and always has been—a Zionist: "In the late 1940s and early 1950s Fast participated in the Peace Movement (*Peekskill, USA,* 1951, Russian translation, 1951), while simultaneously expressing Zionist convictions (*My Glorious Brothers,* a novel from the history of ancient Judea, 1948). After 1956 Fast broke with the progressive movement and published *The Naked God* (1957), an anti-Soviet book."[7]

The fate of Howard Fast is not without precedent. Its general outlines follow quite closely a pattern set two decades earlier by Fast's countryman John Dos Passos. In the 1930s, Dos Passos was not only published very frequently in the USSR; some Soviet critics in fact considered him the most important living foreign writer.[8] Unlike Howard Fast's, Dos Passos's political allegiances underwent a gradual change. Yet there was no corresponding slow cooling of Soviet admiration for the American novelist, which would have been an understandable reaction. As in the case of Howard Fast, the change in Soviet attitudes bore every sign of a sudden administrative decision that was to be strictly enforced:

> Then, at the end of 1936, publication of Dos Passos abruptly ceased. Likewise, he nearly vanished from the pages of Soviet criticism. . . . His opinions had ceased to suit the Communist Party, and so the publication of his works, and critical consideration of them as well, were officially terminated. . . . The repudiation of Dos Passos that took place in 1936 has remained in effect to the present.[9]

As in the case of Orwell and Fast, the *Literary Encyclopedia* acknowledges that some of Dos Passos's early works were of a "progressive" character and had been published in the USSR, while simultaneously minimizing the sincerity of his early political ties. Dos Passos, it turns out, was a mere "fellow traveler [*poputčik*] of the progressive movement" who "broke abruptly with leftist circles after the Spanish Civil War." His later novels, such as the trilogy *District of Columbia,* are called "conservative," while

---

literature, suppresses all mention of Fast.

7. KL, Vol. VII (1972), p. 903. At that time, in fact, Fast's *My Glorious Brothers* was popular in the USSR among Zionist Jews; apparently there were several *samizdat* translations of the novel. A Russian translation of the book was published in Israel in 1975: Govard Fast, *Moi proslavlennye brat'ja* (Jerusalem: Biblioteka "Alija," 1975).

8. Deming Brown, *Soviet Attitudes Toward American Writing,* p. 85.

9. Ibid., pp. 105–6. Only two insignificant items seem to have appeared after that date, a four-page article in a 1944 collection entitled *The Americans and the War,* and a single page in a literary journal. *Problemy literatury S.S.A. XX veka,* p. 431.

*Midcentury* is described as "antidemocratic."[10] A newspaper article printed the same year was much more bellicose in tone. It called Dos Passos a "renegade from the progressive literature of the 1920s and 1930s" infamous for his "fanatical appeals for a struggle against Communism and against Soviet culture."[11]

Of four major European novelists who broke with pro-Soviet causes prior to World War II, one, Arthur Koestler, was simply consigned to oblivion. Unmentioned in the *Literary Encyclopedia,* Koestler, famous as the author of such anti-Stalinist classics as *Darkness at Noon* and *The Yogi and the Commissar,* was a member of the Communist Party from 1931 to 1938, had visited the USSR, and was published there.[12] Ignazio Silone was a founder of the Italian Communist Party; this was duly noted by the *Literary Encyclopedia.* His break with the Party, it suggested, was a result of cowardice. Silone was simply afraid of the Fascists: "Subsequently, in the article "Emergency Exit" (*Un' uscita di sicurezza,* 1949) Silone gave a cynical account of how he became a renegade. . . . Silone's political stance remains strongly anti-Communist."[13]

André Gide was never formally a member of the Communist Party; yet, after his disenchantment with the USSR, Gide was probably more maligned by Soviet and Western Communists than any other "renegade." A fervent admirer of the Soviet Union in 1935, Gide had written at the time:

> In the deplorable state of distress of the modern world, the plan of the Soviet Union seems to me to point to salvation. Everything persuades me of this. The wretched arguments of my opponents, far from convincing me, make me indignant. And if my life were necessary to assure the success of the Soviet Union, I would gladly give it immediately. I write this with a cool and calm head, in full sincerity, through great need to leave at least this testimony, in case death should intervene before I have time to express myself better.[14]

The following year Gide visited Russia as a guest of the Union of Soviet Writers. A Christian, rather than a Communist, defender of the downtrodden and the social outcasts, he was appalled by a number of features of

10. KL, Vol. II (1964), p. 755.

11. *Izvestija,* January 4, 1964. Another, though less spectacular case is that of Pearl Buck whose writings were quite frequently published in the 1930s. The encyclopedia entry (KL, Vol. I [1962], p. 410) recognizes that Pearl Buck appealed for Soviet-American friendship and was an opponent of racism, colonialism, and the armaments race; she was, however, accused of strong and vocal anti-Communism. Most likely, the failure to reprint her novels was due to the fact that Soviet publishers preferred at that time not to disseminate novels that contained warmly sympathetic descriptions of China and her people.

12. Koestler's account of his career as a Communist writer and journalist appears in Richard Crossman (ed.), *The God That Failed* (New York: Harper & Brothers, 1949), pp. 15–75.

13. KL, Vol. VI (1971), pp. 823–24. Presumably, reference is to the essay that appears in Richard Crossman, *The God That Failed,* pp. 76–114.

14. Quoted in *The God That Failed,* p. 173. For Gide's brief account of his disillusionment with the Soviet cause, see ibid., pp. 175–95.

Soviet life, not least the intolerance of dissent, and related his experiences in two books, *Retour de l'U.R.S.S.* and *Retouches à mon retour de l'U.R.S.S.*[15] Gide's defection was never forgiven:

> When he was awarded the Nobel Prize in 1947, Jean Kanapa [a French Communist author and editor—MF] declared that Gide had been disgusted by the Bolsheviks because they were not pederasts. Dominique Desanti, one of the most vehement of the female intellectuals in the Party, did even better in 1949 when she described him, at the age of eighty-one, his face already a death-mask, as surrounded by young admirers who derived from his works the same "liberation" they obtained in the Place Pigalle.[16]

André Gide was also regularly excoriated in the USSR. Upon his death, *L'Humanité,* the French Communist daily, commented: "A corpse has died!"[17] The entry in the *Literary Encyclopedia* notes that Gide was briefly sympathetic to the USSR and that his writings were once published there, but emphasizes their narcissism, amoralism, and antirealism (Gide is described as one of the forerunners of the *nouveau roman* of which Soviet critics disapprove). As for the author himself, he is said to have been an indifferent observer of his country's plight during the Nazi occupation.[18]

André Malraux also "left the democratic struggle after the defeat in Spain," partly because of his "Nietzschean pessimism," but was treated with more consideration, perhaps because he was a cabinet minister in Charles de Gaulle's government with which the USSR was then cultivating closer relations. Prewar publication of his books in the Soviet Union was duly recorded.[19] Some of these, such as *Days of Wrath* and *Man's Hope,*

15. Jürgen Rühle, *Literature and Revolution,* pp. 348–49.

16. David Caute, *Communism and the French Intellectuals,* p. 185. Place Pigalle is notorious for brothels that cater to every taste. Dominique Desanti, author of such scurrilous hatchet jobs as *Masques et visages de Tito,* was herself to become disenchanted with the Communist cause a decade later. After Khrushchev's denunciation of Stalin's crimes in 1956, she "lapsed into a silence that foreshadowed total withdrawal." Ibid., p. 229. Her book *Visages de femmes,* which consists of essays on women revolutionaries such as Louise Michel, Rosa Luxemburg, and Lenin's wife Nadežda Krupskaja, and on Ethel Rosenberg, an American executed on charges of spying for the USSR, was favorably reviewed in *Inostrannaja literatura* (No. 5, 1955) but was not, as far as is known, published in the USSR.

17. David Caute, *The Fellow Travellers,* p. 99. The name Gide, as pronounced and written in Russian, is the same as the word "kike" *(žid).* Mixail Romm, the late Soviet cinema director, recalls how good use was made of this coincidence in an anti-Semitic cartoon in *Krokodil,* the Soviet satirical weekly. Romm's essay was translated into English in *Commentary* (January 1965).

18. KL, Vol. II (1964), pp. 935–36.

19. KL, Vol. IV (1967), pp. 553–54. Just a few years earlier, while relations with de Gaulle's government were still cool, Malraux was described in a Soviet college text as an author "currently honored by the bourgeoisie as one of the most authoritative and 'highly qualified' specialists in anti-Communist literature, as a *maître* of present-day modernism." Z. T. Graždanskaja (ed.), *Istorija zarubežnoj literatury XX veka,* 1963, p. 119. For a time André Malraux was considered in the West as "a communistic chronicler of the times rather than as a truly imaginative novelist." Even after World War II Malraux emphasized that "he was opposing the threat of Stalinism to freedom and to culture rather than Communism as a force for social change." *The Penguin Companion,* Vol. II, pp. 502–3.

which portray Nazism and the Spanish Civil War, could easily be republished were it not for their author's persona. Others would not now be
considered timely, such as *The Conquerors* or *Man's Fate,* both dealing with
the civil war in China. It is unlikely that Soviet publishers would wish at
this time to bring out novels portraying the Soviet Union's friendship for
*either* Chiang Kai-shek *or* Mao Tse-tung. No books by Malraux were
actually reprinted in 1954–64, and there were also none by Silone, Gide, and
Koestler.

Occasionally, "renegades" are "rehabilitated," preferably posthumously.
Richard Wright, the black American writer, described his disillusionment
with Communism in the collection of essays *The God That Failed,* along
with Silone, Gide, and Koestler.[20] His subsequent writings, however, were
not those of an anti-Communist crusader. Wright's central concern remained the plight of America's blacks. Within two years of Wright's death
in 1960, a sixty-page volume of his short stories was issued in 150,000 copies,
while *Eight Men* appeared in 17,000 copies in Estonian. The *Literary Encyclopedia* does record that Richard Wright was once a member of the Communist Party.[21] Clifford Odets was briefly a Party member, but toward the
end of his life, according to the *Theatrical Encyclopedia,* became indifferent
to social concerns and turned to ordinary "bourgeois" drama. Yet Odets
was never a turncoat in the real meaning of the term; a volume of his plays
was republished.[22] Another American playwright, Sidney Kingsley, was
called a "renegade" by the *Theatrical Encyclopedia* for having written the
1951 stage version of Arthur Koestler's "malicious anti-Communist novel"
*Darkness at Noon.* Nevertheless, a few years later there was a new edition
of his play *Dead End,* which "exposes the capitalist way of life that corrupts
and ruins thousands of adolescents, the sons and daughters of the poor. The
street cripples them, transforms them into gangsters, prostitutes and murderers."[23] The Italian novelist Carlo Cassola is the author of *Fausto and
Anna* (1952), a massive novel about romantic and political passions, and
*Les Vieux Compagnons,* which describes a group of Communist workers.[24]
Subsequently, Cassola's ideological ardor cooled; he was even to abandon
social themes altogether.[25] In spite of this, a volume of his writings was
brought out (press run unknown).

The examples of Wright, Odets, and Cassola (and a few others men-

20. Richard Crossman, *The God That Failed,* pp. 115–62.
21. KL, Vol. VI (1971), p. 166.
22. *Teatral'naja ènciklopedija,* Vol. IV (1965), pp. 140–41. Press run unknown. A dissenting
view was that of Boris Izakov who singled out Clifford Odets as a renegade and American
police informer. *Literaturnaja gazeta,* January 3, 1957.
23. KL, Vol. III (1964), p. 26. Press run unknown.
24. *Dictionnaire des littératures,* Vol. I, p. 754.
25. KL, Vol. III (1966), p. 430.

tioned elsewhere) illustrate a phenomenon that is relatively new to highly politicized Soviet publishing. Whereas in the past former Communists were almost never forgiven their desertion from the ranks, and their books would not be likely ever again to see the light of day in the USSR, at present there is greater tolerance. Ex-Party members most likely to benefit from this more permissive attitude are those whose eventual break with the Communist movement was a result of a slow drift, those who were lost to the movement through gradual estrangement rather than a stormy divorce, and preferably long ago. (Ideally, of course, the beneficiary of this kind of "rehabilitation" should be deceased.) Curiously, in cases of such "rehabilitations" Soviet publishers and theatrical directors favor the foreign author's *less* explicitly political works—say, simple exposés of capitalist horrors—rather than those in which their Marxist ideology obviously contained seeds of future treason. When reinstated, such authors are thus downgraded to the rank of critics of bourgeois society; they are not allowed to reclaim their earlier status of politically conscious Communist authors. Another taboo that is no longer scrupulously observed affects quasi-political defectors. Thus, reference was made in an earlier chapter to Manfred Gregor's *The Bridge* which was published in a literary journal; Gregor who now lives in West Germany is a defector from East Germany.[26]

Yet even as some Western authors were forgiven their political transgressions and their works were allowed to reappear in print, the population of the literary limbo was replenished by new sinners. Thus, as already mentioned, in the late 1960s, John Steinbeck was excoriated for approving of the American presence in Vietnam.[27] Karlludwig Opitz, a West German author, was held in considerable esteem in the USSR until the mid-1960s. Thus, his antimilitaristic novel *My General* was printed in 150,000 copies and other works were printed in literary journals.[28] But, as pointed out in the *Literary Encyclopedia,* "Subsequently Opitz's views underwent a radi-

26. East German authors who escaped to the West after 1956 and now live and work in West Germany include, besides Manfred Gregor-Dellin, Gerhard Zwerenz, Peter Jokostra, Christa Reinig, Heinar Kipphardt, and Uwe Johnson. See Jürgen Rühle, *Literature and Revolution,* p. 297. Manfred Gregor's *The Bridge* appeared in *Inostrannaja literatura,* Nos. 10 and 11, 1960. See chapter 5.

27. An article in *Pravda* of February 5, 1967, pointed out indignantly that John Steinbeck "approves without any reservations of the actions of the American butchers [in Vietnam] and heaps insults at those who protest this dirty war."

28. *People, Be on Your Guard,* a strongly political play (originally published in *Geist und Zeit,* No. 3, 1958) was translated in *Inostrannaja literatura* (No. 4, 1959). The play satirizes Western militarists who dream of unleashing a nuclear war; among its villains are European capitalists and American generals. Another attack on militarism, "O du mein Deutschland," appeared in *Znamja,* No. 2, 1961. Later that year Opitz complained to Soviet readers about such unseemly features of life in West Germany as anti-Communist hysteria, tolerance of Nazism, and destitution of writers: "How can one describe all this clericalism, the chauvinists, the American soldiers and the unrepentant Nazis?" *Inostrannaja literatura,* No. 7, 1961, pp. 246–47.

cal change. His later works contain slander of the German Democratic Republic and of Communist ideas."[29] Another recent case is Pierre Daix, a Resistance fighter, former inmate of Nazi camps, and for many years editor of the Communist Party's literary journal *Les Lettres françaises*. His works published in the USSR include *Deep River* (*La Rivière profonde*, 1959, Russian translation, 1961) and *The Murderer* (*Un Tueur*, 1954, Russian translation, 1959), both quite orthodox novels. Yet in 1973 Pierre Daix published *Ce que je sais de Soljénitsyne* (Paris: Seuil, 1973), which not only defended the errant Soviet novelist, then still in the USSR, but also attacked the Soviet Union for its policies of thought control. It is reasonable to assume that Pierre Daix will not be published in the USSR, at least not in the near future.

Still, the overall tendency in Soviet publishing and literary criticism of the post-Stalin period was to broaden rather than to restrict the categories of Western authors considered acceptable, and the literary amnesties were far more numerous than the newly-imposed bans. The republication of Paul Bourget's novel *The Disciple* in 75,000 copies is a case in point. Bourget's French novel, first published in Russia in 1889—the year it appeared in France—can hardly be called "progressive." The *Literary Encyclopedia* notes, "[It] appeared at a time when, after the fall of the Paris Commune of 1871, the French bourgeoisie, seized with fright, attempted to downgrade the status of scientific evidence. Bourget depicts a protagonist whose experiments with the 'mechanism of passions' led him to seduce and ruin a young girl. The novel's message may be reduced to the proposition that scientific thought, which is allegedly inseparable from heartlessness and cynicism, is the opposite of morality and piety." A number of respected literary figures, including Chekhov and Anatole France, did not like the novel. Lenin, however, found it "reactionary, but interesting."[30] Apparently, Lenin's opinion prevailed.

The plays of Heinrich von Kleist, a Romantic and a German nationalist, were long unwelcome in the USSR for much the same reasons as Richard Wagner's operas; the fact that Kleist was held in high esteem in Nazi Germany (as was Wagner) did not help matters. More recently, the *Literary Encyclopedia* observed: "The legacy of Kleist has become the object of an intense ideological struggle. Reactionary bourgeois scholars glorify Kleist as a nationalist or else emphasize the pathological features of his work, viewing him as a forerunner of contemporary modernist drama. . . . Marxist literary scholarship aims at demonstrating the realistic tendencies and humanistic protest against 'German poverty' that is characteristic of Kleist's

29. KL, Vol. V (1968), p. 447.
30. KL, Vol. I (1962), p. 777.

best works."[31] A 10,000-copy edition of Kleist's plays was published in Russian, which partly clears the way to their introduction into the repertory of Soviet theaters. Finally, the relatively restrained, and sometimes even positive, appraisals of the works of Knut Hamsun in Soviet sources in the 1960s suggested that he, too, might ultimately be reinstated among published foreign authors, his collaboration with the Nazis during the occupation of Norway notwithstanding.[32] Indeed, a multivolume set of Hamsun's works appeared in 1970.

An attempt was made in preceding chapters to demonstrate that the reasons for the publication of various Western authors and types of books are often complex and that politics as such is merely one consideration, albeit the most important. We have seen that other factors, ranging from willingness partially to satisfy the public's demand for certain types of reading matter to a desire to provide access to literary masterpieces must be weighed as well. Similarly, the reasons that other books are published not at all, or only very rarely, are sometimes obvious, as in the cases of works by political "renegades" and books whose contents are politically objectionable; in other instances, the considerations are much less clear. In the latter category fall works written in an artistic style that is considered inimical to Socialist Realism—not merely "inferior," but actually menacing—and books conveying a view of reality that is inherently subversive of Socialist Realist canons. We should recall that of the three basic tenets of Socialist Realism, only two—the strong ideological orientation *(idejnost')* and the hortative Communist partisanship *(partijnost')*—are overtly political. The third, *narodnost',* usually interpreted as stylistic accessibility, is not. Yet the third principle of Socialist Realism is enforced just as strictly as the other two, and charges of "formalism"—a common Soviet synonym for artistic complexity and experimentation—are not treated lightly. Literary form is believed to be generally inseparable from the ideological dimension of literature's contents. In Soviet criticism a truly realistic writer is worthy of this honorific only if his works are also ideologically acceptable, or at the very least unobjectionable; conversely, a work that is found ideologically wanting is also unavoidably branded as aesthetically defective. This doctrine explains the formula of "political and artistic decline," of which several instances have been cited earlier, and also the attempts to pin the label of "modernism" on stylistically conventional authors whose poli-

31. KL, Vol. III (1966), p. 597. The "re-evaluation" of Kleist's "controversial works" started in East Germany. *Teatral'naja ènciklopedija,* Vol. III (1964), p. 70. Note the linking of "modernism" with political reaction.

32. KL, Vol. II (1964), pp. 57–58 points with approval to efforts of foreign scholars to salvage the good part of Knut Hamsun's work. Hamsun died in 1952. He was published in the USSR before the war and was well known in prerevolutionary Russia. A twelve-volume set of Hamsun's writings was issued in 1909–10.

tics preclude their publication in the USSR; it also accounts for the reluctance to bring out in the USSR Western writing that is ideologically sound enough, but artistically alien. The latter situation has been, since Stalin's death, a subject of frequent polemics between Western authors, many of them politically leftist but also partial to what they view as revolutionary approaches to art, and the Soviet cultural establishment, which in artistic matters favors old-fashioned bourgeois tastes. (Indeed, Communist politics aside, in painting and in architecture, in drama and in literature, the USSR is probably the most conservative and bourgeois of all Western countries.) At the same time, the Communist and left-wing credentials of some of the foremost representatives of modernist trends in Western literature and the arts make it possible for some Soviet artists and writers to defend, however timidly, the thesis that artistic complexity and experimentation are compatible with Communist orthodoxy in politics.

Why are Soviet authorities so adamantly opposed to formal "difficulty" and experimentation in literature and the arts, to the point of allowing little Western avant-garde writing, theater, painting, and sculpture into the country—to say nothing of not tolerating them in the work of Soviet writers and artists? Perhaps some hint may be found in the following observation by an émigré Soviet musicologist with reference to works by living composers:

> The Party recognizes only two types of music—the "relevant" *(aktualny)* and the "irrelevant" *(neaktualny)*. Irrelevant, or nontopical, music includes music without any accompanying text. Nobody bans it outright, but nobody promotes it either, and it is difficult to have it performed. On the other hand, music accompanied by a text explaining what it is trying to express is considered by the Party to be relevant, topical and important.[33]

Because it destroys artistic devices to which readers and spectators have grown accustomed, formal experimentation in literature, stagecraft, and the representational arts invariably detracts from the clarity of their "message." Traditional modes of expression make for "relevant" *(aktual'noe)* art, while innovation promotes "irrelevance" *(neaktual'nost')*. Thus, traditional realistic writing may be likened to an opera, where the impact of music is complemented by a libretto, costumes, and activity on the stage—all of which may serve as effective vehicles for a "message"—while experimental prose, drama, and verse are closer to recent chamber music, which does not lend itself readily to the task. Experimentation in literature and the representational arts thus impairs their potential as carriers of ideas and reduces their usefulness as educational tools. This consideration is very likely one

33. Michael Goldstein in *The Soviet Censorship*, Martin Dewhirst and Robert Farrell (eds.) (Metuchen, N. J.: The Scarecrow Press, 1973), p. 96.

major reason for the unfriendly attitude of the Soviet authorities (not just "academic" critics, but high government and Party leaders, including, in the period under review, Khrushchev himself) toward "formalism" in literature and the arts; they may view it as an attempt at their depoliticization. That this removal of literature and the arts from effective service as an educational tool would be accomplished not through the traditional open demands for autonomy of the writer and the artist, but rather through an evolution of the *nature* of writing and art, may have provoked the Soviet authorities to view modernist aesthetics as a particularly insidious conspiracy to *steal* literature and the arts from the Soviet cause.

Reference was made in an earlier chapter to the fact that the publication in the USSR of traditional nineteenth-century social realists is enhanced by the Soviet claim that their writings are, in a sense, the foundation for later Socialist Realism.[34] A similar line of reasoning may have argued against the publication of Western authors whose writings can be construed as containing the seeds of future modernism. Henry James is a case in point. He was known in prerevolutionary Russia and was a friend of Turgenev; a translation of *The American* appeared in 1880, and *Washington Square* was published the following year. The evaluation of the American novelist's writings in the *Literary Encyclopedia* is equivocal. On the one hand, *Roderick Hudson, Washington Square,* and *Daisy Miller* are praised for their portrayal of ruthless business sharks and the corrupting power of money. On the other hand, *The American* is said to idealize a millionaire portrayed as an innocent victim of French aristocrats; *Bostonians* "mocks the democratic traditions of American reformers and utopians"; and *Princess Casamassima* contains a "caricature of the revolutionary movement in Europe." Normally, a "mixed" review of this type suggests a selective publication of a foreign novelist's more acceptable works. Not so with Henry James. He was not published in the USSR until 1973.[35] Apparently the reason for this long ostracism is to be sought in the fact that Henry James, a writer "partial to extreme psychologism," was considered a forerunner of "modernism" in general, and in particular of James Joyce and Marcel Proust, who in Soviet criticism form (together with Franz Kafka) the unholy trinity of literary "modernism."[36]

The case of Henry James, which was typical of the Soviet treatment of progenitors of "modernism" during the Stalin era, must be viewed as an extreme exception in more recent times. Since 1960 there has been a significant erosion of the principle of non-publication of "modernist" literature.

34. See chapter 7.
35. *The Aspern Papers* appeared in *Inostrannaja literatura,* No. 7, 1973. An anthology of Henry James was published the following year in 100,000 copies.
36. KL, Vol. II (1964), pp. 646–47.

As is usual in such cases, the first beneficiaries of the more permissive attitude were authors long deceased, and then only those whose amnesty could be justified by references to their other positive qualities, such as "progressive" political views.

A slim, 93-page volume of Arthur Rimbaud's verse appeared in 1960 in 25,000 copies; the translation from the French was by the well-known Soviet poet Pavel Antokol'skij. Like Henry James, Rimbaud bears heavy responsibility for the advent of literary "modernism": "Rimbaud's thesis that formlessness may be conveyed by the formless (which implies acceptance of the possibility of actual disappearance of the artistic image proper) was decisive in the formation of modernist aesthetics."[37] To compensate, much emphasis was given to Rimbaud's hatred of the bourgeoisie, sympathy for the Paris Commune, and particularly to his extreme anticlericalism.[38] A similar pattern is discernible in the reclamation of another French poet, Guillaume Apollinaire: "An anarchistic non-acceptance of the bourgeois world often pushed Apollinaire toward formalist experimentation. . . . Apollinaire's sterile formalist experiments were eagerly continued by the adherents of Dada and Surrealism, but his satirical indictment of the world of capitalism, and the poet's faith in the triumph of 'the dawn over darkness' exerted significant influence on democratic French literature (P. Éluard, L. Aragon)."[39] Linking Apollinaire's name with those of two eminent French Communist authors facilitated his "rehabilitation." An elegant, illustrated 335-page anthology of Apollinaire's verse appeared in 1967 in a large edition of 115,000 copies, under the imprint of the USSR Academy of Science; half the volume consisted of an introduction and annotations.[40]

An early attempt at restoring Charles Baudelaire to the pantheon of publishable writers was made in 1957, at the zenith of the post-Stalin "thaw," by the translator Vil'gel'm Levik. In an introduction to ten pages of new translations of excerpts from Les Fleurs du mal, Levik argued, "He [Baudelaire] was willing to accept even the immoral, provided it was free of the stench of bourgeois philistinism"; Levik supported his statement with a quotation from Maxim Gorky who said of the French poet, "He lived in evil, while loving the good." Levik went so far as to maintain that Baudelaire's so-called decadence was merely highly esoteric, refined, sophisticated poetry.[41] Five years later the Literary Encyclopedia noted that Baudelaire,

37. KL, Vol. VI (1971), p. 251.
38. For a review of the volume see Inostrannaja literatura, No. 2, 1962, pp. 251–53. See also chapter 5.
39. KL, Vol. I (1962), pp. 253–54. Identifying Éluard and Aragon as "democrats" is a genteel political understatement, somewhat like calling a bishop a religious believer. Éluard was and Aragon still is a very prominent French Communist.
40. Gijom Appolliner, Stixi. Perevod M. P. Kudinova, stat'ja i primečanija N. I. Balašova (Moscow: Nauka, 1967).
41. Inostrannaja literatura, No. 3, 1957, pp. 178–81.

who was frequently translated in prerevolutionary Russia, was a poet of many contradictions. While his loss of faith in the possibility of social progress—a result of the fiasco of the Revolution of 1848, in which the poet took an active part—made him "a troubadour of decadence, with its characteristic moral indifference," one must not, the encyclopedia emphasized, lose sight of Baudelaire's sympathy for ordinary people and his hatred of the bourgeoisie. Also, while admitting that Baudelaire's aesthetics were opposed to those of realism, it informed readers that the poet is highly regarded by the French Communists, who in 1946 succeeded in retroactively voiding a French judicial decree that had once declared a collection of Baudelaire's work a menace to public morals.[42] A volume of Baudelaire's verse was published in 1965 in 50,000 copies.[43]

Addressing a conference of Soviet writers in 1950, the eminent novelist and then head of the Writers' Union, Aleksandr Fadeev, complained about the unsatisfactory state of Soviet literary scholarship. As an example, Fadeev singled out a dissertation on Rainer Maria Rilke and Russian literature: "And who is Rilke? An extreme mystic and reactionary in poetry."[44] Fifteen years later a volume of Rilke's verse was brought out in 35,000 copies. While no claims could easily be made for Rilke's advanced political views (he did not even "understand"—a euphemism for "welcome"—the shortlived German Communist revolution of 1918) and there was some truth in Fadeev's claim about Rilke's mysticism, it was presumably the Austrian poet's ties to Russia and Russian literature that influenced the decision of Soviet publishers. Rilke knew some Russian, translated Russian poetry, and corresponded with Boris Pasternak, whose work he influenced.[45]

During his lifetime Albert Camus was *persona non grata* in the USSR for both ideological and artistic reasons. Politically, the problem was clearcut: Camus was no friend of Communism and made no secret of the fact.[46] Nor was Camus much more attractive as a thinker. *The Plague,* to be sure, indicts bourgeois society, but does so "in a decadent hyperbole which transforms it [the indictment] into a repugnance of life itself." In *Exile and the Kingdom* "the problem of man's calling is posed in an overly abstract manner, which hardly conceals the author's political conservatism and

42. KL, Vol. I (1962), pp. 662–63. Much the same views were expressed in *Osnovnye proizvedenija,* 1965, pp. 466–67.
43. Subsequently Baudelaire's poetry began to appear frequently in Soviet journals, in Russian and also in other languages. Thus, a few poems were printed in Ukrainian in *Dnipro,* No. 10, 1967.
44. Cited in Gleb Struve, *Russian Literature Under Lenin and Stalin 1917–1953,* p. 374.
45. KL, Vol. VI (1971), pp. 287–88.
46. A Soviet critic notes: "On the occasion of his acceptance of the Nobel Prize in December 1957, Camus delivered a lecture in Stockholm in which he found it appropriate to heap abuse on Socialist Realism." Z. T. Graždanskaja (ed.), *Istorija zarubežnoj literatury XX veka,* 1963, p. 135.

decadent pessimism."[47] *The Rebel* was said to deny reason as such and was therefore judged to be "polemically directed against Marxism and against the idea of a people's revolution." Taken as a whole, "Camus's writings and philosophy are an inconsistent alloy of humanist and individualistic tendencies which point to the fact that in the age of the people's struggle for Socialism one cannot affirm humanist ideas while at the same time rejecting this struggle."[48] Still, all these serious misgivings notwithstanding, eight years after Camus's death *The Outsider* was printed in a Soviet journal.[49] The choice of the novel may have been influenced by the fact that its portrayal of an indifferent and openly amoral hero is "counterbalanced by the hypocrisy of the church and of the bourgeois court."[50]

Reference was made to the possibility that consistent Soviet disapproval of undue complexity and experimentation in the arts may be linked to the belief that departure from artistic convention inevitably reduces an artistic work's accessibility, and hence also its usefulness as a carrier of ideas. Such an impression is often created by Soviet pronouncements on abstract painting and sculpture or dodecaphonic music. The tone of objections to unconventional modern writing, ranging from *le nouveau roman* to authors in the "theater of the absurd," betrays much stronger apprehensions. Such literature, it is feared, may not only represent wasted opportunity to propagate useful ideas, but, indeed, serve as a carrier for alien and hostile ideas which may slip by undetected masked by the chaos of an unfamiliar stylistic fabric.

A Soviet scholar reports that "many" of Friedrich Dürrenmatt's grotesque tragi-comedies are performed in the USSR.[51] Dürrenmatt's works have also been published in journals and in book form.[52] According to the *Theatrical Encyclopedia*, *The Visit* "satirizes bourgeois mores" (which, in fact, it does), and the Swiss playwright is said to have been hounded by his country's reactionary press for his sympathies for Algeria's Arab insurgents.[53] Yet, throughout the 74-page Soviet monograph devoted to Dürrenmatt's work one senses a feeling of uneasiness and a curious reluctance to endorse wholeheartedly the contents of any of his works: what if their

47. Ibid., pp. 134–35.

48. KL, Vol. III (1966), pp. 351–52. Curiously, the author of this orthodox Soviet article, O. I. Il'inskaja, an intimate of Boris Pasternak, had only recently been released from a Soviet prison.

49. *Inostrannaja literatura*, No. 9, 1968.

50. KL, Vol. III (1966), p. 352.

51. N. S. Pavlova, *Fridrix Djurrenmatt* (Moscow: Vysšaja škola, 1967), p. 3.

52. *The Judge and His Hangman*, a rather contrived detective novel, was printed in *Vokrug sveta*, Nos. 5, 6, and 7, 1966; another, *The Pledge*, appeared in *Inostrannaja literatura*, No. 5, 1966; *A Greek Gentleman Seeks a Greek Lady* was translated in *Novyj mir*, No. 9, 1966; *The Visit* was printed in *Inostrannaja literatura*, No. 3, 1958, and was also published in book form the following year. Pavlova, *Fridrix Djurrenmatt*, p. 18. *The Trap*, a novella, was printed in 1961.

53. *Teatral'naja ènciklopedija*, Vol. II (1963), p. 611.

grotesque form cunningly conceals some harmful ideas? The fact that Dürrenmatt was still alive suggested to the Soviet scholar an even greater degree of caution.[54]

Soviet critics are not overly fond of Eugene Ionesco. They disapprove of his politics, dislike his theoretical pronouncements, and distrust the "message" of even those of his plays that strike a politically "positive" note. Thus, the author of a Soviet textbook was unconvinced by the appearance of a swastika before the final curtain of *The Lesson,* which *could* be interpreted as an attempt to impart a political coloring to the play's long series of senseless murders. The textbook's verdict was merciless: "Ionesco's 'anti-theater' represents an aesthetic embodiment of his conservative convictions. He maintains, for example, that no class struggle is waged in society, that revolution and reaction are the same thing, that everything good and humane lies outside of 'systems' and 'ideologies'."[55] The *Literary Encyclopedia* comments were generally unfavorable but an exception was made for one play: "Ionesco employs the conventions of the grotesque in order to create an impression of an absurdly ridiculous or nightmarish illogism, of the absurdity of human existence. . . . In *Rhinoceros* the dullness of life in a provincial town, which borders on the absurd, becomes objectively a satire on all of contemporary bourgeois society, [a society] in which the bestialization of man is commonplace."[56] The equivocal adverb "objectively" is the standard term in Communist usage denoting an effect not foreseen or desired; thus, there was no intention to present Ionesco as a "progressive" critic of the bourgeois world. A similar reserve was sustained in the *Theatrical Encyclopedia:* strong disapproval of the general premises of the theater of the absurd, and faint praise for *Rhinoceros,* a play in which, it was alleged, a "little man," originally passive, "arrives at an ethical non-acceptance of the deadly rule of Fascist-like monsters."[57] Again, the modifiers ("ethical," "Fascist-*like*") served to restrain the level of approval. Still, the two articles presaged that when a play by Ionesco was finally published in the USSR, it was *Rhinoceros.*[58]

54. Pavlova, *Fridrix Djurrenmatt,* p. 73.
55. Z. T. Graždanskaja (ed.), *Istorija zarubežnoj literatury XX veka,* 1963, p. 136.
56. KL, Vol. III (1966), pp. 159–60.
57. *Teatral'naja ènciklopedija,* Vol. II (1963), pp. 889–90.
58. *Inostrannaja literatura,* No. 9, 1965. The volume of the *Literary Encyclopedia* containing the Ionesco entry, though officially published in 1966, was set in type early in 1965, several months before the appearance of *Rhinoceros.* N. Naumov's postscript to the play interpreted it as an anti-Nazi work: "It is not from hearsay that we know rhinoceroses. Within our memory they stampeded with a victorious roar over the fields of the Ukraine and the vineyards of France, through the streets of Warsaw and Prague." The Soviet critic also discerned a similarity between Ionesco's beasts and the "racists from Alabama." The playwright, Naumov pointed out, agrees that this is *one* valid interpretation of *Rhinoceros.* Ibid., p. 145. Subsequently Ionesco was to disappoint the Soviet Establishment. In 1974 he expressed publicly his support of Israel and, to add insult to injury, joined the editorial board of *Kontinent,* the new literary and political quarterly launched by recent émigrés from the USSR.

272    A DECADE OF EUPHORIA

As pointed out in the Introduction, for all intents and purposes, books read by Soviet citizens are limited to those printed in the USSR; only scholars and specialists have legal access to Western publications. As a result of this situation, Viktor Nekrasov, an eminent Soviet novelist, related that in 1956 he and a few other Soviet writers had to confess to the Italian novelist Alberto Moravia that they had never *heard* of Kafka, much less read his works.[59] At the time of the incident, of course, the writings of Franz Kafka had long since become established classics of world literature. Viktor Nekrasov's story is eloquent proof of the efficacy of the *cordon sanitaire* erected by the Soviet censorship to guard the country's citizenry from the nefarious influences of disapproved works of Western writing.

Not that Kafka, who died in 1924, was equally unknown in all of the countries of the Soviet bloc. Before the war he was read in Eastern Europe both in the German original and in translations, particularly in his native Czechoslovakia. During the Nazi era Kafka's works were proscribed, as were the writings of all Jewish authors. The great postwar revival of interest in Kafka in the West was not reflected in Eastern Europe until 1956 when his works began to be published in Poland at the height of the de-Stalinization of that country's cultural life. Still, for a time, the Soviet Union's cultural authorities remained adamant. In 1959, for example, a Soviet critic reiterated the belief that "in one way or another, Kafka's name is linked to everything that is most reactionary and most hostile to realism in contemporary bourgeois literature," thus simultaneously damning, as customary in Soviet criticism, the writer's art and thought.[60] The pressure to revise Soviet attitudes toward Kafka continued, particularly from Western Communists and friends of the USSR, for whom the Soviet ban on a major Western writer not explicitly anti-Soviet was a great source of embarrassment, supporting anti-Communist claims that rigid censorship continued to exist in Russia even after Stalin's death. In 1962, at the World Peace Congress in Moscow, Jean-Paul Sartre argued that the Soviet bloc's refusal to publish Kafka enabled the West to use Kafka's works as weapons in the Cold War.[61]

Apparently as a result of such pressures from the West and also from the

59. Priscilla Johnson and Leopold Labedz, *Khrushchev and the Arts: The Politics of Soviet Culture 1962–1964*, p. 83. In 1974 Nekrasov, author of the Stalin Prize winning novel *In the Trenches of Stalingrad* and subsequently one of the most active proponents of liberalization, was in effect deported from the USSR. He now lives in Western Europe. Another source claims the incident in question took place in 1958 and identifies Nekrasov's companions as Daniil Granin and the late Vera Panova, both referred to elsewhere in this study. See "The Struggle for Kafka and Joyce: A Conversation between Hans Mayer and François Bondy," *Encounter* (May 1964), p. 83.
60. D. Zatonskij, "Smert' i roždenie Franca Kafki," *Inostrannaja literatura*, No. 2, 1959, p. 212.
61. Priscilla Johnson and Leopold Labedz, *Khrushchev and the Arts*, p. 83. For another version of the incident, see "The Struggle for Kafka and Joyce," *Encounter* (May 1964), p. 83.

Communist intellectuals of Eastern Europe, a conference on Kafka was convened in Czechoslovakia on May 27–28, 1963, largely through the efforts of Professor Eduard Goldstücker of Charles University in Prague. No Soviet delegates were in attendance, but according to a distinguished Polish émigré journalist, it was known that the Soviet cultural administrators favored a partial "rehabilitation" of Kafka on the grounds that his works contained a "premonition of Fascism," a claim that had been advanced earlier to justify a half-hearted "rehabilitation" of Dostoyevsky's *Possessed,* a political novel proscribed during the Stalin era. This stratagem was rejected by the participants of the conference as overly primitive.[62] A number of those present insisted on clearcut answers:

> Ernst Fischer, a Communist writer and critic from Austria, hit home with the question: "Are you going to give Kafka an entry visa?" Fischer and Roger Garaudy, a philosophy professor and leading member of the French Communist Party, helped [?—MF] matters further by attributing the condition of "alienation" which Kafka describes to modern industrial society, rather than to any political system. The Kafka question came up again at the East-West conclave on the novel in July 1963 at Leningrad, where two writers from Czechoslovakia, Jiři Hajek and Ladislav Mnačko, made strikingly effective interventions. Thus, when Kafka was published at last in Moscow, it appeared that Soviet officials had in part been embarrassed into it because *socialist,* and not bourgeois, writers had made an issue of his work.[63]

Actually, Kafka first appeared in the USSR not in Moscow, but in Tallinn. An Estonian translation of one of his more innocuous works, *A Report to the Academy,* was published in 17,000 copies in 1962. Perhaps it was thought that this would cause little harm in Estonia, where Kafka was read before World War II, i.e., prior to the country's annexation by the USSR, and that the language barrier would prevent the book's circulation outside that republic. Two years later Kafka was at long last printed in

62. Gustaw Herling-Grudziński, "Dziennik pisany nocą," *Kultura* (Paris), No. 5/320 (1974), pp. 32–33.

63. Priscilla Johnson and Leopold Labedz, *Khrushchev and the Arts,* pp. 83–84. A brief epilogue is in order on the other *dramatis personae* in the Kafka controversy. The Austrian Communist Fischer and the French Communist Garaudy have both since been denounced as "revisionist" traitors. Goldstücker, prominent in Czechoslovak political life during Dubček's liberal régime, is now an émigré in the West. Mnačko, a non-Jewish Slovak writer, fled the country in 1967 in protest against the régime's anti-Israeli and anti-Semitic policies, and subsequently published an angry novel exposing the evils of Stalinist dictatorship in Eastern Europe. The fate of Jiři Hajek is uncertain. There was, however, the curious and ominous article in *Izvestija,* the Soviet government's newspaper, September 4, 1968, which contained a scurrilous anti-Semitic attack on *another* Jiři Hajek, Dubček's minister of foreign affairs, "exposing" him as a Jewish collaborator with the Nazis whose real, i.e., Jewish, name was Karpeles. Subsequently, *Izvestija* acknowledged its error; the information related had obviously pertained to the writer Jiři Hajek, the defender of Franz Kafka. See my essay "Anti-Semitism as a Policy Tool in the Soviet Bloc," *Soviet Communism and the Socialist Vision,* Julius Jacobson (ed.) (New Brunswick, N. J.: Transaction Books, 1972), pp. 47–48.

Russian, apparently on the assumption that this would put an end to the "unhealthy" interest in his work. The January 1964 issue of *Inostrannaja literatura* published Russian translations of *The Metamorphosis, In the Penal Colony,* and several short tales.[64] Within a year, a volume of Kafka's selected works was brought out by the Progress Publishing House, which specializes in modern foreign books (and books for foreign consumption) rather than fiction written half a century earlier. No information was released on the number of copies printed or on the time required before the volume was issued final clearance in April 1965. The volume's contents were selected by Boris Sučkov, who also wrote the unusually long 60-page introduction.[65] The book included most of the works printed earlier in *Inostrannaja literatura,* such as *The Metamorphosis* and *In the Penal Colony,* a number of novellas and parables, as well as a major novel, *The Trial.* Within a short time the first Russian volume of Kafka was selling on the black market for thirty-five rubles, i.e., over forty dollars at the official exchange rate, which was well above twenty times its official price and more than average weekly Soviet earnings. In a moment of rare candor, this fact was admitted in a Soviet journal.[66]

Sučkov's long introductory essay was a labored attempt to mold Kafka into a standard Soviet image of a not particularly progressive "bourgeois" author whose ideological limitations are occasionally redeemed by truthful portrayals of the seedy and frightening sides of capitalist conditions. Thus, for instance, Kafka's *Amerika* was singled out for some cautious praise because its descriptions of the outer glitter and wealth of the American city were *unconvincing* (although, Sučkov hastened to add, this was merely the result of Kafka's lack of first-hand familiarity with America, rather than of reasoned choice); on the other hand, Kafka's descriptions of child labor in the Hotel Occidental were credited with having "an authentic ring." Even that was accompanied by the disclaimer that "Kafka failed to discern the peculiarities of the newer forms of exploitation and enslavement of man that are characteristic of mature capitalism, with its more elastic and concealed forms of exploitation."[67] Sučkov's treatment of the subject of alienation—

64. Such hopes were, indeed, expressed (as it turned out, prematurely) by a Soviet critic who argued, a few months after the appearance of the "Kafka" issue of the journal, that "a well-grounded and reasoned analysis of the contradictions inherent in Kafka's works, together with the publication of a few of them, have proved much more convincing and effective than the earlier barrage of ringing denunciations." A. Bočarov in *Izvestija,* December 13, 1964.

65. Franc Kafka, *Roman, novelly, pritči.* Perevod s nemeckogo. Sostavitel' i avtor predislovija B. Sučkov (Moscow: Progress, 1965). The late Boris Sučkov was an eminent Soviet specialist in modern Western literature, particularly German.

66. G. Somov, "Princ i niščie," *Molodoj kommunist,* No. 1, 1966, p. 74. The official price of the Kafka volume was one ruble 49 kopeks.

67. Franc Kafka, *Roman, novelly, pritči,* pp. 33–34.

the most vexing problem in the ideological controversy surrounding Kafka
—was impeccably orthodox:

> Alienation is a perfectly real, objective process organically linked to the very
> essence of property-centered capitalist social relations. . . . The process of
> alienation also has clearly spiritual, ideological consequences. It appears
> within consciousness and distorts it, thus placing obstacles in the path of
> consciousness' efforts to comprehend the essence of social relations and to see
> beyond the illusory notions of reality, its true, real contours. Marx empha-
> sized that the most important, indeed the essential, precondition for the
> liquidation of alienation must be a revolutionary restructuring of society.
> . . . Kafka's work reflects with impressive convincingness the bared, concrete
> reality of the enslaving ideological aspect of alienation, which oppresses man-
> kind but completely disregards the opportunities for overcoming it.

Sučkov concluded:

> What then did Kafka contribute to the art of the novel and to twentieth-
> century art generally? An exceptionally acute perception of the tragedy of life
> in bourgeois society, of its fragility and hostility to man. The tragic perception
> of the world grew in Kafka into a blind terror of existence itself.[68]

It is by no means uncommon in the USSR for translated Western literature—and particularly for rarely reprinted old favorites—to sell out very
quickly in the bookstores and soon become available only in the black
market. The case of the Kafka book is somewhat unusual in one respect:
the writer was almost completely unknown only a year earlier when some
of his writings had appeared in a literary monthly. Two factors may have
affected the sudden surge of interest: the particular features of the book itself
and the timing of its publication. (We discount a third, curiosity about a
new foreign author, because by the mid-1960s Soviet readers must have
grown quite accustomed to being introduced to ever larger numbers of
Western writers.)

The late 1950s and the early 1960s saw the great homecoming of hundreds
of thousands, if not millions, of surviving inmates of Stalin's prisons and
concentration camps, a mass migration comparable in physical scope and
psychological impact only to the return of demobilized soldiers at the end
of the war. While the complete text of Khrushchev's "secret" speech of 1956
was not made public, watered-down versions of it were widely known. The
Soviet press was full of materials dealing, if only obliquely, with what were
called "violations of Socialist legality during the period of the cult of person-

68. Ibid., pp. 14–15, 53.

ality," a clumsy euphemism for the crimes of the Stalin era: the mass arrests, wholesale deportations, waves of executions, and vast stretches of the country dotted with jails and labor camps that were to become known in the West some years later as the Gulag Archipelago. In most cases the victims were not formally charged with any specific crimes, or else their trials were a grotesque formality, a macabre game in which all the actors mechanically rehearsed their accustomed parts. Now, decades later, many of the survivors were straggling home. Many, but not all.

The return of the prisoners, the years of police terror, and the inquisition of Stalin's courts were beginning to be mentioned in guarded tones in Soviet literary works, particularly after the Twenty-Second Congress of Communist Party of the Soviet Union in October 1961, at which the decision was taken to remove Stalin's body from the mausoleum on Moscow's Red Square. There were Viktor Nekrasov's short novel *Kira Georgievna,* in which a complacent marriage is shaken by the return from prison camp of the woman's first husband; Vadim Koževnikov's novella *The Fleeting Day (Den' letjaščij),* which recalled the false denunciations to the police of people with the wrong class pedigrees; Leonid Pervomajskij's novel *Wild Honey (Dikij mëd)* in which an innocent victim's widow confronts the policeman who had arrested her husband. Then, in November 1962, came Alexander Solzhenitsyn's *One Day in the Life of Ivan Denisovich,* the understated account of an ordinary prisoner's rather fortunate day in a relatively benign concentration camp. Simultaneously, the first illegal works to circulate in *samizdat* typewritten copies—such as Abram Tertz's *The Trial Begins* and Yuli Daniel's *This Is Moscow Speaking*—suggested that, to paraphrase the once-famous slogan issued on Lenin's passing, Stalin might well be dead but much of his work lives on.[69]

Soviet readers were further sensitized to Kafka's subject matter and style by their recent acquaintance with the plays of Aleksandr Suxovo-Kobylin (1817–1903), one of the most significant literary rediscoveries of the first post-Stalin decade. Suxovo-Kobylin was the author of a trilogy of dramas comprising *Krečinskij's Wedding (Svad'ba Krečinskogo), The Court Case (Delo),* and *The Death of Tarelkin (Smert' Tarelkina).*[70] At least three editions of the trilogy were published—in 1955, 1959, and 1966; the plays were also performed on the stage. There were, in addition, several important critical articles, and at least two book-length monographs, in 1957 and 1961.

69. For a detailed treatment of the subject see Michael Heller, *The World of Concentration Camps and Soviet Literature* (London: Overseas Publication Interchange, 1974). This is the English title page of a Russian book, Mixail Geller, *Koncentracionnyj mir i sovetskaja literatura.*

70. These are now available in English with an excellent introductory essay by Professor Harold B. Segel of Columbia: *The Trilogy of Alexander Sukhovo-Kobylin,* translated and with an introduction by Harold B. Segel (New York: E. P. Dutton, 1969).

The rediscovery of the nineteenth-century Russian playwright in the USSR was important not only for literary reasons. As Harold B. Segel perceptively notes: "For the *Trilogy* is, despite its dramatic structure, a philosophical utterance, a fruition in literary form of philosophical reflection. The humorous characters and scenes, the grotesque and absurd comedy, particularly of the last play, are meant only to relieve and indeed at times heighten, but never obscure this fact."[71]

Suxovo-Kobylin's three plays, his only literary works, were grounded in a shattering personal experience, the unsolved murder of his mistress in 1850 and the periods of arrest and endless court litigation that followed. A unique aspect of the drawn-out case was Suxovo-Kobylin's inability to obtain a verdict that would not only establish his complete innocence in the legal sense, but also fully satisfy public opinion. The author's long existence in the twilight zone between clearcut guilt and absolute innocence is reflected in his plays, particularly *The Court Case* and *The Death of Tarelkin* and imparts to them a strikingly twentieth-century quality, strongly reminiscent of Kafka.[72] *The Death of Tarelkin* is an unusual play; equally unusual is its description in a Soviet source:

> It was the first play in Russian drama to feature as the subject of satirical indictment that mainstay of the state, the police. Suxovo-Kobylin penetrated the secret area that had hitherto been off limits. He portrayed the unbridled powers of the police and the complete defenselessness and vulnerability of persons of all ranks and social standing. . . . The biography of the cynical scoundrel [Raspljuev, one of the characters in the play— MF] was quite logically crowned with attainment of the position of a district police inspector who dreams of "subjecting to arrest one and all" and of "instituting in our fatherland a check on all persons: who are they, in fact?" In *The Death of Tarelkin* Suxovo-Kobylin's satire acquires grotesque forms. Tarelkin's feigning of his own death presented the author with an opportunity to combine the comic with the tragic; sudden turns of action from details of the daily routine to grotesque displacement into nearly surreal planes. Availing himself of devices of the marketplace comedy—*bouffe*, Suxovo-Kobylin recreates the impression of man's extreme vulnerability in the conditions of a police state.[73]

71. Ibid., p. xix.
72. The impression of "contemporaneity" is also strengthened by the trilogy's history, so very much like the odysseys of some literary works in our times. *Krečinskij's Wedding* was written partly abroad and partly in a Russian jail. *The Court Case* was first printed in Germany, in twenty-five copies; it was published in Russia with major cuts and with a title intended to deceive the censorship into believing that it dealt with the distant past, *Times Gone By (Obžitoe vremja)*. See *Teatral'naja ènciklopedija*, Vol. IV (1965), pp. 1137–38. The entire trilogy was published in 1869, (with a "decoy" subtitle, *Kartiny prošedšego*, "scenes from the past"), but staging of the third part was not permitted until 1900.
73. KL, Vol. VII (1972), p. 282.

Compare the above with the following statement from the introductory essay in the Soviet volume of Kafka: "In general, Kafka also shares the view expressed in straightforward manner by his hero [*In the Penal Colony*] who agrees that in the eyes of others, man is always guilty or may be declared guilty."[74]

The parallel between Kafka and Suxovo-Kobylin was noted by a Western scholar, Harold B. Segel, and by at least one Soviet scholar.[75] It is pointed out here in support of our belief that the swift surge of popular interest in Kafka, a newly discovered foreign author, in the mid-1960s was to a large extent a result of the fact that at that time Soviet readers were highly sensitized both to the subject matter and to the manner of Kafka's works. Unlike the writings of many of the proscribed Western authors discussed later in this chapter, Kafka's narrative is simple and clear; it is, indeed, occasionally reminiscent of Leo Tolstoy's parables and Russian folk tales. The world that Kafka's heroes inhabit, however, is chaotic, mysterious, and sinister, reminiscent not only of Solzhenitsyn's and Suxovo-Kobylin's but also, much more significantly, of the oral tales of arrests, interrogations, ludicrous accusations, and nightmarish jails that were then being related in whispers by hundreds of thousands of newly amnestied surviving victims of Stalin's terror.

Kafka's tales of the futility of human efforts to avert the wrath of omnipotent authorities whose cruel whims are unpredictable must have struck many Soviet readers as fantasy that was also—as attested by multitudes of eyewitnesses—documented truth.[76] Thus, for instance, the outline of Kafka's *The Trial* (the Russian translation, incidentally, was entitled *Process*, a near-synonym of Suxovo-Kobylin's *Delo*) would hardly strike a Soviet reader as particularly abstract or contrived. The story of a man charged with an unspecified crime, a man who is wholly innocent yet comes to accept the idea of his guilt and eventual punishment merely because he knows that others *and* the authorities consider him guilty, a story in which the hero's ultimate death is anticlimactic, in which the priest tells Joseph K. that "it is not necessary to accept everything as true, but only to accept

74. Franc Kafka, *Roman, novelly, pritči*, p. 35.
75. *The Trilogy of Alexander Sukhovo-Kobylin*, pp. xlviii–xlix; M. Zlobina, "Zametki o dramaturgii Suxovo-Kobylina," *Novyj mir*, No. 9, 1967, p. 243.
76. In this connection, the following testimony of the German critic Hans Mayer is of some interest:

> I remember I was in Hungary in November, 1956, when the rising took place. After the Russian intervention, people used to tell a story about [the Marxist literary critic] Georg Lukacs: how, when he was arrested, he was taken to Rumania and shut up in some sort of weird castle [!—MF] where he and his fellow-prisoners were treated sometimes like felons and sometimes like guests of honour. After a few days of this, Lukacs is supposed to have said, "So Kafka was a realist after all!"

"The Struggle for Kafka and Joyce," *Encounter* (May 1964), p. 84.

it as necessary"—is reminiscent not only of Arthur Koestler's later novel *Darkness at Noon* (unknown to Soviet readers), but also of the logic of events and the reasoning of many novels by *Soviet* authors that were written for *Soviet* readers. Among those that come to mind are Solzhenitsyn's *The First Circle (V kruge pervom),* Vasilij Grossman's *Forever Flowing (Vsë te čët),* Lidija Čukovskaja's *The Deserted House (Opustelyj dom),* and Evgenija Ginzburg's *Journey into the Whirlwind (Krutoj maršrut).* That these particular works did not actually appear under the imprint of a Soviet publisher but were circulated in *samizdat* does not really matter; they were all *intended* for Soviet readers (some came close to being published) and thus give us grounds to assume that they would have been understood. Furthermore, episodes of this type may be found in published works by Jurij Bondarev, Ilya Ehrenburg, and others. An even more contemporary note may have been detected by Soviet readers in Kafka's *In the Penal Colony,* in which the colony's *previous* commandant is credited with inventing a monstrous machine for punishing prisoners (not that the old commandant was a sadist—he honestly believed that this served the cause of justice and actually benefited the prisoners themselves). Still, the machine, although apparently disapproved of by the present commandant, continues in operation under the new regime. Possible parallels with the Soviet prisons and camps of the mid-1960s are all too obvious.

In recent years no other Western author—and certainly none dead for half a century—received as much unfavorable attention in Soviet literary criticism and general journalism as Franz Kafka. As pointed out earlier, the central theme of this criticism is Kafka's failure to attribute firmly and clearly the nightmare of alienation and despair to capitalism: "Kafka is trying to demonstrate that the enslavement of man *which the writer observes in his bourgeois surroundings,* is not a result of unjust social relations, but is caused by man's organic inability to be free."[77] Hence the charge of Kafka's "pessimism." Yet, as one Soviet critic argued, there is no need to honor Kafka for describing the horror and evil of our times, pointing out that there are other writers who do it just as well or better and suggesting, in effect, that we can really do without Kafka altogether.[78] Kafka's belief in the universality of evil and guilt is "an idea that is not only historically

77. D. Zatonskij, "Smert' i roždenie Franca Kafki," *Inostrannaja literatura,* No. 2, 1959, pp. 209–210. Italics added.

78. The Soviet critic's list of great "pessimistic" authors whom we would do well to read in lieu of Kafka includes Sherwood Anderson, Ring Lardner, Ernest Hemingway, and F. Scott Fitzgerald (particularly *The Great Gatsby*)! Indeed, the critic insists, Kafka's lack of originality is so abysmal, that most of his extravagantly admired attributes may be found not only in such great Russian novelists as Gogol, but even in such minor ones as Aleksej Remizov and Aleksandr Kuprin. See M. [Mixail] Gus, *Modernizm bez maski* (Moscow: Sovetskij Pisatel', 1966), pp. 195–210.

and philosophically false, but is also quite dangerous in practice."[79]

Ironically, Kafka was faulted for his failure to link evil to specific socio-economic conditions at a time when Marxist Soviet historians were trying to explain the evils of Stalinism by such patently un-Marxist devices of "psychohistory" as Stalin's own paranoia and the "cult of personality." A clue to the real objections to Kafka may be found in the strong disapproval with which the Soviet critic cited the claim of Eduard Goldstücker, then still a Communist scholar in good standing in a Soviet-bloc country, to the effect that "Kafka has something to say to us, builders of Socialism."[80] The idea of Kafka's *relevance* to the Soviet world was rightly perceived to be potentially dangerous, encouraging readers of Kafka to form comparisons and parallels which might also include some of those suggested above. It should be noted that such suspicious attitudes extend also to other allegorical and abstract formulations of the human condition in literature, Russian and foreign, old and new, ranging from *Notes from the Underground* to the novels of Albert Camus. It may even suggest some reasons why in Soviet literature itself the Tolstoyan tradition is so strongly favored over the Dostoyevskian. It is unlikely that Kafka will ever be warmly embraced by Soviet critics. Like Dostoyevsky, it will probably require many years for him to earn at least grudging acceptance.[81]

As pointed out, in recent Soviet criticism of twentieth-century Western writing, Franz Kafka, James Joyce, and Marcel Proust regularly emerge as the Unholy Trinity of the pestilence of modernism, sinister in itself and doubly evil because it begot such recent literary abominations as the *nouveau roman* and the repertory of the theater of the absurd. Of the three, Kafka is clearly potentially the most dangerous, since it is his world view rather than his artistic method that is at issue; paradoxically, Kafka while

79. The following was offered as an example of the horrible consequences of Kafka's views: "In the Federal German Republic there was a researcher who determined that the responsibility for the heinous Nazi crimes should be borne by their victims! For the Nazi murders, it turns out, were the realization of secret desires of these victims to murder their own fathers, mothers, sisters, brothers, and children." Ibid., p. 183. Needless to say, no such theories can be traced to Kafka. If anything, they appear to be a vulgarized distortion of Hannah Arendt's controversial book, *Eichmann in Jerusalem* (1963).

80. M. Gus, *Modernizm bez maski*, p. 167.

81. The checkered fortunes of Kafka in Soviet-bloc countries are illustrated by the fact that in May 1973 the Czech Communist weekly *Tribuna* published an article entitled "With Kafka Against Socialism" (Gustaw Herling-Grudzinski, "Dziennik pisany noca," *Kultura* [Paris], No. 5/320, [1974], pp. 32–33). On the other hand, the August 1974 issue of the Soviet monthly *Novyj mir* promised subscribers the publication in 1975 of Kafka's *The Castle*. The latter may well reflect the temporary ascendancy of a "positive" view of Kafka, of which the Soviet critic G. I. Kunicyn appears to be a leading exponent. In Kunicyn's opinion, "Kafka's pessimism stems, on the contrary, *from the fact that he failed to discern the imminence of capitalism's collapse.* This mistake, moreover, neatly 'coincides' with his view of capitalism's (yes, capitalism's) *hostility* to man." G. J. Kunicyn, *Politika i literatura* (Moscow: Sovetskij pisatel', 1973), p. 315. Italics in the original. In Kunicyn's view, Kafka and other "pessimists" and "modernists" should not be viewed as enemies of the Soviet cause. The real danger, in his opinion, are those works of Western literature that propagate a simplistic and complacent view of the capitalist way of life.

most maligned, was also the most recently published. The others had been published decades ago, but have since continued to exist in the USSR only as objects of official scorn: their works remain unavailable. A few chapters from Joyce's *Ulysses* appeared in Russian in 1936, and *Dubliners* was brought out the following year. Boris Sučkov, the author of the introduction to the Kafka volume, wrote of Joyce more in sorrow than in anger: "He squandered his great and original gifts on works that are nearly unreadable; their stylistic peculiarities and their notions of human nature have become the Holy Writ of modern decadence."[82] Occasionally, more moderate voices are heard. Thus, one critic timidly suggested that like Kafka, Joyce, too, revealed "a part of the truth about the anti-human nature of capitalist conditions."[83] At the 1963 Leningrad conference of Soviet and West European writers Ilya Ehrenburg also attempted to strike a conciliatory note: "Can one reject Joyce and Kafka, two great writers who do not resemble one another? To me this is the past, they are historical phenomena. I do not make banners of them, but neither do I make targets of them. . . . Joyce is a writer for writers."[84] Yet the verdict of the *Literary Encyclopedia* was unrelenting:

> The formal experimentalism of the writer earned him the status of one of the pillars [*mètrov*] of modernist literature in its most reactionary manifestations. The influence of Joyce's writings on bourgeois literature of various countries promoted the strengthening of decadent tendencies and led many writers into the dead-end of alogism.[85]

Marcel Proust's *Remembrance of Things Past* was brought out in Russian translation in 1934–38. Since that time Proust has been attacked, but not republished. Boris Sučkov's objection to Proust was rather primitive: Proust's work describes only "a narrow circle of the French bourgeoisie and aristocracy on the eve of World War I"[86]—the kind of argument that might also be used to "discredit," for instance, Tolstoy's *War and Peace* or, *toutes proportions gardées,* Sholokhov's *Silent Don.* At the Leningrad meeting of writers referred to earlier, the eminent Soviet novelist Konstantin Fedin used some heavy irony: "If Soviet novelists were to follow the intuitivism of Proust, consistency would suggest that we resurrect some of our home-grown modernists as well."[87]

Actually, some of the older Russian modernists, such as Andrej Belyj and

82. *Literaturnaja gazeta,* August 31, 1963.
83. D. Zatonskij, "Smert' i roždenie Franca Kafki," *Inostrannaja literatura,* No. 2, 1959, p. 204.
84. Cited in Priscilla Johnson and Leopold Labedz, *Khrushchev and the Arts,* p. 242.
85. KL, Vol. II (1964), p. 655.
86. *Literaturnaja gazeta,* August 31, 1963.
87. Cited in Priscilla Johnson and Leopold Labedz, *Khrushchev and the Arts,* pp. 64–65.

Fedor Sologub, were indeed being resurrected at the time. What obviously worried Fedin was the possibility that some Soviet authors might, indeed, imitate Proust's artistic manner. That this would not be tolerated was made clear by the critic Mixail Gus:

> Kafka's or Proust's attitude toward their milieu is inappropriate for our attitude toward our Socialist milieu because of the fundamental differences between the capitalist world and the Socialist world as a whole, and in particular because *there is no "alienation" in our world.* Thus, the esthetic method of Kafka, Joyce, Musil, and Proust can neither enrich nor "broaden" Socialist Realism.[88]

Strange as this may seem, Proust's unpublished and unavailable writings were the subject of a small book published in 1968. The generally mild tone of the study—and the very fact of its appearance—suggested that some works of Proust may indeed be published in the future, but the overall message was nevertheless an appeal to *oppose* Proust's influence at home and abroad: "Otherwise, one cannot avoid the dead ends in which Marcel Proust's heirs [in the West] find themselves; they have in fact gone so far in their searches of lost time that they propose to create a novel 'starting with nothing, with dust.' "[89]

The attacks on Proust were in reality aimed primarily at his "heirs," as was the criticism of Joyce. The implications of both are quite clear: there must be no *Soviet* followers of Proust or Joyce, since it is felt that their artistic manner is incompatible with good Soviet content.[90] In fact, while the writings of Joyce, Proust, Gide, and Kafka "still retain at least some desire to reflect physical and social reality, their followers, the contemporary modernist extremists, have severed the last links between their art and the real world."[91] They are thus viewed as being quite beyond redemption: their art is no longer capable of serving as a carrier for *any* coherent social ideas. Any, that is, with the one important exception of an implication, an innuendo, an "anti-idea" of sorts. The "modernist extremists," among whom Samuel Beckett is ordinarily pointed to as the most typical and hence the

88. M. Gus, *Modernizm bez maski,* pp. 271–72. Italics added.

89. L. G. Andreev, *Marsel' Prust* (Moscow: Vysšaja škola, 1968), p. 96.

90. A curious parallel may be found in Soviet opposition to the award of the first prize to Federico Fellini's *8 1/2* at the 1963 Moscow Film Festival. The objections centered on the film's structure in which "reality, delirium, and memory" are intertwined, and its overall "pessimism." See *Literaturnaja gazeta,* July 20, 1963. Soviet opposition to the award was the more symptomatic in view of the generally favorable Soviet opinion of Fellini's work. See *Pravda,* June 30, 1963.

91. *Znamja,* No. 2, 1959, p. 235. The author of the article, Lev Kopelev, served, as pointed out earlier, as the prototype for Rubin, the brilliant but dogmatic Communist in Solzhenitsyn's *The First Circle.* A similar view was expressed in the 1960s by Georg Lukacs, in whose *Aesthetics* "Kafka is compared favourably with Beckett, unfavourably with Chaplin." See "The Struggle for Kafka and Joyce," *Encounter* (May 1964), p. 84.

most evil example, readily acknowledge the dismally bleak state of human existence; in fact, they wallow in it. At the same time they adamantly refuse to link it in any way to specific sociopolitical conditions. We *know,* in other words, that the heroes of Beckett and others like him live in capitalist societies, but this is never clearly stated by the authors themselves. Their portraits of human misery are presented, as it were, outside the confines of time and space and thus suggest that no salvation is to be expected from man-induced social changes—to a Soviet Marxist, an insidiously reactionary idea. If human misery cannot be alleviated by social and political reform, then Marxist goals of Socialism and Communism are futile and irrelevant. That is why even Lev Kopelev, an otherwise sophisticated Soviet critic views extreme literary and theatrical "modernism" as cunning *political* conspiracy on the part of Communism's sworn enemies:

> The ruling circles of bourgeois states promote this literature for the sake of their own selfish interests and political calculation. They attempt to pass off the stinking concoctions of Beckett and his ilk as living art. But their writings have nothing in common with true literature. They are not only repugnant, but also dangerous.[92]

Another critic was even more blunt:

> To put it plainly, this abstract pessimism [of the repertory of the theater of the absurd—MF] is reactionary through and through. It profits those whose fingers rest on the push-button of thermonuclear war. *Conviction that the world is "absurd" and its doom inevitable, disarms people in their struggle against the real absurdity of the capitalist system.*[93]

That the political danger allegedly posed by Western "modernist" prose and drama is taken quite seriously is attested by the publication in 1963 of a special study under the auspices of the Soviet propaganda organization "Znanie." Entitled *The Destroyers of the Beautiful: Notes on the Literature of Modernism,* the monograph was apparently intended to serve as an aid for persons preparing lectures on the subject for mass audiences. Its contents were summarized as follows:

92. *Znamja,* No. 2, 1959, p. 236. According to the *Literary Encyclopedia,* "Beckett's work, filled with despair and a sense of the absurdity of existence, is one of the extreme manifestations of modern decadence." KL, Vol. I (1962), p. 500. In the view of the *Theatrical Encyclopedia,* "The grotesque plays of Beckett are filled with moods of pessimism, despair, and void. . . . Beckett's work is symptomatic of the spiritual crisis of the bourgeois intelligentsia of the West." *Teatral'naja ènciklopedija,* Vol. I (1961), p. 488. In the words of a third source: "Is there any hope for man that the world might change, that life might acquire meaning and 'alienation' end? No, answers Beckett with the play *Waiting for Godot."* M. Gus, *Modernizm bez maski,* p. 265.

93. Ibid., p. 13. Italics added.

This popular literary critical essay examines modernism, a harmful, reactionary trend in the bourgeois art of the West. The author makes extensive use
of primary sources and examines the best known works of representatives of
Western modernism (Beckett, Ionesco, and others). The book demonstrates
that this decadent trend, begotten by imperialism and anti-humanist in its
essence, opposes progressive ideas and traditions of realistic art, is hostile to
man, *and serves as a means for distracting the masses from class and social
struggle.* [94]

As pointed out earlier, the paradox of the situation was that Soviet
readers were enjoined actively to despise and beware of a body of writing
with which they were almost wholly unfamiliar. The incongruity of this did
not escape the editors of *Inostrannaja literatura,* and the following note
appeared on p. 191 of its January 1963 issue: "The editorial board's decision
to publish, for the first time in Russian, three self-contained excerpts from
novels by Nathalie Sarraute, Alain Robbe-Grillet, and Michel Butor, these
three 'pillars' of the *nouveau roman* in France, was prompted by the following considerations. Actual samples of the work of these writers are probably
the best testimony of the social narrowness and monotony of artistic devices
of this 'school' which aspires to 'reveal' new principles in literature." This
was followed by a four-page excerpt from Sarraute's *The Planetarium,* six
pages from Robbe-Grillet's *Dans le labyrinthe,* and six pages from Butor's
*Degrees.* Taken out of context and in a meticulously literal translation, they
must, indeed, have appeared as so much gibberish to Soviet readers totally
unfamiliar with any but conventional realistic prose. It is more than likely,
however, that many of these readers might have found even these intention-
ally selected obscure passages from the three French novelists far more
comprehensible, and perhaps even interesting and enjoyable, were it not for
the fact that Soviet schools, publishers, and censors have for decades all but
totally suppressed Russia's *own* tradition of experimental prose. Russians
familiar with such early twentieth-century Russian authors as Boris Pil'-
njak, Yevgenij Zamiatin, and Andrej Belyj—all of them once widely read
in the USSR—would not have found Sarraute, Butor, and Robbe-Grillet
entirely unintelligible. *Inostrannaja literatura*'s ostensibly reasonable pro-
posal that readers make up their own minds about *le nouveau roman* on the
basis of sixteen pages of prose from three unknown Western novelists was
not very different from the "humorous" device used in the late 1940s by the
Soviet satirical journal *Krokodil* to discredit Western painting. The stratagem employed consisted of reproducing, on poor-quality paper and with
terrible ink, some of the more outlandish Western abstract canvases with

94. *Xudožestvennaja literatura* (July–September 1963), p. 90. Italics added. The monograph
was Z. Libman, *Razrušiteli prekrasnogo (Zametki o literature modernizma)* (Moscow: Znanie,
1963).

a brief rhymed pun: *Djadja Sam risuet sam* (Drawings by Uncle Sam Himself). *Inostrannaja literatura*'s gambit was indirectly praised by a Soviet critic three years later.[95] Nevertheless, it does not appear to have been widely emulated, although there were important exceptions: thus, Samuel Beckett's *Waiting for Godot* was published in the October 1966 issue of *Inostrannaja literatura.*

The list of deadly sins which may bar a Western author's publication in the USSR transcends by far the proverbial seven. It includes membership in anti-Soviet political organizations or, more gravely, resignation from pro-Soviet ones. It penalizes for immigration into certain capitalist countries (some, like Israel, more than others) or, worse, emigration from socialist ones. It bars some authors because the unwanted contents of their books are all too clear, turns away others because their contents are ambiguous, and prohibits some which apparently have no intelligible contents at all. As in certain religious traditions, sincere penitence and good deeds may lift the evil decree. As in others, the death of the transgressor is weighty consideration in the eventual annulment of excommunication of his works. And while some sinners are being pardoned and others arrive to take their place, the majority are only being shifted from the inner circles of hell to the more lenient outlying ones without being granted complete absolution.

Some, however, stand to be condemned forever as moral lepers, and Henry Miller seems to be one of them. Significantly, none of the objections to his works are overtly political. Rather, he appears to outrage a Soviet reviewer's moral sense, not only the norms of propriety or prudery, but also the broader context of basic human ethics. In an article entitled "Confessions of an Amoralist," Henry Miller is excoriated for his alleged celebration of selfishness, nastiness, spitefulness, and dishonesty; the charge of "filth" comes almost as an afterthought:

> Miller's "pornoutopia" is reactionary. . . . The anti-humane element of "porn" found its most fitting expression in the writings of Miller. It is for this reason that they lie outside the province of true literature. It is for this very reason that the American writer Henry Miller may be called a foe of man and of civilization itself.[96]

95. "It is quite another matter that the ostrich policy won't do, either. It makes no sense to 'hide' modernist art from the young. After all, forbidden fruit is tempting. It should be shown, but its essence should be revealed, its antihistoricism and sterility." M. Gus, *Modernizm bez maski,* p. 14.

96. M. Tuguševa, "Ispoved' amoralista," *Inostrannaja literatura,* No. 2, 1967, p. 274. The essay is a review of Henry Miller's *The Rosy Crucifixion. Sexus. Plexus. Nexus* (New York: Grove Press, 1965). An English translation may be found in Carl R. Proffer, *Soviet Criticism of American Literature,* pp. 20–23. A delegation of American book publishers visiting the USSR in 1970 reported that the Editor-in-Chief of the Progress Publishing House, which specializes in translations from and into Western languages, "was extremely critical of [Philip Roth's] *Portnoy's Complaint,* we believe for moral reasons." *Book Publishing in the U.S.S.R.,*

Most readers would probably agree that the refined, often lyrical prose of Virginia Woolf bears little resemblance to Henry Miller's often coarse novels or to the grotesque, nightmarish world of Beckett's plays. It is illustrative of the aesthetic sloppiness of the ideologically militant Soviet criticism of Western writing (and it is, alas, this kind that most influences Soviet publishing) that one would never suspect it from a pronouncement by a major Soviet critic of Western literature, which in effect equates the three—a fact made the more important by the unavailability of Virginia Woolf's books: "We know, however, what her [Virginia Woolf's] work represents—flight from reality, irrationalism, pessimism, dehumaniza-tion."[97]

The title of Edward Albee's play comes to mind: *Who's Afraid of Virginia Woolf?*

Why, the "cultural" watchdogs of Soviet readers, that's who.

---

Report of the Delegation of U.S. Book Publishers Visiting the U.S.S.R. October 21–November 4, 1970; August 20–September 17, 1962, 2nd ed., enlarged (Cambridge, Mass.: Harvard University Press, 1971), p. 19.

97. M. Gus, *Modernizm bez maski,* pp. 5–6. An 850-page college textbook of twentieth-century foreign literature devotes 135 pages to British literature without as much as mentioning Virginia Woolf. See Z. T. Graždanskaja, *Istorija zarubežnoj literatury XX veka,* 1963, pp. 404–539.

# CHAPTER
# 9

# *A Problematic Coexistence: Western Culture in Soviet Society*

Statistics cited in earlier chapters attest that however restrictive in selection of titles and discriminatory in the sizes of printings of individual authors and works, the overall quantity of Western writing made available to Soviet readers during the first post-Stalin decade was more than generous. Nevertheless, all indications suggest that the supply has been far from sufficient to satisfy the seemingly insatiable demand, and that the situation continues up to the present. The unusual (and, to the Soviet authorities, somewhat embarrassing) experiment in book exchanging conducted in late 1974 that was described in chapter two is more eloquent testimony to this fact than any statistical data: people of all ages and walks of life were prepared to haul scrap paper over long distances and wait in lines, all in the hope that they might be among the fortunates allowed to take home a volume of Dumas or of Conan Doyle. That the situation was even worse in the early 1950s is suggested by an episode related in Solzhenitsyn's *The First Circle.* A group of imprisoned scientists working in a laboratory and with easy access to well-stocked libraries chances upon a copy of Alexandre Dumas's *The Count of Monte Cristo.* All are impatiently awaiting a chance to read the longed-for novel, and a way is found to hasten the delightful opportunity: the book is torn into sections, and in this manner several men devour it at the same time.[1]

1. Aleksandr Solzhenitsyn, *The First Circle,* translated from the Russian by Thomas P. Whitney (New York: Bantam Books, 1973), p. 195.

The hunger for West European and American books, plays, and films of every description indubitably existed during the Stalin era, but it was only in the more permissive atmosphere of the post-Stalin years that the yearning could be more or less openly expressed. Some privileged intellectuals occasionally resorted to privately-produced translations of Western literary works, all of them quite illegal as is all dissemination of unauthorized works.[2] Ordinary citizens throughout the country flocked in what Soviet newspapers considered alarming numbers to cinemas showing *The Magnificent Seven,* an American Western. Muscovites were more enthusiastic about William Gibson's light comedy *Two for the Seesaw* than the author's countrymen: in 1962, the play was performed simultaneously in *five* theaters of the Soviet capital.[3] In small towns, youthful patrons of libraries had little trouble obtaining political books, of which there were apparently ample supplies, but had great difficulty getting translations of foreign literature: only one request in ten was filled.[4] At the same time, bookstores could not get enough children's books of all kinds, including translations of Western classics. Thus, one bookstore ordered 500 copies of Hans Christian Andersen's *The Steadfast Tin Soldier,* but received only 100; of *Gavroche,* an excerpt from Victor Hugo's *Les Misérables,* 200 copies were ordered and 68 were actually shipped; of Mark Twain's *The Prince and the Pauper,* only 30 arrived of the ordered 100. The worst cut affected *Gulliver's Travels:* the bookstore ordered 200 copies but had to make do with fifteen.[5]

It should be noted that not only are all Soviet books reasonably expensive

2. Thus, Enrico Emanuelli of *Corriere della Sera* reported that at the 1963 conference of European writers a young Soviet author told him: "I felt humiliated by being forced to read Camus's *The Plague* in a typewritten translation. Why won't they let us publish Robbe-Grillet and Nathalie Sarraute?" Gustaw Herling-Grudziński, "Ksiega krzywd," *Kultura* (Paris), No. 12, 1963, p. 31. Solzhenitsyn's reference to a *samizdat* translation of Hemingway's *For Whom the Bell Tolls* was mentioned in chapter 1, note 88.

3. *Sovetskaja kul'tura,* May 21, 1963.

4. In towns with populations below 50,000, the percentages of books that libraries could *not* provide to young readers were as follows:

| Political and popular science | 30 |
|---|---|
| Prerevolutionary Russian literature | 73 |
| Soviet literature | 78 |
| Foreign literature | 90 |

*Kniga i čtenie v žizni nebol'šix gorodov,* 1973, pp. 150–51. The lumping together of popular science with political literature was probably effected in order to conceal the relative lack of interest in propagandistic tracts. One can be confident that the unobtainable books were largely popular science. On June 7, 1962, *Izvestija* reported that on a single day Leningrad bookstores were unable to supply their customers with 8,000 books. Of this number, 3,500 were reference works, 1,400 Soviet prose, 900 foreign literature, and 260 political books. This set of figures demonstrates that the number of *Soviet* literary titles unavailable was more than five times as large as the number of political books, the number of foreign books unavailable was more than three times as large as the number of political books. These figures contradict the assertions of Soviet officials that what the public really clamors for is larger quantities of political writings.

5. *Kniga i čtenie v žizni nebol'šix gorodov,* p. 255.

in terms of Soviet earnings, but in the case of modern Western literature, readers in the USSR have to pay 66 percent more than for books by Soviet authors or for Russian and foreign classics.[6] This means that in spite of the significantly higher prices for contemporary Western writing, the Soviet public was more than willing to buy it. While traditional Russian interest in Western literature was one contributing factor, it clearly was not the decisive one.[7] And conversely, in spite of the profits involved, Soviet authorities were unwilling to supply sufficient quantities even of those Western books that it saw fit to publish, a situation suggesting a degree of uncertainty about the *desirability* of fully satisfying the demand for such reading matter.

In the case of new works by Soviet authors, the Communist Party's utilitarian desiderata become operative, so to speak, long before a manuscript is actually delivered to the publishers. The Union of Soviet Writers sees to it that its members do not lose sight of such requirements, and experienced Soviet writers rarely do, although on occasion direct intervention by the Party is required.[8] The situation is obviously different in the case of books by deceased authors or by authors residing outside the USSR. With the partial exception of commissioned works, the Soviet publishers must evaluate the probable impact on Soviet readers of works that were created by authors quite oblivious to Soviet needs. Still, as Heinrich Böll put it, "the written and particularly the printed word, from the moment it is written and printed, acquires—whether or not so intended by the author—a social concreteness, and exerts an influence on the views of the public, of the society, on the restructuring of the world."[9] That the ideological potential of West European and American literature printed in the USSR was to be harnessed to serve the Soviet cause was explicitly stated in the resolution of the Central Committee of the Communist Party of April 5, 1958:

6. Modern translated foreign fiction, poetry, and drama is sold at the rate of 50 kopeks per "publisher's sheet" (which is the same as an "author's page," i.e., 40,000 letters and spaces, but also includes the title page, annotations, etc.). The rate for Soviet prose and for "collected works of literary classics," which presumably also includes older translated Western writing, is 30 kopeks per "publisher's sheet," B. G. Reznikov, *Rabota prodavca,* 1960, p. 16.

7. In the eighteenth century, the period of the first important cultural contacts with the West, Russian publishers brought out 839 foreign novels in translation as well as 104 original Russian novels; 336 of the former and 55 of the latter were republished at least once. In the nineteenth century, the share of Russian writing increased, but the absolute numbers for both categories were greatly expanded. Among the Western authors most popular with Russia's reading public in the 1820s (when Pushkin was emerging as a major poet) were Radcliffe, Kotzebue, Walter Scott, Cooper, Chateaubriand, and Paul de Kock. M. N. Kufaev, *Istorija russkoj knigi v XIX veke* (Leningrad: Kul'turno-Prosvetitel'skoe Izdatel'stvo "Načatki znanij," 1927), pp. 29, 91.

8. Individual instances as well as general patterns of such interference are cited in most Western studies of Soviet literature, such as Edward J. Brown, *Russian Literature Since the Revolution,* revised ed. (New York: Collier Books, 1969); Gleb Struve, *Russian Literature under Lenin and Stalin, 1917–1953* (Norman: University of Oklahoma Press, 1971); and Harold Swayze, *Political Control of Literature in the USSR: 1946–1959* (Cambridge, Mass.: Harvard University Press, 1962).

9. *Inostrannaja literatura,* No. 3, 1967, p. 207. Cited in KL, Vol. VI (1971), p. 222.

> Resolved, that the principal task of publishers bringing out foreign *belles lettres* is the publication of books that promote the Communist education of the working masses, acquaint them with the classics of world literature, broaden their cultural horizons, and develop their artistic taste; the publication of works that reflect the most important processes of social evolution, the growth of progressive democratic forces, and the people's struggle for peace and democracy. The attainment of these goals requires a strict and thorough-going selection of works by the criteria of their ideological and artistic merit.
> ... The Central Committees of the Communist Parties of the union republics, as well as provincial and regional committees of the Communist Party of the Soviet Union, are herewith instructed to ensure control over the publication of books by foreign authors in local publishing houses.[10]

On June 4, 1959, the same body informed the principal Soviet publisher of modern Western writing that selection of specific titles was not in itself sufficient to accomplish the desired aims. In addition, the publishing house was instructed "to publish, whenever necessary, substantial [*obstojatel'nye*] prefaces and introductory articles, which expose [*raskryvajuščie*] the contents of published books, their merits and shortcomings."[11]

In essence, the didactic functions of non-Soviet and Soviet books, plays, and films were to complement each other. The Soviet works were to teach by positive examples, exhorting their readers and spectators to emulate the actions of their heroes and heroines; the non-Soviet works were to serve as warnings depicting the unseemly features of non-Soviet ways of life. This division of functions was eloquently expressed by a leading figure in the Soviet cinema. Commenting on Fellini's film *La Dolce Vita* and the Soviet *Ballad of a Soldier,* Sergej Gerasimov wrote: "However paradoxical this may at first appear, the two films brought each other into a sharper focus in the eyes of the audiences throughout the world, 'One cannot live this way!' says *La Dolce Vita.* 'This is the way to live!' is the message of *Ballad of a Soldier.*"[12]

Understandably, the message "one cannot live this way" is most effectively distilled from West European and American writing and cinema with contemporary settings, though even literary works written a century ago are expected to produce similar reactions on the premise that the basic features of capitalism have not undergone essential change. Such claims were, for instance, regularly made for the writings of Charles Dickens, which were published in 1954–64 in over twenty million copies. This was found so irritating by the British ambassador to the USSR at the time, Sir William

10. *O partijnoj i sovetskoj pečati, radioveščanii i televidenii,* 1972, p. 450.
11. Ibid., p. 461. The *belles lettres* section of what was then the Foreign Literature Publishing House (Izdatel'stvo Inostrannoj Literatury) was subsequently incorporated into the Progress Publishing House.
12. *Izvestija,* August 13, 1960.

Hayter, that when on the eve of Khrushchev and Bulganin's departure for a state visit to Britain in 1956 he was allowed briefly to address the Soviet people over television, Sir William declared: "I wish, for example, that our two countries were better acquainted with each other's modern literatures. In my country, Dickens is a great, revered, and popular classical writer. Still, he is no more representative of conditions in modern Britain than Dostoyevsky is of present-day Soviet conditions."[13] The more pointed political lessons that Soviet citizens are expected to learn from the reading of Western literature are drawn from modern writing. We shall cite here just a few of the most blunt examples, in which all the *i*'s are dotted and the *t*'s are crossed, remembering, of course, that some of the more outlandish claims are merely Communist rhetoric, not taken seriously by most, and that there may even be cases when these are advanced to provide an excuse for the dissemination of Western literary works of dubious ideological value.[14]

In *The Accident*, a novel by Dexter Masters, an American physicist dies from radiation received as the result of a laboratory mishap. A Soviet translation of the novel was supplied with an introduction by Professor A. Lebedinskij, a corresponding member of the Academy of Medical Science, who took the opportunity to remind his readers that *The Accident* demonstrates the importance of Soviet efforts to secure a ban on nuclear weapons.[15] Jacques Bergier's *Secret Agents Against Secret Weapons*, a documentary novel about the French Resistance in which Nazi rockets intended for use against Britain are sabotaged, was accompanied by a preface in which the author expressed his satisfaction with Soviet achievements in space and also by an editorial note: "In our days, with uneasiness growing throughout the world in connection with the rebirth of West Germany's Bundeswehr as well as of militarist tendencies and revanchist moods, Bergier's book is particularly timely. It reminds us insistently of the dangers of a revival of revanchism and militarism."[16] A review of Mitchell Wilson's *Meeting at a Far Meridian* hinted darkly that the novel was suppressed in the United

13. *Pravda*, March 20, 1956. The British ambassador's grievance was brushed aside two weeks later by V. Jakovlev, vice-chairman of the Soviet society for cultural relations with foreign countries, who wrote that Dickens, Thackeray, Thomas Hardy, and Galsworthy ("insufficiently appreciated in his country") all portray "British customs and national traits that have been preserved up to this time in Britain, a country dedicated to old traditions." *Trud*, April 8, 1956.

14. Thus, for instance, in one foreign play performed in Moscow, a Soviet reviewer assured the public, "impassioned civic motifs are suddenly sounded, angry denunciations of war and Fascism." (*Pravda*, October 27, 1962). The play in question was *Dear Liar*, a rather harmless pastiche of Shavian wit based on G. B. Shaw's romantic correspondence with Mrs. Patrick Campbell. The claim of what may be called "redeeming social value" was probably made to justify the performance of a play that the prudish Soviet reviewer found a bit risqué.

15. *Inostrannaja literatura*, No. 4, 1957, p. 49. The novel was serialized in Nos. 4, 5, and 6 of the journal.

16. *Moskva*, No. 5, 1960, pp. 101–2. The novel was serialized in Nos. 5, 6, and 7 of the journal.

States and then praised the work for demonstrating, quite literally, the healing powers of the Soviet way of life. The novel's central character had been engaged in work that produced America's atomic bomb; as a result of pangs of conscience, he grows depressed and irritable and refuses to sire children. All that, however, changes after a visit to the USSR and contacts with Soviet scientists: "What is it that cured Rennet and restored him to life? Has he become a Marxist or an opponent of the capitalist system? Not at all. But when he came in contact with Soviet people and with the new world that unfolded before him in our country, he could not help feeling the effect of Soviet society's psychological climate. . . . It was all of this taken together that restored Rennet's health."[17]

A review of a Moscow production of Tennessee Williams's *The Glass Menagerie,* a play set in the 1930s, seized on the fact that the dramatist designated the time of the play's action as "Now and the Past": "The cruel world in which the Wingfield family lives is that same cruel world in which the 'average American' goes on living today, with the same melancholy, the same oppressive atmosphere, the same gloomy hopelessness."[18] A 1959 staging of Arthur Miller's *Death of a Salesman* elicited the following comment: "The production . . . portrays the story of Willy Loman's death as a profound social tragedy of present-day America. The salesman's tragic destiny is depicted in the play as a logical consequence of the inhuman laws of the capitalist world. . . . At the same time, Miller's play mercilessly exposes one other side of present-day bourgeois ideology—its lack of ideals, and man's oppressive sensation of the absurdity of his existence."[19] A performance of another of Miller's plays, *The Crucible,* also evoked some contemporary associations:

> Arthur Miller turns to one of the black pages in America's history, the "witch-hunts" in the small town of Salem in the late seventeenth century. And even though the medium of the theater evokes a somber incident from a distant past, the playwright was alluding to the present. It is for that reason that the play is perceived by the audience as a singularly contemporary work in the best sense of the term. . . . "It is paradoxical that today we find ourselves in the same clutches," says Arthur Miller in an authorial comment. And the spectator's eyes behold the heroic shades of Ethel and Julius Rosenberg and other victims of the disgraceful McCarthy era.[20]

The critic's comments are rather startling. *The Crucible* contains no direct references to the Rosenbergs, but Arthur Miller's authorial comment

17. *Izvestija,* June 21, 1961.
18. *Pravda,* June 4, 1968.
19. *Pravda,* July 29, 1959.
20. *Izvestija,* January 10, 1963.

includes many direct observations about the play's relevance to events and practices in the USSR, all of which were suppressed by the Soviet censor- ship.[21]

An editorial in *Literaturnaja gazeta* of February 14, 1957, discerned a common denominator in recent novels by three Western authors: "However we may sympathize with the heroes of Remarque, Hemingway, and Stein- beck [in *A Time to Live and a Time to Die; The Old Man and the Sea;* and *The Pearl*—MF] we know that they are doomed to remain lonely figures without interest in a common cause. We honestly pity them because we are aware that the era of individualism's crash has been with us for quite some time—the era in which everything argues for man's joining in the organized struggle of the working masses." A somewhat similar unity was claimed for a mini-anthology of modern American writing consisting of tales by Hem- ingway, Faulkner, Steinbeck, Saroyan, Robert Bowen, and John O'Hara, the latter two published for the first time in the USSR: "True, all of the items in this selection are somewhat somber in tone and not a single one offers what is known as a happy ending. But such moods, apparently, are not accidental. The fact that they are found in works by very different realistic writers demonstrates once again that the source, the primary cause for such moods is to be sought in the conditions of present-day America."[22]

In the estimate of Soviet publishers and critics, the political usefulness of Western literature is not confined to its documentary value as an exposé of the past and present evils of capitalism. With a little ingenuity, some works (particularly those with elements of science fiction) can be interpreted as prophecies of the even more ominous horrors that capitalism holds in store for mankind in the future. Thus, a translation of Kurt Vonnegut's *Player Piano,* renamed in Russia *Utopia 14,* was published in 215,000 copies. The edition was supplied with an introduction of some twenty pages. Its author was, significantly, not a literary critic, but J. Bestužev-Lada, identified as Doctor of Historical Science, an academic title far more prestigious than the American Ph.D. Judging by the book's publisher, Molodaja gvardija, the volume was intended primarily for young readers. According to the Soviet historian, *Player Piano* offers a valuable glimpse of capitalist society in the near future:

> In economically developed countries, mechanization and automation of pro- duction, particularly in industry and agriculture, annually render millions of jobs superfluous. People are replaced by machines. We have grown accus- tomed to reading about it in science fiction and non-science fiction. And all

21. See chapter 1.
22. *Inostrannaja literatura,* No. 8, 1958, pp. 54–55.

too often we forget that even at this time this process results in tragedy for millions of people. We are even less likely to give much thought to the apocalyptic dimensions that this replacement of man with machine may assume in the next few decades in the developed countries of the West—indeed, is already beginning to assume.[23]

In capitalist conditions, the Soviet historian emphasized, replacement of human labor by machines brings no relief to the working people: "This has always required class struggle and a social revolution." Kurt Vonnegut's oriental potentate was quite right in insisting on calling ordinary Americans "slaves,"[24] and Vonnegut's positive characters were naive in dreaming of a return to an agrarian utopia modeled after the ideas of Thoreau and Emerson.[25] In fact, under capitalism, automation and cybernetics simply pave the way for the establishment of a police state: "This is happening now, and will apparently continue for as long as imperialism and imperialist states continue to exist on the face of the earth."[26] Had Vonnegut's book been written in the olden days, Bestužev mused, its author might have entitled it *A Tale Which Relates How in Conditions of State Monopolistic Capitalism, Cybernetics and Automation (Carried to Their Logical Conclusion) Left No Room for Man on the Face of the Earth.*[27] That is why, in the Soviet historian's estimate, Kurt Vonnegut's novel *Utopia 14 (Player Piano)*

serves as an ideological weapon in the consolidation of forces of progress against those of reaction—*even if this runs counter to its author's subjective views.* It depicts with great artistic power the frightening future with which mankind is threatened by capitalism. It helps rally people to struggle for a better, brighter future. This entitles it [the novel] to a place of honor in modern Western science fiction.[28]

The caveat that a work's political uses need not coincide with its author's views or intentions is occasionally made when far-reaching political claims are advanced by Soviet critics about books by living non-Communist writers; the "objective" political significance of a literary work is thus divorced from the "subjective" views of its creator and hence even a formal disclaimer by the author cannot invalidate it. This rationale made it possible for compilers of an annotated bibliography of recent editions of foreign writing to remind Soviet librarians, schoolteachers, journalists, and professional lecturers on political subjects that

23. Kurt Vonnegut, *Utopija 14* (Moscow: Izdatel'stvo C.K.V.L.K.S.M. "Molodaja gvardija," 1967), p. 6.
24. Ibid., p. 20.
25. Ibid., p. 18.
26. Ibid., pp. 14–15.
27. Ibid., p. 14.
28. Ibid., p. 24. Italics added.

progressive foreign writers are our faithful allies in the struggle against bourgeois ideology. Such wonderful writers as L. Aragon, A. Seghers, E. Hemingway, J. Lindsay, J. Aldridge, V. Prattolini, and other noted cultural figures are well known in the USSR. . . . The current issue of the series *Recent Belles Lettres* recommends quite a few important books that unmask the vices of bourgeois society and the pernicious impact of bourgeois ideas on the human psyche. These works include the novels *The Affair* and *Time of Hope* by the English writer Charles Snow; a volume of short stories by the Spanish author José Maria de Quinto entitled *The Street and Men; The Winter of Our Discontent,* a novel by the well-known American writer J. Steinbeck; *The Mayor of Sanita,* a play by the well-known Italian playwright and film director Eduardo de Filippo; and *The Temple of Satan,* a novel by Wolfgang Schreier, a young writer from the German Democratic Republic.[29]

Sometimes such advice is precise and specific. Thus, another annotated bibliography noted:

The disintegration of contemporary bourgeois society and the collapse of its moral foundations are reflected in John Braine's novel *Life at the Top,* J. P. Marquand's *H. M. Pulham, Esq.,* and A. Moravia's *A Ghost at Noon.* It is advisable to recommend these books to readers in conjunction with sociopolitical books of appropriate content.[30]

Another source was even more explicit and practical:

The books of D. Cusack, G. Greene, H. Böll, A. Seghers, J. Amado provide people with correct notions of events, of the disposition of various social class forces in West Germany, in Latin America, and in other countries. The reading of these books makes much easier the perception and understanding of news found in the press and offers a wealth of associations.[31]

How successful are the attempts to harness the political potential of translated Western literature to serve the Soviet cause? Understandably, an objective and reasonably accurate assessment of the ideological impact of Western culture on the Soviet citizenry is difficult. No independent field work can be undertaken because of the political sensitivity of the subject, while Soviet evidence is not only biased, reflecting often wishful thinking rather than social realities, but also very fragmentary. Thus, in the late 1950s, one Soviet reader wrote: "Whether Steinbeck intended it or not, his

29. *Zarubežnaja literatura (1962): rekomendatel'nyj ukazatel'* (Moscow: Ministerstvo Kul'tury RSFSR, Gosudarstvennaja ordena Lenina Biblioteka SSSR imeni V. I. Lenina, 1963), pp. 3–4. Anna Seghers was an East German novelist. The others are discussed elsewhere in this study, particularly in chapters 6 and 7.
30. *Xudožestvennaja literatura, literaturovedenie, iskusstvo. Rekomendatel'nyj ukazatel' novinok* (October-December 1963), p. 135. For a discussion of the three authors see chapter 6.
31. *Sovetskij čitatel'*, p. 279. See also chapters 6 and 7.

novel *The Pearl* strengthened in me a feeling of sacred and righteous hatred for colonizers and their apostles, and I wanted to stretch out my hand to him as a comrade-in-arms in [common] struggle."[32] Another reader trustingly accepted Upton Sinclair's novel *The Metropolis,* then exactly half a century old, as reliable documentary evidence of what life in America was like in the late 1950s: "Like the overwhelming majority of my countrymen, I have never been in the United States. The author of *The Metropolis,* Sinclair, was an American and I thought I should believe him. He smashed to smithereens the notorious pastoral concept of the 'popular nature of capitalism.' "[33] And the reading of Ellen Dymphna Cusack's *Say No to Death* had the desired effect on a Soviet student: "I was indignant about a social system in which everything is done for the sake of money, in which money is more precious than life."[34]

Still, Soviet authorities are frequently apprehensive about the overall impact of foreign books, plays, and films on the Soviet public, and such apprehensions, in our view, are amply justified.[35] In essence, the undesirable consequences of the wide dissemination of Western cultural materials in the post-Stalin USSR can be traced to two processes. The first is the competition of foreign materials, often spectacularly successful, with domestic cultural products—and the economic and, far more importantly, the ideological implications of this success for those concerned with the political impact of the arts on the Soviet public. The second is the influence of the cultural imports on the quality of Soviet literature and the arts themselves, particularly on those features that affect their function as carriers of Soviet values.

It appears that while the first of these risks was to some extent expected by the Soviet Establishment (after all, this particular danger had always been present and periodically attacked, since significant amounts of literature of non-Soviet origin, particularly the Russian and foreign classics, had been steadily published during the Stalin era as well), the second came as something of a surprise. As a result, the official response to the first menace, that of making available to the Soviet public literary and artistic works deemed damaging to the Communist education of the masses, was relatively reasoned; it could, and did, draw on the Party's experience of earlier years. By contrast, reactions to the second danger, while often violent, betrayed a sense of confusion. While attacks on Soviet writers and artists for ideological errors in their works have an old and inglorious tradition in the USSR,

32. *Inostrannaja literatura,* No. 3, 1957, p. 217. As pointed out, some years later John Steinbeck was excommunicated by the Soviet literary establishment for his support of the American presence in Vietnam.

33. *Trud,* August 30, 1959. Curiously, this letter was printed shortly *after* the Party's denunciation of Upton Sinclair for his doctrinal errors. See chapter 1.

34. O. I. Nikiforova, *Psixologija vosprijatija xudožestvennoj literatury,* p. 140.

35. See Appendix F.

their transgressions *as a large group* were never before openly traced to *imitation* of Western models. This consideration was the more important since the majority of the offenders—writers, playwrights, poets, painters, composers, and filmmakers—were young and thus more reckless than their older colleagues, whose memories of Stalin's treatment of wayward artists were still vivid.

The problem of the ideological and formal influence of Western culture on Soviet literature and the arts during the first ten years following Stalin's death was made more acute by the convergence of several factors. The first and most obvious was the sudden influx into the USSR of a relatively wide variety and large quantities of Western books, plays, films, musical compositions, and, to a lesser extent, paintings and sculpture. The second was the spectacular biological rejuvenation of the Soviet art world. Only recently overwhelmingly dominated by the elderly and the middle-aged, membership rosters of Soviet literary and artistic associations were swollen in the mid-1950s and the 1960s by thousands of young people; and although the USSR did not quite share in the youth cult then in vogue in the West (for a while, a nice contrast was provided by newspaper photographs of the boyish John F. Kennedy and the bald and paunchy Khrushchev), more attention began to be devoted to the young Soviet generation. Various artists' and writers' organizations established separate sections for their younger members. At the same time, a number of periodicals, radio programs, and the like aimed specifically at youthful audiences came into existence.

The young Soviet writers and artists, many of them making their debuts after 1956, were understandably somewhat disoriented by the inconclusive nationwide discussion regarding the ways in which the Stalinist heritage was to be repudiated, and the limits beyond which disavowal of Stalinism implied a dismantling of the Soviet idea itself. Not surprisingly, therefore, many of them avoided identifying themselves with and imitating the pillars of the Soviet literary and artistic establishment, most of whom were, of course, discredited by decades of servile association with some of Stalinism's most repugnant features. This consideration was further reinforced by the then often acknowledged fact that Stalinism's artistic legacy was aesthetically disastrous, consisting largely of countless unreadable novels, embarrassing poems, tedious plays, crudely propagandistic films, contrived oratorios, and naive posters masquerading as serious painting. Thus, in their search for models, many of the younger Soviet authors, artists, and filmmakers turned, not surprisingly, to the newly available West European and American literature, drama, films, music, and painting that were then being advertised in the USSR as the work of "progressive," peace-loving, and anticapitalist artists, many of them friends of the USSR and some even members of Western Communist parties.

The pervasiveness of this phenomenon became apparent in 1962, when *Voprosy literatury,* the country's foremost scholarly journal devoted to Russian as well as foreign literature and literary theory, circulated a questionnaire among a representative sample of the country's younger writers. Two of the six questions to which answers and comments were solicited were: "Which traditions in classical and modern literature do you find congenial? Which searches in artistic form appear to you most promising?" The timing of the questionnaire (it was sent out shortly after the Twenty-Second Party Congress, which marked the highest point in the de-Stalinization campaign) doubtless accounts for the bluntness of some of the responses. Nevertheless, even making some allowances for this coincidence, the answers were most revealing and came to many as a shock. The overwhelming majority of respondents claimed as their masters modern Western authors, Russian and foreign classics, and Soviet authors generally disowned by the establishment. Among the thirty-two returned questionnaires there was hardly a mention of the approved laureates of Soviet letters, both dead and living. Thus, Vasilij Aksënov mentioned Tolstoy and Chekhov, and such maverick Soviet authors as Babel and Platonov, both only recently reinstated as Soviet writers in good standing after many years of a total boycott. According to Aksënov, author of *A Ticket to the Stars* and one of the best of the young prose writers in the USSR, "Hemingway, Faulkner, Böll, and Salinger are also a first-rate school—this in addition to the sheer delight of reading their books."[36] Algimantas Baltakis, a young Lithuanian poet, referred to "men of great heart and mind," among whom were included two Soviet poets, Lugovskoj and Mayakovsky; one Soviet prose writer, Ehrenburg; and four Westerners, Whitman, Neruda, Hemingway, and Éluard.[37] Andrej Voznesenskij, probably the most gifted of the younger Soviet poets, named only a single master whose opinions he had been seeking since boyhood: Boris Pasternak, who had died only recently, scorned by the Soviet literary officialdom.[38] Nikolaj Damdinov, a Burjat writer from distant Inner Mongolia, used the opportunity to attack Vadim Koževnikov's Stalinist potboiler *I Want You to Meet Baluev (Znakom'tes', Baluev):* "Meeting him is no joy. . . . One must not reduce literature to a

36. *Voprosy literatury,* No. 9, 1962, p. 118. In the years that followed Aksënov's extravagant praise of living Western authors, particularly when viewed together with his failure even to mention politely a single Soviet "classic," let alone an older Soviet contemporary, was used as evidence of the alarming state of ideological maturity among young Soviet authors. Still, Aksënov appears to persevere in his errors. Fully a decade later he was taken to task by a Soviet journal for mentioning, in a 1971 short story, a great many foreign poets, including W. H. Auden, Allen Ginsburg, and Lawrence Ferlinghetti. See *Oktjabr',* No. 7, 1972, pp. 189–203.
37. *Voprosy literatury,* No. 9, 1962, p. 120.
38. Ibid., p. 123.

somber list of a person's positive traits."[39] Ivan Drač, a twenty-six year old Ukrainian, referred to some Russian and Ukrainian classics, to the *young* Tyčyna and Ryl's'kyj (i.e., prior to their conversion to Ukrainian Socialist Realism), as well as to Hemingway and Garcia Lorca.[40]

Yevgeni Yevtushenko recanted his anti-American verse written in 1949 at the age of fifteen and added, "As for myself, eclectic as this may seem, I should like to synthesize in my verse some characteristic features of Mayakovsky, Blok, Yesenin, and Pasternak."[41] A long list of foreign authors was provided by the young Armenian writer Perč Zejtuncjan; these included Graham Greene, Arthur Miller, Hemingway, and Saroyan.[42] Anatolij Kuznecov cited "Tolstoy, Jack London, Hemingway,"[43] Šamil Maxmudov, a Bashkir author, cited one Soviet poet, Mayakovsky, and five foreigners—the Indian Tagore, the Turk Hikmet, as well as Whitman, Neruda, and Éluard, then added as an afterthought the "civic-philosophical lyrics" of three rather nonconformist Soviet poets, Martynov, Sluckij, and Smeljakov.[44] Viktor Moskovkin skirted the question, but volunteered his low opinion of the Stalinist "conflictless drama" (i.e., Soviet plays without villains, portraying only differing degrees of virtue) and, blasphemously, criticized Maxim Gorky.[45] Valerij Osipov bluntly declared, "In my view, most promising for quests in artistic form is the legacy bequeathed to future literature by Ernest Hemingway."[46] The Azerbaidzhani Jusif Samedoglu felt a kinship to Turkish writing, as well as to Cervantes, Byron, Tolstoy, Hemingway, Remarque, and Sholokhov, the latter being, incidentally, one of the very few mentions of the officially approved Soviet novelist-laureate.[47] Julian Semënov declared, "Closest to me are the traditions of Pushkin, Dostoyevsky, Chekhov, Hemingway, Remarque, Böll." Only the young Stalinist Vladimir Firsov's report conformed to the requirements of Socialist Realist orthodoxy: his favorite was the crudely propagandistic versifier Isakovskij, whose lyrics are often sung as Soviet military marches.[48]

39. Ibid., p. 128.
40. Ibid., p. 131. Drač also referred to the influence on his work of cinema and of painting, Russian, Soviet, and Western, mentioning Dovženko, Fellini, Vrubel', and Picasso.
41. Ibid., p. 133.
42. Ibid., p. 134. Zejtuncjan also mentioned the painter Modigliani and the film director De Sica.
43. Ibid., p. 140. Kuznecov now lives in the West, as does Naum Koržavin, another of the interviewees.
44. Ibid., p. 144.
45. Ibid., p. 145.
46. Ibid., p. 146.
47. Ibid., p. 152.
48. Ibid., p. 155. A few months earlier, *Voprosy literatury* had circulated another questionnaire among authors of different ages. One of the questions was: "How, in your opinion, can (and should) a Soviet author learn from the classics of Russian and world literature?" The number of published responses was thirty-two, the same as for the questionnaire circulated among young authors. Unlike that questionnaire, however, only two authors had even attempted to provide a reasoned reply. The others offered platitudes (e.g., "don't imitate!"). The

It was merely fifteen years earlier that the problem of Western influences on Russian literature and the arts had been elevated to a major political issue. In the late 1940s one manifestation of the "anti-cosmopolitan" campaign was a concerted attack on literary scholars and art historians who had the temerity to suggest that Russian culture of the past was not entirely original, that the culture which sprang up largely in the nineteenth century was at least in part derivative, owing a measure of its greatness to a successful and creative assimilation of Western Europe's much older cultural traditions. Such self-evident truths and time-honored directions of scholarly inquiry were denounced at that time as "kowtowing to the West" and denigration of Russia's cultural eminence. Stalin's death put an end to the seizure of xenophobia in matters cultural, and in the late 1950s Soviet scholars became once more relatively free to discuss Pushkin's indebtedness to French culture, Byronic elements in Lermontov's verse, and the possible impact of E. T. A. Hoffmann on Gogol.

Doubtless, the more permissive attitude toward studies of cultural contacts and influences across national frontiers during the first post-Stalin decade encouraged young Soviet writers and artists to proclaim openly their admiration for contemporary Western literature and the arts and to emulate them in their own works. This tendency was made to appear the more safe and attractive since, as mentioned, many of the foreign masters were hailed in the USSR as "progressive public figures." A more relaxed attitude toward Western art and writing was also promoted by a number of Soviet authors and scholars of the older generation. Thus, the leading novelist Leonid Leonov wrote in his obituary of Hemingway that "many of his new techniques will find their investigators, interpreters, and followers."[49] P. N. Berkov, an eminent literary scholar, ironically suggested that the alleged contempt of the Soviet public for modernistic writing was not entirely spontaneous.[50] Another veteran novelist, Konstantin Paustovskij, decried the hysteria over some young Soviet people's infatuation with modernism declaring it merely a harmless, if silly, eccentricity.[51] Addressing a 1963 meeting of European writers in Leningrad, Ilya Ehrenburg deplored the

two exceptions were the historical novelist Stepan Zlobin, who pointed to the instructiveness of the novels of Balzac and, to a much lesser extent, of Zola and Maupassant (*Voprosy literatury*, No. 5, 1962, p. 159), and Lev Nikulin, an older novelist known chiefly for his stories about Soviet policemen and detectives. Nikulin replied, however, in his capacity as a member of the editorial board of *Inostrannaja literatura* and his statement did not address itself directly to the question. *Voprosy literatury*, No. 7, 1962, p. 171.

49. *Pravda*, July 4, 1961.

50. "It is surely equally unlikely that any Soviet literary scholar would maintain that the apparent revulsion on the part of the majority of Soviet readers for all kinds of Western avant-garde and anti-realistic art as a whole is also merely an accidental sum total of individual 'tastes'." B. S. Mejlax (ed.), *Xudožestvennoe vosprijatie*, 1971, p. 63.

51. *Literaturnaja gazeta*, May 20, 1959.

Soviet practice of attacking works of Western literature that were unavailable in the USSR and suggested that instead of reading "literary opinions that are based not on a familiarity with the literature proper, but only with literature about that literature," the Soviet public would be better served by translation and publication of some of the controversial books; he added, "I think that one must not be afraid of [literary] experimentation."[52]

Apparently overlooked by the optimists among the young Soviet authors and the liberal older intellectuals was that it was one thing for the Communist Party to permit scholarly debate about the artistic and intellectual impact of nineteenth-century Western Europeans on nineteenth-century Russians, and quite another matter for it to tolerate overt and even acknowledged influences of modern (and frequently living) Western writers and artists, however "progressive" in their politics, on Soviet culture. That the prerogative of exerting political influence on Soviet literature and the arts belongs to the Soviet Communist Party and to it alone is amply demonstrated by the Party's repeated refusals, over the entire span of the history of Soviet literature, to recognize a variety of literary groupings within the USSR, including those with impeccably Communist credentials, as the Party's spokesmen in artistic matters. The Communist Party's control over literature and the arts was to be not only total, but also direct.[53]

The Party's intervention began almost simultaneously with the opening up of Soviet frontiers to Western literature and the arts in the wake of Stalin's death, and its aims were not easy to attain. In essence, it sought to maintain their availability at a controlled level, while minimizing any possible harmful influences on the Soviet public and also insulating against their impact on Soviet arts and letters themselves. The warnings came early and were directed at different areas of artistic expression and also at all levels, from esoteric works to those with mass appeal. That such exhortations continue to the present attests that the dual aim of maintaining controlled

52. Ibid., August 13, 1963. Ehrenburg's predilection for the waging of *Soviet* literary and political battles through ostensible discussion of Western literature was referred to in connection with his essay on Stendhal in *Inostrannaja literatura,* No. 6, 1957. Earlier that year and in the same periodical, Ehrenburg attacked "dogmatists" whose dislike for the irreverent verse of François Villon was complemented by a feeling of spiritual kinship with the *Chanson de Roland* and *The Lay of the Host of Igor,* a medieval Russian epic that was also a great favorite during the Stalin era: "I am, of course, not referring to religion as such, but to the striving of medieval Christianity to rationalize and regulate every aspect of human endeavor, to circumscribe and regiment the world of emotions, to brand as heresy, if not downright witchcraft, not only every departure from the canon, but indeed every manifestation of critical thought." *Inostrannaja literatura,* No. 1, 1957, p. 159. The allusions to Stalinism were all too obvious.

53. The most instructive example of this policy was the Party's refusal to recognize in the early 1930s, the militantly Communist Russian Association of Proletarian Writers (known as RAPP), as its agent in literary matters. The Association was disbanded in favor of an ostensibly "neutral" Union of Soviet Writers which exists to this day and is, of course, directly controlled by the Party. For an excellent account, see Edward J. Brown, *The Proletarian Episode in Russian Literature: 1928–1932* (New York: Columbia University Press, 1953).

availability of Western literature and the arts and preventing their influence on Soviet authors and artists is not easily attained.

As early as 1957 warnings were sounded against inroads being made among Soviet composers by the "modernistic" music of the West; the occasion was the Second Congress of Soviet Composers.[54] Five years later the problem apparently remained unresolved, or so it would appear from the message addressed by the Party's Central Committee on March 27, 1962, to the Third Congress of the same organization. The danger, as the Party saw it, was twofold, but both manifestations were traced to pernicious Western influence. Soviet composers were exhorted to beware of "formalism and pathological modernistic tendencies, which reflect the decay of bourgeois art" and result in overly complex compositions. At the same time, they were told, "Soviet music is also diametrically opposed to those currents of bourgeois pseudo-art that attempt to conceal philistine pseudo-ideology in musical forms pretending to be popular and accessible."[55] Again, the warnings went at least partly unheeded. Within a year, R. K. Ščedrin, secretary of the board of the Composers' Union, inveighed once more against "reactionary trends in music," more specifically "the infatuation with dodecaphony of the present-day West" as well as "the so-called concrete, electronic, and other modernist musical idioms presented in the West as the latest vogue."[56] Himself a conductor and composer, R. K. Ščedrin was in all likelihood taking his cue from an amateur musicologist, Nikita S. Khrushchev, who just three weeks earlier had taken some time off from his other duties to give the country's musicians the benefit of his observations on serious and popular music, on social dancing, and on related matters. The Soviet Prime Minister and Secretary General of the Communist Party was addressing a meeting of musicians, writers, and artists:

> I am fond of some of the songs played by Leonid Utësov's jazz band. But there is also music that makes one sick and turns one's stomach. . . . One can get indigestion from overeating even good food, and one couldn't stand such a large portion of jazz. One felt like running away, except there was nowhere to run to. Music that cannot be understood can only cause irritation. Some people say this is because it is not understood. And there is certainly a kind of jazz that no one can understand and that is repulsive to one's ears. Some of the so-called modern dances that were imported into our country from the West are unacceptable. . . . What some people call modern dancing is just plain obscenity, frenzy, who the hell knows what to call it! . . . It appears that

54. *Sovetskaja kul'tura,* July 16, 1957.
55. *KPSS o kul'ture, prosveščenii i nauke,* 1963, pp. 309–12.
56. *Pravda,* March 27, 1963. The speaker traced some of the problems to the sudden rash of performances of such composers as Hindemith, Bartok, Stravinsky, Britten, Honegger, Poulenc, Milhaud, and Orff. Ščedrin's warnings were supported by another speaker, Aram Khachaturian.

among the younger people in the arts there are some who are trying to prove that melody has no longer any place in music, and that a "new" kind of music is now replacing it, "dodecaphony," a music of noise. It is hard for a normal person to figure out what "dodecaphony" means, but it is most likely the same thing as cacophony. Well, we are going to get rid of all this cacophonic music. Our people cannot use this rubbish in their ideological arsenal.... Our policy in art is one of resolute rejection of abstract art, of formalism and all other bourgeois distortions. This is a policy we have firmly adhered to, adhere to now, and will continue to adhere to.... The press, radio, literature, paintings, films, and plays—all these are our Party's sharp ideological weapons. And the Party will see to it that its weapons are always ready for battle and capable of striking the enemy with utmost precision. The Party will not permit anyone to dull its edge, to weaken its strength.... In literature and in the arts the Party supports only those works that serve to inspire the people to rally their forces.[57]

Just over a year later Khrushchev was removed from office. But seven years after Khrushchev's memorable and colorful address, if one is to judge by a major Soviet composer's speech, the problems remained much the same, as well as the dangers and the proposed remedies. On December 10, 1970, *Pravda* quoted Tikhon Khrennikov as warning that the real objective of the West's modernist music is to "disarm the listener spiritually, contaminate him with germs of pessimism and doubts, and thus distract him from the struggle for social progress."

The first danger signals in Soviet painting traceable to Western influences suggested a two-pronged attack. According to a message sent by the Party's Central Committee to the Congress of Soviet Artists in 1957, the menace to the "optimistic," poster-like Soviet painting came from two directions: the "formalist" (i.e., experimental and complex, including abstractionist painting) and the "naturalistic pseudo-realist," a synonym for realistic art depicting life's less joyous and seamier sides.[58] It seems that the latter tendency was suppressed quickly enough (at least on the surface), because the attacks that followed were nearly all aimed at abstract art, i.e., art that was *overtly* nonpolitical.[59] (A "fable" then circulated in the USSR told of

57. *Pravda,* March 10, 1963.
58. *Pravda,* March 1, 1957.
59. Some abstractionist and other modernist art has for a time penetrated into the USSR through the medium of *Pol'ša,* a Russian-language publication of the Polish Embassy in Moscow, a parallel, as it were, of Poland's role as an intermediary in the influx into Russia of Western European literature in the seventeenth century. After Władysław Gomułka's return to power in October 1956, Soviet-style painting quickly fell into disrepute and Polish artists reverted to Western models; quite understandably, their works were reproduced in the Embassy's Russian journal, one of seven such publications printed by Poland's Ministry of Foreign Affairs in as many languages. The reproduction of abstract paintings in *Pol'ša* was attacked in *Literaturnaja gazeta* on January 26, 1957. A rejoinder by Dorian Płoński, *Pol'ša's* editor-in-chief, emphasized that one cannot be certain who "depicts our epoch more accurately," Picasso or Gerasimov, a stalwart of Stalinist Socialist Realism. Płoński also daringly called the Soviet public's attention to the fact that the Mexican painter D. A. Siqueiros, a Communist

a one-eyed oriental potentate who wished to have his portrait painted. The first painter depicted him as he was, i.e., blinded in one eye, and was promptly beheaded for the sin of "pessimistic naturalism." The second painted the ruler with two eyes, and was banished for "embellishing reality," then the current euphemism for the excessive "optimism" of Stalinist art. Only the third painter satisfied one and all with a canvas of the monarch's perfect profile.)

In Soviet conditions, however, the *absence* of politics is itself political because it implies an unwillingness to embody *any* political message, including the one currently required by the Communist Party. Hence the ferocity of Soviet attacks on abstract art. As early as 1957 a Soviet journal wrote: "Viewed through the eyes of an abstractionist, life appears as phantasmagoric chaos. . . . Some people maintain that this is how the world is seen by man in the nuclear age. . . . This constitutes slander of millions of toilers who struggle relentlessly for democracy and socialism, for peace, and for humanity's happy future."[60] Such early warnings notwithstanding, five years later the President of the Soviet Academy of Arts, Vladimir Serov, found cause to express his grave concern over the "absurd and slavish imitation of bourgeois modernism" on the part of some Soviet painters.[61] Serov's speech was made within days after Khrushchev's notorious visit to an art exhibit during which the then undisputed leader of the Soviet state resorted to crude threats in an attempt to beat some sense into the heads of wayward Soviet painters and sculptors.[62]

Gradually, an official Soviet position crystallized: abstractionism in art was not merely an *alien* concept, but a *hostile* one, an extension of sorts of the old Soviet slogan "who is not with us is against us." On December 17, 1962, Leonid Il'ičëv, chairman of the newly formed Ideological Commission

Party member since 1929, accused Soviet painting of following "dead canons of international academicism," and cited approvingly the then much-advertised Chinese Communist slogan about the need to "let a hundred flowers bloom." Płoński's letter (as well as more attacks on Pol'ša) were printed in *Literaturnaja gazeta,* February 26, 1957. It is worth noting that unrecognized Soviet painters whose attempts to exhibit their work were repeatedly thwarted by the Soviet authorities, most recently in 1974–75, include both abstractionists and "pessimistic" realists. Oskar Rabin is perhaps the most prominent of these painters. A nonconformist Soviet painter is among the central characters in Ehrenburg's 1954 novel *The Thaw,* and such painters are also frequently described in *samizdat* literature.

60. *Sovetskaja kul'tura,* August 24, 1957.
61. *Pravda,* December 9, 1962.
62. A detailed account of Khrushchev's visit to the exhibit on December 1, 1962, can be found in Priscilla Johnson and Leopold Labedz, *Khrushchev and the Arts,* pp. 101–5. Samples of Khrushchev's art criticism include the following observations: "What's the good of a picture like this? To cover urinals with?"; "We aren't going to spend a kopeck on this dog shit"; "The people and government have taken a lot of trouble with you, and you pay them back with this shit"; "My opinion is that you can all go to hell abroad"; "Your paintings just give a person constipation"; "You are stealing from society. You are a parasite"; "Judging by these [artistic] experiments, I am entitled to think that you are pederasts, and for that you can get ten years [of prison]."

of the Party's Central Committee, delivered an address that lasted ten hours. The following excerpts are of some interest:

> We should remember as an immutable truth that art always has an ideological-political bent, that in one way or another it expresses and defends the interests of definite classes and social strata. . . . If we consider the nature of abstract art there can be no two opinions: It does not serve the interests of the working people, it does not express the mentality of the working people, it is designed to cater to the perverted tastes of the satiated.[63]
>
> Socialist Realism provides ample opportunity for a symbiosis as well as for creative competition among the most varied kinds of artists—the champions of romantic generalization, the partisans of the strictly analytical approach, and the followers of other stylistic currents within our art. The existence of this symbiosis is indispensable for the progress of Soviet literature and the arts.
>
> Does this, however, imply our support for a symbiosis and a "peaceful coexistence" of such ideologically opposed artistic trends as Socialist Realism and abstractionism, trends which in the final analysis represent not only contradictory views in aesthetics, but also contradictory positions of political and class nature?
>
> Let us make this perfectly clear. No peaceful coexistence between Socialist ideology and bourgeois ideology has ever existed in the past, nor can it ever exist. . . . The idea of coexistence in the domain of ideology constitutes in reality treason to the interests of Marxism-Leninism and of Socialism.[64]

Attacks on abstractionist art and its perils continued into 1963 and well beyond. Thus, the board of the Writers' Union went on record declaring: "Abstract art dulls human senses, promotes disgust and fear of life, and leads to a moral disarmament of the toiling masses. Abstract art benefits only the forces of anti-Communism and the bourgeoisie."[65] The Soviet Union's titular head of state Nikolai Podgorny bluntly charged that "bourgeois ideologists are attempting to utilize abstract art as a Trojan horse in efforts to undermine the strength of Marxist-Leninist ideology."[66] The controversy continued, with periodic flare-ups provided by arrests and harassment of dissident artists charged with professing abstractionist and modernist heresies. A poignant footnote was provided in the early 1970s when the immediate family of Nikita Khrushchev, the former premier who died in obscurity, discreetly commissioned a tombstone for his grave. The sculptor they chose was Ernst Neizvestny, a "modernist" denounced by the deceased Khrushchev some ten years earlier.

It was in Soviet literature, theater, and cinema that the impact of modern

63. Cited in Ibid., p. 111.
64. *Pravda,* December 22, 1962.
65. *Sovetskaja kul'tura,* April 11, 1963.
66. *Pravda Ukrainy,* April 10, 1963.

Western culture was felt most strongly and provoked most objections. Occasionally, the relationship between the cause and effect was not only clear but also immediate. Thus, according to Leonid Il'ičëv, the Party's ideological chief referred to earlier, "It is worth noting that the so-called 'original' [Soviet] plays frequently make their appearance following the departure of some visiting foreign artists."[67] Similarly clear, in the estimate of the authorities, was the connection between the newly established cultural contacts with the West and the watering down of the ideological content in certain Soviet films: " 'A civic subject? Forget it. No picture based on this kind of script is going to win a prize at Cannes or in Venice.' Catering to the tastes of foreign audiences, worrying whether a motion picture will please the spectators at bourgeois [film] festivals—these things, alas, are still in evidence in the world of the [Soviet] cinema."[68] In an obvious reference to the *Voprosy literatury* questionnaire that was discussed earlier, the staunchly Stalinist writer Anatolij Sofronov declared: "It is disquieting that some of the young [Soviet] authors thoughtlessly copy stylish fads. When discussing their mentors, some of these authors point predominantly to foreign writers, such as Hemingway and Remarque, oblivious to the fact that the *Weltanschauung* of these gifted writers is diametrically opposed to that of our people."[69]

If in the idioms of music and painting alien influences had to be "unmasked," hidden as they were by the puzzling façade of unfamiliar form, in literature, drama, and film the task of exposing alien ideological overtones was considerably simpler. Some of the dangers were plain to see. Thus, foreign influences were blamed for the fact that certain Soviet literary works suggested that in the USSR, too, there existed a "generation gap" and even social injustice; Soviet critics objected to this projection to the USSR of social problems that allegedly existed in capitalist conditions alone.[70] A more complex, and potentially more menacing phenomenon was discerned by Aleksandr Čakovskij, then the editor-in-chief of *Literaturnaja gazeta* and subsequently of *Inostrannaja literatura*. It appears that some Soviet

67. *Sovetskaja kul'tura,* January 10, 1963.

68. Ibid., April 25, 1963.

69. *Komsomol'skaja pravda,* May 8, 1963. Similar apprehensions had been expressed more than a year earlier by Georgij Markov, secretary of the Writers' Union. Markov had referred to Remarque alone. *Literaturnaja gazeta,* December 23, 1961.

70. Objections to the idea that Soviet society is not immune to the problem of a "generation gap" were voiced by the Stalinist novelist Leonid Sobolev (*Literaturnaja Rossija,* April 5, 1963) and were also incorporated in the June 21, 1963, resolution of the Party's Central Committee (*Xudožestvennaja literatura, literaturovedenie, iskusstvo,* April–June 1963, p. 7). On April 10, 1963, *Izvestija* printed a letter to the editor protesting Vladimir Vojnovič's story "I Want to Be Honest," which had appeared in the February 1963 issue of *Novyj mir.* The writer of the letter objected to Vojnovič's insinuations that cheats and careerists flourished in Soviet society, that attempts to expose and uproot them were doomed to failure and that "in our society, *too,* honest people and truth itself find it hard going." Emphasis added.

authors had become attracted to the literary device of "stream of consciousness" which, although venerable enough in the West, was a novelty in the USSR. Čakovskij proceeded to explain the anti-Marxist essence of the "stream of consciousness" technique as a basically Freudian view of reality, in which events follow each other without any *social* logic.[71] Above all, there was the very real danger that if the traditional political categories and criteria employed in Soviet literary criticism were to be replaced, under Western influence, with nonideological ones, this would deal a heavy blow to Soviet literature's political usefulness. As Aleksandr Čakovskij wrote elsewhere, "Articles in our journals abound in such terms as 'humane,' 'emotional alienation,' 'self-contained image,' 'talent as the sole artistic criterion,' 'advanced ideas,' 'lyric emotion,' 'opposition to dogma' and so on, and so forth."[72] Another critic deplored irresponsible talk about "contemporary style" and the potentially destructive idea that in this nuclear age a uniform style in the arts is in order, making ideological considerations irrelevant.[73] President Podgorny also assailed idle chatter about "abstract truth," "universal humanism," "objectivity in literature and the arts," and "absolute freedom."[74] To cite again from Leonid Il'ičëv's marathon speech of December 17, 1962:

> We have no right to underestimate the danger of subversion by bourgeois ideology in the sphere of literature and art, just as in other spheres. The idea of coexistence in the sphere of ideology is in actuality nothing but betrayal of the interests of Marxism-Leninism, of the interests of socialism. And in art we sometimes encounter a retreat from class and Party positions, we sometimes encounter instances of reconciliation with bourgeois ideology. This finds expression, in particular, in a false interpretation of "human nature," in the propaganda of abstract humanism, a kind of evangelical all-forgiveness, as though there were no hostile classes, no capitalism in the world, and no struggle for communism! . . . In our era what is genuinely humanist is what is Communist, since it is in Communist society that the fullest development of the individual takes place, and all the best human traits and qualities are manifested.[75]

Some of the perils discussed above may appear somewhat abstract and even farfetched to a non-Soviet observer (though emphatically not to a Soviet one). An aspect of the ideological erosion of Soviet literature and the

71. *Pravda,* May 7, 1963. It is not impossible that some Soviet authors found the "stream of consciousness" technique appealing precisely for that reason. When social events appear devoid of logic, it may be tempting to describe them as a series of random accidents rather than to impose on them an artificial "social" logic.
72. *Komsomol'skaja pravda,* March 29, 1963.
73. Ivan Anisimov in *Literaturnaja gazeta,* March 30, 1963.
74. *Pravda Ukrainy,* April 10, 1963.
75. Cited in Priscilla Johnson and Leopold Labedz, *Khrushchev and the Arts,* p. 115.

arts by Western cultural imports that may be viewed with some justification as a clear and present danger was the mounting evidence that books, plays, and films by "progressive" Western authors and artists denouncing the criminality of war (indeed, their antimilitarism was often used as a yardstick of their "progressive" nature) promoted pacifist moods among Soviet writers and filmmakers. Some aspects of the problem were discussed earlier;[76] we shall recall here one historical incident that may shed additional light on this clearly sensitive issue.

In 1929 Maxim Gorky sought Stalin's advice as to whether a special journal tentatively entitled *On War (O vojne)* should be launched. In his reply of January 17, 1930, Stalin expressed his opposition to the idea on the grounds that general problems relating to "imperialist" wars (i.e., wars involving capitalist states alone) should be discussed in Soviet political journals already in existence. Stalin's letter continued:

> As to war stories, they will have to be published with great discrimination. The book market is filled with a mass of literary tales describing the "horrors" of war and inculcating a revulsion against *all* war (not only *imperialist,* but *every other kind* of war). These are bourgeois-pacifist stories, and not of much value. We need stories which will lead the reader from the horrors of *imperialist* war to the necessity of getting rid of the *imperialist* governments which organize such wars. Besides, we are not against *all* wars. We are against imperialist wars, as being counter-revolutionary wars. But we are *for* liberating, anti-imperialist, revolutionary wars, despite the fact that such wars, as we know, are not only not exempt from the "horrors of bloodshed" but even abound in them. It seems to me that Voronsky's line in wanting to launch a campaign against the "horrors" of war differs very little from the line of the bourgeois pacifists.[77]

Essentially, the controversy over the treatment of military themes in Soviet literature and films (or, more precisely, a campaign of attacks: no dissenting views were allowed to appear in print) that erupted in 1963 was a result of the dilemma that was formulated in Stalin's letter to Gorky three decades earlier. Stalin was correct in warning that the dissemination of Western antiwar literature within the USSR might produce some undesirable effects. What he could not foresee was that the requirements of a foreign policy of "peaceful coexistence," of various Soviet-sponsored "peace campaigns" (some of them launched within his lifetime and with his bless-

76. See chapter 5.
77. J. V. Stalin, *Works* (Moscow: Foreign Languages Publishing House, 1955), Vol. XII, p. 182. Italics in the original. Aleksandr Voronskij was editor of the influential literary journal *Krasnaja nov'*. For an excellent account of his career and a penetrating analysis of the journal's role in Soviet literary and intellectual history, see Robert A. Maguire, *Red Virgin Soil: Soviet Literature in the 1920's* (Princeton, N. J.: Princeton University Press, 1968).

ings), as well as of the Soviet cultural diplomacy inaugurated by his successors would make wide dissemination of antimilitaristic Western "war stories" unavoidable. As a result, in 1963 the source of the pacifist mood—
Western books and films disseminated in the USSR—could not simply be
removed; at best, it could be contained. The aim of the campaign was to
inoculate Soviet writers and artists against the danger of contamination.

On March 29, 1963, Aleksandr Čakovskij, the editor of *Literaturnaja
gazeta,* addressed a session of the board of the Union of Soviet Writers:

> It has become chic in our literary circles to talk of "de-heroicizing." G.
> Baklanov's tale "An Inch of Ground" and Ju. Bondarev's "The Last Salvos"
> are most frequently singled out as successful examples of the application of
> the "theory of de-heroicizing." . . .
>
> As is commonly known, the theory (if the term must be used) of "de-
> heroicizing" made its debut in world literature after the Imperialist War
> [World War I—MF], which was an unjust war. It was a reaction of progres-
> sive-thinking authors to deceitful official bourgeois propaganda which embel-
> lished that war with a halo of "heroism." It was that which begot Barbusse's
> *Under Fire,* Remarque's *All Quiet on the Western Front,* and Hemingway's
> *A Farewell to Arms.* All that was quite natural and legitimate. *But how can
> one speak of "de-heroicizing" with reference to the Great Patriotic War [World
> War II—MF]? Utterly ridiculous!*
>
> On second thought, one must not dismiss it so easily as merely ridiculous.
> We are dealing here with something far more complex. Politically mature
> people will not fail to discern that all this talk about "de-heroicizing" has the
> same roots, the same "underpinnings," as the notorious debates of 1956–57
> about the proper nature and function of Soviet literature. We may as well be
> frank about it. *All this critical verbiage about "de-heroicizing" and "re-evalua-
> tion" of the concept of "modernity" conceals that same tendency which would
> emasculate literature of its value as propaganda, of its function as an active
> helper of the Party.* [78]

In Čakovskij's estimate, the danger transcended even that of spreading
pacifist moods among the population; the very function of Soviet literature
was at stake. Yet the other pronouncements in the campaign restricted
debate to the pacifist issue alone. The same meeting was addressed by Jurij
Žukov, a noted commentator on foreign affairs:

> Quite a few works have recently appeared in our country that deal with the
> war in what I would call a depressing manner. One reads these works and
> at times one cannot comprehend how we could have won that war. War
> appears in these writings as something quite unsavory, as one continuous
> human slaughter. We must tell the truth about the heroic deeds of our people
> in the Patriotic War [World War II—MF]. Not only about the way our

78. *Komsomol'skaja pravda,* March 29, 1963. Italics added.

brothers died but also why they died, and how, with their deaths, they smashed Fascism.[79]

Another speaker, a much decorated war veteran, a Hero of the Soviet Union, expressed his indignation over the Soviet film *At Your Doorstep (U tvoego poroga);* in that film a Soviet soldier says that "war is not a proper condition of man, it's unnatural." The veteran called this observation "altogether in the spirit of Remarque," adding that the Soviet soldier in the film "should have known that there are different kinds of war, and that our army fights sacred and just wars. . . . That soldier's every gesture and every utterance are filled with gloom, despair, and hopelessness, as if these were not Soviet people, but heroes of the 'lost generation' who found their way into the film from the embittered pages of Remarque."[80]

The campaign was resumed in mid-June of the same year. The level of the attack was escalated; the audience was the Party's Central Committee, and the speaker its ideological chief Leonid Il'ičëv:

> Respect for heroic deeds of the past is indispensable if one is to be inspired to new heroic deeds. Still, in some of the artistic works dealing with the Great Patriotic War [World War II—MF], the central protagonists are not that war's true heroes, but martyrs who die purposeless deaths. The film *At Your Doorstep* and [Bulat Okudžava's] story *Good Luck, Schoolboy! [Bud' zdorov, školjar!]* offer good examples. It is the war's travail and perils that capture our attention in these works. Soviet warriors appear more often as victims than as conscious and courageous fighters against Fascism.
>
> True, the war was hard. But it was first and foremost a great patriotic exploit of the people, of Soviet soldiers steadfast in their devotion to patriotic duty, in their loyalty to the socialist homeland. Depicting them as martyrs is an insult to the memory of the Soviet people's heroism.[81]

Two days later the same newspaper printed an article by General A. A. Episev, head of the Chief Political Administration of the Soviet Army and Navy. The general rebuked unnamed Soviet authors and filmmakers for "belittling the Soviet people's courage and heroism and concentrating primarily on their human weaknesses." Wrote Episev: "Yes, war is indeed the greatest evil. But the war was forced on our people against their will. In

79. *Literaturnaja gazeta,* March 30, 1963.
80. *Komsomol'skaja pravda,* March 31, 1963. According to a Western source, the film was first banned, then released again after much cutting. Harry T. Moore and Albert Parry, *Twentieth-Century Russian Literature* (Carbondale and Edwardsville: Southern Illinois University Press, 1974), p. 146. Other Soviet films criticized for "pacifist overtones in their treatment of military events" included *Peace Unto Him Who Enters* and *Ivan's Childhood. Pravda,* March 23, 1963.
81. *Pravda,* June 19, 1963. Bulat Okudžava's 1961 novella *Bud' zdorov, školjar!,* written in the form of a diary of a very young soldier during World War II, was criticized in the press for "the infantile psychology of its central protagonist." KL, Vol. V (1968), p. 414. The pacifist tone of Okudžava's story is strongly reminiscent of postwar Western writing.

creating their works the authors must, whatever the circumstances, consider the nature of the struggle, the need for our people to defend their freedom and independence with arms in hand."[82]

In February 1964 General Epišev reminded a meeting of Soviet writers: "The note of pacifism that was sounded in a number of books, films, and paintings dealing with the Great Patriotic War [World War II—MF] has been deservedly condemned" as has "the misguided and essentially harmful tendency to belittle the heroism of military events"; the general appealed to the writers to avoid in their works undue emphasis on "pain and suffering, confusion and horrors." The writers were then addressed by the country's Minister of Defense, Marshal Rodion Malinovsky. The Marshal minced no words. After recalling that the Soviet armed forces must be ready "to frustrate any sudden attack by an aggressor and to deliver an instantaneous, crushing retaliatory blow," he turned to artistic matters:

> In certain literary works, in paintings and in films one discerns motifs of pacifism and an abstract rejection of war. Is it right to portray the war that our people fought as nothing but an accumulation of horrors and suffering, to drag into the foreground—and with every naturalistic detail at that—confused little men? Such a one-sided approach to an important theme must be rejected.... We have no right to mechanically graft the ideas of Remarque onto our creative work, thus robbing it of the genuine heroism that is characteristic of our life.[83]

Marshal Malinovsky's words were apparently effective. When a year later, in 1965, on the occasion of the twentieth anniversary of the end of World War II, the scholarly journal *Voprosy literatury* circulated a questionnaire among Soviet authors writing on military subjects, none mentioned Remarque. Konstantin Simonov, a novelist secure in his position, did mention Hemingway but referred to the "delight" of reading *For Whom the Bell Tolls,* not the "pacifist" *A Farewell to Arms.*[84] On the other hand, Leonid Pervomajskij, a writer less secure than Simonov (Pervomajskij is a Jew writing in Ukrainian), dutifully volunteered the observation that Heinrich Böll's novels could not be written by a Soviet author not only on account of differences in their kinds of talent, but first and foremost because of a radically different vision of the world, a vision independent of the writer's personal will."[85] Most of the responding Soviet authors specializing in military subject matter prudently avoided all mention of Western writing.

82. *Pravda,* June 21, 1963.
83. *Krasnaja zvezda,* February 9, 1964.
84. *Voprosy literatury,* No. 5, 1965, p. 52. It is worth noting that Simonov was praising a book that at the time had not been published in the USSR. A censored Russian translation of *For Whom the Bell Tolls* appeared in 1968. See chapter 1.
85. *Voprosy literatury,* No. 5, 1965, p. 43.

Aleksandr Čakovskij's linking of the problem of "de-heroicizing" to the broader question of the nature and function of Soviet literature was apt; it may well be that his argument was not pursued at the time of the campaign against "pacifism" in Soviet literature and the arts in order not to complicate an important issue. Openly didactic, Soviet writing, theater, and films attempt to inspire their audiences with a desire to emulate the exploits of their active central protagonist, the Positive Hero.[86] Čakovskij was therefore correct in viewing the slogan of "de-heroicizing" as a challenge to the basic attributes of Soviet literature and the arts and to their political role in Soviet society.

Germs of the "de-heroicizing" theory were always present in Soviet culture in view of the availability, indeed the inclusion in the school curricula, of the classics of Western writing and, above all, of Russia's own literary masterpieces of the nineteenth century. In contrast to the "heroic" neoclassical period that preceded it, Russian authors of the nineteenth century, when faced with the problem of adjudicating in their works conflicts between the high and the mighty (and the "larger" interests they presumably represented) and the humble and the oppressed, almost invariably cast their sympathies with the latter. Among those writers' proudest creations is the endless gallery of insignificant clerks, martyred peasants, bullied women, tyrannized children, frightened lovers, helpless intellectuals, and doomed rebels. No matter that some of them were (paradoxically, in the estimate of *liberal* critics) "superfluous men"; this did not affect their claims to their creators' sympathies, or those of the Russian reading public.

There can also be no doubt that the call for "de-heroicizing" Soviet literature and the arts that was sounded in the late 1950s and early 1960s was directly and intimately linked to the spectacular, if only partial, demythologizing of the memory of the "greatest hero of all time," the only recently venerated Joseph Stalin. The "supreme hero's" downfall was dramatic and visible to millions. Not only were many of his teachings denounced and renounced. His body was removed from the mausoleum where it had briefly reposed next to Lenin's, and throughout the vast country his monuments were torn down. Thus, the impetus for the "de-heroicizing" tendency can probably be traced primarily to events and conditions within the USSR proper. Nevertheless, the influence of Western writing and the arts must be viewed as an important contributing factor. The impact of Western films is evident, for instance, in the following comments by two leading figures in the Soviet cinema. When asked in 1961 whether he had

86. A thorough and stimulating discussion of the subject with reference to both Soviet literature and its pre-Soviet Russian antecedents is found in Rufus W. Mathewson, Jr., *The Positive Hero in Russian Literature* (New York: Columbia University Press, 1958).

learned anything from the emphatically "anti-heroic" cinema of Italian neo-realism, the Soviet film director Grigorij Chukhrai answered, "Yes, absolutely. . . . The Italian neo-realists were not afraid of showing dirt and dilapidated walls and rags in their films. Life as they show it is hard and full of deprivations, but this background only accentuates the beauty of man."[87] A year later a similar query elicited this answer from the late Mikhail Romm: "I know our youth. I know the impression created by the Italian films. I can underline that this influence was real!"[88] Romm was quick to add that Italian neo-realism "was very close to the Italian Communist Party," and so it was. That, however, did not make its influence on the Soviet cinema, or the impact of its literary counterparts on Soviet writing, any more welcome to the Soviet Establishment.

Among the first to sense the danger was the late Vsevolod Kočetov, then the country's foremost literary exponent of die-hard Stalinist loyalism: "I would say that the worst [Soviet] films and books are produced not just because of ignorance of our people's life. *Rather, they are most often the consequence of a desire among some of us to portray life in the manner in which this is done in the bourgeois West. . . . Undue emphasis on details and failure to discern behind them the essential, heroic features of our people's life result in a distortion of the truth and in forsaking of the method of Socialist Realism.*"[89] In 1962 severe criticism was leveled at Jurij Bondarev's new novel *Silence (Tišina);* Bondarev's transgressions included excessive "de-heroicizing" of the Stalin era, i.e., failure to depict, side-by-side with the darker aspects of the period (descriptions then common in Soviet writing), some of its "heroic" features as well. Thus, one conservative literary journal accused Bondarev of creating a number of "un-heroic" characters including a successful cynic and an eccentric weakling incapable of resisting evil; this was traced to Bondarev's attempts to imitate such living Western authors as Böll, Remarque, Priestley, and Braine.[90] Another journal blamed Remarque alone, but offered some fatherly advice: "The journal version of the novel *Silence* requires some very thorough rewriting."[91]

Attacks on "de-heroicizing" multiplied in the spring of 1963, in the wake of Khrushchev's speech to Soviet artists and writers, referred to earlier in

87. *Izvestija,* July 9, 1961.
88. Cited in Priscilla Johnson and Leopold Labedz, *Khrushchev and the Arts,* p. 100. Among the motion pictures singled out by Romm as "great and unforgettable masterpieces" were Germi's *The Railwaymen* and three films by De Sica, *The Bicycle Thief, Two Coins in the Fountain,* and *Rome, Eleven O'Clock.* Ibid., p. 99.
89. *Pravda,* October 31, 1961. Emphasis added. Ironically, Kočetov's Stalinist address was delivered at the Twenty-Second Congress of the Communist Party, which was the apex of the de-Stalinization drive.
90. *Oktjabr',* No. 9, 1962, pp. 212–13.
91. *Zvezda,* No. 9, 1962, pp. 209–11. The novel had appeared in *Novyj mir,* then the leading "liberal" monthly.

this chapter. On March 30, Aleksandr Kornejčuk, a conservative play-wright of the older generation, assailed nameless young authors for their "so-called de-heroicizing and the denigration of the image of the positive hero," thus clearly linking the two issues; these, in his estimate, were incompatible with socialist ideology.[92] The author of an article in *Sovetskaja kul'tura* on April 18 complained that many of the characters sympatheti-cally portrayed in recent Soviet films were "spiritually shallow" and gener-ally worthless: "The bourgeois theory of de-heroicizing, which aims at the elimination [from the cinema] of strong memorable personages capable of serving as models for emulation by the people, has been a destructive influence on our films." On May 8, Jurij Gagarin, then an international celebrity as one of the first humans to travel in outer space, added his voice to the chorus of detractors of "de-heroicizing": "Why is it, for example, that certain young authors, such as Vasilij Aksënov, choose for heroes of their works characters that are unworthy of emulation? Not only is this abso-lutely wrong; it is even offensive."[93] A more generalized pronouncement on the subject was made three weeks later by S. P. Pavlov, first secretary of the Central Committee of the Young Communist League:

> Certain authors and cinema people have recently decided that discussion of the noble ideas of Communism is, should we say, "in poor taste." Using as an excuse the quest for "the living truth," their attention is diverted with increasing frequency to marginal people isolated from the main currents of life. In the pages of books and on cinema screens we are beginning to encoun-ter sissies and embittered old maids, moods of boredom and of despair. In motion pictures this is occasionally accompanied by [sequences of] "neo-realistic" staircases, littered courtyards, and plaintive songs with the strum-ming of a guitar.[94]

The ideological battles fought over the issue of Western influences on Soviet literature and the arts in the 1960s proved inconclusive, as attested by periodic skirmishes in the years that followed. It is obvious that we are faced here with what may be called, to use a favorite Soviet cliché, an

92. *Literaturnaja gazeta,* March 30, 1963.
93. *Komsomol'skaja pravda,* May 8, 1963. Many of Aksënov's protagonists are, in fact, cynical and disillusioned young people, exponents of the closest Soviet equivalent of the West's "youth culture"; by an amusing coincidence Aksënov, the object of the Soviet cosmonaut's attack, was the author of a novella entitled *Half-Way to the Moon.* To place in perspective the "literary" level of the polemic, Gagarin's query might well be followed up by any number of analogous questions: Is Anna Karenina worthy of emulation? Is Hamlet?
94. *Pravda,* June 21, 1963. "Plaintive songs with the strumming of a guitar" have long been considered in the USSR synonymous with petty bourgeois decadence. (One such guitar-playing "anti-hero," Prisypkin, is the central character of Mayakovsky's comedy *The Bed-bug*). For many years they were associated with the poet Sergej Esenin, whose verse, often filled with longing and despair, remained widely popular, though generally unavailable in print. The genre became fashionable again in the post-Stalin era. Its foremost composer and performer, Alexander Galich, now lives in the West.

"internal contradiction" in the Soviet cultural policies of the post-Stalin era. The dissemination—however selective and controlled—of contemporary Western writing and art, and praise—however guarded and qualified—of its "progressive" features clearly involve the risk that some Soviet authors and artists will choose them as their models. Assuming the inevitability of a degree of continued Western influence on some Soviet authors and artists (influences which, as pointed out, often converge with those of Russia's own prerevolutionary cultural heritage), one can safely predict that the Party will continue to insure that the country's artistic intelligentsia receives regular booster shots of ideological vaccine to immunize it to various strains of Western heresy. Of the continued need for such sanitary measures there can be little doubt; after all, what is perfectly obvious to Communist functionaries may not be entirely apparent to rank-and-file Soviet novelists and filmmakers, to say nothing of ordinary readers. It does require a degree of dialectical skill to understand that Kurt Vonnegut's and Joseph Heller's American soldiers were justified in hating the war, but not so Soviet soldiers in Soviet novels, even though both armies were simultaneously fighting Hitler. Similarly, some mental agility is needed to comprehend that it is praiseworthy to have Alan Sillitoe describe the hovels of Britain and for Alberto Moravia to portray the slums of Italy, but that portraying decaying Soviet tenements is wrong, even though the Soviet authorities remain committed to providing the country with better housing. A measure of polemical legerdemain is a must to maintain a delicately balanced double standard in evaluating essentially parallel material and attitudes in Western and Soviet writing and the arts. And even assuming these talents, the effectiveness of the effort, particularly in its impact on the Soviet public, is very much open to question.

Grave misgivings about the possible impact of Western cultural imports on the Soviet public began to be expressed almost immediately after the adoption of the new policy of closer cultural contacts with the West in the aftermath of Stalin's death. As early as 1956 leaders of the Young Communist League spoke of the pressing need to expose "the pernicious nature of the culture of imperialism."[95] Then, in 1957, a concerted drive was launched to combat the alarming inroads rapidly made by contemporary West European and American plays on the repertories of Soviet theaters, a process made all but inevitable by the incredible devastation wrought on Soviet drama by the literary policies during Stalin's declining years. In their eagerness to bring back to the theaters audiences who had stayed away even from good performances of the Socialist Realist potboilers of the late 1940s and

95. *Sovetskaja Belorussija,* December 22, 1956.

early 1950s (while patronizing revivals of the Russian classics), Soviet theatrical directors and administrators seized on the opportunity to enliven their repertories with recent hits from London, Paris, and New York that seemed, ideologically, harmless enough. Public response was enthusiastic; the cultural bureaucracy was less than elated.

An authoritative pronouncement on the subject of Western plays in Soviet theaters (with some general observations on imported films and translated books) appeared in *Literaturnaja gazeta* on January 3, 1957; the author was Boris Izakov, a prominent commentator on cultural contacts with foreign countries.[96] Izakov took exception to two misconceptions allegedly common in the Soviet literary milieu: "The first is that any [Western] author not directly associated with reactionary pronouncements is *ipso facto* progressive, and that any work depicting ordinary people rather than the bourgeois upper classes is thus democratic. Occasionally our critics are overly generous in awarding such labels as 'progressive' and 'democratic' without adequate justification." Thus, in Izakov's view, there is no such thing as innocent, harmless reading and theater: these serve as a desensitizing narcotic (an opiate for the people?). "It is a mistake," Izakov intoned, "to consider such books, plays, and films merely shallow and superfluous. They are ideologically hostile to us. The avalanche of such materials is part and parcel of the bourgeoisie's cultural offensive." Turning to specifics, Izakov unequivocally assailed the staging in the USSR of Frederick Knott's *Dial M for Murder* and Agatha Christie's *Witness for the Prosecution* as "profoundly alien and ideologically hostile." Marc-Gilbert Sauvajon's French comedy *Tapage nocturne* was dismissed as trash; its portrayal of an immoral capitalist was not accepted by Izakov as adequate compensation. Izakov was also outraged by the publication of a "bloated novel" by Daphne du Maurier, and concluded by warning that translators of Western writing should not forget their "political responsibilities." The campaign against "alien" and "hostile" Western literature and drama continued through 1957 and 1958.[97] Similar, though less spectacular, pronouncements on their perils were also made in the years that followed.

Plays new to the Soviet repertory were not the only ones that required

96. For Boris Izakov's comments on Howard Fast's break with the Communist movement, see chapter 8.

97. Thus, on June 18, 1957, *Sovetskaja kul'tura* assailed Sauvajon's comedy, Knott's thriller, and an old operetta, *A Ball at the Savoy,* as carriers of "bourgeois morality" and cautioned that "ideologists of the bourgeoisie are attempting to disseminate views that are alien to us and to defame our way of life and our Socialist form of government, utilizing to this end their literature and art, their radio and the press." The Party Central Committee's theoretical journal denounced translated Western plays recently performed on the Soviet stage: "Frequently such plays advance the message of harmony among different social classes, extol 'kind' and 'humane' capitalists, and propagate loose morals." *Kommunist,* No. 3 (February 1958), pp. 101–9.

close scrutiny. In the post-Stalin years repeated expressions of concern were voiced in the press over "attempts at a distortion of the ideological and aesthetic message of the classics masquerading as so-called 'new reading.' "[98] One such attempt involving a planned revival of Shakespeare's *Richard III,* thwarted in time by the authorities, was discussed earlier.[99] The stratagem was described in 1968 by Sergej Mixalkov, an orthodox poet and playwright:

> It is hardly a secret that certain theatrical directors stage productions which —however original otherwise—contain quite arbitrary interpretations of the classics, thus provoking an unhealthy agitation among spectators—I said spectators, not the public. It is not the originality of the play's staging that provokes this agitation. This is caused by the political overtones of the modernized lines in the characters' parts that are being addressed directly at the spectators and are aimed at the politically immature. Even if not deliberate and done merely for the sake of cheap theatrics, it bespeaks political and social irresponsibility.[100]

Understandably, Soviet sources are reticent about disclosing concrete instances of undesirable social phenomena directly traceable to the more permissive attitude toward Western cultural imports during the post-Stalin era; there may be a parallel here with the Soviet press policy of systematically suppressing news about traffic accidents, epidemics, and even natural calamities. Nevertheless, occasional items do slip through, and an attempt at piecing them together may be worthwhile.

98. *Pravda,* November 13, 1970.

99. See chapter 1.

100. *Literaturnaja gazeta,* April 3, 1968. Occasionally, such "modernized" interpretations of national classics have serious consequences. It cannot be excluded that Mixalkov's awareness of the peril of politically reinterpreted classics was heightened by events that had occurred in neighboring Poland three months earlier. In January 1968, at performances in Warsaw of a stage adaptation of Adam Mickiewicz's *Forefather's Eve,* the nineteenth-century poem's anti-Russian lines were demonstratively applauded by the audience. The play's closing signalled the beginning of an "anti-Zionist" purge, and ultimately also brought about the downfall of Władysław Gomułka, Poland's leader since 1956.

An interesting, if less dramatic, report of a "modernized" reception of a classic came from Hungary in the summer of 1957, only a few months after the Soviet suppression of the Hungarian revolution. As reported by *Delmagyarorszag* (Szeged) on June 16, 1957: "It has often happened that reactionary forces have tried to place classics of world and Hungarian literature in the service of their political machinations. That is exactly what took place during the performance of [Beethoven's] *Fidelio* in the National Theater of Szeged. Performance after performance, there were groups among the audience who used this glorious masterpiece of Beethoven to stage demonstrations which could not be misunderstood." The manager of the opera house of Hungary's second largest city was surprised that an opera about a revolutionary's successful struggle against oppressors should have provoked such reactions: "All I can say is that perhaps at a time when the people's sentiments were stirred up by counterrevolutionary and fake democratic slogans, the choice of the opera was not very fortunate." Furthermore, "According to *The New York Times* (July 10, 1957, p. 3) the manager of the theater told newspapermen that now 'the real historical background of the opera' would be explained to the audiences. 'In addition, we shall change a few scenes,' he said." *East Europe* (Vol. VI, No. 9, September 1957), p. 41.

That translated Western literature is widely read among young people, and that among college students in particular it is the most popular category of books, were statistically documented in chapter two. Indeed, to cite Sergej Mixalkov:

> Alarming signals are coming from schools and institutions of higher learning. It happens that pupils in the senior grades and even students in philological faculties know more about the problems of the theater of the absurd, about the novel without a hero, about all possible contemporary, bourgeois, reactionary trends in literature and the arts in the West than about the past and present of the literature of their own motherland.[101]

One need not take Mixalkov's testimony on faith; still, it confirms what is suggested by statistical evidence, namely that translated Western writing is read, at least in part, at the expense of Soviet and prerevolutionary Russian literature. Complementing this infatuation with Western writing was a widespread fascination with such cultural and quasi-cultural imports as jazz, rock-and-roll, various kinds of Western dancing, and even sartorial styles. Reported by hundreds of foreign visitors to the USSR, these "fads" were also confirmed by scores of disapproving articles in the Soviet press of the first post-Stalin decade.[102] There was, indeed, historical precedent for treating them seriously. In the eighteenth century, Peter the Great, a wise and farsighted ruler, in an effort to bring Russia closer to Europe, had promoted the wearing of Western clothes. At the same time, Western-style balls were held at the court, and attendance at these was compulsory for certain groups of the upper classes. Some picturesque descriptions of Muscovite boyars watching their daughters dance the minuet with infidel foreigners are given in Aleksej N. Tolstoy's novel *Peter the Great.* In the 1960s, conversely, traditional Russian xenophobia was extended by Party authorities even to Western costume and dances, which were judged both alien and immodest. Indeed, in 1966 the Central Committee of the Young Communist League discerned a new ideological menace, of which Western jazz, fashions, dancing—to say nothing of writing and the cinema—were early but unrecognized harbingers, namely the suggestion that there existed in the West a uniform "youth culture" that observed no class barriers; the threat,

101. *Literaturnaja Rossija,* December 19, 1969. Cited in N. N. Shneidman, *Literature and Ideology in Soviet Education,* p. 45.
102. See, for example, *Komsomol'skaja pravda,* the newspaper of the Young Communist League, April 17, April 26, and June 27, 1957; April 6, 1962; and March 22, 1963. In the latter issue the organization's first secretary S. Pavlov denounced "fools" who accost foreign visitors with pleas for "foreign rags or chewing gum" as well as "ignoramuses" attracted to twist, abstract art, and Western music. See also *Sovetskaja kul'tura,* June 25, 1957; *Izvestija,* September 28, 1958, in which infatuation with jazz was described as protracted illness curable only by "forceful public intervention"; and *Pravda,* December 3, 1962, in which concern about the popularity of jazz among the Soviet youth was expressed by Dmitri Shostakovich himself.

of course, was that the "youth culture" transcended national and political frontiers as well. To combat this heresy, the League's publishing house, Molodaja gvardija, was instructed on March 11, 1966, to exercise greater discrimination in the selection of foreign novels of adventure and science fiction, and on September 1 of the same year the journal *Rovesnik* was advised to publish more material devoted to the role of young people in class struggles abroad—in other words, to show that the young were not a homogeneous social group, but were subject to the usual divisions along class lines.[103]

Not all of the damage done by Western cultural imports was political. Foreign motion pictures, for instance, were occasionally seen as endangering stodgy Soviet morals, with the impressionable young being naturally most vulnerable to such corruption.[104] What was worse, Soviet films imitated Western models, thus compounding the amount of smut on Soviet screens. In 1957 six Soviet schoolteachers dispatched an indignant letter to the editor reporting their embarrassment over some "explicit scenes of intimacy" in a Soviet film they attended with their *eighteen-year-old* charges.[105] The schoolteachers were also shocked by two French productions, *The Charterhouse of Parma* and *The Red and the Black,* probably the more so because both were based on venerable literary classics. Still, they conceded, "Perhaps that is the way they show love in the French movies, but we don't think this should be imitated."[106]

The conflict between Soviet pedagogues and the unscrupulous managers of Soviet motion picture theaters gradually escalated. In 1965, in her presidential address to a convention of the Soviet Teachers' Union, T. P. Januškovskaja demanded that certain films imported from the West be barred from Soviet screens because "they exert a corrupting influence on our young generation."[107] The most interesting report concerned a meeting of factory

103. *Komsomol i molodëžnaja pečat'.* Documenty i materialy s"ezdov i konferencij V.L.K.S.M., plenumov bjuro i sekretariata C.K.V.L.K.S.M (1919–1972). (Moscow: Molodaja gvardija, 1973), pp. 234, 239–40.
104. Adam Ulam, the Harvard political scientist, writes: "All that one can safely say 50 years after the Revolution is that a believer in Victorian middle class values can be heartened by the present scene in the USSR. In what other society are the virtues of thrift, hard work, social cohesion and discipline so greatly encouraged, prudery and decorous public manners strictly enforced, the young and intellectuals kept firmly in their place as in the land of the Soviets?" Adam Ulam, "The Price of the Revolution," *Commentary* (October 1968), p. 81. Cited in Paul Hollander, *Soviet and American Society: A Comparison* (New York: Oxford University Press, 1973), p. 147.
105. The offensive film was not named. Himself an educator, father of young daughters, and a frequent viewer of Soviet films, this writer wishes to go on record as attesting that, whatever their other failings, Soviet motion pictures provide wholesome entertainment for the entire family and, with almost no exceptions, deserve to be rated G.
106. *Komsomol'skaja pravda,* June 28, 1957.
107. *Učitel'skaja gazeta,* February 20, 1965. The problem of excessive puritanism among Soviet schoolteachers was raised in an otherwise undistinguished post-Stalin Soviet film, *And What If This Were Love? (A čto esli èto ljubov'?),* in which two teen-agers are hounded by teachers, parents, and neighbors when their relationship (which actually results in a kiss!) is

workers held in 1968; the subject of discussion was West European and American films. While some of the factual background material was clearly inserted in the newspaper account by the editors, as might also have been the case with some of the suggestions and conclusions, parts of the report appear authentic.[108] Thus, the workers commented that certain Western films were nice; they liked, for instance, *Yesterday, Today, and Tomorrow, It's a Mad, Mad, Mad World,* and *The Teacher from Vigevano.*[109] Others were a mixed bag. Thus, it was said that while *Operation St. Januarius* did satirize religion and gangsters—which was fine—it might also induce Soviet girls to start wearing skirts with shamelessly high hemlines, "above the knees." In general, the workers said, too many naked women were shown in the foreign movies, and one could now see them even in Soviet ones— obviously, an exaggeration. Finally, the workers appeared curiously conversant with the political realities of "cultural exchanges": "Frankly, we don't know the extent of ideological profit we make by showing Soviet movies abroad. All we know about that comes from very confusing accounts in the newspapers. On the other hand, all can see the harm done by some of the movies we import. So who needs such exchanges?"[110]

A strangely old-fashioned, almost anachronistic flavor pervades the Soviet complaints of the 1960s about the corrupting influence on the young of imported films: the French films encouraged immodesty and promiscuity, while the American films bred violence. The chief culprit among the latter was *The Magnificent Seven,* an American Western about Mexican peasants who hire seven *gringo* gunmen to protect them from local bandits who had been periodically raiding their village; the film strikes a subtly ironic note as it shows the *yanqui* desperados gradually becoming tamed by the gentle Mexican farmers. Still, as befits a Hollywood production about red-blooded mounted men in the neighborhood of the Rio Grande, there is a great deal of shooting. An irate Soviet parent counted more than thirty killings in the Russian-dubbed version of the film and proclaimed it as bad as the Tarzan movies of his own youth. What was worse, Soviet children and adolescents began to emulate the activities of the American cowboys on the screen (can it be that the conditioning imparted in Soviet schools to imitate "positive heroes" of books and films had backfired here?). "After leaving the motion

discovered. As one of the students notes, they are told to read books about love in literature courses and are required to discuss love in examination essays, but *falling* in love is a no-no.

108. *Sovetskaja Rossija,* April 17, 1968.

109. It should be remembered, of course, that foreign films shown in the USSR have Soviet-made Russian soundtracks and that objectionable sequences may be cut.

110. The report also noted that the Italians rejected two of the films proposed in the exchange, *Zosja* and *The Iron Flood* (the latter presumably based on Aleksandr Serafimovič's 1924 novel of the same name) and suggested similar selectiveness with regard to Western motion pictures shown in the USSR: "Now, let's have some real reciprocity here!"

picture theater, children began to reenact similar fights, resorting to weapons that could be found in the courtyards and streets. We have a son of our own. Alas, he also saw that movie and is now obsessed with the protagonists of *The Magnificent Seven.* "[111] Apparently, the incident was part of a nationwide phenomenon that gradually acquired dangerous ramifications. Three years later, in 1965, Vadim Tikunov, then the Russian Republic's Minister for the Safeguarding of Public Order, traced ̇much of the problem of juvenile delinquency to the impact on the young of imported Westerns and films about gangsters, citing in particular *The Magnificent Seven, The Black Mask, The Secrets of Paris,* and *There Was Once a Crook.* The republic's chief civil policeman proposed some stringent measures: "A blanket prohibition on the import of foreign motion pictures likely to be damaging to the upbringing of children and adolescents; the establishment of a blue-ribbon commission to consist of representatives of appropriate organizations and government agencies, which will supervise the selection and acquisition of [foreign] motion pictures."[112]

Statistical evidence cited in chapter two suggests that cognitive aspects of literature are the foremost impetus among Soviet readers, and this presumably applies also to translations of Western writing. Yet a degree of skepticism is called for here. As Ilya Ehrenburg put it, "Can it be that hundreds of millions of people read *The Red and the Black* in order to learn what French society was like at the end of the 1820s? Who will dare maintain that *Don Quixote* has been a source of agitation to mankind because it is a satire on the novels of chivalry with which Spaniards were infatuated in the sixteenth century?"[113] This is not to question the authenticity of the statistics. It is more than likely, however, that as a result of the highly utilitarian orientation of literary education in Soviet schools and of Soviet literary criticism as well, a great many respondents felt impelled to cite the most important *utilitarian* reasons, assuming other reasons to be both self-evident and of no great "scientific" importance. Such factors as emotional gratification, aesthetic appeal, to say nothing of ordinary relaxation, let alone "escape," do not rank very high on the Soviet scale of values. There is no exact Russian equivalent of the term "hobby"; it may also be significant that Moscow's central park is officially called a park "of culture and rest" and bears the name of Maxim Gorky. Unlike literary works, foreign films are not considered "high culture," and therefore Soviet re-

---

111. *Izvestija,* June 9, 1962.

112. *Izvestija,* May 28, 1965. Earlier, seeing "a lot of foreign films" and "reading a lot of Remarque" were seen as the likely roots of one cynical Soviet student's admission that his feelings of respect are restricted to "women, gold, honor and wine." Igor Družinin in *Zvezda,* No. 3, 1964. See also Conclusions and Appendix G.

113. Il'ja Erenburg, *Sobranie sočinenij v devjati tomax* (Moscow: Goslitizdat, 1965), Vol. VI, p. 136.

spondents in small towns felt no constraints about telling "scientific" inter-viewers that they attended such films for diversion and escape. Similar reasons were cited with equal frequency with reference to American West-erns and to grandiloquent love stories filmed in India, even though it is arguable that the visual settings of foreign films contain as much "factual information" as the pages of most novels.[114]

It may well be, therefore, that the purely ideological impact of the reading of translated West European and American literature is often superficial, except insofar as Western works compete successfully with the two other major categories of reading, the prerevolutionary Russian classics and So-viet writing. Assuming that the ideological benefits accruing to the Soviet cause from the reading of directly controlled and inspired Soviet literature are generally greater than those that can possibly be obtained even from a carefully selected and interpreted body of writing of Western origin, the net ideological result of the dissemination in the USSR of Western writing (and also drama, cinema, etc.) is probably negative. The negative impact is further reinforced by a number of undesirable side effects inherent in the spread of Western culture, even as efforts are being made to harness its "positive" potential and to assimilate it into the organism of Soviet society, side effects that are relatively rare in the dissemination of conventional Soviet literature.[115] Some of these factors, notably the influence of Western writing and cinema on their Soviet counterparts and consequently also on *their* audiences, were referred to earlier in this chapter and elsewhere. There are others as well.

Thus, for instance, there can be no doubt that many Soviet readers of translated Western literature and viewers of Western motion pictures are probably impressed with what must appear to them as a high standard of

114. *Kniga i čtenie v žizni nebol'šix gorodov,* 1973, p. 79. Occasionally, respondents reported that translated foreign books left them puzzled and irritated and were in any case quite irrelevant to their own experiences. To cite three examples: "What do I need foreign ones for? I live in a Soviet country. The foreign authors' ideas about life are strange to me." (engineer, college educated); "I don't read too many foreign ones. I don't like all those non-Russian names. Also there are words one cannot understand. And their names are hard—it takes you five minutes just to get one name straight. It just burdens your head" (clerical worker, some secondary school); "Foreign authors write about the capitalist way of life. Now, what can capitalism teach you? Every one of our own books does teach you something" (engineer, college educated).

115. We differentiate here between rebellious and unconventional Soviet writing that is occasionally allowed to appear in print at times of ideological permissiveness, such as Vladimir Dudincev's *Not By Bread Alone* during the first "thaw" of 1956 and Solzhenitsyn's *One Day in the Life of Ivan Denisovich* during the second of 1962, and the situation that obtains in the publication in the USSR of writing of non-Soviet origin when decisions must constantly be made about whether a *completed* work's "positive" features outweigh its "negative" factors. With Soviet literature the situation is much simpler. Living Soviet authors are pressured to revise or update their works (or are encouraged by means of financial incentives: thoroughly revised books are considered "new," with corresponding benefits in the scale of royalties), and Soviet censorship takes more liberties with books by deceased compatriots than with those written by foreigners.

living in the West.[116] Paradoxically, this problem is particularly common in works that are otherwise perfectly innocuous ideologically, such as old operettas and filmed musical comedies.[117] While it may be problematic whether rank-and-file Soviet readers would readily discern parallels between, say, abstract problems of social injustice in far-away times and distant lands and concrete issues in their own country,[118] other situations, particularly if shown in modern foreign settings, may make the formation of such analogies all but inevitable. Thus, it is difficult to conceive of a Soviet citizen who would not experience a shock of recognition while reading C. Northcote Parkinson's *Parkinson's Law* or George Mikes's "The Secret of the Success of the Civil Service" and "How to Plan a City," the more so since, while the existence of bureaucracy in the USSR is freely acknowledged and deplored, that same bureaucracy has so far successfully nipped in the bud all attempts in Soviet literature at its collective portrayal.[119] In a contrastingly serious vein, Arthur Miller's *A View from the Bridge,* which raises the painful moral problem of a police informer, was probably read eagerly in the USSR: its translation coincided with the release from concentration camps of many surviving victims of Stalin's informers and the secret police.[120]

Special problems may arise in connection with the dissemination of translated Western literature among the many ethnic minorities of the USSR (which, to reiterate, taken together now constitute close to a majority of the population). While the authorities occasionally hope to achieve spe-

116. In Deming Brown's view the fact that roughly half of all books by American authors printed in the USSR between 1917 and 1960 consisted of works that had been read in Russia before the Revolution, "also reflects political policy. From the standpoint of Party and government, it was safer to print works that described an antiquated America than to print contemporary works, which often depicted conditions of life far superior to those in the Soviet Union." Deming Brown, *Soviet Attitudes Toward American Writing,* p. 316. Professor Brown's observation is essentially true for the earlier periods in Soviet history. In the post-Stalin years such continued Soviet preferences for the older classics of Western literatures were probably also motivated by a desire to avoid books that might suggest parallels rather than contrasts—for instance works describing bureaucratized technological societies, obsolescence of traditional values (such as the work ethic, respect for elders and parents), etc.

117. On July 31, 1968, *Literaturnaja gazeta* described an imaginary Soviet citizen admiring a shining car and a luxurious house in *Sitting Pretty,* a film characterized as an inane American comedy.

118. That *sophisticated* readers from such associations may be readily seen, for instance, from the fact that a Soviet Minister of Culture saw fit to prohibit a performance of Shakespeare's *Richard III* (see chapter 1) or from the complaints about political allusions in "modernized" readings of the classics referred to earlier in this chapter.

119. No genre in Soviet literature has suffered more persecution than satire. Mikhail Bulgakov died before World War II, hounded and unpublished (several of his works were published posthumously in the 1960s); Mikhail Zoshchenko was excommunicated in 1946 for defamation of Soviet Man, dying some years later in obscurity; the works of Il'f and Petrov (such as *The Twelve Chairs* and *Little Golden Calf*) remained unpublished for much of the Stalin era; and Georgij Malenkov's 1952 appeal for Soviet Gogols and Shchedrins met, understandably, with little response. *Parkinson's Law* appeared in *Inostrannaja literatura,* No. 6, 1959, and George Mikes's stories in ibid., No. 5, 1964.

120. It appeared in *Inostrannaja literatura,* No. 4, 1957.

cific objectives by translating certain West European books into individual languages, particular undesirable local reactions can arise as a result. G. O. Zimanas, a senior official in Lithuania's Communist Party, did not go into specifics, but he did intimate in 1958 that "kowtowing to the bourgeois culture of the West" was somehow simultaneously "closely interwoven with survivals of bourgeois [Lithuanian] nationalism" as well as "cosmopolitanism."[121] Decoded from Sovietese rhetoric, this could be rephrased approximately as follows: infatuation with Western culture promotes a feeling of Lithuanian ethnic identity as well as a sense of kinship with world culture, as distinct from Soviet culture alone.

A separate, wide-reaching, and thoroughly documented instance of Western literature's "counterproductive" impact on a large body of Soviet citizens involves the spectacular revival in the 1960s of a fierce and defiant ethnic consciousness among the country's three million Jews, until then seemingly one of the most assimilated and intimidated of all Soviet ethnic communities. As a result of Soviet domestic and foreign policy considerations that need not concern us here, by 1976 over a hundred thousand Soviet Jews had been allowed to emigrate, most of them going to Israel. Conversations by this writer in 1971 with hundreds of these new arrivals revealed the singularly important role that translations of West European and American literature played in the awakening of Jewish national consciousness in the USSR. In conditions where nonfictional materials dealing with the Jewish past and present were almost totally unavailable, translations of Western fiction, poetry, and drama not only filled an emotional need, they were also avidly studied for any factual and quasi-factual information on all subjects of Jewish interest.[122] The range of authors and titles published under official Soviet auspices was exceptionally wide; it included the poetry of Heinrich Heine and *The Diary of Anne Frank, The Merchant of Venice* and Arthur Miller's *Incident at Vichy.* The single most important author in this category was Lion Feuchtwanger; a Soviet textbook printed in the 1960s saw fit to warn students against the "Jewish nationalism" of several of the German novelist's works.[123] Printed Soviet editions were gradually supplemented with illegally circulated unauthorized translations of "numerous novels."[124] Among these were James Michener's *The Source,* Leon Uris's

121. *Voprosy filosofii,* No. 1 (February 1958), pp. 27–38. The phenomenon was also linked to "denigration of the cultures of Soviet peoples."
122. The overall findings of the interviews are summarized in Maurice Friedberg, *Why They Left: A Survey of Soviet Jewish Emigrants* (New York: Academic Committee on Soviet Jewry, 1972).
123. See chapter 7.
124. Roman Rutman, "Jews and Dissenters: Connections and Divergences," *Soviet Jewish Affairs,* Vol. III, No. 2 (1973), p. 32. Rutman, formerly a leading figure in the Jewish movement in Moscow, arrived in Israel late in 1972. He is now on the staff of the School of Engineering at Tel Aviv University.

*Exodus,* and Howard Fast's *My Glorious Brothers.*[125] The unifying feature of the three novels by living American authors was their "Zionist" subject matter: ancient Judea in Fast's, the rise of the modern state of Israel in Uris's, and a combination of these in Michener's. Of the three, Leon Uris's *Exodus* was the most widely read and had the greatest impact. According to Leonard Schroeter, an American lawyer who spent several years in Israel as a senior government official dealing with the problems of Jewish immigrants from the USSR:

> The enormous significance of *Exodus* to the growth and stimulation of the Jewish movement [in the USSR] can hardly be overstated. It has been corroborated again and again by Soviet Jews in the USSR and Israel, and by visitors to the Soviet Union. If ever a book helped make a revolution, the Uris novel about the creation of the Jewish state can be said to have done so. The stories of how *Exodus* went into *samizdat* are varied, but they may all be true, since ideas and tactics in a great movement often develop spontaneously and independently in different places at approximately the same time. . . . In prison camps, one way the inmates occupy their non-working hours is by telling stories. A man with a good memory and a wide reading background may provide the major cultural activity for his fellow-inmates. *Exodus,* as a story, was related in this fashion. Another inmate, impressed with the story, which he had heard a number of times, wrote it from memory when he got out, and in course of time this appeared in 70 to 80 pages in *samizdat* form. The *samizdat* story created a stir, particularly among Zionist groups. Not long after the first version appeared, a second (Zionist) one was issued, deliberately omitting any references to Kitty or romance, and omitting anything not supportive of Zionist ideology. Still later, a third version appeared. This was a translation from the complete English text.[126]

Examples of what the Soviet Establishment would view as instances of "positive" and "injurious" impact of Western literature and the arts on the Soviet social fabric could, of course, be multiplied. At this juncture, however, some tentative general comments may be in order.

In surveying Soviet publishing and criticism of the first post-Stalin decade against the background of the preceding years, the first observation that suggests itself is that the similarities are much stronger than the differences and that although the range of works, authors, subject matter, and styles was significantly widened, the quantitative changes, to paraphrase a Marxist formula, were not of sufficient magnitude to be described as qualitative

125. When Fast was excommunicated in the USSR in 1957, he was, somewhat incongruously, charged with Zionism. A decade later his books were to play a major role in the conversion to Zionism of thousands of Soviet Jews. See chapter 8.

126. Leonard Schroeter, *The Last Exodus* (New York: Universe Books, 1974), pp. 65–66. In Uris's novel, Kitty is a non-Jewish American who does not entirely understand or share the patriotic fervor of her Israeli lover. The Zionist *samizdat* version of *Exodus* suppressed the story for reasons of ideological purity.

ones. The essential features of Soviet publishing and criticism, to say nothing of the censorship, remained essentially stable, though at times they
became more flexible and more permissive (or less efficient?); these shifts,
in turn, could often be traced to the far greater complexity of policy and
practical factors that had now to be reckoned with; we shall return to this
subject in the Conclusions.

During the first post-Stalin decade the Soviet cultural authorities continued to be most hospitable to several categories of West European and
American writing that were discussed in earlier chapters of this study. They
welcomed and promoted old juvenile books—those that build character in
the traditional sense of the term—and those that entertain and, incidentally,
teach the young in the same time-honored wholesome manner. They reprinted on a massive scale authors who exposed the injustices of a cruel and
primitive nineteenth-century capitalism that no longer exists anywhere.
And they disseminated widely books by Party comrades from abroad,
including some whose discipline as members of the movement was questionable, and also books by friends of the USSR and critics of the bourgeois way
of life. These categories are listed here in an approximately descending
sequence of their political "safety." The position of the last group may at
first appear strange; yet it is precisely the books (and sometimes also the
personae) of living left-wing authors from the West that most often cause
concern within the Soviet Establishment and frequently also embittered
controversy. Conversely, repressive and reactionary Soviet policies in literature and the arts are a source of unending embarrassment to French and
Italian Communists, and to other Soviet apologists in the West; thus in
France, their rivals on the Left coined the slogan, *le parti communiste n'est
pas un parti de gauche, c'est un parti de l'Est.* The quip is supported by the
orthodox Communist movement's long record of bitter opposition to leftist
sectarianism, spanning well over half a century from Lenin's denunciation
of "leftist" Communism as a "pediatric disorder," an "infantile disease,"
down to the recent suspicion of West Europe's and America's New Left.

Although opinions differ as to whether Lenin's 1905 article "On Party
Organization and Party Literature" referred to Party journalism or to *belles
lettres,* regardless of Lenin's intentions the essay is treated in the USSR as
the major theoretical pronouncement by the founder of the Soviet state on
*literary* matters, and one of its major points is opposition to "bourgeois-
anarchistic individualism." Yet it is precisely manifestations of "bourgeois-
anarchistic individualism" that are most characteristic of writings by left-
wing authors in the West, including not a few nominal members of the
Communist Party. Such authors may be very critical, even implacably
hostile to what they perceive as the cruelty, selfishness, and irrationality of

capitalism. Still, their values, as expressed in their writings, are decidedly non-Soviet; that these men and women often see themselves as spiritual kin to the Soviet Union, must, one suspects, be considered *their* "internal contradictions." As a rule, books by writers of the "Old Left" (we need not consider the New Left, since its meager literary output is little published in the USSR anyway) emphasize the autonomy of the individual in his clash with hostile society, are skeptical of conventional wisdom, of man-made institutions, and often do not aspire to the acceptance on faith of their own values. Furthermore, except for those by the truly orthodox believers in Party dogma, such writings tend to oppose any authority, despise all wars, hate every nationalism, sympathize with the downtrodden as a matter of principle, and extol rebellion without an overly close scrutiny of its causes and implications. In the West, such books tend to prize spontaneity, champion sexual liberation, downgrade the work ethic, and question the validity of pride in material wealth, the public included. Every one of these attributes runs counter to Soviet practices, if not always to officially proclaimed beliefs. Therefore, wide dissemination of books and other art by Western leftists advocating such principles contributes to the erosion of Soviet values —although, as will be suggested in the Conclusions, this may be partly compensated by other considerations.

The possibility of undermining the politicized conservative aesthetic of Socialist Realism must also be weighed carefully. Hence the incongruity of seeing such devoted friends of the Soviet cause as Diego Rivera and Pablo Picasso or Bertolt Brecht and Sean O'Casey only ritualistically praised in the USSR, but not genuinely accepted, let alone pointed to as proud models for emulation by Soviet artists. Hence also the additional paradox that seemingly mutually exclusive tendencies in modern literature and the arts are assailed in the USSR with almost equal vehemence: the neo-realists of the Italian cinema for their "unselective" and undirected reflection of physical reality, and abstractionism in painting, the *nouveau roman,* and the theater of the absurd for their even more unstructured art, chaotic and open to a wide variety of interpretations and fitting none to the total exclusion of the others. To propose a revisionist heresy: it might not be entirely accidental, nor altogether incongruous that most of Communism's prophets and leaders displayed a preference for solid bourgeois literature and shied away from the revolutionary writing and art of their day. Marx's admiration for the royalist Balzac and for the ancients, Lenin's for the Russian classics, Stalin's (insofar as he was interested in the subject at all) polite nods to traditional high culture, and Khrushchev's fits of rage at modern trends in literature and the arts may all fit a pattern. Can it be that the first two intuitively envisaged a society which, ultimately, would—as all millennarian dreams—reach a stage at which no further evolution would be tolerated, while the latter actually ruled a country in which stability and order were the most prized of virtues?

The corrosive impact of "progressive" modern Western authors may even extend to the tales of their "martyrdom" in capitalist conditions that regularly adorn the pages of Soviet periodicals. They may actually confirm dissident *Soviet* writers in *their* defiance of society. It is not excluded, for instance, that the practice of *Inostrannaja literatura* and other Soviet journals of featuring previously unpublished works by Western authors directly translated from manuscripts sent in by their writers suggested to some dissident Soviet authors the idea of doing the same with *their* writings. On March 24, 1967, the critic Ja. Zasurskij informed readers of *Literaturnaja gazeta* that the American leftist author Albert Maltz, upon realizing the impossibility of getting his "anti-Fascist" *Tale of One January* printed in the United States, sent it to East Germany to be published. Can it be that Maltz's example inspired nonconformist Soviet authors to smuggle *their* manuscripts to America and to West Germany? It so happens that approximately a year or so later such materials were actually appearing in *Novyj žurnal* in New York and in *Grani* in Frankfurt-am-Main.[127]

The end of the first post-Stalin decade, which is essentially the cut-off point of the present study, marks another important development in Soviet society. By the mid-1960s, foreign writing and the prerevolutionary Russian classics ceased to be the only literature of non-Soviet origin available in the USSR, the only literary carriers of non-Soviet values and ideas. The mid sixties also mark the birth of an "unofficial" Soviet literature, much of it surprisingly apolitical in its concerns and attitudes, and "illegal" only because all unauthorized dissemination of any kind of writing is so designated in the USSR. The literary typewritten *samizdat* and the similarly disseminated *magnitizdat* tape recordings of poetry readings and songs grew in importance, variety, and scope in the decade that followed. Ultimately, they became an authentic body of what may be called Soviet counterculture.[128]

127. A suggestion that another book by Albert Maltz may have influenced Solzhenitsyn's *One Day in the Life of Ivan Denisovich* was made in chapter 7, note 192.

128. For some samples of literary *samizdat,* see Abraham Brumberg (ed.), *In Quest of Justice: Protest and Dissent in the Soviet Union Today* (New York: Praeger Publishers, 1970). Illegally circulated poetry and songs are discussed in Gene Sosin, "*Magnitizdat:* Songs of Soviet Dissent," in *Dissent in the U.S.S.R.: Politics, Ideologies, and People,* Rudolf L. Tökés (ed.) (Baltimore: Johns Hopkins University Press, 1975).

# CONCLUSIONS

The impressive expansion in 1954–64 of the publication in the USSR of translations of Western writing (and also, by the way, of editions in the original languages) affected the variety of titles and authors represented, and above all the amounts of such reading made available in Soviet bookstores. The improvement was in many cases dramatic, although as attested by the evidence cited in earlier chapters, even that was insufficient by far. A similar situation prevailed in the country's theaters and movie houses. Obviously, in Soviet conditions the more liberal attitude with regard to European, American, and other literature, drama, and films from the Western world was not a spontaneous development but reflected government policy if not, indeed, explicit directives. Yet almost from the outset, and particularly since the end of the first "thaw," of 1956, there has been a steady stream of reports in the Soviet press, and even a parallel series of official resolutions of the Central Committee, complaining in effect that the new policy has been far too successful, that too many foreign books are printed and sold, that too many Western plays are applauded by Soviet theatergoers, and that too many imported films are filling the country's movie houses. The campaign to banish ideologically objectionable Western drama, discussed in the preceding chapter, continued through 1957 and 1958; still, in 1959 Yekaterina Furtseva, soon to be named the country's Minister of Culture, emphasized that far too often Soviet theaters "stage [translated] plays portraying in false, rosy colors the bourgeois way of life."[1]

The fact that five years later (and after the "purge" of 1963) almost identical conditions were deplored and assailed by two Soviet publications on the same day offers grounds to assume that the problem was not easily resolved, that very likely a precarious compromise was reached between two or more opposed pressure groups.[2] Similarly, a resolution of the Central Committee of the Communist Party of April 5, 1958, formally charged that books of "no ideological and artistic merit, at times with a tendency that is totally unacceptable to Soviet readers" were being published on a large scale. Two examples of such reckless activity were cited: in 1956–57 alone,

1. *Izvestija,* January 30, 1959.
2. *Literaturnaja gazeta,* June 9, 1964; *Sovetskaja kul'tura,* June 9, 1964.

Conan Doyle's descriptions of the adventures of Sherlock Holmes and Dr. Watson were printed in one and a half million copies, and vast quantities of Alexandre Dumas's *Queen Margot* were shipped to the country's bookstores by several publishers at the same time.[3] Two years later, the provincial Saratov University Press, instead of publishing scholarly works (or at least books of local interest appropriate to a city on the banks of the Volga, on the fringes of European Russia), brought out two novels by Erich-Maria Remarque, *Three Comrades* and *A Time to Live and A Time to Die.*[4] A year after the exposure of the Saratov impropriety, the Belorussian State Publishing House printed H. G. Wells's *Mr. Blettsworthy on Rampole Island,* after seeing that a publisher in Moscow had printed a hundred thousand copies of the book.[5] Clearly, neither a small academic publisher nor one located in Minsk would normally dare to so openly defy a formal resolution of the Party's Central Committee. Again, it seems reasonable to assume that *other* resolutions or directives protected them from severe reprisals; we shall return to the problem momentarily. Most striking, however, was the fact that fully sixteen years after the Central Committee's expression of indignation over the publication of such "worthless" and "harmful" books as the works of Conan Doyle and Dumas's *Queen Margot,* precisely these two books were among the fewer than ten titles that were offered late in 1974 to Soviet readers in exchange for scrap paper. And again, there can be no question that this, too, had been cleared with the authorities.[6]

But why the constant irritation of Soviet authorities with the success of Western books, plays, and films among the Soviet public? Were not these, too, made available in the USSR with the blessings of the Party and the government by state-owned publishers, theaters, and movie houses? They were, of course. Apparently, however, the authorities had underestimated their appeal to the Soviet public and also overlooked the elementary fact that the amount of leisure time and money at the disposal of the Soviet citizen are finite, and that time and money spent on translations of Western books and plays and on imported films must, at least in part, come from funds and leisure previously earmarked for Soviet books, plays, and cinema. Again, complaints voiced repeatedly and at different times suggest that a multiplicity of factors involved made a speedy and satisfactory resolution of the problem difficult, if not impossible. Thus, during the 1957–58 cam-

3. *O partijnoj i sovetskoj pečati, radioveščanii i televidenii,* p. 449. The fact that the 1958 resolution was reprinted in this 1972 compilation of documents suggests, as indicated elsewhere in another connection, that it has not been repudiated. Where an earlier decision clearly contradicts a later policy, it is not as a rule republished.

4. *Izvestija,* May 26, 1960.

5. *Izvestija,* December 23, 1961.

6. The 1974 experiment in which books that are difficult to obtain, most of them Western novels, were exchanged for scrap paper was discussed in chapter 2.

paign to reduce the number of Western plays in the repertory of Soviet theaters it was explicitly pointed out on several occasions that the issue was also tied to the fact that theaters produced few Soviet plays and few Russian classics.[7] The inroads made by foreign repertory extended even to the opera. In 1963 a Soviet critic assailed Donizetti's *Lucia di Lammermoor* as a work "offering Soviet people a preposterous tale of family feuds and intrigue among wealthy aristocrats, a tale in which murder, insanity, and suicide are treated as normal." To make matters worse, *Lucia di Lammermoor* and similar foreign operas were staged at the expense of prerevolutionary Russian and Soviet operas: "For every performance of the most frequently performed Soviet opera, there are twenty performances of *La Traviata*, which in turn is shown four times as often as any classical Russian operatic work. With all due respect for great Verdi's genius, a candid question should be posed: are *La Traviata* and operas with similar libretti what builders of Communism really need?"[8]

While statistics were juggled somewhat to impress Soviet readers that such a state of affairs was intolerable (percentages of population were used instead of absolute numbers of viewers, reruns were treated on equal footing with new films), a similar effort was made to make it appear that imported motion pictures were displacing Soviet ones, and that the latter were, in fact, victims of consistent discrimination. Thus, in the city of Groznyj in the Caucasus, *Entry*, an "excellent [Soviet] poetic film," was shown only for two days, while the American musical *Seven Brides for Seven Brothers* and, of course, *The Magnificent Seven* were shown for a long time. Things were no different in the large southeastern city of Nikolaev, where *Entry* and another Soviet feature film, *The Empty Run*, were seen, together, by a mere eight percent of the city's residents, while the imported *Family Talisman* and (again!) *The Magnificent Seven* were shown for two weeks and a month respectively. A revival of *The Ballad of a Soldier* was not given top billing, and a film version of Boris Polevoj's Stalinist classic *The Story of a Real Man* was shown only in a cinema catering to children; but *The Pearl of Santa Lucia, Under the Black Mask,* and *The Medallion of Three Hearts* were shown to large audiences.[9] All that was in 1963, and therefore a

7. See, e.g., *Pravda* March 21, 1957, and August 17, 1958. On January 15, 1957, *Sovetskaja kul'tura* gave a long list of Western plays that were performed in Leningrad at a time when very few Soviet plays were shown. The roll included James Barrie's *What Every Woman Knows*, J. B. Priestley's *Dangerous Corner*, Frederick Knott's *Dial M for Murder*, Marc-Gilbert Sauvajon's *Tapage Nocturne*, as well as stage adaptations of D. Gordon's *The Crime of Anthony Graham* and O. Henry's *The Sixth Floor*. To make matters more intolerable, these were not even the best plays of these particular authors. According to *Sovetskaja kul'tura* there were better plays by Barrie and Priestley than those shown in Leningrad.

8. *Sovetskaja kul'tura*, June 6, 1963. A cautious defense of the Western opera was written in *Izvestija* on June 12, 1963, by I. Petrovskij, rector of Moscow University.

9. *Pravda*, November 24, 1963.

question arises: why, five years later, were such early warnings ignored? Why was Mikhail Romm's *Ordinary Fascism* (a thoughtful, serious film by the way) exhibited 479 times and seen by 118,000 spectators in Gorky Province, while the corresponding figures for a lightweight Western import like *The Queen Chanticleer* were 832 and 233,000, and those for *Some Like It Hot,* a musical comedy starring Marilyn Monroe, were 1,037 showings and 268,000 viewers?[10] We shall return to the question shortly.

Most telling, in a way, and most outspoken, were two articles published within a year of each other by Il'ja Kremlev. The first was published in *Kommunist,* and the second pronouncement on the same subject appeared in *Literaturnaja gazeta.*[11] In the former, Kremlev wrote disapprovingly of the enormous quantities printed of Mayne Reid and Jules Verne, but it was the three million copies of Alexandre Dumas published within less than a year that incensed the Soviet critic: "In terms of paper consumption, this means that the novels relating the adventures of the three musketeers and those of Queen Margot used up nearly twice as much newsprint as the Sovetskij pisatel' Publishing House requires annually for all new Soviet literature." Incomplete data for the first eleven months of 1956 indicated, according to Kremlev, that over a hundred titles by Western authors appeared in a total of 14,500,000 copies (much of it "light reading"), making for an average of 240,000 copies per Western author. The average figure for Soviet writers was less than one-tenth that amount: only 22,000 copies per author.[12] In spite of the fact that his article had appeared in the single most authoritative journal in the USSR and carried the imprimatur of the Party's Central Committee itself, a year later Kremlev still had reasons to note with heavy sarcasm that the country's publishers must have decided that "no Soviet citizen should be without his own Dumas," and that in 1958 Sovetskij pisatel', the largest publisher of Soviet writing, envisaged the publication of 87 new prose works by Soviet authors. Their *combined* press runs would

---

10. *Sovetskaja Rossija,* April 17, 1968.

11. *Kommunist,* No. 8 (June 1957), pp. 123–28; *Literaturnaja gazeta,* May 29, 1958.

12. *Kommunist,* No. 8 (June 1957), pp. 123–28. Eleven years later, the same journal assailed the present writer for having suggested in his *Russian Classics in Soviet Jackets* (1962) that "a typical Soviet novel in 1955–58 was published in an edition of approximately 30,000 copies." The Soviet journalist wrote: "In order to somehow substantiate his deliberately falsified assertion that the works of Soviet writers are printed in wretchedly small editions because the [Soviet] reader prefers the [prerevolutionary Russian] classics, Friedberg pretends to quote 'a source.' Who in America will take the trouble to check, to go through old newspaper files, to compare? They will certainly take his word for it." A. Beljaev, "Sovetskaja literatura i buržuaznye fal'sifikatory," *Kommunist,* No. 12 (August 1968), pp. 112–19.

I owe Mr. Beljaev an apology. My figure of 30,000 copies per typical Soviet novel (which was arrived at after some complex calculations) was, as it turns out, too generous. It should have been 22,000, which would, of course, have strengthened my thesis. While it would have been too much to expect *Americans* to check my figures, one might have hoped that the editors of *Kommunist* (the Soviet Communist Party's theoretical journal!) would have consulted the back files of *their own publication* before printing yet another vituperative attack on Western studies of Soviet literature.

fall below those of the three volumes of Alexandre Dumas in 1955–56.[13]

Why was this state of affairs tolerated during the first post-Stalin decade, and why, indeed, has it been allowed to persist to the present? Why continue a policy that, if one is to believe Soviet sources, helps disseminate alien and hostile ideas among the population, wastes paper that might have been used to print good Soviet novels, displaces Soviet plays and films from the country's stages and movie houses, and, last but not least, exerts a definitely harmful influence on Soviet authors and artists themselves? Why has the policy of wide circulation of Western cultural imports not been abandoned as a mistake, the more so since the failure could (like the indiscriminate planting of corn) have been conveniently blamed by the Brezhnev and Kosygin regime on Khrushchev, deposed from office in 1964, under whom it was in fact inaugurated? The question was, understandably, never openly debated within the USSR. Nevertheless, it appears reasonable to assume that the overall problem of what may be called the cost-benefit ratio of the dissemination of Western writing, drama, and film was examined at some juncture, perhaps on more than a single occasion. It is not inconceivable, for instance, that such a discussion might have taken place, perhaps at one of the Party's Central Committee meetings at which resolutions on various ramifications of the question were adopted.

The issue of Western cultural imports, including translations of older literary works, is clearly relevant to the conduct of Soviet foreign policy— or that aspect of it now called cultural diplomacy—and also to relations with Western Communist parties and various cultural organizations, as well as with influential individual authors. Yet, with rare exceptions, it was hardly ever publicly discussed in that context. In the case of films and visits by musical, theatrical, and dance ensembles, the problem was relatively clearcut as it often (though not always) involved formal exchanges between the Soviet and Western governments.[14] The question that must have been decided was whether the opportunity to have specific Soviet cultural wares displayed in the West was worth the price of allowing similar Western products in the USSR. That this was subject to some hard bargaining goes without saying, but the legitimacy of the transactions itself was plain to see. What is likely, however, is that Soviet diplomats and others regularly concerned with contacts with foreigners probably favor a "softer" line, since

13. *Literaturnaja gazeta,* May 29, 1958. Kremlev was also critical of the fact that the multivolume set of Dickens was printed in 600,000 copies per volume, and that London's "reactionary dime novel," *The Heart of Three,* was included in a set published at 390,000 copies per volume.

14. Academic exchanges also fall in this category. Thus, in the United States, their general limits and framework are negotiated by the Department of State and the Soviet government, but the selection of American participants and support of individual scholarly projects lie within the province of the International Research and Exchanges Board, a nongovernmental academic organization.

a permissive Soviet policy with regard to Western culture in the USSR lends credence to the official stance of "peaceful coexistence" and *détente*. Publication in the USSR of Western authors is widely publicized abroad as evidence of Soviet goodwill, and this, not unreasonably, may be expected to make the atmosphere more conducive to successful negotiations in non-cultural areas, for instance foreign trade.[15] Similarly, Soviet officials charged with liaison with Western nongovernmental bodies (including "friendship societies" and other pro-Soviet groups) may be expected to favor wider publication of Western authors, as may *Intourist*, which deals with foreign tourism in the USSR. Indirectly, the Soviet authorities' desire for acclaim in the West for Soviet culture may also be partly responsible for the often deplored tendencies of Soviet authors and filmmakers to cater to Western tastes.[16] That this cannot always be accomplished without diluting the artistic and ideological orthodoxy expected of Soviet art and letters at home is rather unfairly overlooked. The schizoid reactions include, for instance, criticism within the USSR of certain Soviet authors and works, with resulting restrictions on their availability, along with simultaneous recognition of their usefulness abroad.[17]

Other vested interests within the USSR also undoubtedly act as pressure groups arguing for a wider dissemination of Western cultural imports.

15. Some years ago this writer was present at a meeting with a group of visiting Soviet dignitaries from Central Asia who reeled off impressive statistics on the publication in Uzbek, Turkmen, and other languages of the area of such authors as Mark Twain and Jack London, and demanded to know who among Soviet Central Asian authors were recently translated in the United States. The ensuing tension was relieved when it was pointed out that the older works in some of the languages are known here under different designations (e.g., what is called old Tadzhik literature in the USSR is really classical Persian), and that the works of Turkic folklore are known and studied in the United States. In 1975, by the way, Washington's Arena Stage successfully produced *Ascent of Mount Fuji* of which the Soviet Kirgiz writer Čingiz Ajtmatov was coauthor.

16. There are some interesting inconsistencies in Soviet reactions to Western recognition. Thus, the award of the Nobel Prize for literature to Pasternak was greeted with abuse of the awarding institution; it was recalled, for instance, that the only previous Russian winner of the prize was the bitterly anti-Soviet émigré Ivan Bunin. Shortly thereafter, the same prize was awarded to the staunchly Communist novelist Sholokhov. This time there was pride and rejoicing, and Sholokhov dutifully traveled to Stockholm to receive the award; earlier insults of the Nobel Prize committee were, of course, forgotten. Some years later the same prize was won by Solzhenitsyn, and this brought about a general replay of the Pasternak incident, as did the award, in 1975, of the Nobel Peace Prize to Andrei Sakharov, the leading figure in the unofficial Soviet movement of democratic dissent. However, there was always gratification at the award of Nobel Prizes to nonpolitical Soviet scientists.

17. Thus, for example, two Soviet films, *Andrej Rublev*, about the famous medieval Russian painter of icons, and the strikingly modernistic Ukrainian *Shadows of Forgotten Ancestors*, were strongly criticized within the country and were not widely shown; both, however, were exported abroad where they earned critical acclaim as well as foreign currency. Two young Soviet poets, Andrei Voznesensky and Yevgeni Yevtushenko, have been frequently attacked in the USSR, the first for the "formalism," i.e., modernism, of his verse, and the second for his occasionally unorthodox politics, such as excessively anti-Stalinist verse, a poem condemning anti-Semitism, etc. Both are, however, frequent visitors to the West, on the correct assumption that their appearances *there* are useful to the Soviet cause. Indeed, as suggested earlier, Yevtushenko has in effect inherited the mantle of Ilya Ehrenburg who served in much the same capacity during the Stalin era.

Thus, on October 15, 1954, *Pravda* disclosed that the Soviet translator of George Bernard Shaw's *Pygmalion* was rewarded for his efforts with more than a *million* rubles. The reason was that translators and authors of stage adaptations of prose works were at that time paid the same percentage of box-office receipts as writers of original works.[18] While this was probably an extreme case, it may confidently be assumed that translators from the Western languages act as a lobby favoring the publication of Western writing and performance of Western drama.

The Soviet theaters themselves should also definitely be counted among the proponents of a lenient policy with regard to Western drama and stage adaptations of West European and American prose. The eagerness with which they took advantage of the liberal atmosphere of the two post-Stalin "thaws," of 1956 and 1962, attest to this. The directors and the actors were, no doubt, attracted by an opportunity to perform a wider repertory of modern drama that included plays artistically quite different from the output of Soviet playwrights. At the same time they shared, no doubt, in the admiration for the attribute of Western drama that endears it to Soviet theater administrators, namely its box-office appeal. This, it should be emphasized, was not an entirely selfish consideration. Financial success ranks high among the indicators by which the Soviet authorities judge the performance of theaters; at the same time, Soviet theaters are under constant pressure to stage ideologically worthwhile Soviet drama. The latter, however, are rarely box-office attractions. The need to subsidize, in effect, the politicized Soviet component of their repertories makes the allure of translated Western plays all but irresistible. Building up a repertory that would be ideologically acceptable as well as financially feasible is a balancing act that requires consummate skill, the more so since the authorities' vigilance with regard to either of the two criteria is subject to frequent fluctuations. During the 1957 drive to eliminate from the Soviet theaters' repertory many of the recently introduced Western plays, complaints were occasionally heard that theaters were being unfairly assailed for staging such plays as Frederick Knott's *Dial M for Murder* at a time when Soviet cinemas were allowed to screen third-rate Western thrillers;[19] the protests were probably prompted by what was felt to be both the artistic and financial inequities thus created. Six years later, when the controversy around the problem of Western plays in the theaters' repertory was revived, *Pravda*

18. G. B. Shaw died in 1950, and it is unlikely that any payment was made by the Soviet theaters to his estate. In any case, prior to the Soviet accession in 1973 to the Universal Copyright Convention, they were under no obligation to do so. Thus, the payment to the Soviet translator constituted the only expenditure for the text of the play and may have therefore appeared less extravagant.

19. Such protests were voiced, for instance, at a plenary session of the All-Russian Theater Society. See *Teatr,* No. 3, 1957, pp. 93–99.

reported indignantly on September 3, 1963, that *two* Soviet theaters on tour in Kiev, one from Moscow and the other from the Azerbaidzhani capital of Baku, presented William Gibson's *Two for the Seesaw,* "a work that fails to uncover the profound nature of social contradictions in bourgeois society." Why would good Soviet theaters do a thing like that? *Pravda* revealed the shameful reason: "Difficult though this may be to believe, the name of the game is brazen box-office calculation." That such calculations were a result of demands by the government's own accountants was, of course, bypassed in silence. The consequences of the banishment of many Western plays from the Soviet repertory became immediately apparent. Theaters that had been filled in 1956 and again in 1962 began once more to face the problem of unsold tickets, a predicament sadly remembered from the closing years of the Stalin era. According to *Izvestija,* October 11, 1963, in the previous month Moscow's internationally renowned Art Theater had failed to sell thirty-four percent of its tickets, as had the capital's Pushkin Theater. The percentage of empty seats in the Maly Theater, which specializes in the Russian classics, was twenty-nine; but in the Moscow Drama Theater exactly half of the seats remained unoccupied. The tone of the newspaper article was one of serious concern. Yet the cause was all too obvious: it was the recent purge of the theatrical repertory. It could safely be predicted that slowly but surely such foreign plays would reappear on the Soviet stage, and reappear they did—causing, some years later, a controversy already familiar.

If the Soviet legitimate theaters' partiality for Western cultural imports may be to an extent motivated also by artistic reasons, i.e., the actors' and directors' interest in a more varied and challenging repertory, ordinary commercial considerations explain a similar preference on the part of Soviet movie houses. Thus, the disclosure made by Vadim Tikunov, the Russian Republic's Minister for the Safeguarding of Public Order, directly linking a rise in juvenile delinquency to the showing of certain imported films elicited much reader response.[20] Some of it was summarized in *Izvestija* on August 11, 1965: "Many letters stressed the fact that the personnel of film-rental agencies are concerned first and foremost with box-office receipts, that is with the financial side of the problem, and completely ignore the educational function of motion pictures. It is for that reason that movie houses have been inundated with a muddy avalanche of foreign 'hits' bearing lurid titles. This evoked much surprise, concern, and indignation among readers." At the factory workers' discussion of West European and American films that was also referred to in the preceding chapter and in which

20. The problem of undesirable influences of imported films on the young was discussed in chapter 9.

many imported motion pictures were denounced as a source of ideological subversion and moral decay, the question was posed directly: Why are such films shown? Two reasons were cited. In the first place, they must be exhibited under the terms of film-exchange agreements with foreign countries. The second reason was no less revealing: "In order to earn the amount of cash required of it by the plan, the factory's Palace of Culture must screen box-office hits for fifteen days out of every month."[21] And the "hits" that fill the cash register are apparently not good Soviet films, but Western productions reeking of violence and sex.

Finally, the most influential promoters of Western writing in the USSR are the Soviet editors and publishers themselves. Their predicament is not unlike that of the managers of Soviet theaters: striking a balance between the ideological acceptability of their journals and book lists and also showing a financial profit. The balance, as suggested earlier, is not easily attained, and erring on either side may be dangerous, although, if a choice must be made, it is probably less perilous to err on the side of political orthodoxy. On the other hand, the allure of financial (and popular) success is strong temptation not easily resisted: if another journal (or publishing house) "got away with it," should we not also take the gamble?

Apparently many do. In spite of frequent warnings issued during the first post-Stalin decade, Soviet journals continue the practice of featuring translations from the West European languages in order to boost their circulations. The stratagem, incidentally, is often employed by otherwise conservative periodicals, particularly those whose circulations have been slipping. Thus, on November 20, 1965—that is two years after the doctrinal revivalist meetings of 1963—*Literaturnaja gazeta* took to task three youth publications, *Molodaja gvardija, Sel'skaja molodëž'*, and *Vokrug sveta*, as well as two major literary monthlies, *Neva* and *Moskva*. The offenders had been printing far too many translated novels of adventure and other Western writing in order to enhance their reader appeal. Specifically, *Literaturnaja gazeta* singled out some novels by Graham Greene, and also the memoirs of the popular French singer Edith Piaf which, it claimed, catered to bourgeois tastes. That the transgressions were deliberate and not the result of an oversight may be seen from the fact that five years later Western thrillers by Ellery Queen and Agatha Christie were to be found in such otherwise conservative literary magazines as *Don* and *Neman*.[22] Evidently, no other way was found to satisfy their readers and balance their budgets, thus making compromises with ideological desiderata necessary.

21. *Sovetskaja Rossija,* April 17, 1968.
22. Ellery Queen's "Inspector Queen's Own Case" appeared in *Don,* Nos. 7 and 8, 1970; Agatha Christie's *Destination Unknown* was serialized in *Neman,* a Russian-language literary monthly published in Belorussia (Nos. 1, 2 and 3, 1970).

An imaginary director of a wholesale Soviet book distributing enterprise was described as claiming, in the March 19, 1959, issue of *Literaturnaja gazeta,* that if he were to supply retailers only with books for which there was demand, his job would be simple. He would ship them "only *Home Economics* [i.e., cookbooks—MF] and detective novels." The mythical Soviet business executive was, naturally, exaggerating. Still, as indicated in previous chapters, foreign books, including thrillers, are among the most sought after in Soviet bookstores and libraries, and are always in desperately short supply. Again, the pattern has been much the same: publishers' eagerness to supply the market with foreign books that are virtually guaranteed to make a profit has been periodically denounced by the political authorities as ideologically irresponsible.[23] On April 5, 1958, the Central Committee of the Communist Party excoriated the country's publishers of foreign literature for their "commercial orientation," which resulted in the publication of vast quantities of translations that were not merely ideologically worthless, but actually harmful; the Central Committee reminded the publishers that *"The chief task of publishers of foreign literature is the publication of books which promote the Communist upbringing of the working masses. "*[24] Within months, on September 4, 1958, the publishers were criticized again, this time for accepting subscriptions to multivolume sets (which include a great many West European and American authors) *"without considering the desirability of their mass dissemination. "*[25] Two years later the situation was still unsatisfactory, and on May 31, 1960, the Party's Central Committee passed yet another resolution:

> Many book distributing organizations place orders for books *without any regard for the book buyers' interests. Guided primarily by commercial considerations, they show insufficient initiative in marketing timely literature, particularly political and modern [Soviet] belles lettres. At the same time they place inflated orders for translations of certain foreign authors of no artistic merit.*

The resolution urged book distributors to make every effort to promote the sale of political writings, particularly the classics of Marxism-Leninism,

23. To reiterate: not only do foreign books sell better than most, if not all, other types of books, but the profits accruing to Soviet publishers from their sales are probably greater than from all types of fiction, except only for reprints of the Russian classics. Until 1973, all foreign books and plays were, as far as Soviet publishers and theater directors were concerned, in the public domain. No royalties had to be paid to living foreign authors or to their heirs and estates. Furthermore, the outlays on the translation of new foreign books were more than compensated by the fact that the cost of books falling in the category of "modern foreign literature" was fully two-thirds higher than that of Soviet writing (for which royalties had to be paid!), and of older literature, both Russian and foreign. B. G. Reznikov, *Rabota prodavca v knižnom magazine,* 1960, p. 16.
24. *KPSS o kul'ture, prosveščenii i nauke,* 1963, pp. 243–45. Emphasis added.
25. Ibid., pp. 251–52. Emphasis added.

and of recent works of Soviet literature dealing with contemporary subjects.[26] The truth of the matter was, of course, that the Soviet publishers, guided by perfectly normal "commercial considerations," have been trying to supply the public with books for which there was genuine demand. The Party, however, differentiated between mere demand and the "real" interests of the readers, of which it was the self-appointed arbiter. It is likely that the Soviet publishers would have bowed long ago to the demand that their lists consist largely of politically uplifting Communist reading fare. Yet they cannot do so because they are also required to show a financial profit.[27] And making a profit, as any businessman knows—be he capitalist or "socialist" —often tempts one into compromising with ethics and principles.

One predictable by-product of the wave of criticism and expressions of concern over the undesirable impact of Western cultural imports in the post-Stalin era has been repeated suggestions and demands that the Soviet public be supplied with acceptable Soviet substitutes. Thus, on October 1, 1957, *Sovetskaja kul'tura* wrote that the most effective way to combat the harmful infatuation with Western jazz would be the creation of a sizeable repertory of good Soviet jazz. Igor Moiseyev, the celebrated director of the Soviet folk dance ensemble, suggested in 1962 that the reason for the appeal of rock-and-roll to many young Soviet people is to be sought in the nonexistence of new Soviet dances.[28] The rigidly Stalinist novelist Leonid Sobolev recommended in 1957 that the most effective way to wean young Soviet readers from the books of Conan Doyle would be to provide them with good Soviet thrillers: "People tell me—just look at the thirst for books about spies and criminals! They are literally being read to shreds! In my view this is no cause for rejoicing. They [the Soviet young people—MF] read them out of desperation, because there are no cheerful, noble, moral books about adventures of upright Soviet citizens."[29] A year later the same newspaper for young people continued the campaign against Conan Doyle's Sherlock Holmes, intimating that Soviet readers' admiration for the British sleuth

26. *O partijnoj i sovetskoj pečati, radioveščanii i televidenii,* 1972, p. 466. Emphasis added.
27. The profits, of course, belong to the Soviet state, but "private initiative" has not entirely disappeared from Soviet book publishing. On April 24, 1963, *Izvestija* reported an incident that revealed a degree of ingenuity worthy of Ostap Bender, the immortal Soviet crook from Il'f and Petrov's novels. An audit of the finances of the Kirgiz State Publishing House revealed payments of royalties to such authors as Avicenna (born 980 A.D.), Omar Khayyam (born 1040 A.D.), and Sa'adi (born XII century A.D.). A geographically appropriate parallel would be the sending of checks by a Glasgow or Belfast publisher to one Geoffrey Chaucer.
28. *Izvestija,* May 23, 1962. It was not only rock-and-roll that was found objectionable; so were far more sedate and venerable Western ballroom dances. Thus, on December 1, 1962, Khrushchev commented: "Or take these new dances that are so fashionable now. Some of them are completely improper. You wiggle a certain section of the anatomy, if you'll pardon the expression. It's indecent. As Kogan once said to me when she was looking at a fox-trot, 'I've been married 20 years and never knew this kind of activity is called the fox-trot!' " Priscilla Johnson and Leopold Labedz, *Khrushchev and the Arts,* p. 102.
29. *Komsomol'skaja pravda,* June 6, 1957.

could, with some effort, be channeled in a more constructive direction: it called on Soviet writers to create books about Soviet intelligence agents and secret policemen "boundlessly loyal to their homeland."[30] Similarly, the 1965 pronouncement by Vadim Tikunov, the Russian Republic's Minister for the Safeguarding of Public Order, which blamed the rise of juvenile delinquency in the country on the influx of imported films, contained (side by side with recommendations for measures to be taken to control the import and screening of Western motion pictures) an appeal that "children and adolescents be provided with more opportunities to view motion pictures *that promote patriotic feelings and are rooted in the heroic traditions of our own people.* "[31] What the Soviet Minister was proposing, in effect, was that if Soviet youngsters craved violence on the screen, then instead of American Westerns they should be shown films in which the shooting is done by Soviet soldiers and for a noble cause, and in which the villains are not simple apolitical foreign bandits and gangsters, but recognizable ene- mies of the Soviet people.

Always quick to heed the Party's call, a number of Soviet authors set out to produce Soviet cloak-and-dagger novels, novellas, and short stories with the efficiency that had characterized their earlier concoctions about stern Communist bureaucrats, indefatigable tractor drivers, and wizened old collective farmers. In record time provincial Soviet newspapers were flooded with works which, in the words of the Party Central Committee's resolution of November 18, 1958, "described at length the activities of [anti- Soviet] spies and saboteurs, mysterious murders, various kinds of criminal adventures, and assorted immoral characters." The intentions of the Soviet authors could not be faulted, but the level of performance left much to be desired. The Central Committee demanded that the publication of these obvious imitations of Western thrillers be discontinued.[32] The trouble with many such efforts, a Soviet newspaper noted, was that although they were mildly entertaining (in a crude way, to be sure), they were not sufficiently didactic.[33] The problem with others was their *excessive* didactic success. It was charged, for instance, that Nikolaj Španov's imitations of Conan Doyle had actually *inspired* some young Soviet criminals. Still, this unfortunate fact was not intended to discourage other authors whose creations might

30. Ibid., April 27, 1958. Indeed, on March 31, 1964, the same newspaper printed a suggestion that the beneficent ideological influence of a Soviet James Bond would even extend outside the USSR. Noting the immense popularity of the genre, a later issue of the newspaper (June 10, 1964), appealed that the USSR "use this weapon for our own ends, with dash and skill, use it so that it may hit the enemy in battle without fail."

31. *Izvestija,* May 28, 1965. Other parts of the Minister's pronouncement were discussed in chapter 9.

32. *O partijnoj i sovetskoj pečati, radioveščanii i televidenii,* 1972, pp. 317–18.

33. *Komsomol'skaja pravda,* April 2, 1958. The article described the Soviet characters that populated such stories as "descendants of the Count de Chartreuse and Mr. Westinghouse."

prove more successful: "Whodunits and tales of adventure which unravel the real activities of spies, saboteurs, and criminals can indeed only benefit our readers."[34]

Other responses to official and quasi-official expressions of concern about the impact of Western cultural imports were based on the assumption their appeal was derived not so much from their intrinsic qualities—including their subject matter—as from their "foreignness." Proceeding from that rationale, one newspaper advised that instead of showing objectionable new West European and American films, older foreign films be revived; it recommended, for instance, Charlie Chaplin's *Modern Times* which, in its estimate, "indicts capitalist exploitation."[35] The Central Committee of the Young Communist League tacitly recognized in a 1969 resolution that its journal *Molodaja gvardija* must publish some foreign fiction, but saw no reason why that fiction had to be of Western origin; the journal was directed to print translations of authors from Soviet-bloc and Afro-Asian countries.[36] Finally, there was a renaissance in the 1970s of a genre that had flourished in the USSR during the Cold War, namely Soviet plays with Western settings; much of its success in 1946–53 was due to the public's interest in Western realia, and in the absence of new Western plays, such crudely anti-Western Soviet drama was accepted by many as the best available substitute. Two Soviet plays with American settings opened in Moscow in 1971. Evgenij Ramzin's *Countdown,* staged at the Moscow Art Theater, dealt with America's work on deadly thermonuclear weapons,[37] while *The Three Minutes of Martin Graw,* written by the Soviet foreign correspondent Genrix Borovik, described an alleged conspiracy of Birchites and Klansmen that resulted in the assassination of Martin Luther King.[38]

Assuming the unlikelihood of a complete return to the near-total cultural isolationism of the Stalin era, the Soviet policy of controlled and selective publication of Western writing, particularly by modern authors, of restricted staging of imported plays and limited distribution of foreign films will be continued, and so will the tensions this policy engenders. The tensions are the result of a number of incompatible expectations and mutually exclusive prohibitions, which accompany the implementation of this policy. The Soviet Establishment is in effect, committed to the dissemination, albeit rigidly controlled, of cultural imports from the "bourgeois"

34. *Molodoj kommunist,* No. 11, 1957, pp. 121–24. The unsuccessful Soviet aspirant to Conan Doyle's mantle, Nikolaj Nikolaevič Španov (1896–1961), a former officer in the tsarist air force and subsequently also a Soviet soldier, was the author of many thrillers and novels of adventure. KL, Vol. VIII (1975), p. 780.
35. *Učitel'skaja gazeta,* May 20, 1961.
36. *Komsomol i molodëžnaja pečat',* 1973, p. 259. The resolution was adopted on August 13, 1969.
37. *Izvestija,* March 14, 1971.
38. *Pravda,* June 13, 1971. The play was staged by the Mayakovsky Theater.

world, yet expects these imports to be free of "bourgeois ideology," however indirectly implied. It hails the nonconformist stance of "progressive" Western authors and artists, but refuses to tolerate similar attitudes among Soviet writers, dramatists, filmmakers, and painters. It favors the circulation of cultural imports that are supportive of its political goals, yet also desires to earn money on the transaction, much as Western businessmen would. And conversely, it pressures its publishers, theaters, and cinema managers to show a profit, while also chastising them for making available to the Soviet public West European and American books, plays, and films for which there is genuine demand and which alone can produce such profits.

It may also be reasonably expected that the availability of Western cultural imports will continue to erode, even if only very slowly, some of the artistic rigidities in Soviet literature and the arts and, at times of greater permissiveness, to corrode their ideological purity as well, arguing for greater tolerance with regard to new Soviet literary and artistic production, to the cultural heritage of prerevolutionary Russia, and the formal experimentation of the 1920s.[39]

Most likely, periodic appeals will continue to be made to Soviet authors and artists to produce works that will lessen the need for large scale translation of Western books and production of Western plays, the more so since this will henceforth involve the payment of royalties.[40] It is improbable, however, that a significant body of such writing can be created, that is, books which Soviet readers would freely choose in preference to translations of Western literature. The problem is not one of national traditions in specific genres (there is no intrinsic reason why Russian authors could not produce good thrillers or novels of adventure or bedroom farces), nor, most certainly, of the absence in the USSR of writers as gifted as their Western colleagues. Rather, the impediment is to be sought in certain features en-

39. Some direct admissions by Soviet authors in the 1960s of the influence on their work of modern Western writing were discussed in chapter 9. There are strong indications that the sudden influx of modern Western writing during the first post-Stalin decade facilitated the partial "rehabilitation" in the USSR of Russian authors whose writings had for many years been suppressed as "decadent." Thus, the late Aleksandr Dymšic, a Soviet critic with unassailably orthodox credentials, linked his review of recent Soviet editions of Arthur Rimbaud and Guillaume Apollinaire (who, he insisted, were firmly committed to modernism) to an appeal for a partial lifting of the ban on Russia's own modernists. See *Znamja*, No. 6, 1963, pp. 189–203. Among "modernist" Russian authors whose works reappeared in print during the post-Stalin years were Fëdor Sologub (his *Petty Demon* was printed in the distant Siberian city of Kemerovo with an editorial note explaining that the Symbolist novel about beauty, evil, and the illusory nature of reality is merely a description of the squalor of schools in tsarist Russia), Andrej Belyj (the author of the other great Symbolist novel, *Petersburg*), as well as the poets Marina Cvetaeva and Boris Pasternak. The latter was reinstated only as a poet. His novel *Doctor Zhivago* remains unpublished in the USSR.
40. The same holds true for imported films. In contrast to books and plays, in the recent past these have as a rule either involved payment to Western film companies, or were part of film exchanges with foreign countries.

demic to Soviet writing. Some of these were enumerated in "Aesopian language" in an essay by the late Ilya Ehrenburg that was ostensibly devoted to Stendhal. Thus, Ehrenburg quoted with approval the French novelist's insistence that the role of a writer is to be an observer, not an intruder in life, a stance directly opposed to the activist Soviet definition of a writer as an "engineer of human souls." Stendhal wrote: "If you interfere in life, then you don't see it clearly. It then either causes you too much pain, or brings you too much pleasure."[41] Also attributed to Stendhal was another oblique criticism of a fundamental feature of Soviet writing, namely that overt tendentiousness—even if imposed by society rather than an expression of a writer's personal bias—is ultimately ruinous to literature.[42] And a final quotation from Stendhal clashed head-on with a commandment of Socialist Realism: "One must learn not to flatter anyone—not even the people."[43] It is the obligatory didacticism of the great bulk of Soviet literature, its unconcealed bias, its ideological uniformity, its avoidance of the tragedy of the human condition, of subjects known in prerevolutionary Russian writing as "the accursed questions," its suspicion even of experimentation in artistic form, that set it apart from much of the West's literature of modernity—and also, incidentally, from its own pre-Soviet Russian antecedents.

The need for Soviet substitutes for ideologically objectionable or worthless Western writing is not a recent development, and appeals to Soviet authors to fill this gap have a long history. An eloquent fictional illustration written over forty years ago by the two famous Soviet humorists, Ilya Il'f and Yevgeni Petrov, is reproduced in the Epilogue.[44] "How Robinson Crusoe Was Created" first appeared, incongruously, on October 27, 1932, in *Pravda,* a reflection perhaps of the brief period of disarray that was created that year by the abolition, on Party orders, of all literary groupings then in existence and the creation of a single Union of Soviet Writers.

In Il'f and Petrov's story, an enterprising Soviet editor conceives the idea of commissioning a novel of adventure that would captivate young Soviet readers as much as Daniel Defoe's immortal hero, but that would, in addition, serve as a model for emulation by Soviet children. This, of course, requires that Robinson Crusoe be Soviet. When the manuscript of the commissioned Soviet *Robinson Crusoe* arrives, the editor is dissatisfied because it retains too many features of the British model and, conversely, lacks many elements that are obligatory in Soviet writing. One by one, changes are introduced, which the intimidated Soviet hack meekly accepts.

41. Il'ja Èrenburg, "Uroki Stendalja," *Inostrannaja literatura,* No. 6, 1957, p. 201.
42. Ibid., p. 208.
43. Ibid., p. 212.
44. Il'ja Il'f, Evgenij Petrov, "Kak sozdavalsja Robinzon," *Sobranie sočinenij v pjati tomax,* Vol. III (Moscow: Goslitizdat, 1961), pp. 193–97.

The final product is an ordinary Soviet novel.

A question may therefore be posed: is a Soviet *Robinson Crusoe* possible? The answer is a very hypothetical and qualified yes. A Soviet *Robinson Crusoe* can indeed be created, but only if a Soviet author feels free not to accept all of the corrections and improvements suggested by real-life counterparts of Il'f and Petrov's none-too-fictitious editor. This, however, presupposes a situation where nobody really cares about Robinson Crusoe's citizenship and politics, a prospect that with much understatement may be called remote. It implies a state of affairs in which foreign books, plays, and films can enter the USSR without any prior security clearance, without visas, and once inside the country, move about at will without restrictions and supervision, freely competing with their local counterparts for critical acclaim and public favor.

# EPILOGUE

# *How Robinson Crusoe Was Created*

by Ilya Il'f and Yevgeni Petrov

The editorial offices of the illustrated bi-weekly *Problems of Adventure* were experiencing a shortage of artistic works capable of captivating the attention of youthful readers.

True, there were some works, but not quite the right thing. There was too much of sissy seriousness in all of them. To tell the truth, instead of captivating, they cast a shadow over the souls of youthful readers. And it was captivation that the editor was really after.

At long last they decided to commission a novel with installments.

The office courier was dispatched with a summons to Moldavantsev the writer, and on the following day Moldavantsev was already reclining on the overstuffed sofa in the editor's office.

"You get the idea," the editor was expounding with intensity, "this thing should be engrossing, fresh, and full of interesting adventures. In short, what we are aiming at is a Soviet Robinson Crusoe. The kind no reader can tear himself away from."

"A Robinson—can be done," the writer said succinctly.

"Except we don't want just any plain Robinson, but a Soviet one."

"You bet! What else, Rumanian?"

The writer wasn't much of a talker. One could see at once he was a doer.

And sure enough, the novel was finished on schedule. Moldavantsev did not depart too much from the great original. If it's Robinson you want, Robinson you'll get.

A Soviet young man is shipwrecked. A wave deposits him on an uninhabited island. Alone and defenseless he faces the fierce elements. He is surrounded by danger—wild beasts, lianas, the upcoming monsoon. Still, the perseverance of the Soviet Robinson surmounts all the obstacles that had seemed insurmountable. Three years later he is found by a Soviet searching expedition, and found in top shape. He has tamed nature, built himself a cottage, surrounded it with a green belt of gardens, bred rabbits, made himself a jacket from monkeys' tails, and trained a parrot to wake him with an announcment: "Attention! Off with the blanket, off with the blanket! We begin our morning gymnastics."

"Very nice," said the editor, "and that bit about the rabbits is just great. Quite timely, too. Still, I must say, I am not altogether clear about the central idea of the work."

"Man's struggle with nature," Moldavantsev announced with his customary brevity.

"Yes, but there is nothing Soviet about it."

"What about the parrot? I have him in there instead of a radio. He's an experienced broadcaster."

"The parrot is fine. And the belt of gardens is fine, too. But one gets no feel of Soviet social institutions. Where, for instance, is the local committee? And what about the leading role of the trade unions?"

Suddenly Moldavantsev became agitated. The moment he sensed that the novel might be rejected, his taciturn manner evaporated. He turned eloquent.

"Where can you find a local committee? After all, the island is uninhabited."

"You are quite right, it's uninhabited. All the same, there should be a local committee. I am not a creative artist, but if I were you, I would introduce a local committee. As a Soviet element."

"But the entire plot revolves around the fact that the island is uninhabi . . ."

Suddenly Moldavantsev caught the editor's gaze and stopped short. The gaze was distant and pale, like the sky in March. The writer decided to compromise.

"You have a point," he said, raising his finger. "Why, of course. How could I have overlooked it? Two people are saved in the shipwreck, our friend Robinson and the chairman of the local committee."

"And also two members at large," the editor said icily.

"Ouch!" Moldavantsev squealed.

"Never mind ouch. Two at large, and one woman activist, the membership dues collector."

"Who needs a collector? Who is she going to be collecting membership dues from?"

"Why, from Robinson."

"Let the chairman collect dues from Robinson. It won't do him any harm."

"That's where you are wrong, Comrade Moldavantsev. This is quite intolerable. The chairman of the local committee should not be wasting his time on petty things such as running all over the place collecting dues. We are waging a struggle against such things. He should be devoting his time to serious leadership tasks."

"All right, let's have a dues collector then," Moldavantsev yielded. "This may even do some good. She'll marry the chairman or even Robinson himself. It will make for livelier reading."

"I wouldn't advise that. Don't stoop to the level of dime novels, avoid pathological eroticism. Let her stick to collecting membership dues and keeping them in a safe vault."

Moldavantsev became jittery on the sofa.

"Excuse me, you cannot have a safe vault on an uninhabited island!"

The editor paused.

"Hold it a minute," he said. "In the first chapter you have a wonderful scene. In addition to Robinson and the members of the local committee, the wave also deposits on the island all sorts of objects . . ."

"An axe, a rifle, a surveying compass, a barrel of rum, and a bottle of scurvy remedy," the writer proudly enumerated.

"Cross out the rum," the editor interrupted hastily. "Also, what's that bottle with scurvy remedy? Who needs it? Let's have a bottle of ink instead! And the safety vault is a must."

"You really have a thing about that safety vault! Membership dues may just as well be kept in a hollow of a baobab. Who's going to steal them?"

"What do you mean who? What about Robinson? And the chairman of the local committee? And the members at large? And the commission for the supervision of canteens and general stores?"

"You mean they also got saved?" Moldavantsev asked timidly.

"They did."

Silence ensued.

"Maybe the wave deposited also a table for meetings?" the author inquired sarcastically.

"Wi-thout fail! After all, we must provide people with appropriate working conditions. Say, a water pitcher, a gavel, a tablecloth. The wave may deposit any kind of tablecloth you wish. It may be red, it may be green. I do not restrict artistic creation. But before anything else what you simply must do, my dear fellow, is depict the masses. The broad masses of working people."

"The wave cannot deposit masses," Moldavantsev was becoming obstinate. "This stands in direct contradiction to the plot. Just think about it! All of a sudden the wave deposits on the shore tens of thousands of people! It just makes you laugh."

"Incidentally, a little healthy, optimistic laughter would do no harm," the editor interjected.

"No! A wave cannot do that."

"Why a wave?" The editor was suddenly surprised.

"How else will the masses get to the island? After all, the island is uninhabited?"

"Who said it's uninhabited? You are confusing me. It's all clear. There is an island, or better still a peninsula. It's safer that way. And all kinds of engrossing, fresh, and interesting adventures take place there. Trade union activities are conducted, sometimes insufficiently conducted. The activist woman discovers a number of problems, say in the area of collecting membership dues. She is assisted by the broad masses. Also by the repentant chairman. At the end you may have a general meeting. This would be very striking, particularly from the artistic point of view. And that's it."

"What about Robinson?" Moldavantsev mumbled.

"Oh, yes. It's a good thing you reminded me. I am troubled by Robinson. Get rid of him altogether. He is a senseless, totally unjustified whining character."

"Now I get it all," Moldavantsev said in a funereal voice. "You'll have it by tomorrow."

"Well, good luck. Create. Incidentally, early in the novel you have a shipwreck. Who needs a shipwreck? Let's do it without a shipwreck. It's more engrossing that way. Agreed? All right then. Good-bye!"

Alone in the room, the editor burst out with joyous laughter.

"At long last," he said, "I'll get a true story of adventure, and a really artistic one at that."

*Translated from the Russian by Maurice Friedberg*

# APPENDIXES

## Appendix A
## Soviet Films Based on Works by Western Authors

1918    *Born Not for Money* (based on Jack London's *Martin Eden*); *Thais* (based on a story by Anatole France); *When Do We, the Dead, Arise* (based on Henrik Ibsen); *The Young Lady and the Hooligan* (based on d'Amicis's *Teacher of the Workers*)

1922    *A Specter Is Haunting Europe* (based on Edgar Alan Poe's stories)

1924    *Simple Hearts* (based on Alfred Tennyson's poem "The Saved One")

1926    *According to Law* (based on Jack London's *The Unexpected*)

1927    *Law and Duty* (based on Stefan Zweig's *Amok*)

1928    *The Gadfly* (based on Ethel Voynich's novel of the same name); *Woman from the Fair* (based on Eugene O'Neill's *Desire Under the Elms*)

1929    *The Ghost That Never Returns* (based on Henri Barbusse's *Le Revenant ne revient pas*)

1930    *The Feast of St. Jorgen* (based on Harald Bergstedt's novel of the same name)

1931    *Jimmie Higgins* (based on Upton Sinclair's novel of the same name)

1933    *The Great Comforter* (based on tales by O'Henry); *Harbor of Storms* (based on Honoré de Balzac's *Les Ressources de Quinola*)

1934    *Boule de suif* (based on Guy de Maupassant's novella of the same name)

1935    *Gobseck* (based on an excerpt from vol. 2 of Balzac's *La Comedie humaine*)

1936    *The Children of Captain Grant* (based on Jules Verne's novel of the same name)

1938    *The Oppenheim Family* (based on Lion Feuchtwanger's novel of the same name); *Treasure Island* (based on Robert Louis Stevenson's novel of the same name)

1942    *Tom Canty* (based on Mark Twain's *The Prince and the Pauper*)

1946    *The Fifteen-Year-Old Captain* (based on Jules Verne's *Dick Sand, Boy Captain*); *The White Fang* (based on Jack London's novel of the same name)

1955    *Othello* (based on Shakespeare's play); *The Mexican* (based on Jack London's novella of the same name)

1964    *Hamlet* (based on Shakespeare's play)

Sources: Paul Babitsky and John Rimberg, *The Soviet Film Industry* (New York: Frederick A. Praeger, 1955); V. Ždan (ed.), *Kratkaja istorija sovetskogo kino* (Moscow: Iskusstvo, 1969), pp. 519–90.

# Appendix B
## Popularity Ratings of Prerevolutionary Russian and Soviet Authors as Reported by Soviet Readers in the 1960s

According to a study of the Soviet reading public discussed in chapter 2, popularity ratings for prerevolutionary Russian authors were as follows:

| AUTHOR | AMONG WORKERS, PERCENT | AMONG ENGINEERS AND TECHNICIANS, PER CENT |
|---|---|---|
| Leo Tolstoy | 35 | 41 |
| Pushkin | 18 | 19 |
| Chekhov | 15 | 25 |
| Turgenev | 12 | 13 |
| Lermontov | 11 | 16 |
| Gogol | 8 | 8 |
| Kuprin | 7 | 13 |
| Dostoyevsky | 5 | 8 |
| Nekrasov | 4 | 8 |

Source: *Sovetskij Čitatel'. Opyt Konkretno-sočiologiceskogo issledovanija. Sbornik statej* (Moscow: Kniga, 1968), p. 97.

Arranging the lists in order of popularity, we see that in the case of both groups of readers, there is a close correlation with the list of prerevolutionary authors given below in order of copies printed in the USSR in all languages spoken in that country for the period 1956–62. The full list of ninety-four prerevolutionary Russian authors appears in this writer's essay "Literary Output: 1956–62," *Soviet Literature in the Sixties*, Max Hayward and Edward L. Crowley (eds.) (New York: Frederick A. Praeger, 1964), p. 173.

| POPULARITY AMONG WORKERS | POPULARITY AMONG ENGINEERS AND TECHNICIANS | PUBLISHED 1956–62 |
|---|---|---|
| Leo Tolstoy | Leo Tolstoy | Leo Tolstoy |
| Pushkin | Chekhov | Pushkin |
| Chekhov | Pushkin | Chekhov |
| Turgenev | Lermontov | Lermontov |
| Lermontov | Kuprin* | Turgenev |

| POPULARITY AMONG WORKERS | POPULARITY AMONG ENGINEERS AND TECHNICIANS | PUBLISHED 1956–62 |
|---|---|---|
| Gogol | Turgenev* | Mamin-Sibirjak |
| Kuprin | Gogol** | Nekrasov |
| Dostoyevsky | Dostoyevsky** | Kuprin |
| Nekrasov | Nekrasov** | Dostoyevsky |
| | | Gogol |

*same percentage for Kuprin and Turgenev
**same percentage for Gogol, Dostoyevsky, and Nekrasov

The three lists demonstrate that with the exception of Mamin-Sibirjak (a minor author favored during the Stalin era, known chiefly for his tales for children and novels about the advent of industrial capitalism in the Urals) the same names appear with remarkably similar rankings.

The list of Soviet authors is as follows:

| AUTHOR | AMONG WORKERS, PERCENT | AMONG ENGINEERS AND TECHNICIANS, PERCENT |
|---|---|---|
| Sholokhov | 26 | 30 |
| Lācis | 15 | 15 |
| Gorky | 11 | 16 |
| Simonov | 7 | 14 |
| Fadeyev | 5 | 4 |
| Aleksej N. Tolstoy | 4 | 12 |
| Nikolaj Ostrovskij | 4 | 2 |
| Paustovskij | 1 | 5 |

Source: Ibid.

Except for the Latvian Vilis Lācis, all of the authors on the list are Russian. The divergencies in ratings suggest, among other things, that the better educated engineers and technicians keep up with the latest books (in the late 1950s and early 1960s Simonov published a number of interesting novels and Paustovskij published his memoirs), while workers continue to read authors to whom they were introduced in the school curriculum (e.g., Fadeyev). It is possible, of course, that both groups read Simonov's older war novels and Paustovskij's novels of travel and adventure.

# Appendix C
## Popularity Ratings of Foreign Authors
## Among Subscribers to Literaturnaja gazeta
## in the Late 1960s

In a survey of subscribers to *Literaturnaja gazeta,* classics of foreign literature ranked in order of popularity as follows:

1. Jack London
2. John Galsworthy
3. Honoré de Balzac
4. Theodore Dreiser
5. Stefan Zweig
6. Romain Rolland
7. Franz Kafka
8. William Shakespeare

The most surprising favorite was, of course, Kafka, who had at that time been published only twice, once in a journal and once in book form, just two years earlier.

A similar list of modern authors ranked in order of popularity was as follows:

1. Ernest Hemingway
2. Heinrich Böll
3. Graham Greene
4. Erich Maria Remarque
5. J. D. Salinger
6. John Steinbeck
7. Lion Feuchtwanger
8. André Maurois
9. Kobo Abe
10. John Updike
11. Antoine de Saint-Éxupery
12. Harper Lee
13. William Faulkner
14. Kaufman
15. Georges Simenon
16. Somerset Maugham
17. Ray Bradbury
18. James Aldridge
19. Stanislaw Lem
20. C. P. Snow
21. Truman Capote
22. Ellen Dymphna Cusack
23. Mitchell Wilson

Kobo Abe is Japanese, and Stanislaw Lem, Polish; Kaufman could not be identified. The others were all West European and American authors.

This questionnaire solicited information about likes as well as dislikes, but the latter data were fragmentary. Thus, Hemingway was liked by 12 percent of the respondents and disliked by 2.6; the corresponding figures for Remarque were 9.6 and 0.9.

The data from the questionnaires are cited in *Političeskij dnevnik,* the most intellectual of all the *samizdat* journals to reach the West so far. A collection of eleven issues of the journal was published in the Netherlands in the original Russian: *Političeskij dnevnik, 1964–1970* (Amsterdam: Fond imeni Gercena, 1972). On the questionnaires, see pp. 581–84. The findings originally appeared in *Literaturnaja gazeta,* No. 40, 1968, and No. 19, 1969. See also chapter 2, note 24.

# Appendix D

## Popularity Ratings Among Readers
## Aged 15 to 17 in the 1960s

A list of Soviet authors ranked in order of their popularity with readers fifteen to seventeen years of age was as follows:

| AUTHOR | NUMBER OF RESPONDENTS | PERCENT OF TOTAL |
| --- | --- | --- |
| Sholokhov | 343 | 22 |
| Simonov | 136 | 9 |
| Aleksej N. Tolstoy | 125 | 8 |
| Nikolaj Ostrovskij | 124 | 8 |
| Gorky | 117 | 7 |
| Aleksandr R. Beljaev | 112 | 7 |
| Fadeyev | 88 | 5 |
| Jurij P. German | 86 | 5 |
| Daniil A. Granin | 52 | 3 |
| Paustovskij | 39 | 2 |

Source: *Sovetskij čitatel'*, p. 235.

The three authors read by readers between fifteen and seventeen years of age who did not appear on the list of Soviet writers favored by engineers and technicians are Beljaev, German, and Granin. Aleksandr Beljaev (1884–1942) was one of the founding fathers of Soviet science fiction. Jurij German (1910–68) wrote novels about Soviet physicians and secret policemen; his *Delo, kotoromu ty služis'* and its sequel *Dorogoj moj čelovek* (1957 and 1961) describe "the long road to moral and professional improvement" (KL, Vol. II [1964], p. 137). Daniil Granin (b. 1918) is best known for *Idu na grozu* (1962), a novel about Soviet scientists and engineers.

# Appendix E
## Popularity Ratings of Soviet Authors Among College Students in the 1960s

A list of Soviet authors read by college and university students was as follows (percentages refer to the total sample of 767 respondents):

| AUTHOR | PERCENT |
| --- | --- |
| Sholokhov | 25 |
| Lācis | 17 |
| Gorky | 16 |
| Čingiz Ajtmatov | 10 |
| Paustovskij | 6 |
| Nikolaj Ostrovskij | 6 |
| Fadeyev | 6 |
| Oles' Hončar (Gončar) | 6 |

Source: *Sovetskij čitatel'*, p. 257.

Čingiz Ajtmatov, who writes in both Kirgiz and Russian, is a sensitive and sophisticated prose writer and playwright whose work often successfully blends a lyrical manner with topical subject matter. Oles' Hončar (in Russian, Gončar) is a more conventional Ukrainian novelist: most of his work deals with the war and emphasizes elements of heroism and adventure.

# Appendix F

## Desired Impact of Western Writing:
## A Samizdat Lampoon

As pointed out in chapter 2, "Western Writing and Soviet Readers," Ethel Voynich (1864–1960), a British author who spent the last forty years of her life in the United States, remains to this day widely read in the USSR. Between 1954 and 1964 her novel *The Gadfly* was printed in close to two million copies in fourteen languages, including 25,000 in the original English; its setting is nineteenth-century Italy and its subject is that country's struggle for independence. The novel's long-standing popularity in Russia (published in 1897, it was translated the following year) and its author's personal ties to that country (where she lived between 1887 and 1889) are among the reasons for *The Gadfly*'s status as a major foreign classic in the USSR: "Active participation in the Russian revolutionary movement helped Voynich create the figure of the Gadfly [in Russian, *Ovod*—MF], one of the most striking portraits of a revolutionary in world literature. The Gadfly is contrasted to his father, Cardinal Montanelli. The entire novel is built around the conflict between revolutionary ideas and religion. While unmasking the reactionary nature of religion, Voynich portrays the fearlessness and courage of a fighter who sacrifices his life for an idea. Voynich's novel was a great success in the USA and in England, and it was translated into many languages. Still, it was in Russia that *The Gadfly* found its real homeland and became the favorite book of many generations of progressive youth. It was translated into twenty-two languages of the Soviet peoples, published more than a hundred times in a total of over three million copies, and frequently staged, filmed, and made into operas." KL, Vol. I (1962), p. 1017.

*The Gadfly* is studied in Soviet schools and its hero is often upheld as a model for emulation. The novel is a parodied in a *samizdat* Russian novel recently published in the West. *The Gadfly* relates the story of Manja, an ordinary Soviet girl who volunteers for military service during World War II. Her mother insists that she take along at least some warm woolen socks, but Manja refuses: "Manja is very indignant would Gadfly from the novel by the English author Ethel Voynich do anything like that and Manja was therefore right to be indignant about it but her mother had never read the novel by the English novelist Ethel Voynich and keeps crying bitterly don't cry Mother you should be reading that novel but Mother just keeps on crying she doesn't feel up to reading any novels. . . . [In the army Manja] took care of the wounded and recited to them from memory excerpts from the novel by the English writer Ethel Voynich. . . . [After Manja's heroic death] Mother tells visitors young visitors how on that last night of her life Manja read the novel *The*

*Gadfly* Mother also travels to other cities and people visit her from out of town and Mother often tires but every free moment she rereads the novel *The Gadfly* too bad the English writer Ethel Voynich is dead she would have without fail written about Manja . . ." Evgenij Kušev, "Otryvki iz teksta," *Grani* (Frankfurt/Main), No. 91 (1974), pp. 49–51.

The parody on Ethel Voynich's novel attests to the persistence with which Soviet readers are urged to emulate "positive" literary heroes; its appearance is a reaction to the procedure.

On June 12, 1968, *Izvestija* carried an article by the well-known Soviet novelist Boris Polevoj and by Evgenija Taratuta, a Soviet biographer of Ethel Voynich. The two indignantly refuted a malicious "fabrication" broadcast over the Russian service of the BBC according to which Voynich's revolutionary hero had a most unlikely prototype. As claimed by the BBC, the Gadfly's real-life model was Sidney Reilly, an agent of the British Secret Service who, to add insult to injury, also took part in an anti-Soviet conspiracy. The "outrage" was further compounded by the BBC's gleeful observation that this also implied that one of the foremost positive heroes in all of *Soviet* literature, Pavel Korčagin from Nikolaj Ostrovskij's novel *How the Steel Was Tempered* (where he is described as an admirer of *The Gadfly*), was really aspiring to emulate the exploits of an anti-Soviet British spy. *Izvestija*'s authors attempted to disprove the "canard."

# Appendix G
## Pernicious Influence of Western Writing
## as Seen by the Soviet Military

On rare occasions, criticism of fundamental principles of Soviet literature and the arts and, conversely, admiration of Western writing are linked to ominous events. Thus, on August 27, 1958, *Izvestija* printed an attack on Georg Lukacs's "revisionist" Marxist aesthetics and on a Russian-language book produced in Yugoslavia (presumably for distribution within the USSR), which advocated experimentation in painting. The article gravely recalled that hostile criticism of the principles of Socialist Realism preceded the eruption of the Hungarian "mutiny" of 1956.

A somewhat incongruously alarmist article appeared in the No. 2 (January 1971) issue of *Kommunist vooružёnnyx sil,* the journal concerned with the ideological supervision of the Soviet armed forces; the author, Colonel B. Sapunov, holder of the academic degree of Candidate of Philosophy, was presumably a senior political officer. The colonel warned Soviet soldiers and officers against the danger posed by imported films, quoting the Hollywood producer Darryl Zanuck as saying, "I have repeatedly declared that I consider American motion pictures the best means we can offer for inflicting damage upon Communism." Colonel Sapunov then went on to caution Soviet troops against the French *nouveau roman,* American pop art and jazz, Columbia's professor of Russian literature Rufus Mathewson, the late Boris Pasternak, and Alexander Solzhenitsyn, then still living in the USSR. One particular dead foreign author was singled out for grave accusation:

> The attitude toward the work of Franz Kafka in the Czechoslovak Socialist Republic provides evidence of what the underestimation of modernist tendencies leads to . . . His [Kafka's] name became, as it were, the banner for obliterating all boundries between bourgeois and socialist ideology . . . *This played by no means the least role in the demoralization of some of the intelligentsia of the Czechoslovak Socialist Republic in their move into the camp of the "quiet" counter-revolution.* [Italics supplied; for additional discussion of the author, see chapter 8.]

Having thus linked Kafka to the Czechoslovak "counterrevolution" that some of his readers personally helped crush with their tanks in 1968, the uniformed Soviet philosopher went on: "We cannot ignore the fact that here and there among us there is an excessive preoccupation with the showing of foreign motion pictures. After all, it is no secret that these films, behind an attractive façade, convey open vulgarity and philistine taste and idealize the bourgeois way of life." The article concluded with an impassioned appeal that officers' recreation centers and soldiers' clubs (in the Soviet Socialist army the two are, of course, strictly separate) "conduct extensive and vigorous work in the field of aesthetics and expose bourgeois art." Lest some misapprehension be created that art and aesthetics are matters dealt with by egghead intellectuals or at best commanding officers, the Soviet colonel stressed that "every soldier must become an active fighter here."

The full English text of the article appears in *The Current Digest of the Soviet Press*, Vol. XXIII, No. 4 (February 23, 1971), pp. 9–10, 14.

# INDEX

Salammbô, 89
Salinger, J.D., 68, 73, 199–201
Salminen, Sally, 177
*Salt of the Earth,* 193
Samarin, Roman, 132
Samedoglu, Jusif, 299
*samizdat,* 276, 279, 328, 356–57
Sand, George, 61, 88
Sandburg, Carl, 221
Sardou, Victorien, 101
Saroyan, William, 190–91, 299
Sarraute, Nathalie, 284
Sartre, Jean-Paul, 8, 22, 232–33, 272
Šatunovskij, E., 51
Sauvajon, Marc-Gilbert, 316
*Say No to Death,* 296
Scandinavian authors, 236–39
Ščedrin, R.K., 302
Schallük, Paul, 178
Scherfig, Hans, 239
Schiller, Friedrich, 92
Schnurre, Wolfdietrich, 149
schoolteachers: favorite authors of, 67; criticism of foreign films, 319–22
Schroeter, Leonard, 325
Schultz, James Willard, 119
Sciascia, Leonardo, 177
science fiction, 129–35
Scott, Sir Walter, 127–28
scrap-paper drive, 75–77
Scribe, Eugène, 101
secondary-school pupils' reading preferences, 68–71
second-hand books, 57
*Secret Agents Against Secret Weapons,* 291
Segel, Harold B., 277, 278
Šejnin, Lev, 105
*Sel'skaja molodëž',* 337
Semënov, Julian, 299
Serov, Vladimir, 304
Seton, Ernest Thompson, 112
Sevastikoglu, Georgos, 236
*Seven Brothers,* 91
sexual descriptions, censorship of, 29–32
Shah, M.B., 254
Shakespeare, William: Soviet observance of 400th anniversary, 6; *Richard III,* 51–52, 317; as popular author, 65, 71, 73; *Hamlet,* 85, 94
*Shakespeare, Our Contemporary,* 52
Shaw, George Bernard, 219–21, 335
*The Shield and the Sword,* 105
*Shirley,* 162
*The Shoemakers Nummi,* 9
Sholokhov, Mikhail, 74, 146, 299
Shute, Nevil, 153
*Silas Marner,* 90
Sillitoe, Alan, 21, 40, 46–48, 185
Silone, Ignazio, 260, 262

Silva, Miguel Otero, 175
Simenon, Georges, 76, 107
Simonov, Konstantin, 311
Sinclair, Upton, 54–56, 204, 296
Sinervo, Elvi, 238
Sinjavskij, Andrej (pseud. Abram Tertz), 210, 276
*Sketches by Boz,* 159
Šklovskij, Viktor, 231
*Slaughterhouse-Five,* 29–30, 33, 37
Sluckij, Boris, 299
*A Small Town in Germany,* 36
Smeljakov, 299
Snow, Sir Charles, 32, 34
Sobolev, Leonid, 339
social institutions, Western criticism of, 155–201
Socialist Realism, 156, 207–8, 228–30, 265–67, 327
Sofronov, Anatolij, 306
Solinas, Franco, 177
Sologub, Fëdor, 117, 282
Solzhenitsyn, Alexander: letter to Union of Soviet Writers on censorship, 26–27; *One Day in the Life of Ivan Denisovich,* 153, 276; *The First Circle,* 279, 287
*The Song of Hiawatha,* 92
Soria, Georges, 224
Sovetskij pisatel' publishing house, 332
*Soviet Attitudes toward American Writing,* 1, 4
Soviet reading habits. *See* Reading habits in USSR
Soviet writers: and de-Stalinization, 297–304; master writers most admired by young Soviet writers, 298–99; small press runs for, 332; popularity ratings of, 350–55
Soviet writing: Western preferred over, 63–66; rejected by college students, 74–75, 80, 88; cultural imports' impact on, 296–328; less commericaly successful than Western, 329–44; popularity ratings of, 350–51
Spanish authors, 234–35
Španov, Nikolaj, 340
Spock, Benjamin, 254
stage. *See* plays; theater
Stalin, Josef: his death's effect on censorship, 5, 24–25; his definition of writers, 100; and Mayakovsky, 131; and Rolland, 212; and Barbusse, 213; Khrushchev's denunciation of, 225, 226; victims of Stalinism, 275–76; removal of body from mausoleum, 276; artistic legacy of, 297–98; quoted on literary treatment of military themes, 308; deheroicizing of, 312
Starcev, A.I., 124
Steinbeck, John: Soviet censorship of, 31, 38–39; *Travels with Charley in Search of America,* 38–39, 192; large Soviet printings of,